Contents at a Glance

Introduction   1

Part I: Ethernet, Fast Ethernet, and Gigabit Ethernet   7

   1 Introduction to LANs   9

   2 LAN MAC Addresses   25

   3 Ethernet LAN Structure   41

   4 The Classical Ethernet CSMA/CD MAC Protocol   55

   5 Full-Duplex Ethernet Communication   77

   6 The Ethernet 10Mbps Physical Layer   87

   7 The Ethernet 100Mbps Physical Layer   125

   8 Gigabit Ethernet Architecture   151

   9 Gigabit Ethernet Physical Layer   165

  10 Twisted-Pair Cabling Standards and Performance
      Requirements   183

  11 Auto-Negotiation   203

Part II: Bridging, Switching, and Routing   **223**

  12 Ethernet Bridges and Layer 2 Switches   225

  13 The Spanning Tree Protocol   251

  14 Switches and Multicast Traffic   273

  15 Link Aggregation   291

  16 VLANs and Frame Priority   305

  17 Source-Routing, Translational, and Wide Area Bridges   349

  18 Routing and Layer 2/3 Switches   383

Part III: Other Old and New Technologies   **401**

  19 Token Ring and FDDI Overview   403

  20 ATM Overview   457

  21 ATM LAN Emulation   473

  22 Fibre Channel   501

Part IV: Appendixes   **541**

  A   Physical Layer Encodings for Ethernet, Fibre Channel,
FDDI, and Token Ring   543

  B   Tables   579

  C   Standards Bodies and References   593

  D   Acronym List   597

      Glossary   607

      Index   633

Table of Contents

Introduction 1

Audience 2

Organization 2

    Part I: Ethernet, Fast Ethernet, and Gigabit Ethernet 2

    Part II: Bridging, Switching, and Routing 3

    Part III: Other Old and New Technologies 4

    Part IV: Appendixes 5

Part I: Ethernet, Fast Ethernet, and Gigabit Ethernet 7

1 Introduction to LANs 9

The Birth of Ethernet 9

    Ethernet Characteristics 10

Token Ring 10

Fibre Distributed Data Interface 12

Fibre Channel and ATM 13

Communications Layering Model 13

    LAN Layering Model 14

    LAN Frames 15

Basic LAN Components 16

    Stations and DTEs 17

    LAN Media 17

    Network Interface Card 17

    Device Drivers 17

SNMP, Monitors, and RMON 20

    SNMP Architecture 20

    RMON MIBs 22

    SNMP Transports 22

Standards Body Overview 23

Summary Points 23

2 LAN MAC Addresses 25

Universally Administered MAC Addresses 26

Locally Administered MAC Addresses 27

Broadcast and Group Addresses 27

Individual/Group and Universal/Local Flag Bits 29

Ethernet Address Conventions 29

    Ethernet Multicast Addresses 30

    Traces of Ethernet MAC Addresses 31

Token Ring Address Conventions 32

    Addresses Carried in a Token Ring Information Field 34

    A Trace Showing Token Ring MAC Addresses 34

    Token Ring Functional Addresses 35

FDDI Address Conventions 36
  A Trace Showing FDDI MAC Addresses 36
Summary Points 38
References 39

3   Ethernet LAN Structure   41
Ethernet LAN Architecture 42
  Single Segment Ethernet LAN and CSMA/CD 42
  Using Repeaters to Build Multisegment LANs 44
  Twisted-Pair Cabling and Hub Repeaters 45
  Improving Performance with Bridges 47
  Collision Domains 47
  Leaping to Higher Performance with Switches 48
  Switches and Full-Duplex Operation 50
  Sharing the LAN 50
  The Role of Routers 51
Summary Points 52
References 53

4   The Classical Ethernet CSMA/CD MAC Protocol   55
Classic Ethernet Shared Bandwidth LANs 56
  Preamble and Interframe Gap 56
  The CSMA/CD Protocol 58
  Random Backoff 58
Ethernet MAC Frames 60
  Preamble and Start Frame Delimiter Patterns 60
  Ethernet MAC Frame Size 62
  Relationship Between Frame Size and Collision Domain Size 62
  MAC Frame Formats 63
  Size Modification for Gigabit Ethernet 66
  DIX Ethernet Frame Trace 68
  802.3 LLC/SNAP Frames 68
  802.3 LLC/SNAP Frame Trace 69
  Source of the LLC and SNAP Headers 70
  NetWare over Ethernet 73
Tabulation of Important Ethernet Parameters 74
Summary Points 75
References 76

5   Full-Duplex Ethernet Communication   77
Full-Duplex Architecture 77
  Full-Duplex Parameters 79
  Assuring Backward Compatibility 79
  Handling Congestion 80
  The MAC Control Sublayer 81

MAC Control Frames and PAUSE Frames 81

Implementation 84

Summary Points 84

References 85

6   The Ethernet 10Mbps Physical Layer   87

Baseband Ethernet on Thick Coaxial Cable (10BASE5) 87

Connecting to 10BASE5 Coax 89

Transceiver (MAU) Functions 90

10BASE5 Collision Domain Parameters 92

Practical Problems with 10BASE5 95

Baseband Ethernet on Thin Coax Cable (10BASE2) 95

10BASE2 Collision Domain Parameters 97

Practical Problems with 10BASE2 98

10Mbps Twisted–Pair Ethernet (10BASE-T) 98

10BASE-T Segments 98

Half-Duplex Operation 99

Full-Duplex Operation 104

10Mbps Twisted-Pair Transmission 104

Hub and Switch Connections 106

Twisted-Pair Link Integrity Test 108

Building a Mixed Coax/Twisted-Pair Collision Domain 108

10Mbps on Fiber Optic Cable 110

Features of Fiber Optic Links 110

Fiber Optic Inter-Repeater Link 112

FOIRL Links in a Collision Domain 113

10BASE-FL 114

10BASE-FB 117

Summary of Fiber Distance Specifications 117

The Structure of a Fiber 118

Multimode Transmission 120

Optical Fiber Connectors 121

Summary Points 122

References 124

7   The Ethernet 100Mbps Physical Layer   125

Coexistence and Migration with Auto-Negotiation 127

100Mbps Ethernet on Twisted–Pair Cabling 128

100BASE-TX 128

100BASE-T4 130

100BASE-T2 133

100BASE-FX and FDDI 133

Media Independent Interface 134

100Mbps Collision Domain Diameter 135

    Repeater (Hub) Classes 137

    Collision Domain Configurations 138

    Computing a Special Collision Domain Configuration 140

    Curing the Diameter Problem with Switches 141

100VG-AnyLAN 142

    100VG-AnyLAN Topology 143

    Cables and Connectors for 100VG AnyLAN 143

    Initialization and Port Types 145

    The Medium Access Protocol for One Repeater 147

    The Medium Access Protocol for Two Levels of Repeaters 147

Summary Points 148

References 149

8   Gigabit Ethernet Architecture   151

Gigabit Configurations 153

Full-Duplex Gigabit Ethernet 154

    Full-Duplex Repeaters 155

    Jumbo Frames 157

Half-Duplex Gigabit Ethernet 158

    Modification to Frame Format for Half-Duplex Mode 158

    Frame Bursting for Half-Duplex Operation 159

    1000Mbps Half-Duplex Hubs 161

Summary Points 162

References 163

9   Gigabit Ethernet Physical Layer   165

Features of Gigabit Ethernet 166

    Auto-Negotiation 166

    Bidirectional Gigabit Transmission 166

Physical Characteristics of Gigabit Ethernet 167

1000BASE-X Technology 169

    8B/10B Encoding 169

    1000BASE-SX and LX Transmission: Lasers and VCSELs 170

    Connectors for 1000BASE-SX, 1000BASE-LX, and 1000BASE-LH ..171

    1000BASE-CX Copper Cables and Connectors 173

    Gigabit Interface Converters 174

1000BASE-T Technology 175

1000BASE-T Encoding 175

    Getting the Cable Ready 175

    Encoders, Decoders, and Hybrids 177

    Master/Slave Timing 178

    Auto-Negotiation and Crossover Cable 179

Summary Points 180

References 181

10   Twisted-Pair Cabling Standards and Performance Requirements   183

Cabling Standards Bodies 183

TIA/EIA Categories 184

Wire Features 187

Cabling Layouts 187

Unshielded Twisted-Pair Cabling Performance Parameters 188

Parameters for All Ethernet LANs 189

Parameters for High-Speed LANs 190

Parameter Descriptions 190

Attenuation to Crosstalk Ratio 195

Structural Return Loss and Return Loss 195

Propagation Delay and Time Domain Reflectometry 196

Delay Skew 196

Managing Twisted–Pair Cabling 196

Test Tools 197

The Scope of a Test 198

Testing Fiber Optic Cable 199

Summary Points 200

References 201

11   Auto-Negotiation   203

Auto-Negotiation for Twisted-Pair Interfaces 204

Auto-Negotiation and Ethernet Upgrades 204

Checking and Controlling Interfaces 207

Auto-Negotiation Functionality for Twisted-Pair Interfaces 208

Twisted-Pair Technology Capabilities 208

Negotiating Support for Flow Control 209

Determining Master/Slave Timer Roles 210

Parallel Detection for Twisted–Pair Cabling 210

Exchanging Auto-Negotiation Data across Twisted-Pair Media 210

Message Pages for 1000BASE-T Capabilities 216

Message Codes 217

Auto-Negotiation for 1000BASE-X Interfaces 218

1000BASE-X Auto-Negotiation Implementation 219

Summary Points 220

References 221

Part II: Bridging, Switching, and Routing   223

12   Ethernet Bridges and Layer 2 Switches   225

Main Bridge/Switch Functions 225

Other Bridge Functions 227

Collision Domains 228

Bridged Collision Domains 229

Transparent Bridging 230

Transparent Bridge Internals 234
    Learning 234
    Filtering Table Entries 236
    Static Filtering Information 237
Layer 2 Switch Architecture 242
    Store-and-Forward versus Cut-Through 242
    Parallel Processing with ASICs 243
    Basic Bridge Layer Structure 243
Building Redundancy into a LAN 243
    The Spanning Tree Protocol 244
    Link Aggregation 246
Handling Multicasts 246
    IGMP Snooping and GARP 247
    Functional Structure of a Layer 2 Switch 247
Summary Points 248
References 249

13 The Spanning Tree Protocol   **251**
LAN Structure and SubLANs 252
Protocol Overview 254
    Electing the Root Bridge 254
    Generating the Tree 256
Elements of the Protocol 259
    Port Costs and the Root Path Cost 259
    Root Port, Designated Bridge, and Designated Port 261
    Choosing the Root 262
    Discovering the Root Paths 263
    Topology Changes and Port State Changes 264
    Maintaining the Tree 266
Protocol Messages 266
    The Configuration BPDU 267
    The Topology Change BPDU 270
Summary Points 271
References 272

14 Switches and Multicast Traffic   **273**
Multicasting 274
    The Need to Control Multicasts 275
    IP Multicasts 276
IGMP Snooping 278
    Problems with IGMP Snooping 280
The GARP Multicast Registration Protocol (GMRP) 281
    GMRP Procedures 283
Generic Attribute Registration Protocol 284
    GMRP/GARP Encapsulation and Format 286

Summary Points 288
References 289

15 Link Aggregation   **291**
Using Link Aggregation 292
Link Aggregation Features 293
Link Aggregation Concepts and Procedures 294
Virtual Link MAC Address 295
Link Aggregation Sublayer Structure 297
What a System Needs to Know 297
Link Aggregation Parameters 299
The Link Aggregation Control Protocol 300
Slow Protocols 300
Link Aggregation Control Protocol Messages 300
Frame Distribution and Conversations 302
Summary Points 304
References 304

16 VLANs and Frame Priority   **305**
Virtual LAN Concepts 307
Types of Virtual LANs 308
VLAN Awareness and Ports 308
VLAN Switches 310
Trunks and Tags 310
Access Links 312
Using a Collision Domain as a Trunk 312
Hybrid Links 312
Communicating Between VLANs 314
Independent and Shared Learning 316
The GARP VLAN Registration Protocol 317
VLANs and the Spanning Tree Protocol 318
Implementing VLANs 318
The Default VLAN 319
Static Port-Based VLANs 319
Port- and Protocol-Based VLANs 326
MAC-Address-Based Secure VLANs 328
Processing VLAN Frames 330
Assigning Frames to VLANs via Ingress Rules 330
Forwarding VLAN Frames 332
Configuring VLAN Ports 333
VLANs and Multicasts 334
VLAN Protocol Elements 334
VLAN Identifiers 334
Tagged Frame Formats 335

Assigning Priorities to Frames 339
    IEEE 802 Priority 340
    Forwarding Prioritized Frames 340
    Mapping 802.1 Priorities to Priority Classes 342
GARP VLAN Registration Protocol Details 344
    GVRP Protocol Messages 344
Summary Points 345
References 348

17 Source-Routing, Translational, and Wide Area Bridges   **349**
Source-Routed Bridged LANs 350
    Ring Identifiers and Bridge Identifiers 352
    Route Discovery 353
    Source-Routing Bridge Protocol Elements 356
    Source-Routing Transparent Bridges 360
Translational Bridges 361
    MAC Frame Sizes 362
    Translational Bridging Between Token Ring and FDDI 362
    Translational Bridging Between Transparent Token
      Ring and Ethernet 364
    Translational Bridging Between Source-Routing
      Token Rings and Ethernet 365
Tunneling Token Ring Across Ethernet 366
Structuring a LAN Around a High-Speed Ethernet or FDDI
  Backbone with Tagging 368
    Using Tags in a Transparently Bridged LAN 368
    Using Tags to Translate Source-Routed Frames 370
Remote Bridges 374
    Links Between Bridges 374
    To Bridge or Not to Bridge 375
    Frame Formats on Wide Area Links 376
Summary Points 380
References 381

18 Routing and Layer 2/3 Switches   **383**
Features of Routing 383
    Router Benefits 384
    Network Addresses versus MAC Addresses 384
    Exiting a LAN 386
Routing Procedures 389
    Building Routing Tables 389
    Other Router Functions 392
    Legacy Router Architecture 392
    Layer 3 Switch Architecture 392

Bridge/Routers 394
    Layer 2/3 Switches 394
    Route Once, Switch Many 394
Layer 4 and Application-Layer Switching 396
    Filtering for Security 397
    Prioritizing Traffic 397
    Load Balancing 397
Summary Points 398
References 400

Part III: Other Old and New Technologies   401

19   Token Ring and FDDI Overview   403
Features of Classic Half-Duplex Token Ring 404
    Basic Ring Operation 405
    Active Monitor and Standby Monitor Roles 407
    Functions Performed by the Active Monitor 408
    The Claim Token Election Process 408
    The Beacon Process 409
    The Neighbor Notification Process 409
    Special Servers 410
    Hard and Soft Errors 411
    Joining a Ring 411
    Physical Components for Half-Duplex Token Ring 412
Classic Token Ring Protocol Elements 415
    Addresses 416
    Token Format 416
    General Frame Format 417
    Abort Sequence 421
    Token Ring MAC Protocol Frames 422
    Timers 424
    Token Ring Frame Traces 426
Dedicated Token Ring 431
    C-Ports 432
    Full-Duplex Protocol 434
High Speed Token Ring 437
    Fiber Optic HSTR Lobes 438
Fiber Distributed Data Interface 438
FDDI Topology 439
    Primary and Secondary Rings 441
    Single-Attached Stations and S Ports 443
    Dual-Attached Stations and A and B Port Types 443
    Concentrator M Ports 445
    Wrapping an FDDI Ring 445
    FDDI Media and Encoding 446

FDDI Protocol Elements 447

    Claim Frames and the Target Token Rotation Timeout 448

    Station Management 448

    Beacon Frames 449

    FDDI Frames 450

FDDI Formats 451

    FDDI Token Format 451

    FDDI Frame Format 452

Summary Points 453

References 455

20 ATM Overview   **457**

ATM Concepts 459

    Quality of Service 460

    Concurrent Circuits 462

ATM Architecture 463

The ATM Cell Header 464

    VPI and VCI Numbers 466

    Processing a Cell 467

    Interleaving Cells 468

    AAL5 Frame Format 470

Summary Points 471

References 472

21 ATM LAN Emulation   **473**

Emulated LAN Environments 475

LAN Emulation Clients 477

LAN Emulation Servers 478

    The LAN Emulation Configuration Server 480

    The LAN Emulation Server 483

    The Broadcast and Unknown Server 486

ATM LANE Protocol Elements 488

    ATM Addresses 489

    Initialization with ILMI 490

    LANE Data Frames 490

    LANE Control Frames 494

    Trace of a Join Response Control Frame 496

LANE Version 2 498

Summary Points 499

References 500

22   Fibre Channel   501

        Features of Fibre Channel 502
            Transmission Speeds 503
            Distances, Media, and Connectors 503
        Fibre Channel Equipment and Topology 504
            Fabrics 507
            Loop Switches 507
            Fibre Channel Ports 508
        Fibre Channel Names and Addresses 510
            World Wide Port and Node Names 510
            Port Identifiers (Addresses) 511
        Fibre Channel Levels 512
            Classes of Service 513
            Generic Services 514
            FC-4 Application Mappings 515
        Fibre Channel Data Transfer 515
            8B/10B Encoding and Ordered Sets 516
            Sequences of Frames 516
            Exchanges 518
            Relative Offsets 519
            Logins and Addresses 520
            Well-Known Addresses 521
            Buffers and Credit 521
            Fibre Channel Frame Format 523
        Examples of FC-4 Fibre Channel Use 526
            Encapsulation of IP Datagrams 526
            SCSI over Fibre Channel 529
        Arbitrated Loops 531
            L_Port Addresses 533
            Arbitrated Loop Initialization 534
            Arbitrated Loop Data Transfer 536
        Summary Points 538
        References 539

Part IV: Appendixes   541

    A   Physical Layer Encodings for Ethernet, Fibre Channel,
        FDDI, and Token Ring   543
        Code-Groups and Special Signals 544
        Ethernet 10BASE5, 10BASE2, and 10BASE-T Manchester Encoding 547
        Ethernet FOIRL, 10BASE-FL, and 10BASE-FB 547

100BASE-X Ethernet, FDDI, and CDDI 549
    NRZI Signals for 100BASE-FX and FDDI 550
    MLT-3 Signals for 100BASE-TX and CDDI 551
    4B/5B Code-Groups for FDDI, CDDI, and 100BASE-X 552
Ethernet 100BASE-T4 553
    Ternary Symbols and 8B/6T Encoding 553
    100BASE-T4 Transmission 555
    Special Symbols and Alignment 556
    Translating Between 100BASE-X and 100BASE-T4 in a Hub 558
Ethernet 100BASE-T2 559
    Quinary Symbols and PAM5x5 Encoding 559
1000BASE-X and Fibre Channel 560
    8B/10B Data Encoding 561
    8B/10B Data Code-Group Naming Convention 565
    Special 8B/10B Code-Groups 566
    Ordered Sets of 8B/10B Code-Groups 567
1000BASE-T 568
    Outline of 1000BASE-T Encoding 569
Token Ring 573
    Differential Manchester Encoding 573
    100Mbps Dedicated Token Ring 575
Summary Points 575
References 576

B   **Tables**   **579**
Binary, Decimal, and Hexadecimal Characters 579
8B/6T Tables 580
8B/10B Translation Table 582
References...592

C   **Standards Bodies and References**   **593**
Formal Standards Bodies 593
    IEEE 593
    ANSI 594
    IETF 594
    TIA/EIA 594
    ITU-T 595
    ISO 595
Vendor Groups 595

D   **Acronym List**   **597**

    Glossary   **607**

    Index   **633**

About the Author

Dr. Sidnie Feit is the chief scientist at the Standish Group, a leading research consultancy. An analyst, lecturer, and writer with more than 30 years of data communications and information processing experience, she has designed, tested, and reviewed numerous communications products and assisted in product rollouts. She also has developed training programs in communications technologies for vendors and seminar organizations.

Dr. Feit, who received her B.A., M.A., and Ph.D. from Cornell University, has written many technology manuals and published books, articles, and reports in the areas of data communications, telecommunications, network management, Internet servers, and Internet applications. Her other books include *Wide Area High Speed Networks* (MTP, 1999); *TCP/IP: Architecture, Protocols, and Implementation,* Signature Edition (McGraw-Hill, 1998); and *SNMP: A Guide to Network Management* (McGraw-Hill, 1993).

About the Technical Reviewers

These reviewers contributed their considerable hands-on expertise to the entire development process for *Local Area High Speed Networks*. As the book was being written, these dedicated professionals reviewed all the material for technical content, organization, and flow. Their feedback was critical to ensuring that *Local Area High Speed Networks* fits our readers' need for the highest-quality technical information.

A.G. Carrick has more than a quarter century of experience in information processing. His career spans the spectrum of the industry, including end-user organizations, hardware manufacturers, software publishers, third-party maintenance firms, universities, and research and development firms. His career began with punch-card tabulating machines and proceeded through programming, systems analysis, systems engineering, networking, software development, MIS management, and consulting. He owned a software development firm for seven years, developing software packages for federal, state, and local government agencies; universities; and Fortune 1000 companies; and smaller firms. He now develops software packages, consults about the management and use of computers and networks, and is a lecturer at the University of Texas at Arlington in the Computer Science and Engineering Department.

Gil has written articles for professional journals and for national computer group meetings. He also has been an invited speaker on several occasions at computer professional group chapter meetings and regional computer user group conferences.

Gina Mieszczak is an integration test engineer with 3Com Corporation. She has eight years of experience in the networking/IT industry, including positions in the consulting, retail, and travel industries. Her skills include network and telecommunications troubleshooting, using protocol analyzers, providing technical support, and executing network planning.

Gina is a Cisco Certified Network Associate (CCNA) with technical certifications, including Microsoft MCSE and MCP+I, and she currently is finishing 3Com's Master of Network Science in Remote Access Solutions. She also is currently pursuing the Cisco Certified Network Professional Certification.

Dedication

To my husband, Walter, who kept his patience and good humor.

Acknowledgments

I wish to thank Lisa Thibault, the development editor, who read the full text and made lots of good suggestions. She was my constant email companion, providing encouragement and helping me over bumps in the road. Laura Loveall supervised production and remained good-natured and unfazed when chapters were reordered or figures were replaced. Karen Wachs, the acquisitions editor, helped to keep the project on track.

I also wish to express my gratitude to the technical reviewers, A.G. Carrick, Gina Mieszczak, Lennert Buytenhek, and Murali Rajagopal, who contributed generously of their time and their knowledge. I especially wish to thank A.G. Carrick, who was an inexhaustible source of real-world information, and Gina Mieszczak, who read through the whole text carefully and pinpointed numerous sections that needed clarification.

Network Associates provided current Sniffer Pro monitor software, and Tom Rice of Network Associates supplied many interesting traces and insights. Michael Emerton of 3Com provided some interesting traces of recently developed protocols.

Feedback Information

At MTP, our goal is to create in-depth technical books of the highest quality and value. Each book is crafted with care and precision, undergoing rigorous development that involves the unique expertise of members from the professional technical community.

Readers' feedback is a natural continuation of this process. If you have any comments regarding how we can improve the quality of this book, or otherwise alter it to better suit your needs, you can contact us at www.newriders.com/contact. Please make sure to include the book title in your message and the ten-digit ISBN number, which can be found on the back cover above the bar code.

We greatly appreciate your assistance.

Introduction

Local area network capacity has rocketed upward due to the introduction of Gigabit Ethernet links, cheap 100Mbps Ethernet adapters, and switches whose throughput is accelerated by ASIC hardware. More costly network equipment based on fibre channel architecture is producing even higher performance levels.

Better equipment and higher bandwidths have encouraged a trend toward building bigger LANs. However, a big LAN is prey to bottlenecks, congestion, and broadcast storms. A proliferation of new technologies should help solve these problems by controlling traffic flows, preventing switch congestion, and enabling parallel links to be installed. Some of the new capabilities are astonishing. For example, the GARP VLAN Registration Protocol (GVRP) can assure that a LAN frame addressed to a particular station always is delivered to that station and to no other.

This book introduces modern LAN technologies, explains what they do, and describes how they work. More than 250 figures are included to present concepts in an easy-to-understand manner.

The book includes chapters that follow topics to their full technical depth. However, the material has been organized to allow the reader to explore the topics that are of interest and skip subjects and details that are not currently needed.

Audience

This book is for people who want to understand the technologies that they use and who also want a reference that provides details down to any depth.

You can benefit from this book if you are responsible for planning, implementing, supporting, or troubleshooting local area networks. Consultants, systems engineers, and sales engineers who design corporate networks for clients also can benefit from this information.

The book provides the technical foundation for knowing how and where to deploy multilayer switches. It also describes switch options that network planners and architects can use to make LANs more reliable, to improve performance, and to simplify ongoing maintenance chores.

Organization

The book is organized into four parts. The first part describes classic Ethernet and the new, high-speed versions of Ethernet. The second part describes Layer 2, 3, and 4 switches and application-layer switches. The third part covers Token Ring, FDDI, ATM, and fibre channel LANs. The fourth part provides reference information.

Part I: Ethernet, Fast Ethernet, and Gigabit Ethernet

Chapter 1, "Introduction to LANs," describes and contrasts Ethernet, Token Ring, and FDDI LANs. It presents some general networking background, including descriptions of lower-layer network functions, SNMP network management, and RMON.

Chapter 2, "LAN MAC Addresses," explains how LAN MAC addresses are administered, assigned, and used. It explains the bit-ordering discrepancies between Ethernet, Token Ring, and FDDI MAC addressing.

Chapter 3, "Ethernet LAN Structure," tracks the evolution of Ethernet from CSMA/CD coaxial cable LANs to modern full-duplex switched twisted-pair and fiber optic LANs. It also introduces the role of routers.

Chapter 4, "The Classical Ethernet CSMA/CD MAC Protocol," covers both classic and high-speed half-duplex Ethernet protocols. It describes frame formats and displays traces that illustrate the ways that various types of protocol data are encapsulated.

Chapter 5, "Full-Duplex Ethernet Communication," focuses on full-duplex Ethernet protocols and operations, and presents the full-duplex congestion control protocol.

Chapter 6, "The Ethernet 10Mbps Physical Layer," describes the cables, connectors, transceivers, hubs, switches, and topology restrictions for 10Mbps Ethernet LANs. It includes information needed to integrate legacy LANs with high-speed LANs.

Chapter 7, "The Ethernet 100Mbps Physical Layer," covers all the physical implementations of 100Mbps Ethernet. It provides information on the cables, connectors, hubs, switches, and data encodings that are used for each implementation. It presents a straightforward explanation of half-duplex 100Mbps topology restrictions and Class I and Class II hubs. A sketch of 100VG-AnyLAN is included as well.

Chapter 8, "Gigabit Ethernet Architecture," describes Gigabit LAN configurations, parameters, and mechanisms, including the nonstandard Jumbo frames. It explains the architecture of buffered full-duplex repeaters. Half-duplex Gigabit Ethernet also is presented, along with an analysis of why it is not used.

Chapter 9, "Gigabit Ethernet Physical Layer," covers the physical implementations of Gigabit Ethernet. It provides information on the media, connectors, data encodings, and master/slave roles used for each implementation.

Chapter 10, "Twisted-Pair Cabling Standards and Performance Requirements," is important for network planners and troubleshooters. It describes Category 1-7 cable and cabling layouts. This chapter also provides detailed explanations of the twisted-pair performance parameters used to test for Gigabit Ethernet qualification and gives descriptions of the tools used to test cables. A brief description of some optical cable test parameters is included as well.

Chapter 11, "Auto-Negotiation," describes two families of Auto-Negotiation protocols. The first enables a pair of Ethernet UTP interfaces to negotiate their best set of shared capabilities. The second is used by 1000BASE-X adapters.

Part II: Bridging, Switching, and Routing

Chapter 12, "Ethernet Bridges and Layer 2 Switches," presents the functions performed by Layer 2 switches. It includes an in-depth description of transparent bridge/switch internals and performance characteristics.

Chapter 13, "The Spanning Tree Protocol," explains why a transparently bridged LAN must have a tree structure and how the IEEE 802.1D Spanning Tree Protocol reconfigures the LAN topology after a link or bridge failure.

Chapter 14, "Switches and Multicast Traffic," describes mechanisms that can be used to control multicast traffic in a bridged LAN. It outlines how IGMP snooping and the GARP Multicast Registration Protocol work.

Chapter 15, "Link Aggregation," presents a protocol used to make a set of links that connect two systems operate like a single, aggregated link.

Chapter 16, "VLANs and Frame Priority," is a major chapter that deals with virtual LANs. It describes the different types of VLANs that can be created and gives the purpose of each. This chapter also presents the processing steps performed when a frame passes through a VLAN switch. VLAN protocols (including GVRP) are discussed as well.

Chapter 17, "Source-Routing, Translational, and Wide Area Bridges," describes source-routing, translational, and wide area bridges. It explains how translational switch products overcome the problems that arise when different types of LANs are bridged together.

Chapter 18, "Routing and Layer 2/3 Switches," puts routing and switching in perspective. It walks through a routing procedure to highlight the differences between Layer 3 routing and Layer 2 switching. It briefly discusses the "route once, switch many" philosophy supported in the emerging Multiprotocol Label Switching Architecture (MPLS) standards. Layer 4 switching, application switching, and load balancing are covered as well.

Part III: Other Old and New Technologies

Chapter 19, "Token Ring and FDDI Overview," describes Token Ring and FDDI LANs. A discussion of the classic Token Ring protocols is followed by a description of the newer Dedicated Token Ring protocols, which support full-duplex Token Ring communication and High Speed Token Ring. FDDI topology and protocols also are presented.

Chapter 20, "ATM Overview," lays the groundwork for understanding ATM LANs. It describes ATM service categories, AAL5 frames, and ATM cells. Interleaved cell transmission and ATM Layer 1 switching also are discussed.

Chapter 21, "ATM LAN Emulation," outlines the LAN Emulation (LANE) protocols that are needed to turn ATM into a LAN technology. Addressing, switching, LAN Emulation servers, data frames, control frames, and initialization procedures are covered as well.

Chapter 22, "Fibre Channel," deals with fibre channel, the technology that currently offers the highest LAN speeds. The chapter describes fibre channel features, applications, and equipment. It also covers fabric and arbitrated loop topologies and classes of service. Major elements of the protocol family are presented, and the encapsulation of ordinary user data and SCSI commands and data is described.

Part IV: Appendixes

Part IV starts with an appendix that originally was written as a chapter. Appendix A, "Physical Layer Encodings for Ethernet, Fibre Channel, FDDI, and Token Ring," provides detailed descriptions of the way that data is encoded and signaled onto a medium for Ethernet, fibre channel, FDDI, and Token Ring LANs. It explains mechanisms such as 4B/5B encoding and MLT-3 transmission. The material has been placed into an appendix for easy reference from other chapters. Numerous tables are included as well. Appendix B, "Tables," includes some additional related tables.

Part IV also includes acronyms, a glossary, and pointers to standards groups, consortia, and other information resources.

PART I

Ethernet, Fast Ethernet, and Gigabit Ethernet

1   Introduction to LANs

2   LAN MAC Addresses

3   Ethernet LAN Structure

4   The Classical Ethernet CSMA/CD MAC Protocol

5   Full-Duplex Ethernet Communication

6   The Ethernet 10Mbps Physical Layer

7   The Ethernet 100Mbps Physical Layer

8   Gigabit Ethernet Architecture

9   Gigabit Ethernet Physical Layer

10 Twisted-Pair Cabling Standards and Performance Requirements

11 Auto-Negotiation

CHAPTER 1

Introduction to LANs

A *local area network* (LAN) connects a set of computers so that they can communicate with one another directly. Once upon a time, the term *local* was quite appropriate—early LANs spanned a limited space. A LAN typically connected systems located within a single room or in an area confined within one story of a building.

Gradually, LANs snaked across multiple floors of a building. As time went by, new technologies made it possible for a LAN to span a campus consisting of several buildings, or even to incorporate sites located at great distances from one another.

The Birth of Ethernet

A lot of experimentation took place in the early days of LANs, when a flock of network equipment companies marketed proprietary LAN products. Proprietary technologies locked a customer into using equipment that was manufactured by one vendor.

A watershed event changed the landscape. In the 1970s, Robert Metcalfe and several of his colleagues at the Xerox Palo Alto Research Center (PARC) invented and patented Ethernet. The inventors of Ethernet took the first step along the road to success in 1980, when they decided to publish the Ethernet specification and make it available as an industry standard.

In 1983, 10 megabit per second (Mbps) Ethernet became an *Institute for Electrical and Electronic Engineers* (IEEE) standard. It subsequently also won acceptance by the *American National Standards Institute* (ANSI) and the *International Organization for Standardization* (ISO).

Standardization attracted both vendors and customers to Ethernet. A growing market, customer feedback, and vendor competition created an environment that fostered increasing functionality, improved performance, and decreasing prices.

The original 10Mbps Ethernets ran on coaxial cable media. In the late 1980s, fiber optic implementations were added. Another significant milestone was passed in 1990, when Ethernet over unshielded twisted-pair telephone wire was standardized. This gave an enormous boost to the Ethernet market.

Developers tackled implementation of 100Mbps Ethernet in the early 1990s. When the 100Mbps technology was officially standardized in 1995, products already had been shipping for two years. Instead of resting on its laurels, the IEEE immediately formed a subcommittee to work on 1000Mbps Ethernet. By 1998, the standard was complete, and products hit the market in 1999.

Today's Ethernet LANs operate at 10Mbps, 100Mbps, and 1000Mbps. There are desktop Ethernet interfaces that can run at either 10 or 100Mbps and can be bought for the price of a lunch. At the time of writing, vendors are exploring the possibility of implementing 10 gigabit per second (Gbps, the equivalent of 10,000Mbps) Ethernet.

Ethernet Characteristics

Communicating using the classical Ethernet protocol is like trying to be heard at a dinner party. If there is a break in the conversation, you can jump in and say something. If two people talk at once, however, the transmission fails.

As more people join the party, it gets harder to be heard. The classical protocol includes rules that make it very likely that, in the long run, everyone will get a fair share of the speaking time. However, this protocol is based on a random selection method: There is no absolute guarantee that you will get a fair share of the speaking time within a given time period.

Still, Ethernet has come a long way in the last few years. A full-duplex version of the protocol implemented with modern Ethernet switching equipment enables all participants to transmit and receive at the same time. In other words, everyone at a switched Ethernet dinner party can talk (and hear) at the same time. This is called *full-duplex* LAN communication.

Token Ring

Researchers in IBM's Zurich research lab designed the Token Ring LAN architecture in the early 1980s. IBM laid down a challenge to Ethernet when it introduced Token Ring products in 1985. The Token Ring specification was presented to the IEEE, and Token Ring eventually joined Ethernet as an IEEE, ANSI, and ISO standard.

Token Rings were crafted for predictability, fairness, and reliability. Naturally, these features attracted many users. Almost all IBM mainframe shops used the Token Ring topology, thinking that it would be around for a long time to come if IBM supported it. Token Ring got an extra boost among IBM customers as well: For many years, IBM did not support Ethernet interfaces in most of its computers and networking devices.

As the name suggests, systems in a Token Ring LAN are connected into a ring. The actual layout of a Token Ring LAN is organized very conveniently. Groups of stations are connected to concentrators that can be located in telephone wiring closets. This means that a building can be star-wired for data in much the same way that it is star-wired for telephone service. Figure 1.1 illustrates the layout; the arrows indicate the path that data follows around the ring.

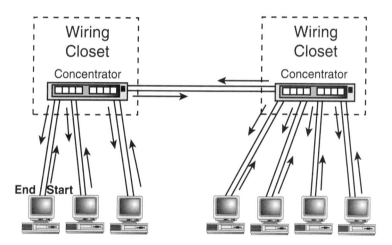

FIGURE 1.1 *TOKEN RING WIRING.*

A special message called a "token" is passed around the ring. When a station receives the token, the station is allowed to transmit data for a limited amount of time. Then it must pass the token on to the next station in the ring. Every station gets an equal opportunity to send data, and there is a limit to the amount of time that can elapse before that opportunity arises.

Classical Token Rings operate at 4Mbps and 16Mbps. The original 4Mbps version ran on shielded twisted-pair cable. Support for unshielded twisted-pair telephone wire was added later.

A 100Mbps version called *High Speed Token Ring* (HSTR) was developed in the late 1990s, and products made their debut in 1998. The 100Mbps Token Ring is useful to customers who wish to improve the performance of their existing Token Ring networks. However, the interfaces are expensive.

A switched, full-duplex version of the Token Ring protocol exists for stations attached to a switch. This means that, as with switched Ethernet, everyone can talk at once. There is no need to circulate a token to control permission to send. However, Token Ring switches are far more costly than Ethernet switches. Furthermore, the arrival of gigabit Ethernet—and the likelihood of a future 10Gbps version—has made many users view Token Ring as a technology of the past. Ethernet is the cheap, scalable solution of the present.

Although IBM continues to support its loyal Token Ring customers, the company now promotes Ethernet for all its platforms. Currently, Token Ring technology is not winning new converts, and many Token Ring shops are gradually migrating over to Ethernet.

Fibre Distributed Data Interface

At a surprisingly early date—1983—work started on what was, at that time, a supernetwork. A *Fibre Distributed Data Interface* (FDDI) network operates at 100Mbps.

The job of designing FDDI was undertaken by the ANSI X3T9.5 task group. Components of the FDDI architecture were described in a series of standards documents whose release was spread across a period of years lasting into the early 1990s.

FDDI was designed with an eye on Token Ring. It has a ring topology, and, like Token Ring, a FDDI ring usually is built around a core ring of concentrators. The FDDI information transfer protocol is closely based on the Token Ring information transfer protocol.

However, the job of physically setting up an FDDI LAN is a far more difficult task than setting up a Token Ring LAN. In addition, FDDI includes some extra protocol elements that are complex and hard to master.

FDDI often has been used as a backbone network when high availability is important. A dual-ring topology optionally can be used at the core of an FDDI network. This dual ring supports automatic recovery from an event such as a broken cable.

An FDDI network can cover a pretty large area. The maximum total path through the network is limited to 200 kilometers (km). However, if the core of the network consists of dual rings, the circumference of the LAN is limited to 100km.

As the name suggests, FDDI originally was designed to run on fiber optic media. An ANSI task group later implemented 100Mbps transmission over twisted-pair copper wire, an important achievement. The copper version is called *Copper Distributed Data Interface* (CDDI). Components taken from FDDI and CDDI transmission technology were reused in 100Mbps Ethernet as well as 100Mbps HSTR.

FDDI provided an ideal backbone for interconnecting Ethernet or Token Ring LANs spread across a campus or spanning sites separated by tens of kilometers.

The downside to using an FDDI network is that it is complex and extremely costly to install. For the most part, the use has been limited to network back-bones. Switched full-duplex implementations of FDDI are available, but they carry a big price tag.

Fibre Channel and ATM

A fibre channel LAN operates at very high speeds and has a topology that is ring-based, switch-based, or a combination of both. The technology initially was used to build *storage area networks* (SANs) that enabled computers to access and share disk or tape storage resources. Increasingly, fibre channel is used to build LANs that interconnect high-performance computers, storage devices, and other peripheral devices.

Asynchronous Transfer Mode (ATM) initially was introduced as a wide area net-working technology. A LAN capability was added later. It enabled ATM sys-tems to communicate with one another—and with Ethernet or Token Ring systems—across a local switch or across a wide area connection.

Fibre channel and ATM have two key features in common:

- Both require a connection to be set up (like setting up a phone call) before a pair of systems can communicate.

- Both support *quality of service*, meaning that error and delay levels can be kept within specified bounds.

Communications Layering Model

In the early 1980s, the ISO began to publish a series of Open Systems Interconnect (OSI) documents that defined standards for data communica-tions. One of these described the OSI layered model for data communications. A simpler model was used by the *Internet Engineering Task Force* (IETF), whose committees produced the TCP/IP communications standards. Figure 1.2 shows the two layered models.

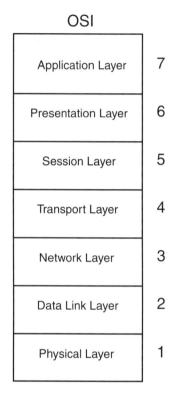

FIGURE 1.2 *THE TCP/IP AND OSI COMMUNICATIONS MODELS.*

LAN Layering Model

LAN technology operates at Layers 1 and 2. The job of Layer 1, the physical layer, is to transmit 0s and 1s across a medium. As indicated in Figure 1.3, LAN physical-layer standards describe the following:

- The characteristics of a physical medium

- The physical signals used to represent digital information

- Other physical specifications, such as the connector types that can be used, the maximum length of a cable, and environmental constraints (such as temperature ranges and freedom from electromagnetic disturbance)

At Layer 2, the data link layer, 0s and 1s are organized into units called *data frames*. LAN data link layer standards describe the following:

- The overall format of a data frame and the meaning of each field that is included in the frame.

- The rules that must be followed to win access to the medium to transmit a frame. These rules define the *media access control* (MAC) protocol.

- The format and interpretation of LAN addresses, which are called *MAC addresses* or *physical addresses*.

> **Note**
> Layer 2 MAC addresses are local. They are meaningful only within one particular LAN. These addresses make it possible to deliver data from one system connected to the LAN to another system on the same LAN.

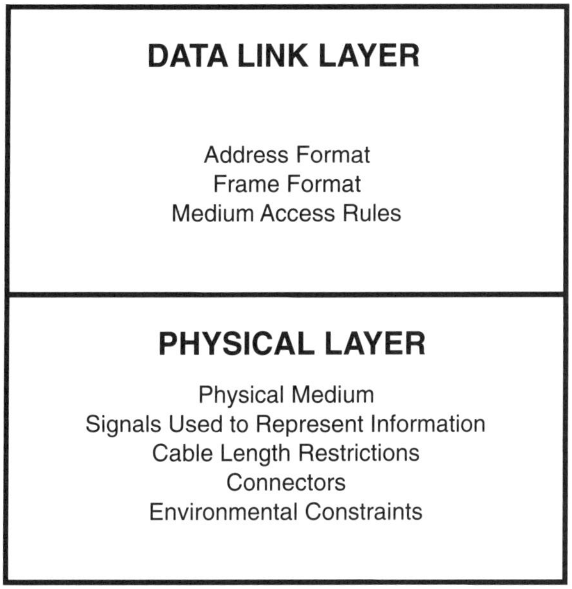

DATA LINK LAYER

Address Format
Frame Format
Medium Access Rules

PHYSICAL LAYER

Physical Medium
Signals Used to Represent Information
Cable Length Restrictions
Connectors
Environmental Constraints

FIGURE 1.3 *LAN LAYERS.*

LAN Frames

Frame formats used for Ethernet, Token Ring, and FDDI are discussed here because they have many features in common. Figure 1.4 shows the general layout of an Ethernet, Token Ring, or FDDI frame.

Each frame has a header that includes a destination and source MAC address. A frame that carries data has an information field.

> **Note**
>
> All Ethernet frames carry data. Some Token Ring and FDDI frames are devoted to special protocol functions—for example, passing the token.

All LAN frames end with a trailer that contains a frame check sequence (FCS) field used to detect transmission errors. The FCS field contains the result of a calculation (called a cyclic redundancy check, or CRC) performed on the remaining bits of the frame. The same calculation is carried out at the destination station; if these answers are not identical, the frame is discarded.

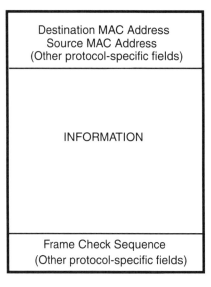

FIGURE 1.4 *GENERAL FRAME LAYOUT*

Basic LAN Components

Some basic terminology is needed before getting started on the in-depth study of LAN technology and protocols. The subsections that follow describe the most fundamental LAN components: stations, LAN media, network interface cards, and device drivers.

> **Note**
>
> Chapter 3, "Ethernet LAN Structure," describes other essential network equipment, including repeaters, hubs, bridges, switches, and routers.

Stations and DTEs

Systems that can originate and receive frames are called *stations*. Stations include client and server computers that exchange data with one another, as well as routers that forward data out of a LAN and transmit data into a LAN.

A system that is a frame originator or receiver also is called *data terminal equipment* (DTE).

> **Note**
>
> It might seem strange to classify a router as a station or DTE. However, a router acts as a source or destination for Layer 2 frame transmissions. When a frame is sent to a router, the router removes the frame header and trailer and processes the content. It then reframes the content and forwards the new frame away from its source LAN and onto a different part of the network.

LAN Media

Many different physical media have been used for LAN communications: coaxial cable, shielded twisted–pair cable, unshielded twisted–pair cable, and fiber optic cable all are in use today. In addition, several wireless technologies have been introduced (infrared, frequency-hopping spread spectrum, and direct sequence spread spectrum).

Network Interface Card

The point of connection between a station (such as a computer) and a LAN medium is called a *network interface*. Network interface functions are performed by a *network interface card* (NIC) that is installed in a station expansion slot. Figure 1.5 contains a rough sketch of a network interface card.

> **Note**
>
> A NIC also is called an adapter or adapter card.

Each network interface card has a unique MAC address. Frames that are sent to a station use the NIC's MAC address to identify the destination. In fact, the MAC address often is referred to as the *NIC address*.

Device Drivers

Each of the many devices used in a computer—such as printers, CD-ROMs, monitor displays, and communications hardware—is controlled by a software program called a *device driver*.

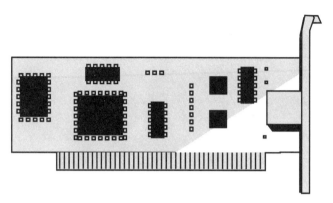

FIGURE 1.5 *A NETWORK INTERFACE CARD.*

Network-layer protocols send and receive data through a network interface by interacting with the device driver that controls the system's NIC. Figure 1.6 illustrates the relationship between the network-layer protocols, the device driver, and the network interface card:

- A network-layer protocol passes outgoing data to the device driver and receives data from the device driver via a standard set of application program interface (API) calls.

- The device driver passes outgoing data to a LAN interface card. It also accepts incoming data from a LAN interface card and passes it to the appropriate network protocol.

> **Note**
>
> For Windows systems, the Network Driver Interface Specification (NDIS) defines the programming interface between network protocols and device driver programs. For Sun Microsystems computers, an API architecture called STREAMS is used.

The device driver and the NIC cooperate in creating the frame headers and trailers that are wrapped around the data that needs to be transmitted.

A different device driver is required for each NIC product because a vendor's device driver communicates with its NIC hardware in a proprietary manner. Suitable device driver software must be supplied by the NIC product vendor.

The benefit of using a standard programming interface between network protocols and a device driver is that the network protocols can function with any NIC that is compatible with the type of station being used. You can replace the current NIC with a new one without making any change to the network protocol software.

However, you must remember to install the device driver software that has been supplied with the new NIC. Even if you bought the new card from the same vendor, it is very likely that the old software will not be capable of "talking" to the new NIC hardware. Vendors are perpetually making design changes to their products to enhance performance and add new features. These changes almost invariably require the card's device driver software to be updated.

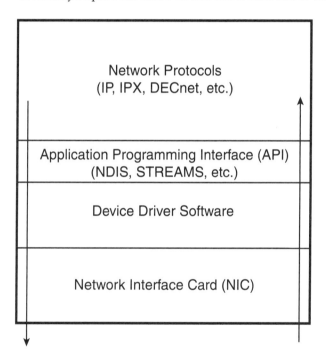

FIGURE 1.6 ROLE OF THE DEVICE DRIVER.

SNMP, Monitors, and RMON

Many of today's LANs contain hundreds—or thousands—of systems. Network management facilities are needed to configure, monitor, and troubleshoot a LAN.

The *Simple Network Management Protocol* (SNMP) is the most widely implemented network management technology. The capability to participate in SNMP is built into virtually every networked device. A *SNMP network management station* can communicate with any device that has been SNMP-enabled.

SNMP originally was created to introduce network management functions into the Internet. It was designed by an Internet Engineering Task Force (IETF) committee; the IETF organization is responsible for developing Internet standards.

Monitors (also called *probes*) are devices that can eavesdrop on LAN activities. A monitor can be configured to watch out for errors or to provide an early warning that trouble is brewing by reporting that some critical threshold has been crossed. Monitors also can capture and analyze protocol traffic, a capability that was used to produce many listings that are displayed in this book.

Remote monitoring (RMON) standards enable an SNMP network management station to cooperate with a network monitor. The main features of SNMP and RMON are outlined in the sections that follow.

SNMP Architecture

SNMP follows a database model. All devices contain information that a network administrator would like to see, including the following:

- Configuration settings
- Status information
- Performance statistics

With the help of an SNMP network management station, an administrator can read this information and then update configuration or status settings.

Figure 1.7 shows the elements of the SNMP model. At the request of applications in the management station, a *SNMP manager* reads or updates management variables at a remote device by sending requests to the device's *SNMP agent*. The manager communicates with an agent using the SNMP protocol.

If a significant event such as a reboot or a serious error occurs at a device, the agent in the device can report it using a message called a *trap*.

Device vendors and third-party software developers enhance the usability of a management station by writing applications that display management information in graphical or pictorial form. For example, the administrator might be shown a picture of a device and be able to troubleshoot or configure a specific component by clicking on it.

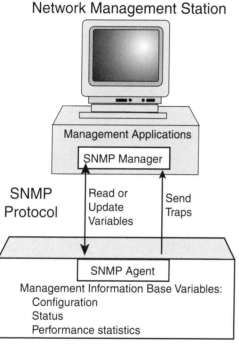

FIGURE 1.7 *THE SNMP MODEL.*

Management Information Base

A collection of network management variables is called a *Management Information Base* (MIB). Examples of MIB variables include these:

- The description of a device

- The number of network interfaces in a device and the type of each interface

- Counts of incoming or outgoing frames

The standardization of MIB variables is an important part of the SNMP effort. A standard MIB variable value has the same format and meaning, independent of which vendor has built the device.

MIB Documents

Many documents describing standard MIB variables have been published as IETF *Request for Comments* (RFC) documents. These are freely available online at the IETF Web site (www.ietf.org). In addition, vendors have written MIBs that describe variables that are specific to their own devices and that are not covered in the standards.

A MIB document includes a set of related definitions that are organized into a unit called a *MIB Module*. These days, as soon as a new technology is introduced, a group of experts writes a MIB Module for the technology.

A major factor in the success of SNMP is that MIB documents are written in a formal language that can be understood by a management station. An administrator simply copies a MIB document to a management station's hard disk and enters a command that adds the new MIB definitions to the set of definitions already understood by the management station. The station then is capable of reading and updating the variables defined in the document.

The usability of a new MIB is enhanced by installing an application that automatically gathers the MIB information and presents it in a succinct form.

RMON MIBs

In the past, a monitor was a standalone device that had to be accessed via its attached keyboard and screen. A series of *remote monitor* MIB documents (RMON MIBs) opened up communication between network management stations and monitors or probes placed in strategic locations within the network. For example, probes can be integrated into switches and routers.

Information gathered by monitors can be retrieved, viewed, and archived at one or more management stations. In addition, monitors can spontaneously report problem situations to management stations. With the help of a network management station application that provides a good user interface to RMON data, communication with monitors becomes a powerful tool.

SNMP Transports

SNMP queries, updates, responses, and trap messages can be carried between systems using any convenient communications protocol. Because SNMP was created to meet Internet needs, the Internet UDP protocol running on top of IP is the most popular transport. However, several other protocols are used to carry SNMP messages, including one that is designed for ATM networks.

Standards Body Overview

Several important standards groups have been mentioned in this chapter:

- IEEE publishes standards related to electronic technologies. Its 802 committee has produced a series of standards documents that describe LAN protocols and LAN physical transmission mechanisms.

- ANSI is a coordinating organization for dozens of specialized U.S. standards organizations and technical committees.

- ISO publishes standards that cover a wide range of interests. International data communications standards are organized under its ISO OSI endeavor.

- The Internet Engineering Task Force (IETF) is responsible for TCP/IP standards. The SNMP standards are maintained and published by the IETF.

Appendix C, "Standards Bodies and References," contains summary descriptions of standards groups and provides pointers to their World Wide Web sites.

The first steps into the world of LANs are now complete. The next chapter will present a detailed study of MAC addresses.

Summary Points

- A LAN connects a set of computers so that they can communicate with one another directly.

- Ethernet, Token Ring, FDDI, fibre channel, and ATM are described in published standards documents.

- Classic Ethernet, Token Ring, and FDDI all were half-duplex protocols— they allowed only one station to transmit successfully at a given time. Currently, switched "full-duplex" implementations of Ethernet, Token Ring, and FDDI enable multiple systems to communicate concurrently.

- Price/performance and an expanding set of usability features have made Ethernet the dominant LAN technology in use today.

- LAN technology operates at the physical and data link layers of the OSI model.

- The job of Layer 1, the physical layer, is to transmit 0s and 1s across a medium.

- At the data link layer, 0s and 1s are organized into frames.

- A MAC address is associated with a network interface card (NIC).

- Every LAN frame has a header that includes a destination and a source MAC address.

- All LAN frames include a frame check sequence (FCS) field that is used to detect transmission errors.

- Systems that can originate and receive frames are called stations or DTEs.

- Network interface functions are performed by a network interface card (NIC).

- Network-layer protocols send and receive data by interacting with an intermediate piece of software called a device driver.

- The Simple Network Management Protocol (SNMP) is supported by almost all network devices.

- Monitors (or probes) are devices that can eavesdrop on LAN activities.

- A Management Information Base (MIB) is a collection of network management variables.

- Remote monitoring (RMON) MIBs enable network management stations to communicate with network monitors.

CHAPTER 2

LAN MAC Addresses

If a computer wants to communicate with another system on its LAN, it needs to identify the target system. Media access control (MAC) addresses (also called *physical addresses*) are used to identify LAN destinations. Every network interface card (NIC) that connects to a LAN must have a MAC address that identifies it uniquely on that LAN.

Unplugging a computer, moving it, and plugging it into a different LAN is a pretty commonplace event. Early on, it was decided that it would be a good idea to assign a unique MAC address to every NIC that is manufactured. That way, a card could be used anywhere without any worry of running into an address conflict.

The IEEE has been given the job of supervising the assignment of unique addresses to NICs. This chapter describes how the IEEE carries out this task and explains how the MAC address space has been divided up and used for different kinds of addresses.

The chapter also includes a discussion of the order in which the bits are transmitted onto a medium for each frame type. This topic is messy and can be tedious. However, it is needed in order to understand problems that can arise when you interconnect different types of LANs into a single LAN. This also enables you to understand one feature of the VLAN headers that are discussed in Chapter 16, "VLANs and Frame Priority."

Universally Administered MAC Addresses

As part of the manufacturing process, each Ethernet, Token Ring, or FDDI LAN adapter card is configured with a MAC address. A LAN MAC address consists of 48 bits (6 bytes). By convention, an address is written as X', followed by six pairs of hexadecimal characters separated by dashes. (The symbol pattern X' stands for "hexadecimal.") For example, the address of the adapter in the computer on which this book is being written is:

X'00-60-08-BD-7C-1E

> **Note**
> Appendix B, "Tables," contains a description of the way that an 8-bit binary string is converted to hexadecimal notation. The appendix contains a tabulation of binary, decimal, and hexadecimal representations of 4-bit quantities.

The IEEE carries out an administrative function that enables vendors to assign globally unique addresses to their adapter products. This works as follows:

- A vendor submits a form to the IEEE and pays a registration fee.

- The IEEE assigns a 3-byte address prefix, called an *organizationally unique identifier* (OUI), to the applicant. For example, the address prefix X'00-60-08 shown previously is owned by 3Com. Xerox owns prefix X'00-00-00, Intel owns X'00-90-27, and Xircom has X'00-10-A4.

The application form and a public list of assigned OUI prefixes are available online at `http://standards.ieee.org/`.

> **Note**
> In the early days of Ethernet, all the prefixes were administered by Xerox and were called block identifiers.

After getting an OUI, a network interface card vendor has the remaining 3 address bytes (24 bits) at its disposal. This means that the vendor can manufacture 2^{24} (16,777,216) NICs with distinct addresses appended to its prefix. These globally unique addresses are called *universally administered MAC addresses*. A vendor can obtain an additional OUI prefix when almost all of its current addresses have been used up.

The IEEE provides a valuable service by overseeing MAC addresses. If you use IEEE universal addresses, you can be sure that the address of a new device added to a LAN will not conflict with the address of any other device on the LAN.

> **Note**
> There have been rumored cases of manufacturing errors that caused duplicate MAC addresses to be produced, but at worst, these are very rare events. The duplicates might be the work of "pirate" clone NIC vendors who pay no attention to the rules. It is a good idea to check that your NICs come from a reputable source.

Locally Administered MAC Addresses

When universally administered addresses are used on a LAN, the MAC addresses look like random jumbles of hex characters. Some LAN administrators prefer to reconfigure each adapter at installation time and assign addresses that have a local interpretation. For example, each address could be split into fields that identify the building, floor, wiring closet, and specific office in which the system has been installed. Knowing the location of a malfunctioning card is helpful when troubleshooting LAN problems.

The IEEE numbering architecture takes this preference into account. A bit in the first address byte is equal to 0 in all universally administered addresses and must be 1 for locally administered addresses.

> **Note**
> Using local addresses imposes an administrative burden. Every card must be manually configured with a MAC address that has a locally defined meaning. If the MAC address corresponds to a station's location, this address must be changed when the station is moved. If a card fails, the staff person replacing the card must remember to configure the replacement correctly when the new one is installed.
>
> The benefit of using a universally administered unique address is that you can attach a system to any LAN without worrying about duplicate MAC addresses.

Broadcast and Group Addresses

An address that identifies a single system is called a *unicast* or *individual address*. A frame sent to a unicast MAC address is targeted at a single destination.

A station attached to a multiaccess LAN has the capability to direct a frame to every system on the LAN. A *broadcast address* is used to do this. All MAC interfaces absorb any frame that is addressed to the broadcast address:

X'FF-FF-FF-FF-FF-FF

This address consists of 48 1-bits.

Sometimes it is convenient to send a frame to a select group of recipient systems. *Group addresses* (also called *multicast addresses*) implement this feature. A bit in the first address byte is equal to 0 for an individual address and 1 for a group destination address.

To set up an adapter so that it will recognize and absorb frames sent to a particular group address, a higher-layer program passes a request to the device driver, which then notifies the adapter to add the new address to its list.

The NIC in Figure 2.1 already has been configured to accept frames addressed to Group-Address-1 and Group-Address-2, in addition to its own unicast address and the broadcast address. The figure shows an application program asking the device driver to add Group-Address-3 to the NIC. A later request could be used to remove a group address from the card.

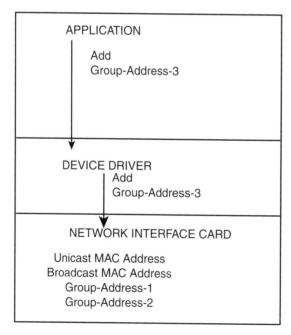

FIGURE 2.1 *Addresses recognized by a NIC.*

Individual/Group and Universal/Local Flag Bits

The two least significant bits in the first byte of a MAC address are the special flag bits that identify whether an address is:

- Individual (0) or group (1)

- Universal (0) or local (1)

Figure 2.2 shows the position of these important bits as they appear when each byte of a MAC address is written in binary with its most significant bit on the left.

Note

This is the normal mathematical order in which the bits in a byte are expressed. See Appendix B.

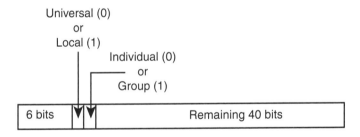

FIGURE 2.2 *Individual/group and universal/local flag bits.*

Ethernet Address Conventions

The IEEE 802.3 committee specified that every byte in an Ethernet frame must be transmitted with the least significant bit first.

Note

This convention sometimes is called little endian order.

Standards do not specify the order in which bits and bytes are stored within a computer. How-ever, a standard does need to spell out the order in which bits and bytes are transmitted. When computers communicate with one another, each needs to know what to expect when bits arrive across a medium.

Note that transmitting the least significant bit first assures that the first MAC address bit that goes onto a wire is the individual/group bit and the second is the universal/local bit.

For example, if X'C2 is the first byte of an address, the first bit that is sent is a 0 (individual address), and the second bit is a 1 (local address). The order of transmission is indicated here by the letters a–h. The bit marked "a" is sent first.

h g f e d c b a ——->
1 1 0 0 0 0 1 0 = X'C2

Ethernet Multicast Addresses

A large number of Ethernet MAC addresses—in fact, half of them—are multi-cast addresses. Multicast addresses are used to send a frame to a group of systems. Recall that the flag that indicates whether an address is unicast or multicast is the least significant bit in the first byte of an address.

When an organization registers and obtains an OUI for unicast addresses, it also can use that OUI for multicast addresses. The organization can define multicast addresses for any purpose that is deemed convenient.

The IEEE 802 committee owns unicast OUI X'00-80-C2. This gives the IEEE the right to define multicast addresses that start with X'01-80-C2. For example, take a look at these addresses and definitions:

X'01-80-C2-00-00-00   Used as a group address for bridges that support the spanning tree protocol

X'01-80-C2-00-01-10   Used as a group address for stations config-ured to receive FDDI status report frames

Digital Equipment Corporation (DEC) owns unicast OUI X'08-00-2B, so it can define multicast addresses that start with X'09-00-2B. DEC has defined many special-purpose multicast addresses. For example, DEC uses X'09-00-2B-00-00-0F as a *local area transport* (LAT) multicast address. LAT is a terminal access protocol that is used in DEC networks. Note that the bits in the first byte (X'09) of these DEC addresses are as follows:

0 0 0 0 1 0 0 **1** ← Least significant bit

Traces of Ethernet MAC Addresses

Every MAC frame has a header that contains the destination and source MAC addresses. The address fields in Listings 2.1, 2.2, and 2.3 were taken from frames captured by a Windows NT Server 4.0 Network Monitor utility. Listing 2.1 shows the address fields in a frame that has been sent from one LAN station to another.

LISTING 2.1 DESTINATION AND SOURCE ADDRESSES IN A UNICAST ETHERNET FRAME HEADER

```
ETHERNET: Destination address : 0020AF3BD450
        ETHERNET: .......0 = Individual address
        ETHERNET: ......0. = Universally administered address
    ETHERNET: Source address : 00A024A6EDE4
        ETHERNET: .......0 = Individual address
        ETHERNET: ......0. = Universally administered address
```

The first byte of both the destination address and the source addresses in Listing 2.1 is X'00. In binary:

$$X'00 = 0000\ 000\mathbf{0} \leftarrow \text{Least significant bit}$$

The least significant bit is 0 in both addresses in Listing 2.1, confirming that they are individual addresses.

The prior bit indicates whether an address is universally administered (0) or locally administered (1). Both of the addresses in the trace are universally administered.

Listing 2.2 shows the addresses for a frame that was broadcast to all systems on the LAN. There is a misleading statement in the third line of the Microsoft protocol analyzer report. Because all bits in the broadcast address are 1, the relevant universal/local bit also is 1. However, the broadcast address is an exception to the rule stating that this means that the address is locally administered.

LISTING 2.2 DESTINATION AND SOURCE ADDRESSES IN A BROADCAST ETHERNET FRAME HEADER

```
ETHERNET: Destination address : FFFFFFFFFFFF
        ETHERNET: .......1 = Group address
        ETHERNET: ......1. = Locally administered address
    ETHERNET: Source address : 00A024A6EDE4
        ETHERNET: .......0 = (Individual address)
        ETHERNET: ......0. = Universally administered address
```

Note

A source address must be a unicast address. After all, some interface sent this frame. The source address must identify which interface it was.

Listing 2.3 shows addresses for a frame with a multicast destination address. An adapter will not absorb frames sent to a particular multicast address unless it has been configured to do so.

A quick check of a list of standard multicast addresses revealed that the frame in the trace is a Hello message directed to a group of routers on the LAN. The originating router sends this message to announce that it is there, alive and well. Each router on the LAN has been configured so that its LAN adapter will accept frames sent to multicast address X'01-00-5E-00-00-05.

LISTING 2.3 DESTINATION AND SOURCE ADDRESSES IN A MULTICAST ETHERNET FRAME HEADER

```
ETHERNET: Destination address : 01005E000005
    ETHERNET: .......1 = Group address
    ETHERNET: ......0. = Universally administered address
ETHERNET: Source address : 00A02456AB6F
    ETHERNET: .......0 = (Individual address)
    ETHERNET: ......0. = Universally administered address
```

Note
The Token Ring and FDDI sections that follow are fairly technical. The reader may wish to skip them now and come back to them later, if needed.

Token Ring Address Conventions

The Token Ring protocol was invented by IBM. IBM had defined many communications protocols prior to designing the Token Ring. For IBM's earlier protocols, the *most significant bit* in each byte was transmitted first This sometimes is call "big endian" order.

IBM did not want to change this practice for the Token Ring protocol. However, IBM also wanted to submit its Token Ring specification to the IEEE.

In its 802.3 standard, the IEEE had specified that the bytes in an Ethernet frame were to be transmitted with the least significant bit first. This was especially important for addresses:

- The first (leftmost) destination address bit that is transmitted must indicate whether it is an individual address (0) or a group address (1).

- The next bit must indicate whether it is a universal (0) or a local (1) address.

IBM's compromise was to:

- Transmit the addresses in the MAC header in the same order as Ethernet addresses with the individual/group bit first

- Transfer the bytes in the information field with the most significant bit first

However, IBM went one step further. The company reinterpreted addresses so that the order of the bits in each address byte was reversed. Reversing converts the least significant bit into the most significant bit.

For example, IBM defined several special multicast addresses (called functional addresses) that are used to identify nodes that perform various types of Token Ring services. Functional addresses start with X'CC (binary 1100 1100). The individual/group bit is the first (most significant) bit of the address. The upper part of Figure 2.3 illustrates the order of Token Ring addresses.

Because a source address always must be an individual address, IBM decided to use the individual/group bit in a source address for a different purpose. IBM used the bit as a flag that indicates whether an additional field containing frame routing information follows. (This field is called the *Routing Information Field*, or RIF, and is explained in Chapter 19, "Token Ring and FDDI Overview.") The lower part of Figure 2.3 illustrates this usage.

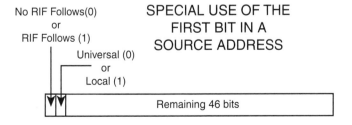

FIGURE 2.3 *Initial bits in a Token Ring address.*

Like Ethernet stations, Token Ring stations recognize X'FF-FF-FF-FF-FF-FF as a broadcast address. The address X'C0-00-FF-FF-FF-FF also is designated as a Token Ring broadcast address. Note that the initial bit of X'CO is a 1, indicating that this is a group address.

Addresses Carried in a Token Ring Information Field

Some protocol messages carry MAC addresses within a frame's information field. For example, TCP/IP stations broadcast *Address Resolution Protocol* (ARP) requests that ask the owner of an enclosed IP address to respond and provide its MAC address.

On a Token Ring, the addresses in these messages are represented (and transmitted) in exactly the same way as in the MAC header.

A Trace Showing Token Ring MAC Addresses

For example, IBM has been assigned OUI X'10-00-5A. Listing 2.4 shows a trace that was obtained with a Network Associates *Sniffer* monitor. The listing shows an ARP message carried in a Token Ring frame.

The source address is reported as IBM1 21D4E2. Later in the message, the full address is displayed as X'08-00-5A-21-D4-E2 in the sender's hardware address field.

The actual NIC address is X'10-00-5A-84-2B-47. The address has been expressed with the bits in each byte reversed, both when its address appears in the Token Ring MAC header and when it reappears inside the ARP data. The transformation is shown as follows. Each byte is translated to bits and is formatted for easy reading with slashes between each group of 8 bits:

```
X'10-00-5A-84-2B-47 =
0001 0000/0000 0000/0101 1010/1000 0100/0010 1011/0100 0111
```

Reversing the order within each byte looks like this:

```
X'08-00-5A-21-D4-E2 =
0000 1000/0000 0000/0101 1010/0010 0001/1101 0100/1110 0010
```

This reversed order is called the *noncanonical* format.

When you examine the actual hexadecimal data that was transmitted, you can see that the source MAC address field is displayed as 88 00 5a 21 d4 e2. The 08 has been converted to 88 because the first bit has been set to 1, indicating that a RIF follows.

LISTING 2.4 TOKEN RING ADDRESSES

```
ARP:
DLC:  ----- DLC Header -----
      DLC:
      DLC:  Frame 31 arrived at  13:35:13.863; frame size is 58 (003A hex)
➡bytes.
      DLC:  FS: Addr recognized indicators: 11, Frame copied indicators: 11
      DLC:  AC: Frame priority 0,  Reservation priority 0,  Monitor count 1
      DLC:  FC: LLC frame,  PCF attention code: None
      DLC:  Destination = Station IBM2  A8EDE3
      DLC:  Source      = Station IBM1  21D4E2
      DLC:
RI:   ----- Routing Indicators -----
(Routing Information Field)
(Other Fields)
ARP: ----- ARP/RARP frame -----
      ARP:
      ARP: Hardware type = 6 (IEEE 802 Network)
      ARP: Protocol type = 0800 (IP)
      ARP: Length of hardware address = 6 bytes
      ARP: Length of protocol address = 4 bytes
      ARP: Opcode 2 (ARP reply)
      ARP: Sender's hardware address = 08005A21D4E2
      ARP: Sender's protocol address = [170.217.24.139]
      ARP: Target hardware address  = 10005AA8EDE3
      ARP: Target protocol address  = [170.217.17.100]
      ARP:
      ARP:
ADDR  HEX     (destination)   *   (source)
0000: 18 40 10 00 5a a8 ed e3 88 00 5a 21 d4 e2 08 c0
0010: 43 e1 43 b0 41 70 aa aa 03 00 00 00 08 06 00 06
0020: 08 00 06 04 00 02 08 00 5a 21 d4 e2 aa d9 18 8b
0030: 10 00 5a a8 ed e3 aa d9 11 64
```

Token Ring Functional Addresses

The Token Ring designers defined 31 *functional address* flags that are used to send frames to a group of systems that play specific roles in a Token Ring network.

Functional addresses are introduced by this 17-bit pattern:

11000000 00000000 0

This translates to X'C0-00, followed by another 0 bit. The first bit in X'C0 shows that these are group addresses, and the second bit shows that these addresses are classified as local addresses. The remaining 31 bits are used as flags that identify the type (or types) of destinations that should absorb the frame. Table 2.1 lists some functional addresses.

A single frame can be sent to multiple groups of systems by setting several flag bits to 1. For example, to send a frame to both an active monitor and a ring parameter server, set the destination address equal to the following:

X′C0-00-00-00-00-03

TABLE 2.1 TOKEN RING FUNCTIONAL MAC ADDRESSES

Function Name	MAC Address
Active monitor	X′C0-00-00-00-00-01
Ring parameter server (RPS)	X′C0-00-00-00-00-02
Ring error monitor (REM)	X′C0-00-00-00-00-08
Configuration report server (CRS)	X′C0-00-00-00-00-10
Source route bridge	X′C0-00-00-00-01-00

FDDI Address Conventions

FDDI information frames are based on Token Ring information frames. As is the case for a Token Ring frame, the information in an FDDI frame is sent with the most significant bit first. And, like Token Ring, the MAC addresses in an FDDI MAC header are expressed in reverse order.

Unfortunately, MAC addresses embedded in an FDDI information field sometimes appear in non-canonical format (bit-reversed, like Token Ring) and sometimes appear in canonical format (not bit-reversed).

- When the FDDI ring interconnects with Token Ring LANs, the non-canonical (bit-reversed) format is used.

- When the FDDI ring interconnects with Ethernet LANs, the canonical format is used.

If both Ethernet and Token Ring LANs are connected to an FDDI LAN, both canonical and noncanonical formats can appear on the FDDI LAN.

A Trace Showing FDDI MAC Addresses

Listing 2.5 is a Network Associates *Sniffer* trace that shows parts of an FDDI frame containing an ARP message that includes MAC addresses in its information field. The actual addresses are:

Destination: X′08-00-20-06-C5-D9

Source: X′08-00-2B-0F-E4-0D

The upper portion of the trace displays the actual addresses, independent of the order of transmission. The reader can see that the MAC header source address is the same as the sender's source address in the ARP part of the trace.

However, the hexadecimal rendition of the trace shows that the address bytes in the MAC header and in the ARP message actually were transmitted in a different manner. For the MAC header, bytes appeared in bit-reversed format:

> Destination: 10 00 04 60 a3 9b
>
> Source: 10 00 d4 f0 27 b0

In the ARP part, the addresses appeared in canonical format:

> Target hardware address: 08 00 20 06 c5 d9
>
> Sender's hardware address: 08 00 2B 0F E4 0D

LISTING 2.5 MAC ADDRESSES IN AN FDDI FRAME

```
ARP: R PA=[128.141.200.5] HA=DEC1  0FE40D PRO=IP
FDDI: ----- DLC Header -----
      FDDI:
      FDDI: Frame 5 arrived at  02:17:27.03635; frame size is 67 (0043
➥hex) bytes.
 . . .
      FDDI: Note: Addresses presented in LSb format
      FDDI:
      FDDI: Destination = Station Sun    06C5D9  (X'08-00-20-06-C5-D9)
      FDDI: Source      = Station DEC    0FE40D  (X'08-00-2B-0F-E4-0D)
      FDDI:
 . . .
(Other Fields)
ARP: ----- ARP/RARP frame -----
      ARP:
      ARP: Hardware type = 1 (10Mb Ethernet)
      ARP: Protocol type = 0800 (IP)
      ARP: Length of hardware address = 6 bytes
      ARP: Length of protocol address = 4 bytes
      ARP: Opcode 2 (ARP reply)
      ARP: Sender's hardware address = 08002B0FE40D
      ARP: Sender's protocol address = [128.141.200.5]
      ARP: Target hardware address   = 08002006C5D9
      ARP: Target protocol address   = [128.141.1.203]
      ARP:

0000: 50 10 00 04 60 a3 9b 10 00 d4 f0 27 b0 aa aa 03
0010: 00 00 00 08 06 00 01 08 00 06 04 00 02 08 00 2b
0020: 0f e4 0d 80 8d c8 05 08 00 20 06 c5 d9 80 8d 01
0030: cb 01 cd 08 01 03 fd 07 f4
```

There are switches that interconnect Ethernets, Token Rings, and FDDI LANs. These switches have to deal with all of the formats and make sense of them. This is messy!

> **Note**
> Chapter 16 describes an IEEE tag header that contains priority and virtual LAN information. This header includes a flag that indicates whether MAC addresses embedded in a frame's information field appear in canonical or noncanonical form. These tags provide a rational solution to a silly problem and are supported in up-to-date equipment.

Summary Points

- Every network interface card (NIC) is assigned a unique 6-byte MAC address.

- Universally unique media access control (MAC) addresses are controlled by the IEEE, which assigns 3-byte organizationally unique identifiers (OUIs) to requesting organizations. An OUI value is used as the first 3 bytes of a unique address.

- Some LAN administrators prefer to assign their own local MAC addresses to NICs.

- A frame whose destination is a broadcast address is sent to every system on a LAN.

- A frame whose destination address is a multicast address is targeted at a group of systems on a LAN.

- Ethernet addresses are transmitted with the least significant bit first. The first bits to be sent are the unicast/group flag and the universal/local flag.

- The most significant bit in a Token Ring information byte is transmitted first. However, addresses are sent with the least significant bit first. To do this, addresses are redefined with a reversed bit order. Addresses appearing in the information field have the same bit ordering as addresses in the MAC header.

- A Token Ring Routing Information Field (RIF) lays out a path from a source to the destination. The first bit in a source address indicates whether a RIF follows.

- FDDI information frames were modeled on Token Ring information frames. The bit ordering for addresses appearing in the information field depends on whether the FDDI LAN interconnects to Token Ring LANs or Ethernet LANs.

References

The IETF Internet Engineering Note (IEN) referenced below contains a playful discussion of the battle between the big-endians and the little-endians.

- IETF IEN-37. "On Holy Wars and a Prayer for Peace." D. Cohen. April 1, 1980.

The following IEEE document tries to clear up the confusion caused by multiple "standard" frame and address formats.

- IEEE Draft Standard 802: Overview and Architecture, 1999.

CHAPTER **3**

Ethernet LAN Structure

In 1980, Digital Equipment Corporation (DEC), Intel, and Xerox published the Ethernet Version 1 specification (also called the *Ethernet Blue Book*). This specification described a 10Mbps LAN that operated across coaxial cable using *baseband* transmission (which means that bits are represented as a series of voltage pulses). An improved version, now called DIX Ethernet or Ethernet Version 2, was published in 1982.

> **Note**
>
> DIX stands for Digital, Intel, and Xerox. Ethernet Version 2 sometimes is written as Ethernet Version II, or simply Ethernet II.

In the meantime, the Institute for Electrical and Electronic Engineers (IEEE) established its 802 committee, tasked with developing and promoting local and metropolitan area network (MAN) standards.

> **Note**
>
> The engineers were not very imaginative when they chose the name of their committee. The 802 committee was formed in the second month (2) of 1980 (80).

In 1981, an 802 subcommittee (called the 802.3 Working Group) got together to compose a standard based on DIX Ethernet. By 1983, when the IEEE standard was officially published, many vendors already had endorsed and accepted both DIX and IEEE Ethernet, and some were shipping products. Sealing its success, the 802.3 standard was adopted by the American National Standards Institute (ANSI) and the International Standards Organization (ISO).

> **Note**
>
> As Chapter 4, "The Classical Ethernet CSMA/CD MAC Protocol," will show, the 802.3 frame format differed slightly from the DIX frame format and imposed a few extra bytes of overhead. Standards advocates have repeatedly declared that the DIX format was dead, but most customers preferred DIX because they got a smidgen of extra throughput by using it. NIC vendors stayed out of the fight and supported both versions on their Ethernet cards.
>
> Finally, in its 1998 update of Ethernet, the IEEE 802.3 committee gave up and incorporated the DIX frame format as one of the acceptable ways of doing business. In fact, the 802 committee used the DIX EtherType to add some useful extensions to Ethernet—frame priority levels and virtual LANs (VLANs). These are described in Chapter 16, "VLANs and Frame Priority." The DIX frame lives!

Ethernet LAN Architecture

Many of the components that make up today's Ethernet LANs were defined in the early years of the original coaxial cable Ethernet LANs. A brief tour of the design of these early LANs is a quick and painless way to introduce Ethernet LAN architecture and terminology.

> **Note**
>
> The purpose of the discussion that follows is to establish some basic terminology and concepts. Many details have been omitted so that some major pieces of the framework can be nailed in place. Later chapters will tell the whole story.

Single Segment Ethernet LAN and CSMA/CD

Figure 3.1 shows a very simple Ethernet LAN made up of several desktop systems and a server attached to a coaxial cable.

A system that wants to send a frame must wait until the medium is quiet—that is, until no other system is sending a frame. Only one frame is allowed to traverse the cable at any given instant. If two stations start to send at the same time, their transmissions will collide, and each will have to wait for a random timeout period before trying again. This set of rules is called *Carrier Sense Multiple Access with Collision Detection* (CSMA/CD).

All the systems listen to the medium and see every frame that is transmitted. Each frame has a header that carries the LAN addresses of its destination and its source.

In Figure 3.1, desktop system A is sending a frame to server C. Server C reads the destination address in the frame's header, recognizes that it matches its own address, and accepts the frame. Systems B and D see the frame but, after examining the destination address, ignore the frame.

The configuration shown in Figure 3.1 is called a *bus topology*. A single cable serves to connect the devices.

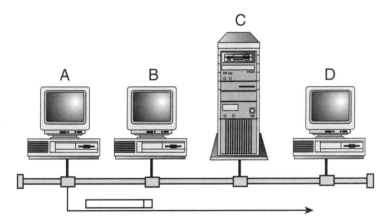

FIGURE 3.1 *Sending a frame on an Ethernet segment.*

The LAN in Figure 3.1 illustrates several concepts:

- The systems are connected to a single coaxial cable bus that is called a LAN *segment*.

- This is a *multiaccess* environment—that is, multiple systems are connected, and a system accesses the medium to send a frame to another system.

- A frame's destination address is examined by every system. This makes it possible to use a broadcast address to send a frame to every station, and to use distinctive multicast addresses to send a frame to a selected group of stations on the LAN.

This often is called a *broadcast multiaccess environment* because many systems are connected to the medium, and each system's network interface "sees" every frame.

Using Repeaters to Build Multisegment LANs

Early LANs tended to be small and compact, but it did not take long before users wanted their LANs to grow. However, the signals that represent zeros and ones grow weak (attenuate) as they propagate through a cable segment. A segment's length must be limited to assure that the signals that it carries are intelligible.

The size of a LAN can be increased by installing one or more *repeaters*. A repeater accepts zeros and ones from one cable segment and transmits them onto one or more other cable segments at full strength. A *repeater* is a physical-layer device.

Note
Hub and concentrator are other names for a repeater. These terms are used for repeaters that connect to more than two segments.

Figure 3.2 shows a coax LAN that has been extended across three segments by adding a repeater. A frame sent by system A will be seen by every device on the LAN. The frame in Figure 3.2 is addressed to system X.

Each LAN segment is connected to a *port* on the repeater. A port is a network interface. In the figure, each repeater port connects to a segment via a short attachment cable.

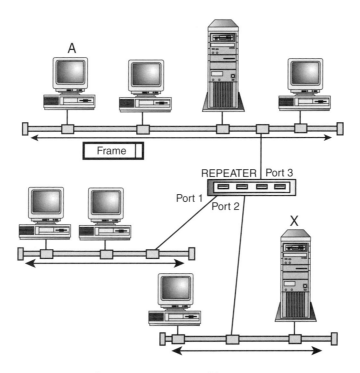

FIGURE 3.2 *Three segments connected by a repeater.*

Twisted-Pair Cabling and Hub Repeaters

Coaxial cable is heavy and stiff, and coax LANs are hard to maintain. For years, telephone companies have used orderly cabling plans based on running unshielded twisted-pair cables from wiring closets to offices. Buildings are full of unshielded twisted-pair cabling.

In the early 1980s, several vendors (led by AT&T) thought that it would make good sense to create a LAN technology that could follow this type of cabling plan and operate over unshielded twisted-pair telephone cable.

The result was *StarLAN*, a 1Mbps twisted-pair LAN. StarLAN was greeted with some initial enthusiasm because a star topology with cables radiating out from a wiring closet made good sense. Using telephone cable was a great advantage because buildings already were wired with telephone cable. However, 1Mbps was just too slow.

Eventually, engineers figured out how to transmit 10Mbps (and later, 100Mbps and 1000Mbps) across unshielded twisted–pair cabling. LAN cabling got a new look—and a new network repeater device—the 10Mbps twisted-pair hub.

The change to twisted-pair cabling and a star topology gave hubs a central role. The hub in Figure 3.3 repeats the bits in a frame transmitted by station A to all the other stations connected to the hub.

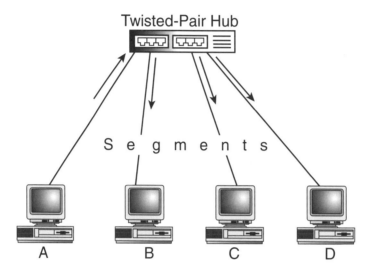

FIGURE 3.3 *Propagating a frame to all stations.*

An important feature of this topology is that there are only two nodes on each cable segment: a computer and the repeater. There are four segments in Figure 3.3, and each connects a computer to the hub.

Note

All that the twisted-pair hub in Figure 3.3 does is to repeat bits from one segment onto another. So, why isn't the device called a twisted-pair repeater?

The answer is "marketing." Early repeaters connected two or three coax segments. Vendors wanted to describe their products using a word that indicated that their products were new. The "hub" products looked different and connected many twisted-pair segments.

Today, the term "hub" sometimes is used for a chassis that contains repeaters along with other network devices. This is unfortunate because it causes confusion and damages the meaning of a convenient piece of networking terminology.

In this book, "hub" will be used to denote a repeater device.

Improving Performance with Bridges

The Ethernet specifications allow 1,024 stations to be attached to a LAN. But when Ethernet bandwidth is a shared commodity, poor performance will make users groan and gnash their teeth long before anywhere near that number of systems has been attached to their LAN.

A *bridge* is a Layer 2 device that takes a lot of the pain out of LAN growth. The three LAN segments in Figure 3.4 are connected by a bridge. Whenever possible, a bridge blocks frames from reaching segments that have no real need to carry them.

For example, if system A in Figure 3.4 wants to send a frame to server C, there is no reason to transmit that frame onto segment 1 or segment 2. If station E wants to send a frame to server H, there is no reason to transmit that frame onto segment 3.

In fact, during a period when users are sending frames to destinations on their own segments, three frames could be in transit at the same time. In other words, for three 10Mbps segments, the available bandwidth would be 30Mbps during that period.

Bridges became popular because they cut down on the traffic that crosses each segment, resulting in more bandwidth for each station on a segment.

Collision Domains

The LAN segments in Figure 3.2 and 3.3 are connected to one another by repeaters. For either of these LANs, a frame transmitted by any station on the LAN will be seen by all stations on the LAN. If two stations send at the same time, their frames will collide. For this reason, a set of segments connected by repeaters is called a *collision domain*.

Note

At any given time, one station (at most) in a collision domain can transmit a frame successfully. If one station talks, the others should be listening. For this reason, CSMA/CD also is called half-duplex Ethernet transmission.

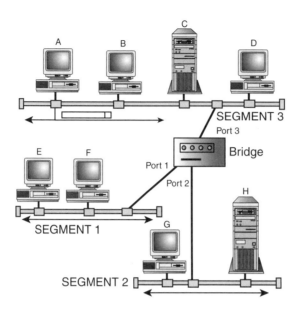

FIGURE 3.4 *Three segments connected by a bridge.*

The bridge in Figure 3.4 splits its LAN into three separate collision domains. Frames with local destinations do not need to be forwarded onto other segments. When a frame must be forwarded, the bridge behaves like a good citizen of the destination collision domain: It listens to check whether the destination medium is available before transmitting the frame. If the medium is busy, the bridge can hold the frame in buffer memory until the medium becomes quiet again.

Administrators appreciated the fact that a bridge could be installed by hooking up the cables and plugging in the power. A bridge eavesdrops on traffic originating on each segment to discover the MAC addresses of the stations on the segment. The bridge creates a table that maps each MAC address to the port through which it is reached. When a MAC address is listed in the bridge table, the bridge will be capable of forwarding frames addressed to that MAC address onto the correct segment. Chapters 12-17 contain a full description of what bridges do and how they do it.

Leaping to Higher Performance with Switches

In 1993, a company named Kalpana introduced LAN *switches*. This was an astonishing event, startling many LAN experts who wondered why they had not thought of it first. A switch is a multiport bridge that can forward several frames at the same time.

Eventually, LAN switches evolved into the popular *Layer 2 switches* in use today. Figure 3.5 shows a set of stations connected to a Layer 2 switch. Twisted-pair or fiber optic cable are the media normally used with a Layer 2 switch.

In Figure 3.5, each link connecting a station to a switch is a separate segment that is bridged to all other segments. The internal architecture of the switch allows many frames to be in transit at the same time, which greatly increases the LAN bandwidth.

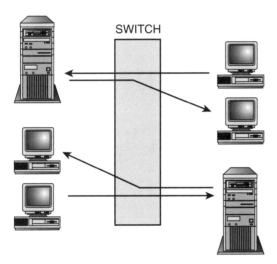

FIGURE 3.5 *A Layer 2 switch.*

> ## Note
> Just as "twisted-pair hub" is an up-market name for a modern repeater, "Layer 2 switch" is an up-market name for a modern bridge. A Layer 2 switch can have numerous ports and uses better hardware technology than the bridges of long ago, but functionally, it is a bridge.
>
> Some modern switches have been loaded with so many extra features and options that the simple plug-and-play installation of earlier times has been lost. Fortunately, there also are simple workgroup switches that still are a breeze to install.

Switches and Full-Duplex Operation

The appeal of multiport switches was enhanced by an addition to the 802.3 standard that gave performance a big boost. As shown in Figure 3.6, when a single station is connected to a switch port, the link between the station and the switch can be used for full-duplex communication. Both systems can transmit and receive at the same time. For example, across a 100Mbps link, the station can transmit frames to the switch at 100Mbps and receive frames from the switch at 100Mbps.

The full-duplex Ethernet MAC protocol is very simple: Either party can send a frame whenever it pleases. CSMA/CD is not needed when full-duplex communication is used.

Note

Full-duplex communication can be used between any systems that are not repeaters. For example, a full-duplex link can be set up between two hosts, two switches (bridges), a switch and a router, or a pair of routers.

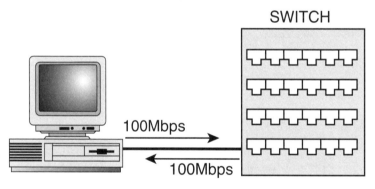

FIGURE 3.6 *Full-duplex communication between a station and a switch.*

Sharing the LAN

LANs are data communications workhorses. A LAN frame can carry traffic that belongs to any type of higher-layer protocol. It is not at all unusual to see a mixture of protocols such as TCP/IP, NetWare IPX/SPX, DECnet, and AppleTalk happily sharing a LAN. Figure 3.7 shows how higher-layer protocols ride on top of Layer 1 and Layer 2 LAN protocols. Many hosts send and receive traffic for several different protocols through a single LAN adapter.

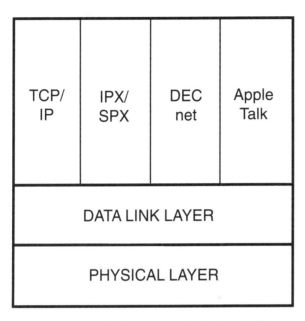

FIGURE 3.7 *Higher-layer protocols sharing a LAN.*

The Role of Routers

It did not take long before users wanted to exchange information with servers located on external LANs dotted across an enterprise—and, with the advent of the Internet, with servers located around the world. Routers make this communication possible.

Figure 3.8 shows two LANs connected by a router. The router also connects these LANs to a long-distance line. This could lead to another site within a company or to the Internet.

A router is a Layer 3 device. Routers have lots of good features. To mention just a few:

- They can connect different types of LANs gracefully.

- Unlike a bridge, a router does not forward LAN broadcast traffic or local LAN multicasts. A sizeable amount of bandwidth can be saved. This is particularly important when the peak load on one of the LANs is close to the LANs capacity.

- They can connect a set of LANs to a set of WAN links of different types—for example, dial-up, leased line, frame relay, or Asynchronous Transfer Mode (ATM).

- They can perform security screening and keep risky traffic off a LAN.

An important thing to keep in mind is that when data from a LAN reaches a router, it has passed through a doorway and left the LAN. The router strips off the MAC frame header and trailer. The protocol data will be encapsulated in a new header and trailer before it is forwarded.

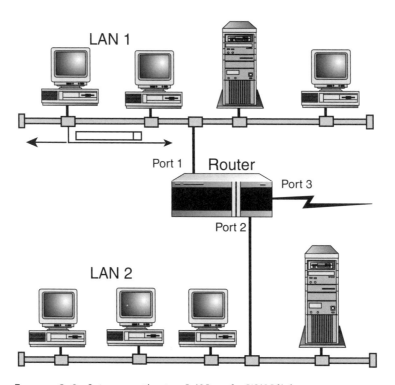

FIGURE 3.8 *Interconnecting two LANs and a WAN link.*

Summary Points

- Although LANs originally were truly local, today a LAN can span a campus or can include multiple sites.

- A LAN operates at the physical and data link layers.

- Cables, communicating computers, repeaters/hubs, and bridges/switches all are LAN components.

- An Ethernet collision domain is made up of end systems, cable segments, repeaters, and hubs. Only one frame can be in transit across a collision domain at any given time.

- The Ethernet Carrier Sense Multiple Access with Collision Detection (CSMA/CD) media access protocol is used on a collision domain. CSMA/CD also is called half-duplex Ethernet communication.

- Bridges and switches increase a LAN's transmission capacity by breaking an Ethernet LAN into multiple collision domains.

- The change from coaxial to twisted-pair cable and from a bus to a star topology was an important step in the evolution of Ethernet.

- When a station is directly connected to a switch, it can communicate in full-duplex mode and can transmit a frame whenever it wishes.

- A single LAN can carry traffic for many different higher-layer protocols.

- A router can connect several LANs to one another and to one or more wide area circuits.

References

The University of New Hampshire's InterOperability Lab (IOL) tests networking products. It provides a home for many vendor consortiums. Each consortium is devoted to a single technology.

The technologies include 100Mbps and Gigabit Ethernet, 100Mbps Token Ring, FDDI, Fibre Channel, 100VG-ANYLAN, virtual LANs (VLANs), bridging, and more. Each consortium member provides platforms representing its equipment and supports the lab's testing activities.

The lab publishes free tutorials and insightful white papers. These are available at http://www.iol.unh.edu/consortiums/fe/index.html

The historic publication that described DIX Ethernet was "The Ethernet—A Local Area Network: Data Link Layer and Physical Layer Specifications." This document was published by Digital, Intel, and Xerox in November 1982.

IEEE Standard 802-1990, "Overview and Architecture," introduces the formal IEEE LAN terminology and architecture. An updated version of this document is in draft form at the time of writing.

CHAPTER **4**

The Classical Ethernet CSMA/CD MAC Protocol

The Ethernet media access control (MAC) protocol is extremely resilient. It has been adapted to a wide range of speeds, media, and changing LAN topologies. The current version of the 802.3 standard (defined in the 1998 edition) can operate at 1Mbps, 10Mbps, 100Mbps, and 1000Mbps.

> **Note**
>
> The 1Mbps StarLAN version of Ethernet introduced in the early 1980s no longer is used and certainly does not qualify as a high-speed LAN technology. It will not be discussed further in this book.

Ethernet media include various grades of coaxial cable, twisted-pair wire, and optical fiber. On twisted-pair or optical fiber, an Ethernet station connected to a switch can operate in full-duplex mode, doubling the potential throughput.

Rules and parameters laid down for the original Ethernet networks have been carried through all the versions. This has supported an astonishing degree of backward compatibility. A LAN administrator can leave stable LAN segments that work well for their users undisturbed, and update or add segments based on newer technologies when higher performance is needed.

This chapter describes the classical CSMA/CD half-duplex Ethernet protocols. Full-duplex Ethernet is described in Chapter 5, "Full-Duplex Ethernet Communication."

Classic Ethernet Shared Bandwidth LANs

Communication on a classic Ethernet LAN is half–duplex. A classic LAN consists of a set of stations that share a fixed amount of bandwidth. Only one frame can be in transit at any given time.

The first physical medium that was used for Ethernet was thick 50-ohm coaxial cable, as is illustrated in the top half of Figure 4.1. Later, Ethernet LANs were constructed by connecting sets of stations to hubs via twisted-pair or fiber optic cables, as is shown in the bottom half of Figure 4.1.

A station sends information to another station by wrapping the information in a MAC frame. A MAC frame is transmitted as a serial stream of bits.

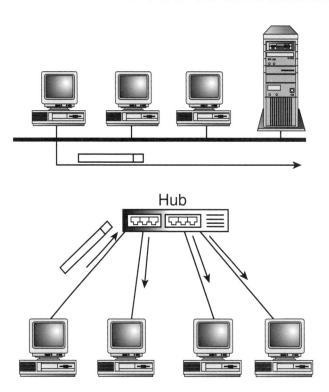

FIGURE 4.1   *Ethernet stations sharing a medium.*

Preamble and Interframe Gap

Every frame is introduced by a special pattern of 1s and 0s called a *preamble*. Figure 4.2 illustrates a series of frame transmissions. The gray areas in the figure correspond to frame preambles. Frame transmissions must be separated by a time interval called the *interframe gap* or *interpacket gap*. The time period between frames can vary, but each period must be at least as long as the interframe gap.

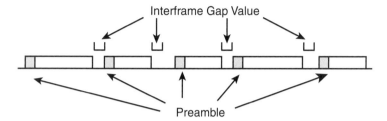

FIGURE 4.2 *Frame preambles and interframe gap spacing.*

The interframe gap period corresponds to 96 bit times (that is, 12 byte times). Thus, the actual time value is different for each speed level. It is:

> 96.000 microseconds (μs) for 1Mbps
>
> 9.600μs for 10Mbps
>
> 0.960μs for 100Mbps
>
> 0.096μs for 1000Mbps

Interframe Gap Shrinkage

The size of the interframe gap between frames can shrink as the frames pass through a repeater. Two factors cause this to happen:

- Variations in network delay can cause irregularities in the times at which frames arrive at a repeater.

- A repeater must lock on to an incoming preamble signal before it can start to retransmit the outgoing preamble and frame bits. The time that it takes to lock on to the signal can vary from frame to frame.

An analogy might help to explain why the gap sometimes shrinks. Suppose that each minute the doorman at a theater allows one customer to enter the lobby to buy a ticket, and normally a customer completes the transaction within 50 seconds. However, customer X walks so slowly that he uses up some of his time on the way to the ticket window. Also, the ticket seller has trouble understanding what customer X wants (that is, the seller has trouble "locking on to the signal"). The result is that the transaction takes 54 seconds. The next customer arrives at the ticket window punctually 6 seconds later—the normal 10-second intercustomer gap has shrunk to 6 seconds.

> **Note**
>
> 802.3 limits the amount of interframe gap shrinkage that is allowed. For example, the standard decrees that the interframe gap must not decrease below 47 bit times for 10Mbps Ethernet, or below 64 bit times for Gigabit Ethernet.
>
> Interframe gap shrinkage is one of the factors that limits the number of repeaters in a collision domain—and, hence, the diameter of a collision domain.

The CSMA/CD Protocol

Stations share a medium by adhering to a very simple media access control (MAC) protocol called *Carrier Sense Multiple Access with Collision Detection* (CSMA/CD). CSMA/CD is based on a few common sense rules:

- **Carrier Sense**—A station listens to the medium all the time. The station can transmit a frame after the medium has been quiet for a period at least as long as the interframe gap.

- **Collision Detection**—Two stations might start to send at roughly the same time. While sending, a station continues to listen, checking whether there is a concurrent transmission that causes its own signal to be garbled.

- **Jamming**—After detecting that a collision has occurred, a sender must continue to transmit bits to assure that all stations will be able to detect the collision. The additional number of bits is called the *jam size,* and it is equal to 32 bits (4 bytes).

- **Waiting**—A station that has participated in a collision must remain silent for a random amount of time before attempting to transmit again.

> **Note**
>
> Almost 10 Mbps throughput can be attained on a CSMA/CD LAN when only one station tries to transmit. However, collisions can reduce the throughput across a busy LAN to 3-4 megabits per second.

Random Backoff

A station that has just experienced a collision knows that there is at least one other system on the LAN that also has a frame to transmit. The station needs to behave in a way that reduces the likelihood that its next attempt to send the frame will cause another collision.

The basic idea is to wait a random time before resending. If the retransmitted frame also experiences a collision, the delay period needs to be stretched out. Specifically, the delay period is a multiple of a parameter called the *slot time*.

> **Note**
> For 10Mbps and 100Mbps, the slot time is equal to 512 bit times (that is, 64 byte times, the time required to send a frame of the smallest legal size). For Gigabit Ethernet, the slot time is 4096 bit times (that is, 512 byte times).

- After one collision, the station randomly "flips a coin" to choose whether to send immediately or wait one slot time.

- If a second collision results, the station randomly picks one of the four integers from 0 to 3 and retransmits after that number of slot times.

- If a third collision occurs, the number of values doubles to the range 0 to 7 slot times.

The doubling continues for up to 10 successive collisions and then levels off at 1,023 slot times. A station retries 16 times before giving up.

Stated in mathematical terms:

- For the nth try, where $n \leq 10$, choose a random number r with:

  $$0 \leq r < 2^n$$

- Retransmit the frame after waiting for the period:

  $$r \times (\text{slot time})$$

The formal name for this procedure is *truncated binary exponential backoff*. It often is referred to less formally as *random backoff*. The number of doublings (10) is called the *backoff limit*. The total number of tries (16) is called the *attempt limit*.

The use of 1,023 slot times might sound like a big interval, but consider the following:

- At 10Mbps, it is equal to .052 seconds.

- At 100Mbps, it is equal to .0052 seconds.

- At 1000Mbps, which has a bigger slot time, the interval is .0042 seconds.

> **Note**
>
> The system (say Station A) that manages to send the first frame after a collision often gets a big advantage. If multiple stations have frames queued up, this frame will be followed by another collision. But this is collision 1 for lucky Station A and collision 2 (with a longer backoff) for the others. The odds are that Station A will get the opportunity to send the next frame too. This will be followed by collision 3 for the others, and they will back off even longer. Lucky Station A often gets to send a long string of frames while other stations wait. This is called the *capture effect*.

Ethernet MAC Frames

As shown in Figure 4.3, an Ethernet MAC frame starts with a header that includes its destination and source MAC addresses. It ends in a frame check sequence (FCS) field that contains a CRC code that is used to detect transmission errors.

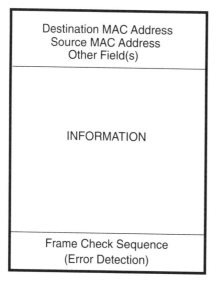

Figure 4.3 *General format of an Ethernet frame.*

Preamble and Start Frame Delimiter Patterns

A station transmits two special bit patterns—a *preamble* and a *start frame delimiter*—prior to sending a MAC frame. Figure 4.4 shows a MAC frame preceded by its preamble and start frame delimiter.

The preamble pattern tells other stations that a frame is on the way and enables the physical layers in the other stations to synchronize their bit timing with the sender's clock by locking on to the signal.

The preamble consists of 7 bytes of alternating 1s and 0s:

10101010 10101010 10101010 10101010 10101010 10101010 10101010

The special *start frame delimiter* (SFD) byte that follows the 802.3 preamble announces that the MAC frame follows immediately. The SFD byte consists of the pattern:

10101011

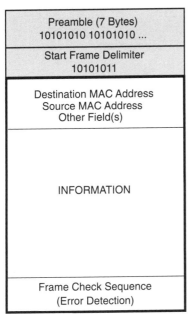

FIGURE 4.4 *Preamble, start frame delimiter, and MAC frame.*

Note

For some speeds and physical media, the frame introducer is somewhat different. The details are in Chapter 6, "The Ethernet 10Mbps Physical Layer," Chapter 7, "The Ethernet 100Mbps Physical Layer," Chapter 8, "Gigabit Ethernet Architecture," and Chapter 9, "Gigabit Ethernet Physical Layer."

Ethernet MAC Frame Size

Limits on the minimum and maximum frame size were established back when Ethernet was developed.

- The minimum MAC frame size was set to 64 bytes. Sometimes the information field in a small frame must be padded to increase the total length of the frame to 64 bytes.

- The maximum frame length was set to 1518 bytes.

> **Note**
>
> A frame that is too short is called a *runt*. Most *runts* are frames that have been chopped off by a collision. Some result from a burst of transmission errors that disrupts the frame.

Relationship Between Frame Size and Collision Domain Size

The original 50-ohm coax Ethernet LANs were allowed to have a maximum diameter of 2500 meters. The minimum MAC frame size was set to 64 bytes (512 bits) to assure that every station would be capable of sensing a collision across a 2500-meter, 10Mbps Ethernet. Figure 4.5 illustrates why the maximum LAN diameter depends on the minimum frame size.

In Figure 4.5, the round-trip time between DTE A and DTE B is assumed to be 514 bit times. This means that it will take 257 bit times for a bit transmitted by DTE A to reach DTE B.

All times in the figure are measured in bit times. The series of events is as follows:

1. At time T=0, DTE A begins to transmit a 512-bit frame.

2. At time T=256, DTE B believes that the medium is free and starts to transmit a frame.

3. At time T=257, bits from DTE A and DTE B have collided. DTE B sends a jam signal.

4. At time T=512, DTE A completes its transmission. It has not yet heard the collision or jam signal. DTE A and other stations that are near it believe that the frame has been sent successfully. DTE A will not back off and try again.

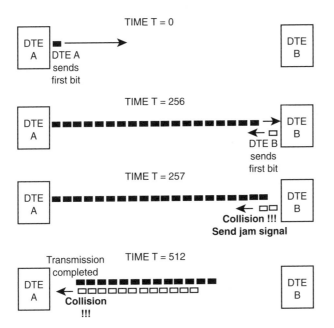

FIGURE 4.5 *Missing collisions when the round-trip time is too long.*

Communication gets completely muddled when collisions cannot be sensed by every station in a collision domain.

MAC Frame Formats

The left side of Figure 4.6 shows the format of the original DIX Ethernet frame. The right side shows the format of the current 802.3 Ethernet frame. The bytes in an Ethernet frame are transmitted top to bottom and left to right. The least significant bit of each byte is transmitted first.

The frame header (destination address, source address, and type or length) occupies 14 bytes, and the FCS trailer occupies 4 bytes. Because the total frame length is limited to 1518 bytes, the maximum size of the information field is 1500 bytes.

Destination and Source Addresses

The first two fields of a frame hold 6-byte destination and source MAC addresses. MAC addresses were described in Chapter 2, "LAN MAC Addresses." The source address is the unicast address of the station that sent the frame. The destination address may be a unicast, multicast, or broadcast address.

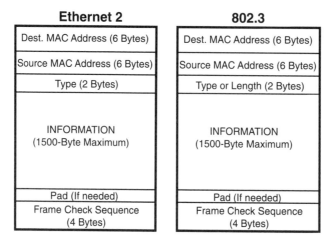

FIGURE 4.6 *Ethernet DIX and 802.3 frames.*

Type or Length

The DIX MAC frame header and the original 802.3 Ethernet MAC frame header were close to identical. They differed only in the use of the 2-byte field that follows the source MAC address.

- For DIX, this field contains a number that identifies the type of protocol unit that is carried in the information field.

- For the original version of 802.3, this field had to carry the length of the information field.

> **Note**
> It is important for a frame to identify the type of protocol information that it carries. When the third field in an Ethernet frame contains the length of the information field, a protocol type identifier must be placed into another header located at the start of the information field.

In spite of the fact that the 802 committee had not blessed the use of the DIX "type" field, users refused to give it up. It worked just fine, and DIX frames did not have to sacrifice part of the information field to identify the protocol being carried. DIX had fewer overhead bytes.

Finally, the use of either a type or a length value in this 2-byte position was absorbed into the 802.3 standard, and the DIX format became part of the official standard.

Ethernet Types

An Ethernet frame is allowed to carry any type of protocol data, and multiple protocols can share a LAN cable. In fact, it is not unusual for a single host to communicate via several different protocols.

When a system receives a frame, it needs to determine what protocol is enclosed so that it can pass the data field to the appropriate processing module. The Ethernet type (also called the *EtherType*) identifies the protocol. A few notable Ethernet types are listed in Table 4.1.

> **Note**
>
> All the Ethernet type values currently in use have decimal values well above 1500, which is the size of the largest Ethernet information field. Thus, a NIC easily can determine whether the type/length field in an incoming frame contains a type or a length value. The hexadecimal representation of 1500 is X'05-DC.

TABLE 4.1 ETHERNET TYPES

Hex Value	Decimal Value	Content of the Data Field
08-00	2048	IP datagram
08-06	2054	Address Resolution Protocol (ARP) message
0B-AD	2989	Banyan VINES
80-9B	32923	AppleTalk data units
80-D5	32981	IBM SNA services over Ethernet
81-37, 81-38	33079, 33080	NetWare data units
86-DD	34525	IP Version 6 datagram
60-03	24579	DECnet Phase IV routing information
60-04	24580	DEC LAT

> **Note**
>
> When DIX Ethernet got started, Xerox Corporation acted as an Ethernet type registration authority. Today, the IEEE acts as the registration authority for companies that want to obtain new Ethernet type numbers. A list of assigned type numbers currently is online at *http://standards.ieee.org/ regauth/ethertype/type-pub.html*.
>
> However, the IEEE lists only names of companies and the type numbers that the companies have been granted. It does not identify the protocols that are associated with these type numbers.

A couple of organizations try to keep track of the current status of protocols and their Ethernet types unofficially, using unverified information
contributed by volunteers. At the time of writing, lists can be found at
`http://www.iana.org/numbers.html` (Choose Ethernet Numbers) and
`http://www.cavebear.com/CaveBear/Ethernet/` (Choose Type Codes).

Size Modification for Gigabit Ethernet

The original Ethernet frame size constraints still hold for the bulk of the traffic
transmitted today. Some extra bytes are added when VLANs are used. VLAN
frame formats are described in Chapter 16, "VLANs and Frame Priority." The minimum size of a transmission had to be changed for half-duplex Gigabit Ethernet.

Warning

At the time of writing, all Gigabit Ethernet implementations are
full-duplex, and this probably will continue to be true in the future. This
means that it is very likely that the discussion that follows is strictly acade-
mic. However, the discussion does shed light on the reasons that half-
duplex CSMA/CD Gigabit Ethernet has not been implemented.

A frame length of 64 bytes is far too small to assure that collisions can be
detected on a Gigabit Ethernet CSMA/CD LAN. At gigabit speed, 512 bit
times is .000000512 seconds. The estimated time required just to get through
the source and destination Gigabit Ethernet DTEs is 864 bit times!

Gigabit Ethernet runs across twisted-pair and fiber optic media. Buildings routinely are wired with 100-meter cable runs. The diameter of a Gigabit Ethernet
collision domain containing a single hub can be expected to be 200 meters. It
takes more than 2000 bit times to cross 200 meters of twisted-pair or optical
cable at Gbps speed.

A sender must continue to transmit for at least the amount of time that it
takes the first byte to travel from its source to its destination. To make this happen at gigabit speed, the minimum size of a transmission must be increased. In
fact, the minimum length of a half-duplex Gbps transmission has been set to
512 *bytes* (4096 bits). This allows more than enough time for a byte to leave
the source DTE, cross 100 meters of cable, pass through a hub, cross another
100 meters of cable, and enter the destination DTE.

Backward compatibility is very important in the Ethernet world, and the half-duplex gigabit problem was solved in a way that preserves backward compatibility. The minimum frame size still is 64 bytes, but extra *carrier extension bytes* are added at the end of a small frame to assure that the transmission reaches the 512-byte level.

Figure 4.7 shows the format of a Gigabit Ethernet frame with appended extension bytes. Note that the frame still must be at least 64 bytes in length, so if a very small amount of data is sent, the transmission might include both pad bytes and extension bytes.

Having to add up to 448 garbage extension bytes to short frames is very wasteful. To mitigate this, Gigabit Ethernet frames can be tied together like freight cars into a long CSMA/CD transmission, raising the efficiency. This is called *frame bursting*.

Note

As was noted earlier, currently all Gigabit Ethernet traffic is sent in full-duplex mode. The CSMA/CD rules do not apply to full–duplex operation, and an extension does not have to be added. Standard full-duplex Gigabit Ethernet is completely backward compatible with classical Ethernet.

However, some vendors support a nonstandard change to the maximum size of a Gigabit Ethernet frame. A Jumbo MAC frame has a size of up to 9018 bytes. The details are explained in Chapter 8.

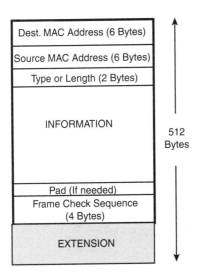

FIGURE 4.7 *A gigabit frame with a carrier extension.*

DIX Ethernet Frame Trace

Listing 4.1 shows a Network Associates Sniffer trace of an Address Resolution Protocol (ARP) message that was transmitted at 10Mbps. Note the following:

- The destination is the broadcast MAC address.

- The source has MAC address X'08-00-14-20-19-82. The OUI X'08-00-14 belongs to Excelan, and the Sniffer has replaced the first 3 bytes of the source MAC address with "Exceln."

- The EtherType for ARP messages is X'08-06.

- An ARP message is short. It is made up of only 28 bytes. The MAC header and frame check sequence contribute another 18 bytes, so the frame size is 46 bytes, which is 18 bytes short of the 64-byte minimum. Hence, 18 pad bytes have been inserted after the ARP data. The frame check sequence (which is not shown in the trace) follows the pad data and is computed against all 60 of the previous 60 bytes.

LISTING 4.1 AN ETHERNET FRAME CONTAINING AN ARP MESSAGE

```
DLC:  Frame 1 arrived at  12:09:34.0000; frame size is 60 (003C hex) bytes.
      DLC:  Destination = BROADCAST FFFFFFFFFFFF, Broadcast
      DLC:  Source      = Station Exceln201982
      DLC:  Ethertype   = 0806 (ARP)
      DLC:
ARP:  ----- ARP/RARP frame -----
      ARP:
          (28 byte ARP message)
      ARP:
      ARP: 18 bytes frame padding
      ARP:
HEX
ff ff ff ff ff ff 08 00 14 20 19 82 08 06 00 01
08 00 06 04 00 01 08 00 14 20 19 82 81 54 19 02
00 00 00 00 00 00 81 54 19 fe 01 01 00 00 26 3d
ea d9 00 00 00 00 6b 69 6c 6c 6a 6f
```

802.3 LLC/SNAP Frames

Extra headers are needed to identify the type of protocol data that is enclosed in an Ethernet frame that conforms to the original 802.3 specification and has a length field. Figure 4.8 shows the common format that is used to identify a protocol that has an assigned EtherType code.

The length field is followed by a 3-byte Logical Link Control (LLC) header and a 5-byte Subnetwork Access Protocol (SNAP) header. The value in the LLC field is X'AA-AA-03. The SNAP header consists of X'00-00-00 followed by the Ethernet type code of the enclosed protocol information. The information field has been cut back to 1492 payload bytes because of the 8 extra header bytes.

The bytes that introduce the Ethernet type (X'AA-AA-03-00-00-00) can be treated like a fixed boilerplate, but the section "Source of the LLC and SNAP Headers," later in this chapter, has more information if you are curious about where these headers came from and what they mean.

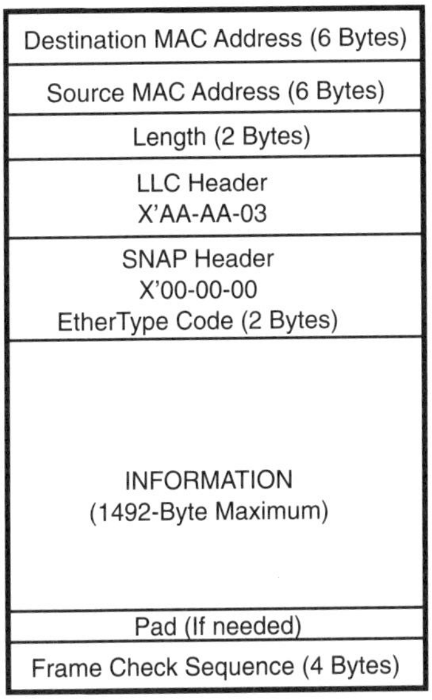

Destination MAC Address (6 Bytes)
Source MAC Address (6 Bytes)
Length (2 Bytes)
LLC Header X'AA-AA-03
SNAP Header X'00-00-00 EtherType Code (2 Bytes)
INFORMATION (1492-Byte Maximum)
Pad (If needed)
Frame Check Sequence (4 Bytes)

FIGURE 4.8 *Format of an 802.3 frame carrying protocol data that has an assigned Ethernet type.*

802.3 LLC/SNAP Frame Trace

Listing 4.2 shows part of a Sniffer trace of a NetWare 802.3 frame that includes LLC and SNAP headers identifying the enclosed protocol information as Novell NetWare data whose Ethernet type is X'81-37.

LISTING 4.2 FORMAT OF AN 802.3 FRAME CARRYING A NETWARE PROTOCOL DATA UNIT

```
DLC:  Frame 12 arrived at  15:36:18.6314; frame size is 118 (0076 hex)
➡bytes.
      DLC:  Destination = Station WstDigD99D41
      DLC:  Source      = Station Intrln02D520
      DLC:  802.3 length = 104
      DLC:
LLC:  ----- LLC Header -----
      LLC:
      LLC:  DSAP Address = AA, DSAP IG Bit = 00 (Individual Address)
      LLC:  SSAP Address = AA, SSAP CR Bit = 00 (Command)
      LLC:  Unnumbered frame: UI
      LLC:
```

continues

Listing 4.2 Continued

```
SNAP:  ----- SNAP Header -----
       SNAP:  (00 00 00)
       SNAP: Type = 8137 (Novell)
       SNAP:
IPX:   ----- IPX Header -----
       IPX:
IPX:   Checksum = 0xFFFF
       IPX:  Length = 96
. . .
HEX
00 00 c0 d9 9d 41 02 07 01 02 d5 20 00 68
03 00 00 00 81 37 ff ff 00 60 . . .
```

Source of the LLC and SNAP Headers

The extra LLC and SNAP headers in Figure 4.8 and Listing 4.2 result from the work of the IEEE 802.2 committee. This committee split the data link layer into two sublayers: a Logical Link Control (LLC) sublayer and a MAC sublayer, as shown in Figure 4.9.

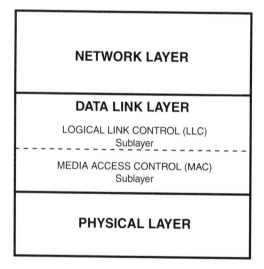

Figure 4.9 *Sublayers of the data link layer.*

The Logical Link Control (LLC) sublayer was designed to serve two purposes:

- Provide a consistent interface between the network layer and the data link layer that is independent of the underlying mode of communication, whether it is Ethernet, Token Ring, FDDI, or a wide area circuit.

- Provide three different types of data link service.

The three service types are

- **Type 1**—Handles transmission of individual PDUs. No extra functions are added to the data link layer.

- **Type 2**—Provides the capability to set up a reliable data link connection with a partner. Data sent across the connection is numbered, and incoming information PDUs must be acknowledged. After a timeout, unacknowledged information PDUs are retransmitted. Type 2 also supports flow control. The Type 2 protocol closely resembles X.25 LAPB.

- **Type 3**—Supports simple command/acknowledge interactions. The arrival of a command PDU requires the recipient to send an acknowledgment PDU. After a timeout, a command PDU that has not been acknowledged is retransmitted.

Type 1 is the predominant data link communication in use today. IBM SNA makes use of Type 2 connections. The author is unaware of any use of Type 3 communication.

LSAPs

A single computer can engage in multiple concurrent data link communications. The 802.2 committee introduced data link layer addresses—called link service access point (LSAP) addresses—intended to help a computer to keep track of different communications flows.

LSAPs appear in LLC headers. Figure 4.10 shows the LLC header format.

- The first field of the header contains the destination service access point (DSAP) number.

- The second field contains the source service access point (SSAP) number.

- The third field contains control information. For Type 1 communication, this is a 1-byte value equal to X'03, which means *unnumbered information*. For Type 2 communication, the control field identifies the type of message (for example, information or flow control). It also carries the numbers used to sequence and acknowledge data.

Setting the DSAP and SSAP equal to X'AA means that a SNAP header follows.

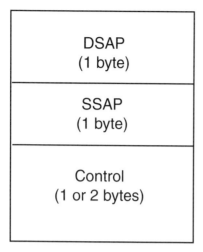

FIGURE 4.10 *Format of the LLC header.*

SNAP Headers

The general format of a SNAP header is displayed on the left side of Figure 4.11. The first 3 bytes contain an organizationally unique identifier (OUI) assigned by the IEEE. The remainder of the SNAP header is designed by that owning organization.

The IEEE assigned the OUI X'00-00-00 to Xerox back in the early days of Ethernet. The right side of Figure 4.11 shows the corresponding SNAP header, which carries a 2-byte EtherType code.

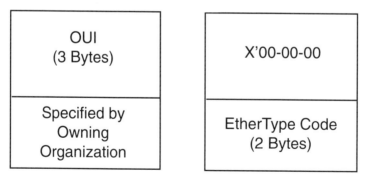

FIGURE 4.11 *SNAP header format.*

NetWare over Ethernet

Packaging data into a frame that has either an EtherType code or a length value, LLC, and SNAP header is a pretty simple job. Unfortunately, Novell generated a fair amount of confusion when it made up two more ways of packaging NetWare IPX protocol data units: its 802.3 "raw" and 802.2 encapsulations.

Novell ended up wrapping its data into frames four different ways: the two standard formats, plus two that it invented. Having four different frame formats makes NetWare the encapsulation king.

Listing 4.3 shows a part of a trace of an 802.3 raw frame containing a NetWare IPX packet. Raw frames were used in the earliest days of the NetWare product. Note that something is missing—there are no 802.2 LLC and SNAP headers that identify the protocol being carried. Because an 802.2 header really is needed in any 802.3 frame that has a length field, the packaging in Listing 4.3 is proprietary.

Breaking the rules seemed a good idea at the time. LANs were small and isolated. If you had NetWare, why would you ever want to run any other protocol on a LAN? And if there is only one protocol, why include a protocol identifier that just adds overhead to each packet?

LISTING 4.3 A NETWARE 802.3 "RAW" FRAME

```
Network Associates Sniffer Trace
DLC:  ----- DLC Header -----
      DLC:
      DLC:  Frame 55 arrived at  17:30:18.8315;
            frame size is 440 (01B8 hex) bytes.
      DLC:  Destination = Station Accton004720
      DLC:  Source      = Station WstDigD6682B
      DLC:  802.3 length = 426
      DLC:
IPX:  ----- IPX Header -----
      IPX:
      IPX:  Checksum = 0xFFFF
      IPX:  Length = 426
      IPX:  . . .
```

It turned out that no protocol is an island and that this actually was not a very good idea. However, placing X'FF-FF into the first field (intended to be used as a checksum field) helps NICs figure out that the frame contains IPX. The NetWare raw encapsulation shares LAN media with other protocols today.

Listing 4.4 shows part of a trace of a NetWare 802.2 encapsulation. Note that the DSAP and SSAP addresses are set to X'E0.

LISTING 4.4 A NETWARE 802.2 FRAME

```
Network Associates Sniffer Trace
DLC:  ----- DLC Header -----
      DLC:
      DLC:  Frame 7 arrived at  15:31:12.6315; frame size is 113 (0071
➥hex) bytes.
      DLC:  Destination = Station WstDigD99D41
      DLC:  Source      = Station Intrln02D520
      DLC:  802.3 length = 99
      DLC:
LLC:  ----- LLC Header -----
      LLC:
      LLC:  DSAP Address = E0, DSAP IG Bit = 00 (Individual Address)
      LLC:  SSAP Address = E0, SSAP CR Bit = 00 (Command)
      LLC:  Unnumbered frame: UI
      LLC:
IPX:  ----- IPX Header -----
      IPX:
      IPX:  Checksum = 0xFFFF
      IPX:  Length = 96
      IPX   .  .  .
```

Tabulation of Important Ethernet Parameters

Table 4.2 summarizes the official Ethernet MAC parameters defined for 1Mbps, 10Mbps, 100Mbps, and 1000Mbps Ethernet.

Note that most of the parameters are the same across all speeds. The interframe gap is the same when it is expressed in bit times. The only exceptional parameter is the Gigabit Ethernet slot time. Recall that this would be relevant only if CSMA/CD Gigabit transmission were used.

TABLE 4.2 ETHERNET MAC PARAMETERS

Parameter	1Mbps	10Mbps	100Mbps	1000Mbps
slotTime	512 bit times	512 bit times	512 bit times	4096 bit times
interFrameGap	96µs	9.6µs	.96µs	.096µs
attemptLimit	16	16	16	16
backoffLimit	10	10	10	10
jamSize	4 bytes	4 bytes	4 bytes	4 bytes
maxFrameSize (without VLAN header)	1518 bytes	1518 bytes	1518 bytes	1518 bytes
minFrameSize	64 bytes	64 bytes	64 bytes	64 bytes*

*A 448-byte extension must be added if half-duplex CSMA/CD is used rather than full–duplex CSMA/CD.

Summary Points

- Classic Carrier Sense Multiple Access with Collision Detect (CSMA/CD) Ethernet also is called half-duplex Ethernet. At any time, only one frame should be in transit.

- Frame transmissions must be separated by a time interval that corresponds to 96 bit times; this is called the interframe gap or interpacket gap.

- The size of the interframe gap between frames can shrink as the frames pass through a repeater.

- After detecting that a collision has occurred, a sender must continue to transmit 32 additional jam bits.

- A station that has participated in a collision must remain silent for a random amount of time before attempting to transmit again. The delay period is a multiple of a parameter called the slot time.

- An Ethernet MAC frame starts with the frame's destination and source MAC addresses and ends with an FCS field that is used to detect transmission errors.

- A station transmits special bit patterns before sending a media access control (MAC) frame.

- The minimum MAC frame size is 64 bytes. The minimum transmission size affects the diameter of a collision domain.

- The third field in an Ethernet frame header identifies either the type or the length of the information field. All of the Ethernet type values currently in use have decimal values well above 1500, which is the maximum-minformation field size.

- If CSMA/CD were used for Gigabit Ethernet, extra extension bits would have to be transmitted at the end of a short frame.

- Extra LLC and SNAP headers that identify the type of protocol data being carried are needed in an Ethernet frame that conforms to the original 802.3 specification and has a length field.

- NetWare traffic has been sent using four different formats: With an EtherType code; in the conventional 802.3 format with LLC and SNAP; 802.3 "raw" which has a length field, but no LLC or SNAP; and 802.2 encapsulation, which has no SNAP, but uses DSAP and SSAP codes as protocol identifiers.

References

The CSMA/CD protocol is defined in Chapters 2, 3, and 4 of

- IEEE Standard 802.3, 1998 Edition. "Carrier Sense Multiple Access with Collision Detection (CSMA/CD) Access Method and Physical Layer Specifications."

CHAPTER 5

Full-Duplex Ethernet Communication

The original Ethernet LANs ran on coaxial cable and used baseband signaling. Only one frame can be in flight across a baseband coax medium at any time. Just as a car pulling onto a road must wait for a break in the traffic before entering, the CSMA/CD rules require a station to wait until the medium is free before it can send another frame. Stations share the medium in a (more or less) fair manner.

However, when LANs are constructed using twisted-pair or optical fiber media connected to switches, the CSMA/CD rulebook can be thrown away. Data can flow from station to station, station to switch, or switch to switch in full-duplex mode.

Full-Duplex Architecture

A twisted-pair or optical fiber segment connects only two nodes. Furthermore, the following are true:

- A system connected to two twisted-pair fibers can send data on one pair and receive data on the other pair.

- A fiber optic adapter connects to two optical fibers. Data is sent on one fiber and received on the other.

The most popular types of cable used for Ethernet clearly have the potential for full-duplex communication.

Stations that are connected to a hub form a CSMA/CD collision domain. The hub repeats bits onto every segment, and only one signal can be in transit at any given time.

However, it is perfectly feasible to send and receive at the same time when stations are connected to a switch. Some vendors realized this quite early and started to market station NICs and switch ports that supported full-duplex operation. Eventually, the 802.3 standards were revised to support this feature. The CSMA/CD discipline no longer is needed or used when full-duplex transmission is in effect.

Figure 5.1 depicts an Ethernet LAN made up of systems connected to a switch and configured for full-duplex communication:

- Each system can send and receive at the same time.

- The CSMA/CD protocol is not applied; there are no collisions.

- A system can send a frame whenever it wants, except for the fact that its frames still must be separated by the interframe gap.

> **Note**
> The advent of full-duplex communication caused CSMA/CD to be called *half-duplex operation*.

SWITCH

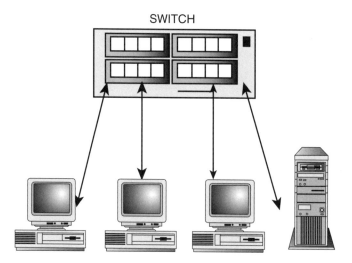

FIGURE 5.1   *Full-duplex communication through a switch.*

This really cranks up the capacity of an Ethernet LAN. For example, a switch with twenty 10Mbps ports has a top capacity of 200Mbps. A switch with twenty 100Mbps ports has a top capacity of 2000Mbps.

> **Note**
>
> The true maximum throughput depends on the capability of the switch to handle a heavy load of traffic. The switch vendor needs to guarantee a generous backplane speed and an adequate supply of buffer memory. The switch must be guaranteed to be "fully non-blocking" to make the grade.

Full-Duplex Parameters

Table 4.2 listed Ethernet MAC parameters. However, only three of these parameters are relevant for full-duplex operation:

- The interframe gap, which is 96 bit times

- The minimum MAC frame size, which is 64 bytes

- The maximum MAC frame size, which is 1518 bytes

These parameters are the same for all speeds: 1Mbps, 10Mbps, 100Mbps, and 1000Mbps.

Assuring Backward Compatibility

Full-duplex operation introduces a compatibility problem because older NICs do not support the feature. When an up-to-date switch port is connected to a hub or to a station with an old NIC card, the switch port must figure out that it must talk to that node in half-duplex mode.

Backward compatibility was established by introducing an *Auto-Negotiation* function that enables nodes to announce their capabilities to one another. If a partner has an old interface and cannot respond to Auto-Negotiation messages, the newer device knows that it must ratchet down to half-duplex (CSMA/CD) communication on that segment. Auto-Negotiation is described in Chapter 11, "Auto-Negotiation."

> **Note**
>
> Auto-Negotiation supports backward compatibility in other ways, too. One of the Auto-Negotiated features is the interface speed.
>
> For example, many hub and switch devices have ports that can operate at either 10Mbps or 100Mbps. When a cable connecting to a station with a 10Mbps NIC is plugged into one of these hub or switch ports, the port operates at 10Mbps. If a new 100Mbps NIC is installed in the station, the speed automatically is negotiated up to 100Mbps.

Handling Congestion

Full-duplex communication gives a big boost to capacity, but it also creates a problem that can degrade network performance. For example, in Figure 5.2, several clients are sending data to a file server at the same time. The switch is incapable of forwarding the frames as quickly as they are arriving.

A switch routinely handles temporary pileups of frames by storing the extra input in buffer memory. If switch memory fills up, however, some frames must be discarded. Usually, discarded frames are retransmitted later by a higher protocol layer. But processing the same frames two or more times reduces the switch's effective throughput and slows end-user response time.

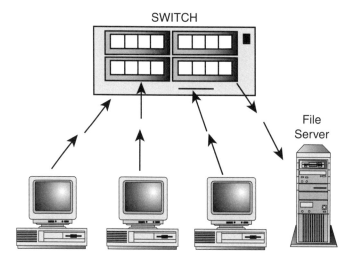

Figure 5.2 *Congestion.*

A switch tries to avoid frame loss by telling attached systems: "Stop while I clean house!" A flow control operation (originally defined in standard IEEE 802.3x and now part of 802.3) does this job.

The party at either end of a full-duplex Ethernet link can ask its partner to stop transmitting frames for a specified length of time. The request is carried in a special PAUSE frame. This is implemented only in a full-duplex environment because it must be possible to ask a partner to pause right away, even while the partner is in the middle of a transmission.

Although support for the PAUSE function currently is an optional feature of the 802.3 standard, Ethernet network interface card and switch vendors have implemented the feature in many of their products.

The MAC Control Sublayer

The 802 committee created an architectural home for PAUSE messages by defining a new *MAC control sublayer*, which is shown in Figure 5.3. Currently, sending and receiving PAUSE messages is the only function performed by this sublayer, but others could be added in the future.

An end system's MAC control sublayer is sandwiched between the MAC sublayer and the Logical Link Control (LLC) sublayer. A switch's MAC control sublayer is sandwiched between the MAC sublayer and the switch frame relaying function.

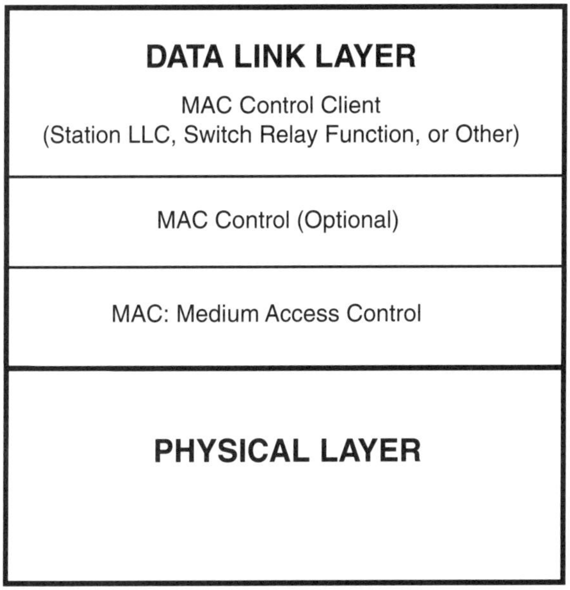

DATA LINK LAYER

MAC Control Client
(Station LLC, Switch Relay Function, or Other)

MAC Control (Optional)

MAC: Medium Access Control

PHYSICAL LAYER

FIGURE 5.3 *The MAC control sublayer.*

MAC Control Frames and PAUSE Frames

Figure 5.4 shows the format of a MAC control frame. MAC control frames have a fixed size of 64 bytes, equal to the minimum frame size. They are identified by an EtherType value of X'88-08. The first field in the MAC control frame data area is a 2-byte operation code that identifies the kind of control data that follows.

The format of the only currently defined MAC control frame, the PAUSE frame, also is displayed in Figure 5.4.

- PAUSE frames are sent to the multicast destination address:

  X'01-80-C2-00-00-01

  The source and destination interfaces both must be preconfigured to accept frames sent to this address.

- The PAUSE operation code is equal to X'00-01.

- A PAUSE frame contains a 2-byte *pause number* that states the length of the pause in units of 512 bit times. For example, at 10Mbps, a value of 1000 translates to 512,000 bit times, or .0512 seconds. The biggest pause number is 65,535, which translates to 3.355 seconds at 10Mbps, .3355 seconds at 100Mbps, and .03355 seconds at 1000Mbps.

- The remainder of the data field is filled with X'00 bytes.

The time needed to clear out buffers might be hard to estimate accurately. The protocol avoids unnecessarily long waits by permitting the pauser to send another PAUSE frame with a 0 wait time to signal that transmission can resume immediately.

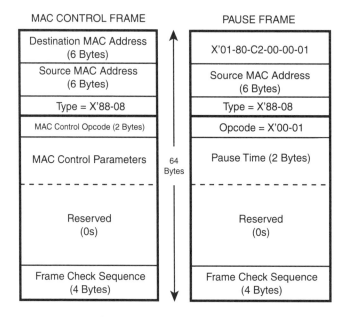

FIGURE 5.4   *The general MAC control frame format and a PAUSE frame.*

The use of PAUSE frames is a feature that needs to be agreed upon by means of the Auto-Negotiation Protocol, described in Chapter 11.

Just to complicate things a little, the partners at the ends of a link can decide to use PAUSE frames to implement flow control in only one direction or in both directions. This actually leads to three choices. For example, in Figure 5.5, station A and switch B could agree that:

- Station A will send PAUSE messages, and switch B will receive them. Station A will flow control switch B, but switch B will not flow control station A.

- Switch B will send PAUSE messages, and station A will receive them. Switch B will flow control station A, but station A will not flow control switch B.

- Both station A and switch B will send and receive PAUSE messages. They will flow control one another.

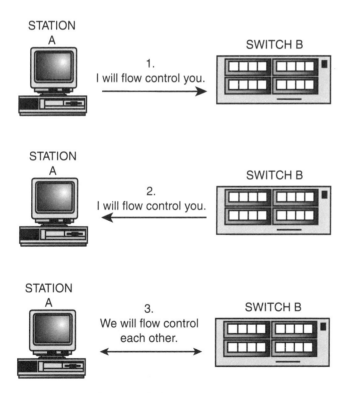

FIGURE 5.5 *Flow control alternatives.*

The first two alternatives are called *asymmetric flow control*. The third alternative is called *symmetric flow control*.

Implementation

The 802.3 flow control specification describes the rules for using PAUSE frames but does not provide any clues as to how a system decides when a PAUSE frame should be sent.

However, a typical implementation is not complicated. For example, the switch in Figure 5.2 usually would be configured with a limit on the amount of buffer memory that is available to hold incoming frames arriving at each of its ports. If the switch has ports capable of operating at more than one speed (for example, 10Mbps and 100Mbps, or 100Mbps and 1000Mbps), more memory can be assigned to the ports currently operating at the higher speed.

In Figure 5.2, there are too many frames heading for the switch. This causes some of the arriving frames to be buffered. When the inbound memory allocation for a port is almost exhausted, the switch sends a PAUSE through that port.

The implementation at an end-user station is straightforward. If the CPU and disk I/O components cannot keep up with the incoming flow of frames, memory allocated for network I/O starts to fill quickly. When a threshold level is exceeded, the system can send a PAUSE frame to its neighboring switch.

Summary Points

- When twisted-pair or fiber optical media is used, data can flow from station to station, station to switch, or switch to switch in full-duplex mode.

- For full–duplex operation, the CSMA/CD protocol is not applied; there are no collisions.

- The parameters relevant for full-duplex operation are the interframe gap, the minimum MAC frame size, and the maximum MAC frame size.

- Backward compatibility with half-duplex interfaces was established by introducing an Auto-Negotiation function that enables nodes to agree on using capabilities that both support.

- Special PAUSE frames tell a partner to temporarily stop sending frames.

- The MAC control sublayer was created to perform PAUSE functions (and other functions that might be defined in the future).

- Traffic control via PAUSE frames can be symmetric or asymmetric (only one party is controlled).

References

The protocols presented in this chapter are defined in

- IEEE Standard 802.3, 1998 Edition. "Carrier Sense Multiple Access with Collision Detection (CSMA/CD) Access Method and Physical Layer Specifications."

Full-duplex operation is discussed in Chapter 4 of the 802.3 standard. The MAC Control sublayer is described in Chapter 31. The PAUSE operation and the format of a PAUSE frame are described in Annex 31B.

CHAPTER 6

The Ethernet 10Mbps Physical Layer

This chapter describes the physical characteristics of Ethernet LANs built using 10Mbps coax, twisted-pair, and fiber optic Ethernet media. Some Ethernet LANs are constructed using a single medium, such as twisted–pair cabling. However, many have been built using a mixture of media types.

Although many people think of coax Ethernet as a technology of the past, a quick check of cabling and components catalogs shows that a market for the technology still exists. There is an installed base of coax LANs that are working well and whose users are satisfied.

It is very unlikely that you will install a new coax Ethernet LAN. However, the architecture and key parameters for Ethernet LANs were defined for the coax LAN environment, so it makes sense to examine the coax environment first. LANs based on thick coax media (called *10BASE5*) and thin coax media (called *10BASE2*) are described in the opening sections of this chapter.

The most common Ethernet LAN medium in current use is twisted–pair cabling, and 10BASE-T LANs are discussed after the coax LANs. The final part of the chapter describes the physical characteristics of fiber optic media and shows how fiber optic cables are integrated into Ethernet LANs.

Baseband Ethernet on Thick Coaxial Cable (10BASE5)

The original Ethernet LAN defined in the 1980s was built from sections of thick, heavy 50-ohm coaxial cable. A LAN *segment* is either a single cable section or is made up of two or more sections joined by connectors (called *barrel connectors* because they are shaped like barrels). The segment at the top of Figure 6.1 is made up of two sections joined by a barrel connector.

A component called a *terminator* is attached to each end of a segment. Each 50-ohm terminator absorbs signals and prevents them from being reflected back into the cable. Coaxial cable should be grounded at exactly one point, and one of the terminators often is selected as the location for the ground connection.

Warning

A defective, loose, or missing terminator kills a LAN. Because of the reflected signals, stations become incapable of locking on to the true signals and receiving incoming data bits.

Multiple coax segments can be connected by repeaters to form a branching bus tree topology like the one shown in Figure 6.1.

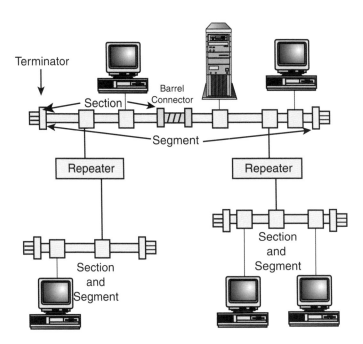

FIGURE 6.1 *A branching bus Ethernet.*

For a thick Ethernet 10BASE5 LAN

- 10 stands for 10 megabits per second (Mbps).

- BASE denotes that data is represented by baseband signals.

- 5 corresponds to the maximum segment length, which is 500 meters.

For baseband transmission, only one signal can be on a cable at any given time. The 0 and 1 bits are transmitted across an Ethernet segment using *Manchester encoding*, which is described in Appendix A, "Physical Layer Encodings for Ethernet, Fibre Channel, FDDI, and Token Ring."

Broadband Ethernet

An alternative *broadband* version of Ethernet was introduced in the early days of Ethernet. In a broadband network, several channels operating on different frequency bands share the cable and multiple transmissions occur in parallel. A broadband Ethernet (which was called 10BROAD36) is implemented as a single long coaxial cable segment.

For a while, the merits of baseband versus broadband were hotly debated. However, stations had to be connected to a broadband LAN by costly frequency modulation transmitters/receivers (*transceivers*), and the connection process required tuning and testing. Baseband became the norm because its transceivers were much cheaper and the installation process was far simpler.

Broadband transmission has resurfaced today in the Internet cable modem service. However, the cable modem networks use proprietary technology that does not adhere closely to the original Ethernet broadband standard.

Connecting to 10BASE5 Coax

Ethernet stations do not connect directly to a 10BASE5 cable. Figure 6.2 illustrates how a network interface card (NIC) connects to the bus. One end of an *attachment unit interface* (AUI) drop cable plugs into the NIC, and the other end plugs into a transceiver. The transceiver also is called a *medium attachment unit* (MAU).

MAU is the term used in the IEEE standards and in some textbooks. However, vendors call their attachment products *transceivers*.

The use of an AUI drop cable is convenient. The thick Ethernet backbone cable can be installed in ceiling or floor ducts. The AUI cable runs from the ceiling or floor to the station.

Note

An AUI cable consists of four individually shielded pairs of wire surrounded by an overall cable shield.

The double shielding makes AUI cable resistant to electrical signal interference. An AUI cable connects to the transceiver and the NIC via 15-pin DB15 connectors.

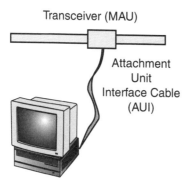

Transceiver (MAU)

Attachment
Unit
Interface Cable
(AUI)

FIGURE 6.2 *Attaching to a coax Ethernet.*

Two styles of thicknet transceivers exist, as is shown on the left side of Figure 6.3. To install an *intrusive* transceiver, the cable segment must be cut and attached to connectors on the transceiver. The well-named *vampire tap* transceiver is nonintrusive; it is clamped onto the cable and connects by piercing the cable.

The right side of Figure 6.3 shows a complete connection between a DTE and a thick Ethernet cable. A station's NIC includes a female D connector. The 15-pin male end of an AUI cable plugs into this, and the opposite female end of the cable plugs into a male D connector on the transceiver.

> **Note**
> Specialized connectors are defined for each of the other media (thin coax, twisted-pair, and optical fiber cabling) discussed in this chapter. However, this initial configuration, consisting of a network interface with a female D connector and an AUI cable connecting to a transceiver, also could be used for each of the media. It is not used because the media-specific NICs are very cheap. Using a separate transceiver would add greatly to the cost.

Figure 6.4 shows a repeater that connects to two coaxial cable segments via two AUI cables.

Transceiver (MAU) Functions

Vendors might have decided to use the name *transceiver* instead of *medium attachment unit* because an MAU does a lot more than attach to a medium. It also sends and receives bits and performs a lot of other functions—for example, when it detects that a frame that it is sending is experiencing a collision, it transmits a jam signal.

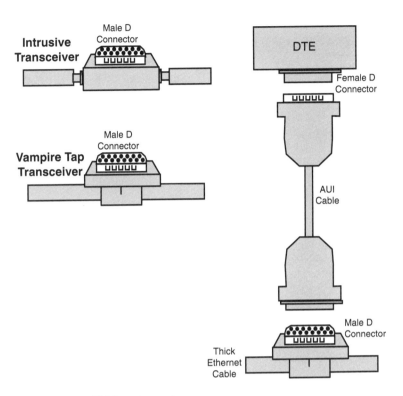

FIGURE 6.3   *Thicknet transceivers.*

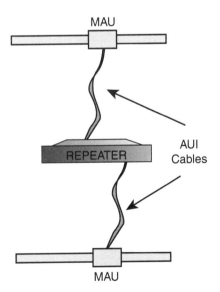

FIGURE 6.4   *Connecting coax segments using a repeater.*

> **Note**
> Station MAUs are not the only ones that send jam signals. When an MAU attached to a repeater detects that the frame that it currently is repeating is experiencing a collision, it has to send a jam signal onto all the other segments to make sure that all stations are alerted to the collision.

A transceiver performs two other worthwhile functions:

- Jabber control
- Signal quality error messages

Jabber Control

Jabber occurs when a station "talks" too long. That is, it transmits continuously for more time than is needed to send a frame of maximum size. This is caused by a malfunction. An 802.3 transceiver controls jabber, cutting off transmission after a time threshold has been exceeded.

Signal Quality Error Messages

After a transceiver has finished transmitting the last bit of a frame, it passes a special signal up to its own station. The signal verifies that the transceiver has done its job and is operating correctly. This mechanism is called the *signal quality error test* (SQE test).

SQE signals are used for two other functions:

- They report collisions.
- They report that improper pulses were sensed on the medium. (This actually might be caused by a fault in the transceiver rather than a problem on the LAN cable.)

The transceiver functions were carried over to the other Ethernet media. Jam transmission, jabber control, and the SQE test function are implemented for baseband coax, broadband coax, twisted-pair, and optical fiber media.

10BASE5 Collision Domain Parameters

A 10BASE5 collision domain is made up of segments connected by repeaters. The important parameters that govern the size and shape of a thick Ethernet collision domain are presented in Table 6.1.

TABLE 6.1 10BASE5 COLLISION DOMAIN PARAMETERS

Parameter or Characteristic	Value
Topology	Branching bus
Type of segment cable	Thick, 50-ohm coax
Connector	"D" with AUI cable and transceiver
Length of an AUI attachment cable	5-50 meters
Maximum length of a segment	500 meters
Maximum propagation delay for a segment	2165 nanoseconds
Maximum number of nodes (stations and repeaters) that can be attached to a segment	100
Minimum distance between two transceivers	2.5 meters
Maximum collision domain diameter	2500 meters
Maximum number of cable segments traversed between a source to a destination	5
Maximum number of repeaters between a source and destination	4
Maximum number of populated segments between a source and destination	3

The placement of stations on a thick coax cable is not arbitrary. The 10BASE5 bus cable (which usually has a yellow or orange jacket) is marked at 2.5-meter intervals with the optimal positions at which transceivers can be attached.

5-4-3 Rule

The last three items in Table 6.1 represent the famous *Ethernet 5-4-3 rule*, which states that any path through a collision domain may:

- Traverse at most five segments

- Go through at most four repeaters

- Cross at most three segments that contain stations

The 5-4-3 rule is illustrated in Figure 6.5. The figure includes seven segments, but this is not a problem—the 5-4-3 rule applies to *paths*. Because of the tree structure, a path between any pair of stations traverses no more than five segments. For example, the path from station A to station B crosses five segments and passes through four repeaters. Only three of these segments are populated with end stations. Similarly, the path from station B to station C crosses five segments, only three of which are populated.

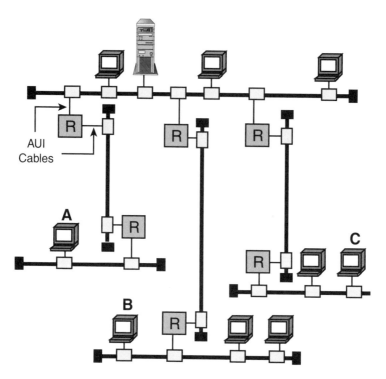

F I G U R E   6.5   *A coax Ethernet LAN extended using repeaters.*

Propagation Delay

The *propagation delay* is the amount of time that elapses when a signal travels from one end of a cable to the other end.

This is the parameter that actually is responsible for the constraints that limit the size of a collision domain. If two or more stations start to transmit at close to the same time, their signals will collide. The network must be small enough so that if multiple stations transmit minimal-sized frames at the same time, all of them will detect the collision. All the receiving stations also must be capable of detecting the collision.

The *network diameter* is the longest path between two points in a collision domain. The five-segment maximum limits the biggest diameter of a 10BASE5 collision domain to 2,500 meters. However, all counts end at a bridge, and bridges can be used to greatly extend the size of a LAN. Chapter 12, "Ethernet Bridges and Layer 2 Switches," has the details.

Note
An Ethernet LAN can include up to 1,024 stations. (Repeaters are not included in this count.)

Unpopulated LAN segments are used as transit links that carry signals from one part of the LAN to another part of the LAN. The diameter of a collision domain can be increased by using fiber optic cable for the unpopulated transit sections. This is discussed later in this chapter.

Practical Problems with 10BASE5

The coaxial cable used for 10BASE5 was hard to work with because it was costly, heavy, and inflexible.

Many organizations started out with small LANs. As PCs and workstations proliferated, a LAN would be extended in a piecemeal fashion, and often an organization would lose track of how much cable was installed and where it was. This made computer moves and changes a big hassle.

LAN growth was difficult as well. New transceivers had to be added carefully at marked locations. Communication across a segment was interrupted whenever an intrusive transceiver was installed or when a new segment bounded by barrel connectors was inserted.

A faulty section of cable, a bad terminator, a loose barrel connector, or a bad transceiver could disrupt communication for everyone on a segment, and the source of the problem was hard to track down.

Baseband Ethernet on Thin Coax Cable (10BASE2)

A new version of coax Ethernet was introduced to overcome some of the problems posed by 10BASE5. This version is built using a lighter, more flexible cable called *thinnet* (or "cheapernet") and is called 10BASE2. As before, *10* means 10Mbps, and *BASE* stands for baseband; the *2* represents 200 meters. However, this is the rounded-up value for the actual maximum segment length, which is 185 meters.

Although AUI cables and external transceivers could be used with 10BASE2, a far less costly configuration became the norm. The transceiver function was integrated onto a NIC that connects directly to the coax bus via a Bayonet Neil-Concelman (BNC) T connector, as is shown in Figure 6.6.

Note

A formal interface called the AUI still exists between the transceiver chip and the other components on a NIC, but this interface is on the card instead of being represented by a cable.

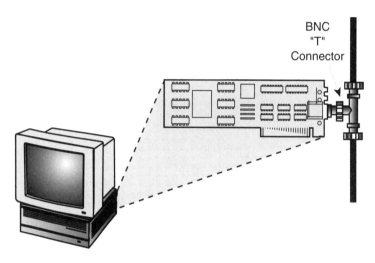

BNC
"T"
Connector

FIGURE 6.6 *Ethernet NIC with integrated transceiver and BNC connector.*

Figure 6.7 illustrates the structure of a 10BASE2 network. A 10BASE2 segment is made up of short lengths of cable connected to one another by BNC T connectors. In other words, a segment is a daisy chain of short cables and BNC Ts.

- For most of the stations, the BNC T is pushed onto a round post extending from the station's 10BASE2 NIC.

- For a few, the NIC may have a female D socket that must be connected to an AUI cable.

The repeater in Figure 6.7 is connected to a pair of transceivers via AUI cables and D connectors. Each transceiver also has a BNC interface.

The tradeoff for the cheaper backbone cable and components, and ease of use is that the coax segments must be shorter. At most, 30 nodes (including both stations and repeaters) can be attached to a thinnet coax segment.

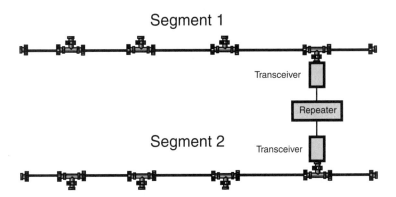

FIGURE 6.7 *Daisy-chained 10BASE2 segments.*

10BASE2 Collision Domain Parameters

Table 6.2 has the vital statistics for a 10BASE2 collision domain. The 5-4-3 rule continues to hold. Therefore, a 10BASE2 collision domain has a maximum diameter of 925 meters. The collision domain size can be increased by using thicknet Ethernet (or optical fiber) for some of the segments, or by introducing bridges.

TABLE 6.2 10BASE2 COLLISION DOMAIN PARAMETERS

Parameter or Characteristic	Value
Topology	Branching bus
Type of segment cable	Thin 50-ohm coax
Connector	BNC
Maximum length of a segment	185 meters
Maximum propagation delay for a segment	950 nanoseconds
Maximum number of nodes (stations and repeaters) that can be attached to a segment	30
Minimum distance between two nodes	.5 meter
Maximum collision domain diameter	925 meters
Maximum number of cable segments traversed between a source and destination	5
Maximum number of repeaters between a source and destination	4
Maximum number of populated segments between a source and destination	3

Practical Problems with 10BASE2

Making room for new stations on a LAN segment is easy: You just insert new sections and additional BNC T connectors. However, communication across the LAN halts while you are doing this.

Furthermore, the simplicity can be a pitfall. Users have been known to disconnect LAN cables while rearranging the furniture in their offices, unaware that they have stopped all LAN traffic dead in its tracks.

As was the case for 10BASE5, faulty sections and bad connectors or terminators can disrupt communications for everyone on a 10BASE2 segment.

10Mbps Twisted–Pair Ethernet (10BASE-T)

It was a banner day for Ethernet when researchers discovered how to cram 10Mbps across unshielded twisted-pair (UTP) cable. In 1990, 10BASE-T became an IEEE standard.

The days of snaking heavy coaxial cable through a building—and, because of moves and changes, often losing track of what actually was hidden in the ceilings and walls—were over. Now a building could be star-wired for data in the same way that it was star-wired for telephony. In many cases, extra wire pairs that already were installed could be used. The label chosen for 10Mbps twisted-pair Ethernet is 10BASE-T. Two wire pairs are used.

10BASE-T Segments

A twisted-pair segment can connect to only two nodes: one at each end of the segment. The maximum 10BASE-T segment size is 100 meters. Figure 6.8 shows several types of 10BASE-T segment connections. At the top, 10BASE-T segments link stations to a hub. The hub is joined to a switch by a 10BASE-T segment, and further segments connect the switch to two servers and to a router. Below that, the figure shows two stations that are directly connected to one another by a 10BASE-T segment. This is perfectly feasible but is not often done.

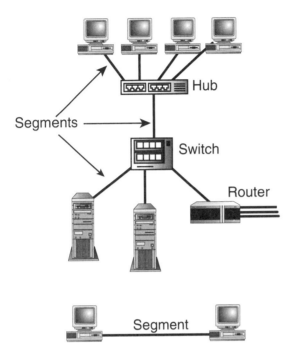

FIGURE 6.8 *10BASE-T segments.*

Half-Duplex Operation

Twisted-pair hubs were introduced to tie several stations into a common collision domain. For example, the hub in Figure 6.9 repeats the bits in a frame transmitted by station A to the other stations connected to the hub. Only one station connected to a hub can transmit at any time. Communication is controlled by the CSMA/CD protocol and is said to be half-duplex.

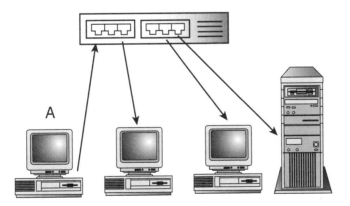

FIGURE 6.9 *Half-duplex communication through a hub.*

10BASE-T Collision Domain Parameters

Table 6.3 displays the parameters for a 10BASE-T Ethernet collision domain. A collision domain is constructed by connecting every station to a hub and interconnecting several hubs. It is important to use twisted-pair cable that meets standard quality requirements. Chapter 10, "Twisted-Pair Cabling Standards and Performance Requirements," discusses various cable *categories* and describes tests that are applied to twisted-pair cables.

The 5-4-3 rule still holds. Because the maximum twisted-pair segment length is 100 meters, the diameter of a collision domain that is constructed using only twisted pair segments is limited to 500 meters, at most.

Note
The diameter of a collision domain that is based predominantly on twisted-pair cabling can be increased by inserting some optical fiber links between hubs. Of course, a very large LAN can be built using switches to interconnect multiple collision domains.

TABLE 6.3 10BASE-T COLLISION DOMAIN PARAMETERS

Parameter or Characteristic	Value
Topology	A tree of stars
Patch cords	Up to 10 meters total
Type of segment cable	2 twisted pairs, Category 3 or better
Connector	RJ-45 jack and plug
Maximum length of a segment	100 meters
Maximum number of nodes that can be attached to a segment	2
Maximum collision domain diameter	500 meters
Maximum number of cable segments traversed between a source and destination	5
Maximum number of repeaters (hubs) between a source and destination	4
Maximum number of populated segments between a source and destination	3

10BASE-T Collision Domain Cabling Topology

The overall topology of a 10BASE-T LAN is a tree of stars, as is illustrated in Figure 6.10. The LAN in Figure 6.10 is constructed around four hubs and is a single collision domain. Each segment is at most 100 meters in length. The longest path through the network passes through four hubs and crosses five segments.

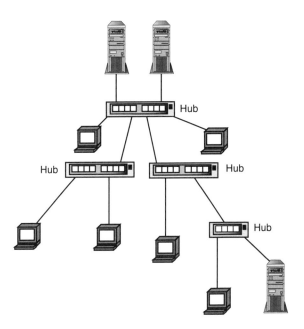

FIGURE 6.10   *A simple 10BASE-T LAN.*

Note
The rule that states that at most three segments along a path can contain stations always holds for a 10BASE-T collision domain. In fact, there are only two stations on any path. All the other nodes along a path are repeaters (hubs).

An unbroken 100-meter run often is used to connect two hubs or to join a hub to a bridge. However, a horizontal cable run between a workstation and a hub normally is broken up into pieces, as Figure 6.11 shows. At the station end, a NIC is connected to a telecommunications outlet by a short cable called a patch cord. Within the wiring closet at the other end, patch cords are used to complete the connection to a specific hub or switch.

Note
A patch cord also is called a *patch cable* or *jumper cord*. A patch cord that connects a user's computer to an outlet often is called a *work area cable*. A patch cord that connects a device to a hub or switch in a wiring closet often is called an *equipment cable*.

A typical breakdown is 90 meters for the long run between the telecommunications outlet and patch panels in the wiring closet and up to 10 meters for the patch cords used at each end. The patch cord connection between the station and the telecommunications outlet normally is limited to a length of 3 meters, at most.

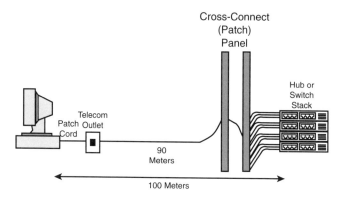

FIGURE 6.11 *Components of a 10BASE-T LAN.*

Patch panels in a wiring closet enable the connections between end-user stations and hubs or switches to be rearranged by unplugging and replugging patch cables.

The patches shown at the top of Figure 6.12 are called *interconnects*. A station is attached to a new hub by unplugging the patch cable from the old hub and plugging it into the new hub. The patches shown in the lower part of Figure 6.12 are called *cross-connects*. Cables connected to the hubs do not need to be touched. An attachment is changed by plugging one end of a patch cord into a different socket. Cross-connects are very convenient. However, they can degrade signals since they introduce more connector hardware into the cable path.

Note
Most NICs bought today operate at either 10 or 100Mbps. A station with a 10/100Mbps adapter can be upgraded to 100Mbps by changing its hub or switch connection so that it attaches to a hub or switch port capable of operating at 100Mbps.

As soon as the new connection is set up, the station's NIC and the hub or switch port automatically perform a negotiation that upgrades the link to the higher speed.

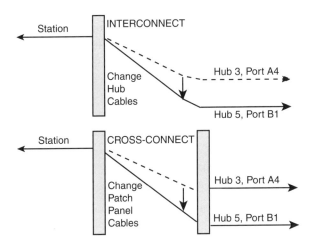

FIGURE 6.12   *Interconnect and cross-connect.*

Figure 6.13 shows a sample layout for a LAN that spans a building. Twisted-pair cabling bundles typically contain 2, 4, or 25 pairs.

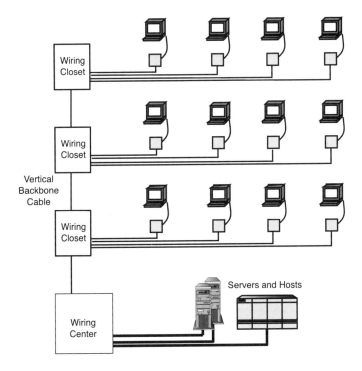

FIGURE 6.13   *Cabling a building.*

Full-Duplex Operation

Many LANs in operation today are built around hubs and half-duplex (CSMA/CD) communication, and they are subject to the CSMA/CD 5-4-3 rule. However, the price of switches has dropped at an astonishing rate, and hubs are destined to gradually fade away from the scene. Because data is sent and received on different pairs, full-duplex transmission is a regular feature of twisted-pair switches. Full-duplex communication was described in Chapter 5, "Full-Duplex Ethernet Communication."

Today's switches operate at 10Mbps, 100Mbps, and 1000Mbps speeds. Up-to-date NICs and switch (and hub) ports support an Auto-Negotiation function that enables peer interfaces to select the speed at which they will operate and to decide whether they will use full-duplex operation. Auto-Negotiation is discussed in Chapter 11.

The advantages of using switches include

- Full-duplex operation for each port

- Bandwidth proportional to the number of ports

- No collisions

- No 5-4-3 rule

The architecture and features of switches are described in Part II, "Bridging, Switching, and Routing."

10Mbps Twisted-Pair Transmission

10Base-T carries data across two twisted pairs of wire. Data is transmitted from a system on one pair and is received on the other pair. The term *twisted-pair* refers to two wires wrapped around each other. For 10BASE-T, the same signal is sent across both of the wires in a pair but with reverse polarity. This means that when a positive voltage is placed on one wire, an equal negative voltage is placed on the other.

There is a good reason for this. A current sent down a copper wire creates an electromagnetic field that induces currents in nearby wires. Some people experience this effect (called *crosstalk*) during a telephone call when they suddenly begin to hear a conversation taking place on another set of wires.

When two wires carrying these reversed signals are twisted around one another, the electromagnetic fields around each wire come very close to canceling each other out. The arrangement is called a *balanced cable*. The more twists per foot, the better this works. The number of twists ranges from 2 to 12 per foot. Figure 6.14 illustrates the relationship between the pairs. The wire labeled Tx+ carries the transmitted signal, and Tx- carries the inverted transmit signal. The wire labeled Rx+ carries the signal that was transmitted from the remote end, and Rx- carries the inverted signal.

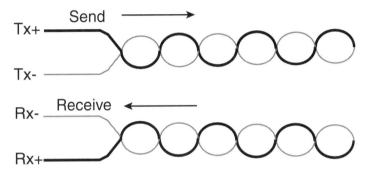

FIGURE 6.14   *Transmit and receive twisted pairs.*

There is another good reason for this paired transmission. If a noise spike occurs along the way, both signals in a pair will be subjected to the same spike. On reception, the inverted signal on the incoming Rx- cable is inverted again. This causes the noise spike to be inverted. The inverted Rx- signal then is added to the Rx+ signal, and the result is that the noise spike cancels itself out.

The two twisted pairs are terminated by a RJ-45 plug at each end. This plug has eight contacts, numbered 1 to 8. Only four are needed, and the ones that are used are:

1	Tx+
2	Tx-
3	Rx+
6	Rx-

Each wire connects a transmit pin at one end to a receive pin at the other end. The top of Figure 6.15 shows the proper matchup. For example, the transmit wire that is attached to pin 1 on the sender side must be attached to pin 3 on the receiver side. The bottom of the figure shows a twisted-pair jack.

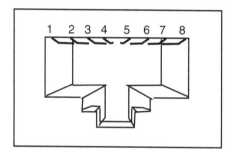

Pin	Name of Signal		Name of Signal	Pin
1	TX+		TX+	1
2	TX-		TX-	2
3	RX+		RX+	3
6	RX-		RX-	6

FIGURE 6.15 *Pin, wire, and jack connections.*

Figure 6.16 shows how a *crossover cable* connects transmit and receive ends.

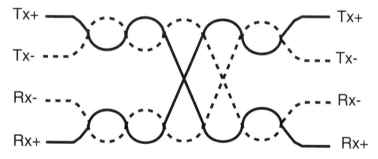

FIGURE 6.16 *Crossover cable wires.*

Hub and Switch Connections

An ordinary garden-variety port that transmits on pins 1 and 2 and receives on pins 3 and 6 is called a *medium dependent interface* (MDI) port. Stations have MDI ports.

You might expect that a crossover cable like the one in Figure 6.16 would be needed between a station and a hub, but hub ports are structured so that the crossover is performed inside the port. These ports are said to be of type *medium dependent interface crossover* (MDI-X). A straight-through cable is used between an MDI port in an end system and an MDI-X port in a hub.

What do you do when a hub has to be connected to another hub? A straight-through cable won't work between two MDI-X ports. Transmit would be connected to transmit and receive to receive. Fortunately, most hubs have a special MDI port that is provided for this purpose. A straight-through cable is used to connect an MDI port on one hub to an MDI-X port on the other hub.

Users prefer not to waste a port on a hub that does not need to be connected to another hub. Many hubs have a special port that is marked MDI/MDI-X. It can be set to MDI or MDI-X by pushing or releasing a button or by moving a slider. Choosing MDI-X lets you connect an end-user station to the port via a straight-through cable. Choosing MDI enables you to connect to an MDI-X port on another hub using a straight-through cable.

> **Note**
>
> The previous discussion also applies to switch ports. End systems connect to MDI-X switch ports via straight-through cables. A switch can be connected to a hub or to another switch via a straight-through cable by using an MDI-X port on one end and an MDI port at the other end.

It is very convenient to be able to use straight-through cables for all your connections. It is all too easy to plug in the wrong type of cable if you have both types lying around.

However, if a hub needs to be connected to more than two hub or switch devices, you could run out of available MDI ports. In this case, you would need to use MDI-X ports at both ends and connect them with a crossover cable.

> **Note**
>
> It is a good idea to buy color-coded cables. All crossover cables should have a characteristic color that stands out, such as hot pink.

Figure 6.17 illustrates valid hub connections.

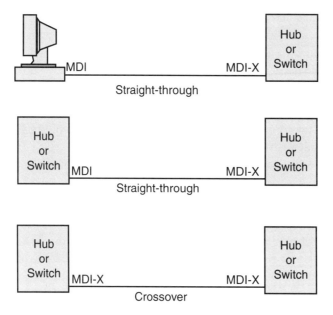

FIGURE 6.17 *Port and cable types.*

Twisted-Pair Link Integrity Test

The fact that data is sent and received across a 10BASE-T link on different wires allowed a useful self-test capability to be introduced. Twisted-pair interfaces detect cable failures automatically by performing an ongoing *link integrity test*. Each interface implements this by sending a special *link integrity signal* across each pair at (approximately) 16-millisecond intervals when the data transmitter is idle.

The signal consists of a special nondata pulse called a *normal link pulse* (NLP). As long as the interface at the other end of the link receives this signal, it knows that the link is working. If no test signal is received during a specified period of time, data transfer through the interface is disabled. Either party can send these test pulses to its partner on its transmit wires as long as its data transmitter is idle.

Building a Mixed Coax/Twisted-Pair Collision Domain

The maximum length of a thick Ethernet segment is 500 meters, and a thin Ethernet segment is, at most, 185 meters long. The length of a twisted-pair segment, however, is limited to 100 meters. Figure 6.18 shows what happens when you build a LAN that mixes 10BASE5 coax and twisted-pair segments. The maximum length of each segment is dictated by its medium type.

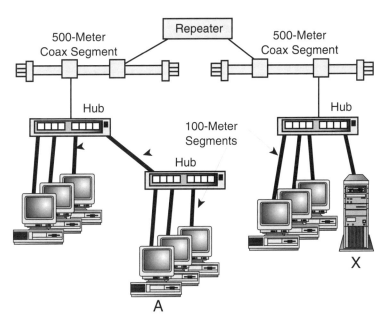

FIGURE 6.18 *Mixed coax and twisted-pair LAN.*

The path from station A to server X passes through four repeaters (three hubs and a coax repeater). It crosses three twisted-pair segments and two coax segments. The thin lines in the figure represent AUI cables. These do not count as segments.

Note

The recommended segment-length restrictions have been established to assure that collisions will be heard by every system. However, it is possible to build LANs that contain some segments that are longer if they are off-set by shorter segments elsewhere. Chapter 13 of the 1998 IEEE 802.3 standard presents a method of calculating whether the delay across the worst path in a network exceeds the permissible bound.

When nonstandard cable lengths are used, it is very important to maintain very detailed documentation of the LAN structure and to flag the exceptions clearly. All LAN administrators need to be kept aware of the exceptions. Otherwise, someone might innocently add a cable that creates a path that is too long. This leads to erratic behavior that is hard to pinpoint and fix. It is a good idea to stick with the normal length restrictions whenever possible!

10Mbps on Fiber Optic Cable

Fiber optic cable easily outperforms copper media. It is capable of carrying a huge capacity for extended distances, and it is not subject to the electromagnetic disturbances that cause distortions and errors in copper wires. No crosstalk problem occurs, either. Optical fiber also offers superior security. Unlike electrical transmission, it does not emit signals that can be captured by electronic eavesdropping equipment.

The use of optical fiber for telecommunications dates back to 1977, when the medium was first used to carry long-distance telephone calls. Fiber optic cable was introduced into the Ethernet local area networking arena in the 1980s.

Ethernet fiber optic links initially were used for long runs of cable within a building or between two buildings. Originally, vendors built proprietary products that satisfied the demand for these long links. In 1987, the IEEE 802.3 committee introduced the 10Mbps *fiber optic inter-repeater link* (FOIRL) standard. FOIRL enabled vendors to build interoperable fiber optic interfaces. A FOIRL link could be used to connect a repeater to another repeater or to a station.

At this time, optical fiber was costly and difficult to work with. Eventually, the price of the cable and components came down, and new connectors made fiber far easier to install and maintain. The medium became increasingly popular, and there was an impetus to update the technology and support even longer cable runs.

The updated set of IEEE 802.3 10Mbps optical fiber standards was dubbed 10BASE-F. 10BASE-F includes three different configurations:

- **10BASE-FL**—An upgrade of FOIRL that interoperates with FOIRL. 10BASE-FL supports station-to-station, station-to-repeater, and repeater-to-repeater links.

- **10BASE-FB**—A specification for repeater-to-repeater backbone links.

- **10BASE-FP**—A specification for a passive optical device designed to interconnect multiple stations. It was not implemented by vendors and will not be described further.

Features of Fiber Optic Links

A fiber optic link is made up of two fibers. A separate fiber is used for each direction of transmission. Figure 6.19 shows how two devices are connected by a link that consists of two fibers.

The carefully layered design of 802.3 interfaces paid off when the IEEE introduced optical fiber. Systems can be connected to fiber by swapping out a
copper medium transceiver and swapping in a fiber optic transceiver.

The upper part of the Figure 6.19 shows a schematic that illustrates flows of
data across two fibers. The lower part shows a station that has a NIC with a
standard 15-pin socket. The station is prepared for fiber optic transmission
by plugging in an AUI cable that connects to a fiber optic transceiver.
(Alternatively, a NIC with an integrated fiber optic transceiver could be
installed in the station.) In the figure, a pair of fiber cables connects the
station to a hub.

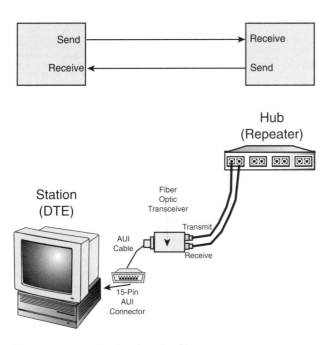

FIGURE 6.19 Send and receive fibers.

FOIRL, 10BASE-FL, and 10BASE-FB interfaces have several features in common
with 10Mbps coax and twisted-pair implementations. These features include

• The use of Manchester encoding to transmit 0s and 1s. Manchester encoding is described in Appendix A.

• Jabber control—that is, the capability to cut off an inappropriate transmission after a time threshold has been exceeded.

- The use of SQE signals to announce collisions and jabbers or other errors to the local system.

- For end stations, the implementation of the SQE test function—that is, an SQE signal that announces the end of each data transmission to the station.

Some features are unique to the optical fiber medium:

- The use of special idle signals. When it is not transmitting data, an optical interface sends a steady stream of special idle signals onto its transmit fiber. This enables the integrity of each fiber to be checked very easily because a signal of some type always should be arriving across a fiber that is functioning properly. The fiber optic link integrity test consists of monitoring the continuous incoming signals.

- A low light-detection function. Any time that the light signal arriving on a fiber is too weak, the interface shuts down its receive data function and sends only idle signals onto its transmit fiber until the incoming signal returns to normal.

- For 10BASE-FB, the capability to send a signal across the transmit fiber that indicates that there is a fault condition on the receive fiber.

Note
For 10BASE-FB, idles are sent in the form of special synchronous signals, which means that the receiver can maintain bit timing using these signals. A consequence is that a 10BASE-FB interface does not have to resynchronize its timing every time a frame arrives. This offers the advantage of reducing the interframe gap shrinkage that occurs when frames pass through a repeater.

Fiber Optic Inter-Repeater Link
The fiber optic inter-repeater link was introduced to connect a repeater to another repeater or to a station across a long and reliable link. Figure 6.20 shows two FOIRL links that span a distance of up to 1000 meters between a pair of copper segments.

A repeater can be converted to an FOIRL repeater by attaching an FOIRL transceiver to the end of an AUI cable. On the left side of Figure 6.20, an AUI cable and transceiver connect each repeater to the optical fiber link.

Vendors also built FOIRL repeaters that contained integrated optical fiber transceivers. In this case, the fiber optic cable is plugged directly into a port on the repeater, as is shown on the right side of Figure 6.20. In either case, the fiber segment can be up to 1000 meters in length.

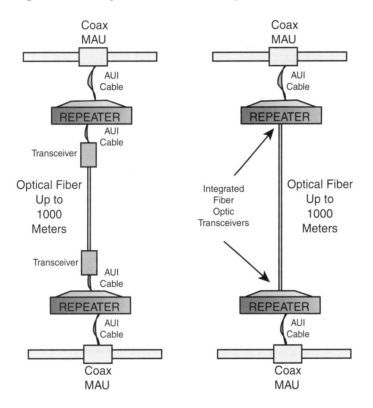

FIGURE 6.20   *A 10Mbps fiber optic inter-repeater link.*

FOIRL Links in a Collision Domain

The maximum length of a particular FOIRL link within a collision domain depends on the topology of the collision domain:

- A FOIRL link on a path with five segments and four repeaters can be 500 meters in length, at most.

- For paths with four segments and three repeaters (or less), a FOIRL link can be any length up to the maximum of 1000 meters.

Figure 6.21 shows a valid configuration for a path (from station A to server X) that traverses five segments and four repeaters (hubs). It includes three 500-meter FOIRL links.

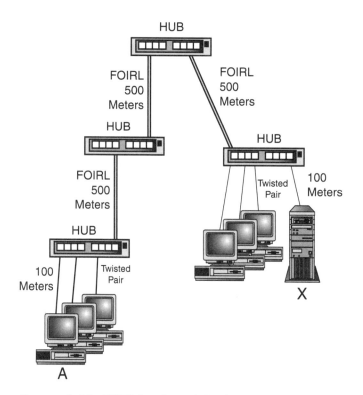

FIGURE 6.21   *FOIRL length restriction for a path with five segments.*

Figure 6.22 shows a valid configuration for a path (from station B to server X) that traverses four segments and three repeaters. It includes two 1000-meter FOIRL links.

10BASE-FL

10BASE-FL is an improved version of FOIRL that

- Is based on more up-to-date connectors and transmission technology.

- Can be used for station-to-station links as well as for repeater-to-repeater and repeater-to-station links.

- Supports links that are up to 2000 meters in length—double the FOIRL distance. (An additional 25-meter AUI cable can be used at each end.)

- Is backward compatible. A 10BASE-FL interface can communicate with a FOIRL interface across a 1000-meter link between repeaters.

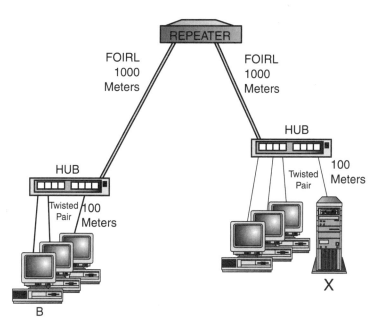

FIGURE 6.22 *1000-meter FOIRL links for a path with four segments.*

A 10BASE-FL link between two DTEs can operate in full-duplex mode. However, Auto-Negotiation is not supported, and both stations must be manually configured for full-duplex operation.

A 10BASE-FL link can be up to 2000 meters long, but the distance must be smaller in a collision domain whose longest path includes three or four repeaters:

- A 10BASE-FL repeater-to-repeater link on a path with five segments and four repeaters can be, at most, 500 meters in length.

- A 10BASE-FL repeater-to-repeater link on a path with four segments and three repeaters can be, at most, 1000 meters in length.

- A 10BASE-FL repeater-to-station link on a path with four segments and three repeaters can be, at most, 400 meters in length.

Figure 6.23 shows an example of a LAN whose longest path crosses three hubs and four segments. Three of the segments are 10BASE-FL links, and the fourth is an FOIRL link. Because there are three repeaters, the repeater-to-station 10BASE-FL links must be limited to 400 meters.

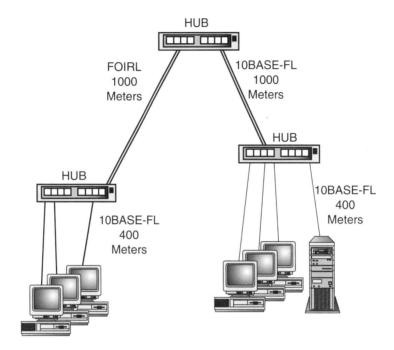

FIGURE 6.23   *10BASE-FL and FOIRL links.*

Any of the FOIRL links in Figures 6.21 and Figure 6.22 can be replaced by a 10BASE-FL link of the same length.

Figure 6.24 shows a 2000-meter 10BASE-FL link that connects a pair of twisted-pair hubs.

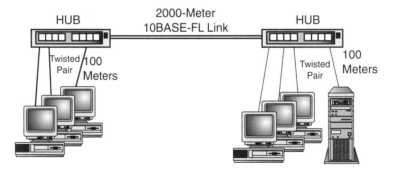

FIGURE 6.24   *A 2000-meter 10BASE-FL link.*

10BASE-FB

As the "B" in the name suggests, 10BASE-FB defines an interface to a backbone link—that is, a 10BASE-FB link is used to connect a pair of repeaters (hubs). A 10BASE-FB link can be up to 2000 meters long, but the distance must be smaller in a collision domain whose longest path includes three or four repeaters:

- A 10BASE-FB link on a path with five segments and four repeaters can be, at most, 500 meters in length.

- A 10BASE-FB link on a path with four segments and three repeaters can be, at most, 1000 meters in length.

A 10BASE-FB link is not longer than a 10BASE-FL link, and 10BASE-FB is less versatile because it cannot be used to connect a station to a repeater. However, 10BASE-FB does have extra features that are useful in a repeater-to-repeater backbone link. The synchronous idles reduce interframe gap shrinkage, and a 10BASE-FB repeater interface can send a special signal to the repeater at the other end of the link to report fault conditions.

Summary of Fiber Distance Specifications

Some distance limitations for FOIRL, 10BASE-FL, and 10BASE-FB segments are summarized in Table 6.4. The three middle columns summarize the length restrictions for a collision domain:

- The usual 5-4-3 rule (at most five segments, four repeaters, and three populated segments) holds when fiber optic segments are added to a collision domain.

- The second column in Table 6.4 shows that a fiber optic segment can be, at most, 500 meters in length if the longest path containing the segment crosses five segments and four repeaters.

- The third column indicates that the length can be increased to 1000 meters if the longest path containing the segment crosses four segments and three repeaters.

- The length of a 10BASE-FL segment that is connected to a DTE is limited to 400 meters if the longest path containing the segment crosses four fiber optic segments and three repeaters, and the length of each repeater-to-repeater link is 1000m.

Keep in mind that these limitations can be lifted by using bridges or switches to reduce the number of segments in paths across a collision domain.

Another alternative is to use an inexpensive *media converter*, which makes two segments behave like one extended segment. The advantage of doing this is that a fiber optic cable can be added to a collision domain without increasing the current segment and repeater count.

TABLE 6.4 10MBPS FIBER OPTIC DISTANCES

Cable	Collision Domain Restrictions			Maximum Length
	Five Segments, Four Repeaters, Repeater-to-Repeater Link	Four Segments, Three Repeaters, Repeater-to-Repeater Link	Four Segments, Three Repeaters, Repeater-to-DTE Link	
FOIRL	500m	1000m	–	1000m
10BASE-FL	500m	1000m	400m	2000m
10BASE-FB	500m	1000m	–	2000m

The Structure of a Fiber

As Figure 6.25 shows, an optical fiber consists of a glass *core* surrounded by another layer of glass that is called *cladding*. One or more layers of protective buffer coating are wrapped around the cladding. A jacket is wrapped around the buffer.

Note

Optical fiber cables also can be made out of plastic, but glass is much preferred. Although plastic is cheaper, it currently supports transmission across only very short cable distances. For example, it can be used for 50- to 100-meter office connections.

Data is transmitted by sending light signals through the core. The cladding material is structured to keep the light within the core. More specifically, the cladding and the core have different *indices of refraction*. The index of refraction of a medium affects the way that light is bent when it strikes the medium. When a ray of light traversing the core strikes the cladding, the difference between the indices causes the light to be bent back into the core.

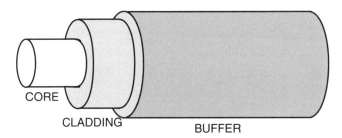

FIGURE 6.25 *Structure of an optical fiber cable.*

The two common types of optical fiber transmission systems are

- **Single mode**—A laser transmits a focused ray of light into a cable whose core has an extremely small diameter: 8–10 micrometers (μm). A single-mode system is capable of carrying enormous amounts of data across long distances, such as tens or hundreds of kilometers. Single-mode fiber is the medium of choice for wide area telecommunications networks. It also is used for gigabit LAN connections.

- **Multimode**—A *light emitting diode* (LED) emits multiple rays of light into a fiber with a larger core, normally 62.5μm. The rays are called *modes*. A multimode system can carry data across distances of up to 2km. Lasers are expensive, and LEDs are cheap. Multimode fiber and LEDs are used for 10Mbps fiber optic implementations.

> **Note**
> There is a third fiber optic transmission system: A Vertical Cavity Surface Emitting Laser (VCSEL) can be used to transmit light signals onto multi-mode fiber. VCSELs are less costly than ordinary lasers and are used for gigabit transmission. VCSELs are discussed in Chapter 9, "Gigabit Ethernet Physical Layer."

Optical fiber cables are described by two numbers separated by a slash. The first number identifies the diameter of the core, and the second is the diameter of the cladding. The standard diameter for cladding is 125μm. The types of fiber used for 10Mbps Ethernet LAN communication are shown here:

Multimode fiber of size 62.5/125μm is the type recommended for 10Mbps Ethernet LANs and is the most popular. The 50/125μm size sometimes is used. 100/140μm and 85/125μm also are acceptable, but their use is rare.

Note
Single-mode fiber is used for higher-speed LANs. Sizes such as 8.3/125µm, 9/125µm, or 10/125µm are commonly used for single-mode fiber. The core is tiny; a human hair has a diameter that is roughly 80µm.

Multimode Transmission

A LED emits multiple rays of light into the core of a multimode fiber. These rays spread out and bounce off the cladding of the multimode cable. This causes some rays to follow a longer path through the cable and arrive later. When the dispersion of the signal becomes too great, the signal is corrupted and cannot be interpreted correctly.

Figure 6.26 illustrates the dispersion of rays through multimode. The upper part of the figure shows the older step index fiber, which has a core whose index of refraction is constant. The lower part of Figure 6.26 shows graded index fiber, whose core index of refraction varies. It is highest at the center and smallest at the edges. The result is that light travels faster near the edges, allowing the rays that traverse longer paths to "catch up" with rays through the center.

Multimode Step Index Fiber

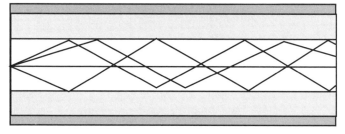

Multimode Graded Index Fiber

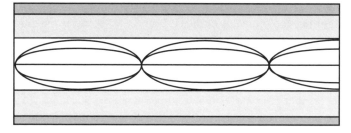

FIGURE 6.26 *Multimode step index and graded index fiber.*

The wavelength of the light tends to vary slightly depending on the distance from the center. The recommended ranges of center wavelengths are

- From 800 to 910 nanometers (nm) for 10BASE-FB and 10BASE-FL

- From 790 to 860nm for FOIRL

Optical Fiber Connectors

Currently, the connector of choice is the *square connector* (SC). A version of this connector is shown in Figure 6.27.

The "bayonet" *straight tip* (ST) *connectors* are recommended in the 10Mbps Ethernet standards documents. They sometimes still are used, and there is a large installed base of these older connectors, which also are shown in Figure 6.27.

> **Note**
> The ST connector is formally called BFOC/2.5 in standards documents. The ST plug connects in a similar manner to a 10BASE2 BNC connector.

A number of vendors have designed connectors that offer some special advantages, such as easy cable termination and a smaller connection footprint. These are referred to as *small form factor* (SFF) connectors. At the time of writing, a TIA committee is reviewing a SG connector, whose clever design makes it inexpensive to manufacture, easy to install, and less likely to pull loose accidentally. In addition, the SG requires half as much space as a duplex SC connector.

Figure 6.27 also displays a *sub miniature type A* (SMA) connector that sometimes is used in Ethernet LANs, and the old *medium interface connector* (MIC) that was defined for use in FDDI LANs and that still is occasionally used in these LANs.

> **Note**
> The SC connector was designed by Nippon Telephone and Telegraph (NTT). AT&T designed the ST connector. 3M and other vendors have contributed to the SG connector design effort.

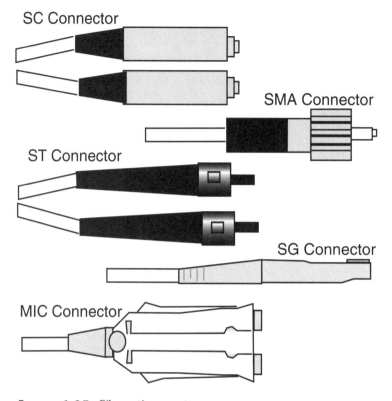

SC Connector

SMA Connector

ST Connector

SG Connector

MIC Connector

FIGURE 6.27   *Fiber optic connectors.*

Summary Points

- A collision domain obeys the 5-4-3 rule: Every path contains at most five segments, four repeaters, and three populated segments.

For coaxial cable LANs

- The original baseband Ethernet LAN defined in the 1980s was built from sections of thick, heavy 50-ohm coaxial cable.

- Only one signal can be on a cable at any given time.

- Stations attach to the medium via attachment unit interface (AUI) cables and transceivers.

- Transceivers send and receive, send jams, control jabber, and detect collisions.

- SQE signals are used to report the completion of a frame transmission, a collision, or improper pulses on the cable.

- Thin (10BASE2) coax is cheaper and easier to work with than thick coax.

- A thin coax segment has a daisy chain structure.

- Systems connect to a 10BASE2 segment via BNC connectors.

A 10BASE-T interface can

- Transmit and receive data

- Participate in a hub-based CSMA/CD collision domain

- Detect collisions

- Perform signal quality error (SQE) tests

- Cut off excessively long transmissions (jabbers)

- Test the link in each direction of transmission via link integrity test pulses

An up-to-date 10BASE-T interface can

- Operate in full-duplex mode across station-to-switch and switch-to-switch links

- Support Auto-Negotiation, which enables it to detect whether its peer supports full-duplex communication and enables the peer to operate at a matching speed

For fiber optic media

- Fiber optic inter-repeater links (FOIRL) were the first standard fiber optic links used for 10Mbps Ethernet.

- 10BASE-FL is an upgrade of FOIRL that interoperates with FOIRL. It supports station-to-station, station-to-repeater, and repeater-to-repeater links.

- 10BASE-FB is a specification for repeater-to-repeater backbone links.

- Fiber interfaces send idle signals between data transmissions. For 10BASE-FB, these are synchronous, and the receiver can use them to maintain bit clocking.

- An FOIRL link can be up to 1000 meters in length. 10BASE-FL and 10BASE-FB links can be up to 2000 meters in length. However, the lengths must be shorter when paths in a collision domain pass through three or more repeaters.

- An optical fiber consists of a core surrounded by another layer called cladding and is wrapped in buffer material and a jacket.

- A link consists of two fibers: one for each direction of transmission.

- The recommended cable for 10Mbps Ethernet fiber links is 62.5/125µm multimode fiber.

- The SC connector currently is the most popular choice, although there is a big installed base of older ST connectors.

References

A detailed description of the Ethernet 10Mbps physical layer can be found in

- IEEE Standard 802.3, 1998 Edition. "Carrier Sense Multiple Access with Collision Detection (CSMA/CD) Access Method and Physical Layer Specifications." Chapters 1–20.

Lantronics has published several Ethernet tutorials online at http://www.lantronics.com/.

ST connectors are described in the standards documents:

- IEC 60874-10. "Connectors for Optical Fibres and Cables: Part 10: Sectional Specification, Fibre Optic Connector Type BFOC/2.5." 1992.

- "TIA Fiber Optic Connector Intermateability Standard 2 (FOCIS-2)."

SC components are described in

- "TIA Fiber Optic Connector Intermateability Standard 3 (FOCIS-3)."

Optical Cable Corporation (http://www.occfiber.com/) has published an excellent set of technology white papers.

CHAPTER 7

The Ethernet 100Mbps Physical Layer

The job of ratcheting up Ethernet speed to 100Mbps was tackled in the early 1990s. In 1993, a group of vendors formed the *Fast Ethernet Alliance* and produced a 100Mbps Ethernet specification that was backward compatible with 10BASE-T and 10BASE-F. They submitted this to the IEEE, and the result (originally published as 802.3u) was absorbed into the 802.3 standard.

Today, Ethernet vendor cooperation continues under the umbrella of the *Fast Ethernet Consortium*. The Consortium sponsors interoperability testing that is performed at the University of New Hampshire InterOperability Lab (IOL) (`http://www.iol.unh.edu/consortiums/fe/index.html`).

The surprising thing about Fast Ethernet is how much of the original structure of Ethernet is retained in its design:

- The minimum and maximum Ethernet frame sizes are unchanged.

- The rules for handling collisions are the same.

The differences are confined to the physical layer. The most significant change caused by increasing the transmission speed is the decrease in the maximum diameter of a collision domain. The reason for this is that at 100Mbps, an Ethernet frame is transmitted in roughly 1/10 of the time required to transmit at 10Mbps. To be sure that a transmitting station detects a colliding frame before the station has sent 64 bytes, the maximum distance between stations also must shrink.

Note

When 100Mbps Ethernet was first considered, there actually were two competing proposals. The Fast Ethernet Alliance championed a backward-compatible version that quickly won acceptance from users. Hewlett-Packard and AT&T advocated a new protocol, 100VG-AnyLAN, that was intended to replace both Ethernet and Token Ring.

The contest between these proposals held up the establishment of a standard for quite a while. Finally, the IEEE accepted Fast Ethernet as part of 802.3 and published 100VG-AnyLAN as a separate standard, 802.12. Despite this, 100VG-AnyLAN did not make much of a dent in the market and is a dying technology.

This chapter deals with 802.3 100Mbps Ethernet. For completeness, the 100VG-AnyLAN protocol is described briefly at the end of the chapter.

Fast Ethernet runs on both twisted-pair copper media and fiber optic cable. As is shown in Table 7.1, three different twisted-pair technologies and one optical fiber technology were defined.

TABLE 7.1 100MBPS ETHERNET TECHNOLOGIES

Technology	Type of Cable	Standard Maximum Cable Length in Meters	Mode of Operation
100BASE-TX	Two pairs of Category 5 unshielded twisted-pair (UTP) cabling or two pairs of IBM Type 1 shielded twisted–pair cabling	100	Half- or full-duplex
100BASE-T4	Four pairs of Category 3 UTP or better	100	Half-duplex only
100BASE-T2	Two pairs of Category 3 UTP or better	100	Half- or full-duplex
100BASE-FX	Two multimode optical fibers	412 half-duplex, 2000 full-duplex	Half- or full-duplex

The first two copper interfaces, 100BASE-TX and 100BASE-T4, and the optical fiber interface, 100BASE-FX, have been implemented as products. 100BASE-T2, however, never made it to the marketplace. The 100BASE-FX fiber optic interface allows for longer cable runs than the twisted-pair implementations.

The physical layer for 100BASE-FX is based on the physical layer of a 100Mbps LAN that has been around for a long time: Fibre Distributed Data Interface (FDDI). 100BASE-TX is based on the physical layer of the copper version of this LAN (CDDI). ANSI standards committee X3T9.5 defined CDDI to introduce twisted-pair transmission into FDDI LANs.

It's confusing enough to sort out the meaning of four different "100BASE" titles, but yet another term sometimes is used. Because 100BASE-FX and 100BASE-TX have a lot in common, this pair of technologies has been dubbed *100BASE-X*.

Coexistence and Migration with Auto-Negotiation

Vendors understand the best way to market Fast Ethernet twisted-pair interfaces. They sell 10/100 twisted-pair adapters that permit an easy migration from 10Mbps to 100Mbps Ethernet. An *Auto-Negotiation* capability was introduced to automate that migration. The Auto-Negotiation Protocol enables an adapter to discover the highest level of functionality that it shares with its peer at the other end of a twisted-pair link.

This is done in two ways. If the interfaces at both ends of a segment are "smart"—that is, capable of performing the Auto-Negotiation Protocol—then the peers exchange messages to announce their capabilities.

If only one of the interfaces is smart, it analyzes incoming signals to recognize a 10BASE-T, 100BASE-TX, or 100BASE-T4 partner. Auto-Negotiation is a requirement for 1000BASE-T interfaces, so link parameters always can be negotiated with a partner whose adapter supports 1000BASE-T.

The 802.3 committee made Auto-Negotiation an optional feature for 10Mbps and 100Mbps devices. So, although all the leading vendors provide it, some products do not. Auto-Negotiation pays for itself by preventing problems that could be very time-consuming to solve, and it certainly should be on the list of essential product requirements.

10/100Mbps twisted-pair NICs are not expensive, and many organizations buy them in bulk. Then an administrator installs a 10/100 card whenever a 10Mbps NIC must be added to a new device or replaced in an old device. This is a good strategy even if some of the hubs and switches that are still in use are old 10Mbps devices.

To upgrade a link originating at a station with a 10/100 NIC to 100Mbps, you just have to connect the other end of the cable to a hub or switch port capable of operating at 100Mbps. Auto-Negotiation partners will select the highest speed supported at both ends.

100Mbps Ethernet on Twisted–Pair Cabling

During the 100Mbps Ethernet development effort, three separate teams of engineers pursued different technical approaches to pushing 100Mbps across twisted–pair cabling. As a result, three distinct twisted-pair physical specifications were written:

- **100BASE-TX**—This version was marketed first and is by far the most popular. It runs across two pairs of wires, either Category 5 UTP cable or IBM Type 1 shielded twisted–pair cable.

- **100BASE-T4**—This version runs across four Category 3 (or better) twisted pairs. Although far less popular than the TX version, it is useful for environments that do not have either Category 5 or shielded twisted-pair cabling. It has some shortcomings, however: The worst is that it does not support full-duplex operation.

- **100BASE-T2**—The goal of this version was complete backward compatibility with 10Base-T—namely, operation at 100Mbps across two pairs of Category 3 (or better) cable. 100BASE-T2 took a long time to develop. In the meantime, 100BASE-TX became well entrenched. A strong and competitive market for 100BASE-TX brought prices down rapidly. 100BASE-T2 required complex engineering that would have made products quite costly. As a result, when the 100BASE-T2 was completed, vendors did not implement the technology. However, its mechanisms used for its physical layer became the basis for gigabit twisted-pair transmission.

All these versions were designed to operate across up to 100 meters of cable.

100BASE-TX

The 100BASE-TX physical layer has a lot in common with 10BASE-T:

- It runs across two twisted pairs.

- A segment length of up to 100 meters is supported.

- Its twisted-pair cables are terminated by RJ-45 connectors, and pin usage is the same for 10BASE-T and 100BASE-TX.

- Transmit wires at one end of the link become receive wires at the other end in the usual crossover fashion.

- Data is transmitted on one cable pair and received on the other pair. As was the case for 10BASE-T, pins 1 and 2 are used to transmit, and pins 3 and 6 are used to receive.

- Full duplex communication can be established between a station and a switch (or on a direct link between two stations).

Some important differences also exist between 100BASE-TX and 10BASE-T:

- 100BASE-TX requires Category 5 unshielded twisted-pair (UTP) cable or IBM Type 1 150-ohm shielded twisted-pair cable.

- A different method is used to encode data onto the wire.

- Link pulses are sent across the link only during initialization. (These pulses are used to transmit autoconfiguration information.) During normal operation, a steady stream of special idle symbols is transmitted between frames.

> **Note**
> Idle symbols are used as interframe filler for all 100Mbps and 1000Mbps technologies that are physically capable of full-duplex transmission. Transmitting idles between frames keeps receive clocks in synch with send clocks at all times. A link problem can be detected immediately because it will result in garbled or weak idle signals.

Use of CDDI Mechanisms

Vendors were able to rush 100BASE-TX to market very quickly because its physical layer was based on the existing CDDI standard. This enabled Fast Ethernet vendors to reuse readily available components when building their products.

> **Note**
> Support for shielded twisted-pair cabling was thrown into the 100BASE-TX standard because it already had been implemented for CDDI LANs.

For CDDI (and FDDI), groups of 4 bits are encoded onto a wire using an encoding scheme called *4B/5B*. This encoding scheme also was used for 100BASE-FX.

The 4B/5B scheme maps 4-bit nibbles to 5-bit patterns of 0s and 1s that are transmitted across the wire. Appendix A, "Physical Layer Encodings for Ethernet, Fibre Channel, FDDI, and Token Ring," has the full details. One of the advantages of this scheme is that there are extra 5-bit patterns that can be used—alone or combined in pairs—as special control codes. Three important patterns are

- **Idle (11111)**—The idle pattern is sent continuously between frames.

- **Start-of-stream delimiter (11000 10001)**—A new frame is introduced by the start-of-stream delimiter.

- **End-of-stream delimiter (01101 00111)**—An end-of-stream delimiter is sent at the end of a frame.

This use of these control codes introduces some significant differences between the 100BASE-TX and 10BASE-T physical-layer protocols. Unlike 10BASE-T, the following is true of 10BASE-TX:

- There is no need to test the integrity of a link using normal link pulses. The continuous idle patterns serve this purpose.

- The first byte of a frame's preamble is replaced by a start-of-frame delimiter.

- An end-of-stream delimiter is transmitted at the end of a frame.

100BASE-T4

The only merit of 100BASE-T4 is that it runs over Category 3 twisted–pair cabling. There still are pockets of Category 3, although most sites have been rewired with Category 5. As was the case for 100BASE-TX, the following is true of 100BASE-T4:

- A segment length of 100 meters is supported.

- The twisted-pair cables are terminated by RJ-45 connectors.

However, there also are several differences between 100BASE-T4 and 100BASE-TX:

- Four twisted pairs are used.

- Full-duplex transmission is not supported.

- Groups of bits are encoded onto the wires using an encoding scheme called 8B/6T. Appendix A describes 8B/6T encoding.

- An interface transmits link integrity pulses across one of the wire pairs when it is not sending data.

Four twisted pairs might sound like a handful, but the cable containing them still can be terminated by RJ-45 plugs. Now, however, all eight pins are used instead of the four pins that are used for 10BASE-T and 100BASE-TX. The total 100Mbps capacity is split into *three* 33 1/3Mbps parts. Just as was the case for 10BASE-T, one wire in a pair carries the normal transmission, while the other wire carries a copy that has been inverted. The way that three of the four pairs are selected to transmit data or receive data looks a little strange at first, but it actually makes very good sense.

Figure 7.1 provides an idea of how it works. Pair 2 always acts as a receive pair, and it also controls what is going on. A system listens on pair 2 to determine whether its partner is transmitting. If the local system is not sending and preamble bits start to arrive on pair 2, pairs 3 and 4 are recruited to act as additional receive pairs for the incoming data.

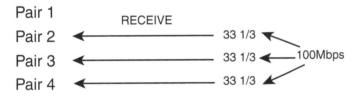

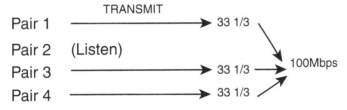

FIGURE 7.1 *100BASE-T4 transmission.*

If the local system has data to transmit, it listens to pair 2 to check that the medium is free. The system then transmits data across pairs 1, 3, and 4. The system continues to listen on pair 2 to detect a collision. If preamble bits arrive on pair 2 while the system is transmitting, a collision is occurring and jamming bits are sent out of the other pairs.

Note the special role of pairs 1 and 2. Pair 1 can only transmit, and pair 2 can only receive. By listening to pair 2, the system finds out whether the medium is free so that it can transmit. If so, pairs 3 and 4 join pair 1 as send pairs. When data is arriving on pair 2, however, pairs 3 and 4 act as receive pairs.

Now you can see why full-duplex operation does not work for 100BASE-T4. Pairs 3 and 4 can be set to work as send pairs, or they can be set to work as receive pairs. There is no way that they can send and receive at the same time.

As was the case for 10BASE-T, wires need to be crossed so that a send wire becomes a receive wire at the other end. The crossover is performed within a hub or switch port, or occasionally by a crossover cable. Figure 7.2 shows the cross-connections between the pins at each end. Note that the pin numbers are not in sequential order. The pin order in Figure 7.2 is the one that normally is displayed because it produces a tidy diagram.

Special start-of-stream and end-of-stream symbol patterns are sent across pairs 1, 3, and 4 to mark the beginning and end of a frame. However, idle symbols are not used. During an idle period, an interface sends link integrity pulses out of TX_D1 and receives them on RX_D2. During initialization, special Auto-Negotiation link pulses are sent and received on the same pairs.

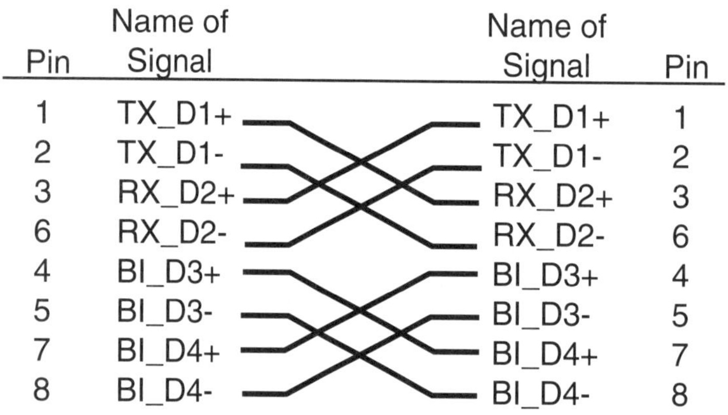

Pin	Name of Signal		Name of Signal	Pin
1	TX_D1+		TX_D1+	1
2	TX_D1-		TX_D1-	2
3	RX_D2+		RX_D2+	3
6	RX_D2-		RX_D2-	6
4	BI_D3+		BI_D3+	4
5	BI_D3-		BI_D3-	5
7	BI_D4+		BI_D4+	7
8	BI_D4-		BI_D4-	8

FIGURE 7.2   100BASE-T4 cross-connections.

100BASE-T2

100BASE-T2 will be discussed only briefly because it has not been implemented in products. 100BASE-T2 differed from 100BASE-TX in the fact that it was designed to run over Category 3 UTP and in its complex encoding scheme (which is sketched in Appendix A). Its implementation required costly digital signal processors and other special electronic components, in contrast with the cheap off-the-shelf components that were used for 100BASE-TX.

Functionally, 100BASE-T2 has some features in common with 100-BASE-TX:

- A segment length of up to 100 meters is supported.

- The Category 3 or better UTP cables are terminated by RJ-45 connectors.

- Data is transmitted on one cable pair and received on the other pair. As was the case for 10BASE-T, pins 1 and 2 are used to transmit, and pins 3 and 6 are used to receive.

- Full-duplex communication can be established between a station and a switch.

100BASE-FX and FDDI

A 100Mbps optical fiber implementation was produced very quickly by borrowing the physical layer from the FDDI physical layer defined by ANSI standards committee X3T9.5. The important characteristics of 100BASE-FX are listed here:

- It runs across a pair of optical fibers. 62.5/125 micron multimode fiber is specified in the 802.3 standard.

- A segment length of up to 412 meters is supported for half-duplex communication. Up to 2000 meters are supported across a full-duplex link.

- The fiber optic cables are terminated by the same SC or ST connectors that were mentioned in Chapter 6, "The Ethernet 10Mpbs Physical Layer" (see Figure 6.27).

- Data is transmitted onto one fiber and received on the other.

- Full-duplex communication can be established between DTEs (that is, a station and a switch, a pair of stations, a pair of switches, a switch and a router, and so on).

As was noted earlier, both 100BASE-TX and 100BASE-FX use the 4B/5B encoding scheme defined by ANSI for the signals that are actually sent across the wire. Just as was the case for 100BASE-TX, three important special patterns are used with 100BASE-FX:

- **Idle (11111)**—The idle pattern is sent continuously between frames.

- **Start-of-stream delimiter (11000 10001)**—A new frame is introduced by the start-of-stream delimiter.

- **End-of-stream delimiter (01101 00111)**—An end-of-stream delimiter is sent at the end of a frame.

Appendix A contains a detailed description of the physical encoding that is used for 100BASE-FX.

Media Independent Interface

An administrator who is preparing a station to participate in a Fast Ethernet LAN must install an appropriate network adapter:

- 100BASE-T4 with an RJ-45 socket for four pairs of Category 3 twisted-pair cabling

- 100BASE-TX with an RJ-45 socket for two pairs of Category 5 twisted-pair cabling

- 100BASE-FX with an ST socket if optical cables with ST plugs have been installed

- 100BASE-FX with an SC socket if optical cables with SC plugs have been installed

Given the number of moves and changes that occur in a typical organization, an administrator could be kept pretty busy pulling adapters out of systems and installing new ones that match the cabling at a new location. For example, a user with a high-powered station that has been communicating via a 100BASE-TX connection might move to a new office and discover that this office is more than 100 meters away from the nearest 100Mbps hub or switch and that the office has been wired with optical fiber.

One way to be ready for situations like this is to install NICs with a *media independent interface* (MII) in systems that are likely to be moved and then to buy hubs and switches that have some MII ports.

When a system has a MII interface, getting ready for 100BASE-T4, 100BASE-TX, or 100BASE-FX transmission is easy: You just get the appropriate type of transceiver and plug it into the MII interface.

Physically, the MII interface is a female 40-pin D connector, as shown in Figure 7.3. Some transceivers have a corresponding 40-pin male connector at one end that plugs directly into the MII. For others, the 40-pin male connector is located at the end of a short cable (up to half a meter in length), as shown in Figure 7.3. The desired physical medium attachment is at the other end of the transceiver.

A MII connector provides flexibility and is useful to meet special needs. However, external transceivers are expensive, and this is not a solution that normally is used for a large number of NICs.

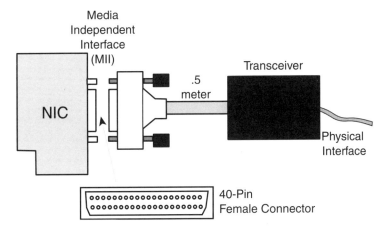

FIGURE 7.3   *A media independent interface (MII).*

Note
Another good solution exists for sites that have a mixture of Category 5 twisted-pair and fiber optic cabling: 100BASE-TX to 100BASE-FX media converters can be deployed to exactly the systems that need them.

100Mbps Collision Domain Diameter

The smallest Ethernet frame is 64 bytes (512 bits) in length. To make sure that every station in a collision domain becomes aware of a collision, the round-trip time between the two stations that are farthest apart must be less than 512 bit times.

At 100Mbps, a round trip of 512 bit times translates to .00000512 seconds. This is not much time!

The speed of light (c) is 299,792,458 meters per second. The speed of electrons through a cable is between .6c and .9c for most cable types. In addition to time spent traversing cables, some time is spent processing bits as they enter and leave each DTE and intermediate repeater. As a result, you can't go very far in 512 bit times. The result is that a 100BASE-T collision domain has a small diameter.

Figure 7.4 illustrates the components of the end-to-end propagation delay for a bit sent from one station to another. The delay is the sum of the times required to

- Transmit a signal through the DTE interface at station A

- Traverse cable 1

- Receive a signal through the incoming hub interface

- Process the signal

- Transmit a signal through the outgoing hub interface

- Traverse cable 2

- Receive a signal through the DTE interface at server X

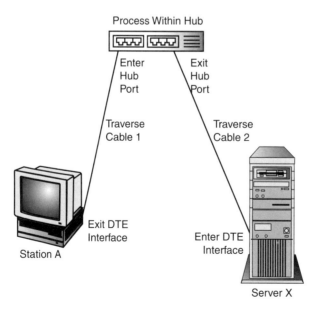

FIGURE 7.4 *Components of 100Mbps transit delays.*

Repeater (Hub) Classes

The 100Mbps time constraints are so tight that the time that it takes to process signals within a hub matters quite a lot. In fact, two different classes of hubs have been defined based on different processing time requirements:

- **Class I**—This type of hub is designed to support a mixture of 100BASE-T4 and 100BASE-X (that is, 100BASE-TX or FX) interface types. Because the signal encodings for 100BASE-T4 and 100BASE-X ports are very different, each incoming signal first must be converted to a bit pattern and then must be recoded into an outgoing signal. This introduces a delay into the forwarding process. The result is that normally only one Class I repeater can be used in a 100Mbps collision domain.

- **Class II**—All hub interfaces are of the same type (either all 100BASE-T4 or all 100BASE-X). Thus, an incoming signal can be repeated directly out of the other ports. The hub forwarding time is fast enough to allow two Class II hubs to be used in a 100Mbps collision domain (although the benefit turns out to be marginal).

Thus, Class II hubs are used when the incoming and outgoing signals are encoded in the same way. That is, a Class II hub can be used in either of these cases:

- Every hub interface is of type 100BASE-TX or of type 100BASE-FX.

- Every hub interface is of type 100BASE-T4.

If two stations are attached to a Class I hub by 100-meter copper cable segments, the time budget is exhausted. There isn't enough time left to traverse another hub.

If all your stations are connected to a hub by shorter cables, you could compute the component delays on your longest path to see whether a second Class I hub could be added. However, this would be risky. If someone later attaches a new station using a longer cable, your entire collision domain would be destabilized. Most administrators follow the conservative course and stick to a single Class I hub.

Note
Before plugging a hub into a LAN, it is important to know which class it is. The IEEE requires vendors to mark a hub with a Roman numeral I or II surrounded by a circle.

Collision Domain Configurations

The figures that follow show distance restrictions for 100Mbps collision domains. The numbers shown for twisted-pair copper cable are based on the use of Category 5 cable. Figure 7.5 illustrates the maximum distances for a DTE-to-DTE connection, such as a link between a pair of switches, a pair of routers, or a station and a switch. Note that a crossover cable needs to be used for a DTE-to-DTE link.

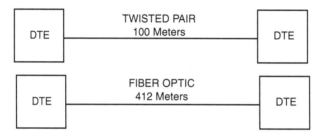

FIGURE 7.5 *DTE-to-DTE half-duplex connections.*

Figure 7.6 shows the maximum distances between DTEs for paths that pass through a Class I hub. Note that the distances depend on the combinations of media that are used.

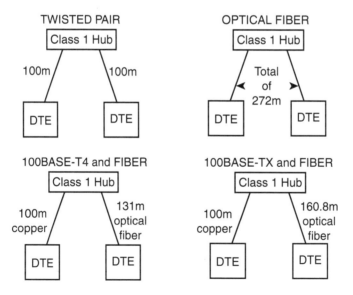

FIGURE 7.6 *Distances for a Class I hub.*

Figure 7.7 shows the maximum distances between DTEs for paths that pass through one Class II hub. The fiber cable lengths are bigger because it takes less time to traverse the hub.

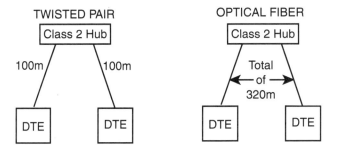

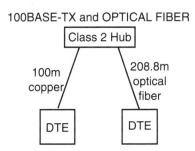

FIGURE 7.7 *Distances for one Class II hub.*

Figure 7.8 shows the maximum distances between DTEs for paths that pass through two Class II hubs. The diameter of the collision domain diameter actually is decreased by the presence of the second hub. It makes more sense to use a stack of hubs that behave like a single hub.

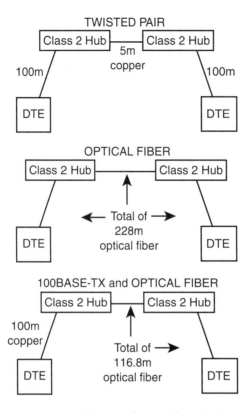

FIGURE 7.8   *Distances for two Class II hubs.*

Computing a Special Collision Domain Configuration

Table 7.2 contains the IEEE 802.3 tabulation of round-trip delay times that can be used to directly calculate maximum collision domain sizes. For more precise values, the IEEE numbers could be replaced by numbers obtained from your specific cable, adapter, and hub vendors.

TABLE 7.2   COMPONENTS OF ROUND TRIP DELAY

Component	Round-Trip Cable Delay in Bit Times Per Meter	Maximum Number of Bit Times
Time to exit/enter two TX/FX DTEs	N/A	100
Time to exit/enter two T4 DTEs	N/A	138
Time to exit/enter one T4 and one TX/FX DTE	N/A	127
Category 3 or Category 4 segment	1.14	114 (for 100 meters)
Category 5 or STP segment	1.112	111.2 (for 100 meters)

Component	Round-Trip Cable Delay in Bit Times Per Meter	Maximum Number of Bit Times
Fiber optic segment	1.0	412 (for 412 meters)
Class I hub	N/A	140
Class II TX/FX hub	N/A	92
Class II T4 hub	N/A	67

To illustrate how Table 7.2 is used, you can verify the value used for the fiber optic cable in the configuration at the bottom of Figure 7.7, which shows the maximum diameter of a collision domain that contains both 100BASE-TX Category 5 copper links and fiber optic links connected to a Class 2 hub.

Assuming that 100-meter copper links will be used, the DTE, copper, and hub delays are:

Enter and leave two TX/FX DTEs	100 bit times
Round trip on 100m Category 5 cable	111.2 bit times
Enter and leave Class II hub twice	92 bit times
Total	303.2 bit times
Time remaining out of 512 bit times for the fiber optic link	208.8 bit times

The round-trip time for fiber optic cable is 1 bit time per meter, so you could use a 208.8-meter fiber optic cable. It actually is desirable to use a fiber optic cable that is 1–5 meters less than 208.8 to keep the round-trip time comfortably under 512 bit times.

Curing the Diameter Problem with Switches

The advent of cheap switches takes the sting out of the collision domain restrictions. You can make a LAN span a large area by connecting many small collision domains with switches.

In the LAN in Figure 7.9, all the desktop systems are connected to a hub by runs of 60 meters or less. A long 250-meter fiber optic run has been connected to a server that is far from the wiring closet.

The round-trip bit times for each component are shown in the figure. The two DTEs account for 100 bit times, the Class II hub uses up 92 during the round trip, the twisted-pair cable accounts for 66.72, and the fiber optic cable accounts for 250. The total is 508.72, which is within the 512 bit-time budget.

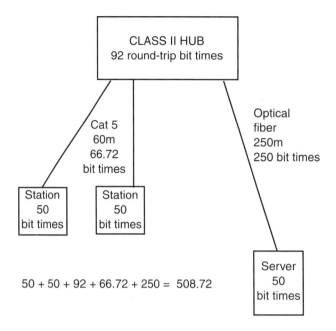

FIGURE 7.9   *A special configuration.*

However, another LAN administrator might innocently plug in a new desktop station using a 100-meter twisted-pair cable run. Missed collisions would lead to some very strange error symptoms, and the problem could be difficult to track down. This situation illustrates the following:

- Switches can be a good investment.

- It is a good idea to stick to the safe, conservative cable-length limits.

- It is very important to document the structure of a LAN carefully, especially if you violate the usual limits.

100VG-AnyLAN

100VG-AnyLAN is a technology that was proposed as an alternative to 100Mbps Ethernet. 100VG-AnyLAN did not succeed in gathering sufficient vendor or customer support to make it into a serious contender. Today, even Hewlett-Packard, its staunchest supporter, offers a meager scattering of VG products that are almost lost within HP's list of Ethernet offerings. The market has cast a deciding ballot for Ethernet.

However, it is easy to see why the IEEE granted 100VG-AnyLAN standards status, publishing it as IEEE 802.12. This is an interesting technology, and it is outlined briefly in the sections that follow.

100VG-AnyLAN Topology

The 100VG-AnyLAN topology is a tree of repeaters that can be nested five levels deep. The repeater at the top of the tree is called the *root repeater*. A three-level LAN is shown in Figure 7.10. In a given 100VG-AnyLAN, all frames conform to either an Ethernet format or a Token Ring format.

The reasoning behind offering a choice of frame formats was to make it easy to create 100VG-AnyLAN islands within an Ethernet shop or within a Token Ring shop, evolving gradually to a pure 100VG-AnyLAN technology. A 100VG-AnyLAN can be connected to adjacent Ethernets or Token Rings via bridges. Figure 7.10 includes a bridge to Ethernet.

Cables and Connectors for 100VG AnyLAN

Several media are supported for repeater-to-DTE links and repeater-to-repeater links. Table 7.3 lists the media that can be used and the length limitations for each type of segment.

RG-45 plugs and sockets are used with the twisted-pair media. SC connectors are used with fiber optic media.

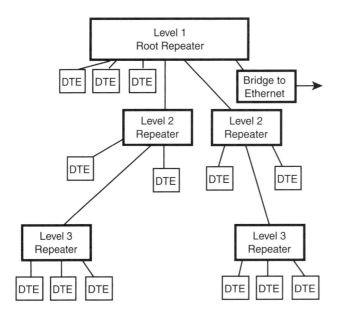

FIGURE 7.10 *Cascading 100VG AnyLAN repeaters.*

TABLE 7.3   MEDIA TYPES AND SEGMENT LENGTHS FOR 100VG-ANYLAN

Medium Type	Segment Length
Four pairs of Category 3 or 4 UTP	100 meters
Four pairs of Category 5 UTP	200 meters
Two pairs of STP	100 meters
One pair of multimode fibers	500 meters with an 800-nanometer transceiver 2000 meters with a 1300-nanometer transceiver

The diameter of a 100VG-AnyLAN can be substantial. However, delays caused by traversing multiple repeaters shrink the diameter. Figure 7.11 shows the largest LANs that can be built using two, three, four, or five levels of repeaters. The diameters range from a maximum of 4 kilometers with two repeaters, to 1 kilometer with five repeaters. The reason that these large diameters can be attained is that collisions do not occur for this technology.

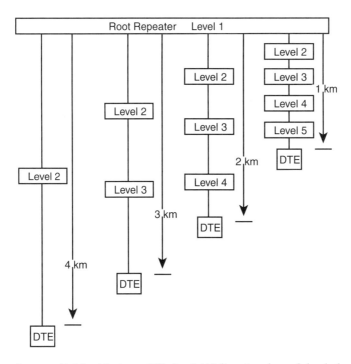

FIGURE 7.11   *Maximum VG-AnyLAN diameters for each level of repeaters.*

Redundant Links

Redundant links can be set up between a pair of repeaters or between a repeater and a DTE. If a primary link fails, an automatic switchover to a secondary link is performed. The recommended configuration for a DTE link is to connect its secondary link to a different upper-level repeater. Thus, connectivity is protected even if an entire repeater fails.

In addition, a second-level repeater can be designated to take over as root if the real root fails. The availability of a root is essential, so this is a prudent feature. However, it provides a more limited recovery capability than that offered by the Spanning Tree Protocol used in Ethernet networks.

Initialization and Port Types

It is easiest to understand how a 100VG-AnyLAN operates by starting off with a LAN that consists of a set of DTEs connected to a single repeater, as shown in Figure 7.12.

Two end-user workstations, a server, a network management station, and a network monitor are attached to the repeater. Station A in the figure has just been plugged in and has started an initialization process.

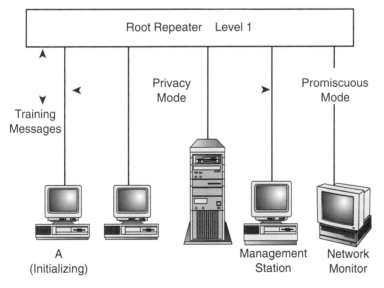

FIGURE 7.12   *A single repeater 100VG-AnyLAN.*

Initialization consists of the exchange of a sequence of special *training frames*. Station A starts the process by announcing the following:

- What its MAC address is

- Whether it is a station or a next-level repeater

- Whether it wishes to receive unicast frames addressed to its own MAC address (*privacy mode*), or wishes to receive copies of all unicast frames (*promiscuous mode*)

- Whether it uses an Ethernet or Token Ring frame format

The upstream repeater responds with indications of the following:

- Whether the requested configuration is compatible with the network

- Whether the node has been accepted as a station or a repeater, or has been refused access

- Whether the node will receive only broadcasts, multicasts, and unicast frames addressed to its own MAC address, or will receive copies of all frames

- Whether the node's MAC address is a duplicate address

- Whether an Ethernet or Token Ring frame format must be used

Note that the repeater learns the MAC address of each connected system during this initialization ("training") process. The normal expectation is that end-user systems will operate in privacy mode. In fact, it is prudent for an administrator to configure each repeater port so that this will be the case. However, in Figure 7.12, exactly one special port has been set up in promiscuous mode so that operations staff can monitor the network.

A VG-AnyLAN repeater performs the following:

- Forwards a broadcast or multicast frame through all ports (except for the one on which it arrived)

- Forwards a unicast frame through the unique port that leads to its destination MAC address, as well as through any promiscuous ports

The Medium Access Protocol for One Repeater

The medium access protocol is called *demand priority*. This means that a system needs to ask its repeater for permission to send a frame and cannot transmit until that permission is granted.

Demand priority supports two priority levels: normal and high. High-priority frames are sent before normal-priority frames.

Referring to Figure 7.12, the repeater performs these tasks:

- Polls each downlink node in round-robin order to find out whether it has a frame that needs to be transmitted, and to determine whether the priority is normal or high

- Grants permission to each high-priority request before granting permission to send normal-priority frames

Note

To prevent lockout, normal frames are promoted to high-priority status after a timeout period so that every frame will get its chance to be sent.

All systems are polled at least once per frame transmission, so the stack of requests is kept up-to-date.

The Medium Access Protocol for Two Levels of Repeaters

The way that polling is carried out in a tree of repeaters is designed so that the LAN will behave like one big repeater. Take the two-level tree in Figure 7.13 for example. If a request is made by DTE 7, which is connected to a lower-level repeater 2, the repeater signals a request to the root. The root will pass control to the lower-level repeater when it is time to grant the port connecting to repeater 2 port permission to send.

For example, if normal requests are made by DTEs 1, 7, 8, and 9, the root repeater will receive the requests via ports 1, 2, and 5.

1. The root grants permission to DTE 1 to send a frame.

2. Moving to port 2, the root delegates authority to repeater 2. Repeater 2 can now schedule a full round-robin cycle of transmissions. It grants permission to send to DTE 7 and DTE 8 in turn.

3. Next, the root delegates authority to repeater 5, which allows DTE 9 to send a frame.

4. The end result is that frames have been sent by DTEs 1, 7, 8, and 9, in that order.

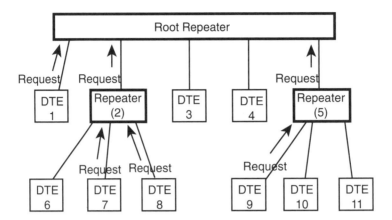

FIGURE 7.13   *Polling and permissions in a tree of repeaters.*

The process works the same way for a deeper tree. When a node transmits a frame, the frame is forwarded to every repeater in the LAN. For example, when DTE 7 transmits a frame, repeater 2 forwards it to the root, which forwards it to the other repeaters.

A broadcast or multicast frame will be delivered through every DTE port. A repeater that recognizes that a unicast destination MAC address belongs to one of its DTE ports forwards the frame through that port. The frame also is sent to any promiscuous DTE connected to the repeater.

Summary Points

- Fast Ethernet runs on both twisted-pair and fiber optic cable.

- 100-meter twisted-pair links are supported for Fast Ethernet.

- 100BASE-FX and 100BASE-TX have a lot in common, and the pair of technologies has been called *100BASE-X.*

- 100BASE-TX runs on two pairs of Category 5 twisted-pair cabling and supports full-duplex operation.

- 100BASE-T4 runs on four pairs of Category 3 twisted-pair cabling and does not support full-duplex operation. Data is transmitted on three pairs, and the fourth is used to sense collisions.

- 100BASE-FX runs on two optical fibers and supports full-duplex operation.

- 100BASE-TX and 100BASE-FX transmission are based on FDDI and CDDI transmission. All these technologies use 4B/5B encoding.

- The goal of 100BASE-T2 was backward compatibility with 10Base-T—namely, operation at 100Mbps across two pairs of Category 3 cable. The technology was not implemented in products.

- Idle symbols are used as interframe filler for 100BASE-TX and 100BASE-FX.

- It is possible to plug a 100BASE-T4, 100BASE-TX, or 100BASE-FX transceiver into a media independent interface (MII).

- The diameter of a Fast Ethernet collision domain ranges from 200 meters to 320 meters, depending on the media and the class of hub that is used.

- A Class I hub supports a mixture of 100BASE-T4 and 100BASE-X links. Only a single Class I hub may be used in a collision domain.

- All the ports on a Class II hub must be of the same type. Two Class II hubs may be used in a collision domain.

- When Fast Ethernet initially was proposed, there was a competing technology called 100VG-AnyLAN. 100VG-AnyLAN is little used today.

- The 100VG-AnyLAN topology is a tree of repeaters that can be nested five levels deep.

References

100Mbps Ethernet is described in

- IEEE Standard 802.3, 1998 Edition. "Carrier Sense Multiple Access with Collision Detection (CSMA/CD) Access Method and Physical Layer Specifications." See Chapters 21–30.

100VG-AnyLAN is described in

- IEEE Standard 802.12, 1998 edition. "Demand-Priority Access Method, Physical Layer and Repeater Specifications."

CHAPTER **8**

Gigabit Ethernet Architecture

100Mbps Ethernet became an IEEE standard in mid-1995. By the end of 1995, a group of vendors had formed the *Gigabit Ethernet Consortium* and had started work on 1000Mbps Ethernet. They worked at a remarkable pace—within 13 months, a specification that described gigabit transmission across multimode and single-mode optical fibers and special shielded copper cables had been written and approved by the IEEE 802.3 committee. One piece was missing, though: a specification for Category 5 twisted-pair cabling. This was published in 1999.

> **Note**
> At the time of writing, work is proceeding on the next step: 10Gbps Ethernet.

The battle between taking a backward-compatible approach versus using a new technology ended when users embraced Fast Ethernet and rejected 100VG-AnyLAN. Engineers working on the Gigabit Ethernet project were determined to make 1000Mbps Ethernet as compatible with the earlier versions as was possible.

The full-duplex version of Gigabit Ethernet is totally compatible with the 10Mbps and 100Mbps versions. However, it was impossible to build CSMA/CD (half-duplex) Gigabit Ethernet that was completely backward compatible. Some changes were needed, and a lot of effort was invested in extending the CSMA/CD protocol so that it could work at gigabit speed.

This effort might have been wasted: At the time of writing no vendors offer half-duplex Gigabit Ethernet; all actual products are designed for full-duplex operation.

There are good reasons for this:

- Extension bytes need to be added to short frames to make CSMA/CD gigabit feasible. Because short frames normally make up a significant portion of LAN traffic, these empty bytes waste bandwidth and reduce throughput.

- Even with frame extension, the diameter of a gigabit collision domain must be quite small to enable all stations to detect collisions.

- Gigabit interfaces are costly. It makes sense to use them in a way that supports the full bandwidth and allows for long cable runs.

Normally, a full-duplex LAN is constructed by attaching stations to switches. However, gigabit switches are expensive. Vendors wanted to offer an additional, less costly alternative. This alternative is a new network device called a *full-duplex repeater* or *buffered distributor*. Full-duplex repeaters are described later in this chapter.

Customers who buy gigabit products are looking for high performance, and some vendors have implemented a *Jumbo frame* feature that improves throughput. The size of a Jumbo MAC frame ranges up to 9018 bytes. Jumbo frames are nonstandard, and there is no sign that the IEEE 802.3 committee is ready to embrace them as part of the Ethernet standard anytime soon. However, the marketplace will make the final decision on whether Jumbos are a good idea.

This chapter concentrates on Gigabit Ethernet architecture and protocols. Full-duplex Gigabit Ethernet is discussed first. Then, for completeness, the adaptations that were needed to implement half-duplex (CSMA/CD) are described.

Chapter 9, "Gigabit Ethernet Physical Layer," deals with gigabit physical implementation issues; Chapter 10, "Twisted-Pair Cabling Standards and Performance Requirements," describes the performance tests required to check cabling systems that will be used for gigabit transmission; and Appendix A, "Physical Layer Encodings for Ethernet, Fibre Channel, FDDI, and Token Ring," outlines the way that data is encoded before it is transmitted.

Gigabit Configurations

Figure 8.1 depicts an environment that benefits from a gigabit link. The servers in the figure are linked to 100Mbps switches. The switches also interconnect communities of workstations. Each 100Mbps switch has one gigabit port, and a gigabit link between the 100Mbps switches provides ample bandwidth for client/server and server/server communications.

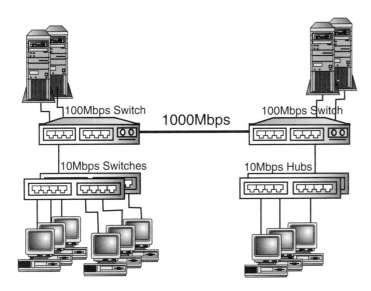

FIGURE 8.1   *Connecting 100Mbps switches with a gigabit link.*

In Figure 8.2, gigabit NICs have been installed in a set of high-performance servers that are connected to a 100/1000Mbps switch. Gigabit NICs also have been installed in client workstations that belong to a workgroup performing network-intensive graphics work. These workstations share the bandwidth provided by a full-duplex (buffered) repeater. A set of 10Mbps switches also connects to the central 100/1000Mbps switch via 100Mbps uplinks.

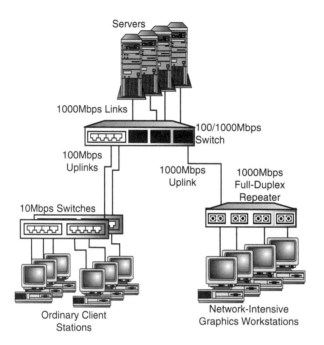

F IGURE 8.2 *Switch and full-duplex repeater connections.*

Full-Duplex Gigabit Ethernet

Full-duplex Gigabit Ethernet is used today. It is entirely natural to use the full-duplex Ethernet protocol because, down at the physical level, both the fiber optic and copper gigabit implementations transmit signals in both directions concurrently. Chapter 9 and Appendix A discuss how this is done.

Full-duplex Ethernet was described in Chapter 5, "Full-Duplex Ethernet Communication." There is nothing complicated about it:

- CSMA/CD is not used. Full-duplex mode is used on links for which there are no collisions.

- A system can send a frame whenever it wants, except for the fact that frames must be separated by an interframe gap and PAUSE requests must be honored.

Full-duplex communication at 1000Mbps is no different from full-duplex communication at 10Mbps or 100Mbps, except for the possible use of nonstandard Jumbo frames. Table 8.1 presents the parameters that are relevant to full-duplex operation.

TABLE 8.1 FULL-DUPLEX ETHERNET PARAMETERS

Parameter	10Mbps	100Mbps	1000Mbps
InterFrameGap	9.6μs (96 bit times)	.96μs (96 bit times)	.096μs (96 bit times)
maxFrameSize (without VLAN header)	1518 bytes	1518 bytes	1518 bytes (9018, if Jumbo frames are supported)
minFrameSize	64 bytes	64 bytes	64 bytes

Full-Duplex Repeaters

The device called a *full-duplex repeater* or *buffered distributor* was designed to overcome the defects of an ordinary hub.

A full-duplex repeater connects to full-duplex links. Like a switch, it can temporarily store incoming frames in buffer memory. Unlike a switch, however, it does not have a filtering table or the high throughput that results from transmitting independent streams of frames in parallel.

A full-duplex repeater performs the following tasks:

- Forwards each incoming frame through all ports other than the one on which it arrived, just as a hub would.

- Connects to each system via a full-duplex link.

- Queues incoming frames and schedules them for transmission in a first-in first-out (FIFO) manner.

- Shares 1000Mbps full-duplex bandwidth (a total of 2000Mbps) among all the connected devices.

- Connects to systems by links whose length is limited by maximum cable distances rather than by collision domain distances.

- Transmits PAUSE frames to impose flow control on endpoint stations whose input queue allocation is almost exhausted. This prevents an overflow situation that would cause frames to be discarded.

The repeater can use flow control for its attached devices, but the devices are not allowed to send PAUSE frames to the repeater.

> **Note**
>
> At the time of writing, gigabit NICs, which require lots of sophisticated electronics, are quite expensive. Adding the memory and processing capability required to build a full-duplex repeater (instead of a hub) is cheap when compared to the cost of the interfaces.
>
> Because many endpoint systems cannot operate at speeds anywhere near the gigabit level, the need to share 2Gbps bandwidth often is not a serious detriment.

Figure 8.3 provides a rough idea of how a full-duplex repeater works. The details of how input and output queues are managed and frame transmissions are scheduled are up to the vendor.

In the figure, each capital letter represents a frame. The alphabetic tags correspond to the order in which the frames arrive at the repeater. In the upper portion of the figure, the input queue for station 1 is almost full. The repeater is sending station 1 a flow control message to pause input for a while.

The lower part of the figure represents the same full-duplex repeater a short time later. Every incoming frame must be queued to all ports except for the one on which it arrived. Frame A currently is in transit to stations 2, 3, and 4, while frame B is queued up to be transmitted to stations 1, 2, and 3. Note that station 4 is transmitting frame G to the repeater at the same time that it is receiving frame A.

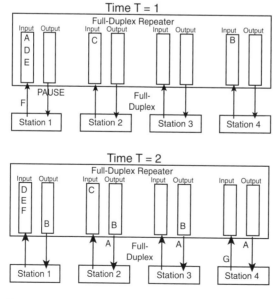

FIGURE 8.3 *A gigabit-per-second full-duplex repeater.*

Jumbo Frames

Lots of full-sized frames are transmitted during a file transfer, Web page download, or other bulk data transfer operation. The maximum MAC frame size is 1518 bytes. The preamble, start frame delimiter, and interframe gap add 20 bytes of protocol overhead. Hence, a total of 12,304 bit times is consumed by each maximum size frame.

Up to 81,274 maximum size frames can be transmitted across a gigabit link in a second. Even more can be sent when there is a mix of frame sizes. A processing overhead is associated with handling each frame, and many computers simply cannot keep up with the number of frames that can arrive across a gigabit link.

Several vendors have decided to solve this problem by introducing non-standard 9018-byte Jumbo frames. The information field in a Jumbo frame contains 9000 bytes, the same number of payload bytes as six maximum-sized ordinary Ethernet frames.

The use of Jumbo frames cuts down on the number of small frames as well as the number of big frames. This is because many of the small frames are sent to acknowledge incoming data. An acknowledgement of a Jumbo takes the place of six acknowledgements for ordinary frames.

Jumbo frames are not really unusually large. Bigger frames are used on 16Mbps Token Rings and across ATM networks.

Effect of Jumbos on Throughput

Jumbos significantly reduce the processing load on computers that transmit and receive frames across a gigabit link. This reduction in processing overhead can result in a large increase in throughput. Systems simply are capable of sending and receiving more data when they have fewer frames to process.

Also, a small—but still significant—improvement in throughput results from the reduction in overhead bandwidth when Jumbo frames are used. A rough calculation provides an idea of its order of magnitude.

- Adding the 18 frame header and trailer bytes to the 20 protocol overhead bytes yields a total of 38 bytes (304 bits) of overhead per frame.

- For a steady stream of 1518-byte frames, this overhead adds up to almost 3,100,000 bytes per second. The overhead is reduced to less than 526,000 bytes per second for a stream of Jumbo frames. This difference can be used to carry extra payload.

Drawbacks and Benefits of Jumbo Frames

The IEEE 802.3 committee has held back on endorsing Jumbos because of fears of interoperability problems. For example, Jumbo frames cannot be used with a buffered repeater unless every repeater port and every NIC connected to the repeater support the feature.

One application that benefits greatly from Jumbo frames is the file access service provided by the Network File Server (NFS) protocol. NFS client and server software is bundled with UNIX computers and is available for PCs. A client computer on a LAN can "mount" a directory located at a NFS file server into its own directory system and then can access files in the directory as if they are local.

Data read from a NFS server is transmitted in 8,192-byte blocks. The TCP/IP User Data Protocol (UDP) often is used to carry these blocks, which must be fragmented into six pieces before they can be sent in conventional Ethernet frames. Fragmentation and reassembly of the blocks imposes a significant burden on both client systems and file servers. No fragmentation is needed when Jumbo frames are used, and this contributes to faster and more efficient file server performance.

Half-Duplex Gigabit Ethernet

Backward compatibility broke down when the 802.3 committee wrote the rules for gigabit hubs operating in a CSMA/CD environment. Some Ethernet protocol elements had to be changed to accommodate half-duplex Gigabit Ethernet.

Half-duplex Gigabit Ethernet is not used at the time of writing, but a description of the protocol elements is included for completeness. The discussion will uncover another reason that motivated vendors to implement only full-duplex Gigabit Ethernet—namely, the small diameter of a gigabit collision domain.

Modification to Frame Format for Half-Duplex Mode

Chapter 4, "The Classical Ethernet CSMA/CD MAC Protocol," presented one of the changes that was needed to implement CSMA/CD (half-duplex mode) at gigabit speed: the addition of extension bits to short frames. A 64-byte (512-bit) frame is on a gigabit medium for far too short a time. Collisions of unextended 64-byte frames cannot be detected in a gigabit collision domain.

Extension bytes need to be added to small frames to keep a MAC frame transmission on the medium for 4,096 bit times (the time to transmit 512 bytes). Figure 8.4 shows a MAC frame that has been extended.

Note

The extension bytes are represented on the physical medium by special nondata symbols. These special symbols enable a receiver to detect exactly where a frame ends and an extension field begins. Appendix A explains how extension symbols are encoded.

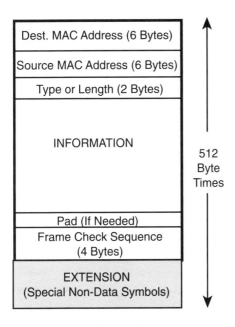

FIGURE 8.4   *A frame with a carrier extension that would be used for half-duplex Gigabit Ethernet.*

Frame Bursting for Half-Duplex Operation

Another adaptation called *frame bursting* or *burst mode* was introduced to reduce the waste caused by transmitting a lot of frame extensions and, hence, to raise the throughput across a gigabit collision domain. As the name suggests, burst mode enables a system to transmit multiple frames in sequence after it has captured the medium.

Figure 8.5 illustrates why this capability was viewed as desirable. The figure shows a 64-byte frame that has the required 448 bytes of carrier extension. Together, the frame and its extension occupy 512 bytes. Adding an initial 8-byte

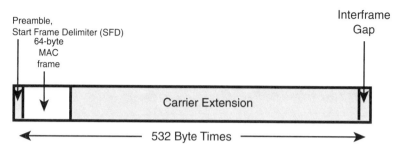

FIGURE 8.5 *Overhead for a 64-byte frame.*

preamble and start-of-frame delimiter and a 12-byte-time interframe gap brings the total up to 532 bytes. Only 12 percent of the utilized bandwidth is occupied by the 64-byte frame.

If you add to this the facts that small frames are commonplace and that collisions bring down the overall bandwidth that is available on a half-duplex gigabit LAN, its price/performance loses all attraction.

Clearly something had to be done. Burst mode was designed to improve half-duplex performance. Figure 8.6 shows how burst mode works:

1. A station with several frames to send transmits the first frame. Extension bits are appended if the frame is less than 512 bytes long.

2. The station continues to send extension bits during the interframe gap time. Other stations recognize that the medium has not been released and do not attempt to transmit.

3. The station sends the next frame. Even if the frame is short, it does not need to be extended. The medium already has been held successfully for enough time to assure that a collision will not occur.

4. If the station still has more frames to send, it again fills the interframe gap with extension bits.

5. The station is allowed to initiate fresh frames until the *burst limit* expires. The burst limit is 8,192 bytes (65,536 bits). Note that an actual transmission can be longer than the burst limit because the sender is allowed to complete a frame that it started to transmit when the burst limit had not yet been exhausted.

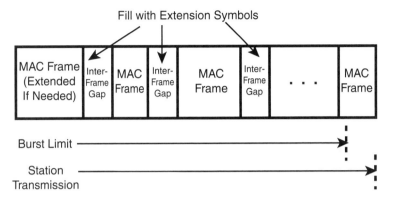

FIGURE 8.6 *Frame bursting in a half-duplex Gigabit Ethernet LAN.*

Even with the added boost provided by frame bursting, half-duplex hubs cannot provide throughput that can compete with the full-duplex repeaters described earlier.

1000Mbps Half-Duplex Hubs

An ordinary half-duplex hub could be used to interconnect a set of gigabit systems into a collision domain in which the overall 1000Mbps bandwidth is shared among the systems. Although these hubs are mythical devices at the time of writing, for completeness, this section discusses the features and limitations of a half-duplex hub implementation.

Tight timing on collision detection squeezed down the diameter of 100Mbps twisted-pair collision domains. The restrictions on the diameter are even more severe at a gigabit per second.

At most, a single hub can be used to connect gigabit devices. Table 8.2 displays the IEEE recommended size for the longest path in a gigabit collision domain for various types of media.

Keeping cable lengths within the conservative limits that are shown will assure that collisions can be detected for a minimum 512-byte transmission. Note that the diameter of a collision domain is quite small even when optical fiber is used.

> **Note**
> The 25-meter shielded copper cables mentioned in Table 8.2 typically are used to interconnect systems located in a computer room—for example, to link a server to a switch or connect a pair of switches to one another.

TABLE 8.2 GIGABIT COLLISION DOMAIN DIAMETERS IN METERS

Configuration	Both UTP	Both Shielded Copper	Both Optical Fiber	Mixed UTP and Fiber	Mixed Shielded Copper and Fiber
One Hub	200 (100+100)	50 (25+25)	220	210 (100+110)	220 (25+195)

The estimated delay for each network component is shown in Table 8.3. Note that it requires 1,840 bit-times simply to process incoming and outgoing bits at DTE and repeater interfaces. Also, a round trip across a 100-meter twisted-pair segment fiber takes roughly the same amount of time as a round trip across a 110-meter fiber optic segment.

TABLE 8.3 GIGABIT NETWORK COMPONENT DELAYS

Network Component	Round-Trip Delay in Bit Times Per Meter of Cable	Maximum Round-Trip Delay in Bit Times
Two DTEs	N/A	864
Category 5 UTP Cable Segment	11.12	1112 (100m)
Special Shielded Copper Cable	10.10	253 (25m)
Fiber Optic Cable Segment	10.10	1111 (110m)
Repeater	N/A	976

Now that the special features of the Gigabit Ethernet protocol have been described, it is time to examine the way that the physical layer was adapted to 1000Mbps speed. Chapter 9 and Appendix A investigate the physical layer in depth.

Summary Points

- The full-duplex version of Gigabit Ethernet is totally compatible with the 10Mbps and 100Mbps versions.

- For full-duplex operation, CSMA/CD is not used, and a system can send a frame whenever it wants, except for the fact that frames must be separated by an interframe gap and PAUSE requests must be honored.

- Stations connect to a device called a full-duplex repeater or buffered distributor via full-duplex links. The stations share the gigabit bandwidth.

- Nonstandard 9018-byte Jumbo frames improve performance by reducing the number of frames that need to be sent, which reduces a station's processing load.

- The half-duplex version of Gigabit Ethernet requires modifications to the protocol. At the time of writing, there are no half-duplex products.

- For half-duplex operation, extension bytes must be added to short frames, bringing their length to 512 bytes.

- Extension bytes are transmitted as special nondata symbols.

- For half-duplex operation, burst mode enables a system to transmit multiple frames in sequence when it has captured the medium.

- Only one hub could be used in a half-duplex Gigabit Ethernet collision domain.

References

A lot of useful information is available at the Gigabit Ethernet Consortium Web site, at `http://www.gigabit-ethernet.org/`.

Gigabit Ethernet standards include

- IEEE Standard 802.3, 1998 Edition. "Carrier Sense Multiple Access with Collision Detection (CSMA/CD) Access Method and Physical Layer Specifications." See Chapters 34, 36, 41, and 42.

- IEEE Standard 802.3ab, 1999. "Supplement to Carrier Sense Multiple Access with Collision Detection (CSMA/CD) Access Method and Physical Layer Specifications—Physical Layer Parameters and Specifications for 1000Mbps Operation Over 4-Pair of Category 5 Balanced Copper Cabling, Type 1000BASE-T."

CHAPTER 9

Gigabit Ethernet Physical Layer

Four standardized physical implementations of Gigabit Ethernet exist:

- **1000BASE-SX**—A fiber optic implementation for a pair of multimode fibers. *SX* corresponds to *short wavelength*. Lasers transmitting light at a wavelength of 850 nanometers (nm) are used.

- **1000BASE-LX**—A fiber optic implementation for a pair of single-mode or multimode fibers. *LX* corresponds to *long wavelength*. Lasers transmitting light at a wavelength of 1300nm are used.

- **1000BASE-CX**—A short shielded copper cable used in wiring closets and equipment rooms. *CX* corresponds to *copper*.

- **1000BASE-T**—An unshielded twisted-pair implementation that operates across four pairs of Category 5 twisted–pair cabling.

The first three were developed concurrently and, as a group, are called 1000BASE-X. They were based on existing fibre channel transmission technology and share a common method of encoding symbols onto a medium.

1000BASE-T, the twisted-pair version of Gigabit Ethernet, utilizes a different and highly complex encoding method, and it required a new transmission technology. The 1000BASE-T implementation includes sophisticated electronics.

Some vendors have extended the 1000BASE-LX single-mode fiber cable length by introducing (currently) nonstandard transceivers. The implementations are dubbed 1000BASE-LH. *LH* corresponds to *long haul*.

Features of Gigabit Ethernet

There are some characteristics that all of the gigabit implementations share in common:

- On initialization or reset, a gigabit interface performs an Auto-Negotiation procedure with its link partner to establish the ground rules for communication.

- After initialization, at the physical level, signals are transmitted concurrently in both directions on a continuous basis.

These features are described in the sections that follow.

Auto-Negotiation

All the gigabit technologies support the exchange of link parameters using an Auto-Negotiation Protocol. The following is true of Auto-Negotiation:

- It confirms that both ends of the link can operate at 1000Mbps.

- It enables each interface to announce whether it wishes to operate in full-duplex or half-duplex (CSMA/CD) mode. Full-duplex mode is used when it is selected by both parties.

- For full-duplex links, it establishes whether PAUSE flow-control frames will be used and whether flow control will be symmetric or asymmetric.

> **Note**
>
> For twisted-pair cabling, Auto-Negotiation also could be used to establish a different speed of operation. At the time of writing, gigabit NICs are significantly more expensive than 100Mbps interface cards. The result is that there appears to be no demand for gigabit-capable adapters that support multiple speeds. However, this could change as prices come down or if 10Gbps adapters are introduced.

Chapter 11, "Auto-Negotiation," has all the details on how Auto-Negotiation works.

Bidirectional Gigabit Transmission

All of the current Gigabit Ethernet technologies are inherently full–duplex. At the *physical* level, signals are transmitted in both directions on a continuous basis. An interface sends idle codes when it is not transmitting a frame. If a gigabit link were configured as a half–duplex link, an interface would have to be inhibited from sending a frame at the same time that it was receiving one.

The fact that the link actually is physically full-duplex undoubtedly contributed to the fact that vendors decided to implement only full-duplex Gigabit Ethernet.

The top portion of Figure 9.1 indicates how 1000BASE-SX or LX transmission operates. A separate fiber is used in each direction. The middle part of Figure 9.1 illustrates a 1000BASE-CX implementation. A separate pair is used in each direction. Frames or special idle symbols are sent across each fiber or wire continuously.

The bottom part of the figure represents 1000BASE-T physical transmission. Four twisted pairs are used. Transmission is bidirectional across each pair. Here again, transmission is continuous with idle symbols being sent between frames.

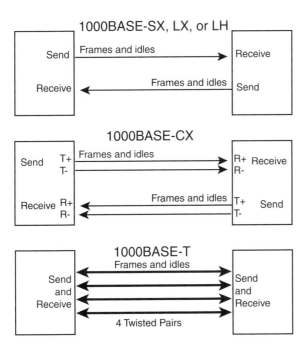

FIGURE 9.1   *Gigabit transmission architecture.*

Physical Characteristics of Gigabit Ethernet

Gigabit Ethernet has been implemented on multimode fiber optic cable, single-mode fiber optic cable, short shielded cables, and unshielded twisted-pair (UTP) cable. Table 9.1 lists the cable length ranges for a variety of gigabit transmission options.

Note that all the short wavelength (SX) implementations and all but one of the long wavelength (LX) implementations, run on multimode fiber. One LX implementation and all LH implementations require single-mode fiber.

The reason that there are several multimode SX and LX entries in the table is that the length of the multimode cable that can be used depends on a cable parameter called the *modal bandwidth*. The modal bandwidth affects the capability of a particular type of multimode cable to transmit information across a given distance. Formally, the modal bandwidth is defined as the worst-case 3-decibel bandwidth that will be achieved by a particular type of cable.

The modal bandwidth is reported in units of MHz × km. To compute the bandwidth in MHz for a given length of cable, the modal bandwidth must divided by the cable length (in km units). For example, the bandwidth in MHz of a 500-meter (.5km) cable with modal bandwidth equal to 500 is: $(500/.5) = 1000$MHz.

> ## Note
>
> *Modal dispersion* is the main factor that determines the modal bandwidth. Modal dispersion results from the fact that many rays of light are emitted into the relatively big core of a multimode fiber. These rays bounce off the cladding of the cable. Some of the rays follow a longer path through the cable and arrive later than others—that is, their arrivals are dispersed. (See Figure 6.26.) A significant amount of modal dispersion interferes with the receiver's capability to interpret incoming signals correctly.
>
> The amount of dispersion that will occur depends on the structure of the cable, the way light is injected, and the length of the cable.

The entry for 1000BASE-LH in Table 9.1 indicates that there is a very broad range of lengths for this nonstandard option. Some 1000BASE-LH transceivers are simply high-quality 1000BASE-LX transceivers whose vendor has guaranteed that transmission will remain reliable across a distance of 10km. Others are proprietary variations of 1000BASE-LX that support very long cables. At the time of writing, there are 1000BASE-LH transceivers that operate across up to 100km of single-mode cable. Some of the lasers that are used for 1000BASE-LH transmit light at wavelengths that are longer than the usual 1300nm LX wavelength.

TABLE 9.1 GIGABIT ETHERNET OPTIONS AND CABLE LENGTHS

Transceiver Type	Cable Type	Diameter of Fiber Core in Micrometers (μm)	Fiber Modal Bandwith (MHz × km)	Cable Range in Meters
1000BASE-CX	Special shielded balanced copper cable	N/A	N/A	0.1–25
1000BASE-SX	MMF	62.5	160	2–220
1000BASE-SX	MMF	62.5	200	2–275
1000BASE-SX	MMF	50	400	2–500
1000BASE-SX	MMF	50	500	2–550
1000BASE-LX	MMF	62.5	500	2–550
1000BASE-LX	MMF	50	400	2–550
1000BASE-LX	MMF	50	500	2–550
1000BASE-LX	SMF	10	N/A	2–5000
1000BASE-LH	SMF	9	N/A	1000–100,000
1000BASE-T	4 UTP	N/A	N/A	100

MMF = multimode fiber, SMF = single-mode fiber, 1000BASE-LH is nonstandard

1000BASE-X Technology

As was the case for 100Mbps Ethernet, an existing transmission technology was reused to speed the development of Gigabit Ethernet. The encoding and the transmission methods already in use for fibre channel technology were adopted for the three 1000BASE-X implementations (100BASE-LX, 100BASE-SX, and 100BASE-CX). This made it possible to reuse existing physical components and helped vendors roll out products quickly.

The sections that follow discuss the encoding method, transmission mechanisms, and connectors for the three 1000BASE-X implementations. 1000BASE-T has very different features and will be described at the end of the chapter.

8B/10B Encoding

For 1000BASE-SX, 1000BASE-LX, and 1000BASE-CX, each byte in a frame is mapped to a 10-bit code prior to transmission. The translation is called *8B/10B encoding.*

> **Note**
> Note that because of 8B/10B encoding, 1,250,000,000 bits per second must be transmitted to send 1000Mbps of data.

The 10-bit codes are called *code-groups*. Note that there are only 256 8-bit patterns, while there are 1024 10-bit patterns. Only a subset of the full number of 10-bit codes needs to be used to represent data bytes. This subset has been selected carefully.

Several reasons exist for performing the translation and using code-groups:

- The code-group patterns that have been selected to represent bytes contain a well-distributed mixture of 0s and 1s. This helps the receiver keep its bit-clocking in synch.

- A balanced mixture of 0s and 1s improves the electrical behavior of copper cables and prevents optical cable lasers from overheating.

- If one or more bit errors occur during data transmission, it is likely that a valid 10-bit pattern will be changed into a 10-bit pattern that does not represent a data byte. Thus, error detection is enhanced.

- There are many extra 10-bit patterns. This makes it possible to define code-group combinations that represent idle signals and frame extension bytes, and mark the beginning and end of a frame.

Details on the exact mapping of bytes to 10-bit code-groups are presented in Appendix A, "Physical Layer Encodings for Ethernet, Fibre Channel, FDDI, and Token Ring."

1000BASE-SX and LX Transmission: Lasers and VCSELs

Gigabit Ethernet runs on both multimode and single-mode optical fiber. Some differences exist between the fiber optic transceivers used for Gigabit Ethernet and the ones that were used for 10Mbps and 100Mbps Ethernet.

Although lasers were used for transmission across long-distance 10Mbps and 100Mbps Ethernet single-mode links, less expensive light emitting diodes (LEDs) were used for 10Mbps and 100Mbps transmission across shorter multimode fiber lines. However, LEDs cannot operate at 1000Mbps. At gigabit speed, lasers are required for multimode fiber as well as single-mode fiber.

Fortunately, there is a type of laser at hand that is quite inexpensive and can be used with multimode fiber: the *Vertical Cavity Surface Emitting Laser* (VCSEL). VCSEL emitters transmitting light whose wavelength is 850nm can support gigabit transmission across cables that are hundreds of meters in length. 850nm laser transceivers are used in the *short wavelength* (SX) implementations.

> **Note**
> The SX wavelength actually varies between 770nm and 860nm, but the products nonetheless are called 850nm transceivers.

The more costly lasers used for data transmission across single-mode fiber are operated at a wavelength of 1300nm for the *long wavelength* (LX) implementation. LX lasers are used with both multimode and single-mode cables. However, even with long wavelength lasers, multimode cable lengths are restricted to at most 550 meters. In contrast, 1000BASE-LX single-mode cables can be thousands of meters in length.

> **Note**
> The LX wavelength actually varies between 1270nm and 1355nm. Even longer wavelengths are being used for some 1000BASE-LH implementations.

LX transmission across multimode fiber requires the help of a special *mode-conditioning patch cord*. This type of patch cord is described in the section "Mode-Conditioning Patch Cords," after the discussion of fiber optic connectors that follows.

Connectors for 1000BASE-SX, 1000BASE-LX, and 1000BASE-LH

The recommended plug for 1000BASE-SX and 1000BASE-LX is a duplex SC connector, depicted in Figure 9.2. It is used for both multimode and single-mode fiber optic gigabit installations. This connector also is used for 1000BASE-LH.

As shown in Figure 9.2, one side of the connector has two flanges that match notches in the outlet boxes.

> **Note**
> As was noted in Chapter 6, "The Ethernet 10Mbps Physical Layer," vendors have designed other connectors that are easy to attach to cables and have a small connection footprint. Work is in progress on a standard SG connector.

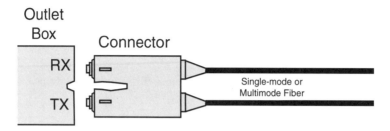

FIGURE 9.2 *A duplex SC fiber optic connector.*

Mode-Conditioning Patch Cords

A problem arises when an LX laser source is aimed at the center of the core of a multimode fiber. Multiple overlapping signals are created, and the receiver may not be able of interpreting incoming signals correctly.

It turns out that offsetting the beam from the center of the multimode core solves the problem. Figure 9.3 shows how this works. An LX laser transmitter is connected to a special *mode-conditioning patch cord* that consists of a single-mode fiber spliced to an off-center position on a multimode fiber. The light beam is aimed into the single-mode end of the spliced fiber.

The type of multimode fiber that is used in the patch cord must be the same type that is used in the attached cable run.

Note

For a mode-conditioning patch cord, the standards recommend that a blue color identifier should be used on the single-mode fiber connector, and a beige color identifier should be used on the other connectors.

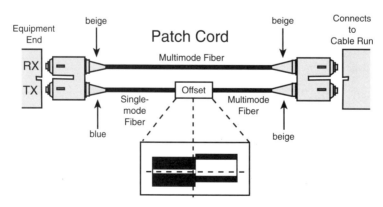

FIGURE 9.3 *A mode-conditioning patch cord.*

1000BASE-CX Copper Cables and Connectors

A special short copper cable was designed for use in wiring closets and computer rooms. Its purpose is to connect two pieces of equipment together via a gigabit link—for example, to connect a server to a switch or to interconnect a pair of routers. 1000BASE-CX cables are sold in pre-assembled form and can be ordered in various cable lengths.

> **Note**
> The fibre channel standard supports a twinax cable as well as this special type of cable.

The 1000BASE-CX cable is a 150-ohm shielded balanced cable that contains four wires. One pair is used to transmit, and the other is used to receive. As was the case for twisted–pair cabling, a positive signal on one wire is balanced by a negative signal on the other wire in the pair. Each pair must be grounded.

The cable is wired in crossover fashion, with a transmit line at one end con-nected to a receive line at the other end. There are two types of connectors, called *style 1* and *style 2*.

Style 1 is the popular 9-pin shielded D-subminiature connector that is shown in Figure 9.4. The connector is male on the cable and female on the receptacle. The figure also shows the pin assignments at each end of a crossover cable.

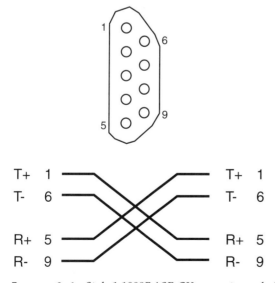

FIGURE 9.4 *Style 1 1000BASE-CX connector and pin assignments.*

The trouble with style 1 is that these 9-pin D connectors are very common, and it would be all too easy to plug one of the ends of a CX cable into an interface that has nothing to do with 1000BASE-CX.

For this reason, the 8-pin style 2 connector, which was designed especially for 1000BASE-CX, is preferred. This is called the *High Speed Serial Data Connector* (HSSDC). Figure 9.5 depicts a style 2 connector and the pin assignments at each end of the crossover cable.

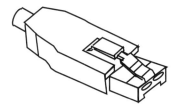

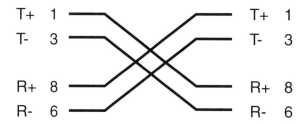

FIGURE 9.5   *Style 2 1000BASE-CX connector and pin assignments.*

Gigabit Interface Converters

Removable outlet boxes called *gigabit interface converters* (GBICs), originally designed for fibre channel interfaces, also are used in Gigabit Ethernet products. The use of GBICs gives both vendors and customers a lot of flexibility. A vendor can build a switch that has slots into which GBICs can be inserted. A customer then can use a slot for any 1000BASE-X technology by plugging in the appropriate GBIC.

Changes are easy. For example, a port can be changed from 1000BASE-SX to 1000BASE-LX by swapping in an appropriate GBIC. Furthermore, GBICs can be replaced without powering off a device.

The GBIC specification was written by a vendor group called the *SFF Committee*. The group originally was formed to design small form factor (SFF) disk drives. After completing its original task, the group took on many other projects.

1000BASE-T Technology

There is a very large installed base of Category 5 unshielded balanced twisted-pair wiring, and the engineers designing Gigabit Ethernet believed that it was very important to create an implementation that could run across 100-meter lengths of high-quality Category 5 cabling terminated by RJ-45 connectors. 1000BASE-T satisfies this need.

Four unshielded twisted pairs (UTPs) are required to attain gigabit bandwidth.

1000BASE-T Encoding

Operating bidirectionally on twisted pairs is a challenge. The encoding used for 1000BASE-T is highly complex. It not only must achieve a balance of 0s and 1s on each cable, but it also must create a balanced electromagnetic condition across all four pairs.

The encoding method consists of several steps:

1. Each byte is scrambled.

2. The scrambled byte is translated to a 4-tuple of special symbols via a mapping called *8B1Q4*.

3. Each symbol is represented on the physical medium by a voltage. Five different voltage levels are used, corresponding to an alphabet of five different symbols. The physical transmission method is called *4-dimensional 5-level pulse amplitude modulation* (4D-PAM5).

More details are presented in Appendix A.

Getting the Cable Ready

A twisted-pair cabling system that will be used for Gigabit Ethernet must satisfy stringent quality requirements. A battery of tests must be applied to ensure that the cabling system can deliver a gigabit load. Chapter 10, "Twisted-Pair Cabling Standards and Performance Requirements," defines the parameters that need to be tested and discusses test tools. Enhanced Category 5 (Category 5E) cabling systems, which are discussed in Chapter 10, consist of high-quality Category 5 cables and connectors that have passed these tests.

New cabling needs to be installed with care. If existing Category 5 cable will be used, it must be tested and recertified, and some changes might be needed to get it to work reliably.

For example, crosstalk from other cables within a bundle ("alien crosstalk") disrupts gigabit transmission, so multiple four-pair sets should not be bundled together. In particular, the 25-pair bundles that are common in many installations cannot be used for Gigabit Ethernet.

In addition, problems are likely to be caused by the following:

- Using too many connectors along the cable path from office equipment to equipment in a wiring closet

- The presence of substandard connectors

- Sloppy installation techniques that result in cable faults or cause loose wire twists near connectors

- The use of poor-quality equipment cables or patch cables

Much of the existing installed Category 5 horizontal cabling will not cause trouble as long as multiple four-pair sets are not bundled together. This is good news because it is a lot easier (and less costly and disruptive) to fix connector and patch cable problems than to pull new horizontal cable.

Five corrective actions are recommended by TIA/EIA TSB-95:

- Replace equipment cords and patch cords with cords constructed from cable that meets the Category 5E specification.

- If the link has a cross-connect, reconfigure the cross-connect as an inter-connect.

- Remove any *transition point* connector. A transition point is a location where flat undercarpet cabling connects to round cabling.

- Replace the work area outlet with an outlet that meets the Category 5E specification.

- Replace a substandard interconnect with an interconnect that meets the Category 5E specification.

Stated succinctly, it helps to use cables and connectors that meet the strict specifications and to reduce the number of connectors along a link to three. Figure 9.6 shows before and after configurations that reduce the number of connectors on a link. The horizontal run in the "before" figure includes a transition point.

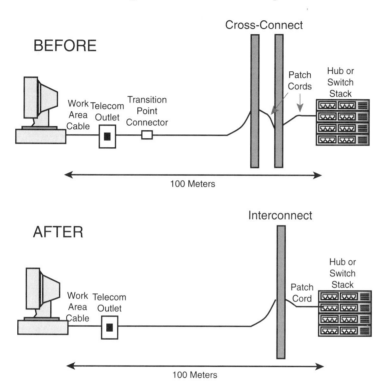

FIGURE 9.6 *Improving signal quality by reducing the number of connectors.*

Encoders, Decoders, and Hybrids

Figure 9.7 illustrates how signals are sent across a 1000BASE-T interface. A triangle containing a T represents a transmit encoder. A triangle containing a R represents a receive decoder. Recall that the encoding process converts a byte into four code symbols. Each of the four pairs carries one of these symbols. The four symbols are transmitted across the four pairs at the same time. Then the 4-tuple is decoded into a byte.

The hybrid component shown in the figure prevents the locally transmitted signals (and any echoed signals that result from reflections) from interfering with the incoming signals that are sent from the far end.

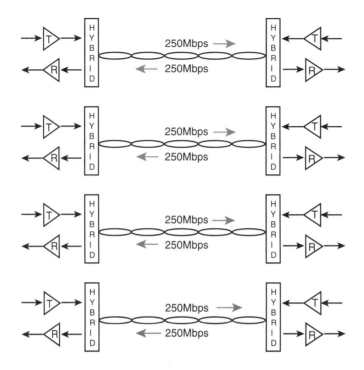

FIGURE 9.7   *1000BASE-T transmission across four twisted pairs.*

Master/Slave Timing

Synchronization of bit timing between partners is especially important because data is being sent and received on the same wire. The bits are synchronized by establishing one end of the link as the timing *master*. The master uses its internal clock for bit timing. The other end is the timing *slave*. It recovers the clock from incoming bits and uses this clocking for its transmission. The master and slave roles either are pre-established by manual configuration or are determined during an Auto-Negotiation interaction.

> **Note**
> If neither side has a preconfigured role, a multiport device (hub or switch) acts as master when communicating with a single-port device. When peers communicate (single-port to single-port, or multiport to multiport) each endpoint generates a random number called a *seed* and sends it to its partner. The party that generates the bigger seed value becomes the master. In the unlikely event of a tie, they start all over. Chapter 11 describes the Auto-Negotiation Protocol in detail.

After Auto-Negotiation is complete, the master initiates a period of *training*. During training, the master sends a sequence of idles that enable the slave endpoint to synchronize its timing with the master. When training is complete, the parties are ready to send data to one another.

Auto-Negotiation and Crossover Cable

Figure 9.7 is slightly misleading because it gives the impression that straight-through cabling is used for 1000BASE-T. In fact, crossovers have to be used for 1000BASE-T, just as for 10BASE-T, 100BASE-TX, and 100BASE-T4.

The reason for this is that, at initialization time, a Gigabit Ethernet interface needs to be capable of exchanging Auto-Negotiation information with whatever type of twisted-pair Ethernet interface is at the other end of the link. Using crossovers makes 1000BASE-T physically compatible with the other twisted-pair Ethernet implementations.

Figure 9.8 illustrates the pin and cable relationships for 1000BASE-T when a MDI interface in a station is connected to an internally crossed-over MDI-X interface in a buffered distributor or switch.

The *BI_D* prefixes labeling each wire stand for *bidirectional data*.

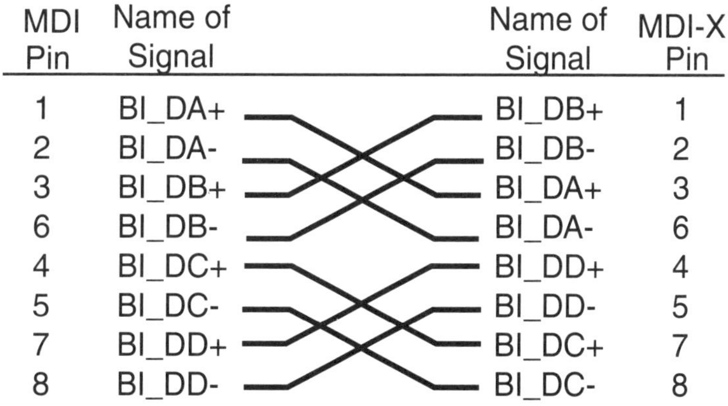

MDI Pin	Name of Signal		Name of Signal	MDI-X Pin
1	BI_DA+		BI_DB+	1
2	BI_DA-		BI_DB-	2
3	BI_DB+		BI_DA+	3
6	BI_DB-		BI_DA-	6
4	BI_DC+		BI_DD+	4
5	BI_DC-		BI_DD-	5
7	BI_DD+		BI_DC+	7
8	BI_DD-		BI_DC-	8

FIGURE 9.8 *Crossover MDI/MDI-X wiring for 1000BASE-T.*

The story of Gigabit Ethernet is not yet complete. Chapter 10 investigates the testing that must be done to qualify twisted-pair cable. Appendix A presents the encodings. Finally, Chapter 11 describes the negotiation that occurs when a link initializes.

Summary Points

- Four different standardized physical implementations of Gigabit Ethernet exist. 1000BASE-SX and 1000BASE-LX are based on fiber optic media. 1000BASE-CX is a shielded copper cable. 1000BASE-T is an unshielded twisted-pair implementation that operates across four pairs of Category 5E wire.

- 1000BASE-SX, 1000BASE-LX, and 1000BASE-CX are based on fibre channel technology. The group is called 1000BASE-X.

- For both the 1000BASE-X and 1000BASE-T physical implementations, frames or idles are transmitted continually in both directions.

- Lasers are used for both multimode and single-mode 1000BASE-X fiber implementations.

- Inexpensive Vertical Cavity Surface Emitting Lasers (VCSELs) support gigabit transmission across multimode cables that are hundreds of meters in length.

- The standard single-mode 1000BASE-LX implementation supports cable lengths ranging up to 5000 meters. Nonstandard 1000BASE-LH implementations support cable lengths ranging up to 100,000 meters.

- 8B/10B encoding, which was introduced for fibre channel, is used for the 1000BASE-X family. Each byte is translated to a 10-bit code-group.

- There are special 8B/10B code-group patterns that represent idles and frame-extension bytes, and they mark the beginning and end of a frame.

- The standard plug recommended for 1000BASE-SX and 1000BASE-LX in the 802.3 standard is a duplex SC connector.

- Overlapping signals are created when a 1000BASE-LX laser beam is aimed at the center of the core of a multimode fiber. The problem is solved by transmitting the light beam into a single-mode fiber mode-conditioning patch cord.

- Two types of connectors exist for 1000BASE-CX cables: a style 1 9-pin D-subminiature and a special style 2 8-pin connector.

- The use of removable outlet boxes called gigabit interface converters (GBICs) provides vendors and users with a lot of flexibility in their 1000BASE-X implementations.

- 1000BASE-T supports 100-meter cables.

- High-quality Category 5E (or better) cabling and connectors must be used for 1000BASE-T. A minimal number of connectors should be used across the link between a station and a repeater or switch.

- The master end of a 1000BASE-T link uses internal timing. The slave end synchronizes with the master.

References

Gigabit Ethernet is defined in

- IEEE Standard 802.3, 1998 Edition. "Carrier Sense Multiple Access with Collision Detection (CSMA/CD) Access Method and Physical Layer Specifications." See Chapters 3, 4, and 34-39.

- IEEE 802.3-ab-1999. "Physical Layer Parameters and Specifications for 1000 Mb/s Operation Over 4-Pair of Category 5 Balanced Copper Cabling, Type 1000BASE-T."

The fibre channel physical layer is described in

- ANSI Standard X3.230-1994 (FC-PH). "Information Technology—Fibre Channel—Physical and Signaling Interface."

SFF information (including the GBIC specification) is available at

```
ftp://fission.dt.wdc.com/pub/standards/sff/spec
```

For complete details of the physical engineering of 1000BASE-X Gigabit Ethernet, see

- Cunningham, David, and William Lane. *Gigabit Ethernet Networking*. Indianapolis, IN: Macmillan Technical Publishing, 1999.

Twisted-Pair Cabling Standards and Performance Requirements

As is the case for the other aspects of data communications, cabling standards are important in order to foster a competitive market for products that do what they are supposed to do. Cabling standards also give test equipment vendors the basis on which to build test products.

Twisted-pair cabling is the most frequently used Ethernet LAN medium. This chapter focuses on twisted-pair cabling requirements and the tests that you must perform to check whether your cable conforms to these requirements. Tests for fiber optic cable are discussed briefly at the end of the chapter.

Cable testing equipment, which is an essential part of a LAN technician's arsenal, can check out the performance parameters that are described in this chapter.

Cabling Standards Bodies

The body that rules United States cabling standards is the Telecommunications Industry Association (TIA) whose parent organization is the Electronic Industries Alliance (EIA). Cabling requirements are described in the *TIA/EIA-568A Commercial Building Telecommunications Cabling Standard*, first published in 1991. This standard has been updated on a regular basis.

A Canadian equivalent of this U.S. standard is called *CSA T529*. The ISO/IEC 11801 standards are followed in Europe and in many other parts of the world. These standards are based partly on TIA/EIA specifications and partly on standards that reflect special European conditions.

A number of organizations influence cabling standards, including the IEEE 803 committee, the ATM Forum, and the Comite Europeen de Normalisation Electrotechnique (CENELEC), among others.

TIA/EIA Categories

The focal point of the standards activity is to define various categories of cabling that are matched to the needs of different applications. A *category number* is a standard rating that is applied to an entire cabling system, which in addition to cable runs, includes outlets, patch cords, panels, connectors, and cross-connect blocks. Rating and testing all of the components of a system makes a lot more sense than focusing only on the cable.

> ### Note
> ISO/IEC and CENELEC use some terminology that differs from the TIA/EIA language. As with TIA/EIA, connectors and cables are rated by category number. However, ISO/IEC and CENELEC use alphabetical *class values* to grade link performance. Class C corresponds to TIA/EIA Category 3 performance, Class D to Category 5, Class E to Category 6, and Class F to Category 7.

Engineers keep reaching for higher capacities for twisted-pair systems, and recently there has been a flurry of work on new cable categories. At the time of writing, seven categories of twisted-pair cable exist, numbered 1, 2, 3, 4, 5, 5E, and 6; discussion of a Category 7 standard already has started as well. A higher number corresponds to better quality cable. The current installed base consists almost entirely of Category 5, 5E, and 3 cable.

Each category above 1 specifies a guaranteed bandwidth measured in megahertz (MHz) that a cable must be capable of transmitting in a dependable manner. (The cable may, in fact, support a higher bandwidth.)

No simple formula maps bandwidth, which is measured as a range of frequencies, into bits per second. Again and again, a clever new transmission technology has raised the number of bits per second that could be sent across a cable with a specified bandwidth.

> **Note**
>
> It is important to think of a category as a standard that you test for, not just as a set of products that you buy. A botched installation can turn the best cable and components into worthless junk. It doesn't take much to botch it—loosening the twists on a cable when adding a connector, pulling the cable with too much force (more than 25 pounds), positioning the cable close to a source of interference such as electric power cables or fluorescent lights, creating too sharp a bend, twisting the cable, or causing a kink.
>
> An entire cable plant must be certified by testing *after* it is installed.

- Category 1 sometimes is referred to as "barbed wire," so you should not expect much from it.

- Category 2 is an improved version that primarily carries digital voice and connects to digital PBX switches.

- Category 3 cable is used in many 10BASE-T LANs. It is made up of two or more pairs of copper wires with each wire wrapped in insulation.

- Category 4 is similar to Category 3, but the quality of the cable and components is somewhat better.

- Category 5 cable is a popular data grade. The quality of the cable and components is better than that of Category 4, and the wires are more tightly wound. Although 100Mbps and Gigabit Ethernet can run on Category 5 UTP cable, problems arise if the entire cable system is not of sufficiently high quality.

- Category 5E was introduced to define the tests that assure that a cable system is capable of supporting Gigabit Ethernet. Some existing Category 5 cable plants have been reclassified as Category 5E after testing.

- At the time of writing, the Category 6 standard still had draft status. However, vendors already sell cables, components, and testers that meet the current draft specifications. Category 6 cable must support a bandwidth of up to 250MHz across 100 meters. It was designed with backward compatibility in mind, so a RJ-45 style connector still is used. Although the components are compatible with Category 5, they must pass tests that require a higher level of quality.

- Category 7, which is aimed at very high transmission capacities, is expected to be a big departure from the other cabling standards. Each twisted–pair segment is shielded, and the cable as a whole also is wrapped in shielding. This cable would be stiff and heavy, and it might turn out to be more costly than optical fiber. Optical fiber can carry far more information than even the best twisted–pair cable.

Note

Most of the copper cable that is sold today is Category 5 or better. Vendors already offer cable that exceeds the performance levels that are targets for Category 6.

While some organizations are moving quickly to install high-performance cable, quite a few sites continue to use Category 3 or thin coaxial cable for their LANs. There still is a small market for Category 3 cable.

The characteristics of each category are summarized briefly in Table 10.1.

TABLE 10.1 UTP CATEGORIES

Category	Bandwidth	Description
1	—	Meets the minimum requirements for plain old telephone service (POTS).
2	—	Sometimes is used for digital PBX or ISDN connections.
3	16MHz	Meets the requirements of 10BASE-T Ethernet, 4Mbps Token Ring, and 100BASE-T4 (as well as voice).
4	20MHz	Meets the requirements of 10BASE-T Ethernet and 16Mbps Token Ring.
5	100MHz	Meets the requirements of 100Mbps Ethernet and, if it passes certification tests, 1000Mbps Ethernet. Also used for CDDI (FDDI over copper).
5E	100MHz	Meets the requirements of 100Mbps and 1000Mbps Ethernet. Category 5E stands for Enhanced Category 5. The cable has passed specified performance tests, and the RJ-45 connector components have been tested and matched to the requirements of high-speed transmission.

Category	Bandwidth	Description
6	250MHz	Currently a draft standard, aimed at 1000Mbps and above. The cable must pass more tests than Category 5E. The RJ-45 connector form is used, but the components satisfy extra performance requirements. Components must be carefully matched.
7	600MHz to 1200MHz	Currently a draft standard, aimed at 1000Mbps and above. Shielded screened twisted-pair cable is used. Each pair is individually shielded. A new connector form is used.

Wire Features

The wire used for a long run of twisted-pair cable is a solid copper cylinder. For Category 1-5E, 100-ohm wire is used. Another feature of the wire is that its diameter is standardized. However, the diameter is reported indirectly, using an inverted measurement called the *American Wire Gauge* (AWG). The AWG value is the inverse of the thickness (in inches) of a wire. For example, the diameter of 24-AWG wire is 1/24 inch. Note that thicker wire has a smaller AWG value.

Category 1-5E LAN cable is predominantly 24 AWG (although 22 AWG was specified as acceptable in the standards). A bigger diameter (such as 23 AWG) might be used for Category 6.

Patch cords, which are used in work areas and wiring closets, need to be flexible. The wire in a patch cord is made up of many thin strands, which makes it far easier to bend. A solid wire cable does not bend easily, fatigues when it is bent, and can be damaged by a bend with too tight a radius.

Cabling Layouts

A typical cabling layout was described in Chapter 6, "The Ethernet 10Mbps Physical Layer." This layout, which conforms to ANSI/TIA/EIA 568-A, specifies a total of 10 meters for equipment cords and patch cords, and a 90-meter cable run between the office telecommunications outlet and cross-connect panels in the wiring closet. An additional detail was added in Chapter 9, "Gigabit Ethernet Physical Layer." A horizontal run can include a *transition point*, which is a location where flat undercarpet cabling connects to round cabling. (See Figure 9.6.)

There are a couple of other cabling layout options (which are specified in ANSI/TIA/EIA TSB 75). One incorporates a *multiuser telecommunications outlet* (MUTO). Up to 24 work area cables (each as long as 20 meters) can run directly from office equipment to a MUTO. The MUTO must be within 70 meters of the wiring closet. Because the MUTO replaces a work area jack, it does not add a connection point to the cable path. However, it often is used to gather pairs together into a 25-pair cable (which should not be done with Gigabit Ethernet).

The other option, called a *consolidation point*, introduces an extra connector into the horizontal run. The horizontal cabling that leads from the telecom outlet to the wiring closet consists of two sections that meet at the consolidation point. The maximum combined length of the two horizontal cable sections is 90 meters.

Up to 24 horizontal cables can meet at a consolidation point. (To compensate for the extra connector, the work area cable must be restricted to a maximum length of 3 meters.) Because this arrangement adds an extra connection point, it can cause problems if used with Gigabit Ethernet connections.

Unshielded Twisted-Pair Cabling Performance Parameters

Cabling performance parameters are not mysterious. They are symptoms that enable you to track down flaws that can distort and ruin the signal on twisted-pair cable. For example:

- The signal might be getting too faint as it traverses the cable.

- The copper wires in a pair might not be twisted tightly all along the cable. This prevents the positive and negative signals in a pair from balancing out and creates an electromagnetic field. This electromagnetic field induces false signals on neighboring cables and may corrupt data transmission.

- Flaws in the cable structure might be causing part of the signal to be reflected back to the source, resulting in problems there.

Expressing performance characteristics as measurable quantities makes it possible to set cable quality standards and use cable-testing equipment to detect faults.

Parameters for All Ethernet LANs

Some basic TIA/EIA test requirements must be satisfied for all twisted-pair cables used for Ethernet LANs. These basic requirements set acceptable levels for the following:

- **Attenuation**—The proportion of power that is lost as a signal traverses a cable. Attenuation is measured in decibels (dB).

- **Near end crosstalk (NEXT)**—The distortion of a weak incoming signal by a strong outgoing signal on a neighboring wire pair. NEXT is measured in decibels.

- **Impedance**—A measure of the opposition to the flow of electricity down the wire. Irregularities in the impedance of a cable, or interconnecting two cables that have different impedance ratings, causes part of an outgoing signal to be reflected back. Impedance is measured in ohms.

A checkup on the health of a cable plant also includes *wiremap testing*. This procedure checks the following for every conductor in a cable:

- Proper pin termination at each end

- Continuity to the remote end

- Crossed pairs or reversed pairs

- Shorts between two or more conductors

- Split pairs (that is, the wires of two different pairs are cross-connected)

The 802.3 specification defines some further wiring constraints needed to assure that Ethernet will function correctly. It specifies maximum values for the following:

- Cable length

- Jitter (that is, variation in the interval between signal transitions)

- Propagation delay

Parameters for High-Speed LANs

Not surprisingly, more stringent requirements must be applied to cable that is used to carry data at gigabit speeds.

Also, a new factor arises for 1000BASE-T Ethernet. 1000BASE-T transmission occurs simultaneously across four twisted pairs. The fact that data is being transmitted at high frequencies across four neighboring wire pairs instead of two creates the potential for severe crosstalk problems.

This led to the establishment of a slew of new parameter definitions and tests. The parameters include

- Far end crosstalk (FEXT)

- Equal level far end crosstalk (ELFEXT)

- Power sum near end crosstalk (PSNEXT)

- Worst pair-to-pair ELFEXT

- Power sum ELFEXT

- Attenuation to crosstalk ratio (ACR)

- Delay skew

- Return loss

Note

Category 5 cable is qualified for use at high speeds by testing that the values of these parameters lie within specified bounds. Currently, the same set of parameters is used to qualify Category 6 cable, but the quality requirements are more stringent.

Parameter Descriptions

Both basic and high-speed performance parameters are described in deeper detail in the sections that follow.

Jitter

At each transmission speed, there is a fixed time interval during which a bit is transmitted. A bit is represented as a variation in the signal sent across a cable— for example, by changing a voltage from high to low or from low to high.

Jitter is a deviation in the periodic interval at which signal transitions occur. Transmission standards set limits on jitter. For example, when tested, a 10BASE-T cable should not exhibit more than 5 nanoseconds of jitter.

Attenuation and Decibels

Attenuation measures the amount of power loss of the electrical signal when it travels through a cable. It is calculated in logarithmic units called decibels (dB). The formula is shown here:

$$\text{Attenuation} = 10 \log^{10}(\text{Power-out}/\text{Power-in}) \text{ dB}$$

Note that if the far end power (the power-out) is 1/10 of the original power (the power-in), the attenuation is

$$10 \log_{10}(1/10) = 10 \log_{10}(10^{-1}) = 10 \ (-1) = -10\text{dB}$$

If the far end power is 1/100 of the power-in, the attenuation is

$$10 \log_{10}(1/100) = 10 \log_{10}(10^{-2}) = 10 \ (-2) = -20\text{dB}$$

The farther a signal travels, the more it attenuates. Thus, attenuation depends on the cable length. Standards documents handle this by stating the value for a specific length (such as per kilometer).

Because the power-out at the far end always is less than the power-in, the attenuation always is negative. The minus sign often is omitted in documents that set attenuation levels. For example, in the statement "Standard 568-A limits attenuation in a Category 5 system to 24dB for a 100MHz signal," it is understood that the measurement actually is –24dB. Note that this means that smaller measurements are good news—they indicate less attenuation.

The attenuation across a cable actually is different at each frequency level. Higher frequencies experience more attenuation.

Note
Temperature and cable diameter also have an effect on attenuation. Attenuation increases as the temperature goes up. Enlarging the diameter of a cable decreases attenuation. This is the reason that a bigger diameter than 24 AWG might be used for Category 6 cable.

Near End Crosstalk

A strong signal transmitted from a station can distort a weak data signal arriving at the station on an adjacent pair of wires. This happens because current flowing through a wire creates an electromagnetic field that induces signals on adjacent wires.

The amount of distortion is measured in decibels and is called the near end crosstalk (NEXT). More precisely, the near end crosstalk is the amount of energy transferred to a weak incoming signal from a strong outgoing signal on an adjacent wire. This amount increases as the frequency level of the transmission increases.

Recall that the same signal is sent across both of the wires in a pair, but with reverse polarity. Twisting the wires tightly causes the two electromagnetic fields to cancel one another. A strong NEXT effect is a symptom that the wires are not twisted properly.

Measuring NEXT

The effect of crosstalk is measured by transmitting a specified signal level on a transmit pair. The near end crosstalk is the proportion of that signal that is transferred to the local receive pair. Figure 10.1 illustrates NEXT. In the figure, a strong outgoing signal induces a NEXT signal on a neighboring pair that could badly distort the weak incoming signal.

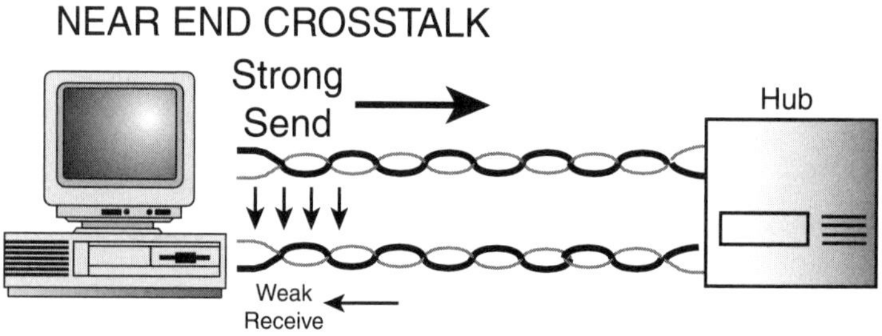

FIGURE 10.1 *A strong outgoing signal inducing NEXT on a neighboring pair.*

NEXT is measured in decibels. You want the NEXT measurement to be small—a small proportion translates to a large negative dB value. As was the case for attenuation, the negative sign commonly is dropped in documentation. For example, the statement "The amount of NEXT between pairs in a four-pair cable should be at least 60dB for a 10MHz link" means that it should be –60dB or less.

NEXT levels are improved by using wire pairs that have been tightly twisted. A certain amount of untwisting is bound to happen near a terminating plug. It is important to make sure that the wires are not untwisted for more than 1/2 inch from the termination point. The use of high-grade plugs and jacks also helps. NEXT is affected by the frequency of the signal and increases as the frequency increases.

Some of the vendors that manufacture high-performance cables conforming to Category 6 performance levels isolate the four pairs from one another using separators called *splines*. Figure 10.2 illustrates one implementation of splines in a sheath containing four twisted pairs. These splines maintain interpair spacing, even when the cable is bent more sharply than it should be. The use of splines reduces near end crosstalk, attenuation, and far end crosstalk.

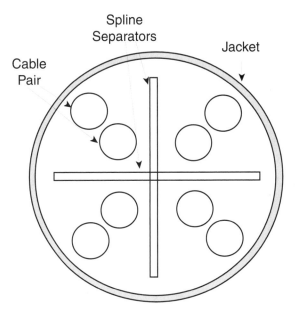

FIGURE 10.2 *Separating twisted pairs within a four-pair cable.*

Far End Crosstalk

Far end crosstalk (FEXT) is the amount of energy transferred to an outgoing signal by an incoming signal on an adjacent wire. Maintaining tight twists and using good connectors at the receive end prevents the FEXT level from getting out of bounds.

Figure 10.3 illustrates FEXT. In the figure, the incoming signal has been attenuated by its trip along the cable, but it still might be capable of inducing noise on an adjacent cable.

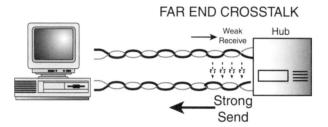

FIGURE 10.3   *A weak incoming signal inducing FEXT on a neighboring pair.*

Measuring FEXT and Computing ELFEXT

Like NEXT, FEXT is measured by transmitting a specified signal level on a transmit pair. The proportion of the signal that is transferred to the transmit pair at the far end then is measured in decibels.

However, this measurement must be adjusted to make it meaningful. The strength of a signal decreases due to attenuation as the signal travels down a length of cable. Thus, the FEXT value depends on the length of the cable and the amount of attenuation.

FEXT is turned into a meaningful measurement by subtracting the attenuation. The result is called the *equal level far end crosstalk* (ELFEXT):

    ELFEXT = FEXT – attenuation

ELFEXT is independent of length and measures a characteristic of a cable product.

PSNEXT, PSELFEXT, and Worst Pair-to-Pair ELFEXT

Four-pair cables are used for 100-BASE-T4 and 1000BASE-T transmission. Every pair causes crosstalk on the three other neighboring pairs. Thus, for pairs A, B, C, and D, the following is true:

- B, C, and D cause near and far end crosstalk on A.

- A, C, and D cause near and far end crosstalk on B.

- A, B, and D cause near and far end crosstalk on C.

- A, B, and C cause near and far end crosstalk on D.

This adds up to a long list of 24 crosstalk measurements. Some combined measurements have been defined to pare the list into a smaller set of numbers that can be used to evaluate a cable:

- Power sum near end crosstalk (PSNEXT)

- Power sum equal level far end crosstalk (PSELFEXT)

- Worst pair-to-pair equal level far end crosstalk

The *power sum near end crosstalk* (PSNEXT) is the sum of the NEXT effects on a pair by the other three pairs. For example, the PSNEXT for pair A is the sum of the near end crosstalk values caused by B, C, and D. There is a separate PSNEXT value for each of the four pairs.

Similarly, there is a separate *power sum equal level far end crosstalk* (PSELFEXT) value for each of the four pairs. The PSELFEXT is the sum of the equal level far end crosstalk (ELFEXT) effects on a pair by the other three pairs. For example, the PSELFEXT for pair A is the sum of the equal level far end crosstalk values caused by B, C, and D.

Finally, the *worst pair-to-pair equal level far end crosstalk* is the biggest ELFEXT effect of one pair on another.

Attenuation to Crosstalk Ratio

The *attenuation to crosstalk ratio* (ACR) is a measurement of the signal to noise ratio at the receive end of a pair. This measurement is expressed in decibels. If the signal is stronger than the noise, the ACR is positive. Bigger ACR values correspond to better signals.

The ACR measurement actually is equivalent to the ELFEXT and can be converted into an ELFEXT value.

Structural Return Loss and Return Loss

If a wire's structure is not uniform, its impedance varies along its length. Changes in impedance cause a signal sent down the wire to lose strength because part of the signal is reflected back to its origin. *Structural return loss* (SRL) is a measure of this loss, expressed in decibels.

Return loss is a measure of the relative amount of a signal that is reflected back to its source. It is related to the uniformity of a cable relative to a given target value for its impedance—100 ohms, in the case of twisted–pair cabling.

Propagation Delay and Time Domain Reflectometry

Recall that the *propagation delay* is the amount of time that it takes a signal to travel from one end of a wire to the other end. Obviously, this depends on the length of the wire and the speed at which electrons travel through the wire.

The propagation delay for a particular type of cable can be computed from a rating called the *nominal velocity of propagation* (NVP). The NVP is the transmission speed along a wire relative to the speed of light in a vacuum. It is expressed as a percentage of the speed of light.

Having a standardized and pretested NVP for a cable enables a network technician to locate a cable fault using a *Time Domain Reflectometry* (TDR) test device. Before testing a cable, the user enters the cable's rated NVP into the device. On command, the test device emits a signal. If there is a fault such as an open cable, short circuit, or bad connection, all or part of the signal pulse will be reflected back.

The test device can estimate the distance to the fault based on the velocity of the signal and the amount of time that elapses between sending the pulse and receiving the reflected signal. TDR tools exist for both coax and twisted-pair cable.

Delay Skew

1000BASE-TX transmits signals across four pairs concurrently. The multiple incoming signals must be synchronized so that they can be recombined into the original signal. A receiver can cope with slight variations in delay, but if too large a difference exists between the propagation times of the pairs, communication will fail.

The *delay skew* is the difference between the propagation delays of the slowest and fastest pairs.

Managing Twisted–Pair Cabling

Changing from coaxial cable to twisted-pair cable did more than rationalize the cabling layout of Ethernet LANs. It improved LAN reliability, availability, and manageability.

A coax bus is vulnerable to cable or connector flaws that can shut down or degrade the performance of the entire LAN. These flaws have always been hard to track down.

Faults still happen in twisted-pair LANs, but the effect of a fault is limited. A cable failure between a hub or switch port and a station affects only that station. Link integrity tests detect a cable failure very quickly. Using an SNMP management station or checking LED lights can pinpoint a trouble spot.

A fault on a link between hubs or bridges temporarily can segment the LAN into two pieces, but each part still can continue to function on its own.

Test Tools

A cable test tool is the LAN technician's best friend. There are basically two types of test tools:

- Continuity/cable testers

- Certification tools

Bulky test devices once were the norm, but now handheld equipment that meets high-quality standards is available.

Continuity/Cable Tester

Called a continuity tester by some vendors and a cable tester by others, these devices offer a helping hand to a someone who is installing a cable in an office or trying to track down a cable fault. The device

- Calculates the total cable length from the office to the hub or switch in the wiring closet

- Performs wiremap tests to verify continuity to the remote end; to check for crossed, reversed, or split pairs; and to make sure that there are no shorts

- Performs TDR tests

Many test products include the components needed to perform a *tone test*. To do this, a *tone test set* is attached to one end of a cable and generates a tone that is transmitted onto a wire. When a separate piece of equipment called a *probe* is placed near a bundle of wires, it can detect which wire in the bundle carries the tone.

Tone test equipment makes it possible to match one end of a cable located in an office to the other end in a wiring closet. It is a valuable tool for installations, for moves and changes, and for tracing faulty wires.

Certification Tool

A certification tool is a high-end tester that can determine whether installed cables meet TIA Category 5, 5E, or proposed Category 6 or 7 requirements. The tool checks the performance parameters automatically.

A product usually also includes the capabilities of a continuity/cable tester as well as optional kits, such as fiber optic test components.

> **Note**
>
> Certification tools differ in their level of accuracy. In fact, standards have been set for the accuracy of their measurements.
>
> The least accurate devices are rated as Level I testers. Level II testers attain a higher degree of accuracy.
>
> Level II-E testers also can calculate quantities such as PSNEXT and ELFEXT needed to qualify Category 5E cables, and Level III testers can check out Category 6 cables.

The Scope of a Test

There are two scopes for tests: *channel* or *permanent link* (also called a *basic link*). These are illustrated in the upper part of Figure 10.4:

- A channel includes all of the cabling system components between a station and a hub or a switch in a wiring closet. It includes up to 90 meters of horizontal cabling, a work area patch cord plugged into an outlet, and cross-connects or interconnects in the wiring closet.

- A permanent link excludes the patch cords. It includes the horizontal cabling and the connectors at each end of the horizontal cabling.

> **Note**
>
> The horizontal cabling portion might include a transition point or a consolidation point.

The lower part of Figure 10.4 shows the components that are included in a channel test. The systems at the ends of the channel have been replaced with test equipment.

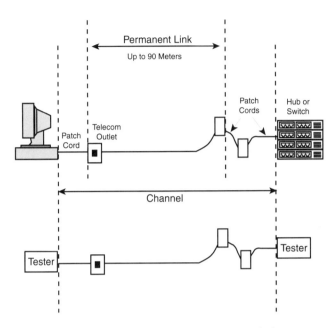

FIGURE 10.4   *Testing a channel or a permanent link.*

Testing Fiber Optic Cable

An understanding of fiber optic cable testing requires more background information than can be included in this book. This section provides a brief discussion of a few of the factors that are involved in testing fiber optic cable.

First of all, there is one boon. Crosstalk, a worrisome problem for twisted-pair media, does not occur for fiber optic media.

Some of the items that must be tested for fiber optic media include:

- **Source optical power**—If the source power is inadequate, information transfer could be error prone or could fail.

- **Signal attenuation**—Most attenuation is caused by scattering of light due to bouncing off the cladding or bouncing off atoms in the glass. Some attenuation is caused by absorption of light by dopants added to the glass. (A dopant is an impurity intentionally added to an optical medium to change its optical properties.) The light then is converted to heat.

- **Wavelength measurement**—Data must be transmitted using specified wavelengths. Less scattering occurs for long wavelengths, so greater cable lengths can be supported with long wavelengths.

- **Cable continuity**—The light used to transmit data is invisible. A cable continuity check is carried out by shining a harmless visible light onto the fiber. This makes bends and breaks visible if the sheath has torn.

> **Note**
> A user should not look into a fiber optic cable while a laser is actively transmitting. Laser energy is high, and exposure to a laser beam can cause blindness.

Cable faults can be located using an optical time-domain reflectometer (OTDR). An OTDR also can measure the amount of light that is being scattered back to the source. However, OTDRs are costly and usually are used only for long-distance single-mode fiber links. A simplified product called a *fault finder* can be used for LANs.

Summary Points

- U.S. cabling standards are published by the Telecommunications Industry Association (TIA) and the Electronic Industries Association (EIA). ISO/IEC standards are used in other parts of the world.

- A category number is a standard rating that is applied to an entire cabling system, which in addition to cable runs, includes outlets, patch cords, panels, connectors, and cross-connect blocks.

- There are seven currently defined categories of unshielded twisted-pair cable, numbered 1, 2, 3, 4, 5, 5E, and 6. A higher number corresponds to better-quality cable.

- Most of the installed base of cable is Category 5 or Category 3. Category 5E and 6 are appropriate for gigabit speeds.

- An American Wire Gauge (AWG) value is the inverse of the thickness (in inches) of a wire. Category 1-5E LAN cable is predominantly 24 AWG.

- All data cable must be tested for impedance, attenuation, and near end crosstalk (NEXT). High-speed LAN cable is checked for equal level far end crosstalk (ELFEXT), power sum near end crosstalk (PSNEXT), worst pair-to-pair ELFEXT, delay skew, and return loss.

- Wiremap testing checks pin termination, continuity, crossed or reverse pairs, shorts, and split pairs.

- A Time Domain Reflectometry test device is used to locate cable faults.

- A continuity and cable tester can calculate cable length, perform wiremap tests, and perform TDR tests. The product usually includes tone test equipment.

- A certification tool is a high-end tester that can determine whether installed cables meet TIA Category 5, 5E, or proposed Category 6 or 7 requirements.

- Fiber optic cable measurements include source optical power, signal attenuation, wavelength measurement, and cable continuity.

References

Copper and fiber cabling performance guidelines are specified in ANSI/TIA/EIA-568, "Commercial Building Telecommunications Cabling Standard," 2000.

Guidelines for field testing Category 3, 4, and 5 UTP cabling can be found in TIA/EIA Technical Service Bulletin 67 (TSB-67), "Transmission Performance Specifications for Field Testing of Unshielded Twisted-Pair Cabling Systems," 1995.

Return loss and ELFEXT link performance parameters are specified in TIA/EIA-TSB-95, "Additional Transmission Performance Guidelines for 4-Pair 100 Ohm Category 5 Cabling," 1999.

Other documents that may be of interest include

- TIA/EIA-569. "Commercial Building Standard for Telecommunications Pathways and Spaces." 1998.

- TIA/EIA-570. "Residential and Light Commercial Telecommunications Wiring Standard." 1997.

- TIA/EIA-606. "Administration Standard for the Telecommunications Infrastructure of Commercial Buildings." 1993.

- TIA/EIA-607. "Commercial Building Grounding/Bonding Requirements." 1994.

- Microtest, Inc. "Field Testing Of High Performance Premise Cabling." 1998.

- "Cabletron Systems Cabling Guide." 1996. http://www.cabletron.com/

- "How to Effectively Manage Your Structured Cabling Infrastructure, An Anixter Technology White Paper." http://www.anixter.com/

CHAPTER 11

Auto-Negotiation

The versatility of Ethernet means that users have many choices of media, speed, and features. This could have turned Ethernet into a configuration nightmare.

Fortunately, automatic negotiation mechanisms were introduced in the mid- to late 1990s. Auto-Negotiation enables a pair of link partners to communicate whenever either end is initialized, reset, or reconfigured. The negotiation enables them to discover an optimal set of mutually supported capabilities.

Currently, two separate Auto-Negotiation technology families exist:

- **10Mbps, 100Mbps, and 1000Mbps twisted-pair interfaces**—Vendors have built single-speed and multispeed twisted-pair interfaces that support Auto-Negotiation. Twisted-pair link partners can negotiate their best set of shared capabilities.

- **1000BASE-SX, 1000BASE-LX, and 1000BASE-CX interfaces**—A uniform Auto-Negotiation Protocol is used by all the devices in this family, but the protocol can be used only when like connects to like (for example, 1000BASE-SX to 1000BASE-SX). Parameters such as the use of full-duplex mode and flow control are negotiated.

This chapter explains twisted-pair Auto-Negotiation first. 1000BASE-X Auto-Negotiation has a subset of the functionality of the twisted-pair version and is discussed at the end of the chapter.

Auto-Negotiation for Twisted-Pair Interfaces

Some of the vendors that built the first 10/100 twisted-pair Ethernet
adapters and hubs created proprietary protocols that enabled link partners
to negotiate and check whether both ends could operate at 100Mbps and
whether both could operate in full-duplex mode.

Users wanted a standard negotiation protocol. The IEEE 802.3 committee acted
quickly and published 802.3u, which was based on National Semiconductor's
NWay negotiation method. IEEE Auto-Negotiation was defined as an optional
feature of 10BASE-T, 100BASE-T4, and 100BASE-TX interfaces. It became a
mandatory part of the 1000BASE-T and 1000BASE-X interfaces that were introduced later.

Twisted-pair Ethernet interfaces that support Auto-Negotiation can automatically determine the following:

- The speed at which they should operate

- Whether both partners are capable of full-duplex mode

- Whether flow control should be used in one direction, both directions,
  or not at all

Auto-Negotiation messages can carry some additional information:

- They can report remote fault conditions.

- They can report vendor-specific or product-specific data.

Auto-Negotiation and Ethernet Upgrades

The capability to automatically negotiate link parameters makes a network
upgrade an easier job.

For example, the devices in Figure 11.1 are connected to a 10Mbps twisted-pair
hub stack. All the systems in this collision domain share the 10Mbps bandwidth. As more stations are added to the LAN in the figure, each station's
share of the bandwidth shrinks. Eventually, the LAN becomes congested and
response time suffers.

Using up-to-date multispeed Ethernet adapters smoothes the path to an
upgrade. Currently, 10/100 adapters are cheap. If the hub in Figure 11.1 is
replaced with a 10/100 hub, performance improves immediately for all the
systems that have 10/100 NICs. Each system will reinitialize and start to
operate at 100Mbps.

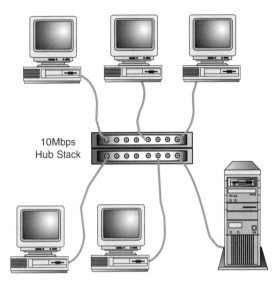

FIGURE 11.1 *Systems connected to a stack of 10Mbps hubs.*

Note

10Mbps segments and 100Mbps segments cannot belong to the same collision domain. A 10/100 "hub" actually contains internal bridging that separates the 10Mbps segments and 100Mbps segments into separate collision domains. Stations with old 10Mbps adapters will share a bandwidth of 10Mbps. Stations with 10/100 adapters will share a bandwidth of 100Mbps.

Pushing performance up again by an order of magnitude is easy. You just replace the hub in Figure 11.1 with a 10/100 switch. A device with a 10/100 adapter immediately gains 100Mbps of full-duplex bandwidth that is dedicated to that device.

Note

The top throughput on a busy collision domain is less than 40 percent of the physical capacity—for example, less than 4Mbps on a 10Mbps LAN. Replacing a hub with a switch gives each station a full-duplex 10Mbps or 100Mbps and can easily increase throughput by a factor of 25 or better.

Moving to higher speeds, Figure 11.2 shows a set of 10/100 switches and a gigabit full-duplex repeater that are connected to a gigabit switch. The gigabit switch has 10 full-duplex ports. This can add up to a 20Gbps capacity.

> **Note**
>
> A switch needs lots of CPU power and big RAM memory resources to han-
> dle full-duplex gigabit traffic on all its ports concurrently. Check vendor
> specifications and test results to verify the actual number of short and long
> frames per second that a gigabit switch can handle.
>
> The buzzword to watch for is nonblocking. This means that the switch can
> deliver all its incoming frames without dropping any, even when frames
> are arriving at all ports at top speed.

Auto-Negotiation eases moves and changes at the gigabit level. For example,
server A in Figure 11.2 shares bandwidth with high-performance stations
attached to the full-duplex repeater on the right. If an increasing number of stations on the left need to access server A and traffic is steadily growing, server A
can be moved to the central gigabit switch. It will immediately have access to a
dedicated full-duplex gigabit bandwidth of its own.

> **Note**
>
> Recall that a gigabit full-duplex repeater also is called a buffered distributor.

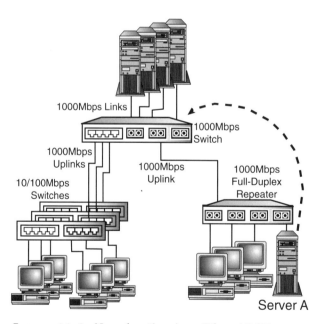

FIGURE 11.2   *Upgrade options in an Ethernet LAN.*

Auto-Negotiation has another benefit: It prevents an inappropriate device from connecting to a LAN. For example, if a user connects a 100BASE-T4 device to a 10BASE-T/100BASE-TX hub and neither the device nor the hub supports Auto-Negotiation, the entire collision domain will be disrupted. However, a hub that supports Auto-Negotiation will refuse to set up a link to an incompatible device and will protect the other stations in the collision domain.

Checking and Controlling Interfaces

A LAN adapter usually has a visible set of LEDs that report the adapter state and status. For example, a green-lit LED marked 100 indicates that 100Mbps has been established on the link and that the link is operational. Sometimes an extra LED blinks when data is being transmitted through the interface. (A steady light indicates that the port is very busy.)

SNMP can be very helpful when you want to check the speed of an interface without walking up to it and looking at LEDs. SNMP also can be used to check the other parameters that have been negotiated for the interface, such as full/half-duplex mode and flow control.

A network administrator can configure a NIC manually (or via SNMP), if there is a reason to do so. This can be applied either of two ways:

- The administrator leaves Auto-Negotiation enabled, but specifies which capabilities will be announced. For example, the administrator might want to force 100BASE-TX and prevent 10BASE-T.

- The administrator specifies the exact behavior that is desired and disables Auto-Negotiation.

Note

Some vendor manuals recommend turning off Auto-Negotiation for router and server ports. Their logic is that it is better to cause the link to die if it cannot operate exactly as you wish (for example, in full-duplex rather than half–duplex mode).

Unfortunately, people make mistakes, and the manually configured interfaces at each end of a link might be incompatible. A sensible alternative is to configure each interface the way you think it should behave and then let it perform Auto-Negotiation so that each end verifies that its partner is compatible. You can check link parameters via a periodic SNMP poll to make sure that you are getting what you expect.

Auto-Negotiation Functionality for Twisted-Pair Interfaces

If a pair of devices connected by a twisted-pair link support Auto-Negotiation:

- Each interface announces the technology choices that it supports.

- Each indicates whether it supports full-duplex communication.

- Each announces its flow control preferences.

A pair of 1000BASE-T interfaces also negotiates to decide which will act as master timer or slave timer for the link. The master uses its own clock, and the slave bases its timing on the incoming data stream.

> **Note**
>
> Currently, 100BASE-T2 is not implemented. In the future, if some vendor builds 100BASE-T2 adapters, these adapters also will perform a master/slave negotiation.

Twisted-Pair Technology Capabilities

The negotiation procedure that is used is quite straightforward:

1. Each party sends its partner a checklist indicating all of the half- and full-duplex technologies that it can support.

2. A set of rules is applied to the values provided by each partner.

3. The outcome of these rules determines the way the link will operate.

Table 11.1 displays the current list of transmission technologies. The choices are listed in order of preference, from highest to lowest. The highest-ranking capability that both link partners have in common is selected. Note that the full-duplex version of a technology always ranks above the half-duplex version.

It might seem odd that the 100BASE-T4 half-duplex version is ranked above the 100BASE-TX half–duplex version. If both partners could support both of these technologies, 100BASE-T4 would be selected. The reason is that 100BASE-T4 can run on Category 3 cable, but 100BASE-TX requires Category 5. The less demanding technology is given preference just in case the cable plant is not up to par.

TABLE 11.1 NEGOTIABLE TRANSMISSION TECHNOLOGIES

Technology	Acceptable Cabling
1000BASE-T full-duplex	Four pairs of Category 5 UTP
1000BASE-T half-duplex	Four pairs of Category 5 UTP
*100BASE-T2 full-duplex	Category 3 UTP
100BASE-TX full-duplex	Two pairs of Category 5 UTP
*100BASE-T2 half-duplex	Category 3 UTP
100BASE-T4 half-duplex	Four pairs of Category 3 UTP
100BASE-TX half-duplex	Two pairs of Category 5 UTP
10BASE-T full-duplex	Two pairs of Category 3 UTP
10BASE-T half-duplex	Two pairs of Category 3 UTP

Not implemented in products

Negotiating Support for Flow Control

Partners that support full-duplex communications will reveal whether they can support flow control messages. Flow control may be symmetric (both partners send PAUSE messages) or asymmetric (only one party sends PAUSE messages).

> **Note**
> Flow control and PAUSE messages were described in Chapter 5, "Full-Duplex Ethernet Communication."

Two bits are used to describe a system's flow control capability, which might be:

- Does not support any flow control capability (00)
- Wishes to send PAUSE messages to the partner, but does not wish to receive them (01)
- Wishes to send and receive PAUSE messages (10)
- Is willing either to send and receive PAUSE messages, or just to receive PAUSE messages (11)

If partner A is capable of sending PAUSE messages and partner B is capable of receiving them, the flow control capability will be enabled for that direction of transmission. If partner B also can send and partner A also can receive, flow control is used in both directions (symmetrically).

Determining Master/Slave Timer Roles

1000BASE-T communications require one partner to act as link master and the other to act as slave. The master uses its local clock to time transmissions. The slave recovers clock timing from the signals received from the master.

Auto-Negotiation chooses the roles based on three rules:

- If an administrator has manually configured one end as master and the other end as slave, the parties will be given these roles.

- If neither side has a preconfigured role, a multiport device (such as a hub or switch) will act as master when communicating with a single-port device.

- If neither is preconfigured and both are single-port or both are multiport, each endpoint generates a random number called a *seed* and sends it to its partner. The party that generates the bigger seed value becomes the master. In the unlikely event of a tie, they start over.

Parallel Detection for Twisted–Pair Cabling

What happens if the interface at one end of the link supports Auto-Negotiation but the other interface does not? A function called *parallel detection* is included in the Auto-Negotiation specification. Parallel detection enables a party to discover whether a non-negotiating partner has a 10BASE-T, 100BASE-T4, or 100BASE-TX interface by examining the signals arriving from the partner.

If the local interface supports the partner's technology, it then can switch to that technology. However, only half-duplex mode can be used, because there is no way to find out whether the partner supports full–duplex communication. The only way to switch the link to full-duplex operation is to configure it manually at both ends and disable Auto-Negotiation at the capable end.

Some vendors have implemented a proprietary feature that enables an interface to detect whether it is attached to properly installed Category 3, 4, or 5 cable. This could affect the choice of speed or prevent a link from being initialized if all permitted options required Category 5 cable.

Exchanging Auto-Negotiation Data across Twisted-Pair Media

How do you exchange configuration data with a twisted-pair link partner if you don't know the speed of the partner's interface or how the partner encodes bits onto the link? And how do you implement it in a way that is backward compatible with old 10BASE-T adapters that were built before there was any need for an autoconfiguration protocol?

The solution that was chosen builds on a low-level mechanism that was introduced with 10BASE-T. Recall that a 10BASE-T interface executes an ongoing cable check by sending a special signal called a link integrity pulse. This pulse is sent periodically (roughly every 16 milliseconds) when the data transmitter is idle.

The link integrity pulse signal also is called a *normal link pulse* (NLP). The top of Figure 11.3 illustrates two NLPs separated by a 16-millisecond idle period.

Old 10BASE-T interfaces continue to operate correctly if a burst of pulses is sent to them instead of a single pulse. A burst is called a *fast link pulse* (FLP). All twisted-pair interfaces capable of performing Auto-Negotiation send FLPs during initialization. Configuration parameters are encoded within each FLP.

A pair of FLPs is illustrated in the middle of Figure 11.3. During Auto-Negotiation, a bundle of FLPs is sent roughly every 16 milliseconds.

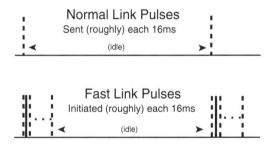

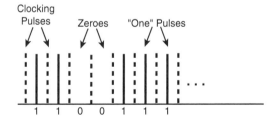

FIGURE 11.3 *NLPs and FLPs.*

Each FLP consists of 33 pulse positions and carries a short 16-bit message. Seventeen odd-numbered pulses are used for clocking. Each of the remaining 16 even-numbered pulse positions represents a data bit:

- The presence of a pulse in an even-numbered position represents 1.

- The absence of a pulse in an even-numbered position represents 0.

The bottom of Figure 11.3 shows a data pattern that starts with 1100111. The lines that represent clocking pulses are dotted to make the data signals stand out. FLPs are roughly 62.5µs apart.

Base Page, Message Pages, and Unformatted Pages

The first 16-bit message is called the *base page*. (Sometimes it is called the *base link code word*.) Additional messages consist of these components:

- An initial *message page* that includes a code that identifies the type of message.

- Depending on the message type, zero, one, or more supplementary *unformatted pages*. The term *unformatted page* is misleading. Each of these pages has a specific format that depends on the type of message.

Format of the Base Page

Figure 11.4 shows the layout of a base page. It includes these components:

- **A 5-bit selector field**—This field identifies the base page type. An Ethernet (802.3) base page is identified by code 00001. (The only other defined type is 802.9. The 802.9 standard defines a protocol for carrying ISDN calls across a LAN.)

- **Technology ability bits**—This field consists of 8 bits that are used to identify supported technologies.

- **ACK bit**—This bit is set to 1 to indicate that at least three copies of the partner's base page have been received.

- **Remote fault (RF) bit**—This bit is set to 1 to signal that there is some kind of link fault.

- **Next page (NP) bit**—If set to 1, this indicates that the originator is willing to exchange one or more additional messages. (For example, an additional message could be used to describe a fault that has been detected.)

Note

An exchange of additional messages occurs only if both the local device and its link partner have set their next page bits to 1 during the base page exchange.

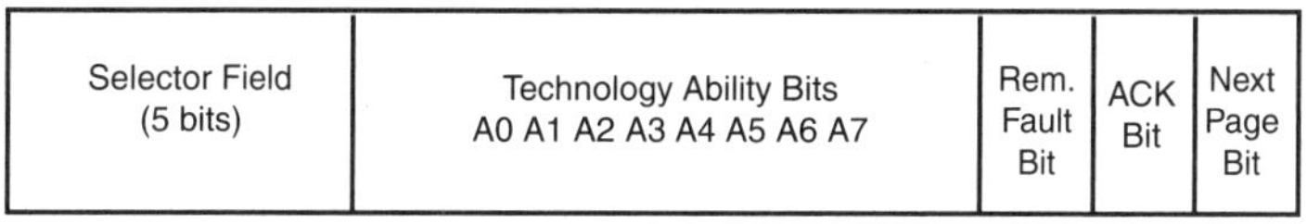

Selector Field (5 bits)	Technology Ability Bits A0 A1 A2 A3 A4 A5 A6 A7	Rem. Fault Bit	ACK Bit	Next Page Bit

FIGURE 11.4 *Format of a twisted-pair base page.*

The meaning of each bit of the base page technology ability field is displayed in Table 11.2. Setting a bit to 1 means that the adapter is willing and able to performing the corresponding technology.

An adapter typically tells its partner that several alternatives are acceptable. For example, a 10/100Mbps adapter can set bits A0, A1, A2, and A3 to 1 to indicate that any of the following are acceptable:

- 100BASE-TX in full-duplex mode

- 100BASE-TX in half-duplex mode

- 10BASE-T in full-duplex mode

- 10BASE-T in half-duplex mode

The first item on this list that is acceptable to the sender's partner will be the one that is chosen. If the partner is picky and can operate only in 100BASE-T4 or 1000BASE-T, the negotiation fails and the link is not set up.

The two PAUSE bits (A5 and A6) were described earlier in the section "Negotiating Support for Flow Control."

TABLE 11.2 TECHNOLOGY ABILITY BIT ASSIGNMENTS

Bit	Technology
A0	10BASE-T
A1	10BASE-T full-duplex
A2	100BASE-TX
A3	100BASE-TX full-duplex
A4	100BASE-T4
A5	First PAUSE bit
A6	Second PAUSE bit
A7	Reserved for future technology

The next four sections contain technical reference material. You may wish to skip ahead to the section entitled "Auto-Negotiation for 1000BASE-X Interfaces."

Format of Message Pages and Unformatted Pages

Note that 1000BASE-T is not mentioned in Table 11.2. 1000BASE-T technology capabilities are announced in an additional message that consists of a message page followed by two unformatted pages.

The upper part of Figure 11.5 shows the general layout of a message page. The first 11 bits of a message page contain a message code that identifies the message type. The remaining 5 bits (from right to left) are described here:

- **Next page bit**—The value is 1 if another page will follow.

- **Message page flag**—This bit is set to 1 if this is a message page.

- **ACK bit**—This bit is set to 1 after receiving at least three copies of a page from the partner.

- **ACK2 bit**—This bit is set to 1 to indicate that the receiver supports the type of message in the received page and can act in accordance with the information that it received.

- **Toggle (T) bit**—This bit alternates between 0 and 1 in the pages that are transmitted and is a very simple message-numbering mechanism. The receiver uses the toggle bit to check that pages are being received in order and without loss. (The initial value of the toggle bit is the opposite of the value of bit A6 in the sender's base page.)

A message page can be followed by zero, one, or more unformatted pages. The lower part of Figure 11.5 shows the layout of an unformatted page. The contents of the first 11 bits depend on the preceding message code. The last 5 bits (from right to left) have the same meaning as the last 5 bits of a message page. The message page flag has value 0 in an unformatted page.

A device indicates that it has no more pages to send by setting the next page bit to 0.

If partner A has sent all of its messages, while partner B has more to send, partner A transmits *null messages* to acknowledge receipt of partner B's messages. A null message is a message page whose message code is 1.

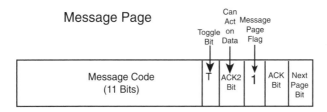

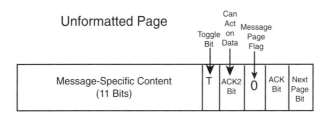

FIGURE 11.5 *Format of message pages and unformatted pages.*

Page Exchange Protocol

The protocol requires pages to be sent multiple times to be sure that they have been received successfully. The steps are shown here:

1. Both systems send their base pages repeatedly with the ACK bit set to 0.

2. After receiving at least three consecutive consistent copies of the partner's base page, a station will transmit several copies of its base page with the ACK bit set to 1.

3. If both partners have set the next page bit to 1 in their base pages, the stations will transmit additional messages.

4. On completion, if both partners have indicated support for a compatible configuration, the link will be established. Otherwise, link setup fails and data cannot be transferred.

Note

The reason for all the repetition is that this is very low-level communication, and no cyclic redundancy check is included in a message. Receiving lots of consistent copies of a message is one way to convince yourself that it is free of errors.

Note that multiple copies of a page are sent out very quickly because a fresh FLP is sent every 16ms. For example, it takes only 96ms to send out six copies of a page.

Message Pages for 1000BASE-T Capabilities

Table 11.3 describes the layout of the three pages that are used to carry 1000BASE-T capabilities. A message code of 8 announces that 1000BASE-T information follows. Bits U3 and U4 on the first unformatted page announce whether the 1000BASE-T interface is willing and able of operating in full-duplex or half–duplex mode.

Bits U0, U1, and U2 determine the master and slave roles for the link partners. Sometimes the "seed" values in the first 11 bits of the second unformatted page must be compared to break a tie.

TABLE 11.3 1000BASE-T MESSAGE PAGES

Bit or Field	Description
Message Page	
First 11 bits	Message code=8; indicates that 1000BASE capabilities follow.
Unformatted Page 1	
U0, U1, U2	Master/slave bits.
U0	1=Master/slave role has been configured manually. 0=Master/slave role has not been configured manually.
U1	If master/slave role has been configured manually (U0=1), then 1=master role and 0=slave role.
U2	If master/slave role has not been configured manually (U0=0), then 1=multiport and 0=single-port.
U3	1000BASE-T full-duplex.
U4	1000BASE-T half-duplex.
U5-U10	Reserved, set to 0.
Unformatted Page 2	
U0-U10	Seed value for master/slave negotiation.

Table 11.4 contains the details of how the master and slave roles are assigned. Basically, it comes down to either assigning the roles (carefully) via manual configuration or leaving the choice open. If the choice is open, a multiport system becomes master and its attached single-port devices assume the slave role. The seed is used to break ties between multiport/multiport or single-port/single-port link partners.

TABLE 11.4 DETERMINING MASTER AND SLAVE ROLES

U0 U1 U2 for Partner A	U0 U1 U2 for Partner B	Outcome
1 1 X	1 0 X	Partner A will be master, and partner B will be slave. (They were manually configured with these roles.)
1 1 X	1 1 X	Not allowed; configuration fails. (Both are masters.)
1 0 X	1 0 X	Not allowed; configuration fails. (Both are slaves.)
0 X 1	0 X 0 or 1 0 X	Partner A is multiport, and partner B either is single-port or has been configured as a slave. Partner A is the master, and partner B is the slave.
0 X 1	1 1 X	Although partner A is multiport, partner B has been manually configured as master and partner A will be slave.
0 X 1	0 X 1	Both are multiport. The partner with the higher seed becomes master.
0 X 0	0 X 0	Both are single-port. The partner with the higher seed becomes master.
Other combination		Autoconfiguration fails.

Message Codes

The previous section described the 1000BASE-T pages that are sent with message code 8. Other message codes have been defined, and several are shown in Table 11.5.

Message code 5 introduces an organizationally unique identifier (OUI) and a data field whose content has been defined by the organization that owns the OUI. Recall that OUIs are 3-byte prefixes administered by the IEEE. (See Chapter 2, "LAN MAC Addresses.")

Message code 6 introduces a *PHY identifier* and a data field whose content is specific to the product with that PHY identifier. A PHY Identifier consists of bits 3-24 of the OUI assigned to an interface manufacturer by the IEEE, followed by a 6-bit manufacturer's model number and a 4-bit manufacturer's revision number. This adds up to a total of 32 bits.

Note

Note that message codes 5 and 6 open up the Auto-Negotiation Protocol to vendor-specific and product-specific enhancements.

TABLE 11.5 MESSAGE CODES

Message Code #	Message Code Description
0	Currently reserved for future enhancements.
1	The code for null messages. The local party sends null messages when it has completed its transmission and the partner is still sending.
2	Reserved for future expansion of the technology ability field. One unformatted page containing a technology ability field follows.
3	Reserved for future expansion of the technology ability field. Two unformatted pages containing a technology ability field follow.
4	Used for describing faults. One unformatted page containing a remote fault code follows. Fault codes include these: 0. Testing the remote fault reporting operation 1. Link loss 2. Jabber 3. Parallel detection fault
5	Organizationally unique identifier tagged message. Four unformatted pages follow. They contain an OUI (spread across three pages) and a data field specific to that OUI.
6	PHY identifier tag code message. Four unformatted pages follow. They contain a PHY identifier and a data field specific to a device with that PHY ID.
7	100BASE-T2 technology message. 100BASE-T2 capabilities follow in two unformatted pages.
8	1000BASE-T technology message. 1000BASE-T capabilities follow in two unformatted pages.

Auto-Negotiation for 1000BASE-X Interfaces

Auto-Negotiation is a mandatory function for 1000BASE-X interfaces. These include the 1000BASE-SX and 1000BASE-LX fiber optic interfaces and the 1000BASE-CX copper interface.

It is physically impossible for incompatible types (for example, 1000BASE-SX and 1000BASE-LX, or 1000BASE-LX and 1000BASE-CX) to communicate across a link, so the technology type is not negotiable. The capabilities that are negotiated include

- Full-duplex or half–duplex capabilities.

- Flow control capability (for a full-duplex link). As was the case for twisted–pair cabling, 2 bits are used to describe whether the system can send and/or receive PAUSE messages.

These Auto-Negotiation messages optionally also can describe remote fault conditions or include vendor- or product-specific data.

1000BASE-X Auto-Negotiation Implementation

1000BASE-X Auto-Negotiation information is not sent in special pulses. Although the information cannot be sent in frames, the bytes that make up an Auto-Negotiation page are transmitted the same way that other data bytes are sent.

Recall that for 1000BASE-X, each data byte is translated into a 10-bit data code-group before it is sent across the medium. In addition to data code-groups, there are several special nondata code-groups that represent idle symbols and mark the beginnings and ends of frames. There also is a special combination of two code-groups that marks the beginning of an Auto-Negotiation page. Figure 11.6 shows how an Auto-Negotiation page is sent across a link.

On arrival, the two introductory code groups are recognized and stripped off. The two code-groups that follow are translated to 2 data bytes. These 2 bytes (16 bits) make up an Auto-Negotiation page.

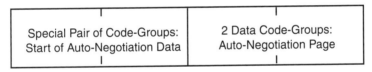

| Special Pair of Code-Groups: Start of Auto-Negotiation Data | 2 Data Code-Groups: Auto-Negotiation Page |

FIGURE 11.6   *Sending an Auto-Negotiation page across a 1000BASE-X link.*

> **Note**
> The translation of bytes into code-groups is explained in Appendix A, "Physical Layer Encodings for Ethernet, Fibre Channel, FDDI, and Token Ring." Details are shown in Table A.9.

Figure 11.6 shows the format of a 1000BASE-X base page:

- The speed must be 1000Mbps, and the partners cannot talk to each other unless their technologies match. Hence, none of the bits are used to set a speed or define a technology.

- A pair of 1-bit flags is used to state whether the interface can operate in half-duplex mode or in full-duplex mode.

- Two pause bits announce whether PAUSE frames are supported and indicate the desired asymmetric or symmetric usage. These are coded exactly as was described earlier, namely:

  00=Do not support any flow control capability.
  01=Wish to send PAUSE messages but not receive them.
  10=Wish to send and receive PAUSE messages.
  11=Willing to send and receive, or just receive.

- Two remote fault bits exist instead of one:

  00=Link OK or device is incapable of fault detection.
  01=Device is going offline.
  10=Link failure.
  11=Auto-Negotiation error; communication not possible.

- The ACK bit is set to 1 if autoconfiguration messages have been received from the partner. (The bit is set after at least three consecutive and matching copies of a page have been received.)

- The next page bit is set to 1 to indicate a willingness to send and receive additional messages.

Succeeding message pages and unformatted pages follow the same format that was shown earlier in Figure 11.5.

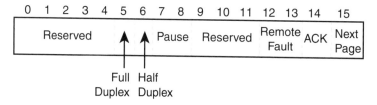

FIGURE 11.7   *Auto-Negotiation base page for 1000BASE-X.*

This implementation has retained as much compatibility with the twisted-pair implementation as was possible.

Summary Points

- Auto-Negotiation enables a pair of link partners to communicate whenever either interface is initialized, reset, or reconfigured and to discover an optimal set of mutually supported capabilities.

- There are two separate Auto-Negotiation technology families: twisted-pair interfaces and 1000BASE-X interfaces.

- Twisted-pair Ethernet interfaces can automatically negotiate transmission speed, half- or full–duplex operation, and use of flow control. In addition, 1000BASE-T and 100BASE-T2 interfaces can negotiate master/slave roles.

- 1000BASE-X interfaces can automatically negotiate half- or full-duplex operation and the use of flow control.

- Both families can use Auto-Negotiation messages to describe a fault or to report vendor- or product-specific information.

- Auto-Negotiation can simplify an administrator's job and ease upgrades.

- Parallel detection enables a party to discover whether a nonnegotiating twisted-pair partner has a 10BASE-T, 100BASE-T4, or 100BASE-TX interface by examining the signals arriving from the partner.

- Auto-Negotiation information is transmitted across a twisted-pair link encoded in fast link pulses (FLPs). Each FLP contains a 16-bit page.

- There are three types of pages: base pages, message pages, and unformatted pages.

- For 1000BASE-X, pages are introduced by a special pair of code-groups.

References

Auto-Negotiation is described in

- IEEE Standard 802.3, 1998 Edition. "Carrier Sense Multiple Access with Collision Detection (CSMA/CD) Access Method and Physical Layer Specifications." Chapters 21, 28, 34, and 37.

For a good introduction to Auto-Negotiation, see

- Verschueren, Ben. "Auto-Negotiation Is Our Friend." University of New Hampshire Interoperability Lab. Available from Internet: http://www.iol.unh.edu/

PART II

Bridging, Switching, and Routing

12   Ethernet Bridges and Layer 2 Switches

13   The Spanning Tree Protocol

14   Switches and Multicast Traffic

15   Link Aggregation

16   VLANs and Frame Priority

17   Source-Routing, Translational, and Wide Area Bridges

18   Routing and Layer 2/3 Switches

CHAPTER 12

Ethernet Bridges and Layer 2 Switches

Chapter 3, "Ethernet LAN Structure," contained a brief sketch of Ethernet bridges. This chapter starts to fill in the picture.

Bridges have been around for a long time. Bridge products evolved into today's *Layer 2 switches*. Functionally, a Layer 2 switch *is* a bridge, but calling it a Layer 2 switch is good marketing. The new title tells a customer that the product has an up-to-date implementation. Compared to the bridge products of the past, today's Layer 2 switches are faster, have more ports, hold more information, have more security options, and sometimes support virtual LANs (VLANs). If the vendors who have made these improvements want to call their products Layer 2 switches, that's okay—but they still are bridges!

The terms *bridge* and *Layer 2 switch* (sometimes shortened to *switch*) are interchangeable in this chapter. The classic term, *bridge*, is used in the initial sections. The functions performed by bridges/Layer-2-switches are described in the IEEE standards documents:

- "802.1D Media Access Control (MAC) Bridges"
- "802.1Q Virtual Bridged Local Area Networks"

Main Bridge/Switch Functions

A bridge carries out three main functions:

- It improves performance by keeping local traffic within a limited part of the LAN.

- It makes it possible to build a mixed-speed LAN. For example, traffic must be bridged between a 10Mbps Ethernet segment and a 100Mbps segment, or a 100Mbps segment and a 1000Mbps segment. Note that a 10/100Mbps or 100/1000Mbps "hub" contains a hidden bridge.

- It extends the area covered by a LAN. The size of a collision domain is limited by rules that restrict cable lengths and the number of repeaters in a path. The scope of these rules ends when a frame reaches a bridge port. The frame makes a fresh start when it is transmitted out another bridge port.

For example, in Figure 12.1 most of the traffic for the workgroup on the left is exchanged between the desktop systems and server B. All systems in the workgroup are attached to 10Mbps hubs.

During the day, a small amount of traffic is directed at database server C, which is connected to a 100Mbps segment. Overnight, workgroup server B is backed up to headquarters file server D, located 500 miles away. In Figure 12.1

- Bridge 1 prevents local workgroup traffic between desktops and server B from being transmitted to the 100Mbps hub on the right or across the wide area link to headquarters.

- Traffic between station A and database server C passes across six segments. However, because the segment count ends and restarts at bridge 1, this path is perfectly acceptable.

- Traffic between workgroup server B and file server D travels far beyond the Ethernet LAN distance limitations that were described in earlier chapters. Bridging makes "local" area networks that span wide-area links completely legitimate.

In earlier times, a LAN bridge was a simple device: You plugged it in, and it did its job. Network administrators loved the simplicity of these products but almost immediately started to ask for extra features that met special needs. Product manuals that originally consisted of instructions on how to unpack the device and plug it in grew thick and full of complicated instructions.

It is the goal of this chapter to enable an administrator to understand today's fully featured Layer 2 switching products and to be able to configure and manage them.

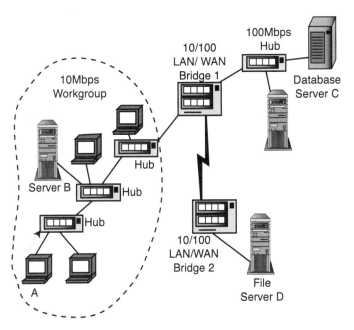

FIGURE 12.1 *Controlling traffic and extending the LAN diameter with a bridge.*

Other Bridge Functions

Bridges have been enhanced with functions that improve performance, security, availability, and manageability. Specific capabilities include

- Preventing some types of frames from being forwarded to parts of a LAN. This is done to eliminate superfluous traffic or to impose some security constraints. An administrator manually configures filtering rules to be applied to frames. Filtering is described in this chapter.

- Eliminating single points of failure by installing backup bridges and creating backup links between bridges. The *Spanning Tree Protocol* (STP) is the most popular backup facility. The Spanning Tree Protocol is introduced in this chapter and is studied in detail in Chapter 13, "The Spanning Tree Protocol."

- Combining a group of links between bridges so they appear to be a single link. This is called *link aggregation*. Aggregating links is preferable to using backup links because the full bandwidth provided by extra links is available during normal operation. Link aggregation is discussed in Chapter 15, "Link Aggregation."

- Setting priorities so that time-sensitive frames can be transmitted quickly. Priority tags are described in Chapter 16, "VLANs and Frame Priority."

- Supporting VLANs, which can group users by their need to communicate with one another and share common data rather than their physical location. VLANs are covered in Chapter 16.

- Supporting network management via the Simple Network Management Protocol (SNMP). High-end products also have a remote monitor (RMON) capability.

Vendors always are trying to get ahead of the pack. To get a competitive edge, some vendors offer new features that are based on proprietary protocols. For example, several vendors have created proprietary solutions that make a set of parallel links behave like a single link. The IEEE 802.1 committee has written a specification (802.3ad) that describes a standards-based way to aggregate links. Some vendors currently offer a modified Spanning Tree Protocol that switches over from a failed component to live backup equipment more quickly. Eventually, this also might become standardized.

When a vendor comes up with a new winning strategy, the advantage usually does not last long. Other vendors are quick to copy the capability. Customers then clamor for a version that works across vendor products. Eventually, it makes sense to cooperate on producing a standard version, and so yet another IEEE subcommittee is convened.

Bridge standards are published in the 802.1 series of publications. Each new subcommittee is given a name that tacks one or more letters onto 802.1. The fact that bridges (that is, Layer 2 switches) are a hot area is reflected in the fact that all of the letters from a to z have been used up. Current committees are named in a new two-letter sequence (aa to az).

Collision Domains

At the outset, it probably is easiest to understand bridge functions in the context of the classic bridges used in traditional coax Ethernets.

A station on a coax LAN segment can see all the frames that are transmitted by any station on its segment. If that segment is connected to other segments by repeaters, it sees every frame that is sent by the stations on *any* of these segments. If two stations start to send at the same time, their frames will collide. This is the reason that a network made up of segments connected to one another by repeaters was called a collision domain.

Figure 12.2 displays a coax-based collision domain made up of three segments. When station A on segment 1 transmits a frame, it is repeated onto segments 2 and 3.

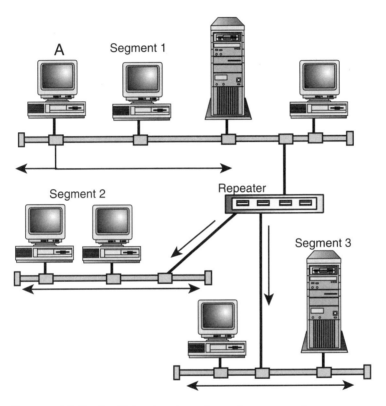

FIGURE 12.2 *A collision domain made up of coax segments.*

Figure 12.3 shows a 10BASE-T collision domain made up of 10 twisted-pair segments connected by hubs. When station A sends a frame, hub 1 repeats it onto all its other segments, including segments that connect to hub 2 and hub 3. Hub 2 and hub 3 each repeat the frame onto all segments except for the one on which it arrived. If two stations transmit frames at roughly the same time, the frames will collide.

Bridged Collision Domains

Bridges partition a LAN into separate collision domains and prevent purely local traffic from leaving a collision domain. If the LAN can be partitioned using bridges so that each workgroup is contained within its own separate

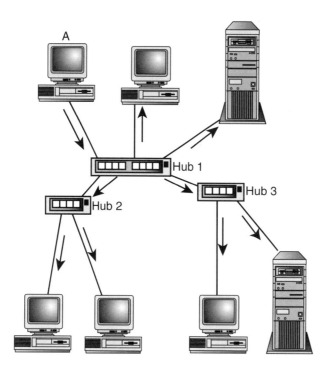

FIGURE 12.3   *A collision domain for twisted-pair segments.*

collision domain, the amount of traffic in each collision domain—and the number of collisions—is reduced appreciably. This translates into more bandwidth for each user and quicker response times.

The bridge in Figure 12.4 partitions a LAN into three collision domains: X, Y, and Z. Figure 12.4 shows a classical Ethernet LAN with a coaxial cable medium.

Segment 1 and segment 2 in Figure 12.4 are connected by a repeater, so these segments make up a single collision domain. This means that if station A and station D start to transmit at roughly the same time, the frames will collide, and both stations will have to back off and try again later. Segment 3 and segment 4 each are separate collision domains.

Transparent Bridging

The bridges that are used in Ethernet LANs are called *transparent* bridges. When a frame is sent from a source in one collision domain to a destination in another, a transparent bridge forwards the frame based on information it has learned by observing the traffic at each port. For example, the bridge in Figure 12.4 learns addresses as follows:

- Through port 1, the bridge can see all the frames that traverse collision domain Y. It records their source MAC addresses.

- Through port 2, the bridge can see all the frames that traverse collision domain Z. It records their source MAC addresses.

- Through port 3, the bridge can see all the frames that traverse collision domain X. It records their source MAC addresses.

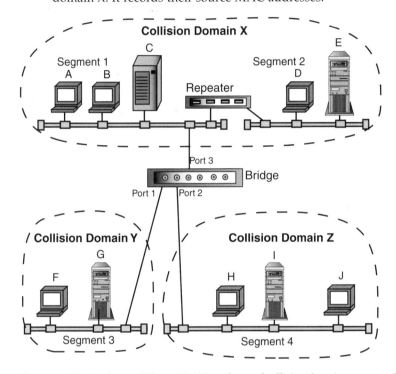

FIGURE 12.4   *A coax Ethernet LAN made up of collision domains connected by a bridge.*

Assuming that all stations in the figure are actively using the network, the bridge will discover the port through which each system is reached. If station A sends a frame to server E, the bridge will ignore it. But if station A sends a frame to server I, the bridge will absorb the frame and transmit it through port 2.

By isolating local traffic, the bridge in Figure 12.4 makes it possible for three frames to be transmitted at the same time. For example, station A could transmit a frame to server E at the same time that server G sends a frame to station F and server I sends a frame to station J.

A Bridge in a Twisted-Pair LAN

Figure 12.5 shows an Ethernet LAN constructed using hubs and twisted-pair cable. The role of the bridge is the same. The two hubs at the top of Figure 12.5 are connected and form a single collision domain. Just as in Figure 12.4, the bridge partitions the LAN into three collision domains. The bridge in Figure 12.5 makes it possible for three frames to be transmitted at the same time.

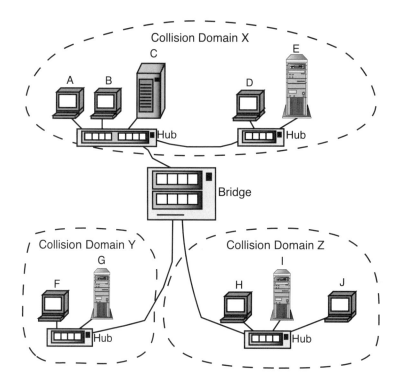

FIGURE 12.5 *A twisted-pair Ethernet LAN made up of collision domains connected by a bridge.*

A Bridge in a Mixed-Media LAN

With a helping hand from bridges, a LAN can be constructed from a mixture of coax segments and twisted-pair segments that operate at different speeds. In Figure 12.6, coax and twisted-pair collision domains are connected by a bridge.

A State-of-the-Art Switched LAN

Figure 12.7 shows a state-of-the-art LAN built using four Layer 2 switches. Each switch port connects to a single segment.

If a workstation or server has an old adapter that operates only in half-duplex mode, its segment will be a collision domain. If a station has an up-to-date adapter, it will operate in full-duplex mode, and CSMA/CD will not be used. A segment that links a pair of switches will operate in full-duplex mode.

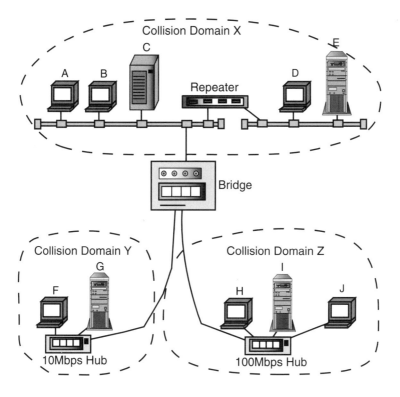

FIGURE 12.6   *A LAN made up of coax and twisted-pair collision domains.*

Note
If each of the 10 systems in the Figure 12.7 had an old adapter that was incapable of full-duplex operation, there would be 10 collision domains in the figure.

The switches amplify the bandwidth available on the LAN by a large factor. Frames can be in transit across every segment at the same time. The throughput is even higher for endpoints that support full-duplex transfer because two frames can be in transit on a segment at the same time: one in each direction.

Note that from the point of view of a switch port, a LAN is divided into two components. One component consists of systems that are reached through that port, and the other component contains the rest of the LAN.

For example, in Figure 12.7, for port 1 on switch 1, the first component consists of station A, and the second is everything else. But for port 1 on switch 3, the first component includes all the systems connected to switch 1 and switch 2, and the second includes all the systems attached to switch 3 and switch 4.

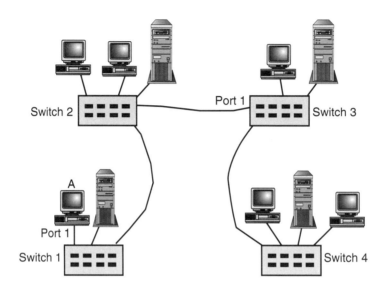

FIGURE 12.7   *A switched twisted-pair Ethernet.*

Figure 12.8 shows what happens when a hub linked to several stations is connected to port 7 on switch 4. That port must now operate in half-duplex CSMA/CD mode.

Transparent Bridge Internals

Now it is time to look inside bridges and find out what makes them tick.

The main function of a bridge is to forward any frame whose source and destination are on different sides of the bridge.

- If the frame's destination is reached through the frame's arrival port, the bridge discards the frame.

- If the frame's destination is not reached through the arrival port, the bridge forwards the frame.

Learning

How does a bridge know where a station with a particular MAC address is located? The method, which is called *learning*, is straightforward:

- The bridge watches all the traffic at each of its ports.

- The bridge notes the source MAC address of each frame and the port at which the frame was observed.

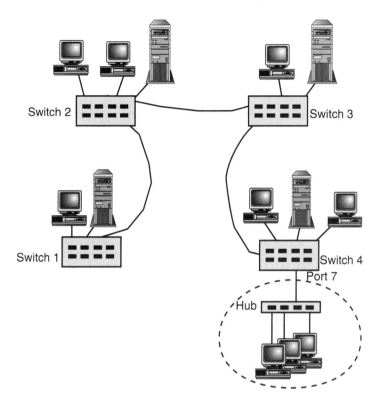

FIGURE 12.8 *Connecting a switch to a hub.*

- The bridge adds what it learns to a table called the *filtering table.* Learned entries also are called *dynamic* entries.

Note

The IEEE name for this table is the filtering database. Vendors have added lots of other names, however. Some use the term forwarding database or forwarding table for the set of dynamically learned entries and use static database or filtering database for the set of manually configured entries.

In a real implementation, a bridge performs a single table lookup to decide how a frame should be handled. The term filtering table has been chosen to represent that table in this book.

Some bridge (Layer 2 switch) products support tables that can hold thousands or tens of thousands of learned entries.

Now the processing steps can be rephrased more accurately:

1. If the frame's destination is in the filtering table and is reached through the arrival port, the bridge discards the frame.

2. If the frame's destination is in the filtering table and its exit port is different from the arrival port, the bridge forwards the frame through the exit port.

3. If the frame's destination is not in the filtering table, the bridge forwards the frame through all ports other than the arrival port.

This reason that this type of bridge is called "transparent" is that you can plug it in and forget it. It is effective, and its actions are invisible to users.

Filtering Table Entries

Table 12.1 shows a few sample learned filtering table entries. Each identifies a MAC address and the number of the port at which the address was observed.

Use of the table is straightforward. For example, if a frame with the destination MAC address shown in the first row (namely, 00-60-08-1E-AE-42) arrives from bridge port 2, the bridge will ignore it. But if a frame with this destination arrives from any other port, the bridge will transmit the frame out port 2.

TABLE 12.1 SAMPLE ENTRIES FROM A BRIDGE FILTERING TABLE

Destination MAC Address	Transmit Port	Status
00-60-08-1E-AE-42	2	Learned
00-60-08-BD-7D-1A	3	Learned
00-90-27-AE-B9-1D	1	Aged out

Note that the third entry in the table is marked "aged out." Every time a bridge observes a MAC address, the bridge restarts a timer associated with its entry. If the station with that address stops sending frames, its entry will time out and be removed from the table.

This makes good sense: There is no point in cluttering the table with MAC addresses for stations that have been shut down for the day, have been given a new NIC, or have been removed from the LAN. A bridge automatically throws out old entries to keep up with the changing LAN environment.

The usual default age-out time is 5 minutes, but this can be changed by the LAN administrator. A short time such as 5 minutes is a good choice if you want to keep the table size as lean as possible. It also assures that traffic will be capable of reaching a system shortly after it has been moved or its NIC has been replaced.

> **Note**
> To make room for new entries, some bridges drop a configured percentage of the oldest filtering table entries when the number of entries nears the table's maximum capacity.

Static Filtering Information

LAN administrators loved the plug-and-play simplicity of transparent bridges, but they promptly demanded an ability to configure and control their bridges. Vendors reacted quickly, giving LAN administrators the ability to selectively control how traffic is forwarded by manually configuring *static* filtering table entries. Static entries do not age out.

Static entries are used for the following purposes:

- To expedite the forwarding of traffic to a server

- To impose security constraints

- To improve performance by blocking out extraneous frames

Using a Static Entry for Efficient Forwarding

You might want to prevent the filtering table entry of an important server from ever aging out of the table. It is easy to do this: You just create a static filtering table entry that maps the server's MAC address to its transmit port.

For example, for the network in Figure 12.9, an entry can state that Web server A (with MAC address 08-00-20-5A-01-6C) is reached via bridge port 2. This prevents the flooding of frames onto other segments that normally would occur if there currently was no dynamic entry for the destination. The result is a reduction in extraneous traffic.

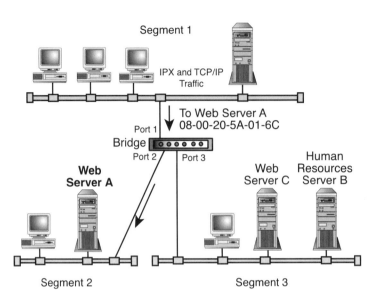

FIGURE 12.9 *Forwarding frames using a static entry.*

Sample Filtering Table Format

Table 12.2 shows an example of how filtering information can be organized into a table. Entry 1 was learned dynamically; through observation, it was learned that MAC address 00-60-08-1E-AE-42 is reached through port 2.

The second entry contains the static forwarding information for Web server A. Any frames arriving from ports other than 2 and addressed to Web server A will be transmitted through bridge port 2.

Entries 3 and 4 are used to control access to the Human Resources Server, and entry 5 is used to cut out excess IPX traffic. These are explained in the sections that follow.

Each entry in Table 12.2 identifies only one outgoing transmit port. However, in general, an entry can list several outgoing ports through which frames should be transmitted. For example, frames sent to a particular multicast address might need to be forwarded through multiple ports.

Table 12.2 Static MAC Address and Filtering Entries

Entry Number	Destination	Protocol	Source Port	Transmit Ports	Status	Comment
1	00-60-08-1E-AE-42	Any	Any	2	Learned	–
2	08-00-20-5A-01-6C	Any	Any	2	Static	To Web server A.
3	00-10-83-34-BA-12	Any	1	None	Static	Protects HR Server from users on segment 1.
4	00-10-83-34-BA-12	Any	2	3	Static	Allows access to HR Server by users on segment 2.
5	Any	IPX	Any	None	Static	All IPX traffic is local to segment 1.

The disadvantage of using a static entry is that the administrator must be very careful to update a system's entry when the system is moved or when its NIC is replaced.

If there is a static entry for a MAC address, no dynamic data is recorded for that MAC address. If the system is moved, the correct dynamic information describing its new location will not be put into the filtering table because of the presence of a static entry.

The filtering table also must be updated if there is a static entry for a system that is removed from the LAN. Otherwise, the table will become clogged with stale, useless data.

Imposing a Security Constraint

Administrators often wish to control the flow of frames across a bridge in order to impose some security rules.

An administrator might want to restrict access to a specific destination MAC address based on the bridge port at which a frame arrives. For example, in Figure 12.10, the LAN administrator wants to prevent all users attached to segment 1 from accessing the Human Resources Server on segment 3, while users on segment 2 are allowed to access the server.

The static information used to protect the Human Resources Server is displayed in entries 3 and 4 in Table 12.2.

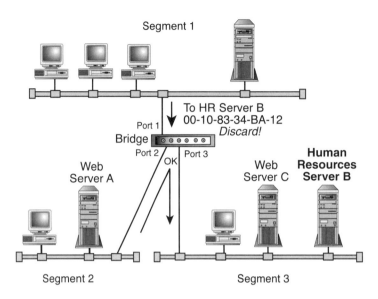

FIGURE 12.10 *Controlling access via a static filtering table entry.*

Improving Performance by Filtering on a Protocol

Many bridge products enable an administrator to control traffic based on the Layer 3 protocol carried in the frame. For example, Figure 12.11 shows that the workgroup systems on segment 1 access a local NetWare file server via IPX. The systems use TCP/IP to connect to the Web servers that are on other segments. The administrator wishes to block IPX traffic from entering or leaving segment 1. There is no valid reason for IPX traffic to flow between this segment and the other LAN segments.

If a frame with an unrecognized destination MAC address that carries IPX information is received at port 1, the bridge will not transmit the frame through ports 2 and 3. However, a frame that carries IP information will be transmitted.

In addition, IPX frames originating on segment 2 or 3 will be blocked from being sent through port 1. Entry 5 in Table 12.2 makes sure that no IPX traffic is carried across the bridge.

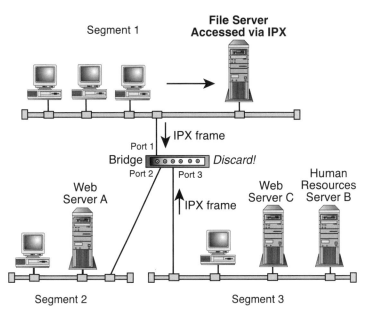

FIGURE 12.11 *Blocking protocol traffic.*

Controlling Traffic Using Other Attributes

Some bridges can impose constraints that are based on other header informa-tion. For example, frames that carry TCP/IP application data have Layer 4 headers that identify the application. Some bridges even can make forwarding decisions based on whether a particular byte pattern appears at some specific location in a frame.

Another option that has become popular is the ability to limit the total number of broadcast or multicast frames that may be forwarded per second.

Note
The IEEE 802.1D bridge standard states that constraints can be based on the source port and destination MAC address. Some vendors added the ability to control traffic using elaborate criteria because some customers wanted this feature. Other vendors offer low-cost products that can filter only on the destination MAC address.

Layer 2 Switch Architecture

What happened that caused vendors to build a new generation of bridge products and invent a new name for them?

- LANs got bigger.

- Bandwidth needs increased.

- Vendors got smarter.

- Hardware got better and cheaper.

The most important hardware innovation was the introduction of low-cost *application specific integrated circuit* (ASIC) chips. The steps in a computer program (or in a group of computer programs) can be converted to hardware logic that is etched onto an ASIC chip. The result is that the programs run a lot faster.

This actually is not a new idea. For years, there have been chips that performed specialized compute-intensive functions such as encryption or data compression. What is new is the ability to design special-purpose chips quickly and produce them relatively inexpensively. The ASIC chips used in switches contain on-chip program logic, a small general microprocessor, and memory. The amount of logic or memory that fits on a chip increases every year.

Store-and-Forward versus Cut-Through

According to the IEEE 802.1D bridge standard, a bridge should process each incoming user frame in a store-and-forward manner. That manner is detailed here:

1. Wait until an entire frame has been received.

2. Check the frame-check sequence, and discard the frame if it has been corrupted.

3. Discard runts that result from collisions, overly long frames, and malformed frames.

4. For a good frame, check the filtering table and, if appropriate, relay the frame through one or more ports.

Operating in store-and-forward mode enables a bridge to weed out a lot of network debris instead of forwarding it.

However, store-and-forward also slows down delivery. Several vendors offer one or both of the following fast-forwarding *cut-through* options:

- Frame transmission starts as soon as the destination address has been received and looked up. Hence, the bits at the head end of a frame will be going out on the wire while the rest of the frame still is being received. This means that frames that are malformed or that have a bad frame check sequence are forwarded until the flaw is discovered.

- Alternatively, frame transmission starts as soon as an initial valid 64 bits have been received. This reduces the chance of forwarding an errored frame because collision fragments and other malformed frames will be detected and discarded.

Some products try to give you the best of both worlds. If the error rate reaches a preset threshold, the switch changes from cut-through to store-and-forward mode.

Parallel Processing with ASICs

Whether store-and-forward or cut-through mode is used, whenever a frame arrives, a bridge must search its filtering table to see whether there is an entry that indicates what should be done with the frame. As the size of LANs has increased, the size of this table also has increased. This is a job for ASICs!

Typically, each switch line card in a Layer 2 switch contains ASICs that process incoming frames. Although the bridge filtering table is supervised and maintained by a central CPU, working copies of the table are loaded into the memory of each ASIC. Table lookups are performed by each ASIC, enabling many lookups to be carried out in parallel. This gives performance a big boost.

For further comments on how frames are processed, see Chapter 18, "Routing and Layer 2/3 Switches," which contains a discussion of Layer 2/3 switch architecture.

Basic Bridge Layer Structure

Figure 12.12 shows the simple protocol structure of a basic bridge. Each port has a physical-layer and MAC-layer component. The bridge performs learning, filtering table lookups, and relaying of frames.

Building Redundancy into a LAN

The effect of a link or bridge failure ranges from a minor inconvenience to a crisis that results in the loss of substantial amounts of productivity. Many users want to build redundancy into their bridged networks to prevent a single point of failure.

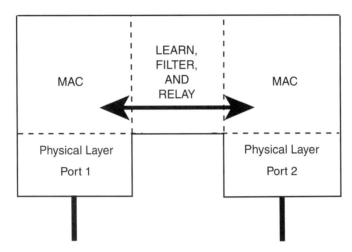

FIGURE 12.12 *Structure of a basic bridge.*

The Spanning Tree Protocol is the standard, universally accepted method of building redundancy into a bridged Ethernet LAN. It enables the bridges in a LAN to activate backup links when connectivity fails.

A second mechanism called *link aggregation* enables a set of links connecting two systems to behave like a single link. If one link fails, its traffic is diverted onto the remaining live links.

The subsections that follow present brief introductions to these technologies. Spanning Tree details are presented in Chapter 13, and link aggregation is discussed in Chapter 15.

The Spanning Tree Protocol

Transparent bridges and redundant paths do not mix. Figure 12.13 shows a simple example. The top part of the figure shows systems connected on a coax LAN. The bottom part shows the same set of systems connected using twisted-pair cabling and hubs. Both versions are bridged in the same way.

If station A transmits a frame addressed to server B on collision domain Y, both bridges will forward this frame onto collision domain Y.

When bridge 2 transmits its copy of the frame, port 2 on bridge 1 observes the frame, reads its source address, and concludes that station A is on collision domain Y. Now bridge 1 thinks that station A is on both collision domain X and collision domain Y! The same thing happens to bridge 2 when port 2 at bridge 2 observes the copy of the frame that was forwarded onto collision domain Y by bridge 1. It does not take long for the whole LAN to fall down in a heap of confusion.

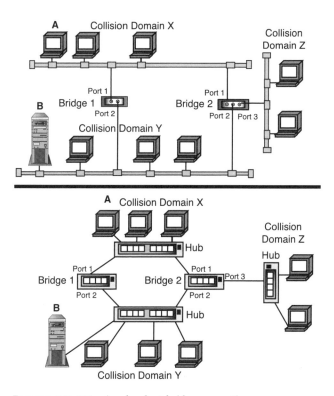

Figure 12.13 *A redundant bridge connection.*

In fact, there can be only one path between any two stations that are on the same Ethernet LAN. Two paths create a loop. A LAN built using transparent bridges can't have any loops in it; it must have a tree structure.

> **Note**
> Bridges are the nodes in the tree.

Fortunately, the Spanning Tree Protocol lets you have your tree and get redundancy, too.

The Spanning Tree Protocol converts a LAN that contains one or more loops into a tree-shaped LAN by blocking redundant bridge ports. To accomplish this, bridges exchange *Bridge Protocol Data Unit* (BPDU) messages that enable them to agree on an initial tree-shaped topology and, after the failure of some component, change the topology to repair broken paths.

In Figure 12.14, a redundant topology has been converted to a tree by blocking port 2 on bridge 2. A blocked port does not forward traffic and does not learn new entries for its bridge's filtering table.

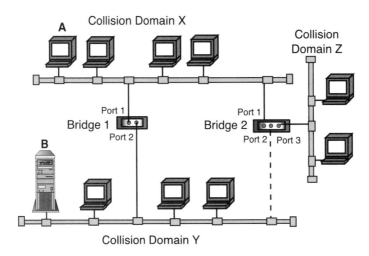

F I G U R E 12.14 *Removing a loop by blocking a port.*

More details about the inner workings of the Spanning Tree Protocol are available in Chapter 13.

Link Aggregation

Several Layer 2 switch vendors offer a product feature that enables several lines to act like a single line. Stated differently, several ports on a switch cooperate and behave like one port. Vendors have several names for this capability: *trunking, port aggregation, inverse multiplexing*, and *link aggregation*. The IEEE has chosen the term *link aggregation*, so that is the one that will be used here.

Link aggregation is illustrated in Figure 12.15. In the figure, four 100Mbps links between switch 1 and switch 2 have been combined into one 400Mbps aggregated link.

The Spanning Tree Protocol treats an aggregated link as a single link.

Handling Multicasts

The bridge learning process improves performance: A unicast frame whose destination has been learned is forwarded only through the port that leads to the destination—it does not get sent onto other parts of the LAN.

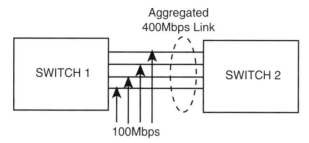

FIGURE 12.15 *Link aggregation.*

An administrator can enter static information that reduces unnecessary unicast traffic even further.

Stemming the flow of multicast frames is another challenge. According to the original rule of multicasting, if even one station on a LAN joins a multicast group, every station on the LAN will see all the frames sent to that multicast group. As multicast applications become more prevalent, following this rule will undo the efficiencies that have carefully been built into the new switch devices.

IGMP Snooping and GARP

Bridge vendors quickly devised a stopgap method called *IGMP snooping* that channels multicast frames to group members. The *Internet Group Management Protocol* (IGMP) is the protocol that TCP/IP systems use to join and leave an IP-based multicast group. Bridges eavesdrop on IGMP messages to build table entries that identify the ports that lead to members of a multicast group.

IGMP snooping is far from ideal, and a long-term solution called the *GARP Multicast Registration Protocol* (GMRP) was defined by an IEEE 802.1 working group. GMRP enables systems that wish to join a multicast group to register with a neighboring bridge. Bridges exchange registration information that assures that multicast frames will be forwarded to group members.

IGMP snooping and GMRP are described in Chapter 14, "Switches and Multicast Traffic."

Functional Structure of a Layer 2 Switch

Bridges originally were designed to either ignore or forward a frame; they were not the sources or destinations of any frames. This changed when features such as the Spanning Tree Protocol, link aggregation, GMRP, and SNMP management were introduced. Bridges exchange protocol traffic with one another and exchange SNMP messages with network management stations.

Figure 12.16 shows the layered structure of a modern Layer 2 switch. Each bridge port has its own MAC address. This enables the bridge port to be the source or destination of a frame.

Link aggregation runs directly on top of the MAC sublayer. However, the messages used in the Spanning Tree Protocol and the GARP Multicast Registration Protocol contain Logical Link Control (LLC) headers, and these protocols operate above the LLC layer.

IGMP snooping runs on top of IP, and SNMP usually runs on top of the User Datagram Protocol (UDP) and IP.

The stage now is set for a presentation of all the protocol details. This is done in the chapters that follow.

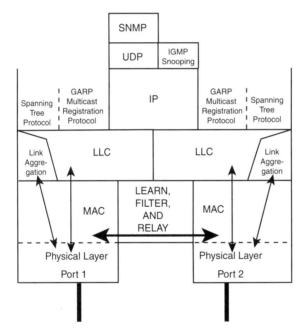

FIGURE 12.16 *Layered structure of a bridge.*

Summary Points

- Layer 2 switches are modern bridge products.

- A bridge improves performance by keeping local traffic within a limited part of a LAN.

- A bridge makes it possible to build a mixed-speed LAN. For example, traffic must be bridged between a 10Mbps segment and a 100Mbps segment.

- A bridge can extend the diameter of a LAN.

- An Ethernet transparent bridge can dynamically record the port through which a MAC address can be reached in a filtering table. This process is called learning.

- Static entries can be configured into a filtering table and used to expedite the forwarding process, impose security constraints, and improve performance by blocking selected frames from entering parts of the LAN.

- LAN availability can be improved by installing backup bridges and backup links. The Spanning Tree Protocol (STP) enables bridges to automatically reconfigure the LAN topology to use backup resources.

- Some bridge products can treat a set of links between a pair of devices like a single link. This is called link aggregation.

- Some bridge products can give priority treatment to preferred frames.

- Some bridge products support virtual LANs (VLANs).

- Bridges eavesdrop on Internet Group Management Protocol (IGMP) messages to build filtering table entries that identify the ports that lead to members of a multicast group.

- The GARP Multicast Registration Protocol (GMRP) enables systems that wish to join a multicast group to register with a neighboring bridge.

- Support for Simple Network Management Protocol (SNMP) is almost universal.

- In high-powered Layer 2 switches, each switch line card contains application specific integrated circuits (ASICs) that process incoming frames. A working copy of the filtering table is loaded into the memory of each ASIC, and many table lookups occur in parallel.

References

Bridge architecture and functions are described in

- IEEE 802.1D. "Local and metropolitan area networks—Common specifications—Media Access Control (MAC) Bridges." 1998.

CHAPTER 13

The Spanning Tree Protocol

The cost of extra equipment often is negligible compared to the cost of a network failure. The usual way to prevent network failures is to install extra equipment and extra network links. However, as discussed in Chapter 12, "Ethernet Bridges and Layer 2 Switches," multiple paths leading to the same LAN destination form loops that cause bridges to crash.

If redundant LAN paths are created, some must be placed in backup mode. If these paths are needed to cope with a network failure, they must be upgraded to active status.

Manually controlling the topology of a big, complicated LAN can be a tough job—especially since several administrators may be allowed to add and remove equipment and make parameter changes independently. It is very desirable to have a protocol that can control LAN topology automatically.

The IEEE 802.1D Spanning Tree Protocol (STP) was designed to do this. The protocol enables the bridges in a LAN to perform the following actions:

- Discover and activate an optimal tree topology for the LAN

- Detect failures and subsequent recoveries, and automatically update the topology so that the "best" tree structure possible is selected at any given time

The topology of the LAN automatically is calculated from a set of bridge configuration parameters that are established by administrators. The tree will be the "best" one that can be constructed using these parameters. If the configuration job is botched, the results might not be the best that actually is possible.

The 802.1D STP has won strong acceptance in the marketplace. This protocol always has been popular for Ethernet LANs, but it is increasingly used in Token Ring LANs as well. The protocol was designed to operate with any type of LAN MAC protocol, not just Ethernet.

> **Note**
>
> Several vendors have created proprietary special purpose variants of the STP. For example, the IBM variant prevents Token Ring explorer frames from following a looped path. (Explorer frames are used to set up a path across a series of Token Ring Source Route bridges. These bridges are described in Chapter 19, "Token Ring and FDDI Overview.") Use of proprietary variants is fading, and these variants will not be discussed in this chapter.

LAN Structure and SubLANs

Bridges (switches) provide the infrastructure that holds the pieces of a LAN together. Each bridge port connects to one of these pieces.

> **Note**
>
> No standard terminology exists for the piece of a LAN that is connected to a bridge port. The term subLAN is used for this purpose in this book.

The LAN pieces (subLANs) look quite different depending on their internal technology. For example, subLAN A, in the upper-left corner of Figure 13.1, is a coax-based collision domain that includes two segments and a repeater. SubLAN B, in the upper-right corner, is a twisted-pair collision domain that is built around two hubs. Note that traffic moving between bridge 1 and bridge 2 must cross subLAN B.

Assuming that all the links in the lower half of the figure are full-duplex links, subLANs C and D in Figure 13.1 are just full-duplex links that connect bridge 2 to bridge 3 and bridge 4. SubLANs E to L are full-duplex links that connect workstations and servers to bridges.

SubLANs A and E to L are called *leaves*, which means that they do not carry traffic from one bridge to another. These subLANs are the "end of the line" and are not very interesting from the point of view of LAN structure.

Figure 13.2 shows the kind of picture that will be used in this chapter to depict LAN structures. All the leaves have been stripped from the LAN. Each subLAN that interconnects bridges is represented by a bar with boxes that represent points of connection.

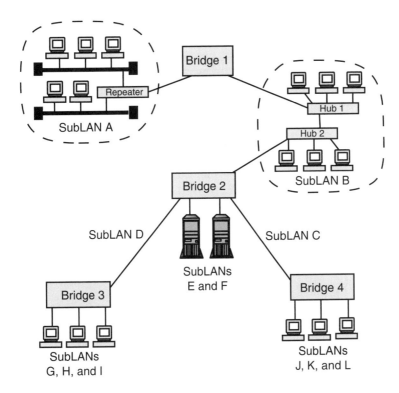

FIGURE 13.1 *Pieces (subLANs) of an Ethernet LAN.*

The bar can represent a subLAN that is a collision domain (as is the case with subLAN B), or the bar may be superimposed on a simple point-to-point link between a pair of bridges (as is the case with subLANs C and D).

Note
If you are trying to understand the LAN skeleton, it does not matter what type of subLAN the bar represents. However, when you are trying to pick parameters that will help the STP set up a good topology, it matters a lot whether a subLAN is a busy 10Mbps collision domain or a full-duplex gigabit link.

Protocol Overview

This section provides a rough understanding of the major spanning tree concepts. Later sections present detailed definitions and describe the protocol mechanisms.

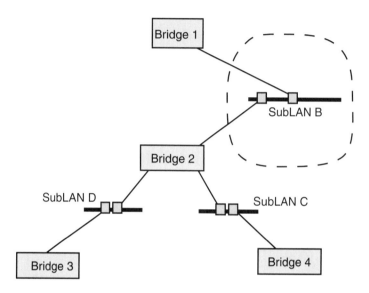

FIGURE 13.2 *The structure of a bridged LAN.*

Electing the Root Bridge

The first step in the STP is to choose a bridge that will act as the *root* of the tree. The tree that is formed will consist of paths that radiate from the root and reach every bridge and every subLAN.

The sample bridged LAN in Figure 13.3 illustrates how a LAN's root bridge is chosen.

- Every bridge is assigned a MAC address that is used as its unique *bridge address*. The customary convention is to reuse the smallest port MAC address as the bridge address. To avoid clutter in the figure, the bridge addresses in Figure 13.3 are written as MAC1, MAC2, and so on.

- Each bridge also is assigned a priority number. The priority number followed by the bridge address is called the *bridge identifier*.

- The root of the tree is the bridge with the smallest bridge identifier. To find the root, select the bridge (or bridges) with the smallest priority number. If there is a tie, compare the bridge (MAC) addresses to break the tie.

Bridges discover which one is the root by exchanging their bridge identifiers. This process is called an *election*. A wise administrator rigs the result of the root election by assigning the lowest priority number to the bridge best suited to be the root and then assigning the next lowest to bridges that can act as backup roots. If an administrator does not assign a specific value to a bridge, its priority will default to 32,768.

In Figure 13.3, bridge 1 has priority number 0 and is the clear winner of the root contest.

> **Note**
> It is convenient to place the root at the top of a LAN structure diagram. This conforms to the usual computer science convention for drawing tree structures.

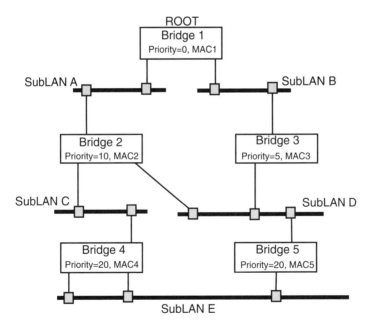

FIGURE 13.3 *Electing the root bridge.*

An administrator should consider several factors when deciding which bridge would be the best one to win the contest for root:

- The root should have a central position in a LAN. As you shall soon see, STP messages flow from the root to all other bridges on a periodic basis. A central position minimizes the distance that these messages must travel.

- The preferred root bridge should be a solid, reliable piece of equipment. If the root bridge fails, another root must be elected. LAN traffic is disrupted during the changeover process.

- The root should be given ample bandwidth by locating it on the backbone of the LAN.

- The root should be located in an area that gets plenty of support and attention.

Generating the Tree

It is desirable to configure bridges so that the Spanning Tree algorithm will choose and activate the paths branching out from the root that deliver the best performance. An easy way to plan for this is to do the following:

- Assign a cost number to each subLAN.

- Compute the cost of a path by adding cost numbers that are assigned to each subLAN traversed by the path. The path that has the least cost is the best.

The process by which cost numbers are configured into bridges will be explained later, in the section "Port Costs and the Root Path Cost." For now, we'll stick to this simple, intuitive model.

Assigning Costs

Table 13.1 shows the cost values recommended by the IEEE. Appropriately, the lowest costs are assigned to subLANs that operate at the highest bandwidths. When you pick a least-cost path, you want it to be the one that provides the best performance.

The table also shows the range of values that can be used by an administrator who wants to fine-tune a cost. For example, a subLAN that consists of a stack of 10Mbps hubs connected to a large and busy workgroup could be assigned a cost value that is greater than 100 (for example, 300); likewise, a subLAN that consists of a single 10Mbps link could be assigned a cost value below 100.

A full-duplex link has more capacity than a half-duplex link, and the cost should reflect this. For example, a half-duplex 10Mbps link connecting a pair of bridges might be rated at 75, while a full-duplex 10Mbps link might be rated at 50.

TABLE 13.1 RECOMMENDED SEGMENT COST VALUES

Link Speed	Recommended Value	Recommended Range
4Mbps	250	100–1000
10Mbps	100	50–600
16Mbps	62	40–400
100Mbps	19	10–60
1Gbps	4	3–10
10Gbps	2	1–5

In Figure 13.4, A and B are 1Gbps Ethernet subLANs, C is a 100Mbps Ethernet subLAN, and D and E are 10Mbps subLANs. The default costs have been assigned to each subLAN.

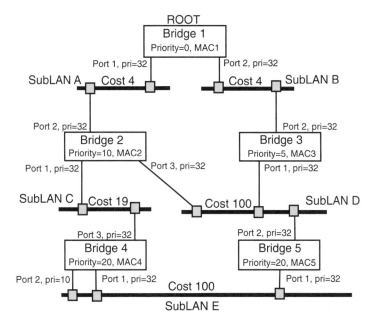

FIGURE 13.4 *Assigning subLAN costs.*

The cost of reaching a bridge is the sum of the costs of the subLANs that are crossed when traveling from the root to the bridge. The cost of reaching a subLAN is the same as the cost of reaching the bridge adjacent to the subLAN on the path from the root.

Optimal Path Example

The discovery of optimal paths starts at the root and works its way through the network. In Figure 13.4

- The cost of the path from the root to bridge 2 is 4.

- The cost of the path from the root to bridge 3 also is 4. Note that both bridges connect to subLAN D, and they provide paths of equal cost from the root to subLAN D. Only one of these paths can be used. The tie is broken by comparing the bridge priorities. Bridge 3 has a smaller priority number and wins.

- The best path from the root to bridge 4 crosses subLANs A and C and has a total cost of 23.

- The best path from the root to bridge 5 crosses subLANs B and D and has a total cost of 104.

- SubLAN E can be reached via bridge 4 (cost 23) or bridge 5 (cost 104). Bridge 4 wins.

Two ports on bridge 4 have been connected to subLAN E to provide a backup in case of port failure. Only one can be active (otherwise, a loop would form), and a preferred port must be chosen.

Every port on a bridge is configured with a priority number. (The default port priority is 32.) In this example, the LAN administrator has ensured that port 2 will be preferred to port 1 by assigning port 2 a smaller priority number. If the priorities had been equal, the smaller port number would have been preferred. The combination of the port priority and the port number is called the *port identifier*.

> ### Note
> Why would anyone care which port on a bridge was used to connect to a subLAN? Keep in mind that the subLAN might be a large collision domain consisting of a cascade of hubs. One of the bridge ports might be connected to a preferred central hub, and the other might be connected to a different hub. The second connection might have been installed to keep at least part of the subLAN connected to the LAN if the central hub failed.

Figure 13.5 shows the tree that results from choosing optimal paths. The dotted lines correspond to blocked ports. Port 3 on bridge 2, port 1 on bridge 4, and port 1 on bridge 5 have been blocked to form the tree. The set of paths that have been selected is called the *active topology*.

Elements of the Protocol

The stage now is set for a closer view of the inner workings of the STP.

Bridges get the information that they need to build an optimal tree topology by exchanging *Bridge Protocol Data Unit* (BPDU) messages. These messages are addressed to the multicast address X'01-80-C2-00-00-00, which the IEEE has assigned to bridges participating in the STP.

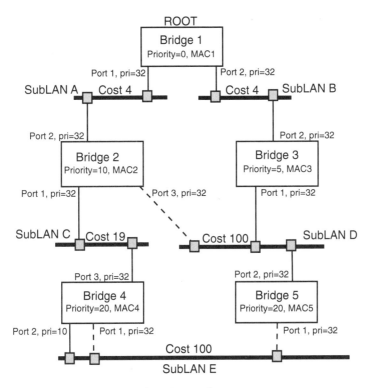

FIGURE 13.5 *Choosing the active topology.*

Port Costs and the Root Path Cost

An administrator must enter configuration data at each bridge—the data does not float around on subLANs. Instead of associating a cost with a subLAN, a corresponding *path cost* is associated with each port. In Figure 13.6, the cost that earlier was associated to each subLAN in Figure 13.5 has been configured as the path cost for each port that connects to the subLAN.

The cost of getting from the root to a bridge is called the bridge's *root path cost*:

- A bridge's root path cost is computed by adding port path cost numbers along the path from the root to the bridge.

- Cost numbers are added only for ports that *receive* frames forwarded from the root to the bridge.

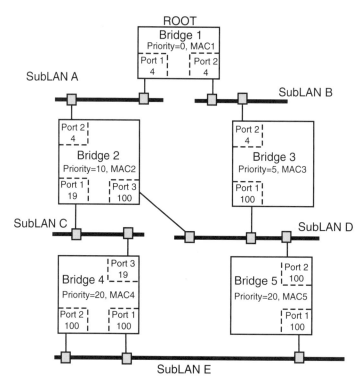

FIGURE 13.6 *Formal path costs associated with ports.*

For example, to compute the root path cost for bridge 4 in Figure 13.6, you would add the following path port costs:

- Bridge 2, port 2 (cost 4)

- Bridge 4, port 3 (cost 19)

The total is 23.

Bridge 1, port 1 and bridge 2, port 1 *send* frames on the path, and their values are *not* added in.

The answers computed using the port costs in Figure 13.6 are exactly the same as the answers computed using the subLAN costs in Figure 13.4. For example, the root path cost for bridge 4 still is 23, and the root path cost for bridge 5 still is 104. Costs for the sending ports along the way are not counted because that would cause each subLAN cost to be counted twice.

The root's own port numbers never get added in, so should an administrator bother to assign cost numbers to the root's ports? The answer is yes. Another administrator might come along and change a bridge priority number somewhere, causing a different bridge to become root. The current root then becomes an ordinary citizen. If no numbers have been assigned to its ports, their costs default to 128. This could warp the topology of the resulting tree.

Although it usually makes sense to assign the same cost to every port that connects to the same subLAN, the rules do not require administrators to do this. Although it might seem illogical, administrators can assign different cost values to different ports that connect to the same subLAN.

Actually, it makes political sense to allow this because, in real life, several administrators might be responsible for configuring bridges in a LAN. Each might control a different set of bridges, and each might have a different opinion about the cost that should be assigned to a port connected to a particular subLAN. The administrators don't have to fight it out. The STP still will work perfectly well even if the numbers are different. However, the administrators might not all agree that the tree that finally is produced by the protocol is "optimal."

Root Port, Designated Bridge, and Designated Port

Some additional definitions are needed before describing in detail how the protocol chooses a root bridge, discovers optimal paths, and updates the tree topology. Some key definitions are listed here:

- **Root port**—The port on a bridge that connects to its best path to the root.

- **Designated bridge for a subLAN**—The bridge that transmits frames coming from the direction of the root onto the subLAN, and that transmits frames from the subLAN toward the root. The designated bridge is on a least-cost path between the subLAN and the root.

- **Designated port**—The single unblocked port that connects a subLAN to its designated bridge.

Choosing the Root

Every bridge starts out with dreams of glory: It assumes that it is the root and is the designated bridge for each subLAN to which it is directly connected.

If multiple ports connect a bridge to a particular subLAN, the port with the smallest priority number is used, and the others are blocked. If the priority numbers are equal, the smallest port number wins.

A bridge that thinks that it is the root multicasts *Configuration BPDUs* onto each subLAN to which it is connected. If another bridge on that subLAN knows better, it transmits a Configuration BPDU onto the subLAN that names its candidate for root—a bridge that has a better (priority, MAC) bridge ID combination.

For example, in Figure 13.3, when bridge 4 initializes, it assumes that it is the root. It soon receives a message from bridge 2 that nominates itself because bridge 2 has a better priority number. However, bridge 2 soon learns that bridge 1 has an even better priority value (0, which is the best possible). Bridge 2 passes that information along in the next BPDU that it sends across subLAN C.

Listing 13.1 shows part of the trace of a Configuration BPDU. In the trace, the sender identifies the priority and MAC number of the bridge that it believes to be the root—namely, itself. This can be seen by comparing the root identifier field with the sending bridge ID field.

The cost of getting from the root to itself is 0, so the sender reports a root path cost of 0. The sender has priority value X'80-00 (32,768), which is the default.

The 2-byte port identifier (X'8002) shows that the port has been assigned the default port priority (X'80, which is decimal 128) and that the sender transmitted the message through port X'02 (decimal 2).

LISTING 13.1 INITIAL FIELDS IN A CONFIGURATION BPDU

```
BPDU: Root Identifier    = 8000.0200000A402C
    BPDU:   Priority        = 8000
    BPDU:   MAC Address     = 0200000A402C
    BPDU:
    BPDU: Root Path Cost    = 0
    BPDU:
    BPDU: Sending Bridge Id = 8000.0200000A402C.8002
    BPDU:   Priority        = 8000
    BPDU:   MAC Address     = 0200000A402C
    BPDU:   Port            = 8002
```

If this bridge receives a BPDU that has a smaller value in its root identifier field, it will accept that system as the new root. Through a series of corrections, all the bridges discover the real root very quickly.

Discovering the Root Paths

After the root has been discovered, it does not take long to generate the rest of the tree. The root multicasts a Configuration BPDU across each of its adjacent subLANs. This BPDU is received by each bridge connected to these subLANs.

Each receiver creates a new Configuration BPDU by

- Replacing the 0 value in the root path cost field with the cost associated with its arrival port. For example, bridge 2 in Figure 13.6 would put a value of 4 in the root path cost field.

- Placing its own identifier in the sending bridge identifier field.

The bridge then sends this updated BPDU onto every subLAN for which it believes it is the designated bridge.

It is possible that another bridge also believes that it is the designated bridge for one of these subLANs. If so, that bridge will send its own BPDU onto the subLAN. Each bridge compares the root path cost value in an incoming BPDU with its own value. The bridge with the smallest root path cost wins. A tie is broken in the usual way, by comparing bridge identifiers.

For example, in Figure 13.6, bridge 2 and bridge 3 send BPDUs onto subLAN D to report identical root path costs of 4. The tie is broken in favor of bridge 3 because its priority number, 5, is the low value.

Updated BPDUs are propagated down the tree until every bridge discovers its root port, its root path cost, and its designated ports. For example, in Figure 13.6

1. Bridge 5 receives the BPDUs sent across subLAN D by bridges 2 and 3, and discovers that adjacent bridge 3 lies on its path to the root. Hence, port 2 is the root port for bridge 5, and its root path cost is 104.

2. Bridge 5 then sends a BPDU that reports its root path cost onto subLAN E.

3. When bridge 5 receives a BPDU from bridge 4 reporting a root path cost of 23, bridge 5 discovers that it is not the designated bridge for subLAN E and that port 1 is not a designated port.

Note

The topology of the tree is completely described by the identity of the root bridge, the root ports, and the designated ports.

The tree is formed by "turning on" the root ports and designated ports, enabling them to forward frames. The other ports are blocked and cannot send or receive data frames, although they will continue to send and receive BPDUs.

Topology Changes and Port State Changes

The tree topology must be recomputed after the failure or recovery of a bridge or a bridge port. One or more blocked ports might need to be placed on active duty.

For example, Figure 13.7 shows how the topology that was established in Figure 13.5 changes after bridge 4 crashes. Port 1 on bridge 5 needs to be unblocked and must learn the MAC addresses of the systems on subLAN E.

Other bridges have to do some relearning as well. For example, before the crash, the following was true:

- Bridge 2 learned the MAC addresses of stations on subLAN E from frames that were travelling up the tree from subLAN E to other subLANs.

- Bridge 2 was forwarding frames sent from subLAN A to subLAN E through its port 1.

After the crash, bridge 2 must unlearn the subLAN E destination addresses quickly. Traffic from subLAN A to subLAN E will have to pass through bridges 1, 3, and 5.

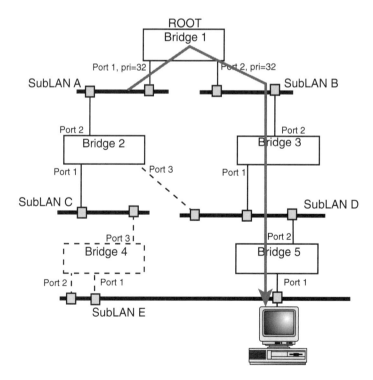

FIGURE 13.7 *Topology changes after a bridge crashes.*

To avoid chaos during a change (for example, while bridge 4 ages out its subLAN E addresses and bridge 5 learns them), a bridge needs to activate a blocked port in stages. First, the port needs to remain quiet until the topology of the new tree has settled down. If both old ports and new ports are functioning at the same time, traffic will circle around looped paths.

Secondly, a port that is unblocking needs to enter a learning phase to discover the MAC addresses that are reached through the port. In fact, during a topology change, all ports in the tree must age out their dynamic filtering table entries quickly and relearn their dynamic address information.

> **Note**
> Recall that the filtering table includes both dynamically learned and manually configured entries.

Table 13.2 displays the complete set of port states and the functions performed while in each state. A *forward delay timer* controls the duration of the *listening* and *learning* states in Table 13.2. This timer also is used to age out dynamic filtering table entries following a topology change.

TABLE 13.2 SPANNING TREE BRIDGE PORT STATES

State	Functions
Disabled	The port is incapable of functioning, either because of equipment failure or action by an administrator.
Blocking	The port can only send and receive BPDUs.
Listening	A timer is set and the port is waiting quietly for a period (the forward delay time) to allow other bridges to discover the new topology. The port continues to send and receive BPDUs.
Learning	After the listening period has expired, the timer is reset to the forward delay time, and the port starts to learn MAC address information and add it to the filtering database. The port continues to send and receive BPDUs.
Forwarding	After the timer has expired, the port is ready to receive and forward frames. The port continues to learn MAC address information that is added to the filtering database and is capable of sending and receiving BPDUs.

> **Note**
> In addition to the functions listed in Table 13.2, every nondisabled port is capable of sending and receiving SNMP network management messages.

Maintaining the Tree

Each bridge records some topology information. For example, it keeps track of the following:

- The identifier of the root bridge
- The bridge's root port
- The bridge's root path cost
- The bridge's designated ports

This information needs to be refreshed periodically.

It is the job of the root to launch a round of information exchanges at regular intervals. The root sends out a fresh Configuration BPDU every time a period called the *hello time* has elapsed. This triggers a cascade of new BPDUs away from the root toward the bottom of the tree, and enables each bridge to validate or update its information.

If a problem prevents Configuration BPDUs from arriving at a bridge, it is very likely that some of the bridge's topology information is out of date. The topology information is discarded if no BPDUs have been received during a timeout period whose value is called the *maximum age*.

The current tree can be disrupted by the failure of a port or of an entire bridge, by administrative changes in configuration data, or by the addition of more equipment. Any bridge that has evidence that the topology information needs to change transmits a *Topology Change Notification* BPDU through its root port. This BPDU is relayed *upward* toward the root. The root reacts by sending out a Configuration BPDU to acknowledge that it has received the Topology Change Notification.

Protocol Messages

Recall that frames containing Bridge PDUs are addressed to the multicast address X'01-80-C2-00-00-00. These frames contain the 3-byte Logical Link Control (LLC) header that is displayed in Figure 13.8. The LLC destination service access point (DSAP) and source service access point (SSAP) addresses both are X'42. The control field value, X'03, means "unnumbered information."

> **Note**
>
> Logical Link Control headers, DSAPs, SSAPs, and control fields were discussed in Chapter 4, "The Classical Ethernet CSMA/CD MAC Protocol," in the section called "LSAPs."

The first 2 bytes of a BPDU contain the protocol identifier X'00-00.

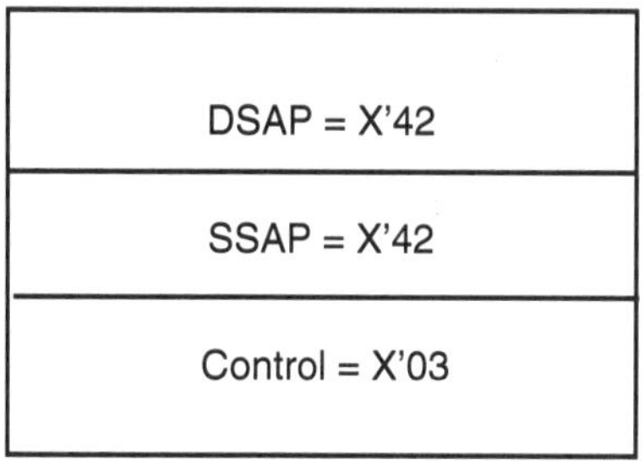

DSAP = X'42
SSAP = X'42
Control = X'03

FIGURE 13.8 *LLC header in BPDU frames.*

The Configuration BPDU

Figure 13.9 shows the layout of a complete Configuration BPDU message. The last three parameters (maximum age, hello time, and forward delay) are values that have been configured at the root bridge. The root announces them to the other bridges to synchronize the actions of the protocol across all the bridges. In particular

- The maximum age is used to time out stale protocol information.

- The hello time sets the interval at which the root sends BPDUs.

- The forward delay times out port state changes.

After the root bridge sends a BPDU containing these values, other bridges save them and copy them into the BPDUs that they transmit. All bridges quickly learn these values, and the bridges are governed by them until a different bridge becomes root.

Every bridge is configured with its own maximum age, hello time, and forward delay. However, a bridge's values are not used unless the bridge becomes the root.

One remaining parameter has not been explained. The value in the message age field starts out at 0 and is incremented at each bridge downstream from the root. An incoming message whose age exceeds the maximum age timer value is discarded.

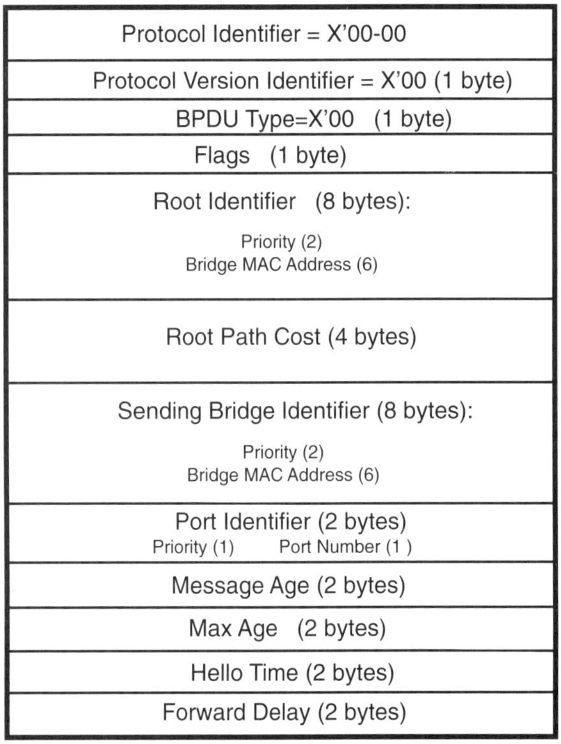

Protocol Identifier = X'00-00
Protocol Version Identifier = X'00 (1 byte)
BPDU Type=X'00   (1 byte)
Flags   (1 byte)
Root Identifier   (8 bytes): Priority (2) Bridge MAC Address (6)
Root Path Cost (4 bytes)
Sending Bridge Identifier (8 bytes): Priority (2) Bridge MAC Address (6)
Port Identifier (2 bytes) Priority (1)   Port Number (1)
Message Age (2 bytes)
Max Age   (2 bytes)
Hello Time (2 bytes)
Forward Delay (2 bytes)

FIGURE 13.9   *A Configuration BPDU.*

Listing 13.2 displays a DIX Ethernet frame that was captured by a Network Associates Sniffer and that contains a Configuration PDU. Note the following:

- The frame's destination MAC address is multicast address X'01-80-C2-00-00-00, which the IEEE has assigned to bridges participating in the STP.

- The message has an LLC header with DSAP and SSAP equal to X'42 and a control field containing X'03, which means "unnumbered information."

- The protocol identifier X'00-00 corresponds to the STP. The protocol version is X'00.

- BPDU type X'00 indicates that this is a Configuration message.

- Only two of the flag bits are used. These bits are employed in the topology change procedure.

- The root identifier includes the root's bridge identifier—that is, its priority number and the MAC address selected to uniquely identify that bridge.

- The sender believes that it is the root and, hence, reports its root path cost as 0 and the message age as 0.

- The sending bridge identifier is the same as the root identifier.

- The sending port's priority and port number are included.

- In this example, a message older than the maximum age of 20 seconds (which is called the *information lifetime* in the trace) should be ignored and discarded. The root will generate a fresh BPDU every 2 seconds.

- The forward delay time in the trace is 15 seconds. This means that it will take a total of 30 seconds for a blocked port to transition through listening and learning states to the forwarding state.

LISTING 13.2 A COMPLETE CONFIGURATION BPDU

```
DLC:  Destination = Multicast 0180C2000000, Bridge_Group_Addr
      DLC:  Source      = Station 0200000A40CC
      DLC:  802.3 length = 38
      DLC:
LLC:  ----- LLC Header -----
      LLC:
      LLC:  DSAP Address = 42, DSAP IG Bit = 00 (Individual Address)
      LLC:  SSAP Address = 42, SSAP CR Bit = 00 (Command)
      LLC:  Unnumbered frame: UI
      LLC:
BPDU: ----- Bridge Protocol Data Unit Header -----
      BPDU:
      BPDU: Protocol Identifier = 0000
      BPDU: Protocol Version   = 00
      BPDU:
      BPDU: BPDU Type = 00 (Configuration)
      BPDU:
      BPDU: BPDU Flags = 00
      BPDU:  0... .... = Not Topology Change Acknowledgment
      BPDU:  .... ...0 = Not Topology Change
      BPDU:  .000 000. = Unused
      BPDU:
      BPDU: Root Identifier   = 8000.0200000A402C
      BPDU:   Priority        = 8000
      BPDU:   MAC Address      = 0200000A402C
      BPDU:
      BPDU: Root Path Cost    = 0
      BPDU:
      BPDU: Sending Bridge Id = 8000.0200000A402C.8002
      BPDU:   Priority        = 8000
      BPDU:   MAC Address      = 0200000A402C
```

```
BPDU:   Port          = 8002
BPDU:   Message Age         = 0.000 seconds
BPDU:   Information Lifetime = 20.000 seconds
BPDU:   Root Hello Time     = 2.000 seconds
BPDU:   Forward Delay       = 15.000 seconds
```

Every field in the Configuration BPDU has a purpose that is clear—except for the sending port priority and the port number. In fact, this information is needed when a bridge talks to itself! If a LAN administrator has hooked up two or more ports on a bridge to the same subLAN (as is the case for bridge 4 in Figure 13.7), there is no way for the bridge automatically to be aware that both ports attach to the same subLAN. Including the sending port identifier in the BPDU reveals what is going on.

For example, bridge 4 in Figure 13.7 is connected to subLAN E via ports 1 and 2. When the bridge transmits a Configuration BPDU out one of the ports—say, port 1—the BPDU will be received by the other port. The bridge will note that it sent this BPDU and then will discover that it has two connections to subLAN E.

The Topology Change BPDU

One more type of BPDU exists. A bridge that has detected a topology change sends a *Topology Change Notification* BPDU up the tree through its root port. Each bridge that receives this type of message also transmits a Topology Change Notification BPDU through its root port. The message makes its way up the tree until a notification reaches the root.

Topology Change BPDUs are short and sweet, as Listing 13.3 illustrates. The message content consists of 5 bytes:

- The protocol identifier, X'00-00 for the STP

- The protocol version, X'00

- The BPDU type, which is Topology Change Notification (X'80)

There are no parameters in the message. The rest of the frame's data area contains 39 bytes of padding.

LISTING 13.3 A TOPOLOGY CHANGE NOTIFICATION BPDU

```
BPDU: ----- Bridge Protocol Data Unit Header -----
    BPDU:
    BPDU: Protocol Identifier = 0000
    BPDU: Protocol Version    = 00
    BPDU:
    BPDU: BPDU Type = 80 (Topology Change)
    BPDU:
DLC: Frame padding= 39 bytes
```

After a Topology Change BPDU has made its way up to the root, the root transmits Configuration BPDUs whose Topology Change Acknowledgement flag is set to 1. This flag notifies all bridges that the change has been seen. The root sends Configuration BPDUs whose Topology Change flag is set to 1 for a period of time equal to the sum of the bridge maximum age and bridge forward delay. This warns all the bridges that they should age out the dynamic entries in their filtering databases quickly, using the forwarding delay as the timeout.

Summary Points

- The IEEE 802.1D Spanning Tree Protocol (STP) was designed to automatically generate a tree-shaped LAN topology that does not contain loops and to update the topology to use backup resources if some active component fails.

- The tree will be the "best" one that can be constructed using the bridge parameters that have been established by LAN administrators.

- The first step in the STP is to choose a bridge that will act as the root of the tree.

- The tree that is formed will consist of paths that radiate out from the root and reach every bridge and every subLAN.

- A bridge identifier is made up of a priority number and the unique bridge MAC address. The root of the tree is the bridge with the smallest bridge identifier.

- The root should have a central position in a LAN, be a solid, reliable piece of equipment, have access to robust bandwidth, and be located in an area that gets plenty of support and attention.

- A port identifier is made up of a port priority and the port number.

- Every port is assigned a path cost.

- A bridge's root path cost is computed by adding port path cost numbers for ports that receive frames along the path from the root to the bridge.

- The port on a bridge that connects to its best path to the root is called the root port.

- The bridge that transmits frames coming from the direction of the root onto the subLAN is called its designated bridge.

- The single unblocked port that connects a subLAN to its designated bridge is called its designated port.

- The root bridge, root ports, root path costs, and designated ports are selected by an exchange of Configuration BPDUs.

- A bridge signals a change by sending a Topology Change BPDU up the tree toward the root.

- There are five port states: disabled, blocking, listening, learning, and forwarding.

- Each bridge is configured with hello time, forward delay, and maximum age parameters that it will advertise if and when it is the root.

References

The Spanning Tree Algorithm and Protocol are described in

- IEEE 802.1D. "Local and Metropolitan Area Networks—Common Specifications—Media Access Control (MAC) Bridges." 1998. Chapters 8 and 9.

CHAPTER **14**

Switches and Multicast Traffic

One of the core functions performed by a bridge is to protect the bandwidth available within a collision domain by blocking off traffic that is not addressed to a station in that domain. Chapter 12, "Ethernet Bridges and Layer 2 Switches," showed that bridges do a good job of channeling unicast frames to their destinations.

Controlling multicast traffic is a more difficult challenge. Multicasting was designed in the days of broadcast-style LANs, and the original assumption was that multicast frames would be visible to every station on a LAN. For today's large and geographically extended LANs, it makes no sense to glut the whole LAN with traffic to deliver a stream of multicasts to one or two stations.

The first mechanism that bridge vendors used to stem the tide was targeted at IP multicast traffic. IP systems send out *Internet Group Management Protocol* (IGMP) messages to notify IP routers that they want to join an *IP multicast group*—that is, that they want to receive IP traffic sent to a particular IP multicast address.

The mechanism that was introduced is called *IGMP snooping*. Bridges eavesdrop on IGMP messages to discover which subLANs contain users that have joined IP multicast groups. IP multicast traffic is delivered across a LAN in frames with multicast destination MAC addresses.

IGMP snooping has some shortcomings. To mention a couple, it imposes a big overhead burden on bridges, and it works only for IP traffic. A better solution was defined by an IEEE 802.1 working group. This group created a Layer 2 protocol that enables a system to register with neighboring bridges. The system asks the bridges to be sure to send it frames that have particular destination multicast MAC addresses.

Registration information is propagated from bridge to bridge across a LAN, and every bridge becomes aware of the ports through which it needs to forward frames addressed to a specific multicast address.

This solution is called the *GARP Multicast Registration Protocol* (GMRP). GMRP provides pinpoint control, enabling bridges to carry multicasts exactly where they need to go. Vendors have welcomed this solution and have been quick to implement it.

> **Note**
>
> GARP stands for the Generic Attribute Registration Protocol. This protocol provides a general registration mechanism for use in a bridged LAN. GMRP was the first protocol that was built on top of GARP.

Both IGMP snooping and GMRP are described in this chapter.

Multicasting

Multicast MAC addresses enable a single frame to be addressed to a group of stations. A multicast address also is called a *group address*, and stations that have been configured to receive traffic addressed to a particular group address are said to be members of a multicast group.

Multicast MAC addresses are used in two ways:

- Standard multicast MAC addresses have been assigned to specific types of devices and or network roles. For example, a multicast sent to destination MAC address X′01-00-5E-00-00-02 is directed to every multicast-capable router on a LAN.

- A pool of addresses is reserved for ad hoc multicast groups. These addresses are used for applications such as conferences, distance learning, or entertainment. An address can be checked out of the pool and used for a limited amount of time.

> **Note**
>
> It is perfectly legitimate for a station that does not belong to a multicast group to send data to a multicast group. In this case, the sender does not accept any frames transmitted to the group address. Think of a lecturer addressing a large group of attendees at a convention—with no questions from the audience allowed! The members of the audience are receivers, but the lecturer is not a receiver.

A network device such as a bridge or router is shipped from the factory with its adapter ready to receive frames sent to standard, device-specific multicast addresses.

Joining an ad hoc multicast is like picking a cable TV channel. The user picks a multicast group, and the user's application software notifies the device driver to join the group.

The Need to Control Multicasts

A LAN multicast adds no special load to a small, broadcast-style LAN. For example, the hub in Figure 14.1 repeats all frames—unicast and multicast—onto every segment. Every station automatically sees every frame. The NIC in a system that has joined a multicast group absorbs frames sent to the multicast group address in addition to those sent to its unicast address. Stations that are not group members simply ignore the multicast frames.

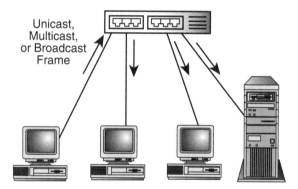

Unicast,
Multicast,
or Broadcast
Frame

FIGURE 14.1 *A hub repeating all frames.*

As LANs have gotten larger, it has become desirable to prevent group frames from chewing up the bandwidth in subLANs that neither contain group members nor are on the path to a subLAN that holds members.

For example, in Figure 14.2, a group of users at site 1 is planning to hold a local electronic conference. All the participants are connected to subLAN A.

There is no reason to forward the group's multicast frames onto subLANs B, C, and D. In fact, sending these frames across the wide area bridge that connects site 1 to remote site 2 would needlessly use up a lot of valuable bandwidth.

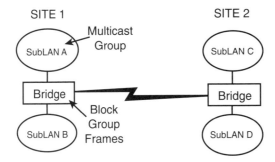

Figure 14.2 *Constraining the scope of multicast frames.*

The need to limit the scope of multicasts has become even more urgent with the growing popularity of connecting LAN stations directly to switch ports. The benefit of a switched LAN is precisely that everybody does *not* have to see all the traffic, enabling multiple independent streams of traffic to flow through the switch. Conventional multicasting, however, requires the frames to be delivered through *every* port in the LAN, even if only one station needs to see the traffic.

Queuing multicast frames to every port can clog up a LAN switch and slow switch performance. Clearly, it is desirable to learn which ports lead to stations that have joined a multicast group, and then forward the frames addressed to that group only through those ports.

You could try to control the forwarding of frames sent to standard, role-based group addresses by manual configuration. However, this will not work very well if your network is growing or changing. In any case, it is not feasible to maintain manual entries for multicast conferences that an organization sets up on an ad hoc basis.

IGMP snooping, which can be used to control IP multicast traffic, was the first mechanism that was developed to control multicasts. It is described in the sections that follow.

The GARP Multicast Registration Protocol (GMRP) is a more effective and reliable method that applies to all multicast traffic, not just IP-based multicasts. GMRP is described later in the section called "The GARP Multicast Registration Protocol." GARP is described in the section, "Generic Attribute Registration Protocol."

IP Multicasts

The TCP/IP protocol suite includes mechanisms that make it possible to set up multicast conferences. IP is a protocol that has broad scope. An IP destination can be far away in a location that is reached by passing through many routers.

The scope of an IP multicast can be one of the following:

- A single LAN

- A private network that includes many LANs

- A group of participants connected by the Internet

A class of IP addresses has been set aside for use as multicast IP addresses. Systems that want to receive traffic sent to a particular multicast IP address form an *IP multicast group*.

Mapping IP Multicast Addresses to Ethernet Multicast Addresses

An IP datagram sent to a multicast IP address must be forwarded onto every LAN that contains an IP multicast group member. When an IP datagram with a 4-byte IP multicast address arrives at a router, the router must stick a 6-byte MAC frame header on the datagram to transmit it onto a LAN. What MAC address should it use?

For Ethernet LANs, there is a simple rule that maps a multicast IP address into a multicast MAC address in a very elegant manner. Figure 14.3 shows the Ethernet MAC address for an IP datagram whose destination is a multicast IP address. The first 3 bytes of the MAC address always are X'01-00-5E.

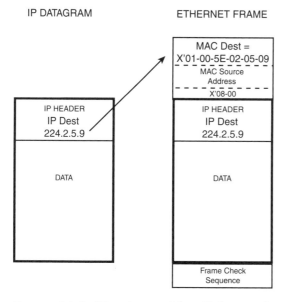

FIGURE 14.3 *Wrapping a multicast IP datagram in an Ethernet frame.*

The last three (decimal) numbers of the multicast IP address are 2.5.9. These translate into hex as X'02-05-09, which is the value in the last 3 bytes of the mapped MAC address shown on the right.

> **Note**
>
> Actually, the first 25 bits of the MAC address always are X'01-00-5E, followed by a 0 bit. The last 23 bits of the multicast IP address get copied into the last 23 bits of the MAC address.
>
> IP multicast addresses start with a number in the range 224–239 and are called Class D addresses.

Mapping IP Multicast Addresses to FDDI Multicast Addresses

The same mapping as shown in Figure 14.3 is done for FDDI, but the address probably will appear in a monitor trace in non-canonical order, which reverses the bits in each byte. (See Chapter 2, "LAN MAC Addresses," for more on non-canonical order.) For FDDI, the address X'01-00-5E-02-05-09 that appeared in Figure 14.3 would look like X'80-00-7A-40-A0-90.

Token Ring and Multicast Addresses

Unfortunately, there is no mapping for Token Ring, which has very limited support for multicasts. All multicast datagrams are placed in frames with functional (reversed-byte) address X'C0-00-00-04-00-00 or, even worse, in frames with broadcast MAC address. A Token Ring station that wants to participate in an IP multicast group must absorb, examine, and discard traffic that has been sent to other multicast groups.

IGMP Snooping

IGMP defines the procedures that enable an IP end system to notify routers on its LAN that it wants to join or leave a particular IP multicast group.

1. A router periodically sends an IGMP query asking whether stations want to join (or continue to be part of) a multicast group.

2. A host that wants to join a group or renew its group membership responds with an IGMP membership report. Membership reports are addressed to the multicast address of the group being joined or renewed.

3. A router listens for these reports and uses them to determine whether at least one station on the LAN wants to receive traffic sent to that multicast address.

Many switch products enable the switch administrator to turn on IGMP snooping, which causes the switch to eavesdrop on these messages. The switch then makes entries in the filtering table, which channels frames addressed to a group to the ports that lead to group members.

Specifically, a port is added to the output list of a filtering table entry for a multicast address if at least one participant is reached via that port.

Figure 14.4 shows the effect of IGMP snooping. The multicast group members in the figure include stations A, B, and C. Station A has sent a frame to the multicast group.

1. By snooping, switch X has discovered that ports 1 and 4 are the only ones that lead to multicast members. Because the frame arrives on port 1, switch X forwards the frame only through port 4. Table 14.1 shows the filtering table entry at switch X.

2. Switch Y has discovered that ports 1, 3, and 5 are the only ones that lead to multicast members. Because the frame arrives on port 1, switch Y forwards the frame only through ports 3 and 5.

3. Switch Z has discovered that ports 1 and 4 are the only ones that lead to multicast members. Because the frame arrives on port 1, switch Y forwards the frame only through port 4.

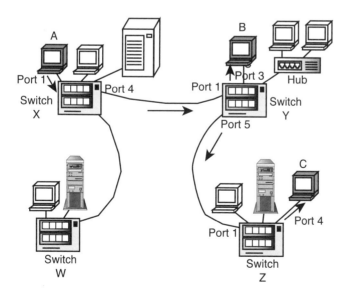

FIGURE 14.4 *Using IGMP snooping to cut out unnecessary multicast traffic.*

TABLE 14.1 ENTRY AT SWITCH X LEARNED VIA IGMP SNOOPING

Destination Address Status	Protocol Comment	Receive Port		Transmit Ports
01-00-5E-02-05-09 Multicast	IP	Any	1, 4	Learned

Figure 14.5 shows the protocol components that are used for IGMP snooping.

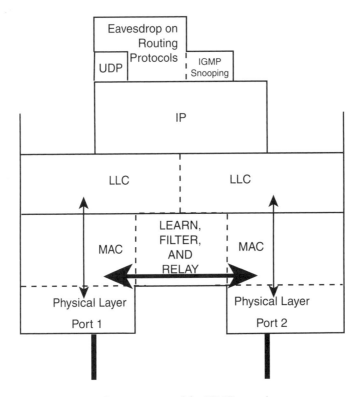

FIGURE 14.5 *Components used for IGMP snooping.*

Problems with IGMP Snooping

A switch that locates multicast recipients via IGMP snooping takes on some CPU-intensive work. Membership reports are sent to the address of the group that the system wants to join. Thus, the switch must examine *every* multicast frame and check whether it contains an IP datagram. If so, the switch must examine the IP header to find out whether the datagram contains an IGMP membership report message.

When a datagram contains a membership report, the switch must create or update a filtering table entry for the multicast address and then make sure that the port on which the frame arrived is included in the list of output ports.

A switch also should forward each multicast frame transmitted by a router to other routers on the LAN that lead to multicast recipients. For example, in Figure 14.6, the stations shown in black belong to the multicast group for address M, and

- Router 1 transmits a frame with destination multicast address M onto the LAN that is surrounded by a dotted line.

- The frame must be forwarded to the member stations attached to switch A and switch B.

- The frame also must be forwarded to router 3, which is attached to a different LAN containing a group member.

To identify which routers lead to recipients, a switch must eavesdrop on router-to-router protocol messages. Unfortunately, lots of different router-to-router protocols are used to exchange this information (including DVMRP, Dense Mode PIM, Sparse Mode PIM, and MOSPF). This starts to get complicated!

> **Note**
> DVMRP stands for Distance Vector Multicast Routing Protocol. PIM stands for Protocol Independent Multicast, and MOSPF stands for Multicast Extensions to Open Shortest Path First.

In addition to being compute-intensive, IGMP snooping has other drawbacks. It does not provide an easy way to identify routers that need to receive frames sent to a particular multicast address. It provides no method for identifying network monitors that want to receive multicast frames for the purpose of troubleshooting. Furthermore, it works only for IP multicasts.

The GARP Multicast Registration Protocol (GMRP)

The *GARP* (Generic Attribute Registration Protocol) *Multicast Registration Protocol* (GMRP) is a general Layer 2 standard that does not have the problems associated with IGMP snooping. It works efficiently and can support multicasts on behalf of any protocol, not just IP. GMRP is described in the 802.1D bridge protocol standard.

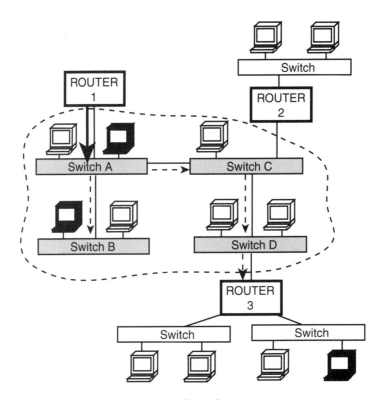

FIGURE 14.6 *Forwarding a multicast frame.*

A system that wants to receive traffic sent to a particular multicast group uses GMRP to register with adjacent switches. GMRP lets hosts, switches, routers, and network monitors actively request the traffic that they want. When GMRP has been implemented, a switch will not forward multicast frames through a port that does not lead to registered recipients.

GMRP makes it possible to channel the transmission of frames addressed to a multicast group onto those subLANs that contain or lie on a path to the systems that need to receive the frames.

Note

The disadvantage of GMRP is that interfaces in all systems that will participate in multicasts must be updated to versions that support GMRP. In contrast, IGMP snooping needs to be supported only in network switches.

Switch performance could be protected by using ASICs to handle the extra processing burden.

GMRP Procedures

A system uses GMRP to register its wish to receive multicast traffic. The system can ask to receive the following:

- Multicast frames addressed to a list of specific multicast MAC address.

- All multicast frames (as long as there is no manual entry preventing some of this traffic from being forwarded). This service is called "all groups" and is likely to be requested by a router or a network monitor.

- All multicast frames for which there are no other filtering table entries that specify whether they should be forwarded. This is called the "all unregistered groups" service.

Figure 14.7 illustrates what happens when an end system registers to receive frames sent to multicast address M. As illustrated in the figure, adjacent switch A adds an entry to its filtering database indicating that frames to address M must be propagated through port 1, which leads to the end system.

Switch A then sends registration messages out its other active ports, indicating that it needs to receive multicasts sent to M. The information propagates across the LAN to all the other switches. Each switch forwards frames addressed to M through the port at which the registration message arrives.

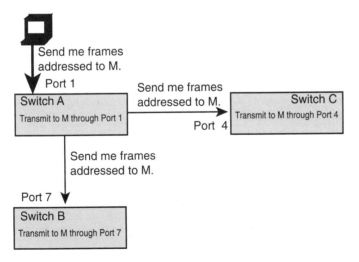

FIGURE 14.7 *Propagating GMRP registration requests.*

A system also uses GMRP messages to announce that it wants to cancel registrations.

> **Note**
> The active ports on a switch are those that have not been blocked by the Spanning Tree Protocol. The fact that the topology is a tree ensures that registration and deregistration messages will not cycle back to the originating switch.

Generic Attribute Registration Protocol

GMRP is one specific application of a more general protocol: the Generic Attribute Registration Protocol (GARP). GARP provides mechanisms that enable a station to register a piece of information with LAN systems that propagate that information through the LAN.

The creators of GARP had multicast registration in the back of their minds as the first way that GARP would be applied. They made GARP general so that it could be used to register other types of requests.

> **Note**
> The GARP VLAN Registration Protocol (GVRP) is a related member of the GARP family. GVRP enables stations to join and leave VLANs.

Like other GARP-based protocols, GMRP is a Layer 2 protocol and can be implemented in NIC drivers. For example, when a system joins a multicast via IGMP, the NIC driver could automatically send a GMRP registration message to adjacent switches. No snooping would be required.

Up-to-date NICs support GMRP. It might be possible to upgrade an older NIC to perform GMRP by means of a device driver software update, if the vendor has made this software available.

The discussion that follows provides a rough idea of how the protocol works. For details, see 802.1D.

- A system that is directly connected to a switch registers for a group by sending two *join* messages.

- A system must refresh its membership by sending fresh joins periodically.

- The station quits by sending a *leave* message.

- If the leave message is lost, the switch will think that the station still wishes to participate. To correct this situation, after an extended period the switch sends a *leaveall* message, announcing that if it does not receive fresh joins soon, it will terminate all registrations on the port.

Figure 14.8 illustrates the procedure.

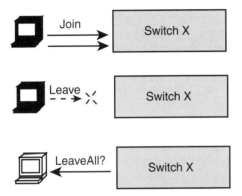

FIGURE 14.8 *Registering and deregistering across a single-station link.*

Figure 14.9 illustrates what happens when multiple stations connect to a switch via a single switch port. Stations A, C, and D want to receive multicasts sent to group M. A hub connects them to a switch port.

- If station A has sent two join messages, there is no need for the others to do so. The hub will send identical multicast frames to all of them.

- If station A decides to quit and sends a leave message, other stations send joins to keep the flow of messages coming.

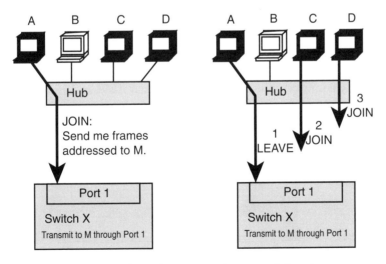

FIGURE 14.9 *Multiple stations connected to one switch port.*

Note

The GARP protocol is designed so that only a couple of joins will be sent even if two or more stations concurrently decide that they need to send joins. The reason for this is that each station delays for a random time before sending a join, which spreads out the transmission times. Because all stations hear the joins as they are sent, no more are needed when two of them have been heard. All stations then can become quiet.

GMRP/GARP Encapsulation and Format

Frames containing GMRP messages (which also are called GMRP protocol data units, or GMRP PDUs) are sent to multicast address X'01-80-C2-00-00-20 and are absorbed by any adjacent bridge port that supports GMRP. A receiver knows that a GARP message contains GMRP information because the message is contained in a frame addressed to the special GMRP multicast MAC address.

GMRP messages are simply GARP messages that carry GMRP attributes. GARP messages are encapsulated in the same way as bridge protocol data units (BPDUs). That is, they are wrapped in frames that contain a 3-byte Logical Link Control (LLC) header with the following:

> DSAP=X'42
>
> SSAP=X'42
>
> Control field = X'03 (unnumbered information)

Figure 14.10 displays the format of a GARP message. A GARP message starts with a 2-byte protocol identifier field equal to X'00-01. This is followed by one or more message blocks. The message closes with a 1-byte end mark equal to X'00.

Each message block consists of an attribute type code, a list containing one or more (event, value) pairs, and an end mark. Separate codes are included for "join" and "leave" events. A value can be either of the following:

- **Group**—The values are MAC multicast addresses.

- **Service requirement**—The value is an ID code that corresponds to either "all groups" or "all unregistered groups."

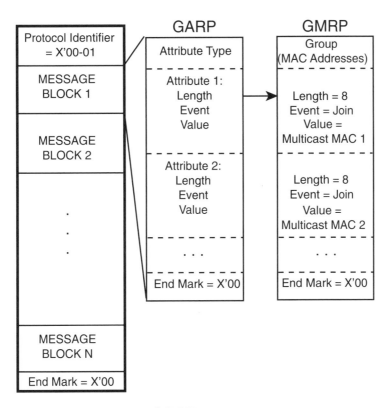

FIGURE 14.10 *GARP and GMRP messages.*

Figure 14.11 shows the protocol-layer components that support GARP and GMRP. GMRP is simpler and more accurate than IGMP snooping and was designed to operate entirely at Layer 2. GMRP also was custom-designed to do the job of optimizing the flow of multicast frames through a LAN.

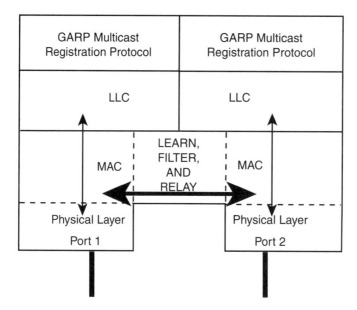

FIGURE 14.11   *Components used for GARP and GMRP.*

Summary Points

- It is a good idea to protect the bandwidth available within a collision domain by blocking off multicast traffic that is not addressed to a station in that domain.

- It is more difficult to block off multicast traffic than to block off unicast traffic.

- IP multicast addresses are mapped into Ethernet or FDDI MAC addresses. The first 25 bits of the MAC address hold a fixed-bit pattern. The last 23 bits of the MAC address are copied from the last 23 bits of the multicast IP address.

- IGMP snooping is one method used to discover which parts of a LAN need to receive multicasts sent to a particular group.

- To perform IGMP snooping, bridges eavesdrop on the IGMP messages that stations use to join and leave multicast groups.

- IGMP snooping is CPU-intensive. It requires a Layer 2 switch to examine the contents of a lot of Layer 3 traffic.

- The GARP Multicast Registration Protocol (GMRP) is a Layer 2 protocol that enables stations to register with bridges and identify the multicast traffic that they want to receive.

- GMRP is built on top of a more general Layer 2 protocol called the Generic Attribute Registration Protocol (GARP).

- GARP provides mechanisms that enable a station to register a piece of information with other LAN systems and then propagate that information through the LAN.

References

GMRP and GARP are described in:

- IEEE 802.1D. "Local and Metropolitan Area Networks—Common Specifications—Media Access Control (MAC) Bridges." 1998. Chapters 10–13.

The router-to-router messages that track the locations of multicast recipients are described in the IETF Request for Comments (RFC) documents that follow:

- **RFC 1075**—Waitzman, D., C. Partridge, and S.E. Deering. "Distance Vector Multicast Routing Protocol." RFC 1075, 1988.

- **RFC 1585**—Moy, J. "MOSPF: Analysis and Experience." RFC 1585, 1994.

- **RFC 2117**—Estrin, D., D. Farinacci, A. Helmy, D. Thaler, S. Deering, M. Handley, V. Jacobson, C. Liu, P. Sharma, and L. Wei. "Protocol Independent Multicast-Sparse Mode (PIM-SM): Protocol Specification." RFC 2117, 1997.

- **RFC 2337**—Farinacci, D., D. Meyer, and Y. Rekhter. "Intra-LIS IP Multicast Among Routers over ATM Using Sparse Mode PIM." RFC 2337, 1998.

- **RFC 2362**—Estrin, D., D. Farinacci, A. Helmy, D. Thaler, S. Deering, M. Handley, V. Jacobson, C. Liu, P. Sharma, and L. Wei. "Protocol Independent Multicast-Sparse Mode (PIM-SM): Protocol Specification." RFC 2362, 1998.

Several draft documents that will update the RFCs listed here are in progress.

CHAPTER 15

Link Aggregation

Link aggregation, sometimes called *trunking*, combines a set of links so that they behave like a single link. A combined set of links is called an *aggregated link*, a *virtual link*, or a *trunk*. A port that participates in link aggregation is called an *aggregation port*.

The capability to aggregate links affords important benefits:

- A high-capacity link can be set up between a pair of systems by combining a group of links.

- The procedure improves network availability. The failure of one underlying link in a group of links causes a reduction in available bandwidth, but the aggregated link continues to function.

In the past, it was common to install extra LAN links for backup purposes. A backup link would be idle unless its primary link failed. This meant that an organization had to invest in bandwidth that was used only in emergencies. Today, one or more backup links can be aggregated with a primary link, and the extra bandwidth can be used all the time.

Because link aggregation is a very useful capability, several vendors have created proprietary aggregation solutions over the past few years. These solutions have been based on vendor-defined protocol message exchanges. This meant that aggregation would work only between systems obtained from the same vendor.

In 1998, the IEEE 802.3ad Link Aggregation Task Force was formed to define a standard procedure for the Ethernet environment. Many vendors have pledged support for the emerging 802.3ad Ethernet link aggregation standard.

Note

At the time of this writing, the 802.3ad standard had not been finalized. The material in this chapter was included because link aggregation is an important function and because the protocol mechanisms that are used appear to be stable. Some product testing already has started.

A multivendor link aggregation standard is a useful addition to the Ethernet protocol family. It provides users with scalable bandwidth and good availability options.

Because the protocol functions can be performed at the device driver level, the protocol can be made available quickly in new drivers, or by updating some existing drivers.

Although Ethernet is the focus of attention for 802.3ad, link aggregation has been introduced into other parts of the network. Some vendors have implemented proprietary link aggregation for FDDI links. In addition, the IETF has defined an aggregation method for point-to-point WAN links called the *PPP multilink protocol*.

Note

The PPP multilink protocol is described in RFC 1990.

Using Link Aggregation

Figure 15.1 shows an example of how aggregated links are used to prevent network bottlenecks. At the top, a pair of full-duplex 1Gbps links between large switches has been aggregated into a virtual full-duplex 2Gbps link. On the right, four full-duplex 100Mbps links leading to a server farm have been aggregated into a virtual full-duplex 400Mbps link. On the left, two 100Mbps full-duplex links leading to a community of 10Mbps workstations have been aggregated.

Link Aggregation Features

Link aggregation can group together a set of full-duplex Ethernet links connecting systems such as:

- A pair of Layer 2 switches

- A Layer 2 switch and a server

- A pair of servers

- A Layer 2 switch and a router

- A pair of routers

The links share the traffic load that is sent between the systems.

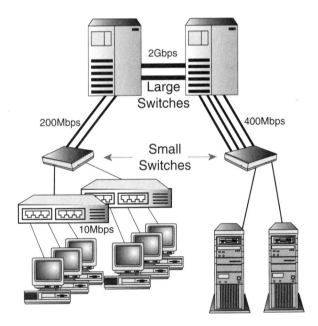

FIGURE 15.1 *Aggregated links.*

Note

All the links in an aggregated group are required to operate at the same speed.

A crucial feature of the protocol is that it combines links between any pair of systems that are capable of using the negotiation procedure defined by the link aggregation standard:

- When an administrator has enabled aggregation, the protocol automatically groups duplicate links to a common destination into one or more virtual links.

- If links are added or removed, or if they fail, the protocol will regroup the links automatically.

An administrator optionally can control and guide link aggregation through manual configuration choices.

Link aggregation is backward compatible. If an older system that does not support the protocol is connected to a newer system that does, the negotiation procedure simply will fail and links will not be aggregated.

For some types of traffic, it is important to deliver frames in the same order in which they were transmitted. The link aggregation protocol includes a simple mechanism that assures that selected streams of frames will be delivered in the same order in which they were sent.

The sections that follow describe link aggregation concepts. Although links between many types of systems can be aggregated, to keep the discussion concrete, this chapter focuses mainly on aggregating links that connect switches. Link aggregation operates in exactly the same way for other systems.

Link Aggregation Concepts and Procedures

Figure 15.2 shows some of the components of the environment in which virtual links exist. The figure shows switches that consist of a chassis, a CPU module, and a set of slots for *line cards*. A line card is an input/output (I/O) card that can be installed in a chassis.

A customer obtains a set of interface ports that support a particular communications technology by installing the appropriate type of line card—for example, Ethernet, Token Ring, FDDI, ATM, or T1. A line card typically provides several communications ports and contains an application specific integrated circuit (ASIC) chip that processes the type of traffic that the line card supports.

The chassis on the left includes a 1Gbps Ethernet line card, a Token Ring line card, two 100Mbps Ethernet line cards, and some other line cards. The separate links that make up a virtual link are called *link segments*. Each link segment must be a full-duplex link.

In the figure, four links on a 100Mbps Ethernet line card on the left connect to a line card at the second switch. Link aggregation has been enabled on the 100Mbps line cards, so the four link segments will be aggregated into a single virtual link.

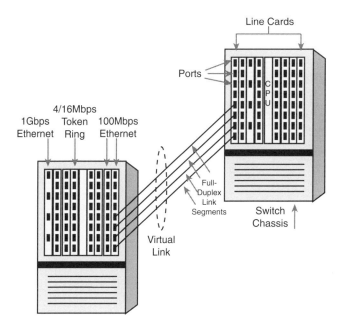

FIGURE 15.2 *Aggregated link environment.*

The maximum number of link segments (or equivalently, the number of ports) on a device that can be aggregated depends on how a vendor has implemented the device, and this differs for each product. For many devices, traffic is processed by an on-card ASIC, and all the ports that are aggregated must be on the same card. Some products allow ports on adjacent line cards to be aggregated. Others limit the total number of ports to some value (for example, 4) and require that they be physically adjacent on a line card.

The restrictions are product-specific. Based on competitive pressure, a vendor might modify a product's architecture to remove some aggregation restrictions to make the product more attractive to customers.

Virtual Link MAC Address

A virtual link must behave just like a real link. This means that a virtual link in an end system (such as a server) must have its own MAC address. User frames sent from the server onto a virtual link carry the MAC address in their source MAC address field. User frames sent to the server across a virtual link contain the MAC address in their destination MAC address field.

Some implementations automatically use the smallest MAC address of the aggregation ports participating in the virtual link as the virtual link's MAC address. Others allow an administrator to configure a MAC address.

Figure 15.3 illustrates the relationship between a virtual MAC and its underlying real links. Frames carrying traffic passed down from higher layers include the virtual MAC address in each frame's source address field.

However, low-level protocol messages are used to set up and maintain the virtual link. These messages are exchanged across each of the underlying link segments. The source address in one of these frames is the real MAC address of the port from which it was sent. These protocol messages are studied later in this chapter, in the section "The Link Aggregation Control Protocol."

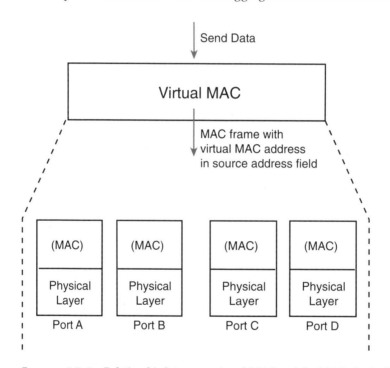

FIGURE 15.3 *Relationship between a virtual MAC and the MACs for its link segments.*

A MAC address also is needed for a virtual link in a switch. The reason for this is that there are some messages that will be originated and received by the switch. For example, SNMP messages, BPDUs, and GMRP messages that are sent and received across a virtual link need well-defined and consistent source and destination MAC addresses.

Link Aggregation Sublayer Structure

Link aggregation adds yet another optional sublayer to the data link layer, as shown in Figure 15.4. The link aggregation sublayer schedules outgoing user frames that have been passed to the virtual MAC onto the real links. In the figure, frames are distributed across four real links. The sublayer also collects and orders incoming user frames for delivery to higher layers.

The link aggregation sublayer is responsible for controlling the aggregation process. It decides which links it should attempt to aggregate, based on configuration information in the local system. The sublayer then carries out a separate negotiation across each real link by sending, receiving, and processing *link aggregation control protocol* (LACP) messages.

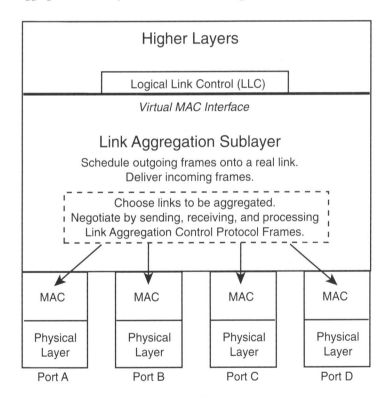

FIGURE 15.4 *Link aggregation architecture.*

What a System Needs to Know

Links connected to switch A in Figure 15.5 are candidates for aggregation. Switch A is connected to switch B by four links and to switch C by two links.

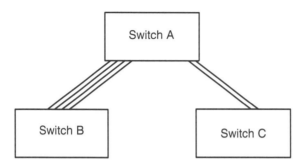

FIGURE 15.5 *Switches capable of aggregation.*

An administrator could configure every switch manually and describe exactly how links should be combined. However, it is better to have a protocol that can do the job automatically. Note that even if an administrator wants to control the configuration, an automatic protocol still is needed to handle changes to the topology caused by line failure and recovery. Automation also is needed to handle cabling changes and the addition of new switches.

In order to aggregate the lines between switch A and switch B in Figure 15.5:

- Switch A must be configured in a way that permits it to aggregate the four links shown on the left.

- Switch A must check that no structural rules will be broken by aggregating these links. (For example, there might be a requirement that links must belong to the same line card and must be adjacent.)

- Switch A must check which of these links are active and determine whether they all connect to the same device (switch B, in this case).

- Switch A must learn whether switch B is willing and able to aggregate these links.

The link aggregation control protocol enables a system to gather information that it needs by exchanging messages with its neighbors across each link segment. After links have been aggregated, the status of each link segment is monitored by means of periodic message exchanges.

Link Aggregation Parameters

Most of the parameters used in link aggregation messages were borrowed from the Spanning Tree Protocol. Recall that a Spanning Tree bridge system identifier consists of the following components:

- A 2-byte priority number.

- A unique MAC address assigned to the system. The system's smallest MAC address normally is used.

Systems other than bridges (for example, routers or servers) that need to aggregate links can be assigned unique system identifiers in exactly the same way.

Similarly, the ports of any participating system can be assigned identifiers with the same structure as the Spanning Tree Protocol port identifiers. That is, a system port ID consists of the following components:

- A port priority value

- The port number

One additional number called a *key* must be assigned to each port. Ports with the same key value have the potential to be aggregated. Ports with the same key are said to belong to a *key group*.

Assigning a set of local ports to a key group does not guarantee that all of them actually can be aggregated successfully. The protocol must comply with these points:

- Apply device-specific rules to determine which of the ports can be aggregated. For example, there might be a limit on the number of ports that can be aggregated, or a requirement that the ports be adjacent.

- Determine whether all the ports in a key group really connect to the same remote system.

- Check which of the remote ports also belong to a common key group.

Protocol messages carry flag parameters that show whether a port can be added to a particular group, and whether it already has been added to the aggregation group.

> **Note**
>
> A lazy administrator could simply assign all ports to the same key group. The protocol will find out what can be aggregated and then will go ahead and group all links that it possibly can. As the protocol discovers groups that can be aggregated, it assigns its own operational keys to them.

The Link Aggregation Control Protocol

This section outlines the major features of the protocol structure. Virtual links are created, monitored, and updated by means of an exchange of protocol messages.

Link aggregation protocol messages are exchanged across each link segment. They belong to real links rather than virtual links. The source address in each of the frames is the source MAC address of the real port from which it was sent.

Slow Protocols

Link aggregation belongs to a family called *slow protocols*. The characteristics of an Ethernet slow protocol are listed here:

- No more than five frames are transmitted in any 1-second period.

- Protocol messages are carried in frames addressed to a special multicast address assigned to the slow protocols. The slow protocols multicast address is X'01-80-C2-00-00-02.

- The EtherType field contains a value assigned to slow protocols. The EtherType value is X'88-09.

The first byte of the information field in a slow protocol frame contains a code that identifies the subtype of slow protocol PDU that follows.

Link Aggregation Control Protocol Messages

Aggregation information is carried in *Link Aggregation Control* PDU (LACPDU) messages, whose subtype value is X'01.

LACP message parameters include

- Local system identifier (priority and system MAC)

- Local port identifier (priority and port number)

- Key assigned to the port

- Local state flags

- Partner system identifier (when it is known)

- Partner port identifier (when it is known)

- Partner key assigned to the port

- Partner state flags

- Timer information

Figure 15.6 illustrates how this information can be used to aggregate links between a pair of switches.

1. At the top of the figure, switch 1 learns that six ports in key group 1 lead to neighbor switch 2.

2. However, at switch 2, the six ports have been configured into two separate key groups. This is because switch 2 is incapable of aggregating more than four ports into a group.

3. Switch 1 and switch 2 agree to aggregate the first four ports.

4. Switch 1 automatically assigns a new key value to the remaining two ports, creating a new key group. After a fresh exchange of messages, these two link segments are aggregated and used as a backup link.

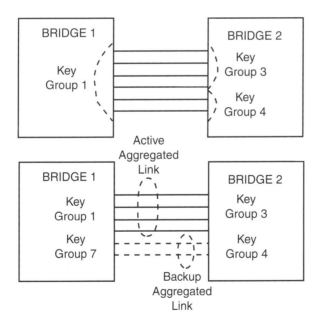

FIGURE 15.6 *Aggregating links between bridges.*

Ongoing protocol messages update the configuration, adding or removing link segments from an aggregated link.

Frame Distribution and Conversations

When a flow of frames is split across multiple link segments, some might arrive out of order. Sometimes being out of order matters—for example, for frames belonging to IBM SNA sessions. In other cases, order does not matter at all. For example, delivering IP data out of order does not cause a problem. The trick is to preserve order when it matters.

A flow of frames that must be delivered without changing their order is called a *conversation*. The frames within a given conversation are delivered in order by the simple expedient of sending the frames through the same port, across the same link segment. The receiver must then be sure to deliver frames that were received by a given port in the order in which they arrived. (However, when these frames are delivered, they can be interleaved with frames received from other ports.)

As shown in Figure 15.7, a link segment can carry several conversations. For example, frames for conversations C2, C6, and C7 have been assigned to the top link segment; C3, C5, and C8 are sent across the middle link segment; and frames for conversations C1 and C4 are sent across the bottom link segment.

Other traffic that does not belong to any conversation can be spread across the three links using any algorithm the vendor wants to apply.

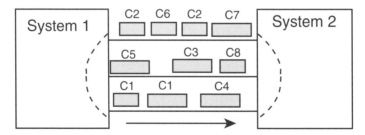

FIGURE 15.7 *Conversations assigned to link segments.*

Many different parameters can be used to define a conversation subflow, including combinations of any the following parameters:

- Source MAC address
- Destination MAC address

- The reception physical port number

- The type of destination MAC address (individual, multicast, or broadcast)

- The type of higher-layer protocol data that is carried in the frame (such as SNA)

- Higher-layer protocol information (such as a destination IP or IPX network identifier)

Switching a Conversation to a Different Link Segment

A critical part of the protocol is the capability to switch a conversation from one link segment to another. This is vital because a conversation's assigned segment might fail, or conversations might need to be redistributed to improve the load balance.

The procedure used to carry out a transition first "flushes" the old link and then switches over. The steps are listed here:

1. Choose a new link segment to be used for the conversation.

2. Stop transmitting frames for the conversation. Discard submitted frames that belong to the conversation until the changeover procedure is complete.

3. Start a timer that lasts long enough to allow all frames belonging to the conversation that already have been transmitted to arrive.

4. If the link segment previously assigned to the conversation still is functioning, send a special marker protocol message through its port. This marker tells the partner that no more frames for the conversation will arrive on this link segment.

5. Wait until either a marker response protocol message is received or the timer expires. The arrival of a marker response speeds up the changeover. When a response has been received, there is no need to wait any longer.

6. Resume frame transmission for the conversation on the new link segment. The recipient will know that a conversation has been switched successfully when it receives a frame with the conversation's defining characteristics at a different port.

Note that there is a cost to a switchover: A few frames might be discarded in Step 2.

Marker and marker response protocol messages have slow protocol subtype X'02. They include fields identifying the originating system and port as well as a transaction ID.

Summary Points

- Link aggregation, which also is called trunking, combines a set of links so that they behave like a single link, which is called a virtual link.

- Link aggregation improves network capacity and availability.

- The link aggregation standard applies only to full-duplex Ethernet links.

- All links in an aggregated group must operate at the same speed.

- The link aggregation control protocol automatically groups links and regroups them after a link addition, deletion, or failure.

- Product-specific restrictions sometimes govern the way that link segments can be aggregated.

- A virtual link must have a MAC address. Some implementations automatically use the smallest MAC address assigned to an aggregation port participating in the virtual link.

- The link aggregation sublayer is responsible for controlling and executing the aggregation process. It decides which links it should attempt to aggregate based on configuration information in the local system.

- A key value is assigned to each port. Ports that have the same key value have the potential to be aggregated.

- Frames that must be delivered in order are assigned to a conversation. All the frames for a particular conversation are transmitted through the same port. The receiver then must deliver them in the order in which they arrived.

- Conversations are defined using parameters such as source or destination MAC address or type of protocol data being carried.

References

Link aggregation is described in

- IEEE 802.3ad. "Aggregation of Multiple Link Segments." 2000.

The IETF has defined a wide area link aggregation protocol in

- Sklower, K., B. Lloyd, G. McGregor, D. Carr, and T. Coradetti. "The PPP Multilink Protocol (MP)." RFC 1990, 1996.

CHAPTER 16

VLANs and Frame Priority

The introduction of efficient bridges (Layer 2 switches) has made it easy to build very large LANs. There are some advantages to letting a LAN grow very large instead of cutting it into separate smaller LANs that are separated by routers:

- Fewer routers are needed. High-capacity routers are more costly than bridges.

- Many administrators feel that routers are more complicated to configure than bridges.

- Bridges forward traffic faster than routers (although current Layer 3 switches—which are routers—are fairly fast).

> **Note**
>
> Keep in mind that by definition, a LAN contains only hubs (Layer 1 wiring concentrators) and bridges (Layer 2 switches). When you go through a router, you have left a LAN.

Building a big physical LAN can pay off in terms of performance gains and equipment savings. With the help of translational switches (which are discussed in Chapter 17, "Source-Routing, Translational, and Wide Area Bridges"), a big LAN can be constructed using a combination of Ethernet, Token Ring, FDDI, and ATM technologies.

Big LANs also cause some problems. In the past, most LAN traffic was local. Traffic could be isolated within small collision domains that were bridged to the rest of the LAN. For example, a bridge could prevent traffic between IPX stations and a local IPX server from leaving its collision domain.

Today the capability to isolate traffic using conventional switches is eroding. Users access far-away servers or belong to project teams whose members are located far apart. Relatively little traffic can be bottled up within a local collision domain.

Furthermore, collision domains are shrinking and gradually disappearing. They are being replaced by individual, full-duplex connections between computers and Layer 2 switches. The methods (described in Chapter 12, "Ethernet Bridges and Layer 2 Switches") used to keep traffic isolated within a collision domain are less relevant and are incapable of controlling much of the traffic on a big modern switched LAN.

Broadcasts are an especially thorny problem. Every higher-layer protocol causes stations to initiate a spattering of broadcasts. When there are hundreds of stations on a LAN, this adds up to a substantial traffic burden. Each broadcast is sent through every port on the LAN, delaying other traffic.

Flooding of ordinary unicast frames is another source of traffic that spreads across a LAN. Recall that if a frame's destination MAC address is not in a switch filtering table, the switch transmits the frame through every port except for the one on which the frame arrived. Except for manually entered MAC addresses, the MAC address of any system that is quiet for a while is removed from all LAN filtering tables.

Security is another issue that concerns some LAN administrators. Some sensitive LAN traffic should not be flooded to all ports on a switch. However, if the community of users who exchange sensitive data is physically dispersed, it is difficult to control where their frames are sent.

The concept of a *virtual LAN* (VLAN) was introduced as a way to control the traffic flows on a physical LAN. A VLAN is made up of a group of systems (such as the computers in a workgroup) that need to communicate with one another. Traffic between these systems stays bottled up within their virtual LAN. This can cut back overall LAN traffic significantly and can improve security.

The groundwork for supporting virtual LANs in a standardized fashion was laid by the IEEE in 802.1Q, "Virtual Bridged Local Area Networks." This chapter describes the concepts and protocols introduced in that standard, as well as many vendor-initiated VLAN features.

This chapter also discusses frame prioritization because the priority and VLAN protocols are closely related. Both are implemented using the same protocol header.

> **Note**
>
> Customers wanted VLANs before VLAN standards were available. Vendors built proprietary solutions, and the solutions varied a lot. Standards now are available, but a lot of dissimilarity still exists in the ways that products work.
>
> Instead of listing every feature that any product might offer, this chapter starts with a standards-based orientation and then presents particularly useful enhancements that are available in product offerings.

Virtual LAN Concepts

VLAN protocols enable an administrator to partition a LAN into multiple virtual LANs. Each VLAN is assigned a number that identifies it uniquely within the LAN.

Multiple VLANs share the switches and links in an underlying physical LAN. However, each VLAN logically behaves like a separate LAN. All of a VLAN's frame traffic (including its broadcasts and multicasts) is confined to the VLAN. This translates to improved performance because the total amount of traffic on the physical LAN can be reduced.

VLANs are constructed around a core set of switches that support the needed functions and protocols. These are called *VLAN-aware switches*, or more simply *VLAN switches*.

> **Note**
>
> VLAN switches are Layer 2 switches—that is, bridges. They are called *switches* in this chapter because most vendors refer to them that way.

Many older switches in the installed base are not VLAN-aware, and not all new switch products support VLANs. Furthermore, the switches that do support VLANs do not necessarily do it in exactly the same way.

Before the completion of the IEEE standard, vendors invested a great deal of effort (and money) in creating proprietary VLAN solutions. Today, a vendor typically has to support its proprietary VLAN protocols along with the standard IEEE VLAN protocols because many customers still use older equipment in the field that runs the proprietary solution.

The IEEE standard defines basic VLAN functionality. Vendors legitimately enhance this in various ways. Standards-based products interoperate at the basic level, but you might lose some attractive add-on capabilities when you connect heterogeneous equipment.

Types of Virtual LANs

A virtual LAN can be created to serve any purpose. It can be long-lived or temporary. For example, a virtual LAN may consist of:

- All users in a common workgroup or project team

- A community consisting of a database server and a set of systems that access the server on a regular basis

- Systems that send and receive traffic for a particular protocol or family of protocols (for example, IP, IPX, NetBIOS, DECnet, or SNA)

- A community of users that belong to a multicast group

- A set of systems whose communication must be isolated because of security concerns

A single LAN can contain a mixture of workgroup, community, protocol, and security-based VLANs.

Each virtual LAN is assigned a number called a *VLAN identifier*. Every frame handled by a VLAN switch is associated with some VLAN.

Note

The scope of a VLAN identifier is an entire physical LAN. A system anywhere in the LAN can be configured to be a member of any VLAN that has been defined for the LAN.

A frame is forwarded based on its VLAN identifier and its destination MAC address. For now, the easiest way to understand how this works is to visualize a separate filtering table for each VLAN identifier. A frame's destination MAC address is looked up in the switch filtering table that contains entries for its VLAN.

VLAN Awareness and Ports

Any end system or switch that performs VLAN functions and protocols is said to be VLAN-aware. A VLAN-aware switch can simply be called a *VLAN switch*.

An end system becomes VLAN-aware when appropriate device driver software is installed and configured. Most current VLANs include few VLAN-aware end systems.

A VLAN environment can be constructed around a single VLAN switch. For example, switch A is the only system in Figure 16.1 that is VLAN-aware.

VLANs 2 and 3 in the figure have been configured by identifying the ports on switch A that lead to systems assigned to each of the VLANs. Specifically, the following is true:

- Every system reached via switch A ports 0, 2, 3, and 7 belongs to VLAN 2.

- Every system reached via switch A ports 1, 4, 5, and 6 belongs to VLAN 3.

No computer is aware that it belongs to a VLAN. In fact, switch B is not aware that it participates in VLAN 2. As part of its normal operation, switch B transmits broadcasts, multicasts, and flooded frames through port 5 to switch A. This traffic arrives at port 7. Switch A identifies every frame arriving at port 7 as a VLAN 2 frame and forwards it accordingly.

From the point of view of switch B, the systems in VLAN 3 do not even exist. Switch A does not forward any VLAN 3 frames to switch B, and switch B only observes and learns the MAC addresses of the VLAN 2 systems attached to switch A.

Note that the entire structure of the VLANs in Figure 16.1 is described by enumerating the ports at switch A that participate in each VLAN. In general, assigning ports to a VLAN is a key configuration step. Later sections contain more information about this.

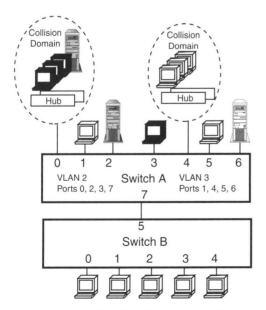

FIGURE 16.1 *VLANs defined at a switch.*

VLAN Switches

Figure 16.2 shows two VLANs that are spread across three switches. Switches A and B both are VLAN-aware. Each supports members of two VLANs.

Switch C does not have to be a VLAN switch to participate in the configuration shown in Figure 16.2 because all of its stations are assigned to VLAN 3. Switch A will make sure that VLAN 3 frames are forwarded to switch C, and will forward frames sent from switch C to VLAN 3 systems.

However, if switch C is a not VLAN switch, an administrator will have limited flexibility in making moves and changes. For example, if the owner of station W is moved to an office that is cabled into switch C, the station cannot be configured into its old VLAN (VLAN 2) unless switch C is changed to a VLAN switch.

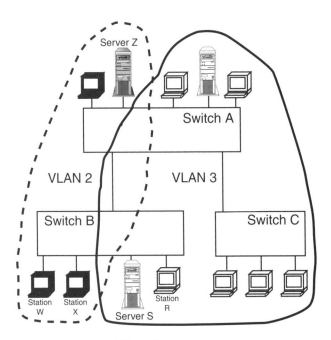

FIGURE 16.2 *VLAN members.*

Trunks and Tags

A link that carries traffic between a pair of VLAN switches is called a *trunk link*. Traffic belonging to any number of VLANs can share a trunk link. In Figure 16.2, VLAN 2 and VLAN 3 share the trunk link between switch A and switch B.

When a frame arrives at a VLAN switch, the switch must determine which VLAN the frame belongs to before the frame can be forwarded. For example, if a unicast or multicast frame from a VLAN 3 system at switch B arrives at switch A, switch A must look up the destination address in the VLAN 3 MAC table.

Switch A needs a way to associate a frame that arrives from switch B with the right VLAN. The solution is illustrated in Figure 16.3. Frames that are transmitted across a trunk between VLAN switches include an extra subheader called a *tag*. A tag includes a frame's VLAN identifier and also contains a priority level for the frame. A frame whose header contains a tag that identifies a VLAN is called a *VLAN-tagged* frame or a *tagged frame*.

Note

Sometimes tags are used only to indicate the priority of frames without identifying VLAN membership. These frames are called *priority-tagged*.

The VLAN identifier field in a priority-tagged frame is set to 0, which stands for "the null VLAN." A frame whose tag contains a nonzero VLAN identifier is called *VLAN-tagged* or just *tagged*. It is assumed that a priority is assigned to a VLAN-tagged frame, even if the priority field happens to be 0.

Thus, frames can be untagged, priority-tagged, or VLAN-tagged.

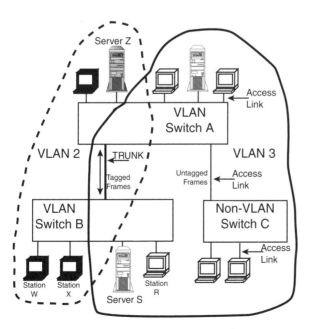

FIGURE 16.3 *A trunk link, tagged frames, and access links.*

Access Links

A link that connects a VLAN-unaware system to a VLAN switch is called an *access link*. Assuming that all the end systems in Figure 16.3 are VLAN-unaware, all the links that connect end systems to the VLAN switches are access links.

Because switch C also is VLAN-unaware, the link between switch C and switch A in Figure 16.3 also is an access link.

Using a Collision Domain as a Trunk

The trunk link in Figure 16.3 is a point-to-point link, which is the most common type of trunk link. However, a collision domain also can be used as a trunk link.

Figure 16.4 shows a set of VLAN bridges that are connected by an FDDI ring that is being used as a trunk. Every system attached to a trunk must be VLAN-aware.

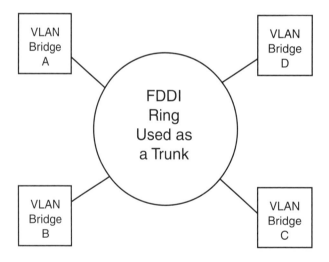

FIGURE 16.4   *An FDDI ring used as a trunk link.*

Hybrid Links

It would not be unusual for a LAN administrator to add some VLAN-unaware application servers to the FDDI ring in Figure 16.4. This would turn the ring into the *hybrid link*, shown in Figure 16.5.

Formally, a *hybrid link* is a collision domain that connects VLAN bridges to one another and also includes VLAN-unaware systems.

The VLAN-unaware systems all must be assigned to a single default VLAN. In this example, VLAN 4 is that default VLAN.

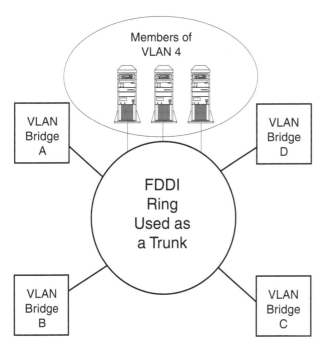

FIGURE 16.5 *A hybrid link.*

Any collision domain could be used as a hybrid link—even a twisted-pair Ethernet collision domain built around a bunch of interconnected hubs. This would be a bit of a mess, though, and it also would negate some of the desirable features supposedly gained by using VLANs.

> **Note**
>
> Every VLAN-unaware system in a hybrid link "sees" all of the frames that are transmitted across the subLAN by every bridge.
>
> However, a tagged frame contains an EtherType code that is not recognized by an ordinary end station. The station will not be capable of interpreting a tagged frame and will discard it (unless the station's owner is using monitor software that captures all frames that are in transit.)

Communicating Between VLANs

The purpose of a VLAN is to control and separate some types of traffic from other types of traffic.

In Figure 16.3, even though the systems on VLAN 2 and VLAN 3 share switches and share the bandwidth on the trunk between switch A and switch B, a system on VLAN 2 cannot communicate with a system on VLAN 3.

In Figure 16.6, switch A has been replaced by a Layer 2/3 switch—in other words, a combined bridge and router. Systems in VLAN 2 and VLAN 3 now can communicate with each other by sending traffic through the router module at bridge/router A.

Because the term *switch* becomes ambiguous when both bridges and routers are present, the Layer 2 switches in the figure are labeled as bridges.

Note that if station X wants to send data to server S:

1. Station X wraps the data in a frame whose destination is the MAC address of its local router, bridge/router A.

2. Bridge B tags the frame and forwards it to bridge/router A.

3. The router removes the frame header and trailer, and creates a new tagged frame whose destination is the MAC address of server S. This frame's tag indicates that it belongs to VLAN 3.

4. The router forwards the frame to bridge B.

5. Bridge B then removes the tag and delivers the frame to server S.

This is a roundabout way to get from X to S! However, this often is exactly what a LAN administrator wants. The administrator might want to place tight controls on who can access what. A router can do a good job of security screening.

However, if stations on VLAN 2 really should be allowed to reach server S directly, there are ways to do it. The usual solution is shown in Figure 16.7. A system can be a member of two or more VLANs. Server S in Figure 16.7 is VLAN-aware and belongs to both VLAN 2 and VLAN 3.

It is smart to add a server to every VLAN whose systems need to access the server. This allows the traffic to be delivered directly, without being routed.

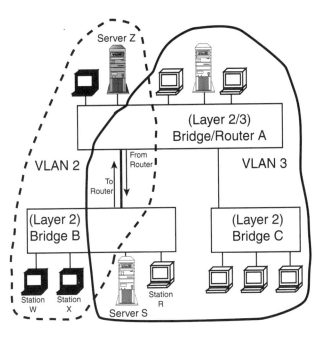

FIGURE 16.6   *Routing traffic between VLANs.*

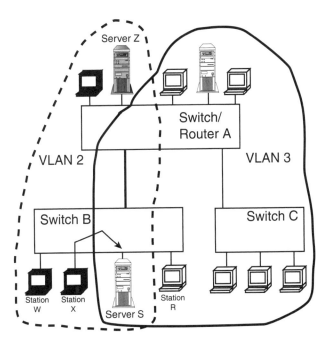

FIGURE 16.7   *Belonging to multiple VLANs.*

> **Note**
> Some vendors support "route once, switch many" mechanisms that enable a switched path to be temporarily opened up between systems that belong to different VLANs after some initial frames have been routed between them.

Independent and Shared Learning

One way to implement VLANs at a switch is to set up a separate filtering table for each VLAN. The switch stores the MAC addresses learned for a VLAN in that VLAN's filtering table. This is called *independent VLAN learning* (IVL).

As was the case in Figure 16.7, systems might belong to more than one VLAN. In this case, it is more efficient to use a single filtering table that contains MAC addresses that have been learned across a group of VLANs—or for all VLANs. This is called *shared VLAN learning* (SVL). Shared learning eliminates some unnecessary flooding of frames.

For example, if independent learning is used for the VLANs in Figure 16.7, the MAC address of VLAN-aware server S might be included in the VLAN 3 filtering table at switch B, but might not yet be in the VLAN 2 filtering table.

The top of Figure 16.8 represents independent switch B filtering tables for VLANs 2 and 3 in Figure 16.7. When a separate VLAN 2 table is used and station X sends a frame to server S, the following occurs:

1. The destination MAC address of server S is not in the VLAN 2 filtering table.

2. The frame must be transmitted through all VLAN 2 ports at switch B other than the port connected to station X.

3. When the frame arrives at switch A, it is forwarded through all the switch ports belonging to VLAN 2 other than the port of arrival.

Frames addressed to server S are flooded in this manner until server S sends a frame to a destination in VLAN 2 and its MAC address is entered into the VLAN 2 filtering table.

However, if shared learning is used for both VLANs in Figure 16.7, then as soon as server S transmits a frame to any destination, its MAC address is entered into the joint filtering table at switch B. This table is depicted at the bottom of Figure 16.8. The entry for server S can be used immediately for all of the VLANs to which it belongs.

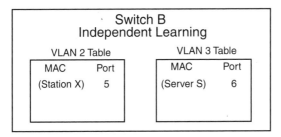

FIGURE 16.8 *Independent and shared filtering tables.*

The GARP VLAN Registration Protocol

Maintaining a big VLAN can be a lot of work. It would be very helpful if a VLAN system could tell its neighbors which VLAN traffic it wants to receive.

In fact, this is exactly what a very valuable member of the VLAN protocol family, the *GARP VLAN Registration Protocol* (GVRP), accomplishes. Using GVRP, a VLAN-aware end system or switch registers with a neighboring switch to join (or leave) a VLAN. Each system periodically updates its registrations automatically. Stale registrations age out after a timeout interval.

> **Note**
>
> GARP, which stands for the *Generic Attribute Registration Protocol*, was introduced in Chapter 14, "Switches and Multicast Traffic." GARP provides a general registration mechanism for use in a bridged LAN.

GVRP propagates VLAN registration information through an entire LAN. Later sections present some GVRP examples and describe the protocol.

> **Note**
>
> A LAN that consists entirely of VLAN-aware end systems and VLAN-aware switches will operate very efficiently if all end systems and switches support GVRP.
>
> Every end system could register and report its location, and this information would be propagated to every switch. The result would be that every unicast frame would be delivered only to its intended destination. No flooding would be required.

VLANs and the Spanning Tree Protocol

A physical LAN either has a tree structure or configures itself into a tree by means of the Spanning Tree Protocol (STP). All VLANs are superimposed on the current active tree structure. This means that VLAN frames cannot be forwarded through ports that have been blocked by the Spanning Tree Protocol.

In a big, complicated LAN containing many switches and backup links, it is possible that one or more VLANs could be chopped into noncommunicating pieces when the Spanning Tree Protocol modifies the LAN topology.

Fortunately, when GVRP is enabled, GVRP messages automatically update VLAN membership information after a change in the Spanning Tree topology. GVRP repairs broken VLAN paths.

Implementing VLANs

The previous sections introduced some major VLAN concepts and features. Now it is time to focus on how VLANs are configured and how switches process VLAN frames.

A VLAN is created by

- Assigning a VLAN identifier

- Defining VLAN members

- Listing the switch ports through which members of the VLAN can be reached

- For each VLAN port, indicating whether frames belonging to a VLAN must be transmitted from the port with or without tags

There are many different ways to define VLAN membership, including the following:

- **Default**—Initially, all ports in a switch belong to the same default VLAN.

- **Port-based**—At each switch, list the ports that belong to the VLAN.

- **Port- and protocol-based**—At each switch, list ports that belong to the VLAN and the types of protocol traffic that can traverse the VLAN.

- **IP address prefix-based**—At each switch, list ports that belong to the VLAN and specify an IP address prefix. The VLAN carries frames for IP systems whose IP addresses begin with the prefix, IP broadcast and multicast frames, and Address Resolution Protocol (ARP) frames that carry queries and responses related to the IP addresses.

- **Port- and GVRP-based**—Create a VLAN by entering the VLAN identifier at one or more switches. Allow computers and switches to join and leave the VLAN via GVRP protocol interactions.

- **Port- and MAC address-based**—At each switch, manually enter (port, MAC address) combinations that describe the systems that belong to the VLAN.

These VLAN types are described in the sections that follow. The types that are supported vary from vendor to vendor.

The Default VLAN

When a VLAN bridge initializes for the first time, all ports automatically are members of the default VLAN. The VLAN identifier of the default VLAN is 1. If no other VLANs are configured on a LAN, the default VLAN equals the whole LAN.

Some administrators delete the default VLAN to assure that no traffic will be forwarded unless it explicitly can be associated with an intentionally defined VLAN.

Static Port-Based VLANs

The most universally supported method of defining a VLAN at a switch is to enter the VLAN ID into a configuration screen and list the switch ports that belong to the VLAN. This is called a *port-based VLAN*.

End systems attached to a simple port-based VLAN do not need to know what VLAN they belong to. The VLAN membership of a frame sent by a station is determined by the access port at which the frame enters the switch.

Figure 16.9 displays a LAN consisting of a single switch with two port-based VLANs. There is no need to tag any frame; the switch easily can separate the traffic for each VLAN.

The benefits of splitting the ports into these two VLANs include

- Broadcast and multicast traffic originated by a system stays within its own VLAN.

- A frame sent to a MAC address that is not in the switch's filtering table is flooded only through ports that belong to its own VLAN.

Note that the systems in Figure 16.9 that belong to VLAN 2 cannot communicate with systems in VLAN 3. (A routing module would have to be added to the switch to allow communication between the VLANs.)

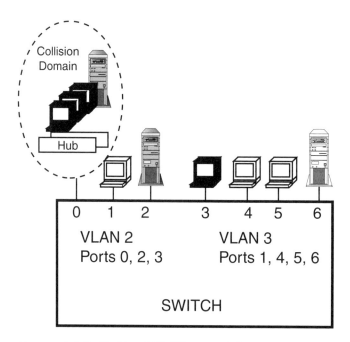

FIGURE 16.9   *Port-based VLANs at a switch.*

Tagging in Static Port-Based VLANs

Port 6 in Figure 16.10 belongs to two VLANs. Now there is a problem: When a frame from the server arrives at port 6, how does port 6 know which VLAN the frame belongs to?

For port-based VLANs, the answer is that frames between the switch and this server need to be tagged. NICs and device drivers that make a system VLAN-aware are available today.

Some NIC vendors enable an administrator to configure VLAN-aware systems from a remote administrator console. New NICs also have security features that make it possible to do this safely.

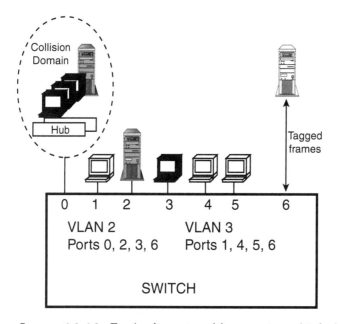

FIGURE 16.10 *Tagging frames to and from a port associated with two VLANs.*

Configuring Trunks for Port-Based VLANs

Figure 16.11 shows a LAN that includes VLAN-aware switches and two trunk links.

Trunk ports are configured in a vendor-specific way. For many products, a trunk port is automatically enrolled in all VLANs that have been configured at its switch; this is the case in Figure 16.11.

For some products, you define every VLAN at every switch, whether there are members at the switch or not. In addition, each trunk belongs to every VLAN. The result is that all broadcasts, multicasts, and flooded traffic for any VLAN are forwarded across all trunks to every switch, whether or not that switch has members in the VLAN.

This negates some of the benefits that VLANs are supposed to provide. A different approach is taken in Figure 16.11. In the figure, a VLAN is defined at a switch only if there are members attached to that switch. The trunks at the switch automatically are added to each of the defined VLANs.

Thus, in Figure 16.11, trunk port 4 at switch A automatically has been added to VLANs 1, 2, and 3. Similarly, trunk ports 3 and 12 at switch B belong to VLANs 1, 2, and 3, while trunk port 2 at switch C belongs to VLANs 3 and 4.

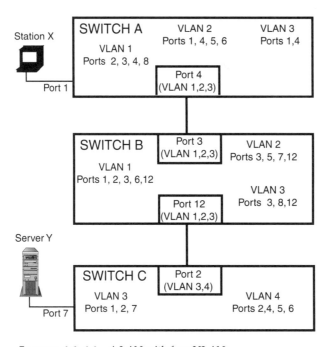

FIGURE 16.11   *A LAN with four VLANs.*

Note that the trunk configuration is not perfect. Switches B and C still will forward some traffic unnecessarily. The following manual changes fix this:

- Remove port 12 at switch B from VLANs 1 and 2. This prevents it from forwarding unwanted broadcasts, multicasts, and floods for VLANs 1 and 2 to switch C.

- Remove port 2 at switch C from VLAN 4. This prevents it from forwarding unwanted broadcasts, multicasts, and floods for VLAN 4 to switch B.

Figure 16.12 shows the result of these changes.

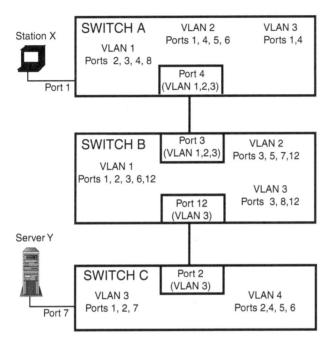

FIGURE 16.12 *A more efficient VLAN configuration.*

Maintaining VLAN Configuration Manually

As a LAN grows and the number of stations and switches increases, the switch configuration chore can become quite burdensome. Vendors provide functions that automate a lot of the work. However, the best way to understand these functions is to look at what life is like without them.

Consider what happens when the user at station X is assigned to a new work-group and must be transferred to VLAN 4. The (unaided) administrator must make the following changes at switch A:

1. Remove VLAN 3.

2. Create VLAN 4. Add port 1 to VLAN 4. (Add port 4 to VLAN 4 if the product does not add it automatically.)

The administrator must make the following changes at switch B:

1. Remove port 3 from VLAN 3. There no longer is any reason to forward VLAN 3 frames to switch A.

2. Create VLAN 4. (Add port 3 and port 12 if the product does not add them automatically.)

The administrator must make the following changes at switch C:

1. Remove port 2 from VLAN 3.

2. Add port 2 to VLAN 4.

This simple example shows that raw VLANs are not necessarily easy to configure! The proprietary vendor solutions enabled switches to exchange enrollment information with one another and automated many of these steps. However, a standard was needed to allow switches from different vendors to interwork. The GARP VLAN Registration Protocol is the standard protocol designed to automate VLAN configuration chores.

Maintaining VLAN Configuration with GVRP

GVRP is most effective in a network made up entirely of VLAN-aware systems. At the time of writing, relatively few end systems are VLAN-aware. However, GVRP still has great value, even when supported by only a backbone of VLAN-aware switches.

Going back to Figure 16.11, when GVRP is used, VLAN information associated with a trunk port defines the VLANs for which the trunk port wishes to receive traffic.

Each trunk port registers with its neighbor, announcing the traffic that it wishes to receive. Each switch propagates these registrations to its neighbors. The result is that a switch port registers a VLAN identifier with a neighbor

1. If there are local members of that VLAN at the switch

2. If the switch has received registrations that announce that there are members of the VLAN that are attached to other switches reached through its ports

For example, in Figure 16.11

1. Port 2 at switch C registers with port 12 at switch B, asking port 12 to forward all frames that belong to VLANs 3 and 4. Switch C has members that belong to these VLANs.

2. Port 3 at switch B registers with port 4 at switch A, asking for all frames that belong to VLANs 1, 2, and 3 because it has local members. It also asks for all frames belonging to VLAN 4 because switch C has requested these frames.

In Figure 16.13, each trunk port is labeled with the identifiers of VLANs whose frames the port has been asked to forward. Note that these numbers apply to *outgoing* traffic only. This forwarding information is stored in dynamic filtering table entries at each switch.

Note that the fact that switch C wants to receive VLAN 4 frames has propagated up to switch A. However, because no system at switch A belongs to VLAN 4, this does not cause any VLAN 4 frames to be sent across from switch A to switch B.

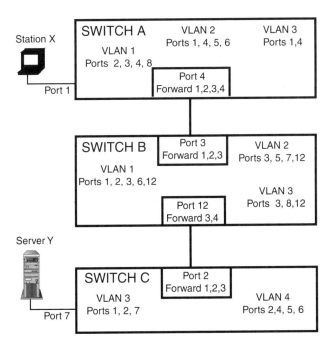

FIGURE 16.13 *VLANs whose frames will be forwarded across trunks.*

Now look at what happens when station X must be transferred to VLAN 4:

1. The administrator deletes VLAN 3 from switch A.

2. The administrator creates VLAN 4 and adds port 1 to it.

3. Port 4 at switch A automatically transmits a GVRP registration stating that it wishes to receive frames sent to VLAN 4.

4. Port 12 at switch B automatically transmits a GVRP registration stating that it wishes to receive frames sent to VLAN 4.

Switches B and C learn that they need to forward VLAN 4 frames toward switch A.

When you consider the effect of moves and changes coupled with the modifications caused by the automatic self-reconfiguration of a LAN via the Spanning Tree Protocol, the argument for using a protocol such as GVRP is especially compelling.

For a LAN in which every system is VLAN-aware, it is possible to use VLANs without doing any manual configuration at switches. Instead, each end system can be configured with the VLAN(s) to which it belongs. End systems register with neighboring switches, and the switches create and remove VLANs based on these registrations.

Some disadvantages arise when doing this. A collision domain attached to one switch port might contain hundreds of end systems. It is easier to configure the switch port than all of these systems.

Issues of security and control also must be considered. However, vendors are dealing with these problems by supporting secure, centralized configuration of endpoint systems.

Port- and Protocol-Based VLANs

Some products support port- and protocol-based VLANs. These VLANs are defined by listing

- The set of ports that belong to the VLAN

- One or more types of protocol traffic that can be carried across the VLAN

A frame belongs to the VLAN if both of the following are true:

- The frame arrives at a switch port that belongs to the VLAN.

- The frame carries traffic for one of the listed protocols.

An identical set of ports can be used to define of two distinct VLANs. For example

- **VLAN 10**—Ports 1, 2, 3, 4, 5. Protocols IP and ARP

- **VLAN 20**—Ports 1, 2, 3, 4, 5. Protocol SNA

More often, a pair of VLANs overlaps at a few ports. For example, VLAN 2 in Figure 16.14 supports IPX traffic, while VLAN 3 carries IP traffic. Ports 2 and 3 at switch A belong to both VLANs.

Although the stations attached to ports 2 and 3 belong to both VLAN 2 and VLAN 3, these stations do not need to support tagging. When a frame arrives at port 2 or 3, switch A can assign it to a VLAN based on its protocol, so tags are not required.

If VLANs 2 and 3 were merged into a single VLAN, IPX broadcasts and multicasts would have to be forwarded to switch B. Furthermore, a frame exchanged between an IPX station and the local IPX server would be flooded to switch B if its destination MAC addresses had timed out and had been removed from the filtering table.

Using the protocol type to separate the traffic flows can cut back substantially on overhead traffic while not imposing a burdensome amount of administration.

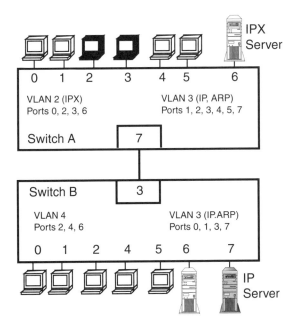

FIGURE 16.14 *Port- and protocol-based VLANs.*

IPX and IP VLANs

A few points must be kept in mind when configuring port- and protocol-based VLANs.

As was noted in Chapter 4, "The Classical Ethernet CSMA/CD MAC Protocol," IPX messages can be encapsulated into LAN frames in several different ways. Your switch product might count each encapsulation as a separate protocol.

It is important to include all of the encapsulations used in your LAN in an IPX VLAN definition. Otherwise, some IPX frames might be discarded by a switch and vanish.

The IP protocol relies on the Layer 2 Address Resolution Protocol (ARP) to translate IP destination addresses into MAC addresses. Hence, an IP VLAN must include the ARP protocol as well.

An IP VLAN usually corresponds to an *IP subnet*. This is a set of systems whose IP addresses start with a prefix that is not used anywhere else in the IP network. The only way for traffic to leave an IP subnet is via a router.

An IP subnet VLAN is configured by specifying the following at each switch:

- The set of ports that belong to the VLAN
- One or more types of protocol traffic
- The IP address prefix that defines the subnet

Traffic is carried between IP subnet VLANs by forwarding it to a router.

MAC-Address-Based Secure VLANs

The most tedious—but also the most secure—way to define VLAN membership at a switch is to list the port and MAC address of every VLAN endpoint system. Some products support this option, which is used to define VLANs that have extra security.

A switch can be configured to discard any incoming frame whose source MAC address is not associated with that port.

A unicast frame will not be delivered unless its destination address and exit port number are enrolled at one of the switches. Unicast frames never need to be flooded to multiple endpoint systems. An endpoint system never sees a frame that it is not intended to receive.

Figure 16.15 illustrates how a switch delivers frames for a secure VLAN. The stations that are displayed in the figure are members of the secure VLAN.

1. A station that has address MAC-2 and is attached to port 1 at switch B transmits a frame to destination address MAC-8.

2. Port 1, MAC-2 is a legitimate member of the VLAN, so the frame is accepted.

3. The destination MAC address (MAC-8) is not currently in a filtering table at switch B.

4. Switch B forwards the frame to switches A and C, but does not forward it through any of its local access ports.

5. Switch A discards the frame. MAC-1 is the only local MAC address on the secure VLAN.

6. Switch C delivers the frame through port 6 to MAC-8.

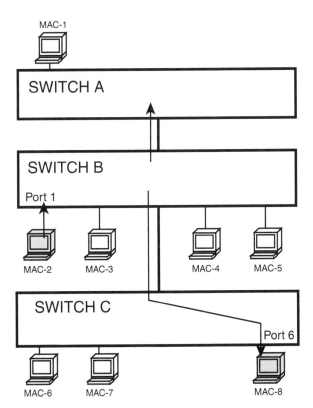

FIGURE 16.15 *Delivering frames on a secure VLAN.*

Processing VLAN Frames

Earlier sections have introduced some of the major VLAN concepts and VLAN types. Now it is time to focus on how VLANs are configured and how switches process VLAN frames.

The cost of reducing broadcast and flooding overhead and controlling user access to parts of a LAN is that some extra processing must be performed by VLAN switches. This processing is controlled by configuration choices made by a LAN administrator.

The purpose of each configuration choice can be better understood after examining the steps that are followed when a switch processes a frame. These steps include

1. Examine each incoming frame and assign it to a VLAN. The rules controlling the assignment process are called *ingress rules*.

2. Check the filtering table to determine the output port or ports.

3. For each output port, verify that the port is a member of the frame's VLAN and check whether the frame needs to be tagged. The output processing procedures are called *egress rules*.

Assigning Frames to VLANs via Ingress Rules

The association of a frame to a VLAN is easy if the arriving frame is tagged and the tag contains a VLAN identifier. However, this does not guarantee that the frame will be forwarded. The frame might have arrived at a port that is not on that VLAN's member list.

An administrator must decide whether the port should be strict and discard the frame, or relaxed and forward the frame. If the port is configured to be strict, a tagged frame is discarded if the port is not on the member list for the frame's VLAN.

An arriving frame that has no tag—or that has just a priority tag—might be discarded. A port optionally can be configured to reject all incoming frames that are not VLAN-tagged.

If an arriving frame that is not VLAN-tagged can be admitted, the switch tries to classify the frame based on VLAN configuration information. The switch tries to make the most specific match:

- If the arrival port belongs to one or more VLANs, the frame is checked to see whether it meets the requirements for membership in any of these VLANs. If not, the frame is discarded.

- If the frame has met the membership criteria for exactly one of the port's VLANs, the frame is assigned to that VLAN.

- If the frame has met the membership criteria for more than one of the port's VLANs, the frame is assigned to the VLAN whose membership requirement is most specific and stringent. The ratings of matches, from most to least specific, are

  - A VLAN defined by (port number, MAC address) combinations

  - A VLAN defined by a port list and an IP address prefix

  - A VLAN defined by a port list and a list of supported protocols

  - A VLAN defined by a port list

Figure 16.16 outlines the decision process. A vendor might vary the procedure slightly, based on special features of its switches.

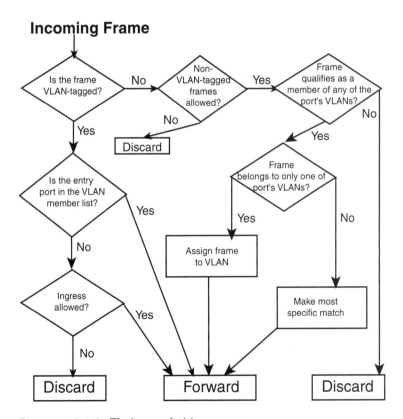

FIGURE 16.16 *The ingress decision process.*

Forwarding VLAN Frames

A VLAN switch follows some basic rules when processing frames that need to be forwarded:

1. When a frame arrives at a switch, its VLAN ID is determined by the ingress rules.

2. If the destination is a broadcast address, the frame is forwarded through every switch port belonging to that VLAN, except for the source port.

3. If the destination is a unicast or multicast address, the set of filtering table entries for that VLAN is searched for a matching destination MAC address. Table 16.1 shows two sample entries in a shared filtering table.

4. For a MAC address-based secure VLAN, if the destination is a unicast or multicast address and is not found in the filtering table, the frame is forwarded through the appropriate trunk ports.

5. For other VLANs, if the destination is a unicast or multicast address and is not found in the filtering table, the frame is forwarded through the switch ports belonging to that VLAN and the appropriate trunk ports.

6. For each exit port, the configuration information for that VLAN port is checked to see whether the frame must be transmitted in tagged or untagged format. Depending on the result, a tag might have to be added or removed. This would require the frame check sequence to be recomputed.

TABLE 16.1 SAMPLE VLAN SHARED FILTERING TABLE ENTRIES

Entry Number	Destination MAC Address	VLAN	Transmit Port(s)	Status
1	00-60-08-1E-AE-42	2	5	Learned
2	08-00-20-5B-31-6D	2, 3	6	Learned

A VLAN filtering table contains

- Static entries for unicast and multicast MAC addresses, manually configured by an administrator

- Dynamic entries for unicast MAC addresses, learned by observing the source MAC addresses of frames arriving at a VLAN port

- Optionally, dynamic entries for multicast addresses, learned via GMRP registrations

- Optionally, dynamic entries for unicast MAC addresses, learned via GVRP registrations

Note

Not all valid frames arriving at a switch need to be forwarded. A switch is the destination for some frames, such as SNMP messages or Bridge Protocol Data Units.

Configuring VLAN Ports

In the previous sections, you saw that an administrator must make several decisions that influence how tightly the scope of a VLAN is controlled. Several configuration decisions are made separately for each port:

- Will this port reject incoming frames that are not tagged?

- Will this arrival port reject an incoming frame if the ingress port does not belong to the VLAN that matches the frame's VLAN classification?

- For a specified VLAN, must frames sent by this port be tagged?

- Will this port accept incoming GVRP registrations for a specified VLAN?

Table 16.2 lists the formal names of these VLAN parameters and summarizes the meaning of each. For the first two parameters, a separate value is assigned to each port. For the rest, a separate value is assigned for each (port, VLAN) combination for which the port belongs to that VLAN.

TABLE 16.2 VLAN PORT CONFIGURATION PARAMETERS

Formal Name of Parameter	Applies to:	Valid Values
Acceptable frame types	Incoming frames at a specific port	Admit only VLAN-tagged frames. Admit all frames.
Enable ingress filter	Incoming tagged frames at a specific port	If yes, check whether the ingress port belongs to a VLAN that matches the frame's VLAN classification. Discard frames for which there is no match. If no, do not check for a match.

continues

TABLE 16.2 CONTINUED

Formal Name of Parameter	Applies to:	Valid Values
Transmit with tag header	Outgoing frames for a specified (port, VLAN) pairing	Yes means that frames for this VLAN must be tagged before being transmitted from the port.
GVRP registration allowed	Incoming registrations for a (port, VLAN) pairing	Yes means that the port will accept registrations for this VLAN.

VLANs and Multicasts

In a LAN environment that supports VLANs, multicasts are isolated within VLANs.

When a multicast frame enters a bridge port, it is subject to the same ingress processing as other frames and either is assigned to a VLAN or is discarded.

The same holds true for the GMRP frames that are used to join or leave multicast groups. When a GMRP frame arrives at a port, the frame either is assigned to a VLAN or is discarded. The join or leave requests in the frame apply to the VLAN that has been associated with the frame.

VLAN Protocol Elements

The IEEE committee that worked on VLANs took advantage of the fact that a new header was about to be added to MAC frames. The tag header actually is used for triple duty:

- It contains a 12-bit VLAN identifier.

- It includes a 3-bit priority value.

- Some LANs are made up Ethernets, Token Rings, and FDDI rings that are connected by bridges that translate between frame formats. A tag header can include information that assists in this translation.

VLAN Identifiers

VLAN identifiers are 12-bit quantities. Hence, they can represent decimal numbers ranging from 0 to 4095. Some of these values are reserved:

- 0 does not correspond to a VLAN. It is called the *null* VLAN ID and is used in a priority-tagged frame to indicate that no VLAN ID has been assigned.

- 1 is the default VLAN ID.

- Values ranging from 2 to 4094 are assigned to VLANs as needed.

- 4095 is reserved.

Vendors typically add their own special rules for using VLAN IDs. A vendor might limit the usable range of numbers.

Every bridge port must belong to one or more VLANs. When a VLAN bridge initializes for the first time, all ports automatically are members of VLAN 1.

Tagged Frame Formats

A receiver must be capable of easily detecting whether a tag has been sandwiched into a frame header. The tag really must stand out, so the VLAN protocol designers had to find a good place to put the tag.

The solution was to introduce a new EtherType value (X'81-00) signaling that a frame has a tag header.

Format of a Tagged Ethernet Frame

Figure 16.17 shows how this works for Ethernet frames:

- The EtherType field, which follows the source MAC address, contains X'81-00. This is the beginning of a tag header.

- The next 2 bytes contain *tag control information* (TCI). This includes the 3-bit priority field, a 1-bit flag called the *Canonical Format Indicator* (CFI), and the 12-bit VLAN identifier field.

- The Ethernet length or type value that was in the frame before it was tagged follows the tag control information.

A tag header adds 4 bytes to the length of an Ethernet frame. If the value of the Canonical Format Indicator flag is 1, another field containing 2 to 30 bytes will be inserted in the frame after the length/type field.

Note
This additional field appears when different types of LANs have been combined using special *translational bridges*. The extra field often contains source routing information. The name of this field is the *embedded routing information field* (E-RIF). The details are explained in Chapter 17.

To accommodate extra tag header bytes, a tagged Ethernet frame is allowed to be longer than an untagged frame.

A legacy LAN interface will not be capable of making much sense out of tagged frames. Some of the frames will be larger than the normal maximum frame size. All will have an EtherType that is unfamiliar. To play it safe, administrators often restrict tagging to frames that pass between a pair of VLAN-aware switches.

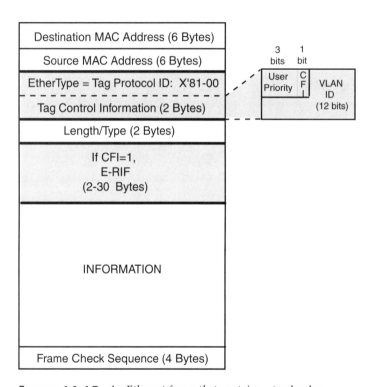

FIGURE 16.17   *An Ethernet frame that contains a tag header.*

Listing 16.1 shows a Sniffer trace of a tagged Ethernet frame carrying an ARP message.

Note that the Ethernet type field carries X'81-00, signaling that a tag follows. The priority value is 0. The VLAN identifier is 2.

LISTING 16.1 TRACE OF A TAGGED ETHERNET FRAME

```
8021Q: VLAN ID = 2

DLC:  ----- DLC Header -----
      DLC:
      DLC:  Frame 1 arrived at  17:29:35.0000; frame size is 60 (003C hex)
      ➥bytes.
      DLC:  Destination = 3COM BD7C18
      DLC:  Source      = 3COM BD7C19
      DLC:
8021Q: ----- 802.1Q Packet -----
      8021Q:
      8021Q: Tag Protocol Type      = 8100
      8021Q: Tag Control Information = 0002
      8021Q:    User Priority        = 0
      8021Q:    VLAN ID              = 2
      8021Q: Ethertype   = 0806 (ARP)
      8021Q:
ARP:  ----- ARP/RARP frame -----
      ARP:
      ARP: Hardware type = 1 (10Mb Ethernet)
      ARP: Protocol type = 0800 (IP)
      ARP: Length of hardware address = 6 bytes
      ARP: Length of protocol address = 4 bytes
      ARP: Opcode 2 (ARP reply)
      ARP: Sender's hardware address = 006008BD7C18
      ARP: Sender's protocol address = [10.0.0.1]
      ARP: Target hardware address  = 006008BD7C19
      ARP: Target protocol address  = [10.0.0.2]
      ARP:
      ARP: 14 bytes frame padding
      ARP:
```

Format of a Tagged Token Ring Frame

Figure 16.18 shows how the tag header is sandwiched into a Token Ring frame. If the frame contains a routing information field, it appears in its normal position after the source MAC address.

An 8-byte LLC/SNAP header follows, ending in the special EtherType protocol identifier X'81-00, which indicates that the next 2 bytes contain tag control information.

The frame's original 5-byte SNAP subheader, which identifies the type of protocol data the frame carries, follows the tag control information.

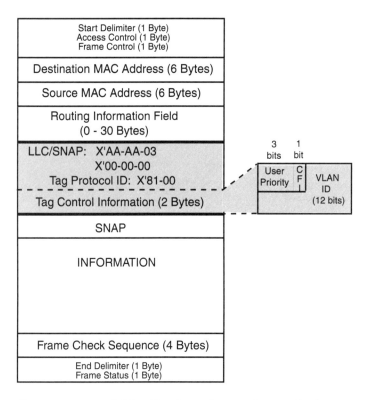

FIGURE 16.18   *A Token Ring frame that contains a tag header.*

Format of a Tagged FDDI Frame

Figure 16.19 shows how the tag header is sandwiched into an FDDI frame. If the frame contains a routing information field, it appears in the normal position after the source MAC address.

An 8-byte LLC/SNAP header follows, ending in the EtherType protocol identifier X'81-00, which indicates that the next 2 bytes contain tag control information. This is followed by the frame's original SNAP subheader.

The main difference between the FDDI format and the Token Ring format is that, like an Ethernet frame, an FDDI frame optionally can include a 2- to 30-byte field that carries some source routing information.

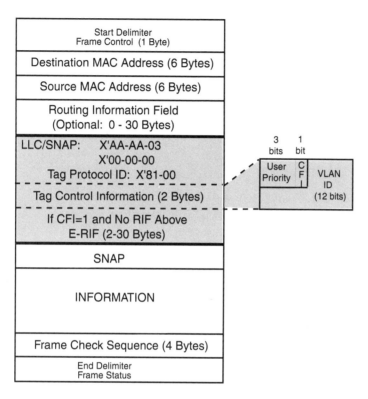

FIGURE 16.19 *An FDDI frame that contains a tag header.*

Assigning Priorities to Frames

Traditional bridges treated all frames the same way—first come, first served. But the importance of user traffic varies. Some carries mission-critical interactive data. Some consists of background file transfers that can tolerate delays.

The capability to prioritize traffic has been high on the customer wish list for quite a long time. Each vendor has met this need in a different way. Some products allow customers to give a type of traffic either high or low priority. Some support many priority classes. Depending on the product, customers may be able to assign traffic to a priority class according to the following:

- Protocol (such as IP, IPX, TCP, UDP, DECnet, or SNA)

- Application (as defined by a TCP or UDP port number, or an IPX socket number)

- Fields in an IP header that state precedence and type of service value

IEEE 802 Priority

The trouble with implementing priorities based on features such as IP type of service or TCP application port number is that a switch must examine the upper-layer protocol data in every frame to find out which type of priority handling the frame deserves.

By introducing a tag header, the IEEE 802.1Q VLAN and priority standard makes it possible to establish the priority once—either at the source host or at the port of entry into the switch adjacent to the host—and write it into the tag header added to the frame.

As Figures 16.17, 16.18, and 16.19 showed, a frame's priority is announced in a 3-bit field in the tag. When translated into decimal, the priority values range from 0 (lowest priority) to 7 (highest priority).

A LAN administrator might wish to prioritize the LAN's traffic without breaking the LAN into smaller VLANs. When priority-tagged frames are used, the tag's VLAN ID field is set to the null value (0), and only the priority bits contain usable information.

Forwarding Prioritized Frames

Bridges/switches were intended to be simple devices (at least, originally). A frame arrives, the bridge checks its filtering table and then forwards the frame accordingly.

Priorities make switch architecture a little more sophisticated. A switch must maintain separate output queues for each priority class that it supports. Figure 16.20 depicts a switch that supports four priority classes. Outgoing frames are lined up in four queues at each port.

Note

Figure 16.20 reflects a logical queuing structure. An actual implementation might make more efficient use of memory by storing a single copy of a frame and maintaining a list of the ports through which it must be sent.

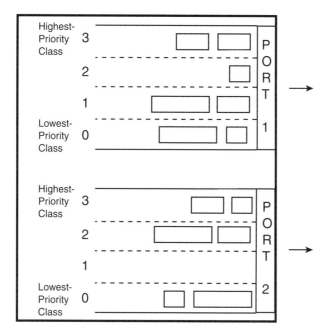

FIGURE 16.20 *Priority queues in a switch.*

Basic rules that can govern the transmission of prioritized frames are listed here:

- Frames in the highest-priority class queue are transmitted first.

- A frame in a lower-priority class queue is transmitted when all higher-level queues are empty.

There is a flaw in these rules, however: If there is a steady stream of high-priority traffic, low-priority traffic might never get sent!

Vendors overcome this flaw in different ways:

- Some vendors promote a frame to the next higher-level queue after a timeout period. Thus, a low-level frame that is blocked will work its way up the ladder.

- Some vendors set maximum transmission time limits for each priority level. When the time limit is reached, the right to transmit is given to the next level down until the lowest level is reached. The process then repeats, starting with the highest priority level.

Note
A frame cannot be queued in a switch for an unlimited amount of time. There is a timeout period after which a frame is discarded.

Mapping 802.1 Priorities to Priority Classes

Supervising a lot of queues adds to the complexity of the software in a switch. Some switches do not prioritize at all and have a single queue for each port. Some have two priority classes, high and low. The example in Figure 16.20 has four priority classes. However, few switches would be expected to set up eight classes and support eight queues.

When a frame that is tagged with a priority value arrives at a switch, the switch must figure out which queue the frame should join. To do this, the switch maps the frame's priority value to one of its supported priority classes. The IEEE has published a table that recommends the way that this should be done. Table 16.3 shows the mapping recommended in Table 8-2 of IEEE 802.1Q.

For example, if the switch does not prioritize (that is, uses only one class) then obviously all frames must be placed in the same exit queue, which has priority class 0. The column headed "1 Class" shows this mapping.

If the switch supports two classes (0 = low, 1 = high), then frames with priority values 0 to 3 go into the low queue (class 0), and frames with priority values 4 to 7 go into the high queue (class 1). The column headed "2 Classes" shows this mapping.

When a switch supports four or more classes, some of the mappings are strange. For example, if the switch supports eight classes

- Priority value 0 maps to class 2

- Priority value 1 maps to class 0

- Priority value 2 maps to class 1

There actually is some logic behind this. Some incoming tagged frames might be arriving from a switch that does not prioritize. That switch sends all of its frames with a single default priority value of 0. Frames with 0 priority values are given a small boost, just in case the 0 means "default" instead of "low." The mapping of the next couple of priority values is adjusted to work around this choice.

TABLE 16.3 MAPPING PRIORITY VALUES TO PRIORITY CLASSES

Number of Switch Priority Classes

Priory Value	1 Class	2 Classes	3 Classes	4 Classes	5 Classes	6 Classes	7 Classes	8 Classes
0	0	0	0	1	1	1	1	2
1	0	0	0	0	0	0	0	0
2	0	0	0	0	0	0	0	1
3	0	0	0	1	1	2	2	3
4	0	1	1	2	2	3	3	4
5	0	1	1	2	3	4	4	5
6	0	1	2	3	4	5	5	6
7	0	1	2	3	4	5	6	7

The priority *class* used in a particular bridge does not affect the priority *value* in a frame's tag. Normally, the frame is forwarded without any change to this value.

However, Figure 16.21 illustrates a case for which the priority value would change. Switch B has only one priority level. All frames arriving at switch A from switch B have priority 0.

The administrator at switch A has manually configured the arrival port so that it will change incoming frame priorities from 0 to 4. Note that according to Table 16.3, these frames will be placed in Class 2 queues at switch A.

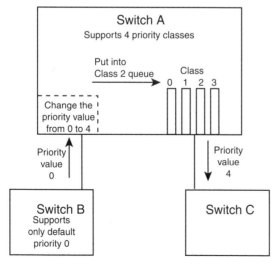

FIGURE 16.21 *Changing the priority value based on switch configuration.*

GARP VLAN Registration Protocol Details

The convenience and power of having a generic registration protocol was confirmed when the second GARP application was introduced. The GARP VLAN Registration Protocol (GVRP) enables systems to register VLAN memberships with an adjacent port. A system sends a `join` message to register.

Bridges propagate their static, port-based VLAN memberships and dynamic VLAN registrations in order to assure that frames transmitted onto a VLAN can reach any VLAN participant.

GVRP enables a system to register at a port and request that frames for one or more VLANs be forwarded to the system. Earlier, in the section "Maintaining VLAN Configuration with GVRP," you saw how GVRP simplifies and automates a large portion of the VLAN configuration effort.

In fact, a VLAN can even be created dynamically by an end-system GVRP registration. The VLAN is deleted when either all participating systems have sent `leave` messages or their registrations have timed out.

The GVRP registration protocol is similar to the GMRP protocol, which was described in Chapter 14:

- A GVRP message contains a list of `join` and `leave` requests.

- Each request contains the identifiers of the VLANs to be joined or left.

When a station registers and joins a VLAN at a port and the port is not currently participating in the VLAN, the following occurs:

- The bridge adds a dynamic VLAN entry for that port.

- The bridge propagates registration information through all ports (other than the source of the registration) that are active for the current spanning tree.

The result of this is that all ports on paths leading to the registered system learn that they need to forward frames belonging to the registered VLAN toward the registered system.

GVRP Protocol Messages

GVRP messages are GARP protocol data units that are sent to multicast MAC address X'01-80-C2-00-00-21, which has been set aside for GVRP use. (Recall that the multicast address used for GMRP was X'01-80-C2-00-00-20.) The messages contain VLAN `join`s and `leave`s.

Figure 16.22 shows the GVRP message format, which is very similar to the GMRP message format shown earlier in Chapter 14 (see Figure 14.10).

> **Note**
> In Figure 16.22, the 4-byte message block length covers a 1-byte length field, a 1-byte event identifier, and a 2-byte attribute value field that contains a VLAN identifier.

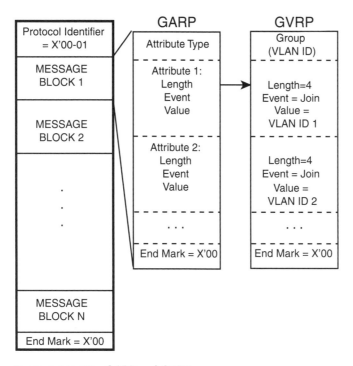

FIGURE 16.22 *GARP and GVRP messages.*

Summary Points

• Building a big physical LAN can pay off in equipment savings and in the capability to include high-bandwidth backbone links.

• Broadcasts and flooded unicast frames can generate a lot of LAN traffic.

• Virtual LANs were introduced as a way to control the traffic flows on a physical LAN.

- Systems that support VLAN protocols are said to be VLAN-aware.

- VLANs can be used to confine traffic within a workgroup, give selected stations access to a server, carry data for specified protocols, or isolate traffic for reasons of security.

- A VLAN can be defined by listing switch ports that participate in the VLAN.

- A link between a pair of VLAN switches is called a trunk. Traffic belonging to several VLANs can share a trunk.

- A link that connects one or more VLAN-unaware systems to a VLAN switch is called an access link.

- A hybrid link is a subLAN (such as an FDDI ring) that connects VLAN bridges to one another and that also connects to VLAN-unaware systems.

- VLAN-tagged frames include a header that contains a VLAN identifier and a priority value.

- The VLAN identifier in a priority-tagged frame contains a null VLAN identifier.

- A router forwards traffic between VLANs.

- Traffic between clients and a VLAN-aware server can be expedited by enrolling the server in multiple VLANs.

- When independent learning is used, a MAC address observed and learned in one VLAN is not shared with other VLANs.

- When shared learning is used, a MAC address observed and learned in one VLAN is shared with other VLANs.

- Using GVRP, a VLAN-aware end system can register with a neighboring switch to join (or leave) a VLAN.

- GVRP propagates VLAN registration information through the entire LAN.

- All VLANs are superimposed on a single active Spanning Tree structure.

- When a VLAN bridge initializes for the first time, all ports automatically are members of a default VLAN whose identifier is 1.

- A static port-based VLAN is the most universally supported type of VLAN. The administrator configures the VLAN ID and the list of switch ports that belong to the VLAN.

- Adding a GVRP registration capability to a port-based VLAN eases VLAN maintenance chores.

- A port-and-protocol VLAN is defined by listing the set of ports that belong to the VLAN and one or more types of protocol traffic that can be carried on the VLAN.

- A MAC address-based VLAN is defined by enumerating (port, MAC address) pairings for the systems that belong to the VLAN. This method is used to improve the security on a VLAN.

- When a frame arrives at a switch port, a set of ingress rules is applied in order to associate the frame with a VLAN.

- The frame is forwarded after looking for a matching MAC address and VLAN identifier in a filtering table.

- In a LAN environment that supports VLANs, multicasts are isolated within VLANs.

- VLAN identifiers are 12-bit quantities and can represent decimal numbers ranging from 0 to 4095.

- The fact that a frame contains a tag header is signaled by the use of a special EtherType value.

- The priority values in a tag can range from 0 to 7. When a frame arrives at a switch, the tag priority value must be mapped to a priority class supported by the switch. The switch priority classes correspond to output queues.

- The GARP VLAN Registration Protocol (GVRP) enables a system to register at a port and request that frames for one or more VLANs be forwarded to the system. GVRP is similar to GMRP.

- A bridge propagates GVRP registration information through all ports (other than the source of the registration) that are active for the current spanning tree.

References

The IEEE priority standard originally was published as 802.1p. It later was incorporated into the joint VLAN and priority standard:

- IEEE 802.1Q. "Virtual Bridged Local Area Networks." 1998.

The GARP VLAN Registration Protocol also is described in 802.1Q.

The Generic Attribute Registration Protocol (GARP) is described in Chapter 12 of the standard:

- IEEE 802.1D. "Media Access Control (MAC) Bridges." 1998.

VLAN implementations vary greatly from vendor to vendor. The best way to get a sense of the capabilities that are available is to check the configuration manuals for products from vendors such as Cisco, 3Com, Nortel, and Cabletron.

Source-Routing, Translational, and Wide Area Bridges

The last few chapters have discussed local area transparent bridges. Transparent bridges are characterized by their capability to learn the MAC addresses that are reached through each port and by the use of the Spanning Tree Protocol to restructure the LAN topology automatically after a component failure.

This chapter introduces source-routing bridges, which IBM designed for its Token Ring networks. Although transparent bridging can be used in Token Rings, source-routing often is preferred. Some LAN administrators install bridges that behave like transparent bridges for some traffic and follow source-routes for other traffic. Bridges that can do this are called (not surprisingly) source-routing transparent (SRT) bridges. They are popular at sites that are migrating from source-route bridging to transparent bridging.

Normally, the terms *routing* and *routes* apply to Layer 3 networking. Here the terms are used at Layer 2. It is unfortunate that IBM introduced this terminology because it has caused some confusion.

Bridging is a Layer 2 function; frame traffic is forwarded based on destination MAC addresses. Routing is a Layer 3 function. Layer 3 traffic is forwarded based on Layer 3 network addresses (such as IP addresses) that are located within network-layer protocol data units. Source-routed traffic actually is bridged traffic.

The advent of Layer 2/Layer 3 switch products has led some vendors to write product documentation that jumbles the functions performed at each layer. To avoid confusion, the terms, *bridge* (instead of Layer 2 switch) and *router* (instead of Layer 3 switch), are used in this chapter. (See Chapter 18, "Routing and Layer 2/3 Switches," for a detailed explanation of the difference between Layer 2 bridging and Layer 3 routing.)

Translational bridging is another technology that is explored in this chapter. Translational bridges relay frames between Ethernet, Token Ring, and FDDI LANs, creating a big, interconnected LAN. To do this, they translate between frame formats and perform many other conversion functions.

The designers of FDDI borrowed a lot from Token Ring technology. For example, the format of an FDDI information frame is almost identical to the format of a Token Ring frame. Furthermore, FDDI frames optionally can be source-routed. Connecting a Token Ring to an FDDI ring is quite straightforward.

However, Ethernet and Token Ring appear to have been designed on different planets. Connecting Ethernet to Token Ring or FDDI is a difficult proposition. In spite of the problems, there have been customers for translational bridges for as long as there have been multiple LAN technologies. A frame can enter a translational bridge formatted for one MAC type (such as Token Ring) and leave the bridge formatted for a different MAC type (such as Ethernet).

The chapter ends with a brief discussion of remote bridges. These bridges unite LANs located at different sites into a single "LAN." Frames are relayed between sites by forwarding them across a wide area connection such as a leased line or a frame relay circuit.

Source-Routed Bridged LANs

In a source-routing bridged LAN, a frame that must pass through one or more bridges to reach its destination carries its travel directions in a *routing information field* (RIF) in the frame header.

Figure 17.1 shows how this works in a Token Ring LAN. Each Token Ring and each source-routing bridge in the figure has been assigned a numeric identifier. By established convention, these are written using hexadecimal characters. To describe the dotted line route from station X to server Y shown in the figure, the instructions in the RIF would say:

1. Enter ring X'201.

2. Cross bridge X'8, and enter ring X'203.

3. Cross bridge X'6, and enter ring X'214.

4. Cross bridge X'3, and enter ring X'180. The destination MAC address is on this ring.

A frame traveling from server Y to station X would follow the same route in the reverse direction.

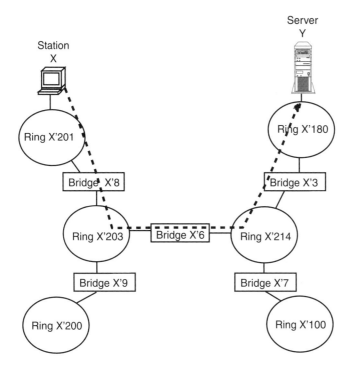

FIGURE 17.1 *Following a source route.*

Before a source route can be used, it must be discovered. The source and destination NICs and intermediate source-routing bridges cooperate to determine a path between a source and a destination. The process is called *route discovery* and is described a little later (in the section "Route Discovery").

Unlike a transparently bridged LAN, there can be multiple active paths through a source-routed LAN.

> **Note**
>
> The method used to set up a source route makes it very likely that the path that is the least busy at setup time is chosen. This means that traffic gets spread across all of the paths that are available. Thus, the technology supports both redundant paths and load balancing.

Figure 17.2 illustrates a source-routed Token Ring LAN. Four paths are shown between station X and server Y.

In the figure, "SRB" stands for source-routing bridge.

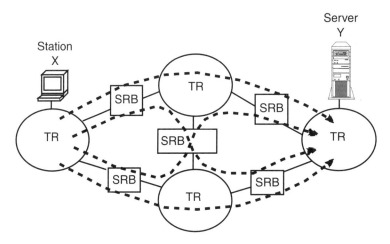

FIGURE 17.2 *A source-routed Token Ring LAN.*

Ring Identifiers and Bridge Identifiers

Each ring in a source-routed Token Ring LAN must be assigned a unique ring number. Each bridge is assigned a bridge number, but bridge numbers do not have to be unique.

Bridge numbers are used to distinguish between two or more "parallel" bridges that connect two rings to one another. The numbers assigned to a set of parallel bridges must be different.

Figure 17.3 illustrates parallel bridges. There are three paths between station X and server Y. The bridge numbers make it possible to distinguish between these paths, indicating which bridge should be crossed.

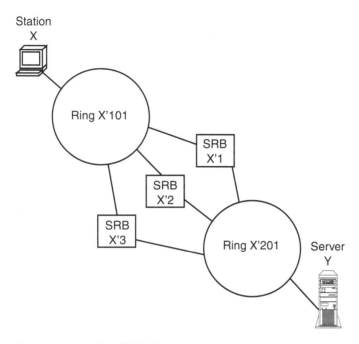

FIGURE 17.3 *Parallel bridges.*

Route Discovery

Route discovery is a two-step process. The source of a communication sends an initial test frame addressed to the targeted destination around its own ring.

> **Note**
>
> Either of two special types of frames—TEST or XID—is transmitted to test whether a destination is on the same ring as the source. If present on the ring, the destination responds with the same type of frame.

If the destination does not respond, the source sends out an *explorer frame* whose job is to discover a path to the destination.

Figure 17.4 illustrates the process.

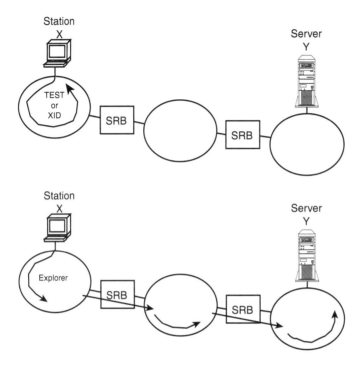

FIGURE 17.4 *Looking for a destination.*

There are two types of explorers:

- The traditional *all-routes-explorer* is flooded across all of the rings in the LAN. Launching a single explorer can cause many explorers to arrive at the destination system.

- A *Spanning Tree explorer* is sent through the active tree that has been established via a Spanning Tree Protocol. Only one explorer can arrive at the destination system.

As an explorer frame progresses through the LAN, each bridge that is crossed adds an entry to a list of rings and bridges that have been traversed by the frame. The information is recorded in the routing information field in the frame header.

The destination system sends the explorer frame (or frames) that it receives back to the source. Each explorer uses its RIF to find its way back, crossing rings and bridges in the reverse order. For an all-routes-explorer, the route in the first explorer that arrives back at the source normally is the one that is cached and used.

The selected route is placed into the headers of subsequent frames sent to the destination.

Most of the intelligence required to make source-routing work is embedded in the source and destination NICs. Source-routing bridges are simple devices that do as they are told. When a source-routing bridge receives an information frame that contains a RIF, it checks the RIF to see if the following combination is on the route:

Arrival ring ID, ID of this bridge, ID of other attached ring

If so, the RIF passes the frame to the exit ring.

> **Note**
> Ethernet end systems cannot participate in source-route bridging. An Ethernet NIC is not capable of performing the route discovery protocol or specifying a route to be followed.

All-Routes-Explorer Frames

If there are multiple paths to a destination, multiple all-routes-explorer frames will be generated. Figure 17.5 shows how this occurs. When an all-routes-explorer frame arrives at a bridge port, the following happens:

- The bridge examines the RIF to see whether the ring attached to the other port already is listed in the RIF.

- If not, the bridge updates the RIF and forwards the explorer onto that ring.

The all-routes-explorer sent from station X to server Y in Figure 17.5 will discover all four of the routes shown in Figure 17.2. That is:

- Ring 1, bridge A, ring 2, bridge C, ring 3

- Ring 1, bridge D, ring 4, bridge E, ring 3

- Ring 1, bridge A, ring 2, bridge B, ring 4, bridge E, ring 3

- Ring 1, bridge D, ring 4, bridge B, ring 2, bridge C, ring 3

Note that when Bridge A sees a frame that has arrived on the route

Ring 1, Bridge D, Ring 4, Bridge B, Ring 2

Bridge A will not forward the explorer onto Ring 1 because Ring 1 already is on the route.

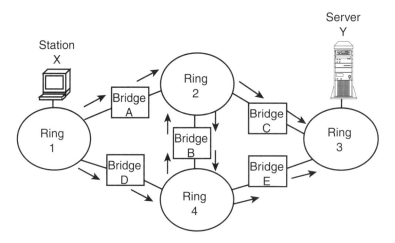

FIGURE 17.5 *Generating multiple explorer frames.*

Spanning Tree Explorer Frames

Spanning Tree explorer frames are used on some source-routed LANs. These explorer frames are forwarded only through ports that are active in the Spanning Tree topology. This means that the unique path that is unblocked at the time the explorer is sent out is the only one that is discovered and cached for communication between the two systems.

Spanning Tree explorers are used in big LANs when there is concern about the amount of traffic that is generated by all-routes-explorer frames. However, this restriction also causes much of the load-balancing benefit that source-routing provides to be lost.

> **Note**
> IBM introduced a proprietary Spanning Tree Protocol that was used solely to prevent all-routes-explorer frames from clogging the LAN.
>
> However, today many sites that use source-routing rely on the IEEE Spanning Tree Protocol for this purpose instead.

Source-Routing Bridge Protocol Elements

A look at some of the source-routing protocol details provides more insight into how source-routing bridges work. An examination of the Token Ring information frame format exposes some of these details.

Figure 17.6 displays the format of a Token Ring information frame that carries traffic for protocols that are identified by an EtherType, such as IP, IPX, AppleTalk, DECnet, DEC LAT, and Banyan VINES. (The LLC field would be different for SNA traffic.)

Frames transmitted onto source-routed LANs contain a routing information field. Frames transmitted onto transparently routed LANs do not contain a RIF.

A simple method is used to indicate whether a frame contains a routing information field. Because a source address always must be an individual address, the individual/group bit in a source address is unused and was recruited for source-routing. This bit is set to 1 to indicate that a RIF follows.

A RIF consists of a 2-byte introducer called a *control field*, followed by the route. The route is made up of a sequence of 2-byte *route descriptors*. Each route descriptor contains a 12-bit ring identifier followed by a 4-bit bridge identifier. The final route descriptor in a RIF contains the destination ring identifier followed by a 0.

> **Note**
> Ring and bridge identifiers are expressed in hexadecimal notation on configuration screens, reports, and traces.

The same RIF format is used for FDDI source routing. For simplicity, the discussion will continue to focus on Token Ring.

Token Ring Frame Trace

Listing 17.1 shows part of a trace of a Token Ring frame. The routing control field indicates that the RIF consists of 8 bytes. This includes the initial 2-byte routing control portion plus three 2-byte route descriptors.

A direction flag in the routing control field indicates whether the route should be followed in the forward or reverse direction. Its value is 0 in the trace, which corresponds to the forward direction. The next value in the control field announces the size of the biggest information field that can be carried on the path.

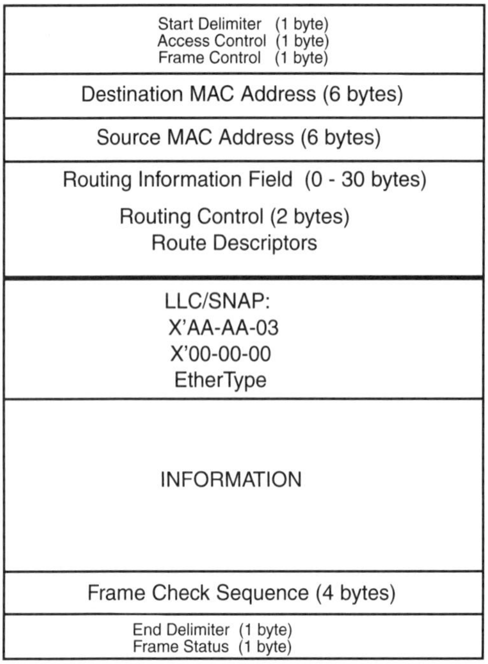

FIGURE 17.6 *A Token Ring information frame.*

Note

The maximum information field size was discovered by the explorer frame that mapped the path. Its value initially was set to the biggest size that the sending device could support. The value is reduced along the way if bridges on the path are limited to smaller sizes.

LISTING 17.1 A TOKEN RING FRAME CONTAINING A ROUTING INFORMATION FIELD

```
DLC:  Destination = Station IBM1  0C892E
      DLC:  Source      = Station IBM2  C9656B
      DLC:
RI:   ----- Routing Indicators -----
      RI:
      RI:  Routing control = 08
      RI:        000. .... = Non-broadcast
      RI:        ...0 1000 = RI length is 8
      RI:  Routing control = 40
      RI:        0... .... = Forward direction
      RI:        .100 .... = Largest frame is 8130
      RI:        .... 000. = Extended frame is 0
      RI:        .... ...0 = Reserved
      RI:  Ring number 416 via bridge 1
      RI:  Ring number 43A via bridge 0
```

```
      RI:  Ring number 43E
      RI:
LLC:  ----- LLC Header -----
      LLC:
      LLC:  DSAP Address = AA, DSAP IG Bit = 00 (Individual Address)
      LLC:  SSAP Address = AA, SSAP CR Bit = 00 (Command)
      LLC:  Unnumbered frame: UI   (X'03)
      LLC:
SNAP: ----- SNAP Header -----
      SNAP:
      SNAP: Type = 0800 (IP)
      SNAP:
IP: ----- IP Header -----
 . . .
```

The route descriptors in Listing 17.1 provide the following directions:

1. Follow ring X'416.

2. Cross bridge X'1, and exit onto ring X'43A.

3. Cross bridge X'0, and exit onto ring X'43E.

4. Look for MAC address IBM1 X'0C892E (X'08-00-5A-0C-89-2E in IBM format, and X'10-00-5A-30-91-74 in IEEE format).

The frame contains the same LLC and SNAP fields that are found in 802.3 LLC frames. The DSAP and SSAP are followed by an LLC control field whose value is X'03. This indicates that this is an unnumbered information frame.

Figure 17.7 illustrates why bridge X'1 on ring X'416 would decide to forward the source-routed frame in Listing 17.1, but bridge X'2 on ring X'416 would not. Each bridge checks whether it is on the route.

Route Discovery Protocol Details

Route discovery is a two-stage process:

1. Check whether the destination is on the same ring as the source.

2. If not, send out an explorer to find the destination.

Many special frames are used in Token Rings and FDDI rings. To execute step 1, a short TEST or XID (exchange identifier) frame is sent out. The first bit of its source address field is set to 0, which means that no RIF is included. This keeps the frame on the local ring.

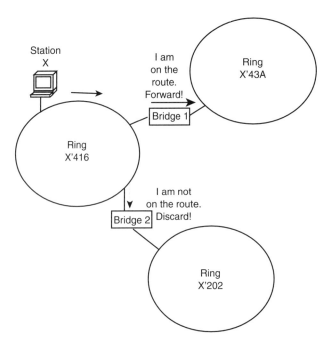

FIGURE 17.7 *Forwarding a source-routed frame.*

> **Note**
> These frame types are identified by the control field in a Token Ring or FDDI LLC header. The LLC control field of a TEST frame is X'E3 or X'F3, and the LLC control field of an XID field is X'AF or X'BF. Recall that the LLC control field for unnumbered information is X'03.

If the destination does not respond, the source issues a TEST or XID for which the first bit of the source address has been set to 1, indicating that a RIF follows. The source inserts the 2-byte RIF routing control field. The first bit of the routing control field is set to 1 to indicate that this frame is an explorer. This causes the frame to be flooded, and it causes bridges along a route to insert ring and bridge numbers.

Source-Routing Transparent Bridges

Source-Routing Transparent (SRT) bridging was introduced to enable a single Token Ring or FDDI LAN to carry both source-routed and transparently bridged traffic. It provides a convenient way to merge source-routed Token Ring (or FDDI) LANs with transparently bridged Token Ring (or FDDI) LANs, or to migrate from one bridging technology to the other.

A Source-Routing Transparent bridge performs source routing for frames that contain routing information fields, and transparent bridging for frames that do not carry routing information. Source-Routing Transparent bridging applies exclusively to LAN technologies that support source routing—namely, Token Ring and FDDI.

Source-Routing Transparent bridges perform the IEEE Spanning Tree Protocol to discover an optimal tree structure. Transparently routed frames cannot be forwarded through blocked ports. However, source-routed frames can be forwarded through any port.

Translational Bridges

One aspect of the move toward building bigger LANs and using fewer routers is that some users are bridging Ethernet, Token Ring, and FDDI LANs to each other. This is being done in spite of some major incompatibilities between these LANs, including differences in the following:

- Frame sizes

- Frame format

- The bit order of the bytes in the frames

- The MAC addresses that are used for LAN multicasts

- Transparent and source-routing bridging

No standard defines exactly how translational bridging should be done, although some standards offer partial solutions that work in particular situations. These partial solutions are augmented by as many proprietary solutions as there are vendors.

Making translational bridges work properly requires some effort when FDDI is involved. Devices throughout a LAN must be configured carefully to prevent incompatibilities that will cause translations to fail. The placement of the bridges that perform translations and the types of traffic that each bridge will process must be planned and implemented carefully.

While considering how much translation should be done, it is good to keep in mind that the processing required to translate a frame from one MAC type to another usually exceeds the processing required to route the frame. Furthermore, it is not easy to troubleshoot translation errors.

Vendors recommend the use of routing for protocols such as IP, IPX, AppleTalk, and DECnet. However, LANs still carry unroutable traffic, such as IBM's classic Systems Network Architecture (SNA) and Digital Equipment Corporation's

(DEC) Local Area Transport (LAT). Sometimes using an existing solid network infrastructure to carry this traffic is the best solution that is available. Barring some compelling need that cannot be met in any other way, translational bridging should be reserved for the hard cases that cannot be routed.

MAC Frame Sizes

One of the problems encountered when translating between Ethernet, Token Ring, and FDDI frames is that these MAC protocols were designed independently, and their maximum frame sizes differ greatly.

Table 17.1 lists the maximum sizes of conventional, untagged frames. Tagging can add from 4 to 34 extra bytes. The maximum frame size that is supported on a particular real Token Ring often is manually set to a value below the levels shown in the table.

Translational bridges cannot perform miracles. If a 4,000-byte Token Ring frame enters a switch, it cannot be forwarded through a standard Ethernet port. A frame is not placed on an output queue if the frame is bigger than the maximum size supported by that output port.

Ethernet, Token Ring, and FDDI LAN frames cannot be fragmented, and there is no way for a frame that is too big to be forwarded using Layer 2 processes.

> **Warning**
> Vendor documentation that blurs the distinction between functions that are performed at Layer 2 and at Layer 3 has caused confusion about fragmentation.

TABLE 17.1 MAXIMUM FRAME SIZES FOR ETHERNET, TOKEN RING, AND FDDI UNTAGGED FRAMES

MAC Type	Maximum Frame Size (Bytes)	Comments
Ethernet	1518	9018 bytes for nonstandard Jumbo frames.
Token Ring 4Mbps 16Mbps 100Mbps	4550 18200 18200	The actual maximum size that is used is configured by an administrator based on the size of the ring, the medium used, and the desired token holding time.
FDDI	4500	This is the limit for Basic mode FDDI, the version that actually is implemented.

Translational Bridging Between Token Ring and FDDI

Token Ring frames and FDDI frames are almost identical, and both can be forwarded using source-route bridging or transparent bridging. Figure 17.8 shows a LAN that is made up of Token Rings connected by an FDDI backbone.

A system can communicate with any other system on the LAN if some conditions are met:

- All systems must use the same type of bridging. Either they all must use source-route bridging, or they all must use transparent bridging.

- All MAC addresses that appear within the information fields of FDDI frames must have the same format—preferably noncanonical—so that no translation from the Token Ring formats is needed.

To understand the last condition, recall that Chapter 2, "LAN MAC Addresses," explained these points:

- For Token Ring, address bytes appear in a bit-reversed (non-canonical) order, both in the MAC header and within the information field.

- For FDDI, address bytes appear in a bit-reversed order in the MAC header. The order used for addresses that appear in the information field may be bit-reversed (non-canonical) or not bit-reversed (canonical). It depends on how the FDDI device driver is configured.

It saves a lot of grief if the FDDI systems use the non-canonical address format within the information field, just as Token Ring systems do. Otherwise, the translational bridges have quite a lot of work to do. The reason for this is that many frames carry addresses within the information field.

Chapter 2 pointed out that Address Resolution Protocol (ARP) frames carry addresses within their information fields. This is far from being the only protocol for which this is the case. For example, NetWare IPX frames carry MAC addresses in their network-layer headers. Messages exchanged between routers for protocols such as RIP or OSPF contain many addresses.

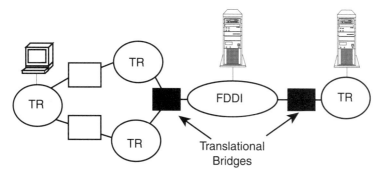

FIGURE 17.8 *Token Rings connected by an FDDI backbone.*

Translational Bridging Between Transparent Token Ring and Ethernet

The price and performance of Fast Ethernet and Gigabit Ethernet have made Ethernet an attractive LAN backbone technology. Figure 17.9 shows Token Rings that are interconnected across an Ethernet. Transparent bridging is used everywhere, and any system can communicate with any other system.

Each translational bridge has to

- Translate between Ethernet and Token Ring frame formats

- Perform conversions between the non-canonical address formats used in Token Rings and the canonical address formats used in Ethernet frames

This LAN is constructed using transparent bridges. The Spanning Tree Protocol would be used to generate a loop-free topology because the LAN contains a looped path.

There are drawbacks to a totally bridged solution:

- The format translations add a lot of overhead.

- Available bandwidth is wasted because redundant links must be blocked by the Spanning Tree Protocol.

Therefore, it makes sense to use Layer 2/3 switches and to route as much of the traffic as possible.

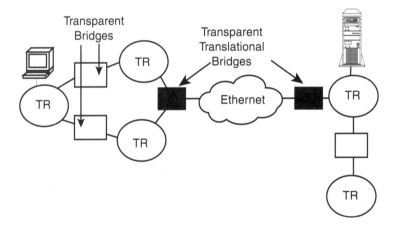

FIGURE 17.9 *Connecting transparent Token Rings to an Ethernet.*

Translational Bridging Between Source-Routing Token Rings and Ethernet

The situation is more complicated if source-routing bridges are used in a Token Ring LAN that is connected to an Ethernet, but some vendors offer proprietary products that can overcome the problems.

Figure 17.10 illustrates what happens. Thanks to the actions of the translational bridge:

- Token Ring systems think that the entire Ethernet is a single Token Ring.

- Ethernet systems think that the Token Ring LAN is an Ethernet.

For traffic from the Token Ring to the Ethernet, the translational bridge

- Responds to explorer frames (The RIF appears to lead to the destination MAC address, but actually it leads to the bridge.)

- Caches RIFs

- Translates incoming Token Ring frames to Ethernet format and forwards the frames

For traffic from the Ethernet to the Token Ring, the bridge

- Translates from Ethernet format to Token Ring format

- Searches its cache for a RIF that leads to the destination MAC address

- If a usable RIF is not found, launches explorer frames to locate the destination and adds the RIF to the cache

For either direction of transmission, the bridge must translate between the non-canonical address formats used in Token Ring information fields and the canonical address formats used in Ethernet frame information fields.

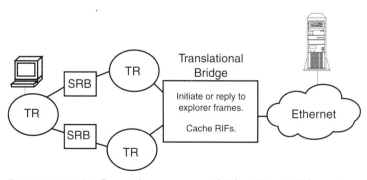

FIGURE 17.10 Connecting source-routed Token Rings to Ethernet.

Tunneling Token Ring Across Ethernet

Sometimes the only reason to connect Token Rings to an Ethernet is to use the backbone bandwidth of the Ethernet. For example, systems on one Token Ring might need to reach an SNA host on another Token Ring, and might have no need to reach any system connected to the Ethernet.

In this case, there is no reason to translate between Ethernet and Token Ring MAC formats because Token Ring and Ethernet systems do not want to communicate with one another.

Several vendors offer proprietary *tunneling* solutions that suit this situation. Figure 17.11 illustrates how it works. The following is true for tunneling bridges:

- The bridges carry each Token Ring frame inside the information field of an Ethernet frame.

- The source and destination MAC addresses on these Ethernet frames are the source and destination MAC addresses of tunneling bridges.

The procedure is very simple if the Token Rings in Figure 17.11 use transparent bridging. In this case, if station X sends an information frame to server Y, the following takes place:

1. The frame is forwarded to bridge A, which checks its filtering table.

2. If server Y's MAC address is in bridge A's filtering table, the entry indicates that the frame must be tunneled to bridge C. Bridge A wraps the Token Ring frame in an Ethernet frame addressed to bridge C and forwards it.

3. If server Y's MAC address is not in bridge A's filtering table, bridge A wraps the Token Ring frame in Ethernet frames that are addressed to bridge B and bridge C, and forwards them.

4. Bridge C forwards the frame onto the ring that leads to server Y.

The procedure is slightly more complicated if the Token Rings use source routing. The Token Rings are fooled into thinking that the Ethernet is a single ring. This procedure is

1. Station X sends out an explorer frame.

2. Bridge A caches the route to station X. It wraps the explorer in Ethernet frames addressed to bridges B and C.

3. Bridges B and C unwrap the explorer and add a "fake" Ethernet ring number and their own bridge numbers to the route. They then forward the explorer into their Token Rings. They also create filtering table entries for station A's MAC address.

4. When server Y returns the explorer to bridge C, bridge C caches the route to server Y and wraps the explorer in an Ethernet frame addressed to bridge A.

5. Bridge A creates a filtering table entry that indicates that server Y is reached via the tunnel to bridge C.

6. Bridge A forwards the frame back to station X.

All systems now are ready to communicate.

This solution has low overhead and is fast. It disposes of the heavy-duty translations that translational bridges must perform. It also avoids the pitfalls that result from glitches in translating between canonical and non-canonical address forms.

The disadvantages of tunneling Token Ring across Ethernet are these:

• Ethernet frame sizes are small. An extra protocol header usually is inserted into the information field of the Ethernet frame to indicate that the content is tunneled Token Ring traffic, making the payload even smaller. This limits the maximum size of the Token Ring frames.

• Solutions are proprietary. All participating bridges must be supplied by one vendor, and there is no guarantee that the vendor will support the solution into the future.

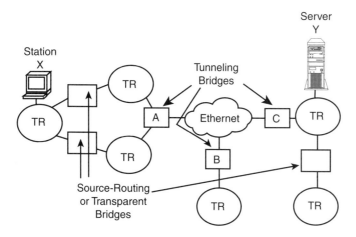

FIGURE 17.11 *Tunneling Token Ring across Ethernet.*

Structuring a LAN Around a High-Speed Ethernet or FDDI Backbone with Tagging

Another option is available to a LAN administrator who wishes to bridge between Ethernet, Token Ring and FDDI LANs. The IEEE 802 VLAN committee introduced VLAN tag features that solve some of the problems encountered in translational bridging between Ethernet, Token Ring, and FDDI.

The IEEE solution supports both transparent LANs and LANs that include source-routed portions. The solution requires frames to be translated, but it offers two advantages:

- It is defined in a standard (802.1Q).

- The tag information explicitly states whether MAC addresses contained in the information field are in canonical or non-canonical format.

Using Tags in a Transparently Bridged LAN

Figure 17.12 shows a transparently bridged LAN that contains Ethernet, Token Ring, and FDDI portions that are interconnected by VLAN-aware transparent bridges.

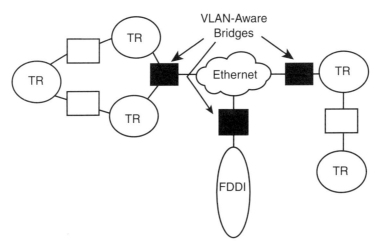

FIGURE 17.12   *VLAN-aware bridges in a transparently bridged LAN with an Ethernet backbone.*

The VLAN-aware bridges insert tag headers into frames that originate in a Token Ring or FDDI system. The frames are sent across the Ethernet in the format shown in Figure 17.13.

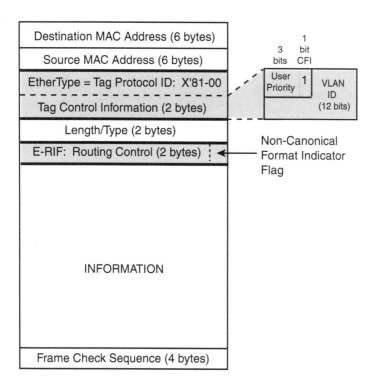

FIGURE 17.13 *Tag information in an Ethernet frame in a transparently bridged LAN.*

The Canonical Format Indicator (CFI) flag in the tag control information is important.

- If the CFI is 0, this is an ordinary tagged Ethernet frame.

- The CFI is set to 1 to indicate that this frame has been translated from Token Ring or FDDI format to Ethernet format, and that an extra embedded routing information field (E-RIF) follows the length/type field.

The E-RIF field is considered to be part of the tag information. In Figure 17.13, the entire E-RIF is just a 2-byte *routing control* field. The values carried for a transparently bridged network are shown in Figure 17.14:

- The initial 3-bit field identifies the routing type, which in this case is transparent.

- A *largest frame* (LF) field indicates, in this case, that the biggest information field is 1470 bytes. This restriction assures that the Token Ring payloads will fit within the Ethernet frame payload areas.

- The final bit is a flag called the Non-Canonical Format Identifier (NCFI). NCFI=0 means that any MAC addresses carried in the information field are in non-canonical form. NCFI=1 means that they are in canonical form.

The NCFI bit takes the mystery out of the most confusing part of the translation process.

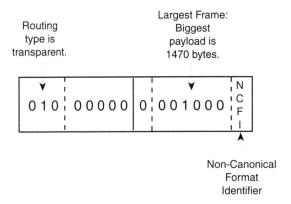

FIGURE 17.14 *The Routing Control field for a frame that originated at a transparent Token Ring or FDDI system.*

Using Tags to Translate Source-Routed Frames

Tagging also can help a high-speed Ethernet or a transparent FDDI ring to be used as a conduit between source-routed Token Ring communities. Figure 17.15 depicts source-routed Token Rings that are connected across an Ethernet or a transparent FDDI ring by VLAN-aware bridges.

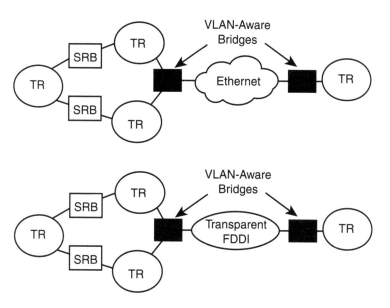

FIGURE 17.15 *VLAN-aware bridges connecting source-routed Token Ring LANs across Ethernet or transparent FDDI.*

Source-routed Token Ring frames are translated to Ethernet format and are sent across the Ethernet in the tagged format shown in Figure 17.16.

The CFI value of 1 indicates that an embedded routing information field (E-RIF) follows the length/type field. In this case, the E-RIF lives up to its name. It includes the route descriptors that were in the routing information field of the original source-routed Token Ring frame before it was translated.

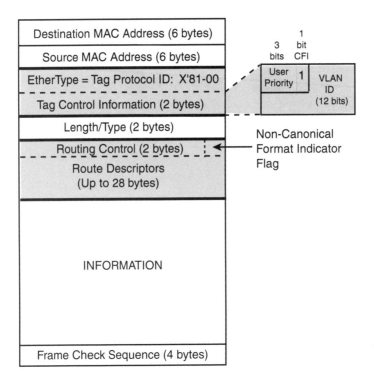

FIGURE 17.16 *An Ethernet frame that carries the information field of a source-routed Token Ring frame.*

Source-routed Token Ring frames are translated and sent across a transparent FDDI LAN in the tagged frame format shown in Figure 17.17.

For either type of backbone, the routing control bytes have the format shown in Figure 17.18. The routing type indicates whether this is an ordinary routed frame (000), an all-routes explorer (100), or a Spanning Tree explorer (110). The next field indicates the length of the E-RIF. The direction bit indicates whether the route should be followed in forward or reverse order.

If the backbone is an Ethernet, the code in the *largest frame* field indicates that the biggest payload is 1470 bytes. If the backbone is an FDDI LAN, the value can range up to 4399 bytes.

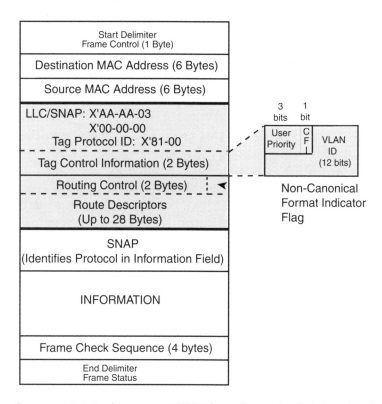

FIGURE 17.17 *A transparent FDDI frame that carries the information field of a source-routed Token Ring frame.*

As before, NCFI=0 means that any MAC addresses carried in the information field are in non-canonical form. NCFI=1 means that they are in canonical form.

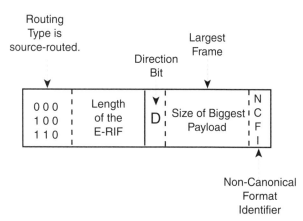

FIGURE 17.18 *The Routing Control field for a frame that originated at a source-routing system.*

Remote Bridges

By definition, a "local" area network was intended to be a network facility covering a limited space, such as a set of offices, a building, or perhaps a campus. But as earlier discussion has shown, the evolution of LANs has been fueled by the desire of users to bend the rules to suit their special needs.

Remote bridges were designed to unite LANs located at different sites into a single LAN. Remote bridges have been used for several reasons. Some protocol traffic cannot be routed, so if local clients needed to cross a wide area link to reach a remote server, bridging was the only alternative. Frequently used non-routable protocols have included IBM SNA, Digital Equipment Corporation Local Area Transport (LAT), and IBM/Microsoft NetBIOS over NetBEUI.

Some network administrators feel that routers are too expensive, too slow, or too complicated to configure. They prefer to bridge all protocols—even routable ones—on principle.

Figure 17.19 shows a pair of LANs connected together by remote bridges to form one large "LAN."

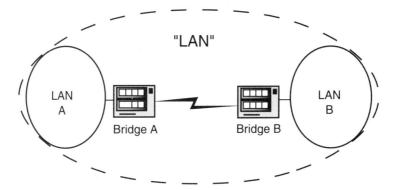

FIGURE 17.19 *Two sites connected by remote bridges.*

Links Between Bridges

LANs can be bridged across a frame relay, ATM, or X.25 circuit; a leased line; a microwave connection; or even a dialup ISDN or POTS line. Some products can aggregate multiple links between a pair of remote bridges so that they behave like a single line.

In some instances, multiple sites are bridged together. Figure 17.20 shows three sites connected by remote bridges. The link between bridge B and bridge C has been blocked by the Spanning Tree Protocol to prevent a loop.

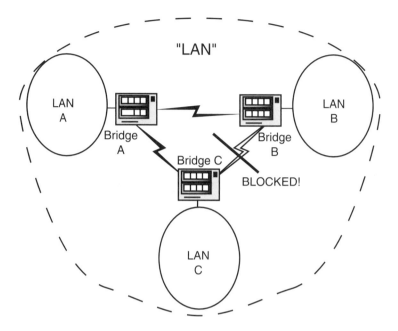

FIGURE 17.20   *Three sites connected by remote bridges.*

To Bridge or Not to Bridge

The absolute need to bridge traffic across wide area links is decreasing. Today, NetBIOS can run over IP and, hence, can be routed. The use of the DEC LAT protocol is in decline as well. However, IBM SNA still is the source of a substantial amount of unroutable traffic.

At the same time, objections against using routers are diminishing. Today's routers are fast, and often less effort is required to set up a router than to configure a bridge to keep unnecessary traffic off the wide area link. This must be done by placing manual entries into bridge filtering tables, or by defining VLANs that control and reduce traffic.

Combined Layer 2/3 switches (bridge/routers) can route most of the traffic and bridge whatever unroutable traffic remains. Unlike bridged traffic, routed traffic can and will use all available links. For example, if the bridges in Figure 17.20 are replaced by Layer 2/3 switches, routed traffic can be sent across the link connecting bridge/routers B and C. Because wide area bandwidth still is costly, it makes sense to use it at all times—not just for backup.

A router forwards exactly the traffic that needs to cross a link, and no more. LAN broadcasts and local multicasts are not forwarded by routers.

In contrast, a bridge forwards a mass of extra traffic. This includes broadcasts and flooded frames whose destination MAC addresses have not yet been learned by the bridge. For example, if all protocols used at sites A, B, and C in Figure 17.20 are bridged, the following would be true:

- ARP broadcasts used to map IP addresses to MAC addresses would be propagated to remote sites.

- NetBIOS name registrations would be broadcast to remote sites.

- NetWare Service Advertisement Protocol (SAP) messages would be broadcast to remote sites.

- If bridge A had not yet learned that system M was located on its local LAN A, a frame addressed to M would be flooded across the remote links.

Another factor to consider is the delay that crossing a wide area link adds to LAN communication. This delay must be taken into account when configuring the timers used for the Spanning Tree Protocol.

Frame Formats on Wide Area Links

An Ethernet, Token Ring, or FDDI MAC frame is bridged across a wide area link by placing the MAC frame into the information field of a WAN frame before sending it across the link. The MAC frame is extracted at the other end and then is forwarded onto the remote LAN.

> **Note**
> The encapsulation of an Ethernet, Token Ring, or FDDI MAC frame inside a WAN frame actually is an instance of tunneling.

Figure 17.21 illustrates what an encapsulation looks like.

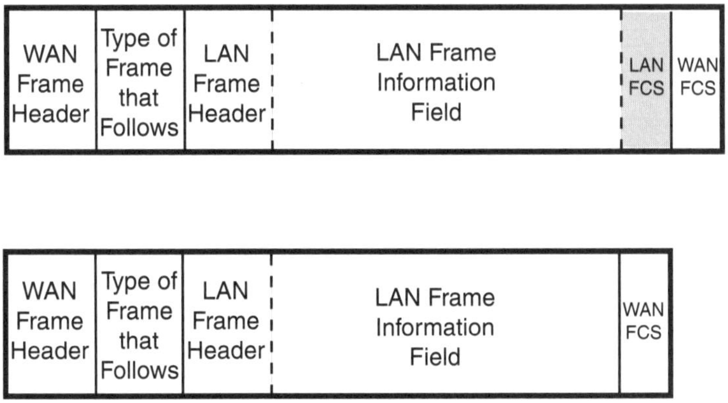

FIGURE 17.21   *Encapsulating a LAN frame within a WAN frame.*

In Figure 17.21, the WAN frame header is followed by a header that indicates the type of data that follows. This data might be a bridged Ethernet, Token Ring, or FDDI frame, or a Bridge Protocol Data Unit (BPDU) used for the Spanning Tree Protocol. Other encapsulated traffic in the mix could include SNA frames and routed protocol data units.

Note that for the encapsulation in the upper part of Figure 17.21, the LAN and WAN frames each contain a frame check sequence (FCS) field. One of these is excess baggage, and for some wide area encapsulations, the LAN FCS can be dropped before the Layer 2 frame is placed into a WAN frame's information field. This is illustrated in the lower part of Figure 17.21. In this case, the WAN frame check sequence is validated when the frame arrives at the remote end of a WAN link. If the frame has not been corrupted, the MAC frame's FCS is recalculated and added before the frame is forwarded onto a LAN segment.

Encapsulation is done a little differently for each wide area technology. Sometimes more than one encapsulation can be used for a particular wide area technology. Table 17.2 lists some encapsulation methods.

TABLE 17.2 WAN ENCAPSULATION FORMATS

WAN Technology	Encapsulation Method	Comments
Point-to-Point line (includes leased lines; switched 56K, ISDN B-channel connections; and ordinary dialup)	Proprietary version of High-level Data Link Control (HDLC)	Proprietary versions of HDLC are designed by vendors.
	Point-to-Point Protocol (PPP)	Defined in a series of IETF standards documents. The basic standard is RFC 1662.
Frame Relay	IETF Multiprotocol over Frame Relay	Often called the RFC 1490 encapsulation by vendors, although the current standard is RFC 2427.
ATM	IETF Multiprotocol Encapsulation over ATM Adaptation Layer 5	Defined in IETF RFC 2684. Similar, but not identical to the encapsulation used for frame relay.
	ATM LAN Emulation	Defined in the ATM Forum LANE specification.
X.25 and ISDN LAPD packets	IETF Multiprotocol Interconnect on X.25 and ISDN in the Packet Mode	Defined in IETF RFC 1356. Similar, but not identical to, the encapsulation used for frame relay.

To provide an idea of what an encapsulated frame looks like, Listing 17.2 shows a Token Ring frame that is encapsulated within a frame relay frame. The frame relay header contains a frame relay data link connection identifier (DLCI). The DLCI is 32, in this case. The frame relay header also includes some flags that are used to report congestion and to indicate whether the frame may be discarded when congestion occurs.

The header after the address field, which starts with X'03-00-80, was defined by the IETF. This is followed by the organizationally unique identifier (OUI) X'00-80-C2, which indicates that a bridged MAC frame is enclosed. The type field value, X'00-09, means that this is a Token Ring frame and that its frame check sequence has been stripped off. (A type field value of X'00-03 would indicate that a complete Token Ring frame that included a frame check sequence was included in the payload.)

LISTING 17.2 A TOKEN RING FRAME ENCAPSULATED WITHIN A FRAME RELAY FRAME

```
FRELAY: ----- Frame Relay -----
      FRELAY:
      FRELAY: Address word = 0801
      FRELAY:  0000 10..  0000 .... = DLCI 32
      FRELAY:  .... ..0.  .... .... = Response
      FRELAY:  .... ....  .... 0... = No forward congestion
      FRELAY:  .... ....  .... .0.. = No backward congestion
      FRELAY:  .... ....  .... ..0. = Not eligible for discard
      FRELAY:  .... ....  .... ...1 = Not extended address
      FRELAY:
FRELAY: ----- Multiprotocol over Frame Relay -----
      FRELAY:
      FRELAY: Control, pad(s) = 0300
      FRELAY: NLPID = 0x80 (SNAP)
      FRELAY:
SNAP: ----- SNAP Header -----
      SNAP:
      SNAP: Vendor ID = IEEE  (OUI X'00-80-C2)
      SNAP: Type = 0009 (802.5)
      SNAP: Pad = 11
      SNAP:
TRING: ----- Token Ring Header -----
      TRING:
      TRING: Physical Control Field :
      TRING: Access Control = 40
      TRING:     010. .... = Priority Bits
      TRING:     ...0 .... = Token Bit
      TRING:     .... 0... = Monitor Bit
      TRING:     .... .000 = Reservation Bits
      TRING: AC: Frame priority 2,  Reservation priority 0,  Monitor count 0
      TRING:
      TRING: Frame Control = 40
      TRING:     01.. ....  = Frame Type (LLC)
      TRING:     ..00 .... = Reserved
      TRING:     .... 0000 = Reserved
      TRING: FC: LLC frame,  PCF attention code: None
      TRING: Destination = Station 0000000060C0
      TRING: Source      = Station 000000006108
      TRING:
LLC:  ----- LLC Header -----
      LLC:
. . .
```

Some trends might make wide area switching grow in popularity instead of fading away. New fiber optic transmission techniques are expanding the bandwidth that can be carried on a tiny optical fiber at an unprecedented rate. Tomorrow's wide area bandwidth price will be a fraction of today's price.

The move to standardize on TCP/IP is gradually eroding the use of unroutable protocols and protocols that have a high density of broadcast traffic. IP version 6 cuts back on IP broadcast traffic.

In addition, ATM LANE, which is discussed in Chapter 21, "ATM LAN Emulation," cuts down on the amount of broadcasting and is designed to blur the difference between wide area and local area communication.

Summary Points

- Transparent bridges learn the MAC addresses that are reached through each port and can participate in the Spanning Tree Protocol, which restructures the LAN topology automatically after a component failure.

- In a source-routing bridged LAN, a frame carries its travel directions in a routing information field (RIF) in the frame header.

- Source routes that cross one or more bridges are discovered by explorer frames.

- An all-routes-explorer frame is flooded across all of the rings in the LAN. When all-routes-explorers are used, multiple active paths can carry traffic to a destination ring.

- Spanning Tree explorer frames are forwarded through ports that are active in the Spanning Tree topology. They are used in big LANs when there is concern about the amount of traffic that is generated by all-routes-explorer frames.

- A routing information field contains a sequence of ring identifiers and bridge numbers.

- Source-routing transparent bridging enables a single Token Ring or FDDI LAN to carry both source-routed and transparently bridged traffic.

- Source-routing transparent bridging provides a convenient way to migrate from source-routed to transparently bridged Token Ring or FDDI LANs.

- Translational bridges relay frames between Ethernet, Token Ring, and FDDI LANs, creating a big, interconnected LAN.

- Translational bridges must overcome major incompatibilities in frame formats, bit order, and transparent versus source-routed bridging.

- It is not difficult to tunnel Token Ring frames across an Ethernet backbone.

- Tagged frames simplify format translation. They enable an Ethernet or FDDI frame to carry a Token Ring frame's payload and routing information field across a transparent Ethernet or FDDI backbone.

- Remote bridges unite Ethernet or Token Ring LANs located at different sites into a single LAN.

- Broadcast traffic can degrade a wide area link between two sites.

- An Ethernet, Token Ring, or FDDI frame is bridged across a wide area link by placing the MAC frame into the information field of a WAN frame.

References

Source-routing is described in Annex C of

- IEEE 802.1D (ISO/IEC 15802-3). "Media Access Control (MAC) Bridges." 1998.

Some of the issues that arise in translating between Ethernet frames that contain a type field and 802.3, 802.5, and FDDI frames are discussed in

- ANSI/IEEE Standard 802.1H (ISO/IEC Technical Report 11802-5). "Media Access Control (MAC) Bridging of Ethernet V2.0 in Local Area Networks." 1997.

VLANs and E-RIFs are described in

- IEEE 802.1Q. "Virtual Bridged Local Area Networks." 1998.

Insight into source-routing bridge configuration parameters can be gained by examining the IETF document:

- RFC 1525. "Definitions of Managed Objects for Source Routing Bridges." E. Decker, K. McCloghrie, P. Langille, and A. Rijsinghani. 1993.

Several IETF RFC documents discuss encapsulations for MAC frames that are transmitted across a wide area link that connects remote bridges:

- RFC 2427. "Multiprotocol Interconnect over Frame Relay." C. Brown and A. Malis. 1998.

- RFC 2684. "Multiprotocol Encapsulation over ATM Adaptation Layer 5." D. Grossman and J. Heinanen. 1999.

- RFC 1356. "Multiprotocol Interconnect on X.25 and ISDN in the Packet Mode." A. Malis, D. Robinson, and R. Ullmann. 1992.

- RFC 1662. "PPP in HDLC-like Framing." W. Simpson, ed. 1994.

- RFC 1990. "The PPP Multilink Protocol (MP)." K. Sklower, B. Lloyd, G. McGregor, D. Carr, and T. Coradetti. 1996.

Descriptions of wide area encapsulations, along with several detailed examples, can be found in

- Feit, Dr. Sidnie. *Wide Area High Speed Networks.* Indianapolis, IN: Macmillan Technical Publishing, 1999.

CHAPTER 18

Routing and Layer 2/3 Switches

This book is primarily concerned with communication between devices that are connected to the same LAN. But it also is important to understand the role and operation of routers, which carry traffic to and from LANs. This is especially true because of the increasing use of Layer 2/3 switches, which bridge some types of traffic and route other types.

This chapter provides an overview of the functions that are performed by routers. It also explains what Layer 2/3/4 and application-layer switches are.

Because of its widespread use, the IP protocol is used as the basis of examples that describe the types of functions that a router performs. Recall that the IP protocol data unit, which consists of a header and payload data, is called a *datagram*.

Features of Routing

A network-layer protocol consists of a network-addressing plan plus a set of procedures performed to deliver data to a destination network address. Routers forward data to its network destination, traversing multiple links along the way.

Several vendors have designed successful proprietary network-layer protocols. IBM SNA, Digital Equipment Corporation's DECnet, Novell's routable IPX/SPX, and routable AppleTalk all have had many loyal adherents. In the end, however, IP, an open standard, won out. Because there is a large installed base of equipment that uses legacy protocols, though, many of today's routers forward one or more of the proprietary traffic flows as well as IP traffic.

Router Benefits

Routers provide total flexibility in building a network topology. As illustrated in Figure 18.1, routers can move data across any series of LAN and wide area links. You can build as much redundancy into a routed network as you want (or can afford).

The IP network layer includes a multinetwork, global addressing plan. This has made the worldwide connection of computers across the Internet possible.

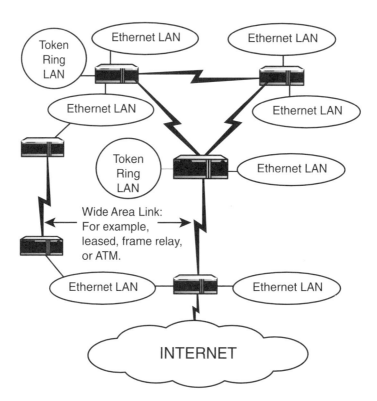

Figure **18.1** *A routed network.*

Network Addresses versus MAC Addresses

A global network-layer address plan is hierarchical, in some ways resembling the telephone number system. In the United States, telephones whose 10-digit numbers start with the same 6-digit prefix are connected to the same switch. IP network addresses that start with the same prefix belong to the same LAN.

An IP system decides whether a destination is on its LAN by comparing its own address prefix with the destination's address prefix.

> **Note**
> The address prefix consists of two parts—a *network number* associated with a whole network, and a *subnet number* associated with systems on a LAN.

If the source and destination address prefixes match, both systems are on the same LAN. The next step is to discover the destination's Layer 2 MAC address.

This step is responsible for a lot of the Layer 2 broadcasts that flood through a LAN. An IP system discovers the MAC address of a destination on its LAN by broadcasting an Address Resolution Protocol (ARP) message that asks the owner of a specified IP address to respond.

For example, in Figure 18.2, station X broadcasts an address resolution request asking the owner of an enclosed IP address to send back the owner's MAC address. When server Y answers, station X caches the MAC address. Station X then is able to wrap IP datagrams addressed to server Y into frames directed to this destination MAC address.

FIGURE 18.2 *ARP MAC address resolution.*

Exiting a LAN

If a destination IP address prefix does not match the source address prefix, a datagram must leave its own LAN to reach its destination. The way that the datagram is launched is

1. Station X looks up the IP address of its local default router. (This either was manually configured, was obtained from a configuration server, or was announced by a router broadcast.)

2. If necessary, station X makes an ARP query to obtain the default router's MAC address.

3. Station A wraps the datagram in a frame whose destination is the router's MAC address and sends it to the router.

4. The router processes the datagram, reframes it and forwards it onward.

Figure 18.3 shows a framed datagram entering a router, being processed and reframed, and leaving. The datagram in this example is being forwarded from an Ethernet LAN to a Token Ring LAN.

The router accepts the incoming Ethernet frame because the frame's destination MAC address matches the MAC address of port 1 at the router. After validating the frame check sequence, the router uses EtherType to identify the kind of protocol data unit that is enclosed—an IP datagram, in this case.

The IP datagram header includes the datagram's destination IP address. The router processes the datagram, looking up the destination IP address in its IP routing table to determine the exit port through which the datagram should be forwarded—in Figure 18.3, this is port 2.

The datagram then is given a completely new frame header and trailer. The frame format depends on the type of segment or link that is connected to port 2, which in this case is a Token Ring segment. The frame check sequence is calculated and placed in the frame trailer.

The source address for this new frame is the MAC address of router port 2. The destination MAC address is the MAC address of the next-hop system, which is either the destination or another router on the path to the destination.

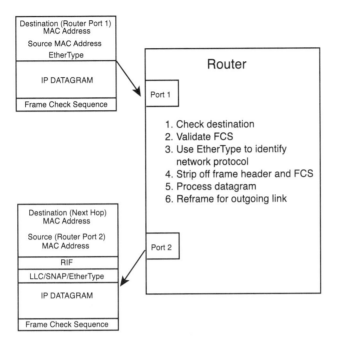

F IGURE 18.3 *A router reframing a datagram.*

Figure 18.4 shows a bird's-eye view of the routed path between station X on an Ethernet and server Y on a Token Ring.

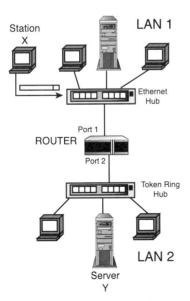

F IGURE 18.4 *Routing a datagram between LANs.*

In contrast, Figure 18.5 illustrates how a Layer 2 switch forwards a frame. In Figure 18.5, both the entrance and the exit ports connect to Ethernet segments. The switch looks up the destination MAC address in the filtering table. The frame is forwarded based on the result.

Note that the entire frame is unchanged—it still has its original source and destination MAC addresses and frame check sequence.

This transaction is a lot simpler than the routing transaction.

> **Note**
>
> Some products give the customer the option of accelerating frames through the switch by using *cut-through* operation, which means that the output port is looked up as soon as a frame's destination address has been received. The switch starts to transmit the initial part of the frame before the complete frame has arrived and, hence, before the frame check sequence can be verified.

The simplicity of a Layer 2 switch enables it to process massive numbers of frames per second. However, if the exit port connects to a Token Ring LAN and the frame format must be translated, the amount of processing rises dramatically.

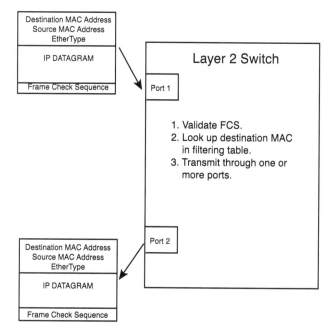

FIGURE 18.5   *A switch forwarding a frame.*

Routing Procedures

The key step in the Layer 3 routing process is a network address table lookup. A router maintains a table that matches address prefixes to output ports.

The specific processing steps that are carried out differ slightly for each of the network-layer protocols. A rough outline that includes most of the steps performed by an IP router follows:

- After discarding the frame header and trailer, the datagram is passed to an IP module for processing.

- The IP header contains a checksum field. The checksum is recalculated, and the datagram is discarded if the outcome does not match the value in the field.

- The IP header includes a field that limits the number of hops that a datagram may traverse. This is decremented, and if the value is 0, the datagram is discarded.

- The header checksum is recalculated and placed into the checksum field.

- A routing table lookup maps the destination IP address in the IP header to the correct output port. That port leads either to a next-hop router or to the final destination.

- Optionally, a list of security screening rules is applied to the datagram. If the datagram fails any test, it is discarded.

- Optionally, a set of rules is applied to assign a priority to the datagram.

- The datagram is wrapped in a fresh frame, which is sent across the next link, either to a next-hop router or to the final destination.

This is quite a lot of processing compared to what a Layer 2 switch (bridge) does.

Building Routing Tables

There is a very direct way to get a routing table into a router—an administrator can type it in. This method is feasible for very small, simple networks.

For more complex networks (such as the one in Figure 18.1), it is best to let the routers do the brainwork. Routers exchange information about the addresses that they can reach. Each router uses this information to build up its routing table. Routing information is updated whenever a change, such as a broken link, occurs.

The router-to-router exchange of routing table information is carried out according to a *routing protocol*. A routing protocol defines the content and format of routing information messages, and the events that cause messages to be sent.

Over the years, many different routing protocols have been created and used for the exchange of IP routing information. The ones used in private networks today include these:

- **RIP version 1**—Obsolete, but still used. It is adequate for very small and simple networks. Router-to-router reports can generate a lot of LAN broadcast traffic. Switchover of traffic from a failed path to a good path can take minutes.

- **RIP version 2**—An improved version that supports more flexible addressing and authentication of router-to-router messages. Broadcasts used for LAN router-to-router reports optionally can be replaced with multicasts. Switchover from a failed path still is slow.

- **Open Shortest Path First (OSPF)**—Scales to very large networks and enables routers to build detailed network maps. The current version is 2. Router-to-router reports consume negligible amounts of traffic. Switchover from a failed path can occur within a few seconds.

- **Internet Gateway Routing Protocol (IGRP)**—The old version of Cisco's proprietary protocol. Router-to-router reports can generate a lot of LAN broadcast traffic. Provides routers with detailed throughput, delay, and reliability information.

- **Enhanced Internet Gateway Routing Protocol (EIGRP)**—The current version of Cisco's proprietary protocol. Router-to-router reports consume negligible amounts of traffic. Switchover occurs fairly quickly. EIGRP provides routers with detailed throughput, delay, and reliability information.

Different divisions in a company might choose different routing protocols. Router vendors accommodate this by enabling a router to run several protocols at the same time, as is done by router A in Figure 18.6. Router A is able to share information with routers in other divisions. All of the information that router A learns from its neighbors contributes to building up its routing table. Note that executing these protocols and updating the routing table consumes CPU cycles.

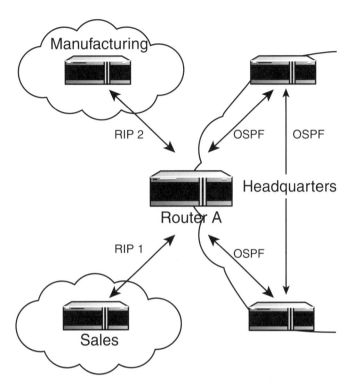

FIGURE 18.6 *Using multiple routing protocols.*

Vendors also support router-to-router protocols that provide information used to forward traffic across the Internet:

- **Exterior Gateway Protocol (EGP)**—Obsolete, but still occasionally used to report the location at which a particular network connects to the Internet.

- **Border Gateway Protocol (BGP)**—A coarse-grained but important protocol for discovering paths across the Internet that lead to a particular network. The current version is 4.

If this is not enough, there also are several choices of router-to-router protocols that are used to build up information used for multicast routing. There are several to choose from:

- Distance Vector Multicast Routing Protocol (DVMRP)

- Dense Mode Protocol Independent Multicast

- Sparse Mode Protocol Independent Multicast

- Multicast OSPF (MOSPF)

Today, just about every router supports IP, but a router might also support additional protocols such as IPX, AppleTalk, or DECnet.

Other Router Functions

Routers often are used as the guardian at the door, keeping unwanted or dangerous traffic out of part of a network. To perform this function, a router is configured with a set of security rules that restrict the traffic that is permitted to pass through the router.

Routers sometimes are given the job of prioritizing traffic and sorting datagrams into queues that get more or less preferential treatment.

For many products, a security or priority rule can be based on fields in the transport layer (Layer 4) header.

Legacy Router Architecture

Legacy routers have a main CPU that carries out the major IP processing steps one datagram at a time. In big networks, routing tables are large, making table searches a compute-intensive activity.

Applying a large number of security or priority rules can bring a legacy router to its knees. Ironically, earlier attempts to prioritize and speed up selected traffic sometimes caused all traffic to be forwarded more slowly.

At busy times, datagrams that are waiting to be processed or to be transmitted onto the next link pile up in memory. When memory usage gets close to capacity, some datagrams need to be dumped. This is the most common cause of datagram loss.

Layer 3 Switch Architecture

Sometimes the communications trade press talks about Layer 3 switches as if they are exotic devices. They are not. They simply are routers, and they do all of the chores that have been described up to this point. They just do their work amazingly faster than the old systems. New technology has boosted Layer 3 switch throughput to tens of millions of packets per second.

The reason that Layer 3 switches are fast is not because someone waved a magic wand and turned routers into hardware automatons. The difference between a conventional router and one of the new switching routers is like the difference between having a job done by a single craftsman versus running a set of efficient assembly lines. All of the old tasks still are done, but now a lot of additional specialized hardware has been introduced, and a lot of the work is done in parallel.

The change to a parallel architecture was made possible by the introduction of low-cost application specific integrated circuit (ASIC) chips. A Layer 3 switch has lots of busy ASIC chips working away, usually one or more per line card. In particular, the CPU-intensive job of searching the routing table is performed in ASICs.

> **Note**
> Chapter 12, "Ethernet Bridges and Layer 2 Switches," noted that ASIC chips also are key components of the architecture of Layer 2 switches.

A Layer 3 switch also still has a central processor. It does chores such as

- Originate outgoing router-to-router messages and process the incoming messages for protocols such as RIP or OSPF, and update the routing table (or tables, if multiple types of network protocols are supported)

- Load copies of the routing table into ASICs, and update these copies as needed

- Provide an administrative user interface for system configuration and management

- Run an SNMP agent process and support remote monitoring (RMON)

Some Layer 3 switches perform security and priority processing in the main CPU.

> **Tip**
> If you are going to apply security or priority rules, it is important to check that these functions are performed in ASICs. If not, performance will be disappointing.

Vendors describe the performance of their systems in terms of packet latency and number of packets per second forwarded. *Packet* is a helpfully vague word: It can stand for *frame* when Layer 2 traffic is being discussed, or any type of network-layer protocol data unit (such as an IP datagram) when Layer 3 is the focus of attention.

The latency is the amount of time that elapses between the time a system receives a packet and the time that the packet is forwarded through a port. The number of packets per second can vary greatly depending on the size of the packets that are being processed. In a second, a system can forward a lot more 64-byte packets than 4000-byte packets. A set of numbers for various packet sizes plus a result for a feasible mix of sizes is a lot more useful than a single measurement.

Keep in mind that the performance benchmarks that are published by vendors usually do not include any security or priority processing.

> **Warning**
> Some vendors provide only ASIC processing for IP traffic and process all other routable protocols in the CPU. If you need to route multiple protocols, the product architecture will make a big difference in the performance that is delivered.

Bridge/Routers

Routers that include a bridging function have been around for a long time. The bridging function was introduced so that routers could forward the unroutable types of traffic. A customer can choose to bridge other routable traffic as well.

Layer 2/3 Switches

Bridges morphed into Layer 2 switches, routers into Layer 3 switches, and bridge/routers (brouters) into Layer 2/3 switches. As before, a customer configures which protocols should be routed and which should be bridged. The difference is that all the actual processing is done a lot faster.

Configuring a Layer 2/3 switch can be a challenge. All the normal router configuration has to be done, along with Layer 2 chores such as VLAN configuration.

Route Once, Switch Many

MAC addresses have meaning only on a single local area network. Routing is needed to direct traffic to globally defined network-layer addresses. However, even for a Layer 3 switch, routing still requires a few microseconds of processing. Considering the multigigabits of bandwidth that are becoming available for both local and wide area networking, this is too much processing time.

For several years, vendors have tried to cut the amount of processing performed by routers to a minimum using proprietary "route once, switch many" techniques.

The introduction of a standard into this arena would be welcome. The IETF is working on a draft for a standard called *Multiprotocol Label Switching Architecture* (MPLS). The basic idea is straightforward:

1. Classify all of the packets processed by a router into numbered Forwarding Equivalence Classes.

2. Assign an incoming packet to its Forwarding Equivalence Class, and prefix a label that carries the corresponding numeric identifier.

3. Switch the packet to a distant router using the label. No other packet processing needs to be performed.

This architecture has several attractive features:

- It can be used with any Layer 3 protocol.

- It can run on top of any type of physical link.

- Traffic can be assigned to a Forwarding Equivalence Class based on factors such as priority or security, as well as destination. Then it can be handled appropriately.

- Label switching is a very simple function and could be performed by inexpensive devices.

Figure 18.7 illustrates a network that has MPLS routers at its core.

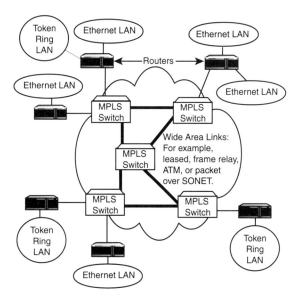

FIGURE 18.7   *An MPLS network.*

Layer 4 and Application-Layer Switching

Figure 18.8 shows the layered protocol model for TCP/IP. Transport layer (Layer 4) and application layer switching currently are applied to TCP/IP traffic.

Layer 3, the network layer, is supposed to include all of the functions needed to get data from its source to its destination. However, some of today's switches peek into the Layer 4 transport-layer header or even into application data during the routing process. The information that a switch gets from the upper layers is used in different ways by each vendor. All of the procedures are proprietary.

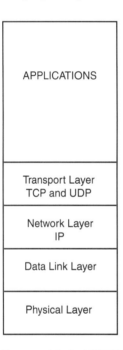

APPLICATIONS

Transport Layer
TCP and UDP

Network Layer
IP

Data Link Layer

Physical Layer

FIGURE 18.8   *TCP/IP Protocol layers.*

IP carries two types of Layer 4 traffic. The Transmission Control Protocol (TCP) is used for applications such as the World Wide Web, file transfer, and email, which require reliable sessions. The User Datagram Protocol (UDP) is used for applications such as SNMP network management and server queries that translate computer names to IP addresses.

A Layer 4 TCP or UDP header contains a number that identifies the application in use. For example, 80 identifies the World Wide Web, 20 and 21 identify file transfer, 25 identifies email, 161 corresponds to SNMP, and 53 corresponds to address queries.

> ## Note
>
> Thanks to Berkeley University researchers who coined the term—these application identifiers are called *port numbers*. This title deserves a top rank in the list of bad network terminology.
>
> Network people use the term *port* for a hardware interface to a switch, router, or computer. A Berkeley port number has nothing to do with hardware; it is an identifier used to name a client or server application that is the endpoint of an exchange of data.

Filtering for Security

Routers have been peeking into Layer 4 for years in order to perform their security filtering function. They frequently grant or deny access to a site or to a LAN based on the source or destination application identified in the transport-layer header.

In addition, by watching for Layer 4 messages that open TCP sessions, a router can allow internal users to open sessions to the outside world, while blocking any attempt that an outsider might make to get in.

Prioritizing Traffic

Layer 4 information can be used in a straightforward way to prioritize traffic. For example, a user could configure a Layer 2/3/4 switch to give preference to World Wide Web TCP traffic and UDP SNMP traffic. The priorities are up to the customer. Some products assure that specified amounts of bandwidth are made available to selected business-critical applications.

Load Balancing

The advent of mammoth Web sites combined with a need to be available 7 days per week and 24 hours per day has inspired many ingenious product solutions. A *load balancer* makes a group of servers (called a *server farm*) look like a single server to the outside world.

A great advantage of this scheme is that if a server fails, the workload is carried by the remaining servers. It also allows for easy growth. New servers can be rolled out as traffic increases.

Figure 18.9 shows a load balancer that fronts an assortment of World Wide Web and file transfer servers. To the outside world, the entire site appears to be a single computer with a single IP address. The load balancer actually is assigning sessions to computers in the farm based on criteria such as

- Application (World Wide Web or file transfer)

- Least busy server or server with best response time

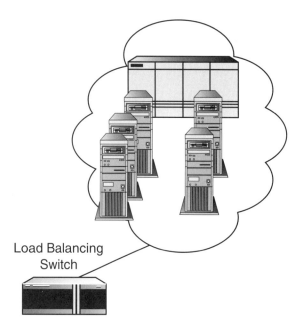

FIGURE 18.9 *A load balancer.*

Some products take this a step further: They perform application-layer switching for the World Wide Web application. This means that they read the Uniform Resource Locator (URL) requested by the client. The request then is routed based on the URL. For example, a URL that points to a "Buy" transaction can be routed to a powerful server that is dedicated to these important transactions.

Summary Points

- A network-layer protocol consists of a network addressing plan plus a set of procedures that are carried out to deliver data to a destination network address.

- A routed network can provide multiple paths to a destination.

- A global network-layer address plan is hierarchical.

- IP addresses that start with the same network and subnet numbers belong to the same LAN.

- An IP system discovers the MAC address of a destination on its LAN by broadcasting an ARP message.

- An IP datagram that is addressed to a destination that is not on the originator's LAN must be transmitted to a router.

- A router performs a routing table lookup to determine the port through which a datagram should be forwarded. A new frame header and trailer must be wrapped around the datagram before it is forwarded.

- Except for very small networks, routers exchange information with one another to build up their routing tables.

- Sometimes routers perform security filtering and prioritize traffic.

- Security and priority rules can be based on the content of a Layer 4 header.

- Layer 3 switches are routers that perform CPU-intensive chores such as searching the routing table in ASIC chips.

- Packet latency is the amount of time that elapses between the time a switch or router receives a packet and the time that the packet is forwarded through a port.

- Bridge/router (brouter) products were the predecessors of Layer 2/3 switches.

- Vendors have introduced many proprietary "route once, switch many" techniques.

- The draft IETF Multiprotocol Label Switching Architecture (MPLS) is an attempt at standardizing "route once, switch many" technology.

- A server farm is a set of servers that have the appearance of a single server to the outside world.

- Load balancers sometimes are called Layer 4 switches because they assign traffic to a server in a server farm by examining Layer 4 headers and evaluating which server is least busy.

- Some load balancers are called application-layer switches because they examine application-layer data to decide which server(s) can process a particular request.

References

A good description of router internals can be found in the IETF standard:

- RFC 1812. "Requirements for IP Version 4 Routers." F. Baker. 1995.

PART III

Other Old and New Technologies

19   Token Ring and FDDI Overview

20   ATM Overview

21   ATM LAN Emulation

22   Fibre Channel

CHAPTER 19

Token Ring and FDDI Overview

IBM has been connecting systems across networks for a long time, and IBM networking always has had a distinctive personality. Much of its early focus was on data entry and data display at remote terminals. IBM equipment was (and still is) used in banks and government offices, and the most important design criterion always has been predictable response time.

The free and easy—and unpredictable—Ethernet LAN environment did not match this requirement. IBM started working on a more controllable LAN technology—Token Ring—in the 1970s. A 4Mbps Token Ring specification was completed in the early 1980s, was submitted to the IEEE for standardization, and was ratified by 1985. Operation at 16Mbps was standardized in 1989. Up to this point, all versions ran on IBM Type 1 shielded twisted-pair (STP) cabling. Unshielded twisted-pair (UTP) cabling was added later.

Performance got a boost when support for full-duplex transmission was added in the 1990s. This feature was called *Dedicated Token Ring* (DTR) because all of the available bandwidth on a link could be dedicated to a single station connected to a DTR concentrator or switch.

Challenged by 100Mbps and 1000Mbps Ethernet, several Token Ring vendors formed the *High Speed Token Ring Alliance* (HSTRA) and wrote a specification for 100Mbps full-duplex Token Ring. NIC and switch products followed quickly.

> **Note**
>
> At the time of writing, the market for high-speed Token Ring products is tepid, and the sponsorship of the High Speed Token Ring Alliance has shrunk to two companies: IBM and Madge.
>
> Conventional 16Mbps half-duplex connections and 32Mbps full-duplex links appear to offer sufficient bandwidth for the desktop connections at most Token Ring sites. When higher-speed desktop, server, or infrastructure connections are needed, some organizations opt for 100Mbps Token Ring switches, while others convert to 100Mbps and 1000Mbps Ethernet or ATM technology.
>
> Token Ring continues to be used at many sites, but it is not winning fresh customers. The technology is in its sunset years.

Features of Classic Half-Duplex Token Ring

A classic Token Ring consists of a set of stations connected in a ring configuration. The stations share the bandwidth provided by the ring.

The physical cabling of a Token Ring looks like a ring of stars, as shown at the top of Figure 19.1. Batches of stations are cabled to concentrators in wiring closets, and the concentrators are connected to one another. The section of cable between a concentrator and a station is called a *lobe*. *Trunk* cables run between concentrators.

It is easier to visualize some aspects of the Token Ring protocols by looking at a stretched-out ring, like the one shown at the bottom of Figure 19.1. Multiple rings can be interconnected by source route bridges or transparent bridges.

A classic Token Ring operates at 4Mbps or 16Mbps. Shielded twisted-pair or unshielded twisted-pair cabling is used for the station cables. Copper or fiber optic segments can be used for the links between concentrators, which are called *trunks*.

Token Ring frames can be big—as large as 18,000 bytes for 16Mbps Token Ring. The use of frames whose size is 4K or more gives Token Ring a definite advantage in throughput over Ethernet.

The classical Token Ring protocol is *half-duplex* because at most one station on a ring can transmit at any given time. Throughput can be kept at a high level on a half-duplex Token Ring because no collisions occur.

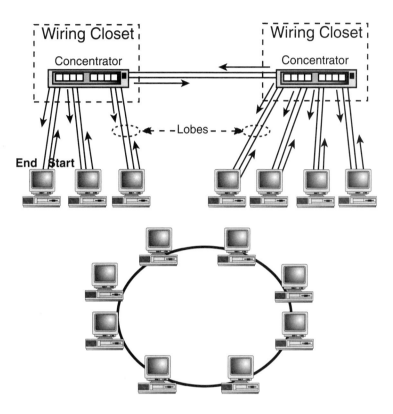

FIGURE 19.1   *Token Ring topology.*

Basic Ring Operation

The idea behind Token Ring operation is straightforward. A special protocol data unit called a *token* circulates from station to station around the ring. A station that has data to send captures (absorbs) the token and transmits a frame followed by some filler bits called an *interframe gap*. The station can continue to transmit frames for a period of time. On completion, it forwards a fresh token to the next station.

A frame is forwarded through each active NIC connected to the ring. Each NIC other than the originator repeats the frame bits onto the next section of cable. A station watches to see whether its own MAC address (or a broadcast address) appears in the destination address field. If so, the destination copies the entire frame into memory, but also continues to repeat the bits onto the next segment.

Eventually, a frame returns to its originator. The originator does not repeat the bits, and this removes the frame from the ring. When its last frame has been removed, the originator transmits a token to the next station.

Figure 19.2 illustrates the procedure. The direction in which data is transmitted is called the *downstream direction*. A station receives bits from its *upstream neighbor* on the ring and sends bits to its *downstream neighbor*.

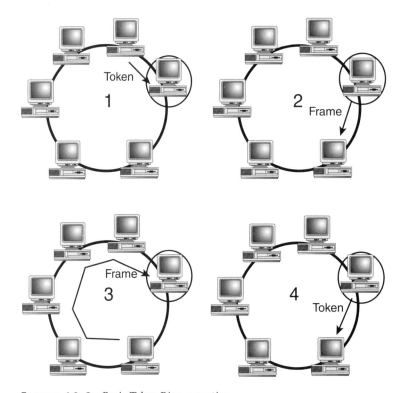

FIGURE 19.2   *Basic Token Ring operation.*

Optionally, some extra throughput can be squeezed out of a 16Mbps Token Ring by using *early token release*. Instead of waiting for its last frame to return, the sender transmits a token right after the interframe gap that follows its final frame.

> **Note**
> Token Ring interframe gaps can be very short. One byte is the minimum allowed at 4Mbps, although 2 bytes are recommended. Five bytes is the minimum at 16Mbps.

Although the basic idea is very simple, quite a lot is involved in keeping the ball rolling around a Token Ring. For example, a station might crash after transmitting a frame. It will fail to absorb its frame and generate a fresh token. A token might be lost due to bit errors. To solve these problems, one station acts as a ring monitor and performs recovery procedures. However, that raises the question of what to do when the monitor crashes. The sections that follow provide the solution.

A station needs to join the ring gracefully when it powers up, and leave it gracefully when it powers down. Unlike Ethernet, the operational parameters are not etched in stone, so a system can get parameters from a configuration server at startup time. Token Ring designers wanted to improve LAN reliability by making it easy to pinpoint trouble spots, so error diagnostic and reporting capabilities were added.

On an Ethernet, there is one type of message: an information frame. Many additional frame types are needed on a Token Ring to support the various ring maintenance functions. This has led to terminology that is different from that used in the Ethernet world:

- The frames that contain user data are called *LLC frames*. As you might expect, these frames contain an LLC header.

- The frames that carry various types of Token Ring protocol messages are called *MAC frames*.

Active Monitor and Standby Monitor Roles

A station on a ring called the *active monitor* watches over the token protocol. If a token has been lost, the active monitor generates a new one. If a frame repeatedly circles the ring, the monitor removes it.

In a classic Token Ring, the active monitor's clock is the ring's master clock. Other stations adjust their bit timing to the timing of incoming bits.

> **Note**
> Many concentrator products built during the last few years actually repeat signals and provide timing to the stations on a Token Ring.

The active monitor is chosen by an election protocol. It periodically announces that it is still doing its job by sending *Active Monitor Present* (AMP) frames.

The other stations attached to the ring act as *standby monitors*. If the "Active Monitor Present" messages cease, the standby monitors participate in an election process and choose a new active monitor.

Functions Performed by the Active Monitor

The first thing a newly elected active monitor station does is clean old data out of the ring by sending a *Ring Purge* frame. A Ring Purge frame is like a yell that says "Quiet down!" Each system that receives the Ring Purge frame resets all of its timers and becomes quiet, simply repeating bits that it is sent. Sending a Ring Purge frame around the ring is called "purging the ring."

After the Ring Purge frame has circled the ring, the active monitor removes it and starts normal operation by transmitting a token.

The active monitor detects the fact that the token has been lost when a timer expires. The active monitor restores normalcy by purging the ring and transmitting a fresh token.

A Token Ring frame header includes a *monitor bit* that initially is set to 0. When a frame passes through the active monitor's NIC, this bit is set to 1. This enables the active monitor to detect whether an incoming frame is coming around for the second time. If so, the active monitor removes the frame from the ring, purges the ring, and initiates a new token.

The Claim Token Election Process

Stations detect that there is no active monitor via a timeout. A station that detects that the active monitor is not functioning properly participates in a monitor election by transmitting a special frame called a *Claim Token* frame. The station, which is called a *transmitter*, repeats its Claim Token frame periodically, sending fill between the frames.

Several stations might detect the problem and become transmitters at the same time. Furthermore, other stations that find out what is going on by receiving a Claim Token frame might have been configured to contend the election by becoming transmitters. They will start to transmit their own Claim Token frames. Any remaining stations stay out of the fray, repeating the Claim Tokens frames that they receive.

The transmitter with the highest MAC address wins the election. The procedure is straightforward: A transmitter that receives a Claim Token frame originating from a station with a bigger MAC address is knocked out of the race and becomes a repeater. Eventually, only one transmitter is left. When that transmitter starts to receive its own Claim Token frames, it knows that it has won.

The Beacon Process

The beacon process identifies the location of a serious fault and initiates some actions that might heal the fault. A station starts to send periodic Beacon MAC frames under the following circumstances:

- A loss of signal occurs, and nothing is arriving from its upstream link.

- Bits are arriving, but the data does not conform to the expected protocol. For example, the data might be a long stream of fill.

- The upstream station has been sending a stream of Claim Tokens for too long.

Other stations repeat the Beacon frames around the ring. The Beacon frames contain the cause of the beacon and the MAC address of the originator's upstream neighbor. If the upstream neighbor receives several Beacons pointing to its address, it removes itself from the ring and tests its NIC to see if there is a problem.

If the transmitter receives its own Beacon frame, the frames are being delivered and the problem has been resolved. The station then initiates the claim token process to elect an active monitor. On the other hand, if the problem has not been resolved when a timeout expires, the station that started the beaconing removes itself from the ring and tests its NIC.

A failure that is caused by a faulty link or a NIC that cannot recognize that it should remove itself must be solved by administrator action. Monitoring the beacon process enables an administrator to isolate the *fault domain*, which consists of three parts:

- The station downstream to the fault, which reports the problem

- The station upstream to the fault

- The equipment between the upstream and downstream systems (cables, concentrators, or repeaters)

The Neighbor Notification Process

A station must know the MAC address of its upstream neighbor to describe a fault domain. In the beaconing process described previously, the beacon transmitter included the MAC address of the upstream neighbor in its Beacon frames.

The *neighbor notification process* enables each station to discover the address of its upstream neighbor. The active monitor periodically starts a neighbor notification process by broadcasting an *Active Monitor Present* (AMP) frame. The process uses some flag bits in the trailers of Token Ring frames. These are called "A" (for *address recognized*) bits and "C" (for *frame-copied*) bits and are set to 0 when a frame is transmitted by its originator.

The first station to receive the frame does the following:

- Sets the A and C bits to 1, and repeats the rest of the Active Monitor Present frame unchanged. (The remaining stations will repeat the Active Monitor Present frame around the ring.)

- Stores the source MAC address in the frame, which is the address of its upstream neighbor.

- Waits for a brief timeout period and broadcasts a *Standby Monitor Present* (SMP) frame.

On receiving a Standby Monitor Present frame whose A and C bits are 0, a station does the following:

- Sets the A and C bits to 1, and repeats the rest of the Standby Monitor Present frame unchanged

- Stores the source MAC address in the frame, which is the address of its upstream neighbor

- Waits for a brief timeout period and broadcasts its own Standby Monitor Present frame

When the active monitor receives a Standby Monitor Present frame whose A and C bits are 0, the cycle is complete. Every station now knows the address of its upstream neighbor.

Special Servers

A ring optionally can include three servers: a *Ring Parameter Server* (RPS), *Configuration Report Server* (CRS), and a *Ring Error Monitor* (REM).

- An initializing station sends a request for parameter values to a Ring Parameter Server. A station can operate with default parameters if no response to a request for parameters arrives.

- A station sends a message to a Configuration Report Server when the station detects that the MAC address of its upstream neighbor has changed.

The Configuration Report Server can send a message to a station telling the station to change its parameters, can ask a station to remove itself from the ring, and can ask a station to provide status information.

- A station periodically reports error counts to a Ring Error Monitor.

Stations send messages to the servers by addressing the frames to well-known multicast functional addresses. For this reason, these servers also are known as the Token Ring *functional servers*.

Functional servers can be spread across different systems or can all be resident at one station. However, a natural place for the servers is at a smart concentrator or a bridge (switch).

Hard and Soft Errors

Some faults disable a ring, while others are transient, causing data to be corrupted for a short time. The Token Ring protocol formally characterizes two types of errors:

- *Hard errors* are defined as faults that prevent frames and/or tokens from circulating around the ring.

- *Soft errors* are defined as faults that cause data corruption but that do not prevent frames and tokens from circulating around the ring.

Hard errors are dealt with immediately by the beacon process. Soft errors are counted and reported. Each station maintains a set of soft error counters and occasionally reports their values to the Ring Error Monitor.

Joining a Ring

When a station is inactive, its lobe cable is bypassed by the concentrator. A station must actively perform an insertion procedure before it can participate in the ring. Five steps are involved:

1. **Test the cable**—The station transmits a series of *Lobe Media Test* frames onto its cable. These frames are sent to the null address, X'00-00-00-00-00-00, and are wrapped back to the station by the concentrator. This enables the station to find out whether its cable is faulty. If the test is successful, the station places a DC current on its cable that causes the concentrator to open its relay and insert the station on the ring.

Note

This is called a *phantom signal* because it does not interfere with the transmission of bits on the same wire.

2. **Make sure that the active monitor is present**—The station sets a timer and watches for evidence that there is an active monitor on the ring. Specifically, it looks for an Active Monitor Present, Standby Monitor Present, or Ring Purge frame. (If none arrives in the timeout period, the station initiates an election by sending Claim Token frames.)

3. **Check for duplicate address**—The station makes sure that no other station on the ring has the same address by sending a Duplicate Address Test frame. If there is a duplicate, the station removes itself from the ring.

Note

For Token Ring networks, locally administered MAC addresses often are preferred to the globally unique manufacturer-assigned MAC addresses. Performing a duplicate address test is an especially wise precaution when locally administered addresses are used.

4. **Learn address of upstream neighbor**—After the station has verified that its address is unique on the ring, it starts to participate in the nearest upstream neighborhood notification processes.

5. **Get configuration parameters**—The station might transmit a Request Initialization frame to the Ring Parameter Server functional multicast address. If there is a Ring Parameter Server, it responds with an Initialize Station or Change Parameters frame. This function rarely is used.

The lobe media test mentioned earlier is used any time that the station needs to test its lobe path as part of an error recovery process.

Removal from the ring is a lot simpler: The station stops applying power to its phantom circuits, which causes the station to be bypassed.

Physical Components for Half-Duplex Token Ring

Figure 19.3 illustrates some of the components of a Token Ring. A Token Ring station must be hooked up to a concentrator to communicate; two stations cannot be directly connected to one another. A classic station is connected to a concentrator by two twisted pairs.

The station receives data on one pair and transmits on the other. The two wire pairs that make up the lobe cable connect to a *trunk coupling unit* (TCU) in the concentrator. When a station is inactive, the TCU bypasses the station's cables. When a station transmits a phantom power current, the TCU closes a relay so that ring data can flow to and from the station.

Originally, shielded twisted-pair cable was used. The cable typically was connected to a station by a 9-pin D-connector, and to a wall outlet by a special IBM connector.

Note
The IBM connectors were well designed, durable, reliable, and virtually "idiot-proof."

Today, the use of unshielded twisted-pair cable and RJ-45 connectors at both the station and wall outlet is common.

Adjacent concentrators are connected by a trunk cable. A pair of optical fibers can be used for a trunk if a very long cable run is needed.

Concentrators are known by a lot of names. IBM has called its concentrators *Multistation Access Units* (abbreviated as MAU or MSAU) and Controlled Access Units (CAUs). Some vendors simply call their products *Token Ring hubs*.

Whatever the name might be, today the main difference between different concentrator products is whether the product's ports are passive or active, and how smart the products are:

- Passive ports just allow signals to pass through. This means that a single section of cable extends from a station NIC, through the TCU, and to the NIC of the next station on the ring.

- Active ports retime and repeat the signal.

- Smart ports retime the signal, repeat the signal, and perform diagnostics, cutting off stations whose NICs try to enter the ring at the wrong speed or that misbehave in some other way.

Smart concentrators support SNMP management variables and SNMP remote monitoring (RMON). RMON makes an enormous amount of information on LAN activity available to a network administrator. Some concentrator products even support troubleshooting via packet capture.

Figure 19.3 shows a standalone concentrator. Internal wiring completes the ring.

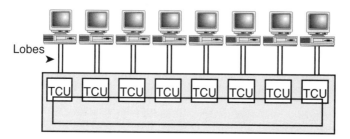

FIGURE 19.3 *A standalone concentrator.*

A concentrator has *ring in* and *ring out* ports that are used to connect to other concentrators. As shown in Figure 19.4, cabling runs from the ring out port of the first concentrator to the ring in port of the second. Several concentrators can be chained together using ring out and ring in ports.

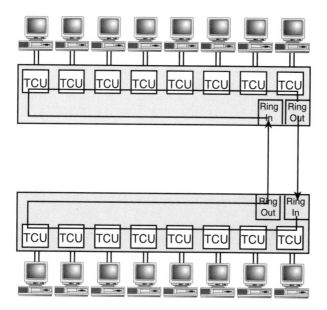

FIGURE 19.4 *Token Ring components.*

IEEE 802.5 suggests a maximum of 250 stations per half-duplex ring. IBM proposed a limit of 260. The actual number that can be supported depends on the quality of the cable and equipment. For example, far fewer stations can be supported when Category 3 unshielded twisted-pair cable is used.

The maximum distance between a station and a concentrator also is quite variable: It depends on whether Category 3 UTP, Category 5 UTP, or STP is used, and on whether the hub ports repeat signals. The cable distance between a station and a hub can be a lot bigger when a hub with active, repeating ports is used. Typical twisted-pair distances for 16Mbps repeated ports are 100 meters for Category 3 unshielded twisted–pair cable, 225 meters for Category 5 cable, and 400 meters for IBM Type 1 shielded-twisted pair cable. (Greater distances are possible at 4Mbps.) Similar length restrictions apply to twisted-pair trunk cables. The length of a trunk cable can range up to 2000 meters when optical fiber is used.

Modern concentrators are very sophisticated. Up-to-date products build an ASIC into each port, giving the port the intelligence that enables it to

- Sense the speed at which an attached station is operating, and refuse entry to the ring if the speed is not compatible

- Identify and bypass lobes that are responsible for a fault

Classic Token Ring Protocol Elements

The sections that follow outline the major features of the classic Token Ring protocol, including

- Token Ring MAC addresses

- The Token Ring format

- LLC frame formats

- MAC frame formats

- Parameters

- Routing information

- Timers

- Types of MAC protocol frames

Addresses

The IEEE LAN addresses described in Chapter 2, "LAN MAC Addresses," are used in Token Rings. However, these addresses are used in a special manner:

- Each address byte is written in reverse order. The first bit of a destination address indicates whether it is an individual address (0) or a group address (1). The second bit indicates whether it is a universal (0) or local (1) address.

- The first bit of a source address is set to 1 to indicate that that a routing information field (RIF) follows.

The broadcast address, X'FF-FF-FF-FF-FF-FF, denotes all stations on the LAN and is used to broadcast an LLC frame. A second address, X'C0-00-00-FF-FF-FF, is used as the broadcast address for Token Ring MAC frames, which carry the messages (such as Active Monitor Present or Beacon frames) that operate the protocol.

Stations use the functional addresses mentioned in Chapter 2 to send protocol messages to the Token Ring functional servers and to other systems that play a special role in the LAN. Functional addresses start with the bit pattern:

11000000 00000000 0

Frequently used functional addresses are reviewed in Table 19.1.

TABLE 19.1 TOKEN RING FUNCTIONAL MAC ADDRESSES

Function Name	MAC Address
Active Monitor	X'C0-00-00-00-00-01
Ring Parameter Server (RPS)	X'C0-00-00-00-00-02
Ring Error Monitor (REM)	X'C0-00-00-00-00-08
Configuration Report Server (CRS)	X'C0-00-00-00-00-10
Source Route Bridge	X'C0-00-00-00-01-00

Token Format

Figure 19.5 displays the format of the token, which is only 3 bytes long. The starting and ending delimiters (which also appear in frames) make it easy to detect where the token (or a frame) begins and ends. The delimiters include special symbols (called J and K) whose encoding on the cable is different from the encoding of 0s and 1s. (Appendix A, "Physical-Layer Encodings for Ethernet, Fibre Channel, FDDI, and Token Ring," has the details.) The I and E bits are explained later, in the section called "Ending Delimiter and Frame Status Fields."

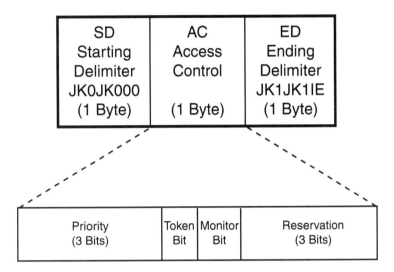

FIGURE 19.5 *Token format.*

The Access Control Field

The access control field that appears in the token also appears in frames. The token bit is 0 in a token and 1 in a frame. The monitor bit starts out as 0 and is changed to 1 when a frame reaches the active monitor NIC. If a frame with the monitor bit equal to 1 arrives at the monitor, the active monitor knows that the frame has cycled all the way around the ring. If this happens, the active monitor purges the ring.

The access control field contains 3 *priority* bits. The Token Ring protocol supports eight levels of priority (numbered from 0 to 7). When a station receives the token, it is allowed to send only frames whose priority level is at least that of the token. A station with high priority frames to send sets the *reservation* bits to the desired priority level. This causes the next token that is released to be set to this requested priority.

General Frame Format

Both user data (LLC) frames and Token Ring protocol (MAC) frames have the format shown in Figure 19.6.

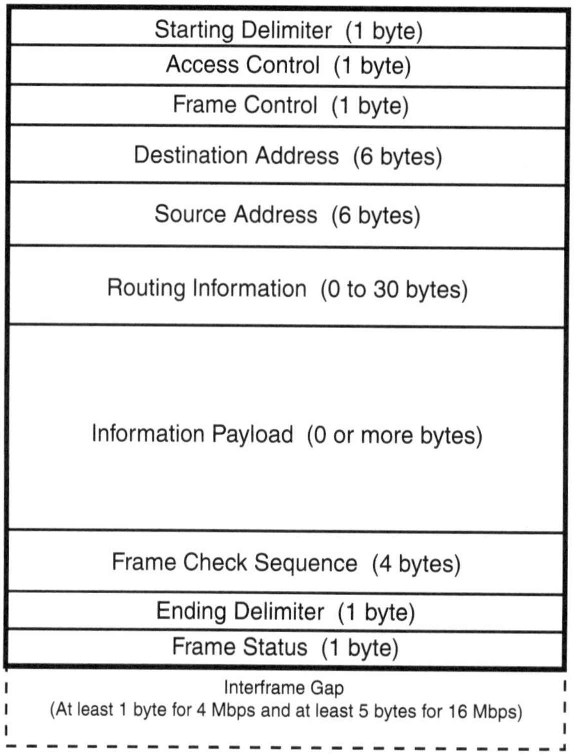

Starting Delimiter (1 byte)
Access Control (1 byte)
Frame Control (1 byte)
Destination Address (6 bytes)
Source Address (6 bytes)
Routing Information (0 to 30 bytes)
Information Payload (0 or more bytes)
Frame Check Sequence (4 bytes)
Ending Delimiter (1 byte)
Frame Status (1 byte)

Interframe Gap
(At least 1 byte for 4 Mbps and at least 5 bytes for 16 Mbps)

FIGURE 19.6 *Token Ring frame format.*

Frame Control Field

The first 2 bits of the frame control field in Figure 19.7 distinguish LLC frames (01) from MAC protocol frames (00). The meaning of the remaining bits depends on this setting. For an LLC frame, the next 3 bits are reserved and the last 3 bits are a user priority that has been passed down by a higher-layer protocol. For a MAC protocol frame, the last 6 bits depend on the type of protocol function that the frame performs.

LLC Frame 0 1	Reserved 0 0 0	User Priority (3 Bits)

MAC Protocol Frame 0 0	Depends on Type of Protocol Function

FIGURE **19.7** *Format of the frame control field.*

Routing Information Field

The routing information field was discussed in Chapter 17, "Source-Routing, Translational, and Wide Area Bridges," but it is reviewed here with a few more details filled in.

A source address must always be an individual (unicast) address, so the first bit in a source address is set to 1 to signal whether the frame includes a *routing information field* (RIF). A routing information field lays out a path from the source to the destination that passes across a series of rings and bridges.

As illustrated in Figure 19.8, the first 2 bytes of the RIF make up the routing control portion, which includes

- The *routing type*. 0XX means that a specific route is provided in the routing descriptor fields. 10X is an all-routes explorer. 11X is a Spanning Tree explorer. (Bits labeled "X" can be either 0 or 1.)

- The *length* of the entire RIF, including the routing control field.

- The *direction bit*, which indicates whether the route should be followed in a forward (0) or reverse (1) order.

- The *largest frame* field, which contains a code that announces the size of the biggest information field that can be carried along the specified path.

The final routing control bit is reserved.

> **Note**
>
> As noted in Chapter 16, "VLANs and Frame Priority," and Chapter 17, in an embedded routing information field (E-RIF), the final bit is used as a non-canonical format identifier (NCFI).

The remainder of the routing information field contains a list of routing descriptors. Each routing descriptor is made up of a 12-bit ring identifier and 4-bit bridge number. A RIF can be 2 to 30 bytes in length.

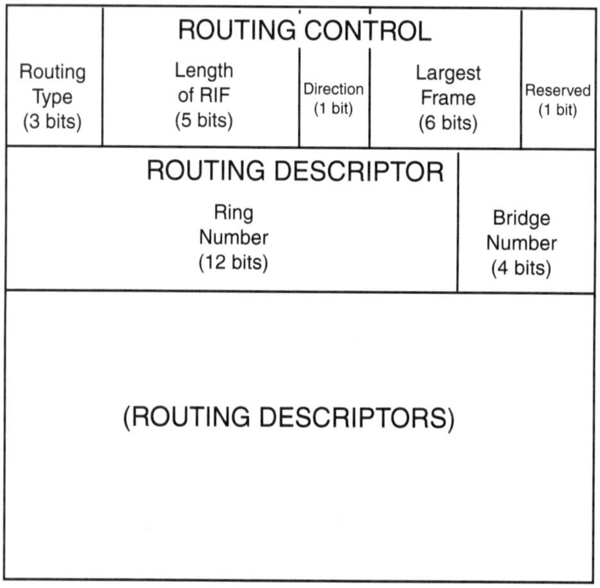

Routing Type (3 bits)	ROUTING CONTROL			
	Length of RIF (5 bits)	Direction (1 bit)	Largest Frame (6 bits)	Reserved (1 bit)
ROUTING DESCRIPTOR				
Ring Number (12 bits)			Bridge Number (4 bits)	
(ROUTING DESCRIPTORS)				

FIGURE 19.8 *Format of a routing information field.*

Ending Delimiter and Frame Status Fields

The ending delimiter, which follows the frame check sequence field, is displayed at the top of Figure 19.9.

When the token holder sends multiple frames, the intermediate frame bit (the I-bit, which is second from the right) is set to 1 in all of the frames except the last. The bit is set to 0 in the last (or only) frame.

The error bit is set to 0 when a token or frame is transmitted. A station sets the value to 1 if it has detected an error (such as an incorrect frame check sequence) while processing the frame.

The frame status field, which is shown at the bottom of Figure 19.9, is located after the ending delimiter. The field includes the useful A and C flag bits. These bits are set to 0 by the transmitting station.

- The "A" stands for *address recognized*. A station on the ring that recognizes the destination address as either its own unicast address or as the address of a group to which it belongs sets both A bits to 1.

- The "C" stands for *copied*. If a station on the ring copies the frame into its memory, it sets both of the C bits to 1.

The A and C bits are duplicated because they are not covered by the frame check sequence calculation. The fact that a pair has consistent values gives some assurance that the bits have not been corrupted.

The remaining bits in the frame status field are not used and are set to 0.

Ending Delimiter

J	K	1	J	K	1	I	E

Frame Status

A	C	0	0	A	C	0	0

FIGURE 19.9 *The ending delimiter and frame status fields.*

Abort Sequence

Sometimes a transmitting station experiences an error condition and wishes to break off before the entire frame has been sent. This is done by transmitting the 2-byte abort sequence that is shown in Figure 19.10. The unexpected arrival of back-to-back start and end delimiters warns a receiving station that the previous frame was not valid.

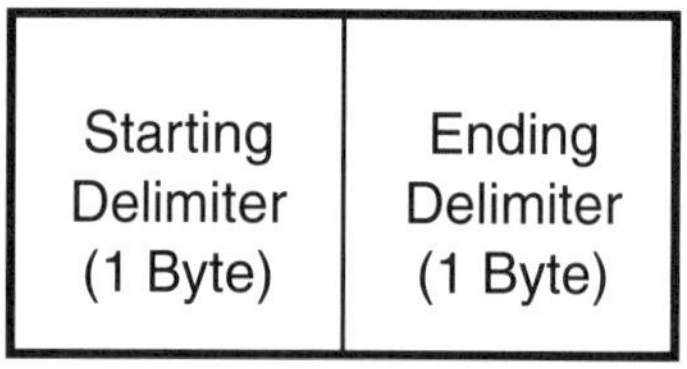

Starting Delimiter (1 Byte)	Ending Delimiter (1 Byte)

FIGURE 19.10   *The abort sequence.*

Token Ring MAC Protocol Frames

Figure 19.11 shows the format of the information field in a MAC protocol frame. The content is a message that formally is called a *vector*. A vector is introduced by length, class, and identifier fields. Two 4-bit codes in the *class field* identify the source and destination system type (such as a pair of stations or a station and a Ring Error Monitor server). The vector identifier number indicates the type of message that is enclosed

Further parameters are carried in *subvector* fields in the vector. The parameters that are included depend on the message type.

Table 19.2 lists types of messages and their identifiers.

Information Field = "Vector"

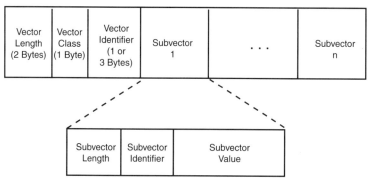

FIGURE 19.11   *Token Ring MAC protocol frame information field.*

TABLE 19.2 TYPES OF MAC FRAME VECTORS

Numeric Identifier	Name	Description
X'00	Response	Sent to acknowledge receipt of a MAC frame or to report an error in a received MAC frame.
X'02	Beacon	Signals that data has stopped flowing from the upstream station.
X'03	Claim Token	Used to elect an active monitor.
X'04	Ring Purge	Transmitted by the active monitor to clear the ring before generating a new token.
X'05	Active Monitor Present	Transmitted by the active monitor to verify its active status and start the neighbor notification process.
X'06	Standby Monitor Present	Transmitted by stations during the neighbor notification process.
X'07	Duplicate Address Test	Transmitted by a station that wants to join the ring. The message is used to check whether the station has a duplicate address.
X'08	Lobe Media Test	Transmitted to check the cable before attempting to join the ring. It is sent to an all-zeroes address.
X'0B	Remove Ring Station	Sent to a station by the Configuration Report Server to force the station's removal from the ring.
X'0C	Change Parameters	Sent to a station by the Configuration Report Server to set the station's operating parameters.
X'0D	Initialize Station	Sent to a station by the Ring Parameter Server to initialize the station's operating parameters.
X'0E	Request Station Addresses	Sent by a management entity to ask for the list of addresses recognized by the station.
X'0F	Request Station State	Sent by a management entity to ask for a station's operational state information.
X'10	Request Station Attachments	Sent by a server or network management system to ask what functions are active at the station.

continues

TABLE 19.2 CONTINUED

Numeric Identifier	Name	Description
X'20	Request Initialization	Sent to the Ring Parameter Server as part of the join process.
X'22	Report Station Addresses	Responds to Request Station Addresses.
X'23	Report Station State	Responds to Request Station State.
X'24	Report Station Attachments	Responds to Request Station Attachments.
X'25	Report New Active Monitor	Sent to the Configuration Report Server by a station that has become the active monitor.
X'26	Report SUA Change	Sent to the Configuration Report Server by a station whose stored upstream neighbor's address has changed.
X'27	Report Neighbor Notification Incomplete	Sent to the Ring Error Monitor by the active monitor to report an error in the neighbor notification process.
X'28	Report Active Monitor error	Sent to the Ring Error Monitor by an active monitor if it detects another active monitor or if another station initiates the claim token process.
X'29	Report Error	Sent to the Ring Error Monitor by a station that is reporting error counts.

Timers

The Token Ring protocol relies on a lot of timers, which are described briefly in Table 19.3. The full details are in Section 3.4 of the IEEE 802.5 specification.

TABLE 19.3 TOKEN RING TIMERS

Type of Timer	Description
Active Monitor	Used by the active monitor. Establishes the interval between Active Monitor Present MAC frames.
Beacon Repeat	Set whenever a station receives a Beacon MAC frame. When it expires, the station can start to transmit Claim Token MAC frames.
Beacon Transmit	Establishes the length of time that a beaconing station should transmit Beacon MAC frames.

Type of Timer	Description
Claim Token	Set when the station starts to participate in the claim token process. If the timer expires, it indicates that the process has failed.
Error Report	Controls error reporting. The timer is set when an initial error occurs. Errors tend to come in bursts, and the station collects errors until the timer expires. The station then reports all of its error counters in a Report Error MAC frame and resets the error counters to 0.
Insert Delay	A timer that controls reinsertion. After a beaconing station has removed itself from the ring, it performs a self-test and rejoins the ring. This timer makes sure that the station refrains from sending data for a period to allow time for reinsertion into the ring to complete.
Join Ring	A timeout on the join process. Enables the station to detect whether a join has failed.
No Token	A timeout that indicates that a token has not appeared within the expected time period.
Queue PDU	Time allowed for queuing an appropriate frame after an event such as receiving an Active Monitor Present or Claim Token MAC frame.
Remove Hold	Time period after insertion when the station cannot request removal. This assures that insertion will complete before a removal is requested.
Remove Wait	Time period after a removal request during which the station must continue to repeat frames.
Request Initialize	Timeout used to detect that a response to the last Request Initialization MAC frame was not received.
Return to Repeat	Timeout that triggers a return to repeat state after a procedure during which a station temporarily stops repeating frames.
Ring Purge	Timeout used to detect a failed ring purge.
Signal Loss	Timeout on the longest valid period during which no signals may arrive. Expiration detects a physical failure.
Standby Monitor	Timeout on receiving an Active Monitor Present MAC frame. Indicates that the active monitor is dead.
Valid Transmission	Timeout used by the active monitor to detect the absence of frames or tokens.
Wire Fault Delay	Timeout that allows a join or reinsertion to complete. This prevents a false wire fault from being diagnosed.
Wire Fault	Defines a sampling period for filtering wire fault.

Token Ring Frame Traces

The sections that follow display Network Associates Sniffer traces of several types of Token Ring frames:

- An LLC frame carrying an IP datagram

- An all-routes explorer frame

- An Active Monitor Present frame

- A Standby Monitor Present frame

- A Claim Token frame

- A Ring Purge frame

- A Report Soft Error frame

Simple LLC Data Frame

Listing 19.1 displays a simple LLC information frame that carries an IP datagram. Only the data link and LLC headers are shown.

The frame status field contains the address recognized (A) and frame copied (c) bits. The first line of the trace reports that this frame was observed before it had been received and repeated by its destination, so these bits still are 0. The priority and reservation bits in the access control field are set to 0, which is the norm. Use of the priority feature is fairly rare.

The frame control field indicates that this is an LLC frame. The LLC header is X'AA-AA-03, indicating that a SNAP subheader follows. The SNAP indicates that the information field carries an IP datagram.

LISTING 19.1 A SIMPLE LLC TOKEN RING FRAME

```
DLC:   FS: Addr recognized indicators: 00, Frame copied indicators: 00
       DLC:   AC: Frame priority 0,  Reservation priority 0,  Monitor count 0
       DLC:   FC: LLC frame,
       DLC:   Destination = Station 3Com2 063841
       DLC:   Source      = Station 3Com2 115176
       DLC:
LLC:   ----- LLC Header -----
       LLC:
       LLC:   DSAP Address = AA, DSAP IG Bit = 00 (Individual Address)
       LLC:   SSAP Address = AA, SSAP CR Bit = 00 (Command)
       LLC:   Unnumbered frame: UI
       LLC:
SNAP:  ----- SNAP Header -----
       SNAP:
       SNAP: Type = 0800 (IP)
       SNAP:
IP:    ----- IP Header -----
```

All-Routes-Explorer LLC Frame

Listing 19.2 shows an all-routes-explorer frame.

The frame control field shows that this is an LLC frame. The destination and source addresses are locally defined rather than universal MAC addresses.

The source address is shown as:

X'40-00-00-00-90-52

However, the actual hexadecimal trace of the source address field is this:

X'C0-00-00-00-90-52

The difference is that the first bit of the source address has been transmitted as 1, to indicate that a routing information field follows. This changes X'4 (0100) to X'C (1100).

The routing information field consists of 10 bytes: the 2-byte routing control portion and four 2-byte routing descriptors.

- The fact that this is an explorer frame (used to discover a route to the destination) is indicated by the first 3 bits of the routing control field. The value of this subfield (100) indicates that this is an all-routes-explorer.

- The direction bit (0) shows that the route still is being built in the forward direction. This also is confirmed by the 0-valued A and C bits in the frame status field.

- The largest frame field shows that 8130-byte frames can be carried on this route.

The frame carries an ordinary NetBIOS payload (a NetBIOS "name recognized" message).

LISTING 19.2 AN ALL-ROUTES-EXPLORER FRAME

```
DLC:  FS: Addr recognized indicators: 00, Frame copied indicators: 00
      DLC:  AC: Frame priority 0,  Reservation priority 0,  Monitor count 0
      DLC:  FC: LLC frame,
      DLC:  Destination = Station 400000000851, BORIS851
      DLC:  Source      = Station 400000009052, KREMLIN1
      DLC:
RI:   ----- Routing Indicators -----
      RI:
      RI:  Routing control = 8A
      RI:       100. .... = All-routes broadcast, non-broadcast return
      RI:       ...0 1010 = RI length is 10
      RI:  Routing control = 40
```

continues

LISTING 19.2 CONTINUED

```
        RI:           0... .... = Forward direction
        RI:           .100 .... = Largest frame is 8130
        RI:           .... 000. = Extended frame is 0
        RI:           .... ...0 = Reserved
        RI:  Ring number 00F via bridge A
        RI:  Ring number 101 via bridge B
        RI:  Ring number 00E via bridge 2
        RI:  Ring number 200
        RI:
  LLC:  ----- LLC Header -----
        LLC:
        LLC:  DSAP Address = F0, DSAP IG Bit = 00 (Individual Address)
        LLC:  SSAP Address = F0, SSAP CR Bit = 00 (Command)
        LLC:  Unnumbered frame: UI
        LLC:
  NETB: ----- NETBIOS Name Recognized -----
```

Active Monitor Present Frame

Listing 19.3 shows an Active Monitor Present frame. The destination address X'C0-00-FF-FF-FF-FF is used for broadcasts of MAC protocol frames (as opposed to LLC information frames).

The address recognized and frame copied bits in the frame status field show that this frame was captured right after it was sent by the active monitor. The first NIC that receives the frame will change these bits from 0 to 1 because the frame has been broadcast.

In the information field, the vector identifier states that this is an Active Monitor Present frame. This is a station-to-station message (which is indicated in the frame's vector class byte).

The physical drop number is a physical location parameter that could be assigned to a station by a configuration server. This parameter is rarely, if ever, set and has default value 0 in the trace.

The final field contains the address of the sender's upstream neighbor. In this case, this is the address of the station that is upstream from the active monitor.

LISTING 19.3 AN ACTIVE MONITOR PRESENT MAC FRAME

```
  MAC: Active Monitor Present
  DLC:  ----- DLC Header -----
        DLC:
        DLC:  Frame 413 arrived at  12:14:10.806; frame size is 32 (0020
        ➥hex) bytes.
        DLC:  FS: Addr recognized indicators: 00, Frame copied indicators:
        ➥00
        DLC:  AC: Frame priority 0,  Reservation priority 0,  Monitor count
        ➥0
```

```
       DLC:  FC: MAC frame,  PCF attention code: Active monitor present
       DLC:  Destination = BROADCAST C000FFFFFFFF, TR_Broadcast
       DLC:  Source      = Station Madge2411430
       DLC:
MAC:   ----- MAC data -----
       MAC:
       MAC:  MAC Command: Active Monitor Present
       MAC:  Source: Ring station, Destination: Ring station
       MAC:  Subvector type: Physical Drop Number 00000000
       MAC:  Subvector type: Upstream Neighbor Address Madge24113FE
       MAC:
```

Standby Monitor Present Frame

Listing 19.4 shows a Standby Monitor Present frame, which is used in the neighbor notification procedure and enables a station to discover its upstream neighbor's MAC address.

The address recognized and frame copied bits in the frame status field show that a prior station has recognized the frame's destination address (which is the MAC broadcast address) and has copied the frame. The monitor bit is 1, indicating that the frame has passed through the active monitor station's NIC. The frame control field identifies this as a Standby Monitor Present frame.

In the information field, the vector identifier states that this is a Standby Monitor Present frame. This is a station-to-station message. The subvectors report the physical drop number (if one had been assigned) and the address of the sender's upstream neighbor.

LISTING 19.4 STANDBY MONITOR PRESENT MAC FRAME

```
MAC: Standby Monitor Present
DLC:  ----- DLC Header -----
      DLC:
      DLC:  Frame 414 arrived at  12:14:10.827; frame size is 32 (0020
      ➥hex) bytes.
      DLC:  FS: Addr recognized indicators: 11, Frame copied indicators:
      ➥11
      DLC:  AC: Frame priority 0,  Reservation priority 0,  Monitor count
      ➥1
      DLC:  FC: MAC frame,  PCF attention code: Standby monitor present
      DLC:  Destination = BROADCAST C000FFFFFFFF, TR_Broadcast
      DLC:  Source      = Station Madge24113FE
      DLC:
MAC:  ----- MAC data -----
      MAC:
      MAC:  MAC Command: Standby Monitor Present
      MAC:  Source: Ring station, Destination: Ring station
      MAC:  Subvector type: Physical Drop Number 00000000
      MAC:  Subvector type: Upstream Neighbor Address Madge2411430
      MAC:
```

Claim Token Frame

Listing 19.5 shows a Claim Token frame. Claim Token frames are used to elect an active monitor.

The first subvector reports the physical drop number. The last variable reports the address of the sender's upstream neighbor.

LISTING 19.5 A CLAIM TOKEN MAC FRAME

```
MAC: Claim Token
DLC: ----- DLC Header -----
     DLC:
     DLC: Frame 86 arrived at  11:12:05.555; frame size is 32 (0020 hex)
     ➡bytes.
     DLC: FS: Addr recognized indicators: 11, Frame copied indicators:
     ➡11
     DLC: AC: Frame priority 0,  Reservation priority 0,  Monitor count 0
     DLC: FC: MAC frame,  PCF attention code: Claim Token
     DLC: Destination = BROADCAST C000FFFFFFFF, TR_Broadcast
     DLC: Source      = Station IBM2  DEC785
     DLC:
MAC: ----- MAC data -----
     MAC:
     MAC: MAC Command: Claim Token
     MAC: Source: Ring station, Destination: Ring station
     MAC: Subvector type: Physical Drop Number 00000000
     MAC: Subvector type: Upstream Neighbor Address IBM2  DEDC89
     MAC:
```

Ring Purge Frame

Listing 19.6 displays a Ring Purge frame. The active monitor transmits a Ring Purge frame to clear out the ring prior to launching a new token.

Again, the sender includes the address of its own upstream neighbor in its information field.

LISTING 19.6 A RING PURGE MAC FRAME

```
MAC: Ring Purge
DLC: ----- DLC Header -----
     DLC:
     DLC: Frame 31 arrived at  19:34:37.775; frame size is 32 (0020 hex)
     ➡bytes.
     DLC: FS: Addr recognized indicators: 00, Frame copied indicators:
     ➡00
     DLC: AC: Frame priority 0,  Reservation priority 0,  Monitor count
     ➡0
     DLC: FC: MAC frame,  PCF attention code: Ring purge
     DLC: Destination = BROADCAST C000FFFFFFFF, TR_Broadcast
     DLC: Source      = Station IBM2  118D9D
     DLC:
MAC: ----- MAC data -----
```

```
MAC:
MAC:   MAC Command: Ring Purge
MAC:   Source: Ring station, Destination: Ring station
MAC:   Subvector type: Physical Drop Number 00000000
MAC:   Subvector type: Upstream Neighbor Address IBM2   12F7EC
MAC:
```

Report Soft Error Frame

Listing 19.7 displays a Report Soft Error frame. Its destination is the functional address of the Ring Error Monitor. The message reports the current values of a station's error counters. The sender resets its counters to 0 after transmitting the report.

LISTING 19.7 A REPORT SOFT ERROR MAC FRAME

```
MAC: Report Soft Error
DLC:   ----- DLC Header -----
    DLC:
    DLC:   Frame 47 arrived at  19:34:39.880; frame size is 48 (0030 hex)
    ➥bytes.
    DLC:   FS: Addr recognized indicators: 00, Frame copied indicators: 00
    DLC:   AC: Frame priority 0,   Reservation priority 0,  Monitor count 0
    DLC:   FC: MAC frame
    DLC:   Destination = Functional address C00000000008, RingError Mon.
    DLC:   Source     = Station IBM2   118D9D
    DLC:
MAC:   ----- MAC data -----
    MAC:
    MAC:   MAC Command: Report Soft Error
    MAC:   Source: Ring station, Destination: Ring Error Monitor
    MAC:   Subvector type: Isolating Error Counts
    MAC:            0 line errors,       0 internal errors,       1
    ➥burst errors
    MAC:            0 AC errors,         0 abort delimiters
    ➥transmitted
    MAC:   Subvector type: Non-Isolating Error Counts
    MAC:            0 lost frame errors,  0 receiver congestion,   0
    ➥FC errors
    MAC:            0 frequency errors,   1 token errors
    MAC:   Subvector type: Physical Drop Number 00000000
    MAC:   Subvector type: Upstream Neighbor Address IBM2   118E9A
    MAC:
```

Dedicated Token Ring

The development of Dedicated Token Ring (DTR) accomplished three important goals:

- It introduced full-duplex operation to Token Rings.

- It enabled vendors to offer standards-based Token Ring switches.

- It set the stage for 100Mbps Token Ring.

Switching and full-duplex operation greatly increased the backbone capacity of Token Ring LANs. DTR enabled multiple stations and classic Token Rings to be attached to a switch, and allowed traffic to flow freely between them. Switches could be connected to stations and to one another by full-duplex links.

DTR shored up the installed base of Token Ring systems. Fortunately for customers, on some Token Ring NIC products the upgrade could be carried out by replacing a device driver and performing a microcode update.

The DTR protocol allows for backward compatibility and supports the classic half-duplex Token Ring protocol as well as full-duplex operation.

Full-duplex Dedicated Token Ring is a point-to-point protocol. Data is not passed around a ring, and there is no token. Just as was the case for full-duplex Ethernet, the complicated protocol elements have been tossed out the window.

Stations connect to a device that vendors call a switch. The specifications call it a DTR concentrator, but neither term totally hits the nail on the head. A DTR product provides switching functions but often also provides the capability to connect a selected set of half-duplex stations into a virtual ring. In the spirit of compromise, DTR concentrators that also support virtual rings are called *Concentrators/Switches* in the sections that follow.

> **Note**
> The full-duplex mode of operation is referred to as *transmit immediate* (TXI) mode. Standards groups never overlook an opportunity to introduce a new acronym, so half-duplex token passing is called *token passing* (TKP) mode.

A DTR Concentrator/Switch is the ideal place for a network management function, and DTR products usually support SNMP management variables and SNMP RMON monitoring variables. A DTR Concentrator/Switch can accumulate information from several Token Rings.

C-Ports

A new type of port, called a *C-Port* (for concentrator port), was defined for use in DTR Concentrator/Switches.

Clearly, a different type of port was needed to support full-duplex DTR stations. But a C-Port also is backward compatible and thus can behave like a classic hub port. A classic Token Ring station's lobe cable can be plugged into the port.

An Ethernet port always is ready for action, whether it is located in a station or in a hub. Classic Token Ring is different. A classic Token Ring hub port waits passively until the station at the end of the lobe cable initiates a ring insertion process.

A C-Port in a Token Ring Concentrator/Switch must be capable of playing a passive role and allowing a station to connect to it. However, it also needs to be capable of playing an active role so that it can initiate the insertion process when it is linked to a port at a classic hub or at a peer DTR switch. This active role is called *station emulation mode*. Figure 19.12 illustrates the versatility of C-Ports; each C-Port is marked with its role.

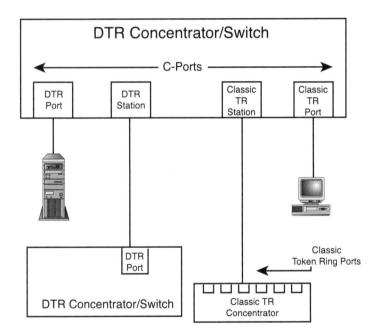

FIGURE 19.12 *C-Port roles.*

The behavior of a Concentrator/Switch port depends on a product's architecture and configuration:

- A DTR station may connect in full-duplex mode. In this case, the station links to a bridging function in the Concentrator/Switch.

- Multiple C-Ports can be combined so that the connected stations appear to share a logical ring. The bridging function interconnects these logical rings with one another and with switched stations.

Concentrator/Switch products usually include both source-routing and transparent-routing bridge capabilities.

Full-Duplex Protocol

In full-duplex mode, many parts of the classic Token Ring are discarded. Data does not circle around a ring, and there is no active or standby monitor role. Some of the frame parameters are unused as well. For example, consider these points:

- The priority, monitor, and reservation bits in the access control field are set to 0 and are ignored. There is no token, so the token bit always is set to 1, meaning "not a token."

- The intermediate frame and error bits in the ending delimiter are set to 0 and are ignored.

Some features have been preserved. The Ring Parameter Server, Configuration Report Server, and Ring Error Monitor Server functions are retained. For example, the servers can provide the following functions:

- A Configuration Report Server can reset the operating parameters in a station or a C-Port.

- A Configuration Report Server can remove a station from the network.

- A Ring Parameter Server can initialize the operating parameters in a station or a C-Port.

- A station or C-Port can report errors to the Ring Error Monitor.

One classical function is retained by introducing a replacement mechanism. Detecting a failed cable and isolating a fault have great value. For a classic station, a long silence on an input cable alerts the station to the fact that there is an upstream fault. But the full-duplex protocol does not have the continuous chatter of an ordinary ring. Frames are sent to or from a station on an as-needed basis, and a frame sent by a station does not cycle back to the station.

A *Heartbeat* MAC frame has been introduced to avoid a complete lull in incoming traffic. Heartbeats are sent periodically by both C-Ports and DTR stations. This enables a long silence to be properly diagnosed as a hard fault. The system that detects the fault transmits a Beacon MAC frame.

The Heartbeat frame has another use as well: It replaces neighbor notification as a way of providing an ongoing check of the neighbor's MAC address.

Joining a Station to a C-Port

A classic station that is connected to a C-Port follows its usual insertion process. C-Ports are backward compatible and support this classic insertion process.

A DTR station or a DTR C-Port in station emulation mode also is backward compatible. It can connect to a conventional Token Ring hub using the classic insertion process.

A DTR station capable of using the new DTR protocol initiates a connection to a C-Port by transmitting a Registration Request MAC frame. This is answered by a Registration Response MAC frame.

The station and C-Port use these frames to announce whether they are configured to operate in half-duplex or full-duplex mode. If they are incompatible, the station will remain in bypass mode but will be able to send an error message reporting the problem to one or more of the Token Ring functional servers.

A station that wants to operate in 100Mbps full-duplex mode can register a request to trade up to this rate of speed. The response code that comes back may accept this speed or indicate that a lower speed must be used.

If registration is successful, the station transmits Lobe Media Test frames to check that the lobe can operate at an acceptable bit error rate. A C-Port repeats test frames back to the station, just as a hub port did for classic Token Ring.

Note

In classic Token Ring, test frames were addressed to X'00-00-00-00-00-00. A new functional address, X'C0-00-00-00-40-00, has been defined as the destination for the DTR Lobe Media Test frames.

Next, the station requests permission to join by sending an Insert Request frame. Then the Concentrator/Switch checks to make sure that the station's MAC address is unique on its logical ring. If all is well, the C-Port sends back an Insert Response frame containing an acceptance. A station connected via twisted-pair cabling places a phantom DC current on its cable, and the join is completed.

DTR MAC Protocol Frames

Table 19.4 lists the MAC frames used in the DTR protocol. Some classic Token Ring frames have been dropped, but several new frames have been added.

TABLE 19.4 MAC FRAMES USED IN THE DTR PROTOCOL

Numeric Identifier	Name	Description
X'00	Response	Sent to acknowledge receipt of a MAC frame or to report an error in a received MAC frame.
X'02	Beacon	Signals an interruption in the data flow on the link.
X'05	C-Port Heartbeat	Sent periodically by a C-Port in port mode. Enables the station to detect whether the link is working, and to learn or verify the MAC address of its neighboring C-Port.
X'06	Station Heartbeat	Sent periodically by a station. Enables its C-Port to detect whether the link is working, and to learn or verify the MAC address of its neighbor.
X'08	Lobe Media Test	Transmitted to check the cable before attempting to join the ring or during hard error recovery.
X'0B	Remove DTR Station	Sent by a Configuration Report Server or network management system to a station's unicast address to force its removal from the network.
X'0C	Change Parameters	Sent by the Configuration Report Server to a C-Port or a station to set its operating parameters.
X'0D	Initialize Station	Sent by the Ring Parameter Server to a C-Port or a station to initialize its operating parameters.
X'0E	Request Station Addresses	Sent to a station by any management entity to ask for the list of addresses recognized by the station.
X'0F	Request Station State	Sent to a station by any management entity to ask for operating state information.
X'10	Request Station Attachments	Sent by any management entity to ask a station or C-Port which functions it performs.

X'11	Registration Request	Sent by a station to register its operating parameters with the C-Port.
X'12	Registration Response	Sent by the C-Port to accept or reject a registration.
X'13	Insert Request	Sent by a station after a successful lobe media test, asking the C-Port to complete the insertion process.
X'14	Insert Response	Sent by the C-Port to accept or reject the insertion request.
X'15	Registration Query	Sent by a C-Port whose station is using the classical Token Ring protocol to invite the station to upgrade to full-duplex mode.
X'22	Report Station Addresses	Responds to Request Station Addresses.
X'23	Report Station State	Responds to Request Station State.
X'24	Report Station Attachments	Responds to Request Station Attachments.
X'29	Report Error	Sent to the Ring Error Monitor to report error counts. It can be sent by a station, a C-Port in station emulation mode, or a C-Port in port mode .

High Speed Token Ring

High Speed Token Ring (HSTR) is a 100Mbps implementation of Dedicated Token Ring. In fact, its official title is *100Mbps Dedicated Token Ring*. Combination 4/16/100Mbps NICs and matching Concentrators/Switches have been available for several years.

The HSTR physical coding and transmission specification was adopted directly from CDDI and FDDI, as were 100BASE-TX and 100BASE-FX Ethernet. The copper implementation runs across two pairs of Category 5 unshielded twisted-pair cabling or two pairs of IBM Type 1 shielded twisted–pair cabling. The fiber optic implementation runs on a pair of multimode fibers. Fiber optic lobes can be used.

Note
A 4B/5B encoding is used for both copper and fiber optic cables. Appendix A has the details.

High Speed Token Ring operates only in full–duplex mode. The MAC protocol used is the full-duplex DTR protocol.

Until the introduction of High Speed Token Ring, switch-to-switch links were limited to full-duplex 16Mbps. The only way to increase this capacity was to use parallel links. This was costly because it occupied several ports on each switch and also was inconvenient. The Token Ring community welcomed the jump to 100Mbps.

Originally, there were hopes for a further jump to gigabit speed, but these were drowned in the rising tide of Ethernet successes. Ethernet won the LAN backbone, and market demand could not support the more advanced Token Ring product.

Fiber Optic HSTR Lobes

In classic Token Ring, a fiber optic cable can be used as a trunk link that connects a pair of concentrators. However, the procedure used to join a station to a ring relied on the use of a phantom current across a copper wire to open the TCU relay, and fiber optic lobes were not supported.

However, it was very desirable to support fiber for the 100Mbps implementation. Hence, an alternative cabling coupling unit and relay management technology were needed. This was engineered in a way that also would work for lower speeds of attachment. The technical problem was solved by defining special, nondata optical signals that a station transmits across an optical fiber to request insertion or to ask for a return to bypass state.

Fiber Distributed Data Interface

Fiber Distributed Data Interface (FDDI) LANs were introduced in the mid-1980s. The technology was developed by the American National Standards Institute (ANSI) X3T9.5 standards committee.

FDDI LANs were designed to operate at high speed, be reliable, and have a large diameter. This made FDDI a popular choice for LAN backbones.

Data is transmitted around a ring at 100Mbps. Systems can be connected by dual rings, and after a break a usable ring path is established automatically. A dual-ring fiber optic network can have a circumference of 100 kilometers.

FDDI truly is a legacy technology that is being replaced by high-speed Ethernet switches.

In place of costly 100Mbps FDDI NICs, there are now cheap 100Mbps Ethernet cards. Instead of FDDI's dual ring and elaborate ring recovery procedures, there are reliable switches and aggregated links. FDDI's large, awkward connectors have been replaced by small and reliable SC connectors. Long distances attainable through the use of optical fiber now are attainable by other LAN technologies using optical fiber.

Several vendors offer LAN switches or routers that include ports that can be connected to FDDI, Ethernet, Token Ring, and ATM segments. This enables the technologies to interwork and also assists in migration between technologies.

FDDI is sketched briefly in the sections that follow.

FDDI Topology

In an FDDI LAN, the nodes that can be the source or destination of data frames are called *stations*. A station has a MAC layer, one or more MAC addresses, and one or more FDDI ports. The stations share the bandwidth provided by the ring.

As was the case for Token Ring, cabling management often is simplified by connecting stations to a concentrator (hub) unit. A concentrator can play its role invisibly. However, it will need a MAC layer and a MAC address if it is going to be configured or supervised via network management messages. In this case, it will have the status of a station, too.

Normally, most stations are connected to concentrators that are attached to a central ring called the *trunk*. Concentrators can be cascaded, making the physical topology of an FDDI network look like a ring of trees, as shown in Figure 19.13.

The path followed by a frame passes through every active station. For example, in Figure 19.13:

1. A frame entering concentrator A flows to concentrator B.

2. The frame flows in and out of each station NIC attached to concentrator B and returns to concentrator A.

3. The frame advances to concentrator C.

4. It flows in and out of each of each station NIC attached to concentrator C and returns to concentrator A.

5. The frame continues around the trunk ring.

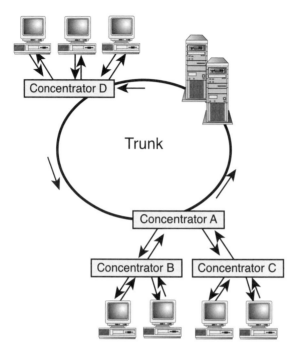

FIGURE 19.13 *FDDI topology.*

Like a Token Ring, an FDDI ring is made up of a series of point-to-point links that connect a station to a station, a station to a concentrator, or a concentrator to another concentrator. Originally, only optical fiber links were used, but copper links were added later.

Separate fibers or wires are used in the transmit and receive directions. Figure 19.14 provides a more detailed view of the path through the tree of concentrators shown at the bottom of Figure 19.13, and it can be seen that data enters each device on one line and exits on a different line.

The path must be adjusted when an additional station—or a lower-level concentrator—is added to the configuration. FDDI adapters make these adjustments automatically. Path control is an important feature of FDDI.

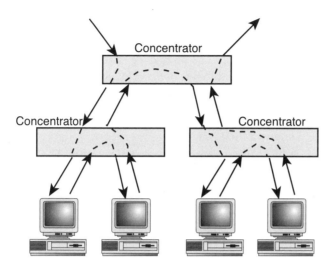

FIGURE 19.14 *A path through an FDDI LAN.*

Primary and Secondary Rings

The trunk can consist of two rings (a dual ring). For a dual ring, during normal operation traffic flows on one of the rings, which is called the *primary ring*. The second ring provides the backup capability and is called the *secondary ring*. If a trunk link on the primary ring fails, the systems adjacent to the break automatically reconfigure the path through the ring and create a new path that includes a mixture of primary and secondary ring links.

Note

The path length around the ring is limited to, at most, 200 kilometers. The dual–ring LAN circumference is restricted to 100 kilometers to ensure that the path length stays within the 200km limit when a break causes both primary and secondary links to be used.

The standard does not set a hard limit on the number of stations that can be attached to an FDDI ring. It does suggest a default maximum of 1000 port attachments. This often is stated as 500 stations.

The maximum time for a bit to circle a maximum-length fiber optic ring that is loaded with stations would be about 2 milliseconds.

The direction of travel on the secondary ring is the opposite of the direction on the primary ring. When a secondary ring is used, frames travel in opposite directions on segments of the primary and secondary rings. For this reason, the primary and secondary rings are said to be *counter-rotating*. In Figure 19.15, the primary ring is shown as the solid outer ring, and the secondary ring is shown as the dotted inner ring.

The top of Figure 19.15 shows a dual ring that connects servers and concentrators. The bottom part of the figure shows another common setup: The dual ring is used as a network backbone and connects to routers and bridges.

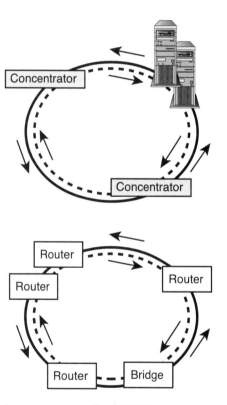

FIGURE 19.15   *Dual FDDI rings.*

Systems that connect to both trunk rings are called *dual-attached*. Other stations are called *single-attached*.

Single-Attached Stations and S Ports

The systems in Figure 19.13 and 19.14 are single-attached. Figure 19.16 shows a detailed view of single-attached port connections. A port that is used for a single-attached connection is called (not-surprisingly) an S Port. Data flows into the port on one line and out on the other line.

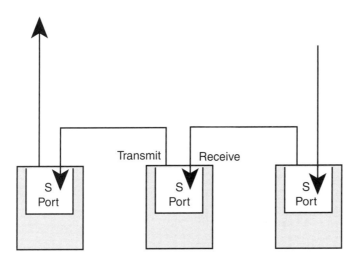

FIGURE 19.16 *Single-attached station ports.*

Dual-Attached Stations and A and B Port Types

The systems in Figure 19.17 are dual-attached and connect to the two rings via two separate ports. Each of these ports has a different type:

- **Type A Port**—The receive line is attached to the primary ring, and the transmit line is attached to the secondary ring. (In brief: primary in, secondary out.)

- **Type B Port**—The transmit line is attached to the primary ring, and the receive line is attached to the secondary ring. (In brief: primary out, secondary in.)

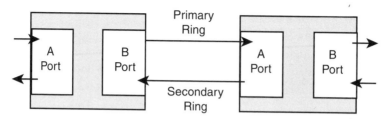

FIGURE 19.17   *Dual-attached station ports.*

Figure 19.18 shows an entire ring to which all stations are dual-attached. The heavy outer line is the primary ring. The primary enters each node at an A Port and exits at a B Port. The thin inner line is the secondary ring. The secondary enters each node at a B Port and exits at an A Port.

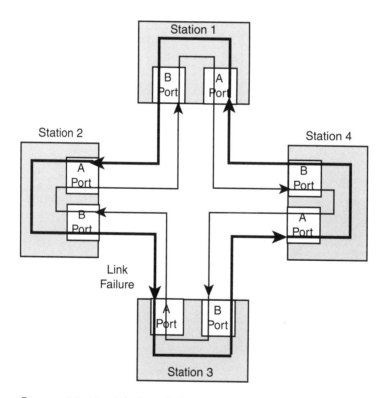

FIGURE 19.18   *A dual-trunk ring.*

Concentrator M Ports

One more type of port that is used in an FDDI ring is illustrated in Figure 19.19. The concentrator in the figure is attached to dual rings via type A and type B Ports. It also is connected to single-attached stations. The concentrator ports that attach to these stations are called *M Ports*.

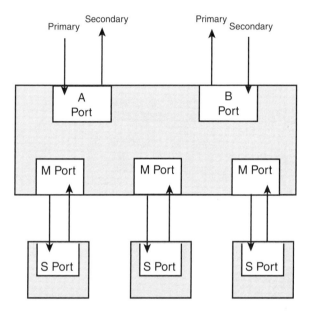

FIGURE 19.19 *M Ports in a concentrator.*

Wrapping an FDDI Ring

The capability of a dual FDDI ring to recover from failed wiring or a failed node is viewed as one of its big advantages. Figure 19.20 shows a ring that has suffered a failure and has recovered.

The problem is solved by creating a ring that contains some segments from the primary ring and some from the secondary ring. This is implemented by changing the path at station 2 and at station 3.

- At station 2, data enters the A Port as usual but exits via the other (secondary) link at that port (instead of through the B Port).

- At station 3, data flows into the B Port (via the secondary link) and then exits as usual via the other (primary) link at that port.

This is called *wrapping* the ring, which means that the secondary ring segment attached to the A Port in station 2 is used to exit that station. This causes traffic to traverse the secondary ring until it enters the B Port in station 3.

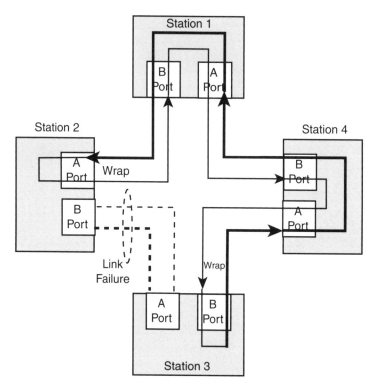

FIGURE 19.20   *A wrapped ring.*

FDDI Media and Encoding

Originally, multimode and single-mode optical fiber were used for all FDDI node-to-node connections. Later, copper links were added, and the copper implementation was called *Copper Distributed Data Interface* (CDDI).

The copper wiring standard is called *Twisted Pair-Physical Medium Dependent* (TP-PMD) and operates over Category 5 unshielded twisted-pair cable or IBM Type 1 150 ohm shielded twisted–pair cable.

The physical media and the encoding method used for FDDI and CDDI were adopted for 100BASE-FX (fiber optic) and 100BASE-TX (twisted-pair) Ethernet, and were discussed briefly in Chapter 7, "The Ethernet 100Mbps Physical Layer." The encoding and transmission mechanisms are described in detail in Appendix A. Just a few of the basic facts are reviewed here.

Data is transformed before it is sent onto an FDDI or CDDI line. Each byte is broken into two 4-bit nibbles. Each nibble is translated to a 5-bit pattern. The encoding scheme is called *4B/5B*.

Extra 5-bit patterns are used (alone or combined in pairs) as special control codes. Special control codes represent the following:

- **Idle (11111)**—The idle pattern is sent continuously between frames.

- **Start-of-stream delimiter (11000 10001)**—A new frame is introduced by the start-of-stream delimiter.

- **End-of-stream delimiter (01101 00111)**—An end-of-stream delimiter is sent at the end of a frame.

FDDI Protocol Elements

As is the case on a Token Ring, stations on an FDDI ring pass a token around. The holder of the token has the right to transmit data for a period of time. The token then is passed to the next station.

FDDI allocates bandwidth to each station in a different manner than the Token Ring protocol. Each station is guaranteed a reserved time quota and is permitted to transmit frames for that time period when it receives the token. Use of the reserved time is called *synchronous transmission*.

There also is an extra amount of time that is loosely shared by the stations. During ring initialization, the stations agree on a *Target Token Rotation Timeout* (TTRT). This is the *average* time that any station expects to wait before it receives the use of the token.

> **Note**
> During normal operation, twice the Target Token Rotation Timeout is the longest time that any station will have to wait.

If a token arrives early, a station can use the extra slack time in addition to its reserved time. This extra time is said to be used for *asynchronous transmission*. Unlike the synchronous transmission time, the asynchronous time is unpredictable.

An ordinary token is called an *unrestricted token*. There also is a *restricted token*. A station uses a restricted token when it wants to have an uninterrupted dialogue with another station during time currently available for asynchronous transmission. The restricted token enables the station to pass control back and forth to its partner, enabling them to send frames to one another.

Claim Frames and the Target Token Rotation Timeout

To get an FDDI ring ready for action, the stations must perform these actions:

- Decide which one will transmit the first token

- Determine the value of the Target Token Rotation Timeout

The stations elect an initial token transmitter and choose the Target Token Rotation Timeout winner by transmitting Claim frames. Each Claim frame includes

- The value that the station would like to use as the Target Token Rotation Timeout. This is a parameter that is preconfigured at each station.

- The sending station's MAC address.

If a station receives a Claim frame whose target timeout is larger than its own, it discards the frame and transmits its own Claim frame. If the time values are tied, the sender with the bigger MAC address wins. Eventually, only one winning station is transmitting claim frames, and the lowest target timeout value has been discovered. This becomes the operational Target Token Rotation Time for the ring.

The winning station then transmits a token, and data transmission can get started.

Station Management

On a Token Ring, all of the ring management functions are performed using MAC frames. An active monitor station has the job of watching for errors and initiating recovery chores.

The work is organized differently on an FDDI ring. There is no active monitor, and every station participates in ring management and recovery using a component called *station management* (SMT).

The station management entity

- Performs all of the steps required to initialize FDDI functions at the station

- Controls the optical bypass of an inactive station

- Tests the integrity of the link to an adjacent node, and performs ongoing monitoring of link errors

- Checks whether the other end of a station port's line is compatible. For example

  - An M Port must connect to an S Port (see Figure 19.19)

  - An A Port must connect to a B Port (see Figures 19.17 and 19.18)

- Inserts an active station into the ring and removes it from the ring

- Initiates the sending of Claim frames

- Performs the wrap (and unwrap) function, changing the port used to transmit or receive as needed

- Is in charge of the station's management information database, which contains its configuration parameters, status values, and performance statistics

Beacon Frames

Beacon frames are used to recover from serious faults, such as a failed link, a reconfigured ring, or a failed claim process. Any station that detects a fault (for example, because of a timeout) transmits a continuous stream of Beacon frames to its downstream neighbor.

The downstream neighbor might be sending its own Beacons. If so, it stops and instead repeats the incoming Beacons. Eventually, only the station that is immediately downstream from the fault is initiating Beacons. This station sends Beacons that carry its upstream neighbor's MAC address.

The Beacons propagate around the ring to the station that is upstream from the fault. This station removes itself from the ring and performs self-tests. If these succeed, it will try to reinsert.

Station management operates the recovery processes. If a ring wrap is needed, station management initiates and supervises the path change.

FDDI Frames

There are four types of FDDI frames:

- LLC frames that carry user data.

- MAC frames that perform important initialization and recovery chores.

- Station management (SMT) frames used to identify upstream neighbors and to perform test and management functions.

- The void frame, which causes receivers to reset their timers to startup values. A void frame is circulated before the ring is reinitialized with Claim frames. The void frame contains no payload.

Table 19.5 lists and describes the two MAC frames.

TABLE 19.5 MAC FRAMES

Frame Type	Description
Claim	Elects the station that will send the first token, and establishes the operational Target Token Rotation Time for the ring
Beacon	Used to announce a serious fault and identify the stations that are upstream and downstream of the fault

Table 19.6 lists the types of station management frames. Note that in contrast to the Token Ring protocol, FDDI neighbor information is propagated using SMT frames.

The FDDI standards were written before the existence of SNMP. Some of the functions formerly performed using SMT frames now are performed using SNMP.

TABLE 19.6 STATION MANAGEMENT FRAMES

Frame Type	Description
Neighbor Information	Enables each MAC to determine its upstream neighbor's MAC address. Also used to detect duplicate MAC addresses. Transmitted every 2 to 30 seconds.
Echo	Used for loopback testing. Can check that the target port, MAC layer, and station management function are operational.
Status Information	Used for Request and Response frames that retrieve basic status information.
Parameter Management	Used to get or set station management parameters.

Frame Type	Description
Request Denied	Indicates that a request was inappropriate or had an incorrect format.
Status Reporting	Notifies FDDI managers of station events and conditions via a status report protocol.

FDDI Formats

The FDDI token and frames were patterned on the Token Ring token and frames, but there are some differences. For example, there is no monitor station on an FDDI ring, and no priority or reservation bits are used, so no access control field is present. Another difference is the use of special characters to delimit frames.

FDDI Token Format

Figure 19.21 shows the format of an ordinary (unrestricted) token. A token must be preceded by four or more idle symbols. The starting and ending delimiters are made up of pairs of special symbols. These are represented by 5-bit code-groups that never are used to represent data bytes.

> **Note**
>
> The starting delimiter code-groups are called J and K.
>
> The 10 bits that actually are transmitted are 1 1 0 0 0 1 0 0 0 1.
>
> A code-group called T is repeated twice to form the ending delimiter for a token.
>
> The 10 bits that actually are transmitted are 0 1 1 0 1 0 1 1 0 1.

The frame control field has a value of X'80 to indicate that this is an ordinary token. (The value X'C0 is used for a restricted token.)

Starting Delimiter	Frame Control	Ending Delimiter
JK Code-Groups	X'80 or X'C0	TT Code-Groups

FIGURE 19.21 *The FDDI token.*

FDDI Frame Format

An FDDI frame is almost identical to a Token Ring frame. A frame can be up to 4500 bytes in length. Figure 19.22 displays the format of an FDDI frame.

The sender transmits a preamble consisting of at least 16 idles before the start of a frame. However, because of differences between the delays between nodes, the number of idles can shrink as the frame is repeated around the ring.

Most of the fields in the FDDI frame should be familiar:

- The starting delimiter is the same as the one used for the token.

- The ending delimiter consists of a single special T symbol instead of a repeated pair.

- The frame control field announces the frame's type (for example, LLC or MAC Claim frame).

- For a user data frame, the information field starts with an LLC header.

- The frame status field consists of three special symbols that are used very much like the status bits at the end of a Token Ring frame. These symbols are used to report error status, address recognized, and frame copied.

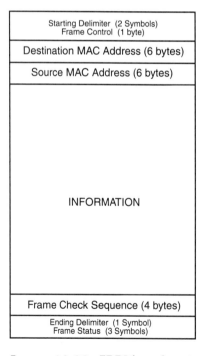

FIGURE 19.22 *FDDI frame format.*

Summary Points

- A classic half-duplex Token Ring consists of a set of stations connected in a ring. The stations share a 4Mbps or 16Mbps bandwidth.

- The physical wiring of a classic Token Ring looks like a ring of stars. Stations connect to concentrators in wiring closets.

- A token circulates around the ring. A station with data to send captures the token, transmits one or more frames, and then sends a fresh token.

- If early token release is used, a sender transmits a token right after the interframe gap that follows its final frame.

- Frames that contain user data are called LLC frames. Frames that carry various types of protocol messages are called MAC frames.

- The active monitor, which is chosen by an election process, watches over the token protocol. Other stations attached to the ring act as standby monitors.

- Standby monitor stations elect a new active monitor by transmitting Claim Token frames.

- A Ring Purge frame clears data out of the ring and is used in several error recovery procedures.

- The Beacon process identifies the location of a fault and initiates some actions that might correct the fault.

- A hard error is a fault that prevents frames and/or tokens from circulating around the ring. A soft error is a fault that does not prevent frames and tokens from circulating around the ring.

- The fault domain for a hard error consists of the station downstream to a fault (which reports the problem), the station upstream to the fault, and the equipment between the upstream and downstream stations.

- The neighbor notification process enables each station to discover the address of its upstream neighbor.

- A ring can include a Ring Parameter Server, a Configuration Report Server, and a Ring Error Monitor. These are called functional servers.

- To join a ring, a station attached via twisted-pair cabling must test the cable, physically get on the ring by transmitting a phantom current, check that an active monitor is present, check that there is no duplicate address on the ring, learn the address of its upstream neighbor, and get its configuration parameters.

- An active concentrator port repeats signals. Up-to-date products provide active ports that can isolate bad lobes, bypass stations that are operating at the wrong speed, and stations whose NICs have other problems.

- The Dedicated Token Ring protocol provides full-duplex switched operation and also supports backward compatibility with classic Token Ring.

- A DTR switch C-Port can connect to a full-duplex station, a half-duplex station, a half-duplex hub, or a C-Port at another switch.

- To connect to a C-Port, a full-duplex station registers, performs a lobe media test, and performs a duplicate address check.

- High Speed Token Ring is a 100Mbps implementation of Dedicated Token Ring. Its physical coding and transmission specification were adopted from CDDI and FDDI.

- FDDI rings were designed to operate at 100Mbps, be reliable, and have a large circumference.

- A dual-ring fiber optic network can have a circumference of 100 kilometers and can connect to 1000 ports.

- A node that can be the source or destination of data frames is called a station. The path followed by a frame passes through every active station.

- Separate fibers or wire pairs are used in the transmit and receive directions.

- Cabling management is simplified by connecting stations to a concentrator.

- Many FDDI LANs look like a ring of trees. The central ring is called the trunk. A trunk can consist of two rings: a primary and a secondary ring.

- Systems that connect to two trunk rings are called dual-attached.

- In the absence of a fault, frames flow from a B Port to an A Port on a primary ring, and from an A Port to a B Port on a secondary ring.

- FDDI runs on multimode fiber, single-mode fiber, Category 5 UTP, and IBM Type 1 STP.

- Data is encoded using 4B/5B translation before it is transmitted.

- Every station has a fixed (synchronous) amount of transmission time and also can use varying amounts of slack (asynchronous) time that occurs when a token arrives earlier than expected.

- Claim frames determine what the value for the target rotation time is and who will send the first token.

- Beacon frames identify the stations that are upstream and downstream from a serious fault.

- Station management performs initialization and error recovery functions.

References

The classic Token Ring protocol is described in

- ANSI/IEEE Std 802.5 (ISO/IEC 8802-5). "Token Ring Access Method and Physical Layer Specifications." 1998.

Dedicated Token Ring and the use of fiber optic lobes are described in

- ANSI/IEEE Std 802.5r and 802.5j. "Token Ring Access Method and Physical Layer Specifications, Amendment 1: Dedicated Token Ring Operation And Fibre Optic Media." 1998.

At the time of writing, the 100Mbps standard still is in draft form:

- 802.5t draft. "Token Ring Access Method and Physical Layer Specifications, 100 Mbit/s Dedicated Token Ring Operation." 1998.

The High Speed Token Ring Alliance Web site is

```
http://www.hstra.com/
```

For a real classic, see

- *IBM Token Ring Network Architecture Reference*. Third Edition (SC3D-3374-D2). New York: IBM Corporation, September 1989.

Major FDDI standards include

- ANSI X3.166. "Fiber Distributed Data Interface (FDDI) Physical Layer Medium Dependent (PMD)." 1989, revised 1995.

- ANSI X3.148. "Fiber Distributed Data Interface (FDDI)—Token Ring Physical Layer Protocol (PHY)." 1988, revised 1994.

- ANSI X3.139. "Fiber Distributed Data Interface (FDDI)—Token Ring Media Access Control (MAC)." 1987, revised 1997.

- ANSI X3.184. "Fiber-Distributed Data Interface (FDDI)—Single-Mode Fiber Physical Layer Medium Dependent (SMF-PMD)." Original 1993, last revision 1998.

- ANSI X3.263 (ISO/IEC CD 9314-10). "FDDI Twisted Pair—Physical Medium Dependent (TP-PMD)." 1995.

- ANSI X3.229. "Fibre Distributed Data Interface (FDDI)—Station Management (SMT)." 1994.

- ANSI X3.184. "Fiber-Distributed Data Interface (FDDI)—Single-Mode Fiber Physical Layer Medium Dependent (SMF-PMD)." 1993, revised 1998.

- ANSI X3.278. "Fibre Distributed Data Interface (FDDI)—Physical Layer Repeater Protocol (PHY-REP)." 1997.

CHAPTER 20

ATM Overview

Asynchronous Transfer Mode (ATM) is a technology that was designed to upgrade the world's public wide area telecommunications networks to a new, higher-speed architecture.

The primary ATM standards body is the *Telecommunications Standardization Sector of the International Telecommunication Union* (ITU-T). The *American National Standards Institute* (ANSI) and the *European Telecommunications Institute* (ETSI) contributed to the ATM effort.

The *ATM Forum*, whose members are equipment vendors and service providers, published interoperability agreements that made it possible to build practical products. The Forum made ATM work by solving the technical problems that arise in real-world use.

ATM was designed to cure the shortcomings of the old, rigid telecommunications structure:

- Lack of scalability
- Inflexible bandwidth options
- Incapability to handle mixed data and voice traffic gracefully

These shortcomings resulted from the age of these networks and from the fact that the legacy telecommunications infrastructure was built for telephone service.

A telephone call is digitized at 64,000 bits per second. This number became the basic building block for the entire system. The other building blocks are carrier lines designed to multiplex telephone call circuits. A T1 carrier provides 24 call circuits, and a T3 carrier provides 672 call circuits.

The whole system depends on time-division multiplexing. A periodic time slot is set aside for each circuit, and complicated multiplexing patterns are used to combine the 672 calls that make up a T3 carrier. Taking apart a T3 bundle and switching its calls into other bundles is a major chore that is done under the gun of tight time slot constraints. Multiplexing and demultiplexing are messy tasks.

ATM was met with enthusiasm because the technology overcomes all of these problems:

- It is scalable and can run at the high speeds provided by today's fiber optic technologies.

- It is flexible; a circuit can be configured with whatever bandwidth meets its transmission requirements.

- It can provide a variety of circuit types that support anything from time-sensitive voice or video traffic to background data transfers.

Today, every major frame relay service runs on top of ATM, and ATM is embedded in Internet backbones.

ATM is a technology that is suitable for local area switches as well as wide area switches. This led to an early euphoric belief that ATM would displace all local area and wide area technologies, and lead to a simplified, homogeneous communications environment.

Cheap 100Mbps Ethernet and Gigabit Ethernet put at least a temporary hold on that dream for the local environment. As for the wide area, customer use of ATM often begins within a service provider's telecommunications network. It is hidden from most end users, who currently prefer to connect to a frame relay service via a leased line. The future success or failure of ATM will be based on the price of equipment and of service, and on how well the technology meets the changing needs of users.

This chapter presents a brief sketch of ATM technology and points out some of its strong points and its weaknesses. Chapter 21, "ATM LAN Emulation," outlines ATM's LAN Emulation protocols and explains how ATM is used to create high-speed "LAN" communities that span great distances.

ATM Concepts

An ATM network is made up of endpoint systems that have ATM NICs and switches that move traffic between the endpoints. An endpoint could be a workstation, a server, or a router. It also might be an Ethernet, Token Ring, or FDDI switch that has an ATM interface.

> **Note**
>
> An SNMP agent or a network server located within an ATM switch also can play the role of an endpoint system.

Figure 20.1 illustrates a big ATM network. As the figure shows, ATM networking is switch-based. Systems are connected to switches, and the switches are connected to each another.

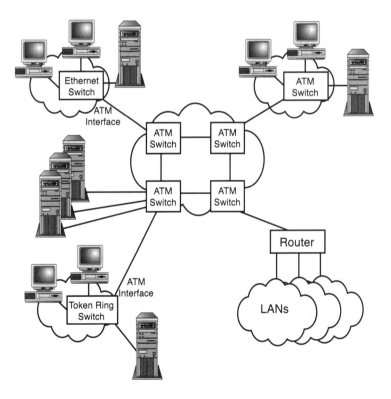

FIGURE 20.1 *An ATM network.*

ATM protocols operate at Layers 1 and 2. Unlike the LAN protocols that have been examined in this book, ATM is *connection-oriented*. This means that a circuit must be set up between the communicating parties before they can transmit data to one another. A circuit can be long-term (behaving like a leased line) or short-term (behaving like a telephone call). A long-term circuit is called a *permanent virtual circuit* (PVC). A short-term circuit is called a *switched virtual circuit* (SVC).

Setting up a switched virtual circuit is like making a telephone call. The caller identifies the called ATM system by providing its ATM number (which actually is called an *ATM address*). ATM numbers used in public networks have the same structure as telephone numbers. There is a lot of flexibility in private network numbering systems. A private network ATM address consists of 20 hexadecimal bytes.

Quality of Service

An Ethernet, Token Ring, or FDDI LAN is like a broad roadway. Systems shoot frames onto the roadway. In an ATM local or wide area network, the roadway is divided into lanes, and groups of lanes provide different categories of service. This is illustrated in Figure 20.2, which shows one direction of traffic. A lot of payload is hauled through the two truck lanes, but traffic in the three automobile lanes can whiz along at a higher speed. At rush hour, of course, the truck and auto lanes can get congested. Furthermore, accidents that prevent some traffic from getting through are not uncommon. The express lanes provide a high-priority service.

In the ATM world, a dual highway is analogous to a communications link. A set of lanes with common characteristics is called a *path*. An individual lane is called a *channel*.

> **Note**
> A circuit is made up of two channels (highway lanes)—one for each direction of traffic.

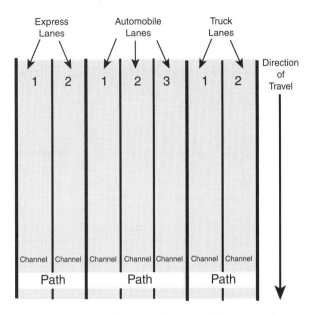

FIGURE 20.2 *Different service categories on a roadway.*

Instead of different service categories for groups of highway lanes, ATM offers different service categories for circuits:

- The Constant Bit Rate (CBR) service provides circuits with a constant bandwidth.

- Real-time Variable Bit Rate (rt-VBR) service delivers a specified average bandwidth and supports applications such as compressed voice or video, which are delay-sensitive.

- Non-real-time Variable Bit Rate (nrt-VBR) service delivers a specified average bandwidth and is suitable for data applications, which are not strongly sensitive to delay.

- Unspecified Bit Rate (UBR) is a best-effort service. It might behave like Internet service—good at some times of the day and sluggish at other times.

- Available Bit Rate (ABR) is a best-effort service that is implemented in a smart way. The service provides continuing feedback that indicates how much bandwidth is available for the sender's use. By throttling back when necessary, senders avoid congesting the network. This prevents traffic from making it halfway through the network and then being thrown away. The result is an improvement in overall throughput for everyone.

A circuit is described by its service category, traffic parameters, and Quality of Service parameters. Traffic parameters include items such as the guaranteed average bandwidth and peak bandwidth for a circuit. Quality of Service parameters include items such as delay, variation in delay (which also is called *jitter*), and percentage of data loss.

> **Note**
>
> The trade press uses the term *Quality of Service* as a blanket term encompassing the combination of service category, traffic parameters, and Quality of Service parameters. This makes it easier for writers to talk about the topic without going into a lot of details.

Concurrent Circuits

You can identify a stream of traffic by identifying the group of lanes and the lane number—for example, automobile lane 3. Each ATM circuit is labeled with a pair of numbers that are called the *Virtual Path Identifier* (VPI) and the *Virtual Channel Identifier* (VCI). The VPI is like the group number, and the VCI is like the lane number within the group.

An ATM interface can support many circuits at the same time. Figure 20.3 illustrates channels for two circuits at an ATM interface. Each pair of channels is inside a path.

> **Note**
>
> By long tradition, when several circuits share a single physical line without being given fixed time slots, they are called *virtual circuits*.
>
> Each circuit is set up with whatever service category, bandwidth, and Quality of Service is needed at a given time. The circuits share an access line that is real and that has a real physical bandwidth capacity.

> **Note**
>
> The ATM technology is very flexible. A virtual circuit can be set up to be one-way only so that there would be a channel in one direction, but not the other.
>
> It also is possible to implement one-way point-to-multipoint circuits. Data sent by a source would be replicated at a switch and sent out on several channels.

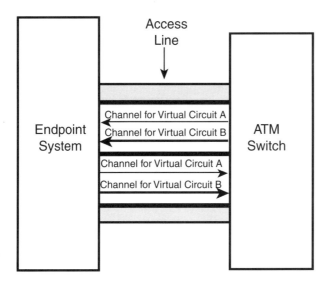

FIGURE 20.3 *Channels for two virtual circuits that share an access line.*

ATM Architecture

ATM operates at Layer 1 and Layer 2. The structure is shown in Figure 20.4.

The ATM data link layer (Layer 2) is called the ATM Adaptation Layer (AAL). The ATM protocol suite includes several protocols that can be used at Layer 2. The one that currently is used for data communications is called AAL5, and that is the one that will be discussed here.

AAL5 frames can be very big. The information field in an AAL5 frame can contain up to 65,535 bytes. However, real implementations generally stick to sizes of 9232 bytes or less.

A higher-layer protocol in an endpoint device passes data to the ATM Adaptation Layer and identifies the path and channel on which the frame should be sent. The ATM Adaptation Layer encapsulates the data into a frame and then slices the frame into 48-byte chunks. It passes each chunk, along with its VPI and VCI identifier, to the physical layer.

The physical layer is divided into two sublayers. The upper sublayer is called the *ATM Layer*. The ATM Layer in an endpoint device adds a 5-byte header to each 48-byte payload, forming a *cell*. It also queues cells in the order in which they will be transmitted.

The lower sublayer is called the *ATM Physical Layer*. This sublayer is responsible for putting cells onto a medium at the sending end and extracting cells from the medium at the receiving end.

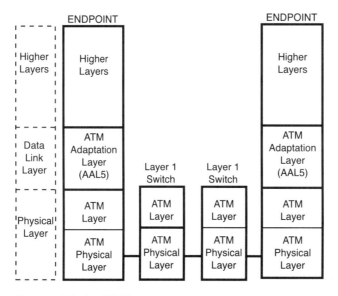

FIGURE 20.4   *ATM Layers.*

It often is mistakenly stated that ATM has cells instead of frames. This is totally wrong. ATM has cells at Layer 1 instead of 1-byte time slots. It has frames at Layer 2 just like any other Layer 2 data protocol.

Earlier chapters discussed Layer 2 and Layer 3 switching. ATM switches operate at Layer 1—only the endpoint systems deal with frames. In Figure 20.4, note that the ATM Adaptation Layer appears only in the endpoint systems. The Layer 1 ATM switches have the job of moving cells through the network as fast as they can.

The ATM Cell Header

Figure 20.5 shows the format of an ATM cell header for a cell that is sent between an endpoint system and its adjacent ATM switch.

Currently, the first 4 bits are unused. Recall that a virtual circuit is identified by its Virtual Path Identifier (VPI) and Virtual Channel Identifier (VCI). The VPI occupies the next 8 bits. When expressed as a decimal number, the VPI value can range from 0 to 255.

The VCI occupies 16 bits. Hence, when expressed as a decimal number, the VCI value can range from 0 to 65,535. In all, there are 16,777,216 possible (VPI, VCI) pairings.

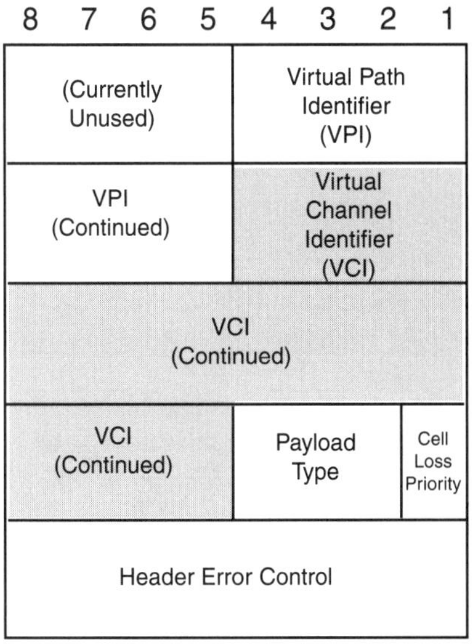

8	7	6	5	4	3	2	1
(Currently Unused)				Virtual Path Identifier (VPI)			
VPI (Continued)				Virtual Channel Identifier (VCI)			
VCI (Continued)							
VCI (Continued)				Payload Type		Cell Loss Priority	
Header Error Control							

FIGURE 20.5 *Cell header sent between an endpoint system and an ATM switch.*

Most ATM cells carry user data, but there also are some diagnostic, test, and network management cells that belong to a special category called operations, administration, and maintenance (OAM).

The 3-bit *payload type* reveals whether a cell contains user data or OAM information as well as some other information that is useful:

• The first bit of the payload type field indicates whether the cell carries user data (0) or OAM data (1).

• For user data, the second bit is set to 1 if congestion is experienced along the path to the destination.

• The third bit is important for AAL5 frames. It is set to 1 to indicate that a cell contains the final segment of an AAL5 frame.

If an ATM switch gets congested, it might be forced to throw away some cells. Cells whose *cell loss priority* bit is set to 1 have a lower priority and are more eligible for discard.

The *header error control* field contains the result of a calculation performed on the previous 4 bytes. The header error control field is recalculated at every switch along the way and at the destination.

If the calculated value does not match the value in the field, the header has been corrupted. In some cases, the header error control value actually can be used to correct a single-bit error. Correction does not work for some physical layers because of the way data is encoded onto the medium. In any case, if the problem was caused by a multibit error, or if correction does not work, the cell is discarded.

VPI and VCI Numbers

The designers of ATM thought big and envisioned networks that would include hundreds or thousands of switches. Each participating system must be assigned an address that identifies where it is located.

However, the VPI and VCI numbers that identify a circuit are completely separate from the ATM address. They have nothing to do with location. They are chosen for convenience at each end when setting up a permanent or switched virtual circuit. As long as a channel has been assigned to a suitable type of path, and as long as the combination of path and channel numbers is unique at the endpoint, any choice is all right.

Thinking in terms of millions of circuits, it would be impossible to try to pick a new (VPI, VCI) combination that was not being used anywhere else in the network. Instead, these numbers have only local significance and can be mapped to a new pairing at every switch in the network.

Figure 20.6 illustrates how this works. Endpoint system A identifies the circuit using VPI=0 and VCI=40. ATM switch 1 knows that the circuit that enters with identifiers (0,40) must leave with identifiers (2,83). ATM switch 2 knows that identifiers (2,83) must be mapped to (0,53) because endpoint system B recognizes the circuit using these numbers.

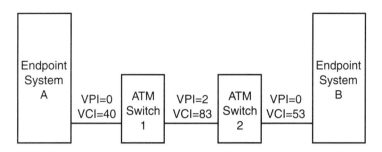

FIGURE 20.6 *Pairs of (VPI, VCI) numbers used along a circuit.*

Processing a Cell

Cell headers are processed by special-purpose chips and can be processed very quickly. At a switch, the most important processing step is a table lookup that maps the incoming port, VPI, and VCI to an outgoing port, VPI, and VCI. Table 20.1 shows a few sample mappings. For example, a cell arriving at switch port 1 with VPI=0 and VCI=45 will be forwarded through port 6 with new VPI=2 and VCI=62.

TABLE 20.1 MAPPING INCOMING CELLS TO OUTGOING CELLS

Incoming			Outgoing		
Port	VPI	VCI	Port	VPI	VCI
1	0	45	6	2	62
1	1	72	3	3	75
2	0	38	3	5	100

After an endpoint passes a cell to an adjacent ATM switch, the size of the VPI field in the cell header is increased to 12 bits, as is shown in Figure 20.7. This means that within the network, path numbers can range from 0 to 4095.

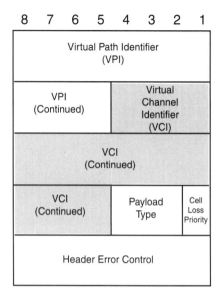

| 8 | 7 | 6 | 5 | 4 | 3 | 2 | 1 |

FIGURE 20.7 *Header of a cell sent between a pair of ATM switches.*

Interleaving Cells

The use of cells makes it easy to build scalable switches that forward traffic at very high speeds. Unlike the old telephony switches, ATM switches do not have to demultiplex and remultiplex complicated patterns of call slot times.

Endpoint systems also gain a big advantage by breaking frames into cells. Frames vary in size from very small to very large. With a conventional Layer 2 or Layer 3 switch, when transmission of a frame starts, all other traffic must wait in line until that transmission is complete.

Figure 20.8 shows traffic that is lined up, waiting for the transmission of a large frame to complete. The small frames at the top arrived in their high-priority queue after transmission of the large frame had begun. Nothing can be done to get the high-priority frames onto the wire until the big frame is out of the way.

The variable sizes of frames make frame delay times very difficult to control and predict.

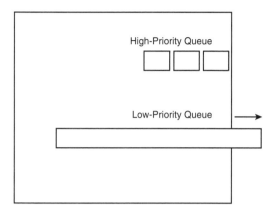

FIGURE 20.8 *Frame delay.*

Figure 20.9 shows cells that are queued up for transmission on three channels. Channel 1 is a high-priority channel. (For example, it might be used for voice.) Channel 2 is used for interactive data, and channel 3 is used for background bulk data transfer.

When data is segmented into cells, it is a lot easier to ensure that a channel gets access to the bandwidth that it has been allocated. The use of cells both minimizes delay and makes delay times far less variable. The high-priority channel 1 cells are not delayed because they can be interleaved into the traffic immediately.

Furthermore, if there is a lull in channel 1 and channel 2 traffic, the extra cells do not have to be wasted; they can be filled with some of the data sent on channel 3. This is the idea behind the unspecified bit rate (UBR) service. A UBR channel usually is assigned some minimum guaranteed rate, but also gets to use leftover bandwidth from other channels.

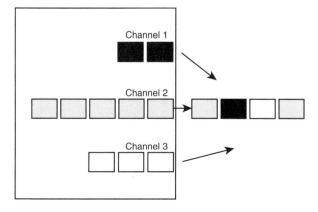

FIGURE 20.9 *Interleaved transmission of cells.*

Using circuits and cells offers several advantages:

- A physical link can be shared by several virtual circuits.

- Each circuit can be assigned the proportion of the bandwidth that the user wants it to have.

- Traffic across a circuit is seen only by its source and destination systems, which enhances security.

- Using cells avoids the variable delays that plague transmission methods based on variable-sized frames.

- Cells are easy to switch, and switch product architects do not have to worry about complicated buffer memory management. Every cell is 53 bytes in length.

Some disadvantages also arise, however:

- With 5 bytes of header for each 48 bytes of payload, cell headers add a 10.4% overhead to data traffic.

- Most local area networks administrators are unfamiliar with ATM technology, making the chore of configuring an ATM LAN endpoint system or switch difficult.

- Converting a system to ATM requires the installation of a relatively costly NIC.

AAL5 Frame Format

Figure 20.10 shows the format of an AAL5 frame. At first view, the format is surprising because there is no frame header. There is a good reason for this. In an ordinary LAN, a header is used to identify a frame's source and destination. In a circuit-based environment, the header is not needed. A circuit must be set up before any data can be transferred. The circuit is identified by its path and channel numbers, which appear in each cell header. No circuit identifier appears in a frame header.

The trailer field contains some important housekeeping information. As was the case for Ethernet, Token Ring, and FDDI, the AAL5 trailer contains the result of a 4-byte cyclic redundancy check function calculation. (This result is stored in the frame check sequence field in an Ethernet, Token Ring, or FDDI frame.)

Recall that the AAL layer slices a frame into 48-byte segments. The pad field is needed because the entire frame must be a multiple of the cell payload size, 48 bytes.

The payload length value enables the receiver to figure out how many pad bytes have been inserted and to verify that none of the cells in the frame have been lost. The end of a frame is marked by setting a flag in the header of its final cell.

The user-to-user byte is reserved for use by a higher-layer protocol. The common part indicator (CPI) currently is just a fill byte, bringing the trailer to a total length of 8 bytes.

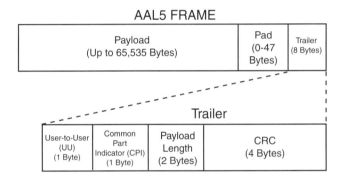

FIGURE 20.10 *Format of an AAL5 frame.*

This brief overview has provided a general idea of the way that ATM works. Chapter 21 looks at the way that ATM has been adapted for use in local area networks.

Summary Points

- ATM originally was designed to upgrade the world's public wide-area telecommunications networks.

- ATM is scalable, flexible, and capable of handling voice, video, and data traffic.

- ATM can be used in local area networks as well as wide area networks.

- An ATM network is made up of a set of ATM switches, and computers, routers, and Layer 2 LAN switches that have ATM interfaces.

- ATM protocols operate at Layers 1 and 2. Layer 2 is called the ATM Adaptation Layer.

- The physical layer is divided into two sublayers, called the ATM Layer and the ATM Physical Layer.

- Several service categories have been defined for ATM. These include Constant Bit Rate (constant bandwidth, such as for uncompressed voice), Real-time Variable Bit Rate (for example, compressed voice or video), Non-real-time Variable Bit Rate (for example, LAN data), Unspecified Bit Rate (best effort), and Available Bit Rate (best effort with feedback).

- An ATM circuit is labeled with a Virtual Path Identifier (VPI) and a Virtual Channel Identifier (VCI).

- Multiple ATM circuits can share the bandwidth on a physical link.

- An ATM cell has a 5-byte header that contains the circuit's VPI and VCI.

- Some diagnostic, test, and network management cells belong to a special category called operations, administration, and maintenance.

- VPI and VCI numbers can be changed at each switch.

- A device transmits a stream of cells. Cells for multiple circuits are interleaved in the stream.

- An AAL5 frame does not have a header. Its trailer contains a CRC value and the length of the payload.

References

The protocol features implemented by endpoint systems and their adjacent switches are described in these ATM Forum documents:

- "ATM User-Network Interface Specification Version 3.1." 1994.

- "ATM Forum Traffic Management Specification Version 4.0." 1996.

The ITU-T I series includes a very large number of documents that relate to ATM.

For a detailed description of ATM networks and ATM protocols, see

- Feit, S. *Wide Area High Speed Networks*. Indianapolis, IN: Macmillan Technical Publishing, 1998.

CHAPTER **21**

ATM LAN Emulation

A set of systems connected to an ATM switch behaves like a bunch of telephones connected to a telephone switch: One instrument talks to another by making a call. This is very different from the way a LAN switch works. A station on a LAN fires off an individual frame to another system—or to all systems—any time it wishes. It does not have to go through a call setup first.

In spite of this vast difference in architectures, the ATM Forum was determined to integrate ATM switches into conventional LANs. The solution is called *LAN Emulation* (LANE).

LANE satisfies these ATM Forum objectives:

- It enables a set of systems that have ATM NICs and are connected to ATM switches to emulate a conventional LAN.

- It enables Ethernet or Token Ring systems connected to ordinary hubs and switches to interact with ATM systems as if they all belong to a conventional LAN.

LANE overcomes another hurdle that is the most important of all: It provides backward compatibility with existing higher-layer protocols and applications. LANE makes it possible for existing network protocols and network applications to run on top of ATM without making changes to any of the software. To the network layer and above, the environment appears to be an ordinary Ethernet or Token Ring.

Note
At the time of writing, LAN Emulation is not supported for FDDI.

Because wide area ATM links can run at speeds that meet or exceed local area connections, it is possible to build a high-performance LAN that spans multiple sites. Clients at one site that access ATM-attached servers at another site can experience remote bandwidth capacity and response time that rivals local bandwidth capacity and response time. Figure 21.1 illustrates a high-speed emulated LAN that spans a wide area ATM connection.

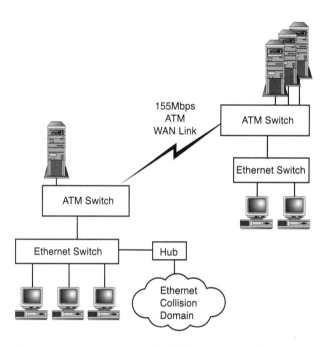

FIGURE 21.1   *An emulated LAN that spans a wide area link.*

The goal of this chapter is to build a good conceptual understanding of LANE, sufficient to comprehend

- The value that LANE can add to a network

- Product descriptions and product documentation

Lots of options and protocol details have been omitted so that the discussion can concentrate on the essentials. Even so, LANE can appear to be quite complicated at first view. However, after you sort out the roles of its various special servers, it turns out to be pretty straightforward.

Emulated LAN Environments

An *emulated LAN (ELAN)* is made up of computers, routers, and bridges that have ATM interfaces and are connected to ATM switches. A single ELAN can span several interconnected ATM switches, and the same set of switches can host several ELAN communities. Each ELAN is identified by a unique name.

There is a close relationship between VLANs and ELANs. An ELAN can be part of a larger VLAN that includes ATM systems and conventional LAN systems. In an environment that uses VLANs, an administrator can configure the ELAN to be part of a particular VLAN.

An ATM NIC is assigned a unique 6-byte MAC LAN address, just like an Ethernet or Token Ring NIC. Having a unique MAC address is an essential requirement to participating in an emulated LAN.

The circuit-based environment is molded into a LAN-like environment through the use of three special emulation servers. These emulation servers make it possible for a MAC frame to get from its source to its destination.

Figure 21.2 shows an Ethernet environment that includes ATM ELAN components. In the figure, Ethernet switches A, B, and C and a pair of central application servers are connected to a backbone ATM switch. The systems attached to the Ethernet switches and to the hubs in the Ethernet collision domain can communicate with one another and with the application servers that are attached to the ATM switch.

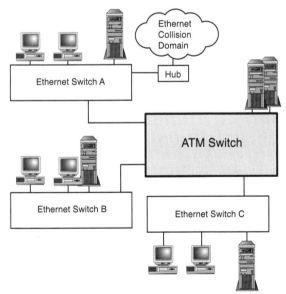

F<small>IGURE</small> **21.2** *An emulated Ethernet LAN environment.*

The Ethernet switches relay traffic between the Ethernet environment and the ATM environment. They are called *proxies* because they relay traffic to and from ATM systems on behalf of the conventional LAN stations.

Figure 21.3 shows a Token Ring environment that includes ATM ELAN components. Token Ring switches A and C, source route bridge B, and a pair of central application servers are directly connected to a backbone ATM switch. The ordinary LAN systems attached to the Token Ring switches and to source route bridge B and its attached rings can communicate with one another and with the application servers that are attached to the ATM switch.

Token Ring switches A and C and source route bridge B are called proxies because they relay traffic between the Token Ring environment and the ATM environment.

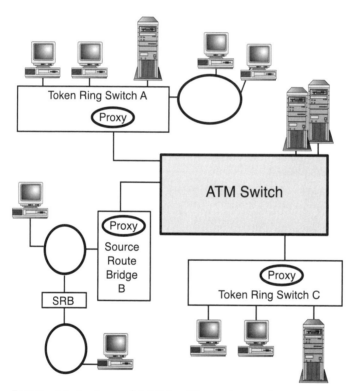

FIGURE 21.3   *An emulated Token Ring environment.*

LAN Emulation Clients

One of the important functions that LANE performs is to hide the underlying ATM layers from the higher protocol layers. This is done by a special device driver that is called a *LAN Emulation Client* (LEC) or a *LANE Client.*

Figure 21.4 shows the location of the LANE Client in an endpoint system's protocol stack. The higher-layer protocol software sends and receives data using *send* and *receive* calls that are part of a standard library of Ethernet or Token Ring device driver calls.

> **Note**
> There are LANE Client device drivers for every major operating system.

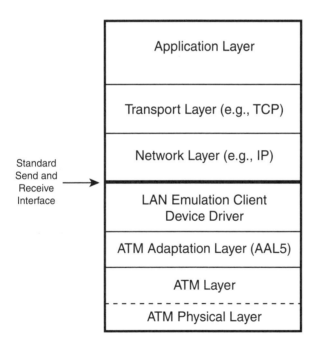

```
                    ┌─────────────────────────────────────┐
                    │         Application Layer            │
                    ├─────────────────────────────────────┤
                    │     Transport Layer (e.g., TCP)      │
                    ├─────────────────────────────────────┤
                    │      Network Layer (e.g., IP)        │
  Standard          ├─────────────────────────────────────┤
  Send and  ──────► │       LAN Emulation Client           │
  Receive           │         Device Driver                │
  Interface         ├─────────────────────────────────────┤
                    │    ATM Adaptation Layer (AAL5)       │
                    ├─────────────────────────────────────┤
                    │            ATM Layer                 │
                    │- - - - - - - - - - - - - - - - - - - │
                    │        ATM Physical Layer            │
                    └─────────────────────────────────────┘
```

FIGURE 21.4 *A LAN Emulation Client in an endpoint system.*

To the upper layers, the LANE Client looks just like an ordinary Ethernet or Token Ring device driver. However, the LANE Client transmits data through an ATM interface and also performs several fairly complicated protocol procedures.

For example, a LANE Client must enroll its system in an ELAN. The enrollment process ties the client to two emulation servers—one that assists with unicast communication and another that handles broadcasts and multicasts.

When an upper layer tells the client to transmit a stream of unicast frames to a destination MAC address, the client

1. Sends a query to the first emulation server asking for the ATM address of the destination.

2. Opens an ATM circuit to the destination.

3. Exchanges frames with the peer system.

When an upper layer tells the client to transmit a broadcast or multicast frame, the client forwards the frame to the second emulation server, which relays the frame to all of the other members of the ELAN.

The sections that follow fill in the details.

LAN Emulation Servers

Three special emulation servers are used to help LAN Emulation clients mimic the behavior of connectionless LAN systems:

- The first (the configuration server) is like the principal of an elementary school, who assigns each incoming student to a classroom (an ELAN).

- The second (the LANE Server) is like the classroom teacher, who takes attendance and keeps track of everyone who is there. This teacher (like a LAN Emulation Server) has got everybody's number.

- The third (the broadcaster) is a gossip. Tell him something, and everybody else will know it immediately.

More formally, the three servers are the

- **LAN Emulation Configuration Server or LANE Configuration Server (LECS)**—Assigns a LAN Emulation Client to a specific emulated LAN.

- **LAN Emulation Server or LANE Server (LES)**—Is in charge of one emulated LAN and keeps track of the MAC addresses and ATM addresses of its members. A LANE client stays connected to this server so that the client can ask for translations from MAC address to ATM address any time that it needs them.

- **Broadcast and Unknown Server (BUS)**—Delivers broadcast and multi-cast frames to stations in the emulated LAN. A client stays connected to this server so that the client can send and receive broadcast and multicast frames at any time.

Figure 21.5 displays another view of the Ethernet ELAN in Figure 21.2 that includes the LANE clients and servers. Figure 21.6 displays another view of the Token Ring ELAN in Figure 21.3 that includes the LANE clients and servers.

Note

In the figures, the three emulation servers are located in the ATM switch. In fact, emulation servers can be located in a switch, router, or endpoint system. The servers also can be spread across different systems.

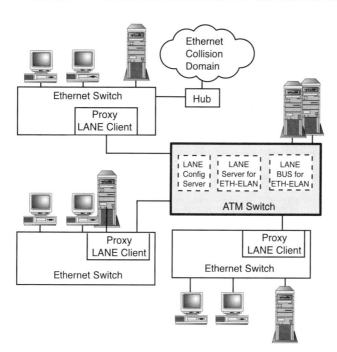

FIGURE 21.5 *Clients and servers in an Ethernet ELAN.*

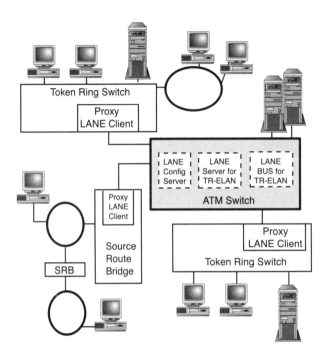

FIGURE 21.6 *Clients and servers in a Token Ring ELAN.*

The LAN Emulation Configuration Server

A LANE Configuration Server does not have a lot to do, but its job is important. The server assigns each LANE client to an appropriate ELAN.

The client interaction with the configuration server is straightforward. The client opens an ATM circuit to the server and announces its own ATM address. Optionally, the client can provide additional parameters that can help the server determine the ELAN to which the client should be assigned. These parameters can include

- The type of ELAN that the client wants to join (Ethernet or Token Ring)

- The name of an ELAN that the client would like to join

- The maximum frame size that the client can support

- The client's MAC address

- A Layer 3 address

The configuration server responds with

- The ATM address of a specific LANE Server

- The type of ELAN (Ethernet or Token Ring) to which the client has been assigned

- The name of the ELAN to which the client has been assigned

- The maximum frame size for the ELAN

A single configuration server can support an entire network, but it also is possible to divide the job among several servers.

Figure 21.7 illustrates a client's interaction with a LANE Configuration Server.

> **Note**
> The special connection used between the client and the configuration server is called a *Configuration Direct Virtual Channel Connection*.

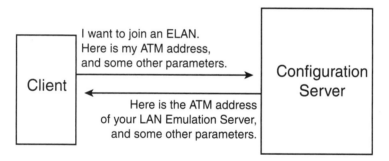

FIGURE 21.7 *Asking the configuration server for the ATM address of a LANE Server.*

Setting Up a Configuration Server

When you understand how clients interact with a configuration server, it is easy to understand what an administrator must do to initialize the server. The administrator must enter one or more pairings:

Name of ELAN   ATM address of ELAN Server

Next, the criteria for assigning clients to an ELAN must be entered. The criteria that can be used are up to each vendor, but the following are reasonable alternatives:

- Enter a single ELAN name, and assign all clients to that ELAN by default.

- Assign a client to an ELAN when the client asks to join that ELAN by name.

- Assign a client to an ELAN based on the client's ATM address. The ATM addresses of all the clients that belong to each ELAN must be entered.

- Set up two ELANs: one for Ethernet and one for Token Ring. Assign a client to an ELAN based on the type of ELAN requested.

Finding the Configuration Server

To get started, a client must figure out how to contact its configuration server.

Three methods can be used:

- Use a "well-known" ATM group address that has been reserved for configuration servers:

  X'4700790000000000000000000000-00A03E000001-00

- Obtain the configuration server's address during system initialization. This is done via the *Integrated Local Management Interface* (ILMI) protocol, which is described later, in the section "Initialization with ILMI."

- When the client system is installed, set up a permanent virtual circuit that automatically is activated whenever the client boots. This circuit must have VPI=0 and VCI=17.

Opening a connection to the well-known ATM address of the configuration server is the method that currently is preferred. When the client contacts the configuration server, the client retrieves the ATM address of its LANE Server.

Note

The format of the preceding 20-byte configuration server address follows an ATM address display convention. The first 13 bytes are grouped together. A hyphen separates this group from the next group of 6 bytes. Another hyphen introduces the final byte.

The LAN Emulation Server

Armed with the address of its LANE server, the client now is prepared to join an ELAN. The first step is to open an ATM connection to the LANE Server.

> **Note**
> This connection is called the client's *control direct virtual channel connection*.

The client and LANE Server then exchange a *join* request and response. The client can include its MAC address with its join request, or, alternatively, the client can announce its MAC address in a separate *register* request after the join has completed.

If the client is located in an Ethernet or Token Ring bridge or switch, it indicates that it is a proxy. It registers its own address but also indicates that it represents other systems whose MAC addresses will not be registered. Traffic will be relayed to those systems via an ATM connection to the proxy.

> **Note**
> Some clients have more than one MAC address. A client can announce multiple MAC addresses in a series of register requests.

In any case, when the join and register steps are complete:

- The server knows the client's ATM address and MAC address(es).

- The client has been given the authoritative values of the LAN type, the maximum frame size, and the name of the ELAN.

- The client might have been assigned a unique 2-byte identifier called the *LAN Emulation Client ID* (LECID). The client includes this identifier (if assigned) in all its information frames. (However, some LAN Servers do not assign these identifiers.)

- The server knows whether the client acts as a proxy for some ordinary LAN systems.

> **Note**
>
> A client system that is a Token Ring source route bridge can register its route descriptor instead of—or in addition to—a MAC address.
>
> Hence, in Token Ring LANE environments, the LANE Server maintains a list of source route bridge route descriptors as well as MAC addresses and ATM addresses.

Figure 21.8 illustrates a join/register transaction.

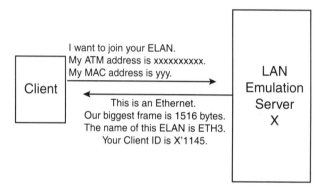

F I G U R E   2 1 . 8 *Joining an ELAN.*

Address Resolution

The LANE Server builds up a database that contains the translations from MAC address to ATM address for systems that have joined its ELAN. This puts it in a perfect position to assist LANE clients that need to map a destination MAC address to a destination ATM address to open up an ATM connection and exchange frames across the connection. The process of discovering the ATM address that corresponds to a MAC address is called *address resolution*.

After joining an ELAN, the client holds on to its initial connection to its ELAN LANE Server. The client sends address resolution requests, which are called *LAN Emulation ARP requests* (LE ARP requests), across this connection and receives LE ARP responses from the server on this connection.

The LANE Server optionally can open a second connection back to the client.

> **Note**
>
> The connection opened by the server is called the *control distribute virtual channel connection.*

This can be an ordinary point-to-point connection. However, a very efficient way for the server to set this up is to use a point-to-multipoint connection.

Figure 21.9 illustrates the way a point-to-multipoint control distribute connection is used. Client A requests the ATM address corresponding to a given MAC address. The server checks and discovers that the MAC address is not listed in its registration database. The server forwards the request on the point-to-multipoint connection. A system that knows the answer will respond.

Note that in Figure 21.9, the system whose MAC address is not in the LANE Server's database is not an ATM system; it is attached to an Ethernet switch. The switch acts as a proxy for its attached systems and responds to the request with its own ATM address.

Client A then can open an ATM connection to the proxy, which will relay traffic to and from the true target system.

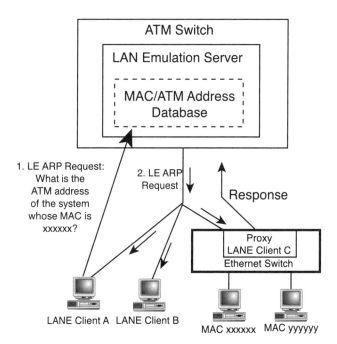

FIGURE 21.9 *Address resolution.*

A LANE Server that does not open these back connections to its clients can relay LE ARP requests to its clients using the ordinary control connections. In this case, a LAN Emulation server that needs to resolve an unknown MAC address might not bother to forward a request to every client, but the server would be sure to forward the request to clients that act as proxies.

The Broadcast and Unknown Server

A client prepares to send broadcasts and multicasts by linking to the Broadcast and Unknown Server (BUS). To get the ATM address of the BUS, the client sends an LE ARP query to its LANE Server, asking for the ATM address of the system corresponding to the broadcast address MAC address X'FF-FF-FF-FF-FF-FF.

When the client receives the ATM address of the BUS, the client opens an ATM connection to the BUS. The client uses this connection to transmit broadcast frames and multicast frames.

> **Note**
> This connection is called the *multicast send virtual channel connection.*

The client can forward other MAC frames to the BUS on this connection. This might be done for protocols that involve very little traffic. For example, a TCP/IP Domain Name server query that translates a computer name such as www.abc.com to an IP address typically is performed using one query frame and one response frame. It would not make a lot of sense to open up an ATM circuit for this small exchange of data.

In addition, sometimes the local LANE Server will not have a destination MAC address in its database and will be incapable of translating it to an ATM address immediately. The client can ask the BUS to flood the frame.

After the client has connected to the BUS, the BUS opens up a separate connection that it uses to deliver broadcast, multicast, or flooded frames to the client.

> **Note**
> This connection is called the *multicast forward virtual channel connection.*

Figure 21.10 illustrates these procedures.

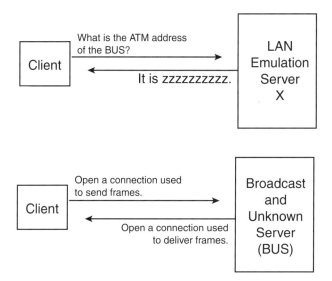

FIGURE 21.10 *Contacting the BUS.*

The bus can deliver broadcasts, multicasts, and flooded frames to its clients very efficiently by using a point-to-multipoint connection as its multicast forward-delivery vehicle. Figure 21.11 illustrates the use of a point-to-multipoint delivery connection.

Note that the BUS in Figure 21.11 is located at an ATM switch, which is a natural place to put it. However, recall that the BUS Server also can be located in a router or an end station.

In the figure, client D transmits a broadcast frame by sending it to the BUS on the multicast send connection. The BUS delivers the frame by sending it out the multicast forward connection. Note that the frame will be delivered to all clients, including client D.

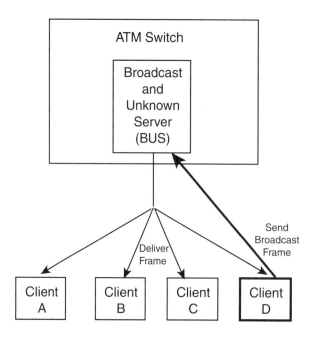

FIGURE 21.11 *BUS delivery via a point-to-multipoint connection.*

ATM LANE Protocol Elements

This section describes the major elements that are used in the LANE protocol, including

- Private ATM addresses

- ATM address initialization via the Integrated Local Management Interface (ILMI)

- The format of LANE data frames

- The functions and format of the control frames that are used in the LANE protocols

Private ATM addresses and ILMI are general ATM protocol elements that are used both outside of and within LANE environments.

The section also includes a trace of a LAN Emulation Ethernet frame.

ATM Addresses

Several formats are defined for ATM addresses, but they all have one trait in common: They are hierarchical. For example, global telephone numbers that identify a country, region, and subscriber number are used as ATM addresses.

Note
These standard numbers are called *E.164 addresses.*

The two address formats most likely to be used in a private ATM network are shown in Figure 21.12. Each consists of 20 bytes. The initial byte indicates the type of address that follows. The address format at the top of Figure 21.12 starts with one of the standard E.164 numbers. This might be a general number that is used to reach the site across a wide area network. This number is followed by 4 bytes that can be used to identify a specific switch at the site.

The next 6 bytes contain an End System Identifier (ESI). A MAC address normally is used as the End System Identifier.

The selector (SEL) byte at the end of each address plays no role in routing a call to an ATM endpoint system; it is an extra byte whose use has not been standardized. The selector byte can be used to select a specific software component that should process incoming ATM frames. For example, it can differentiate among multiple LANE Servers that are collocated at the same node.

The address format at the bottom of Figure 21.12 starts with 12 bytes that an organization can use for hierarchical addressing. For example, subfields could identify an area, a building, and the specific switch to which the endpoint is connected.

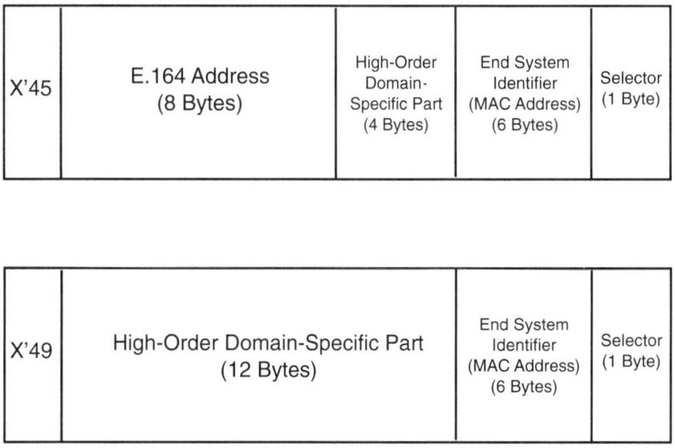

X'45	E.164 Address (8 Bytes)	High-Order Domain-Specific Part (4 Bytes)	End System Identifier (MAC Address) (6 Bytes)	Selector (1 Byte)

X'49	High-Order Domain-Specific Part (12 Bytes)	End System Identifier (MAC Address) (6 Bytes)	Selector (1 Byte)

FIGURE 21.12 *Address formats.*

Initialization with ILMI

ATM makes resourceful use of Simple Network Management Protocol messages to implement a set of procedures called the Integrated Local Management Interface (ILMI). ILMI procedures are not specific to LANE; they are general ATM procedures. At initialization, the following occurs:

1. An endpoint system obtains the first 13 bytes of its ATM address from its switch.

2. The system completes its ATM address by registering its MAC address at the switch.

3. The system and its switch exchange configuration settings and select a common set of parameter values that both support.

4. Optionally, a system also can find out the addresses of the LANE Configuration Server via ILMI.

The switch continues to use ILMI to poll the station periodically to check that the link and the station are still functioning.

ILMI messages are SNMP requests and responses that are carried in AAL5 frames.

> **Note**
> SNMP messages most frequently are carried using UDP and IP. However, in this case, these protocols are not needed. The SNMP messages are packed directly into AAL5 payloads.

LANE Data Frames

Figure 21.13 shows the format of an Ethernet frame that is carried in an AAL5 frame. The AAL5 frame starts with a 2-byte field that contains either the sending client's unique LANE Client identifier or X'00-00. An Ethernet frame follows immediately. The Ethernet frame does not include a frame check sequence; error checking is taken care of by the CRC in the AAL5 frame trailer.

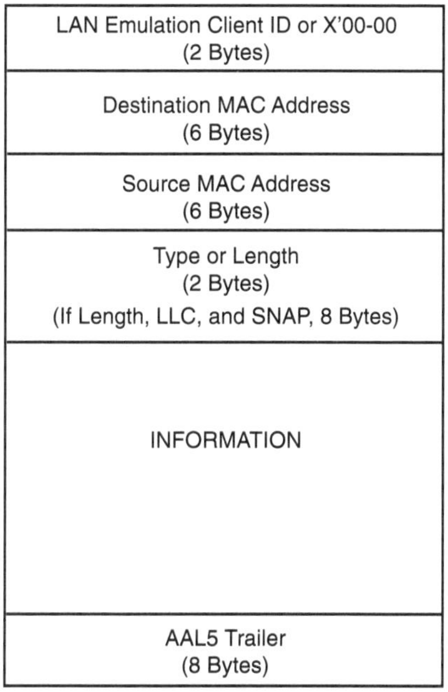

| LAN Emulation Client ID or X'00-00
(2 Bytes) |
| Destination MAC Address
(6 Bytes) |
| Source MAC Address
(6 Bytes) |
| Type or Length
(2 Bytes)
(If Length, LLC, and SNAP, 8 Bytes) |
| INFORMATION |
| AAL5 Trailer
(8 Bytes) |

FIGURE 21.13   *A LANE Ethernet frame.*

Ethernet frames sent between a pair of ATM systems can be bigger than ordinary Ethernet frames. In fact, they can be as large as Token Ring frames. For an 802.3 LLC frame, the length field of an oversized frame must be set to 0. The true size is determined from the length field in the AAL5 trailer.

Using large frames makes good sense when an ATM system communicates with another ATM system. Of course, large frames cannot be used when an ATM system communicates with a conventional Ethernet LAN system.

Listing 21.1 shows a Network Associates Sniffer trace of a LANE Ethernet frame arriving at an endpoint system.

The first part of the trace displays information about the ATM circuit that carried the frame in the trace. The fact that there is a call reference value is a clue to the fact that the frame was carried on a switched virtual circuit. Each call is assigned a call reference number when it is opened.

The Virtual Path Identifier for the circuit is 0, and the Virtual Channel Identifier is 42.

Moving to the AAL5 frame, it starts with the LAN emulation client identifier of the sender, which is X'00-10 (decimal 16). The encapsulated Ethernet frame follows. The frame in the trace contains an LLC and SNAP, but a frame with an EtherType field is equally acceptable. The information portion has been omitted from the listing because it is not of any particular interest. The trailer contains a CRC value and also indicates that the frame payload size was 318 bytes.

Listing 21.1 Trace for a LANE Ethernet Frame

```
ATM: ----- ATM Header -----
     ATM:
     ATM: Frame 3 arrived at  15:26:51.6041; frame size is 336 (0150 hex)
     ↪bytes.
     ATM: Call reference = 175
     ATM: Link = DCE
     ATM: Virtual path id = 0
     ATM: Virtual channel id = 42
     ATM:


LE8023: ----- LAN EMULATION 802.3 -----
     LE8023:
     LE8023: LE Header 0010
     LE8023:
ETHER: ----- Ethernet Header -----
     ETHER:
     ETHER: Destination = Multicast 01000CCCCCCC
     ETHER: Source      = Station Cisco140DC20
     ETHER: 802.3 length = 302
     ETHER:
LLC:   ----- LLC Header -----
     LLC:
     LLC:  DSAP Address = AA, DSAP IG Bit = 00 (Individual Address)
     LLC:  SSAP Address = AA, SSAP CR Bit = 00 (Command)
     LLC:  Unnumbered frame: UI
     LLC:
SNAP: ----- SNAP Header -----
     SNAP:
     SNAP: Vendor ID = Cisco1
     SNAP: Type = 2000 (CDP)
     SNAP:
CDP: ----- Cisco Discovery Protocol (CDP) Packet -----
 . . .
(message contents omitted)
 . . .
ATM:
     ATM: ----- AAL5 Trailer -----
     ATM:
     ATM: 10 pad octets
     ATM: UU    = 0
     ATM: CPI   = 0
     ATM: Length = 318
     ATM: CRC    = 57C64FAE
```

Figure 21.14 shows the format of an encapsulated Token Ring frame. Like the Ethernet frame, it starts with the sender's LANE Client identifier or X'00-00. The Token Ring frame follows. However, a Token Ring access control field serves no purpose in an emulated LAN, so the access control byte is just a placeholder and its content is ignored. The frame control field contains the binary value:

0 1 0 0 0 p p p

Because only user data (LLC) frames make sense for LANE, the first 5 bits are 01000. The last 3 bits are a user priority that has been passed down by a higher-layer protocol.

The remainder of the frame follows the usual Token Ring format, except that, as was the case for Ethernet, the CRC appears in the AAL5 trailer instead of a frame check sequence field.

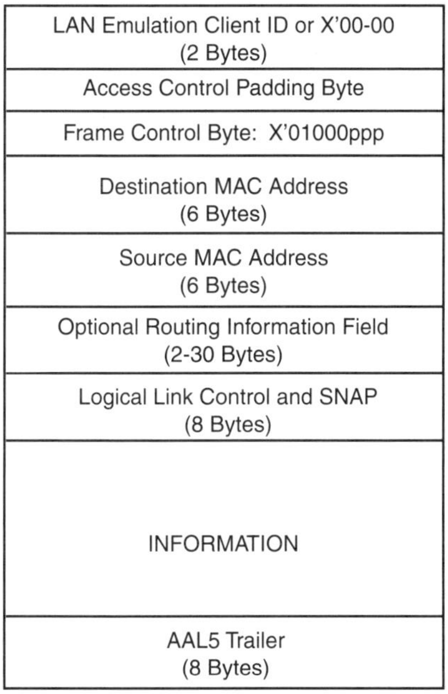

LAN Emulation Client ID or X'00-00 (2 Bytes)
Access Control Padding Byte
Frame Control Byte: X'01000ppp
Destination MAC Address (6 Bytes)
Source MAC Address (6 Bytes)
Optional Routing Information Field (2-30 Bytes)
Logical Link Control and SNAP (8 Bytes)
INFORMATION
AAL5 Trailer (8 Bytes)

FIGURE 21.14 A LANE Token Ring Frame.

LANE Control Frames

The *configuration direct* connection between a client and a LANE Configuration Server, and the *control direct* and *control distribute* connections between a client and its LANE Server are special—they are used to set up and maintain the LANE environment. Ordinary frames are not sent on these connections. These connections carry special control frames that contain a variety of requests and responses.

Table 21.1 lists and briefly describes the LANE control frame types. The table includes some control frame types that have not been discussed elsewhere in this chapter. In the table, "LE" stands for LAN Emulation.

TABLE 21.1 LANE CONTROL FRAMES

Type of Control Frame	Description
LE Configure Request	Sent by a client that wishes to join an ELAN and needs to find out the ATM address of its LANE Server.
LE Configure Response	Provides the address of a LANE Server (and some optional parameters).
LE Join Request	Sent to a LANE Server by a client that wishes to join an ELAN.
LE Join Response	Sent by a LANE Server. If the client has been accepted, the server provides the name of the ELAN, its type, the maximum frame size, and optionally, the client's LANE identifier.
LE Register Request	Sent by a client to register a MAC address or a Token Ring route descriptor.
LE Register Response	Acknowledges the registration.
LE Unregister Request	Sent by a client to withdraw a registration (for example, if it is about to detach from the network).
LE Unregister Response	Acknowledges the unregistration.
LE ARP Request	Sent by a client that wishes to know the ATM address corresponding to a given MAC address. If the LANE server does not know the answer, it will forward the request to clients.
LE ARP Response	Provides the ATM address corresponding to a given MAC address.
Ready Indication	Sent by a caller as soon as it is ready to receive frames on a newly established connection.
Ready Query	Sent by the called party if it has not yet received an expected Ready Indication.

LE Flush Request

Sent by a client to clear out a connection pipeline. The client waits for a response before sending more frames onto the connection.

LE Flush Response

Sent in response to a Flush.

LE NARP Request

Sent by a client to announce that its MAC-address/ATM-address pairing has changed.

LE Topology Request

Sent to its LANE Server by a LANE Client in a transparent bridge. It announces that the client has sent a Configuration BPDU to the BUS and indicates whether a Spanning Tree topology change is occurring. The server forwards the message to other clients.

LAN Emulation Control Frame Format

Figure 21.15 shows the format of a LAN Emulation control frame. Table 21.2 describes the fields in a control frame. Each type of message uses a different subset of the fields, and unused fields are set to zeroes.

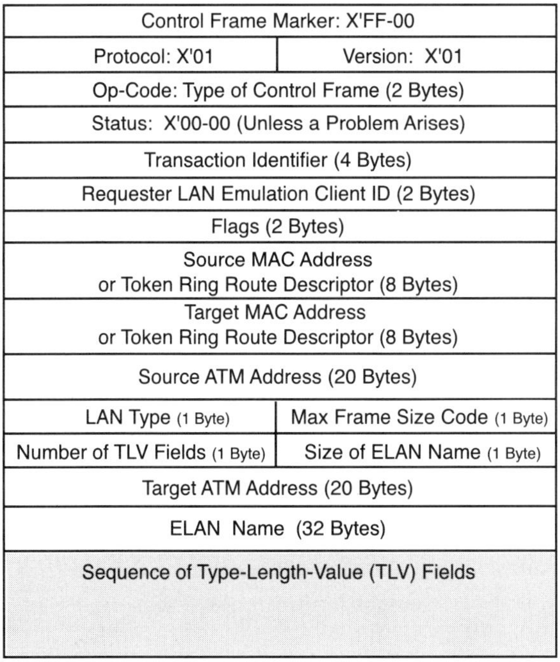

Control Frame Marker: X'FF-00	
Protocol: X'01	Version: X'01
Op-Code: Type of Control Frame (2 Bytes)	
Status: X'00-00 (Unless a Problem Arises)	
Transaction Identifier (4 Bytes)	
Requester LAN Emulation Client ID (2 Bytes)	
Flags (2 Bytes)	
Source MAC Address or Token Ring Route Descriptor (8 Bytes)	
Target MAC Address or Token Ring Route Descriptor (8 Bytes)	
Source ATM Address (20 Bytes)	
LAN Type (1 Byte)	Max Frame Size Code (1 Byte)
Number of TLV Fields (1 Byte)	Size of ELAN Name (1 Byte)
Target ATM Address (20 Bytes)	
ELAN Name (32 Bytes)	
Sequence of Type-Length-Value (TLV) Fields	

FIGURE 21.15 *Format of a LAN Emulation control frame.*

TABLE 21.2 FIELDS IN A LAN EMULATION CONTROL FRAME

Field	Description
Marker	X'FF-00 indicates that this is a control frame.
Protocol	X'01 is used for the ATM LANE protocol.
Version	Identifies the ATM LANE protocol version. Two versions (X'01 and X'02) have been defined.
Op-Code	Identifies the type of control frame, such as a configuration, join, or ARP request.
Status	Set to X'00-00 in requests and successful responses. Reports a problem otherwise.
Transaction-Id	Used to match a response to its request.
Requester-LECID	Is the LAN Emulation Client ID of the client making a request. (It is X'00-00 if the client's identifier is unknown.)
Flags	Used to indicate miscellaneous facts, such as whether the sender is a proxy client in a LAN switch or router.
Source	Is either a MAC address associated with the message source or a Token Ring route descriptor that identifies a client that is a source route bridge.
Target	Is either a MAC address associated with a target system or a Token Ring route descriptor that identifies a destination that is a source route bridge.
Source ATM Address	Is the ATM address of the source.
Target ATM Address	Is the ATM address of the target system (if any).
LAN Type	X'00 is unspecified, X'01 is Ethernet, and X'02 is Token Ring.

Trace of a Join Response Control Frame

Listing 21.2 shows a Network Associates Sniffer trace of a Join Response control frame. The frame arrived on the circuit with VPI=0 and VCI=33. The frame starts with the control frame marker, X'FF-00. Protocol 1 is the LANE protocol, and the version shown is 1. The opcode identifies this as a Join Response frame, and the status code shows that the join was successful.

The Src LAN Dest field carries the requesting client's MAC address. (If the tag in this field were X'00-02 instead of X'00-01, the content would be a source route bridge route descriptor.) The client's ATM address also is shown. The client's MAC address and ATM address have been registered at the server.

The LAN type is Ethernet. The maximum frame size is 1516, and the name of the ELAN is elan43. The message does not include a client identifier, which means that all clients in this ELAN will place identifier X'00-00 at the top of their frames.

LISTING 21.2 TRACE OF A JOIN RESPONSE

```
ATM:
       ATM: Frame 24 arrived at  12:31:24.8874; frame size is 144 (0090
       ➥hex) bytes.
       ATM: Call reference = 10449
       ATM: Link = DCE
       ATM: Virtual path id = 0
       ATM: Virtual channel id = 33
       ATM:
LECTRL: ----- LAN EMULATION CONTROL FRAME -----
       LECTRL:
       LECTRL: Marker       = FF00
       LECTRL: Protocol     = 01
       LECTRL: Version      = 01
       LECTRL: Opcode       = 0102 (JOIN_RESPONSE)
       LECTRL: Status       = 0 (Success)
       LECTRL: Trans ID     = 2091
       LECTRL: Request ID   = 21
       LECTRL: Flags        = 0000
       LECTRL: Src LAN Dest = 000100603E1AF000
       LECTRL:   Tag        = 0001(MAC address)
       LECTRL:   MAC Addr   = 00603E1AF000
       LECTRL: Tar LAN Dest = 0000000000000000
       LECTRL:   Tag        = 0000(not present)
       LECTRL:   MAC Addr   = 000000000000(not present)
       LECTRL: SRC ATM ADDR = 47:0091:8100 0000 0060 3E5C
       ➥EE01:Cisco21AF000:01
       LECTRL: LAN-TYPE     = 01 (Ethernet/IEEE 802.3)
       LECTRL: MAX FRAME SIZE= 01 (1516)
       LECTRL: NUMBER TLVs  = 0
       LECTRL: ELAN NAME SIZE= 6
       LECTRL: TARG ATM ADDR = 0000000000000000000000000000000000000000
       LECTRL: ELAN NAME    = "elan43"
ATM:
       ATM: ----- AAL5 Trailer -----
       ATM:
       ATM: 28 pad octets
       ATM: UU    = 0
       ATM: CPI   = 0
       ATM: Length = 108
       ATM: CRC   = 9BD3AA61 (Correct)
```

LANE Version 2

At the time of writing, LANE version 1 is implemented in products. However, the ATM Forum has published version 2 standards for clients and servers.

Version 2 adds some desirable features to LANE, including

- The introduction of Quality of Service for data connections

- The capability to set up multiple instances of each server type

- An improved method of handling multicast traffic

A LANE client can register the acceptable service categories that it is willing to accept in incoming calls. A caller can set up multiple connections to a destination with each call carrying traffic for a different service category. For example, separate calls could be used for voice, video, and bulk data.

One shortcoming of version 1 LANE is that the Configuration, LANE, and BUS servers are single points of failure. Also, some systems in a widely distributed ELAN must maintain long-distance connections to their servers to participate in the ELAN. At the time of writing, vendors use proprietary methods to overcome these problems.

Version 2 of LANE defines standard protocols that enable servers to communicate with one another and coordinate their activities. An ELAN can be served by multiple LANE Servers that coordinate their MAC-address/ATM-Address databases with one another.

A version 2 BUS has access to a LANE Server's address database. There can be multiple connected BUSes, each responsible for flooding frames to systems that have connected to the BUS. All BUSes for the LAN are listed in the LANE Server database. When a BUS must flood a frame to all nodes, it transmits the frame to its connected clients and to the other BUSes.

A BUS can be "intelligent" as well. A client sometimes passes a frame to the BUS in spite of the fact that the frame's destination MAC address is registered. A version 1 BUS would flood this frame to all clients. An intelligent BUS can forward the frame to its recipient instead of flooding the frame.

Multicasts also are handled inefficiently in LANE version 1 because a multicast frame is forwarded to all clients. In version 2, a client can register its membership in a multicast group. It then can be assigned to a *Selective Multicast Server* (SMS). A Selective Multicast Server opens a point-to-multipoint connection to its clients and forwards a multicast frame addressed to a group to the members of that group.

Summary Points

- LANE enables systems that have ATM NICs and are connected to ATM switches to emulate a conventional LAN.

- LANE enables Ethernet or Token Ring systems connected to ordinary hubs and switches to interact with ATM systems as if they all belong to a conventional LAN.

- LANE makes it possible for existing network protocols and network applications to run on top of ATM without making changes to any of the software.

- An emulated LAN (ELAN) is made up of computers, routers, and bridges that have ATM interfaces and are connected to ATM switches.

- An ATM NIC has a 6-byte MAC LAN address.

- A conventional LAN switch that also has an ATM interface is called a LANE proxy because it relays traffic between the LANE environment and normal LAN systems.

- A LANE Client is a special device driver that hides the underlying ATM communications from higher-layer protocols and applications.

- A LANE Client connects to a LANE Configuration Server to obtain the address of a LANE Server.

- A LANE Client connects to its LANE Server to register its MAC address and to find out the name of its ELAN, the ELAN type, and the maximum frame size. The client also may obtain a unique 2-byte LANE Client ID.

- The LANE Server uses its address database to help LANE Clients map destination MAC addresses to ATM addresses.

- A LANE Client sends and receives broadcasts, multicasts, and flooded frames via its Broadcast and Unknown Server (BUS).

- Private ATM addresses are 20 bytes in length.

- An Ethernet or Token Ring frame is carried inside an AAL5 frame that starts with a 2-byte field containing the sender's unique client identifier or X'00-00. The FCS field is omitted because the AAL5 trailer contains a CRC value.

- Control frames are sent on the *configuration direct* connection between a client and a LANE Configuration Server, and the *control direct* and *control distribute* connections between a client and its LANE Server.

- Version 2 of LANE supports Quality of Service for data connections, the capability to set up multiple instances of each server type, and an improved method of handling multicast traffic.

References

The defining documents for LANE were written by the ATM Forum. In the titles listed here, LUNI stands for LANE User Network Interface and relates to the protocols used between LANE Clients and the special servers. LNNI stands for LAN Emulation Network-to-Network Interface and relates to the protocols that enable the servers to communicate and cooperate with one another.

- AF-LANE-0021.000. "LAN Emulation over ATM, Version 1.0." 1995.

- AF-LANE-0084.000. "LAN Emulation over ATM Version 2—LUNI Specification." 1997.

- AF-LANE-0112.000. "LAN Emulation over ATM Version 2—LNNI Specification." 1999.

The IETF has specified procedures to be used to carry IP traffic across an ATM circuit in the following document:

- RFC 2225. "Classical IP and ARP over ATM." M. Laubach and J. Halpern. 1998.

CHAPTER 22

Fibre Channel

Fibre channel technology was invented to turn a bold thought into reality. The designers believed that the distinction between the LAN protocols and the protocols used to connect a computer to storage peripherals was artificial. They reasoned that if a common technology, physical interface, and protocol framework could be established for both, everyone would benefit:

- Standardized hardware and drivers would lead to lower prices because of economies of scale.

- System costs would decrease because many kinds of devices could be accessed through one high-speed port.

- Technical improvements would be fostered by creating a big market for a standard hardware interface.

Furthermore, fibre channel was designed with a dream wish list of features. It replaces a rat's nest of cables with a clean, switch-based backbone. It supports high-speed transmission. It offers multiple classes of service—including both connection-oriented service that delivers a guaranteed bandwidth across the network and various types of connectionless service. It also offers several quality of service capabilities.

Currently, fibre channel adapters are available for every major computer platform. There is growing use of fibre channel technology to interconnect disk and tape storage resources, and to link up computers in environments that have stringent performance and reliability requirements. At the same time, demand for Gigabit Ethernet hardware, which uses fibre channel components, also is increasing. The result is that the cost of both fibre channel and Gigabit Ethernet technology is decreasing.

> **Note**
> The choice of using the spelling *fibre* instead of *fiber* was intentional. A fibre channel port does not have to be connected to optical fiber; a link can be copper or optical fiber. The word *fibre* projects an image of high-speed and broad bandwidth, whatever the medium might be.

Fibre channel technology was designed to do everything—and to do it any way you want. It is described in a large and rapidly growing bookshelf of standards documents. This chapter presents some of the important ideas and outlines some applications. But of necessity, many details, fine points, and options had to be left out in order to get a description that was in any way intelligible.

Fibre channel standards are published by the American National Standards Institute (ANSI). Much of the work is performed by the T11 standards body of the National Committee for Information Technology Standards (NCITS), which is responsible for device-level interfaces.

Features of Fibre Channel

Fibre channel technology provides a high-speed infrastructure that blends device communication with LAN communication.

It can be used as a new infrastructure for traditional low-level, device-based communications such as the *Small Computer System Interface* (SCSI), the *Intelligent Peripheral Interface* (IPI), and the *High-Performance Parallel Interface* (HIPPI). It also supports the transport of LAN frames carrying high-level protocol data.

Fibre channel's applicability is broad, basically consisting of "things that need to be connected to other things." A single high-speed interface and physical medium can be used to attach a system to a disk controller or a video device, or to carry TCP/IP traffic to a peer application. Specifically, fibre channel standards deal with networking for

- Computer LANs

- Storage area networks (SANs) interconnecting many different types of disk or tape devices

- Audio/video transmission networks

- Real-time systems, such as avionics systems that control every aspect of space rocket flight

Many organizations with large (and growing) data bases and data warehouses have been responsive to fibre channel products that bind together diverse storage resources. The technology supports graceful incremental growth of resources. As a bonus, it allows storage peripheral units to be added or removed without disruption, providing a built-in hot-swapping capability.

Transmission Speeds

The speeds that fibre channel supports are high and keep climbing higher. Table 22.1 shows some currently defined levels. The fractional speeds are used in some older systems. At the time of writing, many "full-speed" switch products are on the market, and higher-speed products are in the pipeline.

The megabit per second (Mbps) speed rate indicates the number of bit signals per second on the medium. The bit rate includes a 20 percent overhead because a byte is translated to a 10-bit code-group pattern prior to transmission. (This is the same 8B/10B translation that was borrowed by 1000BASE-X.)

Fibre channel throughput often is stated in *megabytes* per second (MBps). This is natural, given the frequent application of the technology to storage devices, which measure throughput in bytes per second rather than bits per second.

TABLE 22.1 FIBRE CHANNEL SPEEDS

Title	Megabits per Second (Including Overhead)	Megabytes per Second (Without Overhead)
Eighth Speed	133	12.5
Quarter Speed	266	25
Half Speed	531	50
Full Speed	1062.5	100
Double Speed	2126	200
Quadruple Speed	4252	400

Distances, Media, and Connectors

Supported distances range from 10 meters to 10 kilometers—or further with the help of a single-mode fiber extender.

Fibre channel runs on a special 150-ohm shielded twisted-pair cable (which was reused for 1000BASE-CX Ethernet), 75-ohm twinax coaxial cable, video coaxial cables, and multimode and single-mode optical fiber. Optical fiber is required for the higher 200MBps and 400MBps speeds.

A DB-9 connector is used for shielded twisted-pair cable, and BNC and Threaded-Neil-Councilman Coaxial Cable Connector (TNC) connectors are used for coax. An SC connector is preferred for the optical fiber implementations.

Fibre Channel Equipment and Topology

The communicating devices in a fibre channel network are very diverse. They can be computers, disk drives, printers, scanners, video output systems, and other systems. Because of the multiplicity of end-system types, the devices usually are referred to by the generic term *nodes*. A fibre channel adapter must be installed in each node that participates in a fibre channel network.

Standard fibre channel topologies include

- A simple point-to-point connection between two nodes.

- A set of nodes connected in a ring configuration that is called a *loop*, or, more formally, an *arbitrated loop*. As was the case for classic Token Rings, a loop often is implemented using a hub. Loop bandwidth is shared. Data transmission is half-duplex.

- A set of nodes connected to a switch. Like a LAN switch, a fibre channel switch can support multiple simultaneous communications between pairs of nodes.

- Nodes linked by interconnected switches and arbitrated loops.

Figure 22.1 illustrates point-to-point, loop, and switched topologies. The loop in the figure is implemented by connecting systems to a fibre channel hub. It is becoming routine to use fibre channel loop connections as the communications backplane in disk storage units.

Nodes that belong to a loop share bandwidth (as is done by systems on a Token Ring). Only one node on a loop can transmit data at any given time.

A standalone loop is called a *private loop*. A loop that is attached to a switch is called a *public loop*.

A node communicates through its port via separate transmit and receive wires or optical fibers. This is illustrated in Figure 22.2. The top of the figure shows a connection between a pair of nodes. The middle shows connections between nodes and a switch. The bottom shows some nodes connected into a loop.

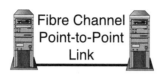

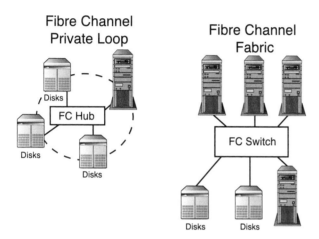

FIGURE 22.1 *Standard fibre channel topologies.*

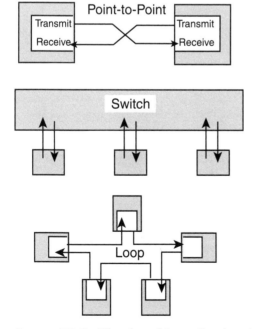

FIGURE 22.2 *Fibre channel transmit and receive lines.*

Figure 22.3 shows a network that consists of interconnected switches and loops. In the figure, several disk devices are connected to public loops.

Switches make up the backbone of a fibre channel network. A loop can have at most one active connection to a switch, so traffic never travels from one switch to another across an intervening loop.

The figure includes a RAID disk system that happens to contain a conventional SCSI interface rather than a fibre channel interface. A SCSI-to-fibre-channel bridge is used to connect the RAID array into the fibre channel network. SCSI commands are part of the fibre channel protocol family, so legacy disk systems can be bridged into a fibre channel network quite easily.

Fibre channel networks have the potential to be quite scalable. Multiple switches can be interconnected to form large networks. However, a lot of work remains to be done on standards (currently at draft status) that deal with path selection and a hierarchical network structure.

Many fibre channel vendors support individual 10km single-mode fiber optic links, and some have announced longer links.

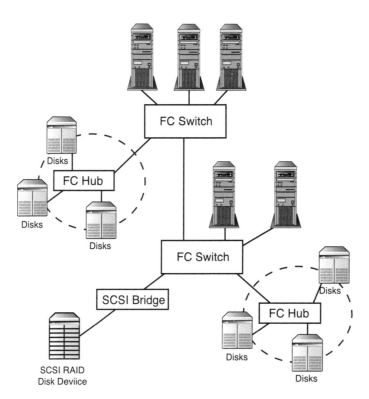

FIGURE 22.3 *A fibre channel network consisting of interconnected switches and loops.*

At the time of writing, work is proceeding on a fibre channel backbone standard that will enable fibre channel switches to be connected across a wide area network. Interfaces are being defined for ATM and SONET.

Fabrics

Fibre channel standards documentation uses the term *fabric* to mean "that to which nodes attach." This term is used in a very confusing manner.

When written in lower case, *fabric* stands for any infrastructure that connects fibre channel nodes to one another. For example, a point-to-point link, an arbitrated loop, or a network with all of the infrastructure in Figure 22.3, including switches and hubs, can be called a fabric.

When written in upper case, technically, a *Fabric* provides switched connectivity between nodes based on 3-byte destination addresses that have been assigned to nodes. It can consist of one switch, many switches interconnected by links, or interconnected switches along with some attached arbitrated loops.

> **Note**
> Unlike an Ethernet LAN or a transparent Token Ring LAN, a Fabric topology can contain any number of paths between nodes.

Vendors call their products hubs, switches, and (see the following section) loop switches, but they also toss the term *fabric* into their documentation.

Loop Switches

An arbitrated loop hub is a simple, limited device that supports half-duplex data communication between attached nodes. Vendors have created a hybrid device called a *loop switch* that boosts bandwidth and allows more complex attachments. A loop switch is designed to improve performance for nodes that have loop interfaces that cannot be attached to a switch.

As shown in Figure 22.4, individual devices, arbitrated loops, and hubs can be connected to a loop switch. Each device believes that it is connected to a real arbitrated loop. However, the loop switch in the figure delivers a full 100 megabytes per second bandwidth through each of its ports. Bandwidth is not shared, and traffic actually is switched between the ports.

If all attached devices are updated to switch-attachable adapters, a loop switch can be converted to a switch.

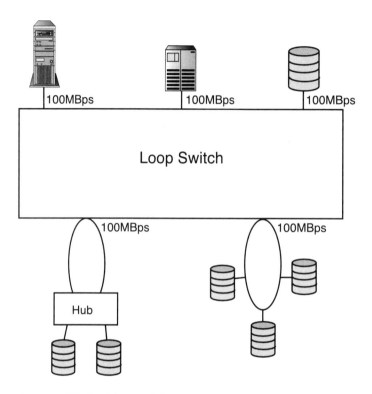

FIGURE 22.4 *A loop switch.*

Fibre Channel Ports

Fibre channel ports have several different roles:

- Nodes in two devices might be connected to form a point-to-point link between the devices.

- A port in a node might connect the node to a switch.

- A port in a node might connect the node to a loop.

- A switch port might connect the switch to a node, to a loop, or to another switch.

A shorthand is used to describe port roles. The shorthand title indicates whether the port is in a node or in a switch and the capabilities that the port has. Table 22.2 lists and describes these titles.

TABLE 22.2 FIBRE CHANNEL PORTS

Type of Port	Description
N_Port	Any node port.
NL_Port	A node port that is connected to an arbitrated loop.
F_Port	A Fabric (switch) port that can be connected to a node.
FL_Port	A switch port that can be connected to an arbitrated loop.
L_Port	An N_Port or F_Port that can perform arbitrated loop functions.
E_Port	A switch expansion port. It can be connected to a port in another switch to form an interswitch link.
G_Port	A switch port that can be connected to a node or to another switch.
GL_Port	A switch port that can be connected to a node, a loop, or another switch.
B_Port	A port on a bridge that connects to an E_Port on a switch.

It is not unusual for every port in a fibre channel switch product to be a GL_Port that is capable of connecting to anything: a node, a loop, or another switch.

Figure 22.5 illustrates N-Ports, F_Ports, NL_ports, and FL_Ports. The hub in the figure acts as a wiring concentrator. The ports in a hub can be passive, but many hub products have ports that repeat bits in order to increase the maximum length of the lobe cables that lead to attached nodes.

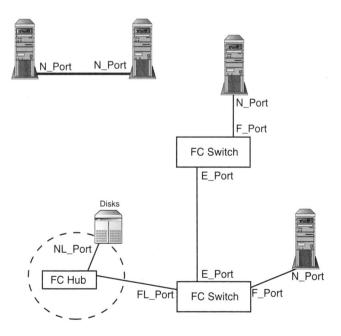

FIGURE 22.5 *Types of ports.*

Fibre Channel Names and Addresses

In conventional LAN technologies, each adapter is assigned a MAC address that identifies it uniquely on a global basis. This MAC address does not indicate where a system is located. On legacy LANs, every frame was placed on a shared medium and was seen by every station, so location did not matter. The fact that this was not a perfect architecture was made clear in earlier chapters, which have described the great efforts that have gone into preventing frames from being flooded across a LAN.

Fibre channel technology was built from the ground up to deliver a frame to its intended destination and to no other node. To do this, it introduces 3-byte addresses that pinpoint the location of every node port.

However, fibre channel also retains the use of globally unique identifiers that are like MAC addresses. Within fibre channel, these serve as *names* that identify a port adapter or a system. These names are used by several higher-layer protocols and also are useful for network management and troubleshooting.

Many fibre channel vendors create unique names in the time-honored manner. A vendor registers with the IEEE, gets a 3-byte OUI, and identifies a specific adapter by adding an additional 3-byte number. These basically are MAC addresses.

Note
Supporting these identifiers makes it easy to run higher-layer protocols that rely on MAC addresses on a system that has a fibre channel adapter.

In addition to IEEE MAC address numbering, several other numbering schemes are used to identify storage units and other devices. All of the numbering schemes have been integrated into an 8-byte naming convention that is described in the next section. The section after that describes fibre channel addresses.

World Wide Port and Node Names

Globally unique names can be assigned to N_Ports, F_Ports, and nodes. These are 8-byte quantities called *world wide port names* and *world wide node names*. Each name consists of

- A 4-bit introducer that identifies a *network address authority* (NAA)

- The name that has been assigned by following the rules of the authority

Table 22.3 describes some of the types of world wide port names.

Note that IEEE names top the list. These 8-byte names contain a 6-byte identifier that has the same form as a MAC address. A company applies for a 3-byte OUI and adds another 3-byte portion so that a port (or node) can be given a unique name.

Fibre channel is different from the other LAN protocols, so the term *MAC* does not quite fit. On the other hand, a title such as "unique address for a field replaceable hardware element" does not lend itself to a graceful acronym.

Zero-bits are used to pad the front of a name that does not fill the 60 bits after the 4-bit introducer. Hence, twelve 0-bits precede a 6-byte IEEE address. The IEEE extended address allows the vendor to use these bits to identify separate ports within a single unit.

TABLE 22.3 WORLD WIDE PORT OR NODE NAMES

Type of Name	Description
IEEE (0001)	Twelve 0-bits followed by a 6-byte IEEE address
IEEE Extended (0010)	A 12-bit address uniquely identifying a F_Port or an N_Port contained in a unit, followed by the 6-byte address of the unit
Locally Assigned (0011)	Assigned by a vendor or via configuration
IEEE Registered Name (0101)	A 3-byte IEEE-assigned company identifier, followed by a 36-bit vendor assigned identifier
CCITT Individual Address (1100)	A 60-bit CCITT address

Port Identifiers (Addresses)

Ports have 3-byte addresses. These addresses are hierarchical, and each byte is a level in the hierarchy:

Byte 1—A domain identifier. This identifies one switch or can be used to identify a set of interconnected switches. If two switches belong to the same domain, there must be a path between them that only passes through switches in that domain.

Byte 2—An area identifier. An area is either a set of ports within and attached to one switch, or an arbitrated loop attached to a switch port.

Byte 3—A port identifier. This identifies a port attached to a switch, a port attached to an arbitrated loop attached to a switch, or a port attached to a private arbitrated loop.

> **Note**
> The addresses of ports attached to a private arbitrated loop start with X'00-00.

An N_Port's 3-byte address formally is called an *N_Port identifier*. Frames are delivered to the port based on this address. Frames are routed to the domain, then targeted to an area, and finally transmitted to the port with a given identifier.

An N_Port obtains its address from the switch to which it is attached during an initialization process that is called a *login*.

This is a sensible arrangement. An N_Port address indicates an actual location. If a node is disconnected from one switch and plugged into another, it will receive a fresh address that reflects its new location.

Wherever it is, a port still retains its built-in world wide port name. This identifies the port adapter uniquely, independently of its location.

Fibre Channel Levels

The topics covered in fibre channel specifications are categorized using five levels, labeled FC-0, FC-1, FC-2, FC-3, and FC-4. Some (but not all) of the levels correspond to protocol layers.

The levels are

- **FC-0**—This level corresponds to the lower part of the physical layer. Its specification defines the characteristics of fibre channel physical media and connectors, and the signals used to place bits onto each medium.

- **FC-1**—This is the part of the physical layer that performs an 8B/10B encoding of data bytes and defines the usage of special code-groups.

> **Note**
> The physical media, connectors, signals, and 8B/10B data encoding used for the 1000BASE-LX, SX, and CX implementations of Gigabit Ethernet were borrowed from fibre channel FC-0 and FC-1.

- **FC-2**—The FC-2 level corresponds to the data link layer. It defines the way that data is packaged into frames and moved from one node to another. It also defines special command signals that provide control functions, such as flow control and error recovery.

- **FC-3**—FC-3 is not a protocol layer. It is a placeholder for functions that are applied across several ports in a node. None have been defined at the time of writing, but one candidate is data striping (for RAID disk arrays).

- **FC-4**—This is the highest level. It defines the way that the various applications that ride on top of fibre channel map onto the fibre channel environment.

Classes of Service

A fibre channel network supports several *classes of service*. These are designed to meet the needs of different types of data transfers. The classes include

- **Class 1**—A service that provides dedicated point-to-point connections. A connection between two nodes has a guaranteed bandwidth. Frames are delivered in order.

- **Buffered Class 1**—A proposed connection-based service that enables ports that operate at different data rates to communicate across a connection. The flow of data is regulated so that the faster port will not overload the slower port.

- **Dedicated Simplex Class 1**—A connection-based service that supports data flow in one direction only. Acknowledgments are sent back via the connectionless Class 2 service.

- **Class 2**—An acknowledged connectionless multiplexing service in a switched network. Some fabric products deliver frames in order, while others deliver frames out of order. The network provides the sender with a notification of delivery or nondelivery, as long as the frame has not been corrupted during transmission across a link.

- **Class 3**—Like Class 2, Class 3 is a connectionless multiplexing service. Some fabrics products deliver frames in order, while others deliver frames out of order. Unlike Class 2, Class 3 does not provide any notification of delivery or nondelivery.

- **Intermix**—This is an optional variation on Class 1 service. It allows a node in a Class 1 connection to exchange Class 2 or Class 3 frames with its connection partner or with other nodes. Bandwidth allocated to the Class 1 connection but unused for that connection can be utilized for the connectionless frames.

- **Class 4 (Fractional Service)**—This connection-oriented service enables a node port to split up its bandwidth and use it for multiple virtual circuits. Virtual circuits can connect to different destinations.

- **Class F (Fabric)**—This connectionless service can be used for control and coordination of the internal behavior of a Fabric. Fabric circuits originate or terminate internally to the fabric.

> **Note**
>
> At the time of writing, most fibre channel switch vendors support Class 2 and Class 3 service.

Generic Services

Several generic services can be provided in a fibre channel network.

The services that are implemented within a particular fibre channel network depend on the network's specific needs. Generic services that have been defined include

- **Directory service**—A directory responds to queries from clients that need address information about the nodes and ports in a region of the Fabric address space. At minimum, a directory maps world wide port names to N_Port addresses. The directory can include other information, such as mappings between MAC addresses or IP addresses and N_Port addresses.

- **Alias service**—Often there are multiple N_Ports that provide access to the same resource. A user can get the same data by connecting to any of these ports. Another way of saying this is that these ports make up a *hunt group*. This is implemented by allowing the ports in the hunt group to share an assigned alias address. A hunt group call is answered by the first free N_Port in the group.

  An authorized client can ask an alias server to add a list of N_Ports to an alias group, remove a list of N_Ports from a group, or return parameters for the alias along with the group of N_Ports that are in the group.

  Another application of the alias service is to support multicasting. A client can add a list of N_Ports to a multicast group or remove them from the group.

- **Time service**—A time server (which is optional) can provide a current time value in response to a query. Multiple time servers that synchronize their values can be provided in the network.

- **Security-key service**—A security-key server enables a pair of clients to be authenticated and to obtain a temporary key that is used to encrypt the data transferred between them.

  To implement this, each client is assigned a secret key, and a copy of this key is stored at the server. On request, the server generates a temporary encryption key and distributes it to the two clients by encrypting it with each client's secret key.

- **Management service**—This is a standard SNMP-based network management service.

A server may be located within a switch or in a node.

FC-4 Application Mappings

FC-4 includes mappings for ordinary data networking and for data transfers that previously were done across a computer-to-device channel. Mappings that have been defined or are in progress include

- Encapsulation of IP and ARP in fibre channel frames. This mapping was defined by the IETF in RFC 2625.

- Small Computer System Interface (SCSI)

- Intelligent Peripheral Interface (IPI)

- Single Byte Command Code Sets (SBCCS)

- High Performance Parallel Interface (HIPPI) Framing Protocol

Two examples of FC-4 functionality are presented later in the sections, "Encapsulation of IP Datagrams" and "SCSI over Fibre Channel."

Fibre Channel Data Transfer

Data is transferred across a fibre channel network in frames. Each frame has a 20-byte header and a trailer that contains a CRC code used to check whether the frame has been corrupted during transmission. The maximum size of a frame payload is 2112 bytes.

8B/10B Encoding and Ordered Sets

The encoding used for fibre channel already has made its appearance in this book. The IEEE 802.3 Gigabit Ethernet working group adopted the fibre channel 8B/10B encoding for 1000BASE-LX, 1000BASE-SX, and 1000BASE-CX. This encoding is described in Appendix A, "Physical-Layer Encodings for Ethernet, Fibre Channel, FDDI, and Token Ring."

Before data is transmitted, each 8-bit byte is translated into a 10-bit pattern called a *code-group* that contains a balanced sprinkling of 0s and 1s. The data code groups used for fibre channel are listed in Table B.3 of Appendix B, "Tables."

Extra 10-bit patterns are used to define special code-groups. Combinations of code-groups (called *ordered sets*) are introduced by a special code group and are used to

- Mark the beginnings and ends of frames

- Provide idle fill between frames

- Signal that the receiver is ready (used for flow control)

- Signal link resets and offline or nonoperational conditions

Each ordered set used for fibre channel consists of four code-groups. Fibre channel ordered sets are listed in Appendix B in Tables B.4, B.5, and B.6:

- Table B.4 displays ordered sets that are used as start-of-frame and end-of-frame delimiters.

- Table B.5 displays ordered sets used as idles and receiver ready signals. These are called *primitive signals*.

- Table B.6 displays the remaining ordered sets. These are called *primitive sequences*.

Sequences of Frames

The basic unit of data transfer is a *sequence* of frames:

- A sequence consists of one or more data frames transmitted in one direction from one N_Port to another N_Port.

- The sending N_Port is called the *sequence initiator*, and the receiver is called the *sequence recipient*.

While a sequence is being transmitted, an associated set of *link control frames* flows back to the sender. These link control frames are used to acknowledge successful delivery, report a delivery problem, perform flow control and buffer management, or send low-level commands to the originating N_Port.

The sequence initiator assigns an identifier to a sequence. This identifier is placed in the header of every frame sent by the initiator and in every response from the recipient.

A sequence often is used to convey a big block of data that does not fit into a single frame. The block is cut into subblocks that can fit into frame payloads. As shown in Figure 22.6, there is a sequence count field in the frame header, and the sequence numbers are used to reassemble the blocks in the correct order and to assure that all subblocks have arrived.

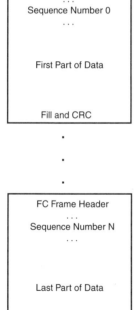

FIGURE 22.6 *Segmenting a large block of data.*

The sequence count number can be reset to 0 at the start of each new sequence, or can continue to increase (until it wraps around from 65535 to 0).

The sender knows that its sequence has arrived safely when the receiver acknowledges the frames in the sequence. Frames can be acknowledged (ACKed) in several ways:

- Each frame can be acknowledged separately.

- Several frames can be acknowledged as a group.

- A single acknowledgment can be sent at the completion of a sequence. This makes good sense when the sequence is used to carry a big block that has been broken into subblocks.

The ACK strategy that will be used is established when a communication is set up between a pair of nodes.

The upper-layer protocol for the communication establishes a policy on what should be done if frames are not transmitted successfully. For example, recovery might require one or more received sequences to be discarded followed by action initiated by the upper-layer protocol. Alternatively, the upper-layer protocol might specify that the receiver should automatically request retransmission after discarding damaged sequences.

Exchanges

An *exchange* corresponds to a data transaction. Formally, an exchange consists of one or more sequences. Two sequences in an exchange cannot be sent concurrently—that is, an exchange is a sequence of sequences.

If all of the sequences are transmitted in the same direction, the exchange is called *unidirectional*. An exchange also can take the form of a two-way conversation, with some sequences flowing in each direction.

Note

A SCSI read of a specified number of disk bytes is an example of an exchange.

Figure 22.7 illustrates unidirectional and bidirectional exchanges.

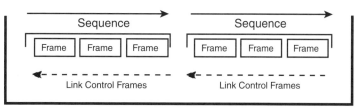

Unidirectional Exchange

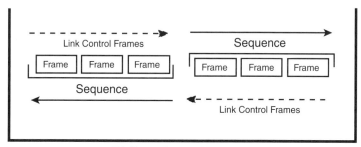

Bidirectional Exchange

FIGURE 22.7 *Frames, sequences, and exchanges.*

A port can participate in multiple exchanges, interleaving the frames that belong to each exchange. A frame header includes an exchange identifier field. Placing a value in this field makes it possible for a receiver to associate the frame with the correct exchange.

Relative Offsets

When data is read from a disk, the reader specifies a starting point for the read. The bytes that are read are measured from this point. A relative offset field in the fibre channel header is used for applications that need to specify an origin and count bytes from that point.

When a relative offset (RO) is used, the origin offset appears in the header of the first frame that is transmitted. In successive frames:

$$RO(n+1) = RO(n) + \text{Length-of-Payload}(n)$$

In other words, the relative offset of the current frame's payload is the previous payload's relative offset plus the length of that payload.

Logins and Addresses

When an N_Port connected to a switch initializes, it performs a login to the switch in order to establish its operating parameters. The parameters that will apply depend on the both port and switch capabilities.

> **Note**
> Although the login protocol is the standard way to establish the environment, a vendor could require that another method, such as static preconfiguration, be used for its product.

Every frame needs a source and destination address. To get started, an N_Port sends its login frames to the special well-known Fabric address X'FF-FF-FE. The N_Port does not yet have a unique 3-byte N_Port address, so it uses X'00-00-00 as its source address.

During login, the N_Port announces parameters such as these:

- Its 8-byte world wide port name and world wide node name. (Note that the node name applies to the whole node, which might have several ports.)

- The total number of buffers it has available for receiving data from the switch.

- The largest frame payload size that it can receive.

- The total number of concurrent sequences for which the N_Port can act as receiver.

- The classes of service that the node wishes to use, and special service characteristics such as

    - Whether the node would like to intermix Class 2 and Class 3 frames with Class 1 connection frames

    - Whether Class 2 or 3 frames must be delivered in order, or if out-of-order delivery is acceptable

The switch F_Port responds with its own set of parameters, describing its buffer resources, supported service classes, and other features.

This is also the time when the switch assigns a 3-byte address (the N_Port identifier) to the N_Port. Frames are routed to the port based on its port address.

A node port might already have been assigned an N_Port identifier on a previous login. In any case, during login, the F_Port either confirms the existing address or assigns a new one to the port.

After an N_Port has logged onto its switch, it is eligible to communicate with other ports. If the N_Port wants to set up a Class 1 or Class 2 communication with a peer, it performs a similar login process to the remote N_Port to establish a class of service and to exchange communication parameters. At the end of a communication, one of the nodes frees up resources by performing a logout.

Well-Known Addresses

Several well-known addresses are used for generic fibre channel destinations. One generic address was already mentioned in the previous section—namely, the destination address used by an N_Port that wishes to send a login message to an adjacent switch port.

The well-known addresses are listed in Table 22.4.

TABLE 22.4 WELL-KNOWN FIBRE CHANNEL ADDRESSES

Address	Description
X'FF-FF-F0 to X'FF-FF-F7	Reserved
X'FF-FF-F8	Alias server
X'FF-FF-F9	Quality of service facilitator—Class 4
X'FF-FF-FA	Management server
X'FF-FF-FB	Time server
X'FF-FF-FC	Directory server
X'FF-FF-FD	Switch controller
X'FF-FF-FE	Switch F-Port
X'FF-FF-FF	Broadcast address

Buffers and Credit

The quality of today's data transmission technology and media is far better than in earlier years. Bit error rates have been falling steadily. Currently, the most common reason for data loss is congestion in a switch or destination system. Congestion causes buffer memory to be exhausted. When there is no place to put incoming data, it must be discarded.

The fibre channel data transmission protocol manages buffers very carefully. Data transfer is modeled as the movement of data from memory buffers in one node to memory buffers in another node. Data in an output buffer is packaged into a frame and transferred to the destination input buffer. The buffer size corresponds to the maximum size of a frame payload.

A *buffer credit system* is used to prevent buffer overflow. During the login process, each party announces the number of buffers that it has allocated to receive frames from its peer. It also announces the biggest frame payload that a buffer can hold.

The current *credit* is the number of free buffers that are available at the receiver. A transmitter must stay within its credit limit. The receiver sends acknowledgments to the transmitter to indicate that data has been received and removed from buffers. This allows the transmitter to send more data.

Two types of buffer credit exist:

- **End-to-end credit**—This is credit offered by a peer N_Port.

- **Buffer-to-buffer credit**—This is credit offered across a single link. This can be a point-to-point link that is a direct connection between a pair of N_Ports, or a link between an N_Port and its adjacent switch port.

Figure 22.8 illustrates credit management for a Class 1 or Class 2 communication. Both end-to-end and buffer-to-buffer credit are illustrated. The transmitting port

- Decreases its end-to-end credit and buffer-to-buffer credit by 1 each time it transmits a frame.

- Increases its buffer-to-buffer credit by 1 each time it gets a *receiver ready* signal. The receiver ready signal is an ordered set.

- Increases its end-to-end credit by 1 for each frame acknowledged by the peer P_Node. An acknowledgment is transmitted as an ACK frame. An ACK might cover multiple received frames.

A dedicated connection is set up for Class 1, and resources always are available all the way to the destination. However, this is not the case for the connectionless Class 2 service. If the fabric cannot deliver a frame, the fabric returns a fabric busy frame, or the destination port returns a port busy frame.

No end-to-end acknowledgement is provided for Class 3 service. Only buffer-to-buffer flow control is provided.

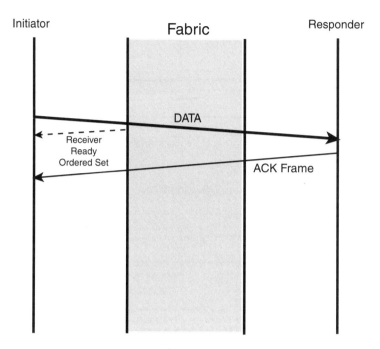

FIGURE 22.8 *Credit for a Class 1 connection.*

Fibre Channel Frame Format

The protocols described in earlier chapters of this book were byte-oriented. Fibre channel transmission is *word-oriented*. Before encoding, a word corresponds to 4 bytes. After 8B/10B encoding, a word consists of four 10-bit code-groups. Some code-groups represent bytes, while others represent ordered sets.

The format of a fibre channel frame is shown at the top of Figure 22.9. As was the case for 1000BASE-X, idle ordered sets are transmitted between frames.

Also, like 1000BASE-X, a frame is bounded by special ordered sets that represent start and end delimiters.

A frame ends with a 4-byte cyclic redundancy check field, just as is the case for conventional LAN frames. If the number of bytes in the payload field is not a multiple of 4, fill bytes are inserted before the CRC.

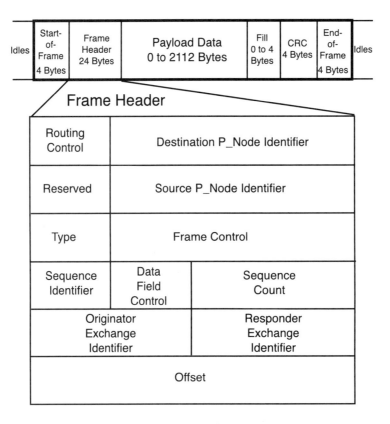

FIGURE 22.9   *Format of a fibre channel frame.*

The lower part of Figure 22.9 shows the format of the 24-byte frame header.

The frame header fields are explained in the following list. Acronyms for the field names are displayed for reference purposes because they often appear in vendor manuals. However, the acronyms will not be used in this text.

- **Routing control (R_CTL, 1 byte)**—Information that indicates the purpose for which the frame is being used. For example, the field can indicate that the frame carries upper-layer protocol data, video data, or control information. Or, the field might indicate that this is a link control frame. Link control frames are used to report acknowledgements or unsuccessful delivery, to perform flow control and buffer management, or to send low-level commands to an N_Port.

- **Destination identifier (D_ID, 3 bytes)**—The N_Port address identifying the port to which the frame is being sent.

- **Source identifier (S_ID, 3 bytes)**—The N_Port address identifying the port that sent the frame.

- **Type (1 byte)**—A code that identifies the type of protocol data carried in a data frame. The specific meaning of the code depends on the value in the routing control field. Sample payloads include link service messages (such as, logon, logout, request credit from peer, or test), LLC/SNAP data frames, SCSI, IPI-3, HIPPI, SNMP, and proprietary vendor video data.

- **Frame control (F_CTL, 3 bytes)**—A field that is packed with useful information. For example, there are subfields that indicate

  - The number of fill bytes in the frame

  - Whether the source of the frame is the originator or responder for the exchange

  - Whether the source of the frame is the initiator or recipient of the sequence

  - Whether this is the first, last, or an internal frame in the sequence

  - For a Class 1 connection, whether the sender wants to terminate the connection

  - Whether the sender has finished its current transmission and is passing the role of sender to its partner

  - Whether the offset field is meaningful and contains a value that describes the relative offset of the frame's payload

- **Sequence identifier (SEQ_ID, 1 byte)**—An identifier assigned to the current sequence by the initiator of the frame sequence.

- **Data field control (DF_CTL, 1 byte)**—Information that indicates whether additional optional headers appear at the beginning of the payload. For example, a special *network header* is included when an IP datagram is enclosed in a fibre channel frame. The section that follows describes the format of this network header.

- **Sequence count (SEQ_CNT, 2 bytes)**—A sequence number assigned to each frame in a sequence. At the end of the sequence, numbering may restart at 0 or continue to increase.

- **Originator exchange identifier (OX_ID, 2 bytes)**—A value assigned by the originator of an exchange. It is used to differentiate between multiple concurrent exchanges.

- **Responder exchange identifier (RX_ID, 2 bytes)**—A value assigned by the responder of an exchange.

Examples of FC-4 Fibre Channel Use

The subsections that follow sketch the way that two upper-layer services are mapped onto an underlying fibre channel network. The examples are

- Transmission of IP and ARP over fibre channel

- SCSI over fibre channel

Encapsulation of IP Datagrams

In the world of TCP/IP, a user identifies a host by a name such as www.yahoo.com. The user's computer gets the host's IP address from a directory server that maps names to IP addresses.

The destination IP address is placed into the header of every datagram sent to the destination host. An IP datagram is delivered to a destination that is attached to a LAN by wrapping the datagram in a frame addressed to the destination MAC address:

- If the source and destination are attached to the same LAN, the source transmits an Address Resolution Protocol (ARP) broadcast, asking the destination with the target IP address to respond and supply its MAC address.

- If the source and destination are not attached to the same LAN, the datagram is forwarded to a router that is attached to the destination LAN. In this case, the router transmits an Address Resolution Protocol (ARP) broadcast, asking the destination to respond and supply its MAC address.

IP datagrams and ARP messages can be carried in fibre channel frames. In a fibre channel network, however, a frame is delivered based on the destination's 3-byte N_Port identifier rather than on its MAC address. Two address translation steps are required before a frame can be transmitted across a fibre channel LAN:

1. IP address to IEEE world wide port name (MAC address)

2. IEEE world wide port name to 3-byte N_Port address

In fibre channel LANs, ARP broadcasts are used to map IP addresses to world wide port names.

A new *fibre channel ARP* (FARP) message was created to resolve 8-byte world wide port names to 3-byte port identifiers.

> **Note**
> FARP optionally can be implemented to perform both steps at once, directly mapping a 4-byte IP address to a 3-byte port address.

A datagram or ARP message that is carried in the payload of a fibre channel frame (or in the payloads of a sequence of frames) must be introduced by a 16-byte network header and an 8-byte LLC/SNAP header. The network header contains the destination and source world wide port names.

Recall that a world wide port name is an 8-byte field that contains

- A 4-bit network address authority (NAA) identifier. For IP and ARP, this is binary 0001, which is the code assigned to the IEEE.

- A 60-bit network address whose format depends on the network address authority. IEEE network addresses consist of 12 bits of 0-padding, followed by a 6-byte MAC address.

> **Note**
> At first glance, using this network header might seem strange. Why not just place an IP datagram into the payload field? However, including these embedded MAC addresses makes it easy to bridge frames between a fibre channel environment and a conventional LAN.

The left side of Figure 22.10 shows a network header followed by an LLC/SNAP header and an IP datagram that is to be encapsulated within one or more fibre channel frames.

The right side of Figure 22.10 shows how a big datagram has been cut into sub-blocks and is carried in a sequence of frames. The first subblock contains the network header and LLC/SNAP. The network header is not repeated in the other subblocks.

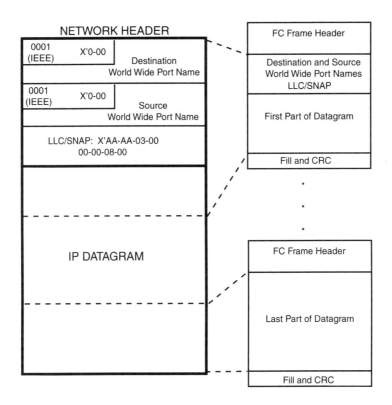

FIGURE 22.10 *Encapsulating an IP datagram in a fibre channel frame.*

The fibre channel encapsulation used for ARP messages is identical to the one used for IP, except for the fact that the LLC/SNAP field is X'AA-AA-03-00-00-00-08-06.

FARP requests and replies are encapsulated directly into fibre channel frames. No network header or LLC/SNAP header is needed.

Note

There is yet another option that can be used for address mappings. IP addresses, world wide port names, and port identifiers could be mapped using a directory service, if one were provided and all nodes were capable of using it.

SCSI over Fibre Channel

The SCSI interface between computers and attached devices has been a popular choice for many computer systems for quite a few years.

The protocol includes many commands that control the flow of data between a computer and an attached device. In the fibre channel implementation, data, commands, and responses to commands are carried between a pair of P_Nodes.

SCSI commands, data, and responses are carried in fibre channel frames. Every SCSI operation starts with a command and ends with a response. The work done as the result of a command is called a *task*. Figure 22.11 illustrates a SCSI device write task. This is implemented as a fibre channel exchange.

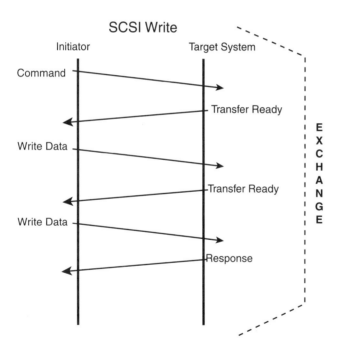

FIGURE 22.11 *A SCSI device write.*

Figure 22.12 shows the format of a fibre channel frame header that introduces a SCSI command frame. Several fields in the header have specially assigned values. For example, the type is X'08 and the frame control field is X'29-00-00.

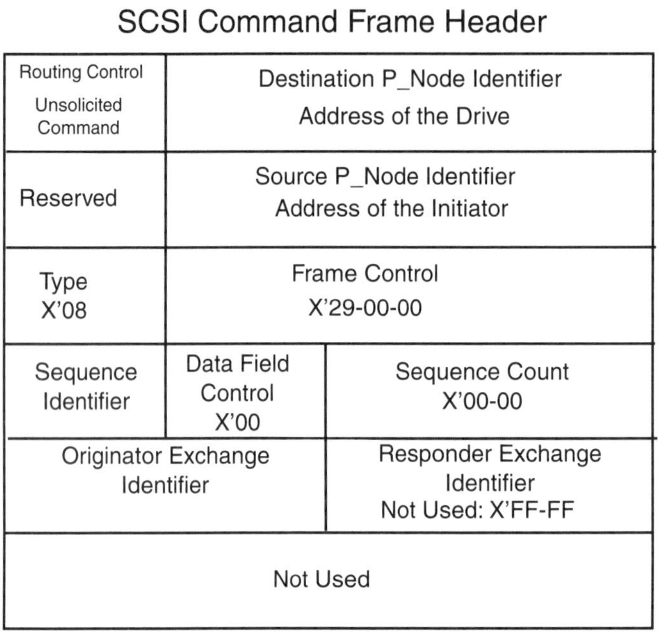

SCSI Command Frame Header

Routing Control Unsolicited Command	Destination P_Node Identifier Address of the Drive	
Reserved	Source P_Node Identifier Address of the Initiator	
Type X'08	Frame Control X'29-00-00	
Sequence Identifier	Data Field Control X'00	Sequence Count X'00-00
Originator Exchange Identifier		Responder Exchange Identifier Not Used: X'FF-FF
Not Used		

FIGURE 22.12 *Format of the fibre channel header for a SCSI command frame.*

Figure 22.13 shows the format of the payload of a SCSI command frame. (Note that the fields are displayed with a 1-byte width, as compared to the 4-byte width used in the display of the frame header.) Fields include

- **Logical unit number**—Picks a specific physical or virtual device at the target.

- **Task attribute**—Indicates the type of queue management that is requested. There are several possibilities—for example, first in, first out or a choice made by the SCSI device based on performance optimization.

- **Terminate task**—Ends the task.

- **Clear auto contingent allegiance**—Returns the drive to normal condition.

- **Target reset**—Clears the command queue for all initiators.

- **Clear task set**—Clears the queue for all initiators.

- **Abort task set**—Clears the commands from this initiator out of the queue.

- **Read data**—Indicates whether data will be transferred to the initiator.

- **Write data**—Indicates whether data will be transferred from the initiator.

- **Command descriptor block**—Contains parameters appropriate to the specific type of command.

- **Data length**—Equals the maximum number of data bytes that will be transferred as a result of this command.

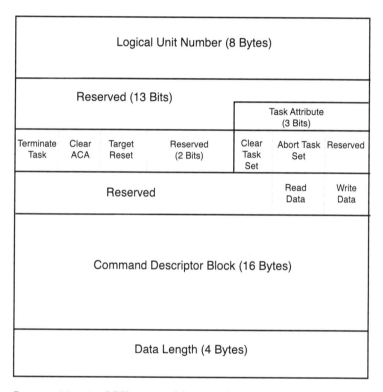

FIGURE 22.13 *SCSI command frame payload.*

Arbitrated Loops

An *arbitrated loop* is made up of a series of nodes connected into a ring. Often a hub is used to organize the cabling.

Like a Token Ring, inactive nodes in an arbitrated loop are bypassed, and a node must perform an insertion process in order to join the loop.

A loop sometimes is built into the backplane of a disk enclosure or some other device chassis. The units that are slotted into the enclosure become active nodes on the loop.

There is an important benefit of the arbitrated loop structure. When a loop is used to link disk units together, connectivity to all remaining disk units is preserved when one or more disk units are removed.

A private (standalone) arbitrated loop can have up to 126 active node ports (NL_Ports). More nodes can be physically attached to the loop, but they would be inactive and their ports would be bypassed. However, a bypassed node can become active when one of the active nodes leaves the loop.

If a switch port (FL_Port) is connected into a loop and becomes active, the loop becomes a public loop. A public loop has one additional port, the switch port (FL_Port). Thus, there can be at most 127 active ports on a public loop.

Figure 22.14 shows the node-to-node connections in a public arbitrated loop. One of the nodes in the figure is inactive. The circuitry automatically causes the node to be bypassed.

Note
Some loop implementations support high availability by connecting the same set of devices together using two separate loops. Of course, each device would need two ports.

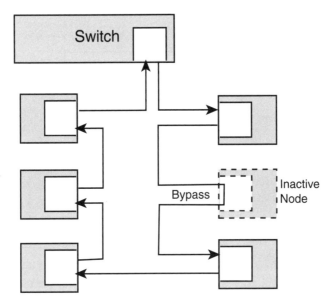

FIGURE 22.14 *A public arbitrated loop.*

L_Port Addresses

A loop port (L_Port) does not log in to a switch. It must obtain its 3-byte address via a different procedure:

- It obtains a 1-byte *arbitrated loop physical address* (AL_PA) through an initialization process.

- If the port is attached to a private loop, the 3-byte port address consists of X'00-00 followed by the AL_PA.

- For a public loop, the fabric port address always has the form X'wx-yz-00. In this case, the first 2 bytes of each loop port address are defined to be X'wx-yz. The third byte is the AL_PA.

An AL_PA is a single byte, and 1 byte translates to decimal numbers ranging from 0 to 255. However, only 127 of these can be used as arbitrated loop physical addresses.

The reason for this is that a byte can be used for an address only if its 10-bit encoding has an equal number of 0s and 1s. There are 134 bytes that meet this requirement, but 7 of them are reserved, leaving 127 useful values.

A low address is desirable because it translates to a high priority. The best AL_PA address of all, X'00, can be held only by a fabric port.

The AL_PA addresses of loop ports are assigned during loop initialization. The initialization process is described in the next section.

Some ports do not care what physical address they are assigned. Others make a bid for a specific address:

- A loop port may "remember" the physical address it got from a previous initialization. If so, it will make an attempt to get it back.

  If the loop is attached to a switch and the port not only got a prior AL_PA but also completed a login to the switch, it has a better chance of getting its old address back. (In this case, the address is called a *fabric-assigned* AL_PA.) However, another port also might be entitled to try to grab that address, and the first port might have to settle for a different address.

- A loop port physical address might have been hard-coded—for example, into the backplane of a disk enclosure. The port will try to get this hard-coded address, but in case of a conflict, it will have to settle for another address.

Arbitrated Loop Initialization

A loop initialization process occurs

- Every time a node is inserted into the loop

- During error recovery

During initialization, a port discovers that it is connected to a loop and realizes that it needs to obtain an arbitrated loop physical address. A port kicks off the procedure by transmitting a series of ordered sets called *loop initialization primitive sequences*. Successive ports transmit these ordered sets onward until they arrive back at the initiator node.

The nodes are now ready to transmit initialization frames, and

1. Select a loop master

2. Make sure that each port gets a unique 1-byte physical address

3. Generate a list of the physical addresses arranged according to each node's position around the loop

Figure 22.15 shows the format of the messages used during loop initialization. Seven different initialization frame types are used in the process. The first frame type is

- **Loop Initialization Select Master (LISM)**—Selects a loop master based on the combination of the 3-byte source port address and 8-byte world wide port name. A fabric port uses X'00-00-00 as its source address in this procedure, so it always wins (when present). All of the loop node ports use source address X'00-00-EF, so on a private loop, the port with the numerically smallest world wide port name wins.

The master is in charge of launching the remaining messages around the loop:

- **Loop Initialization Fabric Assigned (LIFA)**—Gather all fabric-assigned arbitrated loop physical addresses by circulating a bit map. A device can claim an address whose value in the bitmap is 0 by setting the bit to 1.

- **Loop Initialization Previously Acquired (LIPA)**—Recirculate the bit map and gather other previously assigned physical addresses.

- **Loop Initialization Hard Assigned (LIHA)**—Recirculate the bit map and gather hardware-assigned physical addresses.

- **Loop Initialization Soft Assigned (LISA)**—Recirculate the bit map and let each node that has not yet been capable of claiming an address choose the first unused value in the bit map.

- **Loop Initialization Report Position (LIRP)**—Circulate a position map. Each node records its physical address in the first empty slot.

- **Loop Initialization Loop Position (LILP)**—Circulate the completed position map.

If there is a conflict in a fabric-assigned, previously assigned, or hardware-assigned physical address, the node that gets the bit map first sets the bit, and any other node that wanted that address must pick up a new address at the LISA stage.

Routing Control X'22	Destination Node Identifier X'00-00-00 for Fabric Port X'00-00-EF for a Loop Port	
X'00	Source P_Node Identifier X'00-00-00 for Fabric Port X'00-00-EF for a Loop Port	
Type X'01	Frame Control X'38-00-00	
Sequence Identifier X'00	Data Field Control X'00	Sequence Count X'00-00
Originator Exchange Identifier Not Used: X'FF-FF		Responder Exchange Identifier Not Used: X'FF-FF
X'00-00-00-00		
Type of Initialization Frame (4 Bytes)		
World Wide Port Name (8 Bytes) or Port Address Bit Map (16 Bytes) or Port Address Position Map (128 Bytes)		

FIGURE 22.15 *Format of loop initialization messages.*

Arbitrated Loop Data Transfer

The protocols that manage data transfer on a loop are a lot simpler than Token Ring protocols. The reason for this is that several 4-byte ordered set signals are used to manage the loop. These signals take the place of mechanisms such as tokens, purges, claim frames, and active monitors.

A series of 4-byte idle ordered sets is propagated between frame transmissions. A node that wants to communicate replaces the idles with an *arbitrate* signal that includes its own 1-byte AL_PA physical address.

> **Note**
>
> A node's arbitrate signal can be bumped off and replaced by an *arbitrate* signal from a higher priority node (that is, one with a numerically lower AL_PA physical address).

If an *arbitrate* signal circles the loop and returns to the initiator node, the initiator then can start a communication by sending *open* signals that include the 1-byte physical address of the destination. If the communication is to be two-way, the *open* also includes the sender's physical address.

After the *open*, the parties are ready to communicate. When a party wants to terminate the communication, it sends a *close* signal. It can then make the loop available to other nodes or immediately send *open* signals identifying a new partner.

As described so far, this protocol allows one node to grab the loop and monopolize it. There is an optional fairness algorithm that periodically opens up the arbitration process. Also, once a fair node has had its turn, it cannot arbitrate again until it receives an idle.

Table 22.5 describes the special 4-byte signals that are used in arbitrated loop protocols. For several of the signals, the last 2 bytes of the signal contain two physical addresses.

TABLE 22.5 FIBRE CHANNEL ARBITRATED LOOP SIGNALS

Signal	Acronym	Description
Arbitrate	ARBx	The node with address x asks to use the loop. The last 2 bytes of the signal are copies of address x.

Signal	Acronym	Description
Arbitrate (F0)	ARB(F0)	A node tests the loop to see if another node wants to arbitrate. It inserts address X'F0, which is larger than any valid address. Any other node will be capable of replacing X'F0 with its own address.
Open full-duplex	OPNyx	The node with address x notifies the node with address y that it wants to open a two-way circuit.
Open half-duplex	OPNyy	The originator node notifies the node with address y that it wants to open a one-way circuit. The target node cannot send any frames to the originator.
Open broadcast replicate	OPNfr	The initiator announces that all nodes should accept the frames that it will send. The 2 address bytes are X'FF-FF.
Open selective replicate	OPNyr	The initiator prepares a set of nodes to receive a multicast. These messages are sent to each of the destination nodes in turn, asking them to accept the frames that will follow. The "y" is the address of one of the target nodes, and the "r" is X'FF.
Close	CLS	A participant closes an active circuit.
Dynamic half-duplex	DHD	The initiator of a one-way circuit announces that it has no more frames to send.
Mark	MRKtx	This is used for housekeeping functions, such as time synchronization.
Offline	OLS	A node transmits this for a period of time to announce that it is preparing to go offline.
Not Operational	NOS	A node transmits this several times to announce that its port has detected a loop failure or is offline.
Link Reset	LR	A node transmits this several times to initiate the link reset protocol following a link timeout.
Link Reset Response	LRR	A node transmits this several times to indicate that its port has received and recognized link reset signals.
Loop Initialization	LIP	A node initializes the loop, either to join the loop or to recover from a detected problem.
Loop Port Enable	LPEyx	Node x deactivates the bypass circuit at node y. (Node x should be a network management node.)

continues

TABLE 22.5 CONTINUED

Signal	Acronym	Description
Loop Port Enable All	LPEfx	Node x resets the bypass circuits on all ports on the loop.
Loop Port Bypass	LBEyx	Node x closes the bypass circuit at y and prevents the port from actively participating in the loop.

Summary Points

- Fibre channel provides a common infrastructure that can be used to network computers and peripherals together.

- Fibre channel supports protocol data carried in LLC/SNAP frames, SCSI, IPI, and HIPPI, among others.

- Defined speeds range from 12.5MBps to 400MBps.

- Fibre channel can connect one pair of systems across a point-to-point link, a set of systems joined in a loop, or a large switched network (which is called a Fabric).

- Every port has a built-in world wide port name. For example, many ports are assigned IEEE identifiers or IEEE field replaceable hardware unit numbers.

- FC-0 defines cables, connectors, and the signals sent on the medium.

- FC-1 defines the 8B/10B encoding used to translate data bytes into 10-bit code-groups.

- FC-2 is the fibre channel data link layer; it defines the way that data is packaged into frames and specifies the control signals that are used to manage data transfer.

- FC-3 is a placeholder for functions that are applied across several ports in a node.

- FC-4 defines a series of mappings of various applications onto fibre channel—for example, IP and ARP protocol data units or SCSI data and control frames.

- Fibre channel provides several classes of service. The most important are the Class 1 connection-oriented service; Class 2, which is an acknowledged connectionless service; and Class 3, which is an unacknowledged connectionless service.

- Data is transferred in frames. Groups of related frames are organized into sequences. One or more sequences that represent some type of transaction are organized into an exchange.

- A port attached to a switch must perform a login before it can communicate. Its environment parameters are established by the login.

- A port that wants to open Class 1 or Class 2 communication with a target port must log in to the target to establish the parameters for that communication.

- Each port announces the number of receive buffers (the credit) that it is making available to a communication. A node must keep track of its partner's current credit. End-to-end credit is updated by acknowledgement frames.

- An arbitrated loop is made up of a series of nodes connected into a ring. Often a hub or loop switch is used to organize the cabling.

- A standalone loop is called a private loop. A loop that is attached to a switch is called a public loop.

- A loop initialization process occurs whenever a node is inserted into the loop or when error recovery action is needed.

- During loop initialization, the nodes select a loop master, make sure that each port is assigned a unique 1-byte physical address, and generate a list of physical addresses arranged according to each node's position around the loop.

- A loop node requests permission to transmit by replacing idle signals with arbitrate signals.

References

Approved fibre channel references include

- ANSI X3.230. "Information Technology—Fibre Channel Physical and Signaling Interface (FC-PH)." 1994.

- ANSI X3.272. "Information Technology—Fibre Channel—Arbitrated Loop (FC-AL)." 1996.

- ANSI X3.289. "Information Technology—Fibre Channel—Fabric Generic (FC-FG)." 1996.

- ANSI X3.297. "Information Technology—Fibre Channel—Physical and Signaling Interface-2 (FC-PH-2)." 1997.

- ANSI X3.303. "Fibre Channel—Physical and Signaling Interface-3 (FC-PH-3)." 1998.

- ANSI NCITS 321-1998. "Fibre Channel—Switch Fabric (FC-SW)." 1998.

- ANSI NCITS TR-20-1998. "Fibre Channel—Fabric Loop Attachment (FC-FLA)." 1998.

- ANSI NCITS 332-1999, "Fibre Channel—Arbitrated Loop (FC-AL-2)." 1999.

A large number of other references are under development by ANSI committees. Among these are

- "Fibre Channel Link Encapsulation (FC-LE)."

- "Fibre Channel—Fabric Generic Requirements (FC-FG)."

- "Fibre Channel—Switch Fabric-2 (FC-SW-2)."

- "Fibre Channel—Backbone (FC-BB)."

- "Fibre Channel—Virtual Interface (FC-VI)."

- "Fibre Channel—Framing and Signaling Interface (FC-FS)."

- "SCSI Fibre Channel Protocol2 (FCP-2)."

- "Fibre Channel Private Loop SCSI Direct Attach (FC-PLDA)."

- "FCA IP Profile."

Online information is available at the Fibre Channel Industry Association Web site, http://www.fibrechannel.com/; the Fibre Channel Loop Community Web site, http://www.fcloop.org; and the T11 committee Web site, http://www.t11.org/.

The IETF has published a document that standardizes the way that IP is implemented over fibre channel:

- RFC 2625. "IP and ARP over Fibre Channel." M. Rajagopal, R. Bhagwat, and W. Rickard.

A tutorial can be found at the University of New Hampshire interoperability lab Web site:

    http://www.iol.unh.edu/training/index.html

PART IV

Appendixes

A   Physical Layer Encodings for Ethernet, Fibre Channel, FDDI, and Token Ring

B   Tables

C   Standards Bodies and References

D   Acronym List

      Glossary

Physical Layer Encodings for Ethernet, Fibre Channel, FDDI, and Token Ring

This appendix examines the different ways that data is encoded onto a medium for Ethernet, fibre channel, FDDI, and Token Ring LANs.

A detailed acquaintance with encodings is not really needed to install, manage, or troubleshoot a LAN. If an Ethernet or Token Ring chip or a digital signal processor misbehaves, a LAN administrator uses a tester or SNMP to track down the bad NIC, pull it out, and replace it. Many NICs come with lifetime replacement guarantees. Hub and switch products usually are backed by good multiyear guarantees.

A LAN administrator can get along very well without the material in this appendix, which is why it has been included as optional reference material. However, some insights can be gained from a look into physical layer internals. For example, this appendix provides a better understanding of how collisions are detected, explains the delay that occurs within Class I hubs, and clarifies the full-duplex underpinnings of Gigabit Ethernet.

One thing to watch for is the way that encodings are designed to accomplish the following:

- Reduce crosstalk on copper wires by keeping the signal frequency as low as possible

- Prevent an optical fiber from overheating due to a high density of strong light pulses

This is called *promoting dc balance*. The term *dc* actually stands for *direct current*. When applied to both copper and optical fiber, "promoting dc balance" translates roughly to "transmission of almost equal numbers of high and low signals."

Code-Groups and Special Signals

The 0s and 1s in a stream of digital data must be translated into physical symbols that can be impressed onto a medium.

It is natural to visualize the bits in a frame being transmitted across a medium by faithfully copying its 0 and 1 bits into physical representations of 0 and 1— for example, as distinct voltage levels or optical power levels.

The problem with using a high voltage for 1 and a low voltage for 0 is that a receiver has trouble keeping track of where bits begin and end when it receives a long string of 1s or a long string of 0s.

Over the years, several ways of overcoming this problem have been introduced. For example, for 10BASE5, 10BASE2, and 10BASE-T Ethernet, each 0 or 1 is translated into a *Manchester encoded* symbol. Manchester encoding (which is described in the next section) represents bits as *changes* in voltage levels.

Manchester encoding works very well, but it requires a transition between high and low voltage levels for each bit. This is feasible at speeds of up to 16Mbps, but is difficult to implement at higher speeds. The physics of supporting a large number of transitions per second between high and low voltage levels translates into a requirement that the medium support high frequencies and have a big bandwidth capacity (in megahertz).

Engineers have developed several ways to cram more data onto a cable using fewer transitions between high and low voltage levels. One technique translates a set of bits to a bigger set of bits that has a good distribution of 0s and 1s. For example, 4B/5B coding translates each 4-bit pattern to a 5-bit pattern containing a good mix of 0s and 1s. After translation, a 0 can be sent as a "low" and a 1 as a "high" because the bitstream will contain enough transitions to maintain accurate bit clocking.

Another technique that crams more bits per second onto a copper cable is to use more than two voltage levels. Three levels were used for 100BASE-TX and 100BASE-T4. Five levels were introduced for 100BASE-T2 and 1000BASE-T.

Table A.1 summarizes various types of encodings that have been used over the years. These encodings are described in the sections that follow. Some of the encodings that are studied include special control signals in addition to signals that correspond to 0 or 1 data bits. Control signals are delimiters that mark the beginning and end of a frame, or that represent idle symbols that are used as filler between frames.

TABLE A.1 SYMBOL ENCODINGS

Type of LAN	Translation	Symbols	Described As
10BASE5, 10BASE2, and 10BASE-T Ethernet	None	0=High-to-low voltage. 1=Low-to-high voltage.	Manchester encoding
FOIRL and 10BASE-FL Ethernet	None	0=High-to-low optical power. 1=Low-to-high optical power. Special pulse for idle.	Manchester encoding for bits
10BASE-FB Ethernet	None	0=High-to-low optical power. 1=Low-to-high optical power. Additional synchronous signals for idle and fault.	Manchester encoding for bits
100BASE-FX Ethernet and FDDI	4B/5B Map 4-bit nibbles to 5-bit code-groups	0=No transition 1=Alternates between high and low optical power. Special code-groups for idle, start and end of stream, and error conditions.	Non return to zero inverted (NRZI)
100BASE-TX Ethernet and CDDI	4B/5B Map 4-bit nibbles to 5-bit code-groups	Three voltage levels: low, middle, and high. . 0=No transition. 1=Step transitions: low-to-middle, middle-to-high, high-to-middle, middle-to-low, and so on. Special code-groups for idle, start and end of stream, and error conditions	MLT-3, sometimes called NRZI-3
100BASE-T4 Ethernet	8B/6T Map 8-bit bytes to 6-symbol code-groups	Three symbols, labeled [–, 0, +] or [–1, 0, 1] are used. Each symbol is transmitted as a different voltage level.	8B/6T

continues

TABLE A.1 Symbol Encodings

Type of LAN	Translation	Symbols	Described As
100BASE-T2 Ethernet	Map 4-bit nibbles to 2-symbol code-groups	Five symbols labeled [–2, –1, 0, 1, 2] are used. Each symbol is trans-mitted as a different voltage level.	PAM5
1000BASE-SX, 1000BASE-LX, and 1000BASE-CX Ethernet and Fibre Channel	8B/10B Map 8-bit bytes to 10-bit code-groups	1=High optical power or high voltage. 0=Low optical power or low voltage. Special code-groups for idle, extensions, start and end of packet, negotiation, and error conditions.	8B/10B
1000BASE-T Ethernet	8B1Q4 Map 8-bit bytes to 4-symbol code-groups. One symbol is sent on each pair.	Five symbols labeled [–2, –1, 0, 1, 2] are used. Each symbol is trans-mitted as a different voltage level. Special code-groups for idle, extension, start and end of stream, and error conditions.	4D-PAM5
4Mbps or 16Mbps Token Ring	None	0=Transition at start and middle. 1=Transition in middle.	Differential Manchester encoding, with special "J" and "K" symbols
100Mbps Dedicated Token Ring	4B/5B	Same as 100BASE-FX for optical fiber and 100BASE-TX for twisted-pair cable.	NRZI for fiber optic, MLT-3 for copper

Ethernet 10BASE5, 10BASE2, and 10BASE-T Manchester Encoding

Data is transmitted onto 10Mbps coaxial cable and 10Mbps twisted-pair LAN media using a method called *Manchester encoding*. For each 0 and 1 transmitted across the medium:

- The encoded representation of the bit has a voltage transition at its midpoint.

- For a 0-bit, the first half is high and the second half is low.

- For a 1-bit, the first half is low and the second half is high.

Figure A.1 shows the Manchester pattern for 1 0 1 1 1 0 0 1.

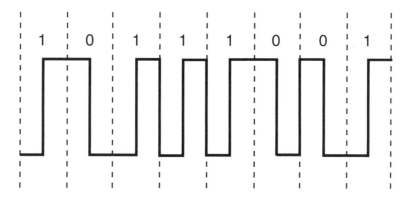

Figure A.1 *Manchester encoding.*

The fact that there is a transition within each bit makes it easy for a receiver to synchronize its timing with the transmitter. If two signals collide on the cable, the transition pattern is broken, enabling systems to detect the collision.

Ethernet FOIRL, 10BASE-FL, and 10BASE-FB

Manchester encoding also is used for 10Mbps Ethernet across fiber optic cable. However, some special signals have been added to the fiber optic specifications to support some useful features.

As noted in Chapter 6, "The Ethernet 10Mbps Physical Layer," whenever data is not being transmitted by a FOIRL or 10BASE-FL interface, the interface sends special idle pulses onto the send fiber.

The idle signal for 10BASE-FB is called a *synchronous idle* and is made up of special clocked symbols. Two new Manchester symbols are defined:

- **Manchester Code Violation Zero (MV0)**—A clocked symbol that is low for a bit duration.

- **Manchester Code Violation One (MV1)**—A clocked symbol that is high for a bit duration.

A synchronous idle is a repeating sequence of symbols:

MV1 MV1 MV0 MV0

A different repeating combination of MV0 and MV1 symbols is used to notify the remote partner that a fault (such as jabber, invalid data, low light, or loss of clocking) has been detected. The remote fault pattern is this:

MV1 MV1 MV1 MV0 MV0 MV0

Figure A.2 shows what the signals look like.

SYNCHRONOUS IDLE

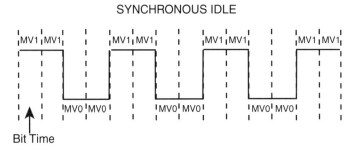

REMOTE FAULT

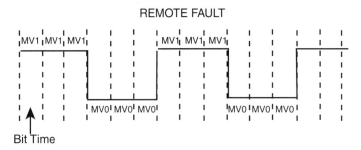

FIGURE A.2 *Synchronous idle and remote fault patterns.*

100BASE-X Ethernet, FDDI, and CDDI

The title 100BASE-X encompasses 100BASE-TX and 100BASE-FX. The 100BASE-X title was coined because even though 100BASE-TX transmits onto twisted-pair cable and 100BASE-FX transmits onto optical fiber, these technologies have a lot in common. The physical layers for 100BASE-FX and 100BASE-TX were derived from the FDDI and CDDI physical layers.

Figure A.3 shows a division of the physical layer into a part that is independent of the medium and a part that is dependent on the medium. The *medium-independent* parts of 100BASE-TX and 100BASE-FX are the same.

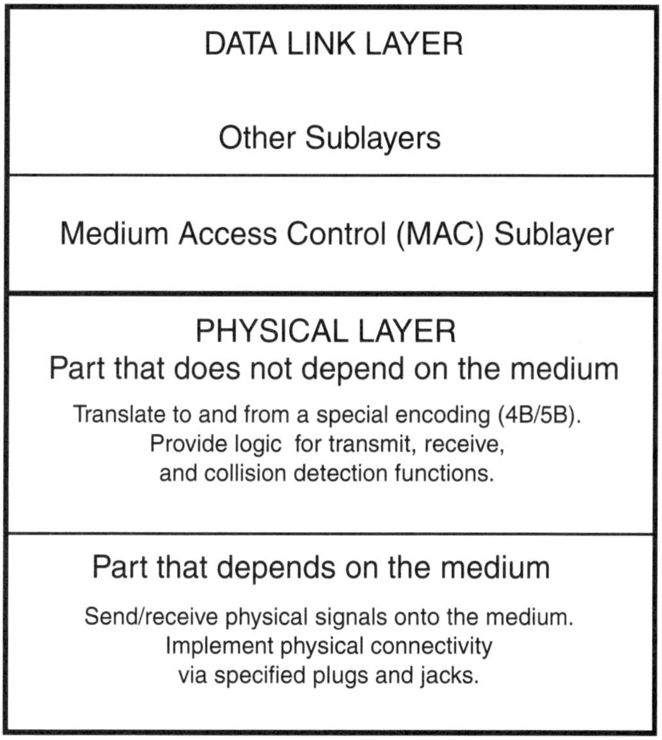

DATA LINK LAYER
Other Sublayers
Medium Access Control (MAC) Sublayer
PHYSICAL LAYER Part that does not depend on the medium Translate to and from a special encoding (4B/5B). Provide logic for transmit, receive, and collision detection functions.
Part that depends on the medium Send/receive physical signals onto the medium. Implement physical connectivity via specified plugs and jacks.

FIGURE A.3   *A view of the physical layer.*

For FDDI, CDDI, 100BASE-TX, and 100BASE-FX, data is prepared for transmission by translating each 4-bit quantity into a 5-bit pattern. This is called *4B/5B translation*.

Before examining exactly how the translation is done, it is helpful to examine the physical signals that are used for 100BASE-FX and FDDI, and for 100BASE-TX and CDDI. The limitations of the two signaling methods are the reason that each nibble must be translated before it is sent.

NRZI Signals for 100BASE-FX and FDDI

100BASE-FX and FDDI operate over two optical fibers. Data is sent on one fiber and received on the other.

Values of 0 and 1 are impressed onto a fiber using *non-return-to-zero, invert-on-one* encoding. This works as follows:

- The 1s are alternatively represented by a high or low signal.

- No change of signal level takes place at a 0.

Figure A.4 displays an NRZI encoding of the bit stream 11010001.

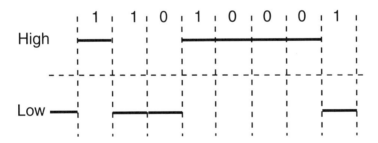

FIGURE A.4   *NRZI-encoded data.*

The problem with NRZI is that when a long string of 0s is transmitted, no transitions occur. This causes the receiver to lose bit time synchronization.

The cure is 4B/5B translation, which converts each 4-bit nibble into a 5-bit code-group that contains at least two 1s. Transmitting these 5-bit code-groups guarantees that there will be two or more transitions whenever a nibble is sent. This enables the receiver to maintain its bit clocking.

MLT-3 Signals for 100BASE-TX and CDDI

Multi-Level 3 encoding (MLT-3) is an efficient signaling method that was introduced for CDDI and adopted for 100BASE-TX. It has a lower bandwidth requirement than the NRZI signaling used for FDDI and 100BASE-FX. This is helpful because Category 5 cable supports far less bandwidth than optical fiber.

Like NRZI, MLT-3 makes a transition for each 1 and stays the same at each 0. However, the transitions are made at three different signal levels. The signal changes one step at a time, as follows:

1. Low to middle

2. Middle to high

3. High to middle

4. Middle to low

The result is that the number of transitions between low and high voltage decreases. (You go all the way from low to high and back to low half as often.) This translates to a lower frequency, which makes it possible to fit 100Mbps onto Category 5 cable with bandwidth to spare and cuts down on crosstalk.

Figure A.5 shows an MLT representation of the bit string 11010001.

Instead of being called low, middle and high, the levels often are represented using these symbols:

[–, 0, +] or [–1, 0, and 1]

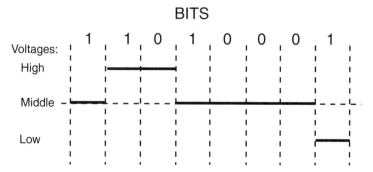

FIGURE A.5 *MLT-3 encoded data.*

MLT-3 presents the same problem as NRZI. No transitions take place when a long string of 0s occurs, and this can cause a receiver to lose bit timing.

The same solution that was applied to NRZI is used here. Each 4-bit nibble is converted to a 5-bit code-group using 4B/5B translation. The combination of 4B/5B translation and MLT-3 signals enables a sender to transmit 100Mbps across a 31.25MHz line.

4B/5B Code-Groups for FDDI, CDDI, and 100BASE-X

Table A.2 shows how the 4B/5B translation is done. The encoding choices have been made so that no 5-bit code has more than two consecutive 0s. When two nibbles are translated in sequence, a few of the 10-bit results contain three consecutive 0s. For example, X'24 translates to 1010001010. However, no sequence of nibbles results in more than three consecutive 0s.

TABLE A.2 4B/5B DATA MAPPINGS

Hex	Binary "Nibble" (4B)	Five Bit Code-Group (5B)
0	0 0 0 0	1 1 1 1 0
1	0 0 0 1	0 1 0 0 1
2	0 0 1 0	1 0 1 0 0
3	0 0 1 1	1 0 1 0 1
4	0 1 0 0	0 1 0 1 0
5	0 1 0 1	0 1 0 1 1
6	0 1 1 0	0 1 1 1 0
7	0 1 1 1	0 1 1 1 1
8	1 0 0 0	1 0 0 1 0
9	1 0 0 1	1 0 0 1 1
A	1 0 1 0	1 0 1 1 0
B	1 0 1 1	1 0 1 1 1
C	1 1 0 0	1 1 0 1 0
D	1 1 0 1	1 1 0 1 1
E	1 1 1 0	1 1 1 0 0
F	1 1 1 1	1 1 1 0 1

Only 16 of the 32 possible 5-bit patterns are needed to represent data nibbles. Some of the remaining patterns have been assigned to special code-groups. Table A.3 describes these special code-groups.

Code-groups I, J, K, T, and R are called *control codes*. Code-group H is a *code violation* that is used to signal a collision or error condition. Code-group Q is used for some special physical connection-management signals needed for FDDI and CDDI.

The idle code-group (I) is sent continuously between frames and enables a system to check the integrity of its receive pair on an ongoing basis. The two-code start-of-stream delimiter (JK) is sent in place of the first preamble byte. The end-of-stream delimiter (TR) marks the completion of the transmission of a frame.

TABLE A.3 SPECIAL 5B CODE-GROUPS

Name	Code-Group	Use for Ethernet	Use for FDDI/CDDI
I	1 1 1 1 1	Idle symbol, sent as filler between frames	Idle symbol, sent as filler between frames
J	1 1 0 0 0	First half of a start-of-stream delimiter	First half of a start-of-stream delimiter.
K	1 0 0 0 1	Second half of a start-of-stream delimiter	Second half of a start-of-stream delimiter.
T	0 1 1 0 1	First half of an end-of-stream delimiter	One T is used as a data frame end delimiter. Two T symbols are used as a token end delimiter.
R	0 0 1 1 1	Second half of an end-of-stream delimiter	
H	0 0 1 0 0	Used to indicate a collision or error condition	Used for special physical connection management signals.
Q	0 0 0 0 0		Used for special physical connection-management signals.

Ethernet 100BASE-T4

100BASE-T4 runs on four pairs of Category 3 twisted-pair cable. An efficient encoding is needed to pack 100Mbps onto Category 3 cable.

Ternary Symbols and 8B/6T Encoding

As with 100BASE-TX, three different signal levels are used for 100BASE-T4. Instead of following fixed steps from low-to-middle, middle-to-high, and so on, however, the voltage levels are used as symbols that can appear in any order. These are called *ternary symbols*.

As was the case for MLT-3, the voltage levels correspond to these ternary symbol labels:

[−, 0, +] or [−1, 0, and 1].

Each 8-bit byte is mapped to a unique code-group consisting of six ternary symbols. There are $2^8 = 256$ different 8-bit patterns, but there are $3^6 = 729$ different 6-symbol code-groups, so more than enough code-groups are available. The code-groups that have been selected to represent data bytes are those that contain an equal or almost equal number of positive and negative symbols.

The translation is called 8B/6T. Table A.4 shows just a few of the 8B/6T-byte translations. The full translation table appears in Appendix B, "Tables" (see Table B.2).

TABLE A.4 SOME SAMPLE 8B/6T BYTE TRANSLATIONS

HEX	Binary Byte	6T Code-Group
00	0 0 0 0 0 0 0 0	+ − 0 0 + −
01	0 0 0 0 0 0 0 1	0 + − + − 0
02	0 0 0 0 0 0 1 0	+ − 0 + − 0
03	0 0 0 0 0 0 1 1	− 0 + + − 0
04	0 0 0 0 0 1 0 0	− 0 + 0 + −
05	0 0 0 0 0 1 0 1	0 + − − 0 +
06	0 0 0 0 0 1 1 0	+ − 0 − 0 +
07	0 0 0 0 0 1 1 1	− 0 + − 0 +
08	0 0 0 0 1 0 0 0	− + 0 0 + −
09	0 0 0 0 1 0 0 1	0 − + + − 0
0A	0 0 0 0 1 0 1 0	− + 0 + − 0
0B	0 0 0 0 1 0 1 1	+ 0 − + − 0
0C	0 0 0 0 1 1 0 0	+ 0 − 0 + −
0D	0 0 0 0 1 1 0 1	0 − + − 0 +
0E	0 0 0 0 1 1 1 0	− + 0 − 0 +
0F	0 0 0 0 1 1 1 1	+ 0 − − 0 +
58	0 1 0 1 1 0 0 0	+ + + 0 − −
59	0 1 0 1 1 0 0 1	+ + + − 0 −
5A	0 1 0 1 1 0 1 0	+ + + − − 0

Inverting 6T Data Code-Groups

Each 6T data code-group displayed in Table A.4 contains either an equal number of + and − symbols, or has one more + than − symbol. This also holds true for the entire data code-group table in Appendix B.

If these symbols were sent as is, dc balance would be lost over time. The dc balance for a wire pair is restored by following rules that invert some of the code-groups sent on that twisted-pair cable:

1. Compute the weight of each code group by adding its symbols. Every code-group has a weight of 0 or 1. For example, the weight of (+++−−0) is 1.

2. Between frames, set the cumulative weight for the twisted-pair cable to 0.

3. If the weight of the current data code-group is 0, do not change the cumulative weight.

4. If the weight of the current data code-group is 1 and the cumulative weight is 0, set the cumulative weight to 1.

5. If the weight of the current data code-group is 1 and the cumulative weight is 1, set the cumulative weight to 0 and reverse the signs of the symbols in the code-group.

100BASE-T4 Transmission

For 100BASE-T4, data is transmitted across three pairs of wires. The sender listens for incoming data on the remaining pair to detect a collision.

Figure A.6 illustrates the data flows. The diagram at the top shows the flow when the system on the left receives data. The diagram on the bottom shows the flow when the system on the left is the sender.

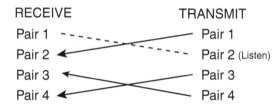

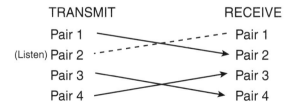

FIGURE A.6   *100BASE-T4 data flows.*

Each byte is translated into a 6T ternary code-group and is sent across one of the pairs. Bytes are assigned to the three pairs in round robin fashion.

Figure A.7 illustrates how this is done. (Note that data flows from right to left in this figure.) In the figure, the first byte is translated to a 6T code-group and is sent across pair 4. The code-group for the next byte is sent across pair 1, and the code-group for the byte after that is sent across pair 3. The sequence then cycles back to pair 4. The sender listens to its pair 2 to check for collisions.

The vertical dotted lines on the right side of Figure A.7 indicate that the transmission times of each 6T code-group are staggered. Thus, as is shown by the vertical dotted lines on the left, a 6T code-group arriving on pair 4 is followed by a code-group on pair 1, and finally one on pair 3. This enables incoming bytes to be collated into their original order at the receiving end. The next section shows how this gets synchronized at the beginning of a frame.

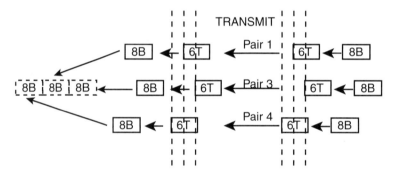

FIGURE A.7 *Transmitting bytes of data for 100BASE-T4.*

A total of $33^1/3$Mbps must be transmitted across each wire. After converting each 8-bit quantity to six symbols, the rate becomes $^6/8(33^1/3) = 25$ million symbols per second. Because of a reduced number of high-low transitions required in the code-groups that are used, the bandwidth that actually is required is only 12.5MHz per wire.

Special Symbols and Alignment

As was the case with the 4B/5B encoding used for 100BASE-X, some 6T patterns are used for special purposes. For 100BASE-T4, special patterns are used to mark the beginning and end of each frame.

Figure A.8 shows how a start-of-stream, data, and end-of-frame pattern is encoded and sent across three wires. Data flows from right to left in this figure; the leftmost bits are transmitted first.

The top of the figure shows that bytes sent across each pair arrive at different times. the lower part of the figure shows the special symbol patterns that are sent at the beginning and end of each transmission. These patterns are distinct from the code-groups that represent data bytes:

- Sixteen startup symbols are transmitted on pair 4, which will carry the code-group that represents the first byte of data.

- Eighteen startup symbols are sent on pair 1, which will carry the code-group for the second data byte.

- Twenty startup symbols are sent on pair 3, which will carry the code-group for the third data byte.

- For each pair, the pattern (+−−+) precedes the first data code-group that is sent across the pair.

The different lengths that are used for the startup patterns set up the staggered arrival times for the 6T code-groups. The arrival times are staggered by two symbol times. This enables the receiver to keep the incoming code-groups in order and collate them correctly. Specifically, code-group 1 arrives two symbol times before code-group 2, which arrives two symbol times before code-group 3, which arrives two symbol times before code-group 4, and so forth.

The length of the frame being transmitted determines which wire pair carries the last data code-group. The last data code-group in Figure A.8 happens to be sent on pair 3. The special pattern (++−−00) signals the end of data. Other special terminating patterns appear on pairs 4 and 1.

The lower part of Figure A.8 shows the names that have been given to groupings of start and end patterns. These patterns and the acronyms and names that have been assigned to them are shown in Table A.5.

TABLE A.5 SPECIAL 6T PATTERNS

Name	Coding	Description
SOSA	+ − + − + −	Start-of-stream-A. Used to represent a preamble byte.
SOSB	+ − + − − +	Start-of-stream-B. Used as a start-of-stream delimiter.
P3	+ −	Preamble 3. Contains preamble bits.
P4	+ − + −	Preamble 4. Contains preamble bits.
EOP1	+ + + + + +	End-of-packet-1. Signals the end of a frame.

continues

TABLE A.5 CONTINUED

Name	Coding	Description
EOP2	+ + + + − −	End-of-packet-2.
EOP3	+ + − − 0 0	End-of-packet-3.
EOP4	− − − − − −	End-of-packet-4.
EOP5	− − 0 0 0 0	End-of-packet-5.
Bad-Code	− − − + + +	Sent when there has been a transmission error.

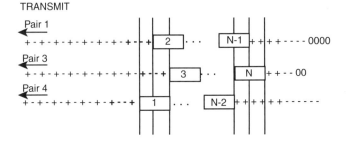

FIGURE A.8 *Transmitting a frame using 100BASE-T4.*

> **Note**
>
> Special dc balance rules are applied to the special 6T patterns. For example, SOSA, SOSB, and Bad-Code never are inverted.

Translating Between 100BASE-X and 100BASE-T4 in a Hub

The 4B/5B encoding used for 100BASE-TX or 100BASE-FX is very different from the 8B/6T encoding used for 100BASE-T4.

A Class II hub that supports either 100BASE-X or 100BASE-T4 exclusively can forward each incoming symbol without further processing. However, a Class I hub that supports both 100BASE-X and 100BASE-T4 interfaces must convert between these encodings. For example, if data is arriving on a 100BASE-X port, the port must accumulate 10 symbols, convert them to 8 bits, and then reconvert them to a 6T code. This is what causes the extra delay in a Class I hub.

Ethernet 100BASE-T2

100BASE-T2 never was implemented in products. Nonetheless, the technology is of some interest because much of it was borrowed for 1000BASE-T, so it will be described here briefly.

Like 100BASE-T4, 100BASE-T2 was designed to run on Category 3 or better wiring. However, unlike 100BASE-T4, 100BASE-T2 requires only two twisted-pair cables and supports full-duplex links as well as half-duplex operation.

A station with a 100BASE-T2 interface could be connected to a half-duplex environment by linking it to a hub, or it could run in full-duplex mode when connected to another station or a switch.

A 100BASE-T2 link actually always physically operates in a full-duplex manner. After an autoconfiguration negotiation that establishes the properties of the link, steady streams of symbols flow across each wire pair in both directions.

Idle symbols are sent between data transmissions. The start and end of each frame are marked by special start-of-stream and end-of-stream delimiters.

Quinary Symbols and PAM5x5 Encoding

Three voltage levels were used for 100BASE-T4. Five were needed for 100BASE-T2. The symbols corresponding to the five different voltage levels are labeled [–2, –1, 0, +1, +2] and represent *quinary symbols*. Transmission of data using several voltage levels is called pulse amplitude modulation (PAM). Because there are five voltage levels, the transmission method is called 5-level pulse amplitude modulation, or PAM5.

A pair of quinary symbols such as (+1, –2) or (0, –1) is used to represent 4 data bits (a nibble). Because there are 16 four-bit patterns and 25 quinary symbol pairs, a mapping of 4 bits into 2 symbols can be done easily. The extra pairs of quinary symbols can be used to represent idles, frame delimiters, and error codes.

Each outgoing 4-bit quantity is scrambled and then is translated to a pair of quinary symbols using a complicated mapping algorithm. The combined mapping and transmission procedure is called PAM5×5.

> **Note**
>
> If you are curious about the mapping, see Chapter 32 of IEEE 802.3 for the details. But be forewarned: The details are very messy.

The box at the top of Figure A.9 represents the conversion of 4 bits to two quinary symbols (An, Bn). The lower part of the figure shows two symbols being transmitted across the two pairs at the same time. The label BI_DA stands for "bidirectional data A," and BI_DB stands for "bidirectional data B." When pair (An, Bn) is received, it is mapped to 4 bits and is unscrambled.

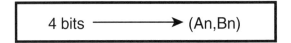

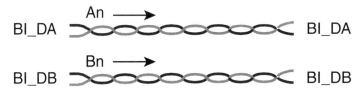

FIGURE A.9   *Encoding and transmitting quinary symbols.*

The rate across each pair is 25 million symbols per second, giving a total of 50 million symbols per second. Each pair of symbols maps to 4 bits, resulting in the 100Mbps data rate. The same number of symbols is sent in the reverse direction simultaneously.

1000BASE-X and Fibre Channel

1000BASE-X is a title that applies to three technologies: 1000BASE-SX, 1000BASE-LX, 1000BASE-CX. These technologies were based on existing fibre channel transmission standards. The 8B/10B encoding method introduced for fibre channel is used for 1000BASE-SX, 1000BASE-LX, and 1000BASE-CX.

As the name 8B/10B suggests, each byte is translated to a 10-bit pattern that has a good distribution of 1s and 0s. After translation, a very simple transmission method is used to send the 10-bit pattern. On optical fiber, a 1 is transmitted as a high optical power level, and a 0 is a low optical power level. High and low voltages are used on copper.

8B/10B Data Encoding

The designers of fibre channel and 1000BASE-X wanted a better balance of 0s and 1s than was obtained by the 4B/5B coding used for FDDI and 100BASE-X. At gigabit speed, maintaining bit clocking is a greater challenge than at 100Mbps. On the other hand, too many transitions produces a signal that has too high a frequency. This can heat up an optical fiber or create a magnetic disturbance around copper. The 8B/10 encoding that is used provides a sufficient number of 1s while keeping the average number of transitions down.

There are 256 8-bit patterns and 1024 10-bit patterns. This means that data code-groups can be chosen from a big pool of 10-bit patterns. To ensure that there is a good distribution of 1s and 0s on the medium, the 10-bit code-groups that have been selected contain the same—or almost the same—number of 1s and 0s. Namely, they contain one of these values:

- Five 1s and five 0s

- Four 1s and six 0s

- Six 1s and four 0s

It is desirable to avoid too many bunched-up 1s or 0s, so the following rules hold true:

- No data code-groups containing the strings 11111 or 00000 are used.

- Only four data code-groups containing the string 1111 are used.

- Only one data code-group contains the string 0000.

The beginning and end of each 10-bit code-group also was designed to avoid long strings of 0s and 1s being produced when two patterns occur in sequence. For example, if the patterns shown below were sent in sequence, there would be six consecutive 0s in the bit stream:

0110111**000 000**1110110

In fact, this will not happen. Joining two 10-bit code-groups never produces more than five consecutive 1s or five consecutive 0s.

The final problem to be solved is to be sure that over time, roughly the same number of 0s and 1s is sent across the medium. There is no way to predict exactly what data bytes will occur in a user's frames. Byte after byte of one data stream might map to patterns with four 1s, while another stream might map to a long string of patterns with six 1s.

The solution was to provide two different 10-bit code-groups to represent each byte.

- If one code-group has six 1s, the other has four.

- If one code-group has five ones, the other also has five.

The basic idea is that the code-group that is used to represent the current byte is chosen based on the distribution of 1s and 0s in the previous code-group. The goal is to balance out the number of 1s and 0s.

Table A.6 displays a few of the translations from bytes to code-groups. Note that in the table, each 10-bit code-group is written as a 6-bit subblock, a space, and a 4-bit subblock.

Note

The 8B/10 code was created by combining older 5B/6B and 3B/4B codes. The 6-bit subblock comes from the 5B/6B code. The 4-bit subblock comes from the 3B/4B code.

Suppose that the current byte is X'03 and has been translated to its code-group with six 1s:

    110001 1011

If X'05 followed, this would be balanced by choosing the code-group with four 1s:

    101001 0100

But suppose that X'04 now follows. Both of its code-groups contain five 1s. However, the prior code-group ended with 0100, which has a lot of 0s, so the best choice is the one that starts with some 1s:

    110101 0100

As you might have guessed, a set of rules enables a computer to decide which code-group should be selected to balance out the flow of 0s and 1s.

Relationship between the Code-Group Columns

At first glance, Table A.6 looks like gibberish, but there is a method to its madness. The first code-group for each byte appears in column 3, and the second code-group appears in column 4. The code-groups in column 4 are computed from the code-groups in column 3.

Each 10-bit code-group is written as a 6-bit subblock, followed by a 4-bit subblock. If a subblock is unbalanced, the corresponding subblock in the second code-group is formed by inverting each of its bits.

For example, the column 3 code-group for X'00 is 100111 0100. 100111 is unbalanced because it has four 1s and two 0s. When each 1 is inverted to 0 and each 0 to 1, you get 011000 as the first subblock of the second code-group. Similarly, 0100 has one 1 and three 0s, so the second subblock of the column 4 code-group ends in 1011.

Checking out another entry, the first code-group for X'0E is 011100 1011. The initial 6-bit subblock is balanced and, hence, will not be inverted. The 4-bit subblock is not balanced and must be inverted. The resulting second code-group is 011100 0100.

Exceptions to this rule exist for some subblocks with equal numbers of 0s and 1s. Because of the bunching of 1s and 0s, 6-bit sub-blocks 111000 and 000111, and 4-bit sub-blocks 1100 and 0011 are viewed as unbalanced and become inverted to one another.

TABLE A.6 SAMPLE 8B/10B MAPPINGS

Hex Value	Binary Byte	10-bit Code-Group Used When Current RD Is −	10-bit Code-Group Used When Current RD Is +
00	00000000	100111 0100	011000 1011
01	00000001	011101 0100	100010 1011
02	00000010	101101 0100	010010 1011
03	00000011	110001 1011	110001 0100
04	00000100	110101 0100	001010 1011
05	00000101	101001 1011	101001 0100
06	00000110	011001 1011	011001 0100
07	00000111	111000 1011	000111 0100
08	00001000	111001 0100	000110 1011

continues

TABLE A.6 CONTINUED

Hex Value	Binary Byte	10-bit Code-Group Used When Current RD Is –	10-bit Code-Group Used When Current RD Is +
09	00001001	100101 1011	100101 0100
0A	00001010	010101 1011	010101 0100
0B	00001011	110100 1011	110100 0100
0C	00001100	001101 1011	001101 0100
0D	00001101	101100 1011	101100 0100
0E	00001110	011100 1011	011100 0100
0F	00001111	010111 0100	101000 1011

Rules for Choosing an 8B/10B Code-Group

The current code-group always is rated as either negative or positive. More formally, it is said to have a *negative running disparity* (RD–) or a positive running disparity (RD+). After the current running disparity has been calculated, the code-group for the next byte is chosen from the RD– or RD+ column based on the result.

At powerup, a transmitter's running disparity is set to negative (–). Thus, the first code-group that is transmitted is chosen from the RD– column.

The running disparity of the current code-group is computed in a two-step process. The running disparity is computed at the end of the first subblock, and then again at the end of the second subblock. This final value is the one assigned to the code-group. The rules follow.

Running disparity at the end of a 6-bit sub-block is positive if one of the following is true:

- There are more 1s than 0s.

- The subblock is 000111.

- The subblock is not 000111, but it does have an equal number of 0s and 1s, and the previous code-group had positive running disparity.

Running disparity at the end of a 6-bit sub-block is negative if one of the following is true:

- There are more 0s than 1s.

- The subblock is 111000.

- The subblock is not 111000, but it does have an equal number of 0s and 1s, and the previous code-group had negative running disparity.

Running disparity at the end of a 4-bit sub-block is positive if one of the following is true:

- There are more 1s than 0s.

- The subblock is 0011.

- The subblock is not 0011, but it does have an equal number of 0s and 1s, and the prior 6-bit sub-block had positive running disparity.

Running disparity at the end of a 4-bit sub-block is negative if one of the following is true:

- There are more 0s than 1s.

- The subblock is 1100.

- The subblock is not 1100, but it does have an equal number of 0s and 1s, and the previous 6-bit sub-block had negative running disparity.

These rules put a lot of weight on what happens in the terminating 4-bit subblock. The running disparity of the entire code-group is positive if this subblock has more 1s or is 0011. The running disparity of the entire code-group is negative if this subblock has more 0s or is 1100. The only time the previous subblock (and possibly the previous code-group) matters is for the patterns 1010, 1001, 0101, and 0110.

8B/10B Data Code-Group Naming Convention

Each 8B/10B data code-group has been assigned a name that is derived (in a rather peculiar manner) from the binary representation of the original byte.

First, a byte is split into a 3-bit part and a 5-bit part. The name of the byte's data code-group is:

D(decimal value of 5-bit part).(decimal value of 3-bit part)

For example, to get the name of the code-group for X'24, write the binary for X'24 in two batches as:

001 00100

The code-group name is D4.1. Table A.7 contains more examples.

TABLE A.7 EXAMPLES OF 8B/10B DATA CODE-GROUP NAMES

Data Code-Group Name	Hex Value	Binary
D0.0	00	000 00000
D1.0	01	000 00001
D2.0	02	000 00010
D3.0	03	000 00011
D4.0	04	000 00100
D11.0	0B	000 01011
D12.0	0C	000 01100
D13.0	0D	000 01101
D14.0	0E	000 01110
D0.1	20	001 00000
D1.1	21	001 00001
D2.1	22	001 00010
D3.1	23	001 00011
D4.1	24	001 00100
D10.1	2A	001 01010
D11.1	2B	001 01011
D12.1	2C	001 01100
D13.1	2D	001 01101
D14.1	2E	001 01110

Special 8B/10B Code-Groups

Many 10-bit patterns do not represent data bytes. Some of these are used for special, nondata code-groups. Table A.8 displays these code-groups; their names are introduced by a K instead of a D.

TABLE A.8 SPECIAL 8B/10B CODE-GROUPS

Special Code-Group Name	Hex Value	Binary	10-bit Code-Group Used When Current RD Is −	10-bit Code-Group Used When Current RD Is +
K28.0	1C	000 11100	001111 0100	110000 1011
K28.1	3C	001 11100	001111 1001	110000 0110
K28.2	5C	010 11100	001111 0101	110000 1010
K28.3	7C	011 11100	001111 0011	110000 1100

Special Code-Group Name	Hex Value	Binary	10-bit Code-Group Used When Current RD Is −	10-bit Code-Group Used When Current RD Is +
K28.4	9C	100 11100	001111 0010	110000 1101
K28.5	BC	101 11100	001111 1010	110000 0101
K28.6	DC	110 11100	001111 0110	110000 1001
K28.7	FC	111 11100	001111 1000	110000 0111
K23.7	F7	111 10111	111010 1000	000101 0111
K27.7	FB	111 11011	110110 1000	001001 0111
K29.7	FD	111 11101	101110 1000	010001 0111
K30.7	FE	111 11110	011110 1000	100001 0111

Ordered Sets of 8B/10B Code-Groups

The special code-groups are used to form code sequences called *ordered sets*. Table A.9 displays the layouts of the ordered sets. Each is introduced by a special code-group and consists of one, two, or four code-groups.

- The /S/ and /T/ codes start and terminate a frame. The /R/ code represents extension bytes for half-duplex Gigabit Ethernet.

- The /V/ code signals a collision or other error.

- Idles are sent between frames. /I1/ is sent if the current running disparity is positive. It converts the running disparity to negative. When the RD is negative, a stream of I2s is sent.

At initialization, the partners send each other an alternating series of C1 and C2 ordered sets. These carry Auto-Negotiation parameters within 16-bit units. (See Chapter 11, "Auto-Negotiation," for information about Auto-Negotiation.)

The K28.5 code-group that introduces idle sequences and configuration ordered sets has this form:

(RD+) 0011111010   or   (RD−) 1100000101

These code-groups start with a special 7-bit string that is called a *comma*. The comma is defined as either of the following:

0011111   or   1100000

This string is found only in K28.5, K28.1, and K28.7. Because of the way that data code-groups have been designed, neither 7-bit comma string will ever occur as part of a 10B data stream. Also, K28.1 and K28.7 currently are unused. Hence, the only time a comma ever will appear is in a K28.5 code-group.

This is very useful. When a receiver locates a comma pattern, it has found the beginning of a K28.5 Auto-Negotiation or idle code-group. It now knows exactly where each of the succeeding code-groups begins. A receiver uses the comma to lock onto code-group boundaries during Auto-Negotiation and to resynchronize the boundaries when idles are sent.

TABLE A.9 ORDERED SETS OF 8B/10B CODE-GROUPS

Name	Purpose	Number of Code-Groups	Encoding
/C/	Auto-Negotiation		Alternating /C1/ and /C2/
/C1/	Configuration 1	4	/K28.5/D21.5/16-bit-config
/C2/	Configuration 2	4	/K28.5/D2.2/16-bit-config
/I/	IDLE		Correcting /I1/, preserving /I2/
/I1/	IDLE 1	2	/K28.5/D5.6/
/I2/	IDLE 2	2	/K28.5/D16.2/
Frame Encapsulation			
/R/	Carrier Extend	1	/K23.7/
/S/	Start of Packet	1	/K27.7/
/T/	End of Packet	1	/K29.7/
/V/	Error Propagation	1	/K30.7/

1000BASE-T

The design of 1000BASE-T borrowed several features from 100BASE-T2.

- A 1000BASE-T link physically operates in a full-duplex manner.

- After an autoconfiguration negotiation that establishes the properties of the link, steady streams of symbols flow across each wire pair in both directions.

- Idle symbols are sent between data transmissions.

- The start and end of each frame are marked by special delimiters.

1000BASE-T operates bidirectionally across four twisted pairs. A complex encoding and lots of extra electronic components have been introduced to accomplish full-duplex gigabit transmission.

Crosstalk can become a serious problem when signals are continuously being sent across a bundle containing four cables. One mechanism that helps is to scramble data before it is sent. Scrambling produces bit streams that do not generate very high-frequency signals on any of the four cables. A high frequency on one cable would produce electromagnetic radiation that would affect the other cables.

After scrambling, each byte is translated to four symbols. One symbol is transmitted across each of the four twisted pairs. Figure A.10 illustrates this procedure. The box at the top of Figure A.10 represents the conversion of an 8-bit byte to four symbols labeled (An, Bn, Cn, and Dn). The "n" represents symbol time period number n.

The lower part of the figure shows one symbol being transmitted across each of the pairs at the same time. When the four symbols (An, Bn, Cn, and Dn) are received, they are mapped to 8 bits and are unscrambled.

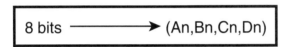

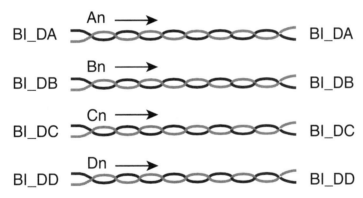

FIGURE A.10 *Transmitting the symbols that make up a byte.*

The "BI_D" prefix in the four labels at the left (BI_DA, BI_DB, BI_DC, and BI_DD) stands for "bi-directional data."

Outline of 1000BASE-T Encoding

After scrambling, bytes are encoded using a method called *8B1Q4*. The title indicates that each 8-bit pattern is translated to a code-group made up of four symbols. Each symbol can be one of the following:

[–2, –1, 0, +1, +2]

For example, a code-group combination such as (0, –1, +1, 0) or (–2, –1, +1, 0) can be used to represent a data byte. Each of the symbols [–2, –1, 0, +1, +2] is represented on the twisted-pair medium as a different voltage level.

> **Note**
>
> The five voltage levels are –1V, –.5V, 0V, .5V, and 1V.

The physical transmission method is called *4-dimensional 5-level pulse amplitude modulation (4D-PAM5)*. The 4D part refers to the fact that four symbols are sent at the same time. The PAM5 part means that there are five voltage levels.

With five choices for each symbol, 625 different four-symbol code-group combinations can be produced. This provides a lot of flexibility in the way that the 256 8-bit data bytes can be represented.

Lots of extra code-groups exist, and some of these are used to represent idles, start-of-stream delimiters (SSDs) at the beginning of a frame, end-of-stream delimiters (ESDs) after a frame, error indications, and (for short frames and half-duplex transmission) carrier extension bytes.

Figure A.11 illustrates the format of a stream of codes that is sent across the four pairs. Idle symbols are sent between frames. A pair of special SSD codes replaces the first two preamble bytes. The remainder of the preamble and the MAC frame are translated into data codes. If there is no frame extension, two CSReset code-groups follow. Two ESD code-groups terminate the frame transmission.

> **Note**
>
> If half-duplex transmission was supported and a frame included an extension, the CSReset code-groups would not be present. A series of CSExtend code-groups would represent the frame extension bytes. These would be followed by two ESD code-groups.

The translation of a data byte into (An, Bn, Cn, Dn) symbols requires several steps:

- Perform a calculation whose inputs are a data byte and a set of scrambling bits to produce a 9-bit word. The method that is used is complex, and the 9-bit word depends not only on the value of the source byte, but also on where that byte appears in the data stream.

- Perform a table lookup that maps the 9-bit word to a four-symbol code-group.

- Apply a formula that adjusts the sign of some of the symbols to balance out positive (+) and negative (–) transmissions on each cable.

The operations on the data must be reversed at the receiving end.

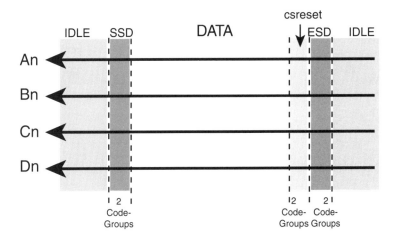

FIGURE A.11 *1000BASE-T transmission.*

Note

The code-groups that are used have been chosen carefully so that they are well separated from each other. Because of the spread between code-groups and the encoding rules that are used, a receiver actually is able to correct some invalid code-groups on arrival and replacing them with the original valid ones. This is called forward error correction.

Table A.10 displays a few of the mappings of 9-bit quantities to four-symbol groups. However, the values shown are not the final symbols that will be transmitted; they are the symbols just before the final sign correction is applied.

The full set of mappings from 9-bit quantities to four-symbol groups can be found in Tables 40-1 and 40-2 of IEEE Standard 802.3ad.

Table A.11 contains code-groups that are used for special functions. A frame is introduced by SSD1 SSD2. It is terminated by ESD1, followed by one of the ESD2 codes. Several patterns represent idles, CSReset ESD2, CSExtend, and a transmit error. The choice depends on the current state of the translation algorithm.

TABLE A.10 SAMPLE 1000BASE-T ENCODINGS

Scrambled 9-bit Word	An, Bn, Cn, Dn Prior to Final Sign Adjustment
000000000	0, 0, 0, 0
000000001	–2, 0, 0, 0
000000010	0, –2, 0, 0
000000011	–2, –2, 0, 0
010000000	0, 0, +1, +1
010000001	–2, 0, +1, +1
010000010	0, –2, +1, +1
010000011	–2, –2, +1, +1

TABLE A.11 SPECIAL CODE-GROUPS PRIOR TO FINAL SIGN ADJUSTMENT

Special Function	Code-Groups
SSD1	(+2, +2, +2, +2)
SSD2	(+2, +2, +2, –2)
Idle	Any pattern of 0s and –2s. For example: (0, 0, 0, 0) (–2, 0, 0, 0) (0, –2, 0, 0) (–2, 0, –2, 0) (–2, 0, –2, –2) (–2, –2, –2, –2)
CSReset (Even)	(+2, –2, –2, +2) (+2, +2, –1, –1) (–1, +2, +2, –1) (–1, +2, –1, +2)
CSReset (Odd)	(+2, –2, +2, –1) (+2, –2, –1, +2) (–1, –2, +2, +2) (+2, –1, –2, +2)
ESD1	(+2, +2, +2, +2)
ESD2	(+2, +2, +2, –2) (+2, +2, –2, +2) (+2, –2, +2, +2) (–2, +2, +2, +2)
CSExtend (Even)	(+2, 0, 0, +2) (+2, +2, +1, +1) (+1, +2, +2, +1) (+1, +2, +1, +2)
CSExtend (Odd)	(+2, 0, +2, +1) (+2, 0, +1, +2) (+1, 0, +2, +2) (+2, +1, 0, +2)
CSExtend Error (Even)	(–2, +2, +2, –2) (–1, –1, +2, +2) (+2, –1, –1, +2) (+2, –1, +2, –1)
CSExtend Error (Odd)	(+2, +2, –2, –1) (–2, +2, –1, +2) (–1, +2, +2, –2) (+2, –1, +2, –2)
Transmit Error	(+2, +2, 0, +1) (0, +2, +1, +2) (+1, +2, +2, 0) (+2, +1, +2, 0)

This exposition has only skimmed the surface of the 1000BASE-T encoding process, which is extremely complex. A complete description would constitute a Master's thesis in engineering!

Token Ring

Differential Manchester encoding is used for classical 4Mbps and 16Mbps Token Rings. It is described in the subsection that follows.

The encoding used for 100Mbps Token Ring is identical to that used for 100BASE-X Ethernet. This helped Token Ring vendors roll out products quickly and kept costs down through reuse of existing components.

Differential Manchester Encoding

Differential Manchester encoding is a variation on the Manchester encoding used for 10Mbps Ethernet LANs. It is used for 4Mbps and 16Mbps Token Ring LANs.

Bits are represented using transitions between high and low voltages for twisted-pair cabling, or high and low light levels for optical fiber.

- For a 0, there are transitions at both the beginning and the middle of the bit.

- For a 1, there is a transition only at the middle of the bit.

What's "different" about Differential Manchester encoding is that the coding used for a symbol depends on the previous symbol. Figure A.12 shows the two ways that the string 1 0 1 1 0 0 0 1 can be encoded. For the upper encoding, the previous symbol ended at a high level. For the lower encoding, the previous symbol ended at a low level.

Note the single transition located in the middle of each 1-bit (either high-to-low or low-to-high) and the two transitions for each 0-bit (one at the start and one in the middle).

Two additional symbols labeled J and K are used in Token Ring transmissions. The J and K symbols appear only within the starting delimiter at the beginning of a frame and the ending delimiter at the end of a frame. Figure A.13 displays the starting and ending delimiter bytes, and shows how the J and K symbols are encoded within them.

- The J symbol has no transitions.

- The K symbol has one transition at the beginning of the bit.

As was the case for the 0s and 1s, the coding of a J or K depends on the previous symbol.

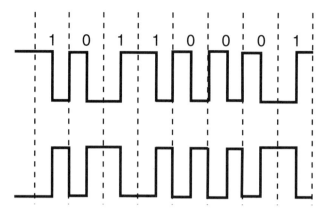

FIGURE A.12 *Differential Manchester encoding of 0s and 1s.*

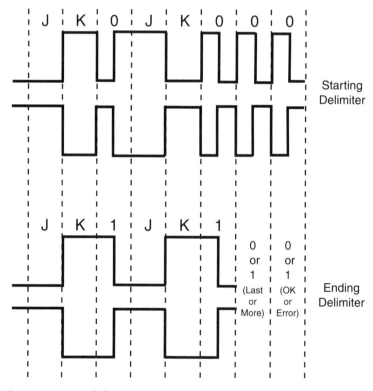

FIGURE A.13 *Delimiters containing J and K symbols.*

The starting delimiter pattern enables a receiver to lock onto byte and bit boundaries, synchronize timing, and receive the rest of the frame accurately.

As Figure A.13 shows, the value of the last 2 bits can vary. In fact, each of these bits reports some important information. They are called the *intermediate frame bit* and the *error-detected bit*.

- The intermediate frame bit is set to 1 to indicate that this is a multiple-frame transmission and that at least one more frame follows. It is set to 0 if this is an individual frame or if it is the last one in a multiple-frame transmission.

- The error-detected bit is set to 1 if any type of error has been found (such as an incorrect frame check sequence).

100Mbps Dedicated Token Ring

100Mbps High Speed Token Ring (HSTR) can operate in a full-duplex switched environment. The data encoding and bit transmission methods were borrowed from CDDI and FDDI, just as was the case for 100BASE-X Ethernet. That is, each 4-bit nibble is translated to a 5-bit code-group. NRZI transmission then is used for optical fiber and MLT-3 for copper.

The shielded twisted-pair wire traditionally used for Token Ring LANs is supported in addition to unshielded twisted-pair and fiber optic media.

Summary Points

- Manchester encoding is used for 10BASE5, 10BASE2, 10BASE-T, FOIRL, 10BASE-FL, and 10BASE-FB.

- For Manchester encoding, there is a voltage (or optical power) transition in the middle of each bit. At high speeds, this would produce a high-frequency signal.

- For 100BASE-FX Ethernet and FDDI, each nibble is translated to a 5-bit code-group that has a sufficient number of 1-bits. Non return to zero inverted (NRZI) transmission is used. This means that 1-bits are transmitted by alternating between high and low optical power levels, but no power change occurs for a 0-bit.

- For 100BASE-TX Ethernet and CDDI, each nibble is translated to a 5-bit code-group that contains at least two 1-bits. Each 1-bit is encoded as a step between three voltage levels. No voltage change occurs for a 0-bit.

- For 100BASE-T4 Ethernet, each byte is mapped to a code-group made up of six symbols chosen from [–, 0, +]. Bytes are transmitted in a staggered order across three twisted pairs.

- For 1000BASE-SX, 1000BASE-LX, and 1000BASE-CX Ethernet and fibre channel, each byte is translated to a 10-bit code-group that has a balanced distribution of 1s and 0s. A 1-bit is transmitted as a higher optical power or higher voltage. A 0-bit is transmitted as a low optical power or low voltage.

- For 1000BASE-T Ethernet, each byte is translated to four symbols chosen from [–2, –1, 0, +1, +2].

- Differential Manchester encoding is used for 4Mbps or 16Mbps Token Ring. For a 0, there are transitions at both the beginning and the middle of the bit. For a 1, there is a transition only at the middle of the bit.

- 100Mbps Token Ring on twisted-pair cabling or optical fiber uses the same transmission techniques as 100BASE-TX and 100BASE-FX.

- Many of the Ethernet technologies support full-duplex Ethernet. These include 10BASE-T, 10BASE-FL, 100-BASE-FX, 100BASE-TX, 100BASE-T2 (not implemented), 1000BASE-SX, 1000BASE-LX, 1000BASE-CX, and 1000BASE-T.

References

Most of the encodings described in this appendix are defined in: IEEE Standard 802.3, 1998 Edition, "Carrier Sense Multiple Access with Collision Detection (CSMA/CD) Access Method and Physical Layer Specifications." The chapters in the standard that describe specific encodings are the following:

- Chapter 9 describes FOIRL.

- Chapter 14 describes 10BASE-T.

- Chapters 15, 17, and 18 describe 10BASE-F.

- Chapters 24–26 describe 100BASE-X.

- Chapters 36, 38, and 39 describe 1000BASE-X.

- The 4B/5B translations are found in Table 24-1 of 802.3.

- The 8B/6T translations are in Annex 23A of 802.3.

The encoding for 1000BASE-T is described in: IEEE Standard 802.3ab. "Physical Layer Parameters and Specifications for 1000Mbps Operation Over 4-Pair of Category 5 Balanced Copper Cabling, Type 1000BASE-T," 1999.

This document contains Chapter 40 of the 802.3 standard. The 9-bit to 4-symbol mappings are found in Tables 40-1 and 40-2.

FDDI is described in the following:

- ANSI X3.139. "Information Systems—Fiber Distributed Data Interface (FDDI)—Token Ring Media Access Control (MAC)," Original in 1987; last revision in 1997.

- ANSI X3.148. "Information Systems—Fiber Distributed Data Interface (FDDI)—Token Ring Physical Layer Protocol (PHY)," Original in 1988; last revision in 1994.

- ANSI X3.166. "Fiber Distributed Data Interface (FDDI) Physical Layer Medium Dependent (PMD)," Original in 1989; last revision in 1995.

The Copper Distributed Data Interface (CDDI) is described in:

ANSI X3.263. "Fibre Distributed Data Interface (FDDI)—Token Ring Twisted Pair Physical Layer Medium Dependent (TP-PMD)," 1995.

Several useful documents can be found at
`http://www.iol.unh.edu/training/ index.html`

For example:

- Frain, John. "1000BASE-X Physical Coding Sublayer (PCS) and Physical Medium Attachment (PMA) Tutorial," 1998.

- Noseworthy, Bob. "1000BASE-T PCS Functional Basics and Overview," 1998.

Differential Manchester encoding is described in Chapter 5 of:

ANSI/IEEE Standard 802.5. "Token Ring Access Method and Physical Layer Specifications," 1998.

APPENDIX **B**

Tables

This appendix contains a miscellaneous set of tables that augment the tables in Appendix A, "Physical-Layer Encodings for Ethernet, Fibre Channel, FDDI, and Token Ring." They include

- Four-bit binary "nibbles" and their decimal and hexadecimal equivalents

- The full set of 8B/6T byte translations used for 100BASE-T4 data transmission

- The full set of 8B/10B byte translations used for 1000BASE-X and fibre channel data transmission

- Fibre channel ordered sets

Binary, Decimal, and Hexadecimal Characters

The normal mathematical order for a string of binary bits is to place the most significant bit on the far-left end of the string. (This sometimes is called *big-endian* order.)

A string of 8 binary bits is converted to a pair of hexadecimal characters by breaking the byte into two 4-bit groups (called *nibbles*) and converting each to a hexadecimal symbol in the range 0-F. For example:

Binary 1 1 0 0 = 8(1) + 4(1) + 2(0) + 1(0) = 12 = X'C

Binary 0 0 1 0 = 8(0) + 4(0) + 2(1) + 1(0) = 2 = X'2

Hence:

Binary 1 1 0 0 0 0 1 0 = X'C2

Table B.1 displays the mapping between sets of 4 binary bits, their decimal value, and their hexadecimal representation.

TABLE B.2 BINARY, DECIMAL, AND HEXADECIMAL REPRESENTATIONS

Binary	Decimal	Hexadecimal
0 0 0 0	0	0
0 0 0 1	1	1
0 0 1 0	2	2
0 0 1 1	3	3
0 1 0 0	4	4
0 1 0 1	5	5
0 1 1 0	6	6
0 1 1 1	7	7
1 0 0 0	8	8
1 0 0 1	9	9
1 0 1 0	10	A
1 0 1 1	11	B
1 1 0 0	12	C
1 1 0 1	13	D
1 1 1 0	14	E
1 1 1 1	15	F

8B/6T Tables

Table B.2 presents the full set of 8B/6T translations between bytes and ternary symbols used for 100BASE-T4 data transmission.

TABLE B.2 100BASE-T4 8B/6T DATA BYTE TRANSLATION TABLE

Hex	6T Code-Group	Hex	6T Code-Group	Hex	6T Code-Group	Hex	6T Code-Group
00	+ − 0 0 + −	20	0 0 − + + −	40	+ 0 + 0 0 −	60	0 − 0 + + 0
01	0 + − + − 0	21	− − + 0 0 +	41	+ + 0 0 − 0	61	0 0 − + 0 +
02	+ − 0 + − 0	22	+ + − 0 + −	42	+ 0 + 0 − 0	62	0 − 0 + 0 +
03	− 0 + + − 0	23	+ + − 0 − +	43	0 + + 0 − 0	63	− 0 0 + 0 +
04	− 0 + 0 + −	24	0 0 + 0 − +	44	0 + + 0 0 −	64	− 0 0 + + 0

Hex	6T Code-Group	Hex	6T Code-Group	Hex	6T Code-Group	Hex	6T Code-Group
05	0 + − − 0 +	25	0 0 + 0 + −	45	+ + 0 − 0 0	65	0 0 − 0 + +
06	+ − 0 − 0 +	26	0 0 − 0 0 +	46	+ 0 + − 0 0	66	0 − 0 0 + +
07	− 0 + − 0 +	27	− − + + + −	47	0 + + − 0 0	67	− 0 0 0 + +
08	− + 0 0 + −	28	− 0 − + + 0	48	0 0 0 + 0 0	68	− + − + + 0
09	0 − + + − 0	29	− − 0 + 0 +	49	0 0 0 − + +	69	− − + + 0 +
0A	− + 0 + − 0	2A	− 0 − + 0 +	4A	0 0 0 + − +	6A	− + − + 0 +
0B	+ 0 − + − 0	2B	0 − − + 0 +	4B	0 0 0 + + −	6B	+ − − + 0 +
0C	+ 0 − 0 + −	2C	0 − − + + 0	4C	0 0 0 − + 0	6C	+ − − + + 0
0D	0 − + − 0 +	2D	− − 0 0 + +	4D	0 0 0 − 0 +	6D	− − + 0 + +
0E	− + 0 − 0 +	2E	− 0 − 0 + +	4E	0 0 0 + − 0	6E	− + − 0 + +
0F	+ 0 − − 0 +	2F	0 − − 0 + +	4F	0 0 0 + 0 −	6F	+ − − 0 + +
10	+ 0 + − − 0	30	+ − 0 0 − +	50	+ 0 + − − +	70	− + + 0 0 0
11	+ + 0 − 0 −	31	0 + − − + 0	51	+ + 0 − + −	71	+ − + 0 0 0
12	+ 0 + − 0 −	32	+ − 0 − + 0	52	+ 0 + − + −	72	+ + − 0 0 0
13	0 + + − 0 −	33	− 0 + − + 0	53	0 + + − + −	73	0 0 + 0 0 0
14	0 + + − − 0	34	− 0 + 0 − +	54	0 + + − − +	74	− 0 + 0 0 0
15	+ + 0 0 − −	35	0 + − + 0 −	55	+ + 0 + − −	75	0 − + 0 0 0
16	+ 0 + 0 − −	36	+ − 0 + 0 −	56	+ 0 + + − −	76	+ 0 − 0 0 0
17	0 + + 0 − −	37	− 0 + + 0 −	57	0 + + + − −	77	0 + − 0 0 0
18	0 + − 0 + −	38	− + 0 0 − +	58	+ + + 0 − −	78	0 − − + + +
19	0 + − 0 − +	39	0 − + − + 0	59	+ + + − 0 −	79	− 0 − + + +
1A	0 + − + + −	3A	− + 0 − 0 +	5A	+ + + − − 0	7A	− − 0 + + +
1B	0 + − 0 0 +	3B	+ 0 − − + 0	5B	+ + 0 − − 0	7B	− − 0 + + 0
1C	0 − + 0 0 +	3C	+ 0 − 0 − +	5C	+ + 0 − − +	7C	+ + − 0 0 −
1D	0 − + + + −	3D	0 − + + 0 −	5D	+ + 0 0 0 −	7D	0 0 + 0 0 −
1E	0 − + 0 − +	3E	− + 0 + 0 −	5E	− − + + + 0	7E	+ + − − − +
1F	0 − + 0 + −	3F	+ 0 − + 0 −	5F	0 0 − + + 0	7F	0 0 + − − +
80	+ − + 0 0 −	A0	0 − 0 + + −	C0	+ − + 0 + −	E0	+ − 0 + + −
81	+ + − 0 − 0	A1	0 0 − + − +	C1	+ + − + − 0	E1	0 + − + − +
82	+ − + 0 − 0	A2	0 − 0 + − +	C2	+ − + + − 0	E2	+ − 0 + − +
83	− + + 0 − 0	A3	− 0 0 + − +	C3	− + + + − 0	E3	− 0 + + − +
84	− + + 0 0 −	A4	− 0 0 + + −	C4	− + 0 + −	E4	− 0 + + + −
85	+ + − − 0 0	A5	0 0 − − + +	C5	+ + − − 0 +	E5	0 + − − + +
86	+ − + − 0 0	A6	0 − 0 − + +	C6	+ − + − 0 +	E6	+ − 0 − + +

continues

TABLE B.2 CONTINUED

Hex	6T Code-Group	Hex	6T Code-Group	Hex	6T Code-Group	Hex	6T Code-Group
87	− + + − 0 0	A7	− 0 0 − + +	C7	− + + − 0 +	E7	− 0 + − + +
88	0 + 0 0 0 −	A8	− + − + + −	C8	0 + 0 0 + −	E8	− + 0 + + −
89	0 0 + 0 − 0	A9	− − + + − +	C9	0 0 + + − 0	E9	0 − + + − +
8A	0 + 0 0 − 0	AA	− + − + − +	CA	0 + 0 + − 0	EA	− + 0 + − +
8B	+ 0 0 0 − 0	AB	+ − − + − +	CB	+ 0 0 + − 0	EB	+ 0 − + − +
8C	+ 0 0 0 0 −	AC	+ − − + + −	CC	+ 0 0 0 + −	EC	+ 0 − + + −
8D	0 0 + − 0 0	AD	− − + − + +	CD	0 0 + − 0 +	ED	0 − + − + +
8E	0 + 0 − 0 0	AE	− + − − + +	CE	0 + 0 − 0 +	EE	− + 0 − + +
8F	+ 0 0 − 0 0	AF	+ − − − + +	CF	+ 0 0 − 0 +	EF	+ 0 − − + +
90	+ − + − − +	B0	0 − 0 0 0 +	D0	+ − + 0 − +	F0	+ − 0 0 0 +
91	+ + − − + −	B1	0 0 − 0 + 0	D1	+ + − − + 0	F1	0 + − 0 + 0
92	+ − + − + −	B2	0 − 0 0 + 0	D2	+ − + − + 0	F2	+ − 0 0 + 0
93	− + + − + −	B3	− 0 0 0 + 0	D3	− + + − + 0	F3	− 0 + 0 + 0
94	− + + − − +	B4	− 0 0 0 0 +	D4	− + + 0 − +	F4	− 0 + 0 0 +
95	+ + − + − −	B5	0 0 − + 0 0	D5	+ + − + 0 −	F5	0 + − + 0 0
96	+ − + + − −	B6	0 − 0 + 0 0	D6	+ − + + 0 −	F6	+ − 0 + 0 0
97	− + + + − −	B7	− 0 0 + 0 0	D7	− + + + 0 −	F7	− 0 + + 0 0
98	0 + 0 − − +	B8	− + − 0 0 +	D8	0 + 0 0 − +	F8	− + 0 0 0 +
99	0 0 + − + −	B9	− − + 0 + 0	D9	0 0 + − + 0	F9	0 − + 0 + 0
9A	0 + 0 − + −	BA	− + − 0 + 0	DA	0 + 0 − + 0	FA	− + 0 0 + 0
9B	+ 0 0 − + −	BB	+ − − 0 + 0	DB	+ 0 0 − + 0	FB	+ 0 − 0 + 0
9C	+ 0 0 − − +	BC	+ − − 0 0 +	DC	+ 0 0 0 − +	FC	+ 0 − 0 0 +
9D	0 0 + + − −	BD	− − + + 0 0	DD	0 0 + + 0 −	FD	0 − + + 0 0
9E	0 + 0 + − −	BE	− + − + 0 0	DE	0 + 0 + 0 −	FE	− + 0 + 0 0
9F	+ 0 0 + − −	BF	+ − − + 0 0	DF	+ 0 0 + 0 −	FF	+ 0 − + 0 0

8B/10B Translation Table

Table B.3 displays the 8B/10B (8-bit to 10-bit) translations between data bytes and 10-bit code-groups that are used for 1000BASE-SX, 1000BASE-LX, 1000BASE-CX, and fibre channel transmission.

Table B.3 uses conventions that were used in the 802.3 standards:

- The binary form of each 8-bit data byte is written with the most significant bit at the left.

- Each binary 10-bit code-group is written with the least significant bit at the left.

- Each 10-bit code-group is written as a 6-bit subblock followed by a 4-bit subblock.

The name assigned to a data code-group is based on the two parts of the binary expression and is

D(decimal value of 5-bit part).(decimal value of 3-bit part)

There are two ways to translate each byte, depending on whether the current running disparity (RD) is negative or positive. Appendix A explains how the running disparity is calculated.

TABLE **B.3** 8B/10B CODE-GROUPS

Data Code-Group Name	Hex Value	Binary	Code-Group Used When Current RD Is −	Code-Group Used When Current RD Is +
D0.0	00	000 00000	100111 0100	011000 1011
D1.0	01	000 00001	011101 0100	100010 1011
D2.0	02	000 00010	101101 0100	010010 1011
D3.0	03	000 00011	110001 1011	110001 0100
D4.0	04	000 00100	110101 0100	001010 1011
D5.0	05	000 00101	101001 1011	101001 0100
D6.0	06	000 00110	011001 1011	011001 0100
D7.0	07	000 00111	111000 1011	000111 0100
D8.0	08	000 01000	111001 0100	000110 1011
D9.0	09	000 01001	100101 1011	100101 0100
D10.0	0A	000 01010	010101 1011	010101 0100
D11.0	0B	000 01011	110100 1011	110100 0100
D12.0	0C	000 01100	001101 1011	001101 0100
D13.0	0D	000 01101	101100 1011	101100 0100
D14.0	0E	000 01110	011100 1011	011100 0100
D15.0	0F	000 01111	010111 0100	101000 1011
D16.0	10	000 10000	011011 0100	100100 1011

continues

TABLE B.3 CONTINUED

Data Code-Group Name	Hex Value	Binary	Code-Group Used When Current RD Is –	Code-Group Used When Current RD Is +
D17.0	11	000 10001	100011 1011	100011 0100
D18.0	12	000 10010	010011 1011	010011 0100
D19.0	13	000 10011	110010 1011	110010 0100
D20.0	14	000 10100	001011 1011	001011 0100
D21.0	15	000 10101	101010 1011	101010 0100
D22.0	16	000 10110	011010 1011	011010 0100
D23.0	17	000 10111	111010 0100	000101 1011
D24.0	18	000 11000	110011 0100	001100 1011
D25.0	19	000 11001	100110 1011	100110 0100
D26.0	1A	000 11010	010110 1011	010110 0100
D27.0	1B	000 11011	110110 0100	001001 1011
D28.0	1C	000 11100	001110 1011	001110 0100
D29.0	1D	000 11101	101110 0100	010001 1011
D30.0	1E	000 11110	011110 0100	100001 1011
D31.0	1F	000 11111	101011 0100	010100 1011
D0.1	20	001 00000	100111 1001	011000 1001
D1.1	21	001 00001	011101 1001	100010 1001
D2.1	22	001 00010	101101 1001	010010 1001
D3.1	23	001 00011	110001 1001	110001 1001
D4.1	24	001 00100	110101 1001	001010 1001
D5.1	25	001 00101	101001 1001	101001 1001
D6.1	26	001 00110	011001 1001	011001 1001
D7.1	27	001 00111	111000 1001	000111 1001
D8.1	28	001 01000	111001 1001	000110 1001
D9.1	29	001 01001	100101 1001	100101 1001
D10.1	2A	001 01010	010101 1001	010101 1001
D11.1	2B	001 01011	110100 1001	110100 1001
D12.1	2C	001 01100	001101 1001	001101 1001
D13.1	2D	001 01101	101100 1001	101100 1001
D14.1	2E	001 01110	011100 1001	011100 1001
D15.1	2F	001 01111	010111 1001	101000 1001
D16.1	30	001 10000	011011 1001	100100 1001
D17.1	31	001 10001	100011 1001	100011 1001

Data Code-Group Name	Hex Value	Binary	Code-Group Used When Current RD Is −	Code-Group Used When Current RD Is +
D18.1	32	001 10010	010011 1001	010011 1001
D19.1	33	001 10011	110010 1001	110010 1001
D20.1	34	001 10100	001011 1001	001011 1001
D21.1	35	001 10101	101010 1001	101010 1001
D22.1	36	001 10110	011010 1001	011010 1001
D23.1	37	001 10111	111010 1001	000101 1001
D24.1	38	001 11000	110011 1001	001100 1001
D25.1	39	001 11001	100110 1001	100110 1001
D26.1	3A	001 11010	010110 1001	010110 1001
D27.1	3B	001 11011	110110 1001	001001 1001
D28.1	3C	001 11100	001110 1001	001110 1001
D29.1	3D	001 11101	101110 1001	010001 1001
D30.1	3E	001 11110	011110 1001	100001 1001
D31.1	3F	001 11111	101011 1001	010100 1001
D0.2	40	010 00000	100111 0101	011000 0101
D1.2	41	010 00001	011101 0101	100010 0101
D2.2	42	010 00010	101101 0101	010010 0101
D3.2	43	010 00011	110001 0101	110001 0101
D4.2	44	010 00100	110101 0101	001010 0101
D5.2	45	010 00101	101001 0101	101001 0101
D6.2	46	010 00110	011001 0101	011001 0101
D7.2	47	010 00111	111000 0101	000111 0101
D8.2	48	010 01000	111001 0101	000110 0101
D9.2	49	010 01001	100101 0101	100101 0101
D10.2	4A	010 01010	010101 0101	010101 0101
D11.2	4B	010 01011	110100 0101	110100 0101
D12.2	4C	010 01100	001101 0101	001101 0101
D13.2	4D	010 01101	101100 0101	101100 0101
D14.2	4E	010 01110	011100 0101	011100 0101
D15.2	4F	010 01111	010111 0101	101000 0101
D16.2	50	010 10000	011011 0101	100100 0101
D17.2	51	010 10001	100011 0101	100011 0101
D18.2	52	010 10010	010011 0101	010011 0101

continues

TABLE B.3 CONTINUED

Data Code-Group Name	Hex Value	Binary	Code-Group Used When Current RD Is −	Code-Group Used When Current RD Is +
D19.2	53	010 10011	110010 0101	110010 0101
D20.2	54	010 10100	001011 0101	001011 0101
D21.2	55	010 10101	101010 0101	101010 0101
D22.2	56	010 10110	011010 0101	011010 0101
D23.2	57	010 10111	111010 0101	000101 0101
D24.2	58	010 11000	110011 0101	001100 0101
D25.2	59	010 11001	100110 0101	100110 0101
D26.2	5A	010 11010	010110 0101	010110 0101
D27.2	5B	010 11011	110110 0101	001001 0101
D28.2	5C	010 11100	001110 0101	001110 0101
D29.2	5D	010 11101	101110 0101	010001 0101
D30.2	5E	010 11110	011110 0101	100001 0101
D31.2	5F	010 11111	101011 0101	010100 0101
D0.3	60	011 00000	100111 0011	011000 1100
D1.3	61	011 00001	011101 0011	100010 1100
D2.3	62	011 00010	101101 0011	010010 1100
D3.3	63	011 00011	110001 1100	110001 0011
D4.3	64	011 00100	110101 0011	001010 1100
D5.3	65	011 00101	101001 1100	101001 0011
D6.3	66	011 00110	011001 1100	011001 0011
D7.3	67	011 00111	111000 1100	000111 0011
D8.3	68	011 01000	111001 0011	000110 1100
D9.3	69	011 01001	100101 1100	100101 0011
D10.3	6A	011 01010	010101 1100	010101 0011
D11.3	6B	011 01011	110100 1100	110100 0011
D12.3	6C	011 01100	001101 1100	001101 0011
D13.3	6D	011 01101	101100 1100	101100 0011
D14.3	6E	011 01110	011100 1100	011100 0011
D15.3	6F	011 01111	010111 0011	101000 1100
D16.3	70	011 10000	011011 0011	100100 1100
D17.3	71	011 10001	100011 1100	100011 0011
D18.3	72	011 10010	010011 1100	010011 0011
D19.3	73	011 10011	110010 1100	110010 0011

Data Code-Group Name	Hex Value	Binary	Code-Group Used When Current RD Is –	Code-Group Used When Current RD Is +
D20.3	74	011 10100	001011 1100	001011 0011
D21.3	75	011 10101	101010 1100	101010 0011
D22.3	76	011 10110	011010 1100	011010 0011
D23.3	77	011 10111	111010 0011	000101 1100
D24.3	78	011 11000	110011 0011	001100 1100
D25.3	79	011 11001	100110 1100	100110 0011
D26.3	7A	011 11010	010110 1100	010110 0011
D27.3	7B	011 11011	110110 0011	001001 1100
D28.3	7C	011 11100	001110 1100	001110 0011
D29.3	7D	011 11101	101110 0011	010001 1100
D30.3	7E	011 11110	011110 0011	100001 1100
D31.3	7F	011 11111	101011 0011	010100 1100
D0.4	80	100 00000	100111 0010	011000 1101
D1.4	81	100 00001	011101 0010	100010 1101
D2.4	82	100 00010	101101 0010	010010 1101
D3.4	83	100 00011	110001 1101	110001 0010
D4.4	84	100 00100	110101 0010	001010 1101
D5.4	85	100 00101	101001 1101	101001 0010
D6.4	86	100 00110	011001 1101	011001 0010
D7.4	87	100 00111	111000 1101	000111 0010
D8.4	88	100 01000	111001 0010	000110 1101
D9.4	89	100 01001	100101 1101	100101 0010
D10.4	8A	100 01010	010101 1101	010101 0010
D11.4	8B	100 01011	110100 1101	110100 0010
D12.4	8C	100 01100	001101 1101	001101 0010
D13.4	8D	100 01101	101100 1101	101100 0010
D14.4	8E	100 01110	011100 1101	011100 0010
D15.4	8F	100 01111	010111 0010	101000 1101
D16.4	90	100 10000	011011 0010	100100 1101
D17.4	91	100 10001	100011 1101	100011 0010
D18.4	92	100 10010	010011 1101	010011 0010
D19.4	93	100 10011	110010 1101	110010 0010
D20.4	94	100 10100	001011 1101	001011 0010

continues

TABLE B.3 CONTINUED

Data Code-Group Name	Hex Value	Binary	Code-Group Used When Current RD Is –	Code-Group Used When Current RD Is +
D21.4	95	100 10101	101010 1101	101010 0010
D22.4	96	100 10110	011010 1101	011010 0010
D23.4	97	100 10111	111010 0010	000101 1101
D24.4	98	100 11000	110011 0010	001100 1101
D25.4	99	100 11001	100110 1101	100110 0010
D26.4	9A	100 11010	010110 1101	010110 0010
D27.4	9B	100 11011	110110 0010	001001 1101
D28.4	9C	100 11100	001110 1101	001110 0010
D29.4	9D	100 11101	101110 0010	010001 1101
D30.4	9E	100 11110	011110 0010	100001 1101
D31.4	9F	100 11111	101011 0010	010100 1101
D0.5	A0	101 00000	100111 1010	011000 1010
D1.5	A1	101 00001	011101 1010	100010 1010
D2.5	A2	101 00010	101101 1010	010010 1010
D3.5	A3	101 00011	110001 1010	110001 1010
D4.5	A4	101 00100	110101 1010	001010 1010
D5.5	A5	101 00101	101001 1010	101001 1010
D6.5	A6	101 00110	011001 1010	011001 1010
D7.5	A7	101 00111	111000 1010	000111 1010
D8.5	A8	101 01000	111001 1010	000110 1010
D9.5	A9	101 01001	100101 1010	100101 1010
D10.5	AA	101 01010	010101 1010	010101 1010
D11.5	AB	101 01011	110100 1010	110100 1010
D12.5	AC	101 01100	001101 1010	001101 1010
D13.5	AD	101 01101	101100 1010	101100 1010
D14.5	AE	101 01110	011100 1010	011100 1010
D15.5	AF	101 01111	010111 1010	101000 1010
D16.5	B0	101 10000	011011 1010	100100 1010
D17.5	B1	101 10001	100011 1010	100011 1010
D18.5	B2	101 10010	010011 1010	010011 1010
D19.5	B3	101 10011	110010 1010	110010 1010
D20.5	B4	101 10100	001011 1010	001011 1010
D21.5	B5	101 10101	101010 1010	101010 1010

Data Code- Group Name	Hex Value	Binary	Code-Group Used When Current RD Is −	Code-Group Used When Current RD Is +
D22.5	B6	101 10110	011010 1010	011010 1010
D23.5	B7	101 10111	111010 1010	000101 1010
D24.5	B8	101 11000	110011 1010	001100 1010
D25.5	B9	101 11001	100110 1010	100110 1010
D26.5	BA	101 11010	010110 1010	010110 1010
D27.5	BB	101 11011	110110 1010	001001 1010
D28.5	BC	101 11100	001110 1010	001110 1010
D29.5	BD	101 11101	101110 1010	010001 1010
D30.5	BE	101 11110	011110 1010	100001 1010
D31.5	BF	101 11111	101011 1010	010100 1010
D0.6	C0	110 00000	100111 0110	011000 0110
D1.6	C1	110 00001	011101 0110	100010 0110
D2.6	C2	110 00010	101101 0110	010010 0110
D3.6	C3	110 00011	110001 0110	110001 0110
D4.6	C4	110 00100	110101 0110	001010 0110
D5.6	C5	110 00101	101001 0110	101001 0110
D6.6	C6	110 00110	011001 0110	011001 0110
D7.6	C7	110 00111	111000 0110	000111 0110
D8.6	C8	110 01000	111001 0110	000110 0110
D9.6	C9	110 01001	100101 0110	100101 0110
D10.6	CA	110 01010	010101 0110	010101 0110
D11.6	CB	110 01011	110100 0110	110100 0110
D12.6	CC	110 01100	001101 0110	001101 0110
D13.6	CD	110 01101	101100 0110	101100 0110
D14.6	CE	110 01110	011100 0110	011100 0110
D15.6	CF	110 01111	010111 0110	101000 0110
D16.6	D0	110 10000	011011 0110	100100 0110
D17.6	D1	110 10001	100011 0110	100011 0110
D18.6	D2	110 10010	010011 0110	010011 0110
D19.6	D3	110 10011	110010 0110	110010 0110
D20.6	D4	110 10100	001011 0110	001011 0110
D21.6	D5	110 10101	101010 0110	101010 0110
D22.6	D6	110 10110	011010 0110	011010 0110

continues

TABLE B.3 CONTINUED

Data Code-Group Name	Hex Value	Binary	Code-Group Used When Current RD Is −	Code-Group Used When Current RD Is +
D23.6	D7	110 10111	111010 0110	000101 0110
D24.6	D8	110 11000	110011 0110	001100 0110
D25.6	D9	110 11001	100110 0110	100110 0110
D26.6	DA	110 11010	010110 0110	010110 0110
D27.6	DB	110 11011	110110 0110	001001 0110
D28.6	DC	110 11100	001110 0110	001110 0110
D29.6	DD	110 11101	101110 0110	010001 0110
D30.6	DE	110 11110	011110 0110	100001 0110
D31.6	DF	110 11111	101011 0110	010100 0110
D0.7	E0	111 00000	100111 0001	011000 1110
D1.7	E1	111 00001	011101 0001	100010 1110
D2.7	E2	111 00010	101101 0001	010010 1110
D3.7	E3	111 00011	110001 1110	110001 0001
D4.7	E4	111 00100	110101 0001	001010 1110
D5.7	E5	111 00101	101001 1110	101001 0001
D6.7	E6	111 00110	011001 1110	011001 0001
D7.7	E7	111 00111	111000 1110	000111 0001
D8.7	E8	111 01000	111001 0001	000110 1110
D9.7	E9	111 01001	100101 1110	100101 0001
D10.7	EΛ	111 01010	010101 1110	010101 0001
D11.7	EB	111 01011	110100 1110	110100 1000
D12.7	EC	111 01100	001101 1110	001101 0001
D13.7	ED	111 01101	101100 1110	101100 1000
D14.7	EE	111 01110	011100 1110	011100 1000
D15.7	EF	111 01111	010111 0001	101000 1110
D16.7	F0	111 10000	011011 0001	100100 1110
D17.7	F1	111 10001	100011 0111	100011 0001
D18.7	F2	111 10010	010011 0111	010011 0001
D19.7	F3	111 10011	110010 1110	110010 0001
D20.7	F4	111 10100	001011 0111	001011 0001
D21.7	F5	111 10101	101010 1110	101010 0001
D22.7	F6	111 10110	011010 1110	011010 0001
D23.7	F7	111 10111	111010 0001	000101 1110

Data Code-Group Name	Hex Value	Binary	Code-Group Used When Current RD Is −	Code-Group Used When Current RD Is +
D24.7	F8	111 11000	110011 0001	001100 1110
D25.7	F9	111 11001	100110 1110	100110 0001
D26.7	FA	111 11010	010110 1110	010110 0001
D27.7	FB	111 11011	110110 0001	001001 1110
D28.7	FC	111 11100	001110 1110	001110 0001
D29.7	FD	111 11101	101110 0001	010001 1110
D30.7	FE	111 11110	011110 0001	100001 1110
D31.7	FF	111 11111	101011 0001	010100 1110

Table B.4 lists ordered sets that are used for fibre channel frame delimiters. SOF stands for *start of frame*, and EOF stands for *end of frame*. A start of frame always follows a series of idles, and the running disparity after an idle always is negative. When an end of frame occurs, the running disparity could be negative or positive. Different ordered sets are used depending on the running disparity.

TABLE B.4 ORDERED SETS USED FOR FIBRE CHANNEL DELIMITERS

Purpose	Running Disparity	Ordered Set
SOF Connect Class 1	−	K28.5 D21.5 D23.0 D23.0
SOF Initiate Class 1	−	K28.5 D21.5 D23.2 D23.2
SOF Normal Class 1	−	K28.5 D21.5 D23.1 D23.1
SOF Initiate Class 2	−	K28.5 D21.5 D21.2 D21.2
SOF Normal Class 2	−	K28.5 D21.5 D21.1 D21.1
SOF Initiate Class 3	−	K28.5 D21.5 D22.2 D22.2
SOF Normal Class 3	−	K28.5 D21.5 D22.1 D22.1
SOF Activate Class 4	−	K28.5 D21.5 D25.0 D25.0
SOF Normal Class 4	−	K28.5 D21.5 D25.1 D25.1
SOF Initiate Class 4	−	K28.5 D21.5 D25.2 D25.2
SOF Fabric	−	K28.5 D21.5 D24.2 D24.2
EOF Terminate	−	K28.5 D21.4 D21.3 D21.3
	+	K28.5 D21.5 D21.3 D21.3
EOF Disconnect-Terminate Class 1 or Class 4	−	K28.5 D21.4 D21.4 D21.4
	+	K28.5 D21.5 D21.4 D21.4
EOF Abort	−	K28.5 D21.4 D21.7 D21.7
	+	K28.5 D21.5 D21.7 D21.7

continues

TABLE B.4 CONTINUED

Purpose	Running Disparity	Ordered Set
EOF Normal	–	K28.5 D21.4 D21.6 D21.6
	+	K28.5 D21.5 D21.6 D21.6
EOF Disconnect-Terminate-	–	K28.5 D10.4 D21.4 D21.4
Invalid Class 1 or Class 4	+	K28.5 D10.5 D21.4 D21.4
EOF Normal-Invalid	–	K28.5 D10.4 D21.6 D21.6
	+	K28.5 D10.5 D21.6 D21.6
EOF Remove Terminate	–	K28.5 D21.4 D25.4 D25.4
Class 4	+	K28.5 D21.5 D25.4 D25.4
EOF Remove Terminate	–	K28.5 D10.4 D25.4 D25.4
Invalid Class 4	+	K28.5 D10.5 D25.4 D25.4

Table B.5 lists fibre channel ordered sets that are called *primitive signals*.

TABLE B.5 ORDERED SETS FOR FIBRE CHANNEL PRIMITIVE SIGNALS

Purpose	Running Disparity	Ordered Set
Idle	–	K28.5 D21.4 D21.5 D21.5
Receiver Ready	–	K28.5 D21.4 D10.2 D10.2
Virtual Circuit Ready Class 4	–	K28.5 D21.7 VC_ID VC_ID

*VC_ID= Virtual Circuit Identifier

Table B.6 lists fibre channel ordered sets that are called *primitive sequences*.

TABLE B.6 ORDERED SETS FOR FIBRE CHANNEL PRIMITIVE SEQUENCES

Purpose	Running Disparity	Ordered Set
Offline	–	K28.5 D21.1 D10.4 D21.2
Not Operational	–	K28.5 D21.2 D31.5 D5.2
Link Reset	–	K28.5 D9.2 D31.5 D9.2
Link Reset Response	–	K28.5 D21.1 D31.5 D9.2

References

Table B.2 is based on Table 23A-1, the 100BASE-T4 8B6T code table, which is in Annex 23A of IEEE Standard 802.3, 1998 Edition. Table B.3 is based on Table 36-1, the *Valid Data Code-groups* table, in Chapter 36 of the same standard.

Table B.4 is based on Table 24, *Frame Delimiters*, in the 1994 ANSI specification, "Fibre Channel Physical and Signalling Interface (FC-PH)," as updated by version 2 (FC-PH-2) in 1996. Table 24 is located in Chapter 11, Section 4. Table B.5 is based on Table 25, *Primitive Signals*, and Table B.6 is based on Table 26, *Primitive Sequences*, in the same fibre channel standards documents (FC-PH and FC-PH-2).

APPENDIX C

Standards Bodies and References

Adherence to standards is very important in the local area network arena. It is rare to find a workplace computer that is not attached to a network, and users take it for granted that computers, networked peripherals, hubs, switches, and routers will interwork without a hitch.

Vendors support standards while retaining their right to innovate. Successful innovations usually find their way into the standards at a brisk pace.

In several areas, standards are driven by vendor associations. Some of these vendor groups are sources of free technology information that can be accessed via the Internet.

Formal Standards Bodies

The formal LAN standards bodies are presented in the sections that follow. Then the vendor groups are described.

IEEE

The *Institute for Electrical and Electronics Engineers* (IEEE) 802 committee is responsible for most of the standards that deal with local area networks.

The IEEE Web site is

```
http://www.ieee.org/
```

IEEE LAN standards documents are not free. They can be ordered online at the IEEE Web site. For a catalog listing, see `http://standards.ieee.org/catalog/contents.html`. Prepaid subscriptions that enable a user to download documents from the Web site are available.

A few references can be downloaded from the IEEE Web site free of cost. A list of assigned organizationally unique identifiers (OUIs) is available at this URL:

```
http://standards.ieee.org/regauth/oui/oui.txt
```

Other useful material can be reached from this URL:

```
http://standards.ieee.org/regauth/oui/tutorials/
```

ANSI

The *American National Standards Institute* (ANSI) is responsible for publishing FDDI and fibre channel standards.

The ANSI Web site is

```
http://www.ansi.org/
```

ANSI documents are not free. They can be purchased at the Web site. ANSI standards usually are republished as ISO or ITU-T standards.

IETF

The *Internet Engineering Task Force* (IETF) is responsible for creating and implementing standards for the Internet. Much of its work is related to updating or enlarging the TCP/IP protocol suite. The IETF has published many standards relating to

- Encapsulating IP traffic in LAN frames

- SNMP Management Information Bases (MIBs) for LAN technologies

Preliminary and final IETF standards are published in documents called *Requests for Comments* (RFCs). IETF documents are free and can be obtained from this Web site:

```
http://www.ietf.org/
```

RFC documents can be located easily from this search page:

```
http://www.rfc-editor.org/rfcsearch.html
```

TIA/EIA

The Electronic Industries Alliance (EIA) is the parent organization for a number of standards groups, including the Telecommunications Industry Association (TIA). Several important TIA/EIA standards relate to premise cabling.

The TIA is a national trade organization and accredited ANSI standards organization whose members provide communications and information technology products and services. Information is available at the organization's Web site:

```
http://www.tiaonline.org/
```

You can search for documents at the TIA Web site. However, the documents actually are purchased from Global Engineering Documents:

```
http://global.ihs.com/
```

ITU-T

The *International Telecommunications Union—Telecommunication Standardization Sector* (ITU-T) is responsible for the basic networking standards relating to ATM.

The ITU's World Wide Web site is

```
http://www.itu.int/
```

ITU-T documents are not free. They can be purchased at the Web site.

ISO

The International Organization for Standardization (ISO) was created to promote international trade and cooperative advances in science. The International Organization for Standardization Web site is

```
http://www.iso.ch/
```

ISO documents are not free. They can be purchased through member country organizations.

Vendor Groups

Specific vendor groups of interest include the following:

- The Gigabit Ethernet Alliance was formed to promote industry cooperation in the development of Gigabit Ethernet. Several white papers are available at their Web site,
  ```
  http://www.gigabit-ethernet.org/
  ```

  Standards must be obtained from IEEE.

- The High Speed Token Ring Alliance was formed by leading Token Ring vendors. Their Web site provides some technology white papers:
  ```
  http://www.hstra.com/whitepapers.html
  ```

  Standards must be obtained from the IEEE.

- The ATM Forum was formed to promote the use of ATM. The Forum originated many ATM standards, including the ATM standards relating to LAN Emulation. Free technical specifications are available at this site:

  http://www.atmforum.com/

- The National Committee for Information Technology Standards (NCITS) was formed to produce market-driven, voluntary consensus standards for storage devices, multimedia, programming languages, and security. Its T11 committee is responsible for fibre channel. The latest revisions of fibre channel draft documents are available at this site:

  http://www.t11.org/

- The Fibre Channel Industry Association Web site provides some overviews of the technology and is located at
  http://www.fibrechannel.com/

Many vendor consortiums have been formed to promote interoperability testing for each of the major LAN technologies. The University of New Hampshire's InterOperability Lab (IOL) publishes a list of consortiums at

  http://www.iol.unh.edu/consortiums/

The IOL performs testing that is sponsored by the consortiums. The IOL also publishes excellent tutorials.

Frequently asked questions (FAQ) documents relating to LAN technologies can be reached from the following Web page:

  http://www.faqs.org/faqs/by-newsgroup/comp/

APPENDIX D

Acronym List

AAL5   ATM Adaptation Layer 5

ABR   Available Bit Rate (ATM)

ACK   ACKnowledge

ACR   attenuation to crosstalk ratio

AL_PA   arbitrated loop physical address (fibre channel)

AMP   Active Monitor Present (Token Ring)

ANSI   American National Standards Institute

ARE   all-routes explorer frame (source routing)

ARP   Address Resolution Protocol

ASIC   application specific integrated circuit

ASN.1   Abstract Syntax Notation One (SNMP)

ATM   Asynchronous Transfer Mode

AUI   attachment unit interface (Ethernet)

AWG   American Wire Gauge

BER   bit error rate

BNC   Bayonet Neil-Concelman

BOOTP   Bootstrap Protocol (TCP/IP)

BPDU Bridge Protocol Data Unit

BPS bits per second

BUS Broadcast and Unknown Server (LANE)

CATV Community Antenna Television

CAU Controlled Access Unit (Token Ring)

CBR Constant Bit Rate (ATM)

CDDI Copper Distributed Data Interface

CENELEC Comite Europeen de Normalisation Electrotechnique

CFI Canonical Format Indicator (VLANs)

CMIP Common Management Information Protocol

CMIS Common Management Information Service

CRC cyclic redundancy check

CRS Configuration Report Server (Token Ring)

CSMA/CD Carrier Sense Multiple Access with Collision Detection (Ethernet)

DA destination address

DAS dual attachment station (FDDI)

dB decibel

DCE data circuit-terminating equipment

DIX Digital, Intel, and Xerox

DMD differential mode delay

DRD destination route descriptor (Token Ring)

DSAP destination service access point

DTE data terminal equipment

DTR Dedicated Token Ring

EIA Electronic Industries Alliance

ELAN emulated LAN (ATM)

ELFEXT equal level far end crosstalk

EMI electromagnetic interference

E-RIF embedded routing information field

ESD end-of-stream delimiter

FC fibre channel

FCS frame check sequence

FDDI Fibre Distributed Data Interface

FEXT far end crosstalk

FID filtering identifier

FIFO first in first out

FLP fast link pulse (Auto-Negotiation)

FMI fiber optic medium interface (Token Ring)

FOIRL fiber optic inter-repeater link (Ethernet)

FTP foil twisted pair

GARP Generic Attribute Registration Protocol

GbE Gigabit Ethernet

GBIC gigabit interface converter

Gbps gigabits (billions of bits) per second

GID GARP Information Declaration

GIP GARP Information Propagation

GMII gigabit media independent interface

GMRP GARP Multicast Registration Protocol

GVRP GARP VLAN Registration Protocol

HDLC High-level Data Link Control

HIPPI High Performance Parallel Interface

HSSDC High Speed Serial Data Connector

HSSI High Speed Serial Interface

HSTR High Speed Token Ring

Hz hertz

IEC International Electrotechnical Commission

IEEE Institute of Electrical and Electronic Engineers

IETF Internet Engineering Task Force

IFG interframe gap

IGMP Internet Group Management Protocol

ILMI Integrated Local Management Interface (ATM)

IP Internet Protocol

IPI Intelligent Peripheral Interface

IPG interpacket gap (Ethernet)

ISDN Integrated Services Digital Network

ISO International Organization for Standardization

IV initialization vector

IVL independent VLAN learning

km kilometers

LACP Link Aggregation Control Protocol

LACPDU Link Aggregation Control Protocol Data Unit

LAG Link Aggregation Group

LAN local area network

LANE LAN Emulation

LAT local area transport

LB-LAN locally bridged local area network

LEC LAN Emulation Client

LECID LAN Emulation Client ID

LECS LAN Emulation Configuration Server

LED light emitting diode

LES LAN Emulation Server

LFSR   linear feedback shift register

LLC   Logical Link Control

LME   Layer Management Entity

LSAP   link service access point

MAC   media access control

MAN   metropolitan area network

MAU   medium attachment unit (Ethernet)

MAU   Multistation Access Unit (Token Ring)

Mbps   megabits (millions of bits) per second

MBps   megabytes per second

MDI   medium dependent interface

MDI-X   medium dependent interface crossover

MHz   megahertz

MIB   Management Information Base (SNMP)

MIC   medium interface connector

MII   medium independent interface

MLT-3   Multi-Level 3 encoding

MM   multimode

MMF   multimode fiber

MPLS   Multiprotocol Label Switching Architecture

MPOA   Multiprotocol Over ATM

MUTO   Multiuser Telecommunications Outlet

MSAU   Multistation Access Unit (Token Ring)

MSDU   MAC service data unit

NAA   network address authority

NBF   NetBEUI Frame Protocol

NCFI   noncanonical format indicator

NCITS   National Committee for Information Technology Standards

NDIS   Network Driver Interface Specification

NEC   National Electrical Code

NetBEUI   NetBIOS Extended User Interface

NetBIOS   Network Basic Input/Output System

NEXT   near end crosstalk

NIC   network interface card

NLP   normal link pulse (10BASE-T Ethernet))

NOS   network operating system

NP   next page

nrt-VBR   non-real-time variable bit rate (ATM)

NRZI   non-return-to-zero, invert-on-one

NTT   Nippon Telephone and Telegraph

NVP   nominal velocity of propagation

ORD   optical receive data

OSI   Open Systems Interconnect

OSPF   open shortest path first

OTD   optical transmit data

OTDR   Optical Time Domain Reflectometer

OUI   organizationally unique identifier

PAM   pulse amplitude modulation

PCI   Peripheral Component Interconnect

PCS   Physical Coding Sublayer

PDU   protocol data unit

PHY   physical layer

PICS   Protocol Implementation Conformance Statement

PLS   physical layer signaling

PMA physical medium attachment

PMD Physical Medium Dependent

PMI Physical Medium Independent

POTS Plain Old Telephone Service

PPP Point-to-Point Protocol

PSELFEXT power sum equal level far end crosstalk

PSNEXT power sum near end crosstalk

PVC permanent virtual circuit

PVID Port VLAN Identifier

QoS Quality of Service

RB remote bridge

RD route descriptor (bridge)

REM Ring Error Monitor (Token Ring)

RF remote fault

RFC Request for Comments (IETF)

RFI radio frequency interference

RI routing information (bridge)

RIF Routing Information Field (bridge)

RII Routing-Information Indicator (bridge)

RIP Routing Information Protocol

RMAC Repeater Medium Access Control (100VG AnyLAN)

RMON remote monitor (SNMP)

RPS Ring Parameter Server (Token Ring)

rt-VBR Real-time Variable Bit Rate (ATM)

SA source address

SAID security association identifier

SAN storage area network

SAP   service access point

SC   square corner

SCSI   small computer system interface

ScTP   Screened Twisted-Pair

SDU   service data unit

SEL   selector byte (ATM)

SFD   start frame delimiter

SFF   small form factor

SILS   Standard for Interoperable LAN/MAN Security

SM   Single-mode

SMA   sub miniature type A

SMF   single-mode fiber

SMI   Structure of Management Information (SNMP)

SMIB   Security Management Information Base

SMP   Standby Monitor Present (Token Ring)

SMS   Selective Multicast Server

SMT   station management (FDDI)

SNA   Systems Network Architecture

SNAP   Subnetwork Access Protocol

SNMP   Simple Network Management Protocol

SQE   signal quality error

SRB   source routing bridge

SRL   structural return loss

SRT   source-routing transparent (bridge)

SSAP   source service access point

SSD   start-of-stream delimiter

SSTP   screened/shielded twisted pair

ST straight tip (fiber optic connector)

STE Spanning Tree Explorer (bridge)

STP shielded twisted pair (cabling)

STP Spanning Tree Protocol (bridges)

SVC switched virtual circuit

SVL shared VLAN learning

TBPS terabits (1000 billion bits) per second

TCI tag control information

TCP Transmission Control Protocol

TCU Trunk Coupling Unit (Token Ring)

TDR Time Domain Reflectometer

TIA Telecommunications Industry Association

TKP Token Passing Protocol

TNC Threaded-Neil-Councilman Coaxial Cable Connector

TPID Tag Protocol Identifier

TTRT Target Token Rotation Timeout (FDDI)

TXI Transmit Immediate Protocol (Token Ring)

UBR Unspecified Bit Rate (ATM)

UDP User Datagram Protocol (TCP/IP)

UP unformatted page (Auto-Negotiation)

USOC Universal Service Order Code

UTP unshielded twisted pair

VCI Virtual Channel Identifier (ATM)

VCSEL Vertical Cavity Surface Emitting Laser

VID VLAN identifier

VLAN virtual LAN

VPI Virtual Path Identifier (ATM)

WAN wide area network

Glossary

Numerals

1BASE5 Obsolete 1Mbps version of Ethernet over twisted-pair cables, also called StarLAN.

4B/5B An encoding used for 100BASE-X Ethernet, FDDI, CDDI, and some ATM physical layers.

5-4-3 rule Restriction on a coax Ethernet that states that a frame can traverse at most five segments, go through at most four repeaters, and cross at most three segments that contain stations.

8B1Q4 An encoding used for 1000BASE-T Ethernet.

8B/6T An encoding used for 100BASE-T4 Ethernet.

8B/10B An encoding used for 1000BASE-CX, 1000BASE-FX, 1000BASE-TX, and fibre channel. Each byte is translated to a 10-bit pattern before it is transmitted.

10BASE2 10Mbps Ethernet over thin 50-ohm coaxial cable.

10BASE5 10Mbps Ethernet over thick 50-ohm coaxial cable.

10BASE-F A generic term for 10BASE-FB, 10BASE-FL, and 10BASE-FP Ethernet over fiber optic cable.

10BASE-FB Specification for 10Mbps Ethernet repeater-to-repeater fiber optic backbone links.

10BASE-FL Specification for a 10Mbps fiber optic link that can be used for station-to-station, repeater-to-repeater, and repeater-to-station links.

10BASE-FP An unimplemented specification for a passive optical device designed to interconnect multiple 10Mbs Ethernet stations.

10BASE-T 10Mbps Ethernet over two pairs of Category 3 or better unshielded twisted-pair cabling.

10BROAD36 A broadband coax implementation of Ethernet that uses frequency modulated transceivers.

100BASE-FX 100Mbps Ethernet over fiber optic cable.

100BASE-T General term for 100Mbps Ethernet over twisted–pair cable.

100BASE-T2 Unimplemented IEEE 802.3 specification for 100Mbps Ethernet over two pairs of Category 3 or better cabling.

100BASE-T4 100Mbps half-duplex Ethernet over four pairs of Category 3, 4, or 5 unshielded twisted-pair (UTP) wire.

100BASE-TX 100Mbps Ethernet over two pairs of Category 5 unshielded twisted-pair or shielded twisted-pair.

100BASE-X General term for 100BASE-FX and 100BASE-TX.

100VG-AnyLAN A technology that competed with 100Mbps Ethernet and was published as a separate standard (802.12).

1000BASE-CX Gigabit Ethernet over specialty shielded copper cable assemblies.

1000BASE-LH Nonstandard long-haul implementation of Gigabit Ethernet over single-mode optical fiber.

1000BASE-LX Gigabit Ethernet using long-wavelength laser devices over multimode and single-mode fiber.

1000BASE-SX Gigabit Ethernet using short-wavelength laser devices over multimode fiber.

1000BASE-T Gigabit Ethernet over Category 5 unshielded twisted-pair copper cabling.

1000BASE-X General term for 1000BASE-CX, 1000BASE-LX, and 1000BASE-SX.

A

access link A link that connects VLAN-unaware systems to a VLAN switch.

active monitor A Token Ring station that supervises the ring and recovers from problems such as loss of the token and repeatedly circulating frames.

adapter Network interface card.

Address Resolution Protocol (ARP) A procedure that is used to map a higher-layer protocol address into a low-layer protocol address (for example, to map an IP address to a MAC address).

agent *See* SNMP agent.

all-routes explorer (ARE) A Token Ring frame that records a route to a destination by traversing every loop-free path through a bridged Token Ring LAN.

American Wire Gauge (AWG) Inverse measure of the thickness (in inches) of a wire. For example, the diameter of 24 AWG wire is 1/24 inch.

application-layer switch A routing switch that takes application-layer data (such as a World Wide Web URL) into account when making forwarding decisions.

application-specific integrated circuit (ASIC) chip A processing chip that contains program logic implemented as hardware.

arbitrated loop A set of fibre channel ports connected into a ring.

asymmetric flow control For full-duplex Ethernet, the capability of one station to send PAUSE frames to its partner, who is not allowed to send PAUSE frames.

asynchronous bandwidth For FDDI, an extra period of time that a station can use to transmit data if the token returns to the station early.

Asynchronous Transfer Mode (ATM) A method of transmitting information that is organized into cells. Also, a virtual circuit service based on ATM technology.

ATM Adaptation Layer 5 (AAL5) An ATM data link layer.

ATM Broadcast and Unknown Server (BUS) A server that delivers broadcast and multicast frames to stations in an emulated LAN.

ATM Integrated Local Management Interface (ILMI) A protocol based on SNMP, used to initialize an ATM station and monitor the link connecting the station to a switch.

ATM LAN Emulation Configuration Server (LECS) A server that assigns a LAN Emulation Client to a specific emulated LAN.

ATM LAN Emulation (LANE) A set of mechanisms that enable an ATM station to emulate a conventional Ethernet or Token Ring LAN station.

ATM LAN Emulation Client (LEC) A special device driver that hides the under-lying ATM layers from the higher protocol layers.

ATM LAN Emulation Server (LES) A server that is in charge of one emulated LAN and that keeps track of the ATM addresses and MAC addresses of its members.

ATM layer Upper part of the physical layer, responsible for adding a 5-byte cell header to each 48-byte payload and queuing cells in the order in which they will be transmitted.

attachment unit interface (AUI) For 10Mbps Ethernet, the interface between communications electronics in a station and a transceiver. This can be implemented as a cable or as an internal interface within a NIC.

attenuation The loss of signal strength that occurs as information traverses a medium. Attenuation is expressed in decibels.

attenuation to crosstalk ratio (ACR) A measurement of the signal to noise ratio at the receive end of a pair, expressed in decibels.

Auto-Negotiation A protocol that enables Ethernet systems at the ends of a twisted-pair or optical fiber segment to negotiate configuration parameters such as speed, half- or full-duplex mode, and use of flow control.

Available Bit Rate (ABR) A best-effort ATM service that provides continuing feedback that tells the sender how much bandwidth is available for the sender's use.

B

backoff For CSMA/CD Ethernet, a period of time that a station must wait before retransmitting after participating in a collision. The period is a randomly selected multiple of the slot time.

balanced cable A metallic cable designed with symmetric transmission elements so that their induced magnetic fields will cancel each other out.

base page The first 16-bit message exchanged during Ethernet Auto-Negotiation. Also called the base link code word.

baseband   Communication via pulses serially impressed on a medium. Only one signal can be on the medium.

Bayonet Neil-Concelman (BNC)   A type of connector used for thinnet Ethernet.

Beacon frame   A frame transmitted by a station on a Token Ring or FDDI ring that has detected a ring failure.

bit error rate (BER)   The number of bits received in error divided by the total number of bits received.

bridge   A LAN device that operates at Layer 2 (the data link layer). A bridge interconnects two or more LAN segments and selectively forwards LAN frames between segments.

bridge address   A MAC address used to uniquely identify an entire bridge.

bridge identifier   A priority number followed by the bridge address.

bridge port cost   A cost value assigned by an administrator.

bridge port identifier   The combination of an assigned port priority and the port number.

Bridge Protocol Data Unit (BPDU) messages   Spanning Tree Protocol messages that enable bridges to agree on an initial tree-shaped topology and, after the failure of some component, change the topology to repair broken paths.

bridge root path cost   A value computed by adding path cost numbers for receive ports along the path from the root to the bridge.

bridge root port   The port on a bridge that connects to its best path to the root.

bridge/router   A device that routes some traffic and bridges the rest. A Layer 2/3 switch.

broadcast   The act of sending a frame addressed to all stations.

brouter   *See* bridge/router.

buffer   A unit of memory, used for the temporary storage of data.

buffered distributor   A special repeater used for Gigabit Ethernet. Each system is connected to the repeater by a full-duplex link. Also called a full-duplex repeater.

bus   A network topology that connects devices via a shared cable.

C

canonical format   The format of a data frame in which the bytes of any MAC addresses conveyed in the user data field have the same bit ordering as in the hexadecimal representation.

Canonical Format Indicator (CFI) flag   A flag in a tag header that indicates whether the frame contains an embedded routing information field (E-RIF).

carrier extension   For half-duplex Gigabit Ethernet, the addition of nondata symbols to the end of frames that are less than 512 bytes in length.

Carrier Sense Multiple Access with Collision Detection (CSMA/CD)   The medium access protocol used for classical half-duplex Ethernet. A station waits until the medium is free before transmitting. If two stations transmit concurrently, a collision occurs, and each station pauses before retransmitting. *See* backoff.

category   A classification system used to differentiate between grades of twisted-pair cable.

chassis   An enclosure that contains slots for a set of network cards.

certification tool   A high-end tester that can determine whether installed cables meet TIA Category 5, 5E, or proposed Category 6 or 7 requirements.

channel   For a cable, includes all the cabling system components between a station and a hub or switch in a wiring closet.

cladding   A cylinder of glass that surrounds the core of a fiber optic cable.

Claim Token frame   A Token Ring frame used in a procedure that elects an active monitor station.

Class 1   A fibre channel service class that provides dedicated point-to-point connections with guaranteed bandwidth.

Class 2   A fibre channel service class that provides acknowledged connectionless communication.

Class 3   A fibre channel service class that provides unacknowledged connectionless service.

Class I repeater   A 100Mbps Ethernet repeater that translates between data encodings. This introduces a delay into the forwarding process, and the result is that normally only one Class I repeater can be used in a collision domain.

Class II repeater   A 100Mbps Ethernet repeater that attaches only to stations that use compatible data encodings. At most two Class II repeaters can be used in a collision domain.

classic Token Ring concentrator   A device that connects to multiple stations and forms all or part of the backbone of a Token Ring.

classic Token Ring station   A station that operates in token-passing mode.

coaxial cable section   A single length of coaxial cable.

coaxial cable segment   A single cable section, or two or more sections joined by connectors, terminated at each end.

code-group   A set of symbols that represent data or control information. For example, for 100BASE-X Ethernet, FDDI, CDDI, and some ATM physical layers, every 4-bit nibble is translated to a 5-bit pattern before it is transmitted, and special 5-bit patterns represent idles and mark the start and end of a frame.

collision   In Ethernet, the disruption of communication that occurs when multiple systems transmit at the same time.

collision domain   A set of Ethernet segments connected by repeaters. If two systems transmit at the same time, a collision will occur.

comma   In 1000BASE-X, a special 7-bit pattern (either 0011111 or 1100000) that is part of an 8B/10B code-group and is used for the purpose of code-group alignment.

concentrator   A device used to organize LAN cabling. Cables run from a system in a work area to a concentrator in a wiring closet or computer room.

Configuration BPDU   A bridge protocol data unit used to select a Spanning Tree root, establish parameters, and maintain the tree topology.

configuration report server (CRS)   A Token Ring server that assists in monitoring and controlling the stations on the ring.

consolidation point   A wiring concentrator that introduces an extra connector into the horizontal run.

Constant Bit Rate (CBR)   An ATM service that provides circuits with a constant bandwidth.

Copper Distributed Data Interface (CDDI)   The copper (twisted-pair) version of FDDI.

core   The central cylinder in a fiber optic medium.

C-Port   A port in a dedicated Token Ring concentrator.

credit   Buffer allocation system that provides flow control for Class 1 and Class 2 fibre channel communications.

cross–connect   A physical connection between patch panels or punch-down blocks. Cross-connects are used to manage the cable topology.

crossover cable   A cable whose wires cross so that a transmit pin at one end is connected to a receive pin at the other end.

crosstalk   A signal induced on a wire by a signal on a neighboring wire.

cut-through bridge   A bridge that starts to transmit a frame before it has received the entire frame.

cyclic redundancy check (CRC)   A value used to detect transmission errors. It is calculated by applying a mathematical formula to the bits in a frame and is appended to the frame.

D

data circuit-terminating equipment (DCE)   Equipment that connects data terminal equipment to a service network.

data link layer   The layer above the physical layer, in which 0s and 1s are organized into frames.

data terminal equipment (DTE)   A communicating system that can be the source or destination of data.

DECnet   A set of proprietary networking protocols designed by Digital Equipment Corporation (now part of Compaq).

Dedicated Token Ring (DTR)   An updated version of Token Ring that can support full-duplex operation.

delay skew   The difference between the propagation delays of the slowest and fastest pairs in a four-pair cable.

designated bridge for a subLAN   The bridge that transmits frames coming from the direction of the root onto the subLAN.

designated port   The single unblocked port that connects a subLAN to its designated bridge.

destination service access point address   *See* link service access point (LSAP) address.

device driver   A software program that controls a device used in a computer, such as a printer, CD-ROM, monitor display, or network interface card.

differential Manchester encoding   The physical encoding method used for 4Mbps and 16Mbps Token Ring. Bits are represented using transitions between high and low signals. For a 0, there are transitions at the beginning and the middle of the bit. For a 1, there is a transition only at the middle of the bit.

differential mode delay (DMD)   For multimode fiber, the creation of multiple overlapping signals that can make it impossible for a receiver to interpret an incoming signal correctly.

downstream neighbor   For Token Ring or FDDI, the adjacent neighbor to which a station transmits and forwards frames.

dual attachment station (DAS)   A system that is connected to both rings in an FDDI dual-ring configuration.

E

egress rules   The rules applied to an outgoing frame at a VLAN switch to determine whether the frame can be transmitted through a port and whether the frame needs to be tagged.

embedded routing information field (E-RIF)   A field used in some VLAN frames that have passed through a translational bridge.

emulated LAN (ELAN)   A set of systems that have ATM NICs and perform protocols that emulate the behavior of conventional LAN systems.

equal level far end crosstalk (ELFEXT)   A measurement of far end crosstalk that removes the difference in attenuation that results from using different cable lengths.

Ethernet   A family of LAN protocols operating at 10Mbps, 100Mbps, and 1000Mbps.

EtherType code   A 2-byte code used to identify the type of protocol data carried by a frame.

exchange   For fibre channel, transmission of sequences of frames that make up a transaction of some kind.

explorer frames   For Token Ring, frames used in the route discovery protocol in a source-routing LAN. Two types exist: all-routes-explorer frames and Spanning Tree explorer frames.

extension bits   For half-duplex Gigabit Ethernet, nondata symbols added to the end of frames that are less than 512 bytes in length.

F

F_Port   A fibre channel fabric port.

fabric   The infrastructure of a fibre channel network (for example, networked switches).

far end crosstalk (FEXT)   The distortion of an outgoing signal by an incoming signal on an adjacent wire, measured in decibels.

Fast Ethernet   A nickname for the 100Mbps version of Ethernet.

fast link pulse (FLP) burst   A sequence of pulses used to transmit the 16-bit messages used for Ethernet Auto-Negotiation on a twisted pair medium.

FC-0   A fibre channel level that corresponds to the lower part of the physical layer.

FC-1   A fibre channel level that performs 8B/10B encoding of data bytes and defines the usage of special code-groups.

FC-2   A fibre channel level that corresponds to the data link layer.

FC-3   A fibre channel level for services that are provided across multiple ports in a single node.

FC-4   A fibre channel level that defines the way that the various applications that ride on top of fibre channel map onto the fibre channel environment.

FCS field   A field at the end of a frame that contains the result of a calculation (called a cyclic redundancy check, or CRC) performed on the remaining bits of the frame.

fiber optic inter-repeater link (FOIRL)   An early implementation of 10Mbps Ethernet across a fiber optic link between two repeaters.

fibre channel (FC)   A local area technology for high-speed communication between networked computers and peripherals.

Fibre Distributed Data Interface (FDDI)   A 100Mbps, local area network based on optical fiber segments and a token-passing protocol.

filtering database   A table in a transparent bridge, used to determine how frames should be forwarded. It can include manually entered static entries, entries that the bridge learned by observing the frames at each port, and entries learned via the GARP Multicast Registration Protocol (GMRP).

filtering table   *See* filtering database.

flooding   Action by a bridge that does not know the port through which a frame's destination MAC address is reached. The bridge transmits the frame through all ports except for the one on which it arrived.

FLP burst   *See* fast link pulse (FLP) burst.

FOIRL   *See* fiber optic inter-repeater link (FOIRL).

forwarding table   *See* filtering database.

frame   A data link layer protocol data unit.

frame bursting   For half-duplex Gigabit Ethernet, the capability to send a sequence of frames before giving up control of the medium.

frame check sequence (FCS) field   *See* FCS field.

Frame Relay   A wide area virtual circuit service.

full-duplex   A mode of operation that enables a pair of systems connected by a link to transmit frames to one another at the same time.

full-duplex repeater   *See* buffered distributor.

functional addresses   For Token Ring LANs, addresses that identify nodes that perform various types of special services.

G

GARP Multicast Registration Protocol (GMRP)   A protocol that enables systems to register their multicast memberships with bridges.

GARP VLAN Registration Protocol (GVRP)   A protocol that enables a VLAN-aware end system or switch to register with a neighboring switch to join (or leave) a VLAN.

Generic Attribute Registration Protocol (GARP)   A protocol that provides a general registration mechanism for use in a bridged LAN.

Gigabit Ethernet   1000Mbps Ethernet. It currently is implemented in full-duplex mode only.

gigabit interface converter (GBIC)   A transceiver used to connect a Gigabit Ethernet port to a specific medium.

gigabit media independent interface (GMII)   A Gigabit Ethernet adapter interface to which different types of GBIC transceivers can be attached. This provides choice in the media to which a system can connect.

H

half-duplex   A mode of operation that allows only a single station to successfully transmit a frame at a given time.

hertz (H2)   Electrical wave frequency in cycles per second. One hertz (Hz) equals one cycle per second.

High-Level Data Link Control (HDLC)   A frame encapsulation and protocol used across wide area point-to-point links.

high performance parallel interface (HIPPI)   A high-performance interface standard defined by ANSI, typically used to connect supercomputers to peripherals and other devices.

High Speed Serial Interface (HSSI)   A physical-layer interface for serial communications between a DTE (for example, a router) and a DCE (for example, a DSU/CSU) that supports up to 52Mbps.

High Speed Token Ring (HSTR)   The 100Mbps version of Token Ring.

hub   A Layer 1 repeater device used to provide connectivity between DTEs.

hybrid link   A subLAN that connects VLAN bridges to one another and that also includes VLAN-unaware systems.

I–K

idle   A special signal sent between frames, used with several LAN transmission technologies.

IGMP snooping   Eavesdropping on IGMP messages by bridges to identify the ports that lead to members of a multicast group.

impedance   A measure (in ohms) of the opposition to the flow of electricity down the wire.

independent VLAN learning   The development of a separate filtering table for each VLAN.

ingress rules   The rules used by a switch to assign an incoming frame to a VLAN.

Internet Engineering Task Force (IETF)   A group responsible for defining and implementing the TCP/IP suite of protocols that is used on the Internet.

Internet Group Management Protocol (IGMP)   A protocol that TCP/IP systems use to join and leave an IP-based multicast group.

Internet Protocol (IP)   The Layer 3 IETF protocol that routes traffic from its source to its destination.

interframe gap   The gap required between the end of an Ethernet frame and the start of transmitting the next frame. For example, for Ethernet, the interframe gap is 96 bit times. (Also called the interpacket gap.)

invalid frame   A frame that either does not contain an integral number of bytes, is too short or too long, or carries an invalid CRC value.

jabber   A condition wherein a station transmits for a period of time longer than the maximum permissible frame length, usually due to a fault condition.

jam bits   In Ethernet, a series of 32 randomly selected bits that are sent after a transmitter detects a collision to assure that all stations hear the collision.

jitter   Time variation in the rate at which bits, cells, or frames are delivered.

Jumbo frame   A nonstandard Ethernet frame implemented by some Gigabit Ethernet vendors. Its size ranges up to 9018 bytes.

L

LAN Emulation (LANE)   *See* ATM LAN Emulation (LANE).

Layer 2 switch   An up-to-date implementation of a bridge.

Layer 3 switch   An up-to-date implementation of a router.

Layer 4 switch   A switch that makes forwarding decisions that take Layer 4 protocol information into account.

Layer 2/3 switch   *See* bridge/router.

light emitting diode (LED)   A device used to transmit signals across multimode fiber optic cable.

line card   An input/output (I/O) card that can be installed in a chassis.

link   The transmission path between any two interfaces connected by a cable segment.

link aggregation   The capability to combine a group of links so that they behave like a single link.

Link Aggregation Control Protocol (LACP)   A protocol that enables link partners to discover the set of links that connect them and convert groups of links to an aggregated link.

link aggregation conversation   A flow of frames that must be delivered without changing their order. All frames are transmitted across the same link segment.

link code word   A 16-bit Auto-Negotiation message encoded into a fast link pulse (FLP) burst.

link integrity test signal   A periodic pulse sent across twisted-pair cable to test the cable when the data transmitter is idle.

link segment   A link that is part of an aggregation.

link partner   The device at the opposite end of a link segment from the local station.

link service access point (LSAP) address   An 802.2 address that appears in a LLC header, intended to identify a source or destination of a flow of data.

LLC frame   A frame containing a Logical Link Control header and user data.

load balancer   A device that makes a group of servers have the appearance of a single server.

lobe cabling   Two twisted pairs of cables used to connect a Token Ring station to a trunk coupling unit (TCU) in a concentrator.

local area network (LAN)   A network that connects a set of computers so that they can communicate with one another directly.

local area transport (LAT)   A nonroutable Digital Equipment Corporation protocol used for terminal access across a network.

Logical Link Control (LLC) sublayer   The portion of the data link layer that supports media-independent data link functions and uses the services of the MAC to provide services to the network layer.

Logical Link Control (LLC) header   A header that contains a source and destination service point addresses and a control field.

Locally Administered MAC address   A MAC address that is assigned to a network interface card by an administrator, replacing the vendor's unique address.

loop switch   A fibre channel device that connects to individual devices, arbitrated loops, and hubs. Multiple devices can transmit and receive data concurrently.

M

MAC address A Layer 2 address associated with a network interface card. It is used for LAN source and destination addresses.

MAC sublayer The portion of the data link layer that wraps outgoing data into frames, checks the CRC for incoming frames, and includes the protocols that control access to the medium.

Management Information Based (MIB) A collection of SNMP network management variables.

Manchester encoding A method of encoding bits onto a medium. There is a voltage transition in the middle of each bit. A 0 has a transition from high to low, and a 1 has a transition from low to high.

media access control address *See* MAC address.

media access control sublayer *See* MAC sublayer.

media converter A device that connects segments for two different media (such as twisted-pair to fiber optic cabling) making the two segments behave like one extended segment.

medium dependent interface (MDI) port A port that transmits and receives via the standard pin connections. Computer adapters or transceivers have MDI ports.

medium dependent interface crossover (MDI-X) port A hub port that reverses the role of the send and receive pins, allowing a straight-through cable to be used between the port and a station

media independent interface (MII) A 100Mbps adapter interface to which different types of transceivers can be attached. This provides choice in the media to which a system can connect.

medium attachment unit (MAU) A transceiver that is used to connect a repeater or data terminal equipment (DTE) to a transmission medium.

medium The material on which the data may be transmitted. STP, UTP, and optical fibers are examples of media.

message page (MP) An Auto-Negotiation message that contains a message code.

MIB Module An organized set of related SNMP definitions within a MIB document.

modal bandwidth   The worst-case 3dB bandwidth that will be achieved on a particular type of multimode cable.

modal dispersion   Dispersion of the arrival times of rays emitted into a multi-mode fiber. A large dispersion makes it impossible for the receiver to interpret incoming signals correctly.

mode-conditioning patch cord   A special patch cord that consists of a single-mode fiber spliced to an off-center position on a multimode fiber. It is used to funnel an LX laser signal into a multimode fiber core.

monitor   A device (also called a probe) that can eavesdrop on LAN activities.

multicast address   An address used to identify a group of systems to which frames will be forwarded.

Multi-Level 3 encoding (MLT-3)   A signaling method that is used for 100BASE-TX and CDDI. It uses three signal levels.

multimode fiber   Optical fiber cable with a relatively wide core (62.5 or 50 microns) that allows multiple rays of light to follow different paths through the core.

Multiprotocol Label Switching Architecture (MPLS)   A "route once, switch many" network protocol.

multiuser telecommunications outlet (MUTO)   An office wiring concentrator.

N

N_Port   A fibre channel node port.

N_Port identifier   A 3-byte address that identifies the location of a port.

National Electrical Code (NEC)   A specification that applies to all facility wiring in the United States.

near end crosstalk (NEXT)   The distortion of a weak incoming signal by a strong outgoing signal on a neighboring wire pair. NEXT is measured in decibels.

Network Addressing Authority   An organization, such as the IEEE, responsible for administering the distribution of unique names or addresses.

network diameter   For a collision domain, the length of the longest path between two points.

Network Driver Interface Specification (NDIS)   A Microsoft specification for a generic device driver for network adapters.

network interface card (NIC)   A hardware component installed in a system expansion slot that enables the system to send data onto a medium and receive data from the medium. A NIC also is called an adapter.

network interface   The point of connection between a station (such as a computer) and a LAN medium.

next page   In Ethernet Auto-Negotiation, any page transmitted subsequent to a base page.

nibble   A group of 4 data bits that is half of a byte.

nominal velocity of propagation (NVP)   The transmission speed along a wire relative to the speed of light in a vacuum.

non-canonical format   The format of a data frame in which the octets of MAC addresses conveyed in the user data field have the same bit ordering as in the bit-reversed representation.

non-canonical format identifier (NCFI) flag   A flag in an E-RIF. NCFI = 0 means that any MAC addresses carried in the information field are in non-canonical form.

non-real-time variable bit rate (nrt-VBR)   An ATM service delivers a specified average bandwidth and is suitable for data applications, which are not strongly sensitive to delay.

nonreturn to zero, invert on ones (NRZI)   An encoding used for 100BASE-FX and FDDI. Ones are alternatively represented by a high or low signal. There is no change of signal level at a 0.

normal link pulse (NLP)   The periodic pulse used for a link integrity test signal, which checks whether the link is working.

NWAY   An Auto-Negotiation protocol introduced by National Semiconductor that became the basis of the 802.3 Auto-Negotiation protocol.

O

Open Shortest Path First (OSPF)   A network routing protocol.

Open Systems Interconnect (OSI) model   A layered model for data communications, defined by an International Organization for Standardization committee.

optical time-domain reflectometer (OTDR)   An optical fiber test tool that locates fiber faults.

ordered set   A single special code-group or a combination of special and data code-groups that represent a signal such as an idle or the start of a frame.

organizationally unique identifier (OUI)   A 3-byte code assigned by the IEEE, usually for use as a MAC address prefix.

P–Q

packet   A generic term used for a Layer 2 frame or a Layer 3 protocol data unit.

page   A 16-bit message used for Auto-Negotiation.

PAM5x5   A coding technique that represents 4 bits as a pair of symbols selected from five signal levels. The levels are represented as (–2, –1, 0, +1, +2).

parallel detection   In Auto-Negotiation, the capability to detect whether a non-negotiating partner has a 10BASE-T, 100BASE-T4, or 100BASE-TX interface by examining the signals arriving from the partner.

passive concentrator   A type of Token Ring concentrator that contains no active elements in the signal path of any lobe port—that is, it does not repeat the signals.

patch cord   A short, flexible cable terminated with connectors.

patch panel   A cross-connect designed to accommodate the use of patch cords. It facilitates administration of moves and changes.

PAUSE operation   A flow control protocol used across a full-duplex Ethernet link. A system sends a PAUSE frame to ask its partner to stop sending frames for a specified period of time.

permanent link   Includes the horizontal cabling and the connectors at each end of a horizontal cable.

permanent virtual circuit (PVC)   For ATM, a long-term preconfigured circuit.

phantom signal   A low-level direct current transmitted by a Token Ring station. It causes the concentrator to open its relay and insert the station into the ring.

physical address   *See* MAC address.

physical layer (PHY)   The layer that interfaces with the transmission medium and transmits and receives bits.

Physical Coding Sublayer (PCS)   A sublayer that contains the functions to encode data into code-groups that can be transmitted over the physical medium.

Physical Medium Dependent (PMD) sublayer   The portion of the physical layer responsible for interfacing to the transmission medium.

plenum cable   Fire-retardant cable that can be carried in air ducts.

Point-to-Point Protocol (PPP)   An encapsulation and protocol defined by an IETF task force and used across point-to-point wide area links.

port-based VLAN   A VLAN defined by a list of bridge ports. All systems reached through those ports belong to the VLAN.

power sum equal level far end crosstalk (PSELFEXT)   The sum of the equal level far end crosstalk (ELFEXT) effects on a pair by the other three pairs.

power sum near end crosstalk (PSNEXT)   The sum of the NEXT effects on a pair by the other three pairs.

preamble   An introductory set of signals transmitted before an Ethernet frame, used to synchronize timing on a LAN.

primary FDDI ring   The ring around which frames flow during normal operation.

priority classes   Priority levels corresponding to the output queues at a port.

priority-tagged frame   A frame that contains a header that carries a null (0) VLAN identifier and a priority value.

private loop   A standalone fibre channel arbitrated loop.

propagation delay   The amount of time that elapses when a signal travels across a cable or across an entire path.

protocol   A set of rules that govern communication.

protocol data unit (PDU)   Information delivered as a unit between peer entities that contains control information and, optionally, data.

public loop   A fibre channel arbitrated loop connected to a switch.

punch-down block   A twisted-pair wiring panel for which each wire is placed in a pin and then punched into place, stripping the insulation and making a connection in the process.

purging   A Token Ring state that occurs when the active monitor has detected a ring error and is returning the ring to an operational state by transmitting Ring Purge frames.

Quality of Service parameters   ATM parameters that relate to delay and reliability requirements.

quinary symbols   Symbols corresponding to five different voltage levels that are labeled [–2, –1, 0, +1, +2]. Quinary symbols are used for 1000BASE-T transmission.

R

random backoff   *See* backoff.

real-time variable bit rate (rt-VBR)   An ATM service that delivers a specified average bandwidth and supports applications such as compressed voice or video, which are delay-sensitive.

registration   The exchange of information between a dedicated Token Ring station and its concentrator port that is required to initiate transmission between the devices.

remote bridges   Bridges that unite separate Ethernet, Token Ring, or FDDI LANs located at different sites into a single LAN. Remote bridges are connected by a wide area connection.

remote monitoring (RMON)   Standards that enable an SNMP network management station to interwork with a network monitoring component in a system.

repeater   A physical-layer device that accepts signals from one cable segment and transmits them onto one or more other cable segments at full strength. (Also called a hub or repeating concentrator.)

resistance   A measurement (in units called ohms) of the degree to which a conductor resists the flow of direct current in an electronic circuit.

return loss   A measure of the relative amount of a signal that is reflected back to its source.

ring error monitor (REM)   A server that receives ring error data from Token Ring stations.

ring in port   A Token Ring concentrator port that receives signals from the main ring path on the trunk cable.

ring out port   A Token Ring concentrator port that transmits signals to the main ring path on the trunk cable.

ring parameter server (RPS)   A Token Ring server that is responsible for initializing a set of operational parameters in a station on a Token Ring.

Ring Purge frame   A frame used to clear data out of a Token Ring as part of an initialization or recovery procedure.

riser cable   Cable to be used in vertical shafts.

root (of a Spanning Tree)   The bridge with the smallest bridge identifier.

route descriptor   A subfield of the routing information field that identifies a segment and bridge on the network path. The route between a pair of communicating systems is represented by a series of descriptors.

route discovery   A protocol that uses explorer frames to discover a path to a destination in a source routing LAN.

router   A device that forwards Layer 3 protocol data units. A router can interconnect multiple local area networks and WAN links with one another. Also called a Layer 3 switch.

routing information field (RIF)   A field in a Token Ring or FDDI frame header in which information describing the route between the communicating systems is stored.

Routing Information Protocol (RIP)   A network routing protocol.

routing protocol   A network protocol that enables routers to exchange information used to build their routing tables.

running disparity   A parameter having a value of + or –, representing the imbalance between the number of ones and zeros in a sequence of 8B/10B code-groups.

S

scrambling function   A transformation applied to outgoing bits to improve the balance between transmitted 1s and 0s. The function is reversed at the receiving end.

screened twisted-pair (ScTP)   Four UTP pairs, with a single foil or braided screen surrounding all four pairs in order to minimize the effect of EMI radiation.

screened/shielded twisted-pair (SSTP)   Four twisted pairs, where each pair is shielded and a shield surrounds all four pairs.

secondary FDDI ring   A backup FDDI ring. After a fault, segments on the secondary ring will be integrated into a usable path.

segment   A copper or optical fiber between two devices. Device types include DTEs, repeaters, bridges, and routers.

shared VLAN learning   The use of a single filtering table that contains MAC addresses that have been learned across a group of VLANs, or for all VLANs.

shielded twisted-pair (STP)   Cable for which each twisted pair of wires is shielded to prevent electromagnetic interference. Sometimes a shield also is placed around the entire cable bundle.

signal quality error (SQE) message   A signal sent across an AUI cable or an internal circuit from a transceiver to its parent DTE or repeater. It is used to announce a collision or to indicate that improper signals have been detected on the medium.

signal quality error (SQE) test   An ongoing check that a transceiver is working. The transceiver sends an SQE signal across an AUI cable or internal circuit whenever it finishes transmitting a frame.

Simple Network Management Protocol (SNMP)   A widely used network management protocol.

single-attachment FDDI station   A station attached to only the primary ring of an FDDI LAN.

single-mode fiber   An optical fiber with a narrow core (8 to 9 microns) that allows light to travel along only one path.

slot time   The minimum number of bit times in a valid half-duplex Ethernet transmission. It is 512 bit times for transmission rates up to 100Mbps, and 4096 bit times for 1000Mbps Ethernet.

SNAP header   A frame header field that identifies the type of protocol data that is being carried.

SNMP agent   Software component in a managed device that participates in SNMP.

SNMP manager   Software component in a network management station that reads or updates management variables at a remote device by sending requests to the device's SNMP agent.

source-routing bridge (SRB) A bridge that is used in a source-routing LAN.

source-routing LAN A bridged LAN in which a frame that needs to be bridged contains a field that describes the route that the frame will traverse.

source-routing transparent (SRT) bridge A bridge that can perform both source-routing and transparent bridging.

source service access point address *See* link service access point (LSAP) address.

Spanning Tree explorer (STE) frame A type of source routing explorer frame that traverses the LAN following only valid Spanning Tree paths.

Spanning Tree Protocol (STP) A protocol that makes it possible to eliminate points of failure by installing backup bridges and backup links. The protocol automatically reconfigures the LAN topology after a failure.

square corner (SC) A popular type of fiber optic connector.

start-of-stream delimiter A delimiter sent at the beginning of a 100BASE-X, FDDI, or CDDI frame.

standby monitors All Token Ring stations other than the active monitor. Any station is capable of taking over the active monitor role if the active monitor fails.

StarLAN A 1Mbps twisted-pair Ethernet LAN introduced by AT&T.

start frame delimiter (SFD) A special bit pattern sent before the first byte of an Ethernet frame.

station A device attached to a LAN that is capable of transmitting and receiving data.

station management (SMT) A software component in an FDDI station that performs initialization, testing, and error recovery functions.

straight tip (ST) A type of fiber optic connector.

store-and-forward bridge A bridge that waits until it has received an entire frame before it starts to forward the frame.

structural return loss (SRL) A measure of signal loss caused by difference in impedance along a wire, expressed in decibels.

SubLAN In an Ethernet LAN, a collision domain or point-to-point link.

Subnetwork Access Protocol (SNAP) header   *See* SNAP header.

synchronous bandwidth   For FDDI, a guaranteed reserved time quota during which a station can transmit frames.

switch   *See* Layer 2, Layer 3, or Layer 4 switch.

switched virtual circuit (SVC)   For ATM, a virtual circuit set up on demand.

symmetric flow control   For full-duplex Ethernet, the capability of a station at either end of the link to send a PAUSE frame to its partner.

T

tagged frame   A frame that contains a header that carries a VLAN identifier and a priority value. Also called a VLAN tagged frame.

Target Token Rotation Timeout (TTRT)   The average time that an FDDI station expects to wait before it receives the use of the token.

TCP/IP   A popular family of communications protocols, originally designed for use on the Internet.

terminator   For a coax Ethernet LAN, hardware attached to the ends of a coax segment. A terminator absorbs signals and prevents them from being reflected back into the cable.

Time Domain Reflectometer (TDR)   A tool used to track the location of cable faults.

Token Passing Protocol (TKP)   Use of the classical Token Ring protocol, which permits a station that has captured a token to transmit data in a Dedicated Token Ring environment.

Token Ring   A LAN technology originated by IBM and standardized as IEEE 802.5.

token   A special sequence of symbols passed from station to station that is used to control access to a LAN medium.

tone test set   A device that is attached to one end of a cable and generates a tone that is transmitted onto a wire. It is used to discover the matching end of a cable.

Topology Change Notification BPDU   A BPDU transmitted toward the root by any bridge that has evidence that the topology information needs to change.

transceiver   A hardware component that transmits signals onto a medium and receives them from the medium. Also called a medium attachment unit (MAU).

transition point   A location where flat undercarpet cabling connects to round cabling.

translational bridge   A bridge that connects LAN components that use different MAC protocols (for example, Ethernet and Token Ring).

Transmit Immediate Protocol (TXI)   For dedicated Token Ring, the capability to transmit data without waiting to capture a token.

transparent bridge   A bridge that forwards a frame based on information in its filtering database.

trap   A message that an SNMP agent sends to report a significant event (such as a reboot or a serious error that occurs at a device).

truncated binary exponential backoff   *See* backoff.

trunk coupling unit (TCU)   A device that couples a Token Ring station to the main path around the ring. A TCU provides the mechanism for inserting a station into the ring and removing it from the ring.

trunking   A term sometimes used for link aggregation.

tunneling   Encapsulating one type of frame inside the data field of another frame.

twisted-pair link   A twisted-pair cable plus connecting hardware.

U

unformatted page (UP)   A message that is part of an Auto-Negotiation exchange. Its content depends on the message code in a prior message page.

unicast address   An address that identifies a single network interface card.

universally administered MAC address   An address assigned to a network interface card by a manufacturer that has obtained a block of unique identifiers from the IEEE.

unshielded twisted-pair cable (UTP)   A cable in which wires are paired and twisted around each other. Usually four pairs are bundled into a single cable. The cables are graded by categories ranging from 1 to 7.

Unspecified Bit Rate (UBR)   A best-effort ATM service.

upstream neighbor   For Token Ring or FDDI, the adjacent neighboring station that transmits and forwards frames to the station.

User Datagram Protocol (UDP)   A connectionless protocol in the TCP/IP family, used to send standalone messages.

V

Vertical Cavity Surface Emitting Laser (VCSEL)   A low-cost laser used for gigabit transmission across multimode fiber.

Virtual Channel Identifier (VCI)   An identifier for an ATM virtual channel. VCIs appear in ATM cell headers.

virtual LAN (VLAN)   A group of systems (such as the computers in a workgroup) that need to communicate with one another, and protocols that restrict the delivery of virtual LAN frames to members of the VLAN.

Virtual Path Identifier (VPI)   An identifier for an ATM virtual path. VPIs appear in ATM cell headers.

VLAN-aware switch   A switch that is capable of participating in VLAN protocols. Also called a VLAN switch.

VLAN trunk   A link that carries traffic between a pair of VLAN switches. It can carry traffic for multiple VLANs.

W–Z

wide area network (WAN)   Communications facilities such as point-to-point links or frame relay service networks that carry data across large distances.

wiremap testing   A procedure that checks wires for proper pin termination, continuity, crossed pairs, shorts, and split pairs.

world wide port name   A unique 8-byte global identifier assigned to a fibre channel port.

worst pair-to-pair equal level far end crosstalk   The biggest equal level far end crosstalk (ELFEXT) effect of one pair on another.

Index

Symbols

1Mbps StarLAN Ethernet, 55
4B/5B data mappings, 552-553
5-4-3 rule, 93
802.1D standard. *See* **Spanning Tree Protocol**
802.3 standard
    Ethernet, 42
    Ethernet MAC frames, 68-69
8B/10B encoding, 169-170, 560-566, 568
    fibre channel data transfers, 516
    naming conventions, 565-566
    ordered sets, 567-568
    running disparity, 564-565
    special code-groups, 566
8B/10B translation table, 582-591
8B/6T byte translations, 553-555
8B/6T translations between bytes and ternary symbols, 580-582
10BASE-FB, 110-112, 117
    Manchester encoding, 547-548
10BASE-FL, 110, 114-116
    Manchester encoding, 547-548

10BASE-FP, 110
10BASE-T
    full-duplex operation, 104
    half-duplex operation, 99
        collision domain cabling topology, 100-102
        collision domain parameters, 100
    hubs, 106-107
    Manchester encoding, 547
    segments, 98
    switches, 106-107
    twisted-pair link integrity test, 108
    twisted-pair transmission, 104-106
10BASE-T (10Mbps twisted-pair Ethernet), 98
10BASE2, 87, 95-96
    collision domain parameters, 97
    Manchester encoding, 547
    problems with, 98
10BASE5, 87-88
    collision domain parameters, 92-93
        Ethernet 5-4-3 rule, 93
        propagation delay, 94-95

connecting to, 89-90
Manchester encoding, 547
problems with, 95
transceivers, 90-92
10Mbps FOIRL (fiber optic inter-repeater link), 110
10Mbps Twisted-Pair Ethernet. *See*
10BASE-T, 98
100BASE-FX, 126
FDDI, 133-134
physical layer encodings, NRZI
signals, 550
100BASE-T2
physical layer encodings, 559
PAM5x5 encoding, 559-560
twisted-pair cables, 128, 133
100BASE-T4
physical layer encodings, 553
8B/6T byte translations, 553-555
data transmission, 555-556
special patterns, 556-558
translating to 100BASE-X in hubs,
558-559
twisted-pair cables, 128-132
100BASE-TX, 127
physical layer encodings, MLT-3
signals, 551-552
twisted-pair cables, 128-129
CDDI, 129-130
100BASE-X, 127
physical layer encodings, 549-550
4B/5B data mappings, 552-553
translating to 100BASE-T4 in hubs,
558-559
100Mbps collision domains, 135-136
configurations, 138-141
hubs, 137
switches, 141-142
100Mbps Ethernet, 125-127, 134. *See also*
Fast Ethernet
Auto-Negotiation, 127
collision domains, 135-136

configurations, 138-141
hubs, 137
switches, 141-142
twisted-pair cables, 128
100BASE-T2, 128, 133
100BASE-T4, 128-132
100BASE-TX, 128-130
**100Mbps High Speed Token Ring
(HSTR), physical layer encodings, 575**
100VG-AnyLAN, 126, 142, 147-148
cables, 143-144
connectors, 143-144
initializing, 145-146
redundant links, 145
topology, 143
1000BASE-CX. *See* **1000BASE-X**
1000BASE-LH, 165
1000BASE-LX. *See* **1000BASE-X**
1000BASE-SX. *See* **1000BASE-X**
1000BASE-T, 165, 175
bit timing synchronization, 178-179
cables, 175-177
crossover cables, 179
encoders/decoders/hybrids, 177-178
encoding, 175
message pages, master/slave
roles, 216
physical layer encodings, 568-573
1000BASE-X, 165, 169
8B/10B encoding, 169-170
Auto-Negotiation, 218-220
connectors, 171-172
copper jumper cables, 173-174
gigabit interface converters (GBICs),
174-175
lasers, 170-171
mode-conditioning patch cords, 172
physical layer encodings, 8B/10B
encoding, 560-566, 568
1000Mbps. *See* **Gigabit Ethernet**

A

A-ports, FDDI, 443

AAL (ATM Adaptation Layer), 463

AAL5, ATM, 470-471

abort sequences, Token Ring
  protocol, 421

ABR (Available Bit Rate), ATM, 461

access control fields, token format, 417

access links, VLANs, 312

ACR (attenuation to crosstalk ratio), 195

Active Monitor Present (AMP)
  frames, 407
    Token Ring protocol, 428-429

active monitors, Token ring, 407
    functions of, 408
    protocol, 424

active topology, 258

adapters, fibre channel adapters, 504

address resolution, LES, 484-486

Address Resolution Protocol (ARP), 34

addresses
    address resolution, 484-486
    ATM addresses, 460
      LANE, 489
    broadcast addresses, 28
    Ethernet addresses, conventions,
      29-30
    Ethernet MAC addresses, 30
      traces of, 31-32
    Ethernet MAC frames, 63
    FDDI
      conventions for, 36
      MAC addresses, 36-38
    fibre channel, 510
      port identifiers, 511-512
    fibre channel data transfers, 520-521
    group addresses, 28
    L_Port, 533
    MAC addresses. See MAC addresses

multicast addresses, 274. See also
  multicasting
NICs, 28
Token Ring
    conventions for, 32-34
    functional address flags, 35-36
Token Ring protocol, 416
unicasts, 27

advantages
    of cells, 470
    of circuits, 470
    of routers, 384

aggregated links, 291-292. See also link
  aggregation

aggregation ports, 291

aggregation. See link aggregation

alias service, fibre channel, 514

all-routes-explorer frames, 354
    LLC, Token Ring protocol, 427-428
    route discovery, source-routing
      bridged LANs, 355

AL_PA (arbitrated loop physical
  address), 533

American Wire Gauge (AWG), 187

AMP (Active Monitor Present)
  frames, 407
    Token Ring protocol, 428-429

ANSI (American National Standards
  Institute), 9, 23, 457, 594
    ATM, 457
    fibre channel, 502

application specific integrated circuit
  (ASIC) chips, 242, 294, 393
    parallel processing, 243

application-layer switches, load
  balancing, 397-398

application-layer switching, Layer 4, 396

arbitrate signal, 536

arbitrated loop physical address
  (AL_PA), 533

arbitrated loop signals, 536-538

arbitrated loops, 531-532
    data transfers, 536
    fibre channel, 504

initializing, 534-535
L_Port addresses, 533
architecture
ATM, 463-464
full-duplex Ethernet, 77-79
of Layer 3 switches, 392-394
of legacy routers, 392
SNMP, 20-21
MIB, 21
MIB documents, 22
ARP (Address Resolution Protocol), 34
ASIC (application specific integrated circuit) chips, 242, 294, 393
parallel processing, 243
assigning
frame priorities, 339
forwarding, 340-341
IEEE 802.1Q, 340
frames to VLANs via ingress rules, 330-331
asymmetric flow control, 84
asynchronous transmission, 447
attachment unit interface (AUI), 195
ATM (Asynchronous Transfer Mode), 457-459
AAL5, 470-471
advantages of circuits and cells, 470
architecture, 463-464
channels, 460
concurrent circuits, 462
LANE. *See* LANE
paths, 460
protocols, 460
Quality of Service, 460-462
virtual circuits, 462
ATM Adaptation Layer (AAL), 463
ATM addresses, 460
LANE, 489
ATM cell headers, 464-466
AAL5, 470-471
cells
interleaving, 468-469
processing, 467

VCI numbers, 466
VPI numbers, 466
ATM data link layer, 463
ATM Forum, 596
ATM Layer, 463
ATM Physical Layer, 464
attempt limit, 59
attenuation, 189
cabling performance parameter, 191
fiber optic cabling, 199
attenuation to crosstalk ratio (ACR), 195
AUI (attachment unit interface), 89
Auto-Negotiation, 79, 203
100Mbps Ethernet, 127
1000BASE-T, 179
1000BASE-X interfaces, 218-220
Gigabit Ethernet, 166
master/slave timing, 178-179
twisted-pair interfaces, 204
controlling, 207
Ethernet upgrades, 204-207
exchanging data across twisted-pair media, 210-212
flow control, 209
functionality, 208
master/slave timer roles, 210
message codes, 217-218
parallel detection, 210
transmission technologies, 208-209
Available Bit Rate (ABR), 461
AWG (American Wire Gauge), 187

B

B-ports, FDDI, 443
backoff limit, 59
backward compatibility, full-duplex Ethernet, 79
bandwidth
Ethernet, shared bandwidth, 56
modal bandwidth, 168
TIA/EIA cabling standards categories, 184

barrel connectors, 87

base link code word, 212-213

base pages, 212

format of, 212-213

Beacon frames, FDDI, 449

beacon process, Token Ring, 409

Beacon Repeat, Token Ring
protocol, 424

Beacon Transmit, Token Ring
protocol, 424

BGP (Border Gateway Protocol), 391

bidirectional. *See* full-duplex

big-endian order, 579

binary characters, 580

bit timing synchronization, 1000BASE-
T, 178-179

BPDU (Bridge Protocol Data Unit)
messages, 259, 266-267

Configuration BPDUs, 262-270

root path discovery, STP, 263

Topology Change Notification BPDU,
270-271

bridged identifiers, source-routing
bridged LANs, 352

bridges. *See also* Layer 2 switches

BPDU messages, 259, 266-267

Configuration BPDU, 267-270

Topology Change Notification
BPDU, 270-271

compared to Layer 2 switches, 225

designated STP, 261

Ethernet LANs, 47

filtering table entries, 236-237

functions of, 225-228, 234

LAN structure, 252-254

learning process, 234, 236

multicasts, 246-247

IGMP snooping, 247

port costs, STP, 259-261

redundancy, 243-244

link aggregation, 246-247

STP, 244-246

remote bridges. *See* remote bridges

root bridge election, STP, 254-256

root path discovery, STP, 263

root port, STP, 261

root selection, STP, 262

routers, Layer 2/3 switches, 394

separating collision domains, 229-231

source-routing bridged LANs. *See*
source-routing bridged LANs

SRT bridges, 349

static filtering table entries, 237

efficient forwarding, 237-238

filtering constraints, 241

protocol filtering, 240-241

sample format, 238-239

security constraints, 239-240

topology changes, STP, 264-266

translational bridges. *See* translational
bridges

translational bridging. *See*
translational bridging

transparent bridges, 230-231

mixed-media LANs, 232-233

switched LANs, 232-235

twisted-pair LANs, 231-232

tree generation, STP, 256-259

tree maintenance, STP, 266

broadband Ethernet, 89

broadcast addresses, 28

Broadcast and Unknown Server (BUS),
479, 486-488

broadcast multiaccess environments, 44

broadcasts, 306

buffer, fibre channel data transfer,
521-522

buffer credit system, fibre channel data
transfers, 521-522

Buffered Class 1, fibre channel classes
of service, 513

buffered distributors, 155-156

building routing tables, 389-392

burst mode, half-duplex Gigabit
  Ethernet, 159-161
BUS (Broadcast and Unknown Server),
  479, 486-488

C

C-ports
    DTR, 432-433
    joining stations to, 435
cable testers, 197
cables
    100VG-AnyLAN, 143-144
    1000BASE-T, 175-177
    copper jumper cables, 1000BASE-CX,
      173-174
    crossover cables, 1000BASE-T, 179
    fiber optic cable. See fiber optic cable
    Gigabit Ethernet, 167-169
    mixed coax/twisted-pair cables, 108
    thinnet, 95
    trunk, 404
    twisted-pair cables
        100Mbps Ethernet, 128
        parallel detection, 210
    twisted-pair cabling, 45
cabling
    fiber optic, testing, 199-200
    layouts, 187-188
    performance parameters, 188-189
        attenuation, 191
        attenuation to crosstalk ratio
          (ACR), 195
        delay skew, 196
        FEXT (far end crosstalk), 193-195
        high-speed LANs, 190
        jitter, 190
        NEXT (near end crosstalk), 192-193
        propagation delay, 196
        return loss, 195
        structural return loss (SRL), 195
    standards bodies, 183-184

STP, 403
TIA/EIA categories, 184-187
twisted-pair
    faults on, 196-197
        scope of tests, 198-199
        test tools, 197-198
    UTP, 403
    wire features, 187
Canonical Format Indicator (CFI), 335
Canonical Format Indicator (CFI)
  flag, 369
carrier extention bytes, 67
Carrier Sense Multiple Access with
  Collision Detection. See CSMA/CD
Category 1 cabling, 185
Category 2 cabling, 185
Category 3 cabling, 185
Category 4 cabling, 185
Category 5 cabling, 185
Category 5E cabling, 185
Category 6 cabling, 185
Category 7 cabling, 186
CAUs (Controlled Access Units), 413
CBR (Constant Bit Rate), ATM, 461
CDDI (Copper Distributed Data
  Interface), 13, 446
    100BASE-TX, 129-130
    physical layer encodings, 549-550
        4B/5B data mappings, 552-553
        MLT-3 signals, 551-552
cell lose priority, ATM cell headers, 465
cells
    advantages of, 470
    ATM cell headers
        interleaving, 468-469
        processing, 467
certification tools, 198
CFI (Canonical Format Indicator), 335
CFI (Canonical Format Indicator) flag,
  369
channels
    ATM, 460
    scope of cabling tests, 198

circuits
    advantages of, 470
    ATM, concurrent circuits, 462
    virtual circuits, 462
cladding optical fibers, 118
Claim frames, FDDI, 448
Claim Token, Token Ring protocol, 425
Claim Token frames
    Token Ring, 408
    Token Ring protocol, 430
Class 1, fibre channel classes of
    service, 513
Class 2, fibre channel classes of
    service, 513
Class 3, fibre channel classes of
    service, 513
Class 4 (Fractional Service), fibre
    channel classes of service, 514
Class F (Fabric), fibre channel classes of
    service, 514
class fields, 422
Class I hubs, 137
Class II hubs, 137
classes of service, fibre channel levels,
    513-514
coaxial cable, 45
code-groups, 516
    8B/10B encoding, 169-170
code-groups, 516. See also ordered sets
collision domain, Gigabit Ethernet, 162
collision domain cabling topology,
    10BASE-T (half-duplex operation),
    100-102
collision domain parameters
    10BASE-T, half-duplex operation, 100
    10BASE2, 97
    10BASE5, 92-93
        Ethernet 5-4-3 rule, 93
        propagation delay, 94-95
collision domains, 228-230, 306
    100Mbps, 135-136
        configurations, 138, 140-141
        hubs, 137
        switches, 141-142

Ethernet LANs, 47-48
Ethernet MAC frames, size, 62-63
fiber optic distances, 118
FOIRL links, 113-114
mixed coax/twisted-pair, 108
separating with bridges, 229-231
as trunk links, 312
common part indicator (CPI), 471
communicating between VLANs, 314
communications layering model, 13
    LAN frames, 16
    LAN layering model, 14
compatibility, full-duplex Ethernet and
    half-duplex Ethernet, 79
components
    of LANs, 16
        device drivers, 17-19
        DTE, 17
        media, 17
        NIC, 17
        stations, 17
    of Token Ring, 412-415
concentrator ports. See C-ports
Concentrator/Switch ports, 433
concentrators/switches, 432
concurrent circuits, ATM, 462
Configuration BPDUs, 262
    STP, 267-270
configuration direct connection, 494
configuration direct virtual channel
    connection, 481
Configuration Report Server (CRS), 410
configuration servers
    finding, 482
    setting up, 481
configurations of
    100Mbps collision domains, 138-141
    Gigabit Ethernet, 153-154
configuring
    port-based VLANs
        maintaining configurations
            manually, 323-324
        maintaining configurations
            with GVRP, 324-326

trunks for port-based VLANs,
321-322
VLAN ports, 333-334
congestion, full-duplex Ethernet, 80-81
connecting to 10BASE5, 89-90
connections
configuration direct, 494
configuration direct virtual channel
connection, 481
control direct, 494
control direct virtual channel
connection, 483
control distribute, 494
control distribute virtual channel
connection, 484
multicast forward virtual channel
connection, 486
multicast send connection, 487
multicast send virtual channel
connection, 486
connectors
ST connectors, 121
1000BASE-X, 171-172
100VG-AnyLAN, 143-144
fiber optics, MIC, 121
fibre channel, 503
SC, 121
**consolidation point (cabling
layout), 188**
Constant Bit Rate (CBR), ATM, 461
continuity testers, 197
**control codes, physical layer
encodings, 552**
control direct connections, 494
**control direct virtual channel
connection, 483**
control distribute connections, 494
**control distribute virtual channel
connection, 484**
control frames
Join Response control frames, 496-497
LAN Emulation, 495-496
LANE, 494-495

control signals, 545
Controlled Access Units (CAUs), 413
controlling
multicasts, 275-276
twisted-pair interfaces,
Auto-Negotiation, 207
conventions
for Ethernet Addresses, 29-30
for FDDI addresses, 36
for Token Ring addresses, 32, 34
conversations, LACP, 302
switching to different link
segments, 303
Copper Distributed Data Interface.
See **CDDI**
**copper jumper cables, 1000BASE-CX,
173-174**
costs
assigning to subLANs, 256-257
port costs, STP, 259-261
CPI (common part indicator), 471
**credit, fibre channel data transfer,
521-522**
crossover cables, 1000BASE-T, 179
crossovers, 107
crosstalk, 104
CRS (Configuration Report Server), 410
CSA T529 standard, 183
**CSMA/CD (Carrier Sense Multiple
Access with Collision Detection),
43, 47, 58**
Ethernet, 58
**cut-through mode, Layer 2 switches
compared to store-and-forward mode,
242-243**
cut-through operations, 388

D

data field control frame header fields, fibre channel frame format, 525
data frames, LANE, 490-493
data terminal equipment (DTE), 17
data transfers
  arbitrated loops, 536
  fibre channel, 515
    8B/10B encoding, 516
    addresses, 520-521
    buffer credit system, 521-522
    exchanges, 518-519
    frame format, 523-526
    frame sequences, 516, 518
    logins, 520-521
    ordered sets, 516
    relative offsets, 519
data transmission, 100BASE-T4 (physical layer encodings), 555-556
dB (decibels), 191
dc balance, restoring, 555
decibels (dB), 191
decimal characters, 580
decoders, 1000BASE-T, 177-178
Dedicated Simplex Class 1, fibre channel classes of service, 513
Dedicated Token Ring. See DTR
delay, Gigabit Ethernet network components, 162
delay skew (cabling performance parameter), 196
delimiters, fibre channel (order sets), 591-592
demand priority, 100VG-AnyLAN, 147-148
Dense Mode Protocol Independent Multicast, 391
designated bridges, STP, 261
designated ports, STP, 261
destination identifier frame header fields, fibre channel frame format, 524
device drivers, LAN, 17-19

Differential Manchester encoding, Token Ring, 573-575
Digital, Intel, and Xerox (DIX), 41
directory service, fibre channel, 514
disadvantages of tunneling Token Ring across Ethernet, 367. See also problems
dispersion, modal, 168
distance specifications, fiber optic cable, 117-118
Distance Vector Multicast Routing Protocol (DVMRP), 391
distances, fibre channel, 503
DIX (Digital, Intel, and Xerox), 41
DIX Ethernet, 41, 65
  Ethernet MAC frames, tracing, 68
downstream direction, Token Ring, 406
DTE (data terminal equipment), 17
DTR, 432
  C-ports, 432-433
  full-duplex protocols, 434
    joining stations to C-ports, 435
    MAC frames, 436-437
DTR (Dedicated Token Ring), 431
dual-attached stations, FDDI, 443-444
DVMRP (Distance Vector Multicast Routing Protocol), 391

E

E-RIF
  source-routed frames, 371
  transparently bridged LANs, 370
early token releases, Token Ring, 406
EGP (Exterior Gateway Protocol), 391
egress rules, VLAN frames, 330
EIA (Electronic Industries Alliance), 183, 594
EIGRP (Enhanced Internet Gateway Routing Protocol), 390
ELAN (emulated LAN), 475
  MAC addresses, 475
  Token Ring, 476

ELFEXT (equal level far end
  crosstalk), 194
encapsulating
    GARP, 286-287
    GMRP, 286-287
    IP datagrams, FC-4, 526-528
encoders, 1000BASE-T, 177-178
encoding
    1000BASE-T, 175
    FDDI, 446-447
encodings (physical layer), 543-544
    4B/5B data mappings, 552-553
    100BASE-T2, 559
        PAM5x5 encoding, 559-560
    100BASE-T4, 553
        8B/6T byte translations, 553-555
        data transmission, 555-556
        special patterns, 556-558
        translating to 100BASE-X in hubs,
          558-559
    100BASE-X, 549-550
    1000BASE-T, 568-573
    1000BASE-X, 8B/10B encoding,
      560-566, 568
    CDDI, 549-550
    FDDI, 549-550
    Manchester encoding, 547
        fiber optic cable, 547-548
    MLT-3 signals, 551-552
    NRZI signals, 550
    Token Ring, 573
        100Mbps High Speed Token
          Ring, 575
        Differential Manchester encoding,
          573-575
    types of signal encoding, 544-546
ending delimiters, frame format of
  Token Ring protocol, 420
Enhanced Internet Gateway Routing
  Protocol (EIGRP), 390
EOF (end of frame), 591
equal level far end crosstalk
  (ELFEXT), 194

equipment, fibre channel, 504
Error Report, Token Ring protocol, 425
error-detected bit, Differential
  Manchester encoding, 575
errors, Token Ring, 411
Ethernet
    1Mbps StarLAN, 55
    802.3 standard, 42
    10BASE-T. See 10BASE-T
    10BASE2. See 10BASE2
    10BASE5, 87-88
        connecting to, 89-90
    10BASE5. See 10BASE5
    100Mbps. See 100Mbps Ethernet
    bridges
        compared to Layer 2 switches, 225
        filtering table entries, 236-237
        functions of, 225-228, 234
        learning process, 234, 236
        multicasts, 246-247
        redundancy, 243-247
        static filtering table entries, 237-241
        transparent bridges, 230-235
    broadband, 89
    characteristics of, 10
    collision domains, 228-230
        separating with bridges, 229-231
    CSMA/CD, 58
    DIX Ethernet, 65
    fiber optic cable, 110
    full-duplex, 10, 77
        architecture, 77-79
        backward compatibility, 79
        congestion, 80-81
        MAC control sublayer, 81-84
        parameters, 79, 155
        PAUSE frame implementation, 84
    Gigabit Ethernet
        1000BASE-LH, 165
        1000BASE-T, 165, 175-179
        1000BASE-X, 165, 169-175
        Auto-Negotiation, 166
        configurations, 153-154

full-duplex, 154-158, 166-167
half-duplex, 158-162
physical characteristics, 167-169
references, 181
specification, 151-152
half-duplex, 78
history of, 9-10
interframe gaps, 56-57
shrinking, 57
LANE frame, 490-492
Layer 2 switches
compared to bridges, 225
hardware innovations, 242
layer structure, 243-244, 247-248
parallel processing, 243
store-and-forward compared to
cut-through mode, 242-243
Manchester encoding, 547
parameters, tabulating, 74
random backoff, 58-59
shared bandwidth, 56
tagged frames, 335-337
translational bridging between
source-routing Token Ring, 365
translational bridging between
Transparent Token Ring, 364
tunneling Token Ring across, 366-367
upgrades, twisted-pair interfaces
Auto-Negotiation, 204-207
Ethernet 5-4-3 rule, 93
Ethernet addresses, conventions, 29-30
Ethernet Blue Book, 41
Ethernet LANs, 42
bridges, 47
collision domains, 47-48
full-duplex operations, 50
hub repeaters, 46
multisegment LANs, repeaters, 44
routers, 51-52
sharing LANs, 50
single segment Ethernet LANs, 42-44
switches, 48-50
twisted-pair cabling, 45-46

Ethernet MAC addresses, 30-32
Ethernet MAC frames, 60
DIX Ethernet, tracing, 68
format, 63-64
addresses, 63
Ethernet types, 65
Gigabit Ethernet, modifying sizes,
66-67
LLC headers, 70-71
LSAPs, 71
LLC/SNAP frames, 68-69
NetWare, 73-74
preambles, 60
size, frame size versus collision
domain size, 62-63
size of, 62
SNAP headers, 70-72
start frame delimiters, 60-61
Ethernet multicasts, mapping to IP
multicast addresses, 277
Ethernet Version 1 specification, 41
Ethernet Version 2, 41
EtherType, 65
exchanges, fibre channel data transfers,
518-519
exchanging data across twisted-pair
media, Auto-Negotiation, 210-212
exiting LANs, 386-388
explorer frames, 353
extension bytes, half-duplex Gigabit
Ethernet, 158-159
Exterior Gateway Protocol (EGP), 391

F

fabrics, fibre channel, 507
far end crosstalk (FEXT), 193-195
Fast Ethernet, MII, 134-135
Fast Ethernet Alliance, 125
Fast Ethernet Consortium, 125
Fast Ethernet. *See* 100Mbps Ethernet

fast link pulse (FLP), 211
FC-0, fibre channel levels, 512
FC-1, fibre channel levels, 512
FC-2, fibre channel levels, 512
FC-3, fibre channel levels, 513
FC-4
  fibre channel, 515, 526
    encapsulating IP datagrams,
      526-528
    versus SCSI, 529-531
  fibre channel levels, 513
FDDI (Fibre Distributed Data
  Interface), 12-13, 438-439
  100BASE-FX, 133-134
  addresses, conventions for, 36
  encoding, 446-447
  formats, 451
    frame format, 452
    token format, 451
  history of, 12
  MAC addresses, 36-38
  media, 446-447
  physical layer encodings, 549-550
    4B/5B data mappings, 552-553
    NRZI signals, 550
  rings, wrapping, 445
  stations, 439
  tagged frames, 338
  topology, 439-440
    A-ports, 443
    B-ports, 443
    dual-attached stations, 443-444
    M-ports, 445
    primary rings, 441-442
    S-ports, 443
    secondary rings, 441-442
  translational bridging between Token
    Ring, 362-363
FDDI frames, 450
FDDI multicasts, mapping to IP
  multicast addresses, 278
FDDI protocols, 447-448
  Beacon frames, 449
  Claim frames, 448

SMT, 448-449
Target Token Rotation Timeout, 448
features
  of fibre channel, 502-503
    transmission speeds, 503
  of link aggregation, 293-294
FEXT (far end crosstalk), 193-195
fiber optic cable, 110
  10BASE-FB, 117
  10BASE-FL, 114-116
  distance specifications, 117-118
  fiber optic links, 110-112
  FOIRL, 112
  FOIRL links, 113-114
  Manchester encoding, 547-548
  structure of fiber, 118-119
fiber optic cabling, testing, 199-200
fiber optic HSTR lobes, 438
fiber optic inter-repeater link (FOIRL),
  112. See also 10Mbps FOIRL
fiber optic links, 110-112
fiber optics
  connectors, 121
  multimode fiber, transmitting, 120-121
fibre channel, 501-502
  8B/10B encoding, 560-566, 568
    naming conventions, 565-566
    ordered sets, 567-568
    running disparity, 564-565
    special code-groups, 566
  addresses, 510-512
  arbitrated loop signals, 536-538
  arbitrated loops, 531-532
    data transfers, 536
    initializing, 534-535
    L_Port addresses, 533
  classes of service, 513-514
  data transfers, 515
    8B/10B encoding, 516
    addresses, 520-521
    buffer credit system, 521-522
    exchanges, 518-519
    frame fromat, 523-526
    frame sequences, 516, 518

logins, 520-521
　ordered sets, 516
　relative offsets, 519
equipment, 504
FC-4, 515, 526
　encapsulating IP datagrams,
　　526-528
　versus SCSI, 529, 531
features of, 502-503
　transmission speeds, 503
levels, 512-513
　classes of service, 513-514
　generic services, 514-515
loops, 504
names, 510
primitive sequences, order sets, 592
primitive signals, order sets, 592
topologies, 504, 507
　fabrics, 507
　loop switches, 507
　ports, 508-509
world wide node names, 510-511
world wide port names, 510-511
fibre channel adapters, 504
fibre channel delimiters, order sets,
591-592
Fibre Channel Industry
Association, 596
fibre channel ports, 508-509
Fibre Distributed Data Interface.
See FDDI
filtering for security, Layer 4, 397
filtering constraints, bridges (static
filtering table entries), 241
filtering protocols, bridges (static filter-
ing table entries), 240-241
filtering table entries, bridges, 236-237
finding configuration servers, 482
flag bits, MAC addresses, 29
flags, Token Ring addresses, 35-36
flow control, 83-84
　twisted-pair interfaces,
　　Auto-Negotiation, 209

FLP (fast link pulse), 211
FOIRL (fiber optic inter-repeater
links), 112
　Manchester encoding, 547-548
FOIRL links, fiber optic cables, 113-114
format
　of base pages, 212-213
　of Ethernet MAC frames, 63-64
　　addresses, 63
　　Ethernet types, 65
　of FDDI, 451
　　frame format, 452
　　token format, 451
　of message pages, 214
　of unformatted pages, 214
forwarding
　prioritized frames, 340-341
　traffic, static filtering table entries,
　　237-238
　VLAN frames, 332-333
frame bursting, 67
　half-duplex Gigabit Ethernet, 159-161
frame control field, frame format of
Token Ring protocol, 418
frame control frame header fields, fibre
channel frame format, 525
frame distribution, LACP, 302
frame format
　FDDI, 452
　fibre channel, 523-526
　remote bridges, wide area links,
　　376-380
　Token Ring protocol, 417
　　ending delimiters, 420
　　frame control field, 418
　　frame status fields, 421
　　RIF, 419-420
Frame Relay, encapsulating Token Ring
frames, 379
frame sequences, fibre channel data
transfers, 516-518
frame status fields, frame format of
Token Ring protocol, 421

frames, 14
   AMP, 407
   assigning priorities, 339
      forwarding, 340-341
      IEEE 802.1Q, 340
   assigning priorities to, mapping
     802.1Q priorities to priority classes,
     342-343
   Beacon frames, FDDI, 449
   BPDU messages, 266-267
      Configuration BPDU, 267-270
      Topology Change Notification
       BPDU, 270-271
   Claim frames, FDDI, 448
   Claim Token frames, 408
   collision domains, 228-230
      separating with bridges, 229-231
   control frames
      Join Response control frame,
       496-497
      LANE, 494-496
   data frames, LANE, 490-493
   Ethernet MAC frames. *See* Ethernet
    MAC frames
   explorer frames, 353
      all-routes-explorer, 354-355
      Spanning Tree explorer, 354
      Spanning Tree explorer frames, 356
   extension bytes, half-duplex Gigabit
    Ethernet, 158-159
   FDDI, 450
   format of Token Ring protocol, 417
      ending delimiters, 420
      frame control field, 418
      frame status fields, 421
      RIF, 419-420
   Heartbeat MAC frames, 434
   LAN frames, 16
   link control frames, 517
   LLC frames, 407
   Lobe Media Test, 411
   MAC frames, 407
      DTR full-duplex protocols, 436-437
      translational bridges, 362
   multicasts. *See* multicasts, 247
   parallel processing, Layer 2
    switches, 243
   PAUSE, 80-84
      implementation, 84
   priority-tagged, 311
   remote bridges, wide area links,
    376-380
   Ring Purge, 408
   SMP, 410
   Token Ring MAC protocol frames,
    422-424
   VLAN frames. *See* VLAN frames
full-duplex Ethernet, 10, 77
   architecture, 77-79
   backward compatibility, 79
   congestion, 80-81
   MAC control sublayer, 81-84
   parameters, 79, 155
   PAUSE frame implementation, 84
full-duplex Ethernet MAC protocol, 50
**full-duplex Gigabit Ethernet, 151,
   154-155**
   full-duplex repeaters, 155-156
   Jumbo frames, 157-158
   physical transmission, 166-167
full-duplex operations
   10BASE-T, 104
   Ethernet LANs, 50
full-duplex protocols, DTR, 434
   joining stations to C-ports, 435
   MAC frames, 436-437
full-duplex repeaters, 155-156
full-duplex Token Ring, 12
**functional address flags, Token Ring,
   35-36**
functions of active monitors, 408

G

GARP (Generic Attribute Registration Protocol), 274, 284-285, 317
encapsulating, 286-287
joins, 286
GARP Multicast Registration Protocol. *See* **GMRP**
GARP VLAN Registration Protocol. *See* **GVRP**
GBICs (gigabit interface converters), 174-175
Gigabit Ethernet
1000BASE-LH, 165
1000BASE-T, 165, 175
bit timing synchronization, 178-179
cables, 175-177
crossover cables, 179
encoders/decoders/hybrids, 177-178
encoding, 175
1000BASE-X, 165, 169
8B/10B encoding, 169-170
connectors, 171-172
copper jumper cables, 173-174
GBICs, 174-175
lasers, 170-171
mode-conditioning patch cords, 172
Auto-Negotiation, 166
configurations, 153-154
full-duplex, 154-155
Jumbo frames, 157-158
physical transmission, 166-167
repeaters, 155-156
half-duplex, 158
burst mode, 159-161
extension bytes, 158-159
hubs, 161-162
MAC frames, modifying sizes, 66-67
physical characteristics, 167-169
references, 181
specification, 151-152

Gigabit Ethernet Alliance, 595
Gigabit Ethernet Consortium Web site, 163
gigabit interface converters (GBICs), 174-175
gigabit NICs, 156
GMRP (GARP Multicast Registration Protocol), 247, 274, 281
encapsulating, 286-287
multicasts, 283
group addresses, 28, 274. *See also* **multicast addresses**
GVRP (GARP VLAN Registration Protocol), 284, 317, 344
join messages, 344
leave messages, 344
maintaining VLAN configurations, 324-326
messages, 344-345

H

half-duplex Ethernet, 78
full-duplex compatibility with, 79
half-duplex Ethernet transmission. *See* **CSMA/CD**
half-duplex Gigabit Ethernet, 151, 158
burst mode, 159-161
extension bytes, 158-159
hubs, 161-162
half-duplex operation, 10BASE-T, 99
collision domain cabling topology, 100-102
collision domain parameters, 100
half-duplex Token Ring. *See* **Token Ring**
hard errors, Token Ring, 411
hardware innovations, Layer 2 switches, 242
header error control field, ATM cell headers, 466

headers, IP datagrams, 386
Heartbeat MAC frames, 434
hexadecimal characters, 580
high-speed LANs, cabling performance
   parameters, 190
HIPPI (High-Performance Parallel
   Interface), 502
history
   of Ethernet, 9-10
   of FDDI, 12
   of Token Ring, 10, 403
HSTR (High Speed Token Ring), 11,
   403, 437-438, 595
   fiber optic HSTR lobes, 438
HSTRA (High Speed Token Ring
   Alliance), 403
hub repeaters, Ethernet LANs, 46
hubs
   10BASE-T, 106-107
   Class I, 137
   Class II, 137
   classes of 100Mbps collision
      domains, 137
   half-duplex Gigabit Ethernet, 161-162
   Token Ring hubs, 413
   translating between 100BASE-X and
      100BASE-T4 encodings, 558-559
hybrid links, VLANs, 312-313
hybrids, 1000BASE-T, 177-178

I

IBM, Token Ring, 10
identifiers
   N_Port identifier, 512
   VLAN identifiers, 334
IEEE (Institute for Electrical and
   Electronics Engineers), 9, 23, 593
   MAC addresses, universally
      administered, 26
IEEE 802 VLAN committee, 368

IEEE 802.1D standard. See Spanning
   Tree Protocol
IEEE 802.1Q, mapping to priority
   classes, 342-343
IEEE 802.1Q priority, prioritizing
   frames, 340
IETF (Internet Engineering Task Force),
   13, 23, 594
IGMP (Internet Group Management
   Protocol), 247, 273
IGMP snooping, 247, 273, 278-280
   multicasts, controlling, 276
   problems with, 280-281
IGRP (Internet Gateway Routing
   Protocol), 390
ILMI (Integrated Local Management
   Inteface), 488
   LANE, initializing, 490
impedance, 189
implementing VLANs, 318-319
improving bridge performance, Ethernet
   LANs, 47
independent VLAN learning (IVL), 316
indices of refraction, fiber optics, 118
individual addresses, 27
individual/group flag bits, 29
information fields, Token Ring
   addresses, 34
ingress rules, VLAN frames, 330-331
initializing
   100VG-AnyLAN, 145-146
   arbitrated loops, 534-535
   LANE with ILMI, 490
Insert Delay, Token Ring protocol, 425
Institute for Electrical and Electronics
   Engineers. See IEEE
Integrated Local Management Inferface.
   See ILMI
Intelligent Peripheral Interface (IPI), 502
interframe gaps, 56-57, 405
   shrinking, 57
interleaving cells, ATM cell headers,
   468-469

intermediate frame bit, Differential
Manchester encoding, 575
Intermix, fibre channel classes of
service, 513
International Organization for
Standardization (ISO), 9, 595
International Telecommunications
Union—Telecommunication
Standardization Sector (ITU-T), 595
Internet Engineering Task Force. *See*
IETF
Internet Gateway Routing Protocol
(IGRP), 390
Internet Group Management Protocol.
See IGMP
interoperability issues, Jumbo
frames, 158
InterOperability Lab (IOL), 596
intrusive transceivers, 90
inverting 6T data code-groups, 555
IOL (InterOperability Lab), 596
IP datagrams
FC-4, encapsulating, 526-528
headers, 386
IP multicast groups, 273
IP multicasts, 276
mapping to Ethernet multicast
addresses, 277
mapping to FDDI multicast
addresses, 278
IP subnets, 328
IP VLANs, 328
IPI (Intelligent Peripheral
Interface), 502
IPX VLANs, 328
ISO, 23
ISO (International Organization for
Standardization), 9, 595
ISO/IEC 11801 standards, 183

ITU-T (International
Telecommunications Union—
Telecommunication Standardization
Sector), 595
ATM, 457
IVL (independent VLAN learning), 316

J-K

jabber, transceivers, 92
jam size, 58
jitter, 462
cabling performance parameter, 190
join messages, GVRP, 344
Join Response control frame, 496-497
Join Ring, Token Ring protocol, 425
joining
rings, Token Ring, 411-412
stations to C-ports, 435
joins, 483
GARP, 286
Jumbo frames, 157
Gigabit Ethernet, 152
interoperability issues, 158
throughput, 157
jumpers, 173. *See also* copper jumper
cables

key groups, 299
keys, 299

L

L-Port, addresses, 533
LACP (link aggregation control
protocol), 297-300
conversations, 302
switching to different link
segments, 303

frame distribution, 302
messages, 300-302
slow protocols, 300
LACPDU (Link Aggregation Control PDU), 300
LAN Emulation Clients. *See* **LECs**
LAN Emulation Configuration Server. *See* **LECS**
LAN Emulation control frame, 495-496
LAN Emulation Server. *See* **LES**
LAN emulation servers, 478-479
BUS, 486-488
LECS, 480-482
LES, 483
address resolution, 484-486
LAN Emulation. *See* **LANE**
LAN frames, 16
LAN layering model, 14
LAN MAC addresses, 25
locally administered, 27
universally administered, 26
LAN media, 17
LANE (LAN Emulation), 473
ATM addresses, 489
control frames, 494-495
data frames, 490-493
Ethernet frame, 490-492
ILMI, initializing, 490
Join Response control frame, 496-497
protocol elements, 488
Token Ring frame, 493
LANE Clients. *See* **LECs**
LANE Configuration Server. *See* **LECS**
LANE Server. *See* **LES**
LANE version 2, 498
LANs (local area networks), 9
components of, 16
device drivers, 17-19
DTE, 17
media, 17
NIC, 17
stations, 17

Ethernet LANs. *See* Ethernet LANs
Ethernet. *See* Ethernet
exiting, 386-388
security, 306
sharing, 50
source-routing bridged LANs. *See* source-routing bridged LANs
subLAN structure, 252-254
tagging, 368
transparent bridges, tagging, 368-370
largest frame (LF), 370
lasers, 1000BASE-X, 170-171
Layer 2 switches, 49. *See also* **bridges**
bridges, 394
compared to bridges, 225
hardware innovations, 242
layer structure, 243-244
layered structure, 247-248
parallel processing, 243
store-and-forward compared to cut-through mode, 242-243
Layer 3 switches
architecture of, 392-394
bridges, 394
Layer 4
application-layer switching, 396
load balancing, 397-398
security, filtering, 397
traffic, prioritizing, 397
layouts, cabling standards, 187-188
learning process, bridges, 234-236
leave messages, GVRP, 344
leaveall messages, GARP, 284
leaves (subLANs), 252
LECs (LAN Emulation Clients), 477-478, 480-482
LECS (LAN Emulation Configuration Server), 478
legacy routers, architecture, 392
LES (LAN Emulation Server), 478, 483
address resolution, 484-486

levels of fibre channel, 512-513
  classes of service, 513-514
  generic services, 514-515
LF (largest frame), 370
line cards, link aggregation, 294
link aggregation, 227, 246-247, 291-292
  features of, 293-294
  line cards, 294
  parameters, 299
  sublayers, 297
  switches, 297-298
  virtual link MAC addresses, 295-296
Link Aggregation Control PDU
  (LACPDU), 300
link aggregation control protocol.
  See LACP
link control frames, 517
link integrity signals, 108
link integrity test, 108
link service access points (LSAPs), 71
links
  access links, 312
  between remote bridges, 374
  fiber optic inter-repeater links, 112
  fiber optic links, 110-112
  hybrid links, 312-313
  redundant links, 100VG-AnyLAN,
    145
  trunk links, 310
listings
  Configuration BPDU, 269-270
  Configuration BPDU initial fields, 262
  Topology Change Notification
    BPDU, 270
LLC (Logical Link Control), 70
  all-routes-explorer frames, Token
    Ring protocol, 427-428
LLC data frame, Token Ring
  protocol, 426
LLC frames, 407
  Ethernet MAC frames, 68-69
  tracing, 69-70

LLC headers, Ethernet MAC frames,
  70-71
  LSAPs, 71
load balancers, 397
load balancing Layer 4, 397-398
Lobe Media Test frames, 411
lobes, 404
  fiber optic HSTR lobes, 438
local area networks. See LANs
locally administered MAC addresses, 27
Logical Link Control. See LLC
logins
  fibre channel data transfers, 520-521
  N_Port identifier, 512
loop initialization primitive
  sequences, 534
loop switches, fibre channel, 507
loops
  arbitrated loops. See arbitrated loops
  fibre channel, 504
  private loops, 504
LSAPs (link service access points), 71

M

M-ports, FDDI, 445
MAC (media access control) protocol, 15
MAC addresses, 15
  ELAN, 475
  Ethernet, 30-32
  FDDI, 36-38
  flag bits, 29
  locally administered, 27
  Token Ring, 34-35
  universally administered, 26-27
  versus network addresses, 384-385
  virtual link MAC addresses, link
    aggregation, 295-296
MAC control sublayer, 81-84
MAC frames, 407
  Active Monitor Present, 428
  Claim Token MAC frames, 430

DTR, full-duplex protocols, 436-437
Ethernet MAC frames. *See* Ethernet
  MAC frames
FDDI, 450
Report Soft Error MAC frames, 431
Ring Purge MAC frames, 430
sizes of translational bridges, 362
Standby Monitor Present frames, 429
VLANs, 334
**MAC-address-based secure VLANs,
  328-329**
**Management Information Base
  (MIB), 21**
management service, fibre channel, 515
Manchester encoding, 547
  fiber optic cable, 547-548
mapping
  802.1Q priorities to priority classes,
    342-343
  IP multicasts
    to Ethernet multicast
      addresses, 277
    to FDDI multicast addresses, 278
master/slave roles, 1000BASE-T, 216
master/slave timer roles, twisted-pair
  interfaces (Auto-Negotiation), 210
master/slave timing, 1000BASE-T,
  178-179
**MAU (medium attachment unit), 89-90,
  See also transceivers**
**MAU or MSAU (Multistation
  Access Units), 413**
**MDI (medium dependent
  interface), 106**
**MDI-X (medium dependent interface
  crossover), 107**
media
  FDDI, 446-447
  fibre channel, 503
Media access control addresses. *See*
  MAC addresses
media access control (MAC)
  protocol, 15

media independent interface. *See* MII
medium access protocol. *See* demand
  priority
**medium attachment unit (MAU), 89-90.
  See also transceivers**
medium dependent interface (MDI), 106
**medium dependent interface crossover
  (MDI-X), 107**
medium interface connector (MIC), 121
message code 5, 217
message code 6, PHY identifier, 217
message code 8, 217
**message codes, twisted-pair interfaces
  (Auto-Negotiation), 217-218**
message pages, 212
  1000BASE-T, master/slave roles, 216
  format of, 214
messages
  GVRP, 344-345
  LACP, 300-302
Metcalfe, Robert, Ethernet, 9
**MIB (Management Information
  Base), 21**
MIB documents, 22
MIC (medium interface connector), 121
MII (media independent interface), 134
  Fast Ethernet, 134-135
**mixed coax/twisted-pair collision
  domains, 108**
**mixed-media LANs, transparent
  bridges, 232-233**
**MLT-3 signals, physical layer encodings,
  551-552**
modal bandwidth, 168
modal dispersion, 168
**mode-conditioning patch cords,
  1000BASE-X, 172**
monitor bits, 408
monitors, 20
MOSPF (Multicast OSPF), 392
**MPLS (Multiprotocol Label
  Switching), 395**
**MSAU or MAU (Multistation Access
  Units), 413**

multiaccess environments, 43
multicast addresses, 28. *See also* group
  addresses
    Ethernet, 30
multicast forward virtual channel
  connection, 486
multicast MAC addresses, 274-275
Multicast OSPF (MOSPF), 392
multicast send connection, 487
multicast send virtual channel
  connection, 486
multicasting, 274-275
multicasts
    bridges, 246-247
        IGMP snooping, 247
    controlling, 275-276
    GMRP, 283
    IP multicasts, 276
        mapping to Ethernet multicast
          addresses, 277
        mapping to FDDI multicast
          addresses, 278
    Token Ring, 278
    VLAN frames, 334
multimode fiber
    fiber optics, 119
    transmitting, 120-121
Multiprotocol Label Switching
  Architecture (MPLS), 395
multisegment LANs, Ethernet (building
  with repeaters), 44
Multistation Access Units (MAU or
  MSAU), 413
MUTO (multiuser telecommunications
  outlet), cabling layout, 188

N

NAA (network address authority), 510
names, fibre channel, 510-511
naming conventions, 8B/10B encoding,
  565-566

NCFI (noncanonical format
  identifier), 370
NCITS (National Committee for
  Information Technology
  Standards), 596
    fibre channel, 502
NDIS (Network Driver Interface
  Specification), 18
near end crosstalk (NEXT), 189, 192-193
negative running disparity, 564
neighbor notification process, Token
  Ring, 409-410
NetWare, Ethernet MAC frames, 73-74
network address authority (NAA), 510
network addresses versus MAC
  addresses, 384-385
network diameters, 94
Network Driver Interface Specification
  (NDIS), 18
network interface card. *See* NICs
network numbers, 385
NEXT (near end crosstalk), 189, 192-193
NFS (Network File Server), Jumbo
  frames, 158
nibbles, 550, 579
NICs (network interface cards), 17
    addresses, 28
    gigabit NICs, 156
NLP (normal link pulses), 108, 211
No Token, Token Ring protocol, 425
nodes, 504
noncanonical format identifier
  (NCFI), 370
normal velocity of propagation
  (NVP), 196
nrt-VBR (non-real-time Variable Bit
  Rate), ATM, 461
NRZI signals, physical layer
  encodings, 550
NVP (normal velocity of
  propagation), 196
N_Port identifiers, 512
    fibre channel data transfers, 520-521

O

OAM (operations, administration, and maintenance), 465
offsets, relative offsets (fibre channel data transfers), 519
Open Shortest Path First (OSPF), 390
Open Systems Interconnect (OSI), 13
operation of Token Ring, 405-407
operational keys, 300
optical fiber connectors, 121
optical fiber. *See* fiber optic cabling, fiber optics
optical time-domain reflectometer (OTDR), 200
optimal paths, subLANs, 258-259
order sets
    fibre channel, 592
    fibre channel delimiters, 591-592
ordered sets
    8B/10B encoding, 567-568
    fibre channel data transfers, 516
originator exchange identifier frame header fields, fibre channel frame format, 526
OSI (Open Systems Interconnect), 13
OSPF (Open Shortest Path First), 390
OTDR (optical time-domain reflectometer), 200
OUIs (organizationally unique identifiers), 26

P

packets, 393
page exchange protocol, 215
PAM5x5 encoding, 559-560
parallel detection, twisted-pair interfaces (Auto-Negotiation), 210
parallel processing, Layer 2 switches, 243

parameters
    cabling performance, 188-189
        attenuation, 191
        attenuation to crosstalk ratio (ACR), 195
        delay skew, 196
        FEXT (far end crosstalk), 193-195
        high-speed LANs, 190
        jitter, 190
        NEXT (near end crosstalk), 192-193
        propagation delay, 196
        return loss, 195
        SRL, 195
    Ethernet, tabulating, 74
    full-duplex Ethernet, 79, 155
    link aggregation, 299
paths
    ATM, 460
    optimal paths, subLANs, 258-259
PAUSE frames, 80-84
payload type, 465
performance, cabling performance parameters, 188-189
    attenuation, 191
    attenuation to crosstalk ratio (ACR), 195
    delay skew, 196
    FEXT (far end crosstalk), 193-195
    high-speed LANs, 190
    jitter, 190
    NEXT (near end crosstalk), 192-193
    propagation delay, 196
    return loss, 195
    structural return loss (SRL), 195
permanent links (scope of cabling tests), 198
permanent virtual circuit (PVC), 460
phantom signals, 412
PHY identifier, message code 6, 217
physical addresses. *See* MAC addresses
physical characteristics, Gigabit Ethernet, 167-169

physical layer encodings, 543-544
4B/5B data mappings, 552-553
100BASE-T2, 559
PAM5x5 encoding, 559-560
100BASE-T4, 553
8B/6T byte translations, 553-555
data transmission, 555-556
special patterns, 556, 558
translating to 100BASE-X in hubs,
558-559
100BASE-X, 549-550
1000BASE-T, 568-573
1000BASE-X, 8B/10B encoding,
560-568
CDDI, 549-550
FDDI, 549-550
Manchester encoding, 547
fiber optic cable, 547-548
MLT-3 signals, 551-552
NRZI signals, 550
Token Ring, 573
100Mbps High Speed Token
Ring, 575
Differential Manchester encoding,
573-575
types of signal encoding, 544-546
physical transmission, full-duplex
Gigabit Ethernet, 166-167
port costs, STP, 259-261
port identifiers, fibre channel, 511-512
port numbers, 397
port states, STP, 265
port-based VLANs, 319-320, 326-328
maintaining configurations manually,
323-324
maintaining configurations with
GVRP, 324-326
tagging, 320
trunks, configuring, 321-322
ports
100VG-AnyLAN, 145-146
C-ports, DTR, 432-433

Concentrator/Switch ports, 433
designated STP, 261
fibre channel, 508-509
VLAN ports, configuring, 333-334
VLANs, 308-309
positive running disparity, 564
power sum equal level far end crosstalk
(PSELFEXT), 195
power sum near end crosstalk
(PSNEXT), 195
PPP multilink protocol, 292
preambles, Ethernet MAC frames, 60
primary rings, FDDI, 441-442
primitive sequences, 516
fibre channel, order sets, 592
primitive signals, 516
fibre channel, order sets, 592
prioritizing
frames, 339
forwarding, 340-341
IEEE 802.1Q, 340
traffic, Layer 4, 397
priority classes, mapping 802.1Q
priorities, 342-343
priority-tagged frames, 311
private loops, 504
probes, monitors, 20
problems
with 10BASE2, 98
with 10BASE5, 95
with IGMP snooping, 280-281
procedures for routing. *See* routing
procedures
processing
cells, ATM cell headers, 467
VLAN frames. *See* VLAN frames
promoting dc balance, 544
propagation delay (cabling performance
parameter), 196
protocol filtering, bridges (static filtering
table entries), 240-241
protocol-based VLANs, 326-328

protocols
ARP, 34
ATM, 460
BGP, 391
Dense Mode Protocol Independent
Multicast, 391
DVMRP, 391
EGP, 391
EIGRP, 390
FDDI. *See* FDDI protocols
full-duplex protocols, DTR, 434
GARP. *See* GARP
GMRP, 247, 281
IGMP, 247, 273
IGRP, 390
LACP, 297-298, 300
slow protocols, 300
LANE. *See* LANE
MOSPF, 392
OSPF, 390
page exchange protocol, 215
PPP multilink protocol, 292
RIP version 1, 390
RIP version 2, 390
slow protocols, LACP, 300
source-routing protocols, 356-357
route discovery, 359
Token Ring, 358-359
Token Ring frame trace, 357
STP, 244-246, 251-252
BPDU messages, 266-271
designated bridges, 261
designated ports, 261
port costs, 259-261
root bridge election, 254-256
root path discovery, 263
root port, 261
root selection, 262
topology changes, 264-266
tree generation, 256-259
tree maintenance, 266
Sparse Mode Protocol Independent
Multicast, 392
TCP, 396

Token Ring, 415. *See also* Token Ring
protocol
UDP, 396
VLAN protocols. *See* VLAN protocols
proxies, 476
**PSELFEXT (power sum equal level far
end crosstalk), 195**
**PSNEXT (power sum near end
crosstalk), 195**
public loops, 504
purging the ring, Token Ring, 408
PVC (permanent virtual circuit), 460

Q

Quality of Service, 462
ATM, 460-462
Queue PDU, Token Ring protocol, 425
quinary symbols, 559-560

R

random backoff, 59
Ethernet, 58-59
real-time Variable Bit Rate (rt-VBR), 461
receiver ready signals, 522
redundancy, bridges, 243-244
link aggregation, 246-247
STP, 244-246
redundant links, 100VG-AnyLAN, 145
references, Gigabit Ethernet, 163, 181
registers, 483
**relative offsets, fibre channel data
transfers, 519**
REM (Ring Error Monitor), 410
remote bridges, 374
deciding to bridge, 375-376
links between bridges, 374
wide area links, frame formats,
376-380

remote monitor MIB (RMON MIB), 22
remote monitoring (RMON), 20
Remove Hold, Token Ring protocol, 425
Remove Wait, Token Ring protocol, 425
repeaters, 137. *See also* hubs
    collision domains, 228-230
    demand priority, 147-148
    Ethernet LANs, 44
    full-duplex, 155-156
Report Soft Error frames, Token Ring
    protocol, 431
Request Initialize, Token Ring
    protocol, 425
responder exchange identifier frame
    header fields, fibre channel frame
    format, 526
restoring dc balance, 555
return loss (cabling performance
    parameter), 195
Return to Repeat, Token Ring
    protocol, 425
RFC (Request for Comments)
    documents, 22
RIF (Routing Information Field), 33,
    350, 419
    frame format of Token Ring protocol,
        419-420
Ring Error Monitor (REM), 410
ring identifiers, source-routing bridged
    LANs, 352
Ring Parameter Server (RPS), 410
Ring Purge, Token Ring protocol, 425
Ring Purge frames
    Token Ring, 408
    Token Ring protocol, 430-431
rings
    FDDI, wrapping, 445
    joining Token Ring, 411-412
RIP version 1, 390
RIP version 2, 390
RMON (remote monitoring), 20
RMON MIB (remote monitor MIB), 22

roles
    master/slave roles, 1000BASE-T, 216
    of master/slave timer, twisted-pair
      interfaces Auto-Negotiation, 210
root bridges, election (STP), 254-256
root path costs, STP, 259-261
root paths, discovery (STP), 263
root port, STP, 261
roots, selection (STP), 262
route descriptors, 357
route discovery, 351
    source-routing bridged LANs, 353-355
      all-routes-explorer frames, 355
      Spanning Tree explorer frames, 356
    source-routing protocols, 359
route once, switch many techniques,
    394-395
routers
    advantages of, 384
    bridges, Layer 2/3 switches, 394
    Ethernet LANs, 51-52
    legacy routers, architecture of, 392
routing, 383
    LANs, exiting, 386-388
    Layer 3 switches, architecture, 392-394
    Layer 4, 396
      filtering for security, 397
      load balancing, 397-398
      prioritizing traffic, 397
    network addresses versus MAC
      addresses, 384-385
    route once, switch many techniques,
      394-395
routing control frame header fields,
    fibre channel frame format, 524
Routing Information Field. *See* RIF
routing procedures, building routing
    tables, 389-390, 392
routing tables, building, 389-392
RPS (Ring Parameter Server), 410
rt-VBR (real-time Variable Bit Rate),
    ATM, 461
running disparity, 8B/10B encoding,
    564-565

S

S-ports, 443
SC (square connector), 121
scopes of tests, twisted-pair cabling, 198-199
SCSI (Small Computer System Interface), 502
    fibre channel, 502
    versus fibre channel, 529-531
secondary rings, FDDI, 441-442
security
    LANs, 306
    Layer 4, filtering, 397
    static filtering table entries, 239-240
security-key service, fibre channel, 515
segments
    10BASE-T, 98
    collision domains, 228-230
        separating with bridges, 229-231
Selective Multicast Server (SMS), 498
sequence count frame header fields, fibre channel frame format, 525
sequence identifier frame header fields, fibre channel frame format, 525
sequences of frames, fibre channel data transfers, 516, 518
server farms, 397
servers
    configuration servers
        finding, 482
        setting up, 481
    CRS, 410
    LAN emulation servers, 478-479
        BUS, 486-488
        LECS, 480-482
        LES, 483-486
    REM, 410
    RPS, 410
    Token Ring, 410-411
services, fibre channel levels, 514-515
SFD (start frame delimiter), Ethernet MAC frames, 60-61

shared VLAN learning (SVL), 316
sharing LANs, Ethernet LANs, 50
shielded twisted-pair (STP) cabling, 403
short-term circuit (SVC), 460
shrinking interframe gaps, 57
Signal Loss, Token Ring protocol, 425
signal quality error messages, transceivers, 92
signal quality error test (SQE), 92
signals
    arbitrated loops, 536-538
    control signals, 545
Simple Network Management Protocol. See SNMP
single segment Ethernet LANs, 42, 44
single-attached connections (S-ports), 443
single-mode fiber, fiber optics, 119-120
size
    of Ethernet MAC frames, 62
    of Gigabit Ethernet, Ethernet MAC frames, 66-67
slot times, 59
slow protocols, LACP, 300
Small Computer System Interface. See SCSI
SMP (Standby Monitor Present) frames, 410
SMS (Selective Multicast Server), 498
SMT (station management), FDDI, 448-449
SMT frames, FDDI, 450
SNAP (Subnetwork Access Protocol), 68
    Ethernet MAC frames, 68-69
SNAP frames, tracing, 69-70
SNAP headers, Ethernet MAC frames, 70-71
    LSAPs, 72
SNMP (Simple Network Management Protocol), 20
    architecture, 20-21
        MIB, 21
        MIB documents, 22

network management station, 20
transports, 22
snooping, IGMP. *See* IGMP snooping
SOF (start of frame), 591
soft errors, Token Ring, 411
source identifier frame header fields,
fibre channel frame format, 525
source routed frames, translating with
tags, 370-371, 373
source-routing bridged LANs, 350-352
bridge identifiers, 352
protocol elements, 356-357
route discovery, 359
Token Ring, 358-359
Token Ring frame trace, 357
ring identifiers, 352
route discovery, 353-355
all-routes-explorer frames, 355
Spanning Tree explorer frames, 356
SRT bridging, 360
source-routing protocols, 356-357
route discovery, 359
Token Ring, 358-359
Token Ring frame trace, 357
source-routing Token Ring,
translational bridging between
Ethernet, 365
source-routing transparent (SRT)
bridges, 349
Spanning Tree explorer frames, 354
route discovery, source-routing
bridged LANs, 356
Spanning Tree Protocol (STP), 244-246,
251-252, 318
BPDU messages, 266-267
Configuration BPDU, 267-270
Topology Change Notification
BPDU, 270-271
designated bridges, 261
designated ports, 261
port costs, 259-261
root bridge election, 254-256
root path discovery, 263

root port, 261
root selection, 262
topology changes, 264-266
tree generation, 256-259
tree maintenance, 266
VLANs, 318
Sparse Mode Protocol Independent
Multicast, 392
special code-groups, 8B/10B
encoding, 566
special patterns, 100BASE-T4 (physical
layer encodings), 556, 558
specifications, Gigabit Ethernet, 151-152
splines, 193
SQE (signal quality error test), 92
square connector (SC), 121
SRL (structural return loss), 195
SRT (source-routing transparent)
bridges, 349
SRT bridging, source-routing bridged
LANs, 360
ST (straight tip) connecotrs, 121
standalone loops, 504
standards, cabling standards
layouts, 187-188
performance parameters, 188-196
ruling bodies, 183-184
TIA/EIA categories, 184-187
wire features, 187
standards bodies, 23
ANSI, 594
IEEE, 593
IETF, 594
ISO, 595
ITU-T, 595
TIA/EIA, 594
Standby Monitor, Token Ring
protocol, 425
Standby Monitor Present (SMP)
frames, 410
Token Ring protocol, 429
standby monitors, Token Ring, 408
StarLAN, 45

start frame delimiter (SFD), Ethernet MAC frames, 60-61
start of frame (SOF), 591
static filtering table entries, bridges, 237
  efficient forwarding, 237-238
  filtering constraints, 241
  protocol filtering, 240-241
  sample format, 238-239
  security constraints, 239-240
station emulation mode, 433
station management (SMT), 448-449
stations
  dual-attached stations, FDDI, 443-444
  FDDI, 439
  joining to C-ports, DTR, 435
  LANs, 17
  single-attached stations, FDDI, 443
store-and-forward mode, Layer 2 switches compared to cut-through mode, 242-243
STP (shielded twisted-pair) cabling, 403
STP. *See* **Spanning Tree Protocol**
straight tip (ST) connectors, 121
structural return loss (SRL), 195
structure
  of optical fiber, 118-119
  subLANs, 252-254
subLANs
  assigning costs to, 256-257
  optimal paths, 258-259
  structure, 252-254
sublayers, link aggregation, 297
subnet numbers, 385
Subnetwork Access Protocol. *See* **SNAP**
subvector fields, 422
SVC (short-term circuit), 460
SVL (shared VLAN learning), 316
switched LANs, transparent bridges, 232-235
switches. *See also* **Layer 2 switches**
  10BASE-T, 106-107
    full-duplex operation, 104
  100Mbps collision domains, 141-142
  Ethernet LANs, 48, 50

  full-duplex Ethernet, 77-79
    congestion, 80-81
  Layer 2/3, 394
  Layer 3, 392-394
  link aggregation, 297-298
  loop switches, fibre channel, 507
  maximum throughput, 79
  route once, switch many techniques, 394-395
  VLAN switches, 310
  VLANs, 307
switching conversations to different link segments, 303
symmetric flow control, 84
synchronization of bit timing, 1000BASE-T, 178-179
synchronous idle, 548
synchronous transmission, 447

T

tables, VLAN filtering tables, 332
tabulating Ethernet parameters, 74
tag control information (TCI), 335
tagged frame formats, VLAN protocols, 335
  tagged Ethernet frames, 335-337
  tagged FDDI frames, 338
  tagged Token Ring frames, 337
tagging
  LANs, 368
  port-based VLANs, 320
  source-routed frames, translating, 370-373
  transparently bridged LANs, 368-370
tags, VLANs, 310
Target Token Rotation Timeout, FDDI, 448
TCI (tag control information), 335
TCP (Transmission Control Protocol), 396

TCU (trunk coupling unit), 413
TDR (Time Domain Reflectometry), 196
Telecommunications Industry
    Association (TIA), 183, 594
Telecommunications Standardization
    Sector of the International
    Telecommunication Union. *See* ITU-T
terminators, 88
ternary symbols, 553-555
test tools for twisted-pair cabling, 197
    certification tool, 198
    continuity tester, 197
    scope of tests, 198-199
testing fiber optic cabling, 199-200
thick coaxial cable. *See* 10BASE5
thinnet, 95
throughput
    Jumbo frames, 157
    maximum, 79
TIA (Telecommunications Industry
    Association), 183, 594
TIA/EIA (Telecommunications Industry
    Association/Electronic Industries
    Alliance), 594
TIA/EIA cabling standards categories,
    184-187
Time Domain Reflectometry (TDR), 196
time service, fibre channel, 515
timers, Token Ring protocol, 424-425
TKP (token passing) mode, 432
token format
    FDDI, 451
    Token Ring protocol, 416
        access control fields, 417
token passing (TKP) mode, 432
Token Ring, 11-12, 404
    active monitors, 407
        functions of, 408
    addresses
        conventions for, 32, 34
        functional address flags, 35-36
    beacon process, 409
    Claim Token frames, 408

components of, 412-415
CRS, 410
DTR, 431
ELAN, 476
encapsulating within Frame Relay
    frames, 379
errors, 411
full-duplex, 12
history of, 10, 403
HSTR, 437-438
    fiber optic HSTR lobes, 438
joining rings, 411-412
LANE frame, 493
LLC frames, 407
MAC addresses, 34-35
MAC frames, 407
multicasts, 278
neighbor notification process, 409-410
operation of, 405-407
physical layer encodings, 573
    100Mbps High Speed Token
        Ring, 575
    Differential Manchester encoding,
        573-575
REM, 410
Ring Purge frames, 408
RPS, 410
servers, 410-411
source-routing protocols, 358-359
standby monitors, 408
tagged frames, 337
translational bridging between FDDI,
    362-363
tunneling across Ethernet, 366-367
Token Ring frames, source-routing
    protocols, 357
Token Ring hubs, 413
Token Ring MAC protocol frames,
    422-424
Token Ring protocol, 415
    abort sequences, 421
    addresses, 416
    frame format, 417

ending delimiters, 420
frame control field, 418
frame status fields, 421
RIF, 419-420
frame traces, 426
Active Monitor Present frame,
428-429
Claim Token frames, 430
LLC all-routes-explorer frame,
427-428
LLC data frame, 426
Report Soft Error frames, 431
Ring Purge frames, 430-431
Standby Monitor Present
frames, 429
MAC addresses, 416
MAC protocol frames, 422-424
timers, 424-425
token format, 416
access control fields, 417
tokens, 405
tone tests, 197
**tools, test tools for twisted-pair cabling,
197-199**
topologies
100VG-AnyLAN, 143
active, 258
changes, STP, 264-266
fibre channel, 504, 507
fabrics, 507
loop switches, 507
ports, 508-509
tree maintenance, STP, 266
topology
FDDI, 439-440
A-ports, 443
B-ports, 443
dual-attached stations, 443-444
M-ports, 445
primary rings, 441-442
S-ports, 443
secondary rings, 441-442

**Topology Change Notification BPDU,
STP, 270-271**
**TP-PMD (Twisted Pair-Physical
Medium Dependent), 446**
tracing
Ethernet MAC frames, DIX
Ethernet, 68
LLC frames, 69-70
SNAP frames, 69-70
traffic
assigning priorities, 339
IEEE 802.1Q, 340
Layer 4, prioritizing, 397
training master/slave timing, 179
training frames, 100VG-AnyLAN, 146
transceivers, 89-90
10BASE5, 90-92
jabber, 92
signal quality error messages, 92
transferring data, 515. *See also* **data
transfers**
transition point (cabling layout), 187
**translating source-routed frames with
tags, 370-371, 373**
translational bridges, 361-362
MAC frame sizes, 362
translational bridging, 350
between source-routing Token Ring
and Ethernet, 365
between Token Ring and FDDI,
362-363
between Transparent Token Ring and
Ethernet, 364
**Transmission Control Protocol
(TCP), 396**
transmission speeds, fibre channel, 503
**transmission technologies, twisted-pair
interfaces (Auto-Negotiation), 208-209**
transmission, 555-556
transmit immediate (TXI) mode, 432
transmitters, Claim Token frames, 408
transmitting multimode fiber, 120-121

transparent bridges, 230-231
    filtering table entries, 236-237
    functions of, 234
    learning process, 234, 236
    mixed-media LANs, 232-233
    static filtering table entries, 237
        efficient forwarding, 237-238
        filtering constraints, 241
        protocol filtering, 240-241
        sample format, 238-239
        security constraints, 239-240
    switched LANs, 232, 234-235
    twisted-pair LANs, 231-232
Transparent Token Ring, translational
    bridging between Ethernet, 364
transparently bridged LANs, tagging,
    368-370
transports, SNMP, 22
trees
    generation, STP, 256-259
    maintenance, STP, 266
truncated binary exponential backoff.
    See random backoff
trunk coupling unit (TCU), 413
trunk links
    collision domains, 312
    VLAN switches, 310
trunks, 291, 404
tunneling Token Ring across Ethernet,
    366-367
Twisted Pair-Physical Medium
    Dependent (TP-PMD), 446
twisted-pair, 104
twisted-pair cables, 100Mbps
    Ethernet, 128
        100BASE-T2, 128, 133
        100BASE-T4, 128, 130-132
        100BASE-TX, 128-130
twisted-pair cabling. See also cabling
    Ethernet LANs, 45-46
    faults on, 196-197
    scope of tests, 198-199

    test tools, 197
        certification tool, 198
        continuity tester, 197
twisted-pair interfaces,
    Auto-Negotiation, 204
    controlling interfaces, 207
    Ethernet upgrades, 204-207
    exchanging data across twisted-pair
        media, 210-212
    flow control, 209
    functionality of, 208
    master/slave timer roles, 210
    message codes, 217-218
    parallel detection, 210
    transmission technologies, 208-209
twisted-pair LANs, transparent bridges,
    231-232
twisted-pair link integrity test,
    10BASE-T, 108
twisted-pair segments, 10BASE-T, 98
twisted-pair transmission, 10BASE-T,
    104-106
TXI (transmit immediate) mode, 432
Type frame header fields, fibre channel
    frame format, 525
types of VLANs, 308, 319

U

UBR (Unspecified Bit Rate), ATM, 461
UDP (User Datagram Protocol), 396
unformatted pages, 212
    format of, 214
unicasts, 27
unidirectional exchanges, 518
universal/local flag bits, 29
universally administered MAC
    addresses, 26-27
upstream neighbors, Token Ring, 406
User Datagram Protocol (UDP), 396
UTP (unshielded twisted-pair) cable,
    98, 403

V

Valid Transmission, Token Ring protocol, 425
vampire tap transceivers, 90
VCI (Virtual Channel Identifier), 462
    ATM cell headers, 466
VCSEL (Vertical Cavity Surface Emitting Laser), 119, 171
vectors, 422
vendor groups, 595-596
virtual circuits, 462
virtual LANs. *See* **VLANs**
virtual link MAC addresses, link aggregation, 295-296
virtual links, 291
Virtual Path Identifier. *See* **VPI**
VLAN filtering tables, 332
VLAN frames, 330
    egress rules, 330
    forwarding, 332-333
    ingress rules, 330-331
    multicasts, 334
VLAN identifiers, 334
VLAN ports, configuring, 333-334
VLAN protocols, 334
    tagged frame formats, 335
        tagged Ethernet frames, 335-337
        tagged FDDI frames, 338
        tagged Token Ring frames, 337
VLAN switches, 307-310
    trunk links, 310
VLAN tag features. *See* **tagging**
VLAN-aware, 308-309
VLAN-aware transparent bridges, 368
VLANs (virtual LANs), 306-308
    access links, 312
    awareness of, 308-309
    communicating between, 314
    default VLAN, 319
    GVRP, 317

    hybrid links, 312-313
    implementing, 318-319
    IP VLANs, 328
    IPX VLANs, 328
    IVL, 316
    MAC frames, 334
    MAC-address-based secure VLANs, 328-329
    port-based VLANs, 319-320, 326-328
        configuring trunks, 321-322
        maintaining configurations manually, 323-324
        maintaining configurations with GVRP, 324-326
        tagging, 320
    ports, 308-309
    protocol-based VLANs, 326-328
    STP, 318
    SVL, 316
    switches, 310
    tags, 310
    trunk links as collision domains, 312
    types of, 308, 319
VPI (Virtual Path Identifier), 462
    ATM cell headers, 466

W-Z

wavelength, fiber optic cabling, 199
Web sites
    Gigabit Ethernet Consortium, 163
    vendor groups, 595-596
wide area links, remote bridges (frame formats), 376-380
Wire Fault, Token Ring protocol, 425
Wire Fault Delay, Token Ring protocol, 425
wire features, cabling standards, 187
wiremap testing, 189
world wide node names, fibre channel, 510-511

world wide port names, fibre channel,
  510-511
worst pair-to-pair equal level far end
  crosstalk, 195
wrapping FDDI rings, 445

Books for Technology Professionals

Windows NT/2000

Windows NT Automated Deployment and Customization
by Richard Puckett
1st Edition
$32.00
ISBN: 1-57870-045-0

Learn time-saving advice that helps you install, update, and configure software on each of your clients without having to visit each client. This book includes reference material on native NT tools, registry edits, and third-party tools.

Windows NT Shell Scripting
by Tim Hill
1st Edition
$32.00
ISBN: 1-57870-047-7

A complete reference for Windows NT scripting, this book guides you through a high-level introduction to the shell language itself and the shell commands that are useful for controlling or managing different components of a network.

Windows NT and UNIX Integration
by Gene Henriksen
1st Edition
$32.00
ISBN: 1-57870-048-5

This book provides you with an all-in-one guide to integrating NT and UNIX in the same network. It begins with the fundamentals of both NT and UNIX and then proceeds with discussions of file sharing, proven solutions to the problems related to printing in an integrated environment, and more.

Windows NT Device Driver Development
by Peter Viscarola and W. Anthony Mason
1st Edition
$50.00
ISBN: 1-57870-058-2

This title begins with an introduction to the general Windows NT operating system concepts relevant to drivers. Then, it progresses to more detailed information about the operating system, such as interrupt management, synchronization issues, the I/O Subsystem, standard kernel mode drivers, and more.

Windows NT Heterogeneous Networking
by Steven B. Thomas
1st Edition
$40.00
ISBN: 1-57870-064-7

A complete reference for internetworking all major systems with Windows NT, both at the OS and protocol levels, this book tells you how to successfully develop an enterprise model as well as how to optimize hardware, domain controllers, and enterprise service traffic.

Windows NT/2000 Thin Client Solutions: Implementing Terminal Services and Citrix MetaFrame
by Todd Mathers
2nd Edition, Summer 2000
$45.00
ISBN: 1-57870-239-9

This authoritative resource provides proven strategies for analyzing, testing, and implementing scalable thin client systems. Coverage includes server, network, and client planning; tips on avoiding traps during Terminal Server implementation; best uses of thin client technology in corporate and ASP environments; and the latest updates to Citrix MetaFrame 1.8.

Win32 Perl Programming:
The Standard Extensions
by Dave Roth
1st Edition
$40.00
ISBN: 1-57870-067-1

See numerous proven examples and practical uses of
Perl in solving everyday Win32 problems. This is the
only book available with comprehensive coverage of
Win32 extensions where most of the Perl functionality
resides in Windows settings.

Windows NT Domain
Architecture
by Gregg Branham
1st Edition
$39.95
ISBN: 1-57870-112-0

This book contains the in-depth expertise that is necessary to both truly plan a complex
enterprise domain and reconfigure current domains.
It includes discussion of important domain design
considerations in preparation for Windows 2000.

Windows 2000 Server: Planning
and Migration
by Sean Deuby
1st Edition
$40.00
ISBN: 1-57870-023-X

*Windows 2000 Server: Planning and
Migration* can quickly save the NT professional
thousands of dollars and hundreds of hours. This title
includes authoritative information on key features of
Windows 2000 and offers recommendations on how
to best position your NT network for Windows 2000.

Windows 2000 Quality
of Service
by David Iseminger
1st Edition
$45.00
ISBN: 1-57870-115-5

Windows 2000 Quality of Service teaches
network engineers and administrators how to define
traffic control patterns and utilize bandwidth in their
Windows-based networks.

Windows NT Applications:
Measuring and Optimizing
Performance
by Paul Hinsberg
1st Edition
$40.00
ISBN: 1-57870-176-7

This book offers developers crucial insight into the
underlying structure of Windows NT as well as the
methodology and tools for measuring, and ultimately
optimizing, code performance.

Windows 2000 and Mainframe
Integration
by William Zack
1st Edition
$40.00
ISBN: 1-57870-200-3

Windows 2000 and Mainframe Integration
provides both mainframe and Windows computing
professionals with the practical know-how to build
and integrate Windows 2000 technologies into their
current environment.

Windows Script Host
by Tim Hill
1st Edition
$35.00
ISBN: 1-57870-139-2

Windows Script Host is one of the first books published about this powerful tool. The text focuses on system scripting and the VBScript language using objects and server scriptlets, and includes numerous ready-to-use script solutions.

KDE Application Development
by Uwe Thiem
1st Edition
$39.99
ISBN: 1-57870-201-1

This book takes a no-nonsense approach to writing applications using the KDE and Qt KDE. Focusing on such essentials as KTsp configuration and maturation, localization and internationalization, application documentation, the automated make process, and development tools, *KDE Application Development* is for the Linux developer inexperienced with GUI or desktop programming and for the GUI developer learning to create Linux applications.

Windows NT/2000 Native API Reference
by Gary Nebbett
1st Edition
$50.00
ISBN: 1-57870-199-6

Windows NT/2000 Native API Reference offers the first comprehensive look at the undocumented APIs. This essential reference enables you to develop debuggers, analysis tools, and run-time libraries; determine whether expected but seemingly missing functionality is absent or just not officially documented; and discover the API changes that accompanied the release of Windows 2000.

Windows NT/2000 ADSI Scripting for System Administration
by Thomas Eck
1st Edition
$45.00
ISBN: 1-57870-219-4

Simplify redundant and solve challenging administrative tasks with *Windows NT/2000 ADSI Scripting for System Administration*. A supply of Visual Basic code segments to streamline the majority of tasks performed on Windows NT/2000, IIS, and Exchange Server is just the beginning of what this book has to offer. Its COM-based approach enables you to implement solutions in VB, ASP, and WSH. The techniques and code provided have been proven in one of the world's largest financial institutions.

Programming

Handbook of Programming Languages, Volume I
Edited by Peter Salus
1st Edition
$49.99
ISBN: 1-57870-008-6

This is the most comprehensive source on the principal object-oriented languages. It covers languages from Smalltalk to Java with explanations of the languages' histories, descriptions of their syntax and semantics, how-to information and tips, and pointers to potential traps.

Handbook of Programming Languages, Volume II

Edited by Peter Salus
1st Edition
$49.99
ISBN: 1-57870-009-4

The four most important imperative languages are covered in this title: Fortran, C, Turbo Pascal, and Icon. Evaluate them to find the best imperative language for your purpose at hand, and learn how these languages are related to each other historically and syntactically.

Handbook of Programming Languages, Volume III

Edited by Peter Salus
1st Edition
$49.99
ISBN: 1-57870-010-8

Beginning with Jon Bentley's discussion of little languages, this book continues to discuss languages "specialized to a particular problem domain"—such as Perl, sed, awk, SQL, Tcl/Tk, and Python.

Handbook of Programming Languages, Volume IV

Edited by Peter Salus
1st Edition
$49.99
ISBN: 1-57870-011-6

This book begins with the functional programming group, descended from John McCarthy's LISP of the late 1960s, and moves on to discuss its offspring: Emacs Lisp, Scheme, Guile, and CLOS.

Smart Card Developer's Kit

by Scott B. Guthery and Timothy M. Jurgensen
1st Edition
$79.99
ISBN: 1-57870-027-2

This is all the practical information a computing professional needs to write programs that use and run on smart cards. Smart card communications and commands, SDKs, terminal-side and card-side APIs, security, financial applications, and e-commerce are all covered in this title.

Exchange & Outlook: Constructing Collaborative Solutions

by Joel Semeniuk and Duncan Mackenzie
1st Edition, Spring 2000
$40.00
ISBN: 1-57870-252-6

Beginning with the advantages of collaborative solutions, this instructive resource proceeds to the tools and strategies you should use in applying them to your environment. *Exchange & Outlook: Constructing Collaborative Solutions* gives you the practical examples and advice you need to extract the most functionality from the Microsoft toolset.

Autoconf, Automake, and Libtool

by Ben Elliston, et al.
1st Edition, Fall 2000
$34.99
ISBN: 1-57870-190-2

This book is the first of its kind, authored by Open Source community luminaries and current maintainers of the tools, it teaches developers how to boost their productivity and the portability of their applications using GNU autoconf, GNU automake, and GNU libtool.

Delphi COM Programming

by Eric Harmon
1st Edition
$45.00
ISBN: 1-57870-221-6

Delphi COM Programming offers a practical exploration of COM to enable Delphi 4 and 5 developers to program component-based applications. Typical real-world scenarios, such as Windows shell programming, automating Microsoft Agent, and creating and using ActiveX controls, are explored. Discussions of each topic are illustrated with detailed example applications.

Networking

Wide Area High Speed Networks

by Dr. Sidnie Feit
1st Edition
$50.00
ISBN: 1-57870-114-7

Networking is in a transitional phase between long-standing, conventional wide area services and new technologies and services. This book presents current and emerging wide area technologies and services, makes them understandable, and puts them into perspective so that their merits and disadvantages are clear.

ASDL/VSDL Principles

by Dr. Dennis J. Rauschmayer
1st Edition
$44.99
ISBN: 1-57870-015-9

ASDL/VSDL Principles provides the communications and networking engineer with the practical explanations, technical detail, and in-depth insight needed to fully implement ASDL and VSDL. Coverage includes the fundamentals of the transmission theory and crosstalk in the outside plant, including the details of modeling and simulating the expected performance of ADSL and VSDL under different operating conditions.

DSL

by Dr. Walter Y. Chen
1st Edition
$54.99
ISBN: 1-57870-017-5

DSL is ideal for computing professionals who are looking for information on new high-speed communications technologies and information on the dynamics of ADSL communications in order to create compliant applications. Get calculation examples for all signal environments, coverage of ADSL, and a multitude of other xDSL technologies.

Gigabit Ethernet Networking

by David G. Cunningham, Ph.D., and William G. Lane, Ph.D.
1st Edition
$50.00
ISBN: 1-57870-062-0

Gigabit Ethernet is the next step for speed on the majority of installed networks. Explore how this technology will allow high-bandwidth applications such as the integration of telephone and data services, real-time applications, thin-client apps such as Windows NT Terminal Server, and corporate teleconferencing.

Supporting Service Level Agreements on IP Networks

by Dinesh Verma
1st Edition
$50.00
ISBN: 1-57870-146-5

An essential resource for network engineers and architects, *Supporting Service Level Agreements on IP Networks* will help you build a core network capable of supporting a range of service levels. You'll also learn how to create SLA solutions using off-the-shelf components in both best-effort and DiffServ/IntServ networks. See how to verify the performance of your SLA—as either a customer or a network service provider.

Directory Enabled Networks

by John Strassner

1st Edition

$50.00

ISBN: 1-57870-140-6

Directory Enabled Networks (DEN) is a specification for managing networks through centralized control. Written by the creator of the technology, *Directory Enabled Networks* is a comprehensive resource on the design and use of DEN. The book provides practical examples, along with a detailed introduction to the theory of building a new class of directory enabled applications that will solve networking problems.

Understanding Public-Key Infrastructure

by Carlisle Adams and Steve Lloyd

1st Edition

$50.00

ISBN: 1-57870-166-X

This book is a tutorial on, and a guide to the deployment of, public-key infrastructures (PKIs). It covers a broad range of material related to PKIs, including certification, operational considerations, and standardization efforts as well as deployment considerations. Emphasis is placed on explaining the interrelated fields within the topic area to assist those who will be responsible for making deployment decisions and architecting a PKI within an organization.

Intrusion Detection

by Rebecca Gurley Bace

1st Edition

$50.00

ISBN: 1-57870-185-6

Written by a former key figure in the National Security Agency, this guide to the field of intrusion detection covers the foundations of intrusion detection and system audit. *Intrusion Detection* provides a wealth of information, ranging from design considerations to how to evaluate and choose the optimal commercial intrusion detection products for a particular networking environment.

Designing Addressing Architectures for Routing and Switching

by Howard C. Berkowitz

1st Edition

$45.00

ISBN: 1-57870-059-0

One of the greatest challenges for network design professionals is making the users, servers, files, printers, and other resources visible on their network. This title equips the network engineer or architect with a systematic methodology for planning the wide area and local area network "streets" on which users and servers live.

Understanding and Deploying LDAP Directory Services

by Timothy A. Howes, Ph.D., Mark C. Smith, Ph.D., and Gordon S. Good

1st Edition

$50.00

ISBN: 1-57870-070-1

This comprehensive tutorial provides the reader with a thorough treatment of LDAP directory services. Minimal knowledge of general networking and administration is assumed, making the material accessible to intermediate and advanced readers. The text is full of practical implementation advice and real-world deployment examples to help the reader choose the path that makes sense for the specific organization.

Differentiated Services for the Internet

by Kalevi Kilkki

1st Edition

$50.00

ISBN: 1-57870-132-5

Differentiated Services, an IETF standards effort, is one of the few technologies enabling networks to alter traffic patterns to suit the needs of a particular application. With the help of *Differentiated Services for the Internet*, you will understand the potential of DiffServ traffic-handling mechanisms to create a more robust, versatile, and efficient Internet infrastructure.

Switched, Fast, and Gigabit Ethernet, Third Edition

by Robert Breyer and
Sean Riley
3rd Edition
$50.00
ISBN: 1-57870-073-6

Switched, Fast, and Gigabit Ethernet,
Third Edition is the one and only
solution needed to understand and
fully implement this entire range of Ethernet innovations. Acting as both an overview of current technologies and hardware requirement and a hands-on, comprehensive tutorial for deploying and managing Switched, Fast, and Gigabit Ethernet networks, this guide covers the most prominent present and future challenges network administrators face.

Wireless LANs: Implementing Interoperable Networks

by Jim Geier
1st Edition
$40.00
ISBN: 1-57870-081-7

Wireless LANs covers how and why to migrate from proprietary solutions to the 802.11 standard, and it explains how to realize significant cost savings through wireless LAN implementation for data collection systems.

LDAP: Programming Directory-Enabled Applications

by Timothy A. Howes, Ph.D.,
and Mark C. Smith
$44.99
ISBN: 1-57870-000-0

This overview of the LDAP standard discusses its creation and history with the Internet Engineering Task Force as well as the original RFC standard. LDAP also covers compliance trends, implementation, data packet handling in C++, client/server responsibilities, and more.

The DHCP Handbook

by Ralph Droms, Ph.D.,
and Ted Lemon
1st Edition
$55.00
ISBN: 1-57870-137-6

The DHCP Handbook is an
authoritative overview and expert
guide to the setup and management of a DHCP server. This title discusses how DHCP was developed and its interaction with other protocols, explaining how DHCP operates, its use in different environments, and the interaction between DHCP servers and clients. Network hardware, inter-server communication, security, SNMP, and IP mobility are also discussed. Included in the book are several appendices that provide a rich resource for networking professionals working with DHCP.

Designing Routing and Switching Architectures for Enterprise Networks

by Howard C. Berkowitz
1st Edition
$55.00
ISBN: 1-57870-060-4

This title provides a fundamental understanding of how switches and routers operate, enabling readers to effectively use them to build networks. The book walks network designers through all aspects of requirements, analysis, and deployment strategies; strengthens readers' professional abilities; and helps them develop skills necessary to advance in their profession.

Quality of Service in IP Networks

by Grenville Armitage
1st Edition
$50.00
ISBN: 1-57870-189-9

With increased Internet traffic,
data, audio, and video applications
have become more vulnerable to costly delivery delays and packet losses. Quality of Service (QoS) is a standards effort to provide consistent levels of service despite these delivery problems. *Quality of Service in IP Networks* provides network engineers and architects with an understanding of the key technologies and techniques that will enable Internet QoS.

Software Architecture and Engineering

Designing Flexible Object-Oriented Systems with UML
by Charles Richter
1st Edition
$40.00
ISBN: 1-57870-098-1

Designing Flexible Object-Oriented Systems with UML details the UML, which is a notation system for designing object-oriented programs. The book follows the same sequence that a development project might employ, starting with requirements of the problem using UML use case diagrams and activity diagrams. The reader is shown ways to improve the design as the author moves through the transformation of the initial diagrams into class diagrams and interaction diagrams. The author continues offering tips and strategies for improving the design and ultimately incorporating concurrency, distribution, and persistence into the design example.

Constructing Superior Software
Paul C. Clements, et al.
1st Edition
$40.00
ISBN: 1-57870-147-3

This title presents a set of fundamental engineering strategies for achieving a successful software solution with practical advice to ensure that the development project is moving in the right direction. Software designers and development managers can improve the development speed and quality of their software by using this book, and they can improve the processes used in development.

A UML Pattern Language
Paul Evitts
1st Edition
$45.00
ISBN: 1-57870-118-X

While other books focus only on the UML notation system, this conceptualizes and illustrates their use through patterns. It provides an integrated, practical, step-by-step discussion of UML patterns with real-world examples to illustrate proven software modeling tehniques.

**MACMILLAN
TECHNICAL
PUBLISHING
U·S·A**

Advanced Information
Cutting-Edge Technologies

Books from MTP Offer Advice and Experience

Technology Series

The *Technology Series* is a comprehensive and authoritative set of guides to the most important computing standards of today. Each title in this series is aimed at bringing computing professionals closer to the scientists and engineers behind the technological implementations that will change tomorrow's innovations in computing. These titles are written and reviewed by those responsible for creating the technology and writing the standards.

Network Architecture and Development Series

The *Network Architecture and Development Series* is a complete set of guides that provides computing professionals with the unique insight of leading experts in today's networking technologies. Each volume explores a technology or set of technologies that is needed to build and maintain the optimal network environment for any organization or situation.

Circle Series

The *Circle Series* is a set of guides for the growing community of advanced, technical-level networking professionals who work with operating systems such as Linux, UNIX, Windows NT, and Windows 2000 as architects, developers, or administrators. Each title focuses on a single component or problem set discussed within the framework of the related technologies. The *Circle Series* provides network designers and programmers with detailed, proven solutions to their problems.

How to Contact Us

Visit Our Web Site

www.newriders.com
On our Web site, you'll find information about our other books, authors, tables of contents, indexes, and book errata. You can also place orders for books through our Web site.

Email Us

Contact us at this address:
nrfeedback@newriders.com
- If you have comments or questions about this book
- To report errors that you have found in this book
- If you have a book proposal to submit or are interested in writing for New Riders/MTP
- If you would like to have an author kit sent to you
- If you are an expert in a computer topic or technology and are interested in being a technical editor who reviews manuscripts for technical accuracy

nrmedia@newriders.com
- For instructors from educational institutions who want to preview New Riders/MTP books for classroom use. Email should include your name, title, school, department, address, phone number, office days/hours, text in use, and enrollment in the body of your text along with your request for desk/examination copies and/or additional information.
- For members of the press who want to review copies of New Riders/MTP books. Email should include your name and the publication or Web site you work for.

Write to Us

New Riders/MTP
201 W. 103rd St.
Indianapolis, IN 46290-1097 USA

Call Us

Toll-free (800) 571-5840 + 9 + 4511
If outside U.S. (317) 581-3500. Ask for New Riders/MTP.

Fax Us

(317) 581-4663

We Want to Know What You Think

To better serve you, we would like your opinion on the content and quality of this book. Please complete this card, and mail it to us or fax it to 317-581-4663.

Name _____

Address _____

City _____ State _____ Zip _____

Phone _____

Email Address _____

Occupation _____

Operating system(s) that you use ____ _____

What influenced your purchase of this book?

❑ Recommendation ❑ Cover Design
❑ Table of Contents ❑ Index
❑ Magazine Review ❑ Advertisement
❑ MTP's Reputation ❑ Author Name

How would you rate the content of this book?

❑ Excellent ❑ Very Good
❑ Good ❑ Fair
❑ Below Average ❑ Poor

What do you like least about this book? Check all that apply.

❑ Content ❑ Writing Style
❑ Accuracy ❑ Examples
❑ Listings ❑ Design
❑ Index ❑ Page Count
❑ Price ❑ Illustrations

How do you plan to use this book?

❑ Quick reference ❑ Self-training
❑ Classroom ❑ Other

What do you like most about this book? Check all that apply.

❑ Content ❑ Writing Style
❑ Accuracy ❑ Examples
❑ Listings ❑ Design
❑ Index ❑ Page Count
❑ Price ❑ Illustrations

What would be a useful follow-up book for you? _____

Where did you purchase this book? _____
_____

Can you name a similar book that you like better than this one, or one that is as good? Why?
_____
_____

How many MTP books do you own? _____

What are your favorite computer books? _____
_____

What other titles would you like to see us develop? _____
_____

Any comments for us? _____
_____

Fold here and tape to mail

New Riders Publishing/MTP
201 W. 103rd St.
Indianapolis, IN 46290